Second Canadian Edition

The Gendered Society Reader

Edited by **Michael S. Kimmel** • **Amy Aronson** • **Amy Kaler**

OXFORD
UNIVERSITY PRESS

OXFORD
UNIVERSITY PRESS

8 Sampson Mews, Suite 204, Don Mills, Ontario M3C 0H5
www.oupcanada.com

Oxford University Press is a department of the University of Oxford.
It furthers the University's objective of excellence in research, scholarship,
and education by publishing worldwide in

Oxford   New York

Auckland   Cape Town   Dar es Salaam   Hong Kong   Karachi
Kuala Lumpur   Madrid   Melbourne   Mexico City   Nairobi
New Delhi   Shanghai   Taipei   Toronto

With offices in

Argentina   Austria   Brazil   Chile   Czech Republic   France   Greece
Guatemala   Hungary   Italy   Japan   Poland   Portugal   Singapore
South Korea   Switzerland   Thailand   Turkey   Ukraine   Vietnam

Oxford is a trade mark of Oxford University Press
in the UK and in certain other countries

Published in Canada
by Oxford University Press

Library and Archives Canada Cataloguing in Publication

The gendered society reader / editors, Michael Kimmel, Amy Aronson, and Amy Kaler.—2nd Canadian ed.

Includes bibliographical references.
ISBN 978-0-19-543371-5

1. Sex role—Textbooks. 2. Sex differences (Psychology)—Textbooks. 3. Gender identity—
Textbooks. 4. Sex discrimination—Textbooks. 5. Equality—Textbooks.
I. Kimmel, Michael S. II. Aronson, Amy III. Kaler, Amy, 1966–

HQ1075.G467 2011   305.3   C2011-900192-6

Cover image: Brand New Images/Getty

Oxford University Press is committed to our environment.
This book is printed on permanent (acid-free) paper ∞.

Printed and bound in Canada

1 2 3 4 — 14 13 12 11

Contents

              Intersections of Gender, Race, and Class   408
              Sepali Guruge, Nazilla Khanlou, and Denise Gastaldo

Chapter 40   Genderbashing: Sexuality, Gender, and the Regulation of Public Space   420
              Viviane K. Namaste

Chapter 41   The White Ribbon Campaign: Involving Men and Boys in Ending Global
              Violence against Women   429
              Michael Kaufman

              Questions for Critical Thought   438

              Acknowledgments   439

Preface to the Canadian Edition

Editing the second Canadian edition of *The Gendered Society Reader* has been a pleasure and a challenge. The pleasure rested in the chance to read widely and to familiarize myself with the liveliness and curiosity that characterizes the best gender research in Canada today. The challenge lay in the difficulty of choosing among the wide array of relevant texts. For every text chosen for inclusion, many others could not be chosen. This was especially true for the two new sections on media and on social movements.

The challenge also lay in moving into a textual space already delineated by Michael Kimmel, one of the most prominent international figures in gender studies. My changes to this book have inevitably altered this space in directions of my own choosing, but I believe I've been able to retain his sense of gender as something that saturates the social world, differentiating the experiences of men and women and manifesting itself in actions, relationships, ideas, and dreams. I also believe I've retained Dr Kimmel's sense of hope and possibility for the transformation of gender, creating a better, more humane world for everyone, male and female alike.

In editing the Canadian version, I used several criteria in choosing texts to include. The most obvious criterion was that the texts had to be Canadian; they had to deal with the lives and experiences of Canadians, and ideally also be written by a Canadian author. I focused on the nationality of the texts not because I wanted to fill some arbitrary quota for Canadian content, but because I wanted to enable students to take a critical, analytical look at the country in which their own gendered subjectivities are being formed. I wanted to avoid the problem my own students often complain about: the tendency to universalize American experiences and to treat the United States as the norm for the entire world.

This desire on my part is consistent with the broader feminist imperative to question all universalizing tendencies, and to attempt to decentre the centres of power—including academic power—in our writing, thinking, and teaching. There is no question that Canada and the United States are similar in many ways when it comes to the workings of gender, but it's important not to take this similarity for granted, and to look for gender at work in the social world around us, rather than just gazing across the border.

Along the same lines, I have prioritized qualitative accounts of lived experience over heavily quantitative texts. I don't think that qualitative research is somehow better or truer than quantitative studies, but I do think that qualitative work offers undergraduates a way, at least partially, to get inside the life-worlds of gendered subjects, including those who are gendered differently than the students themselves. Qualitative work also enables readers to get a sense of the complex intersections of gender and other social categories, such as race, socioeconomic class, sexuality, and bodily status, all of which shape the experience of being gendered in subtle but powerful ways.

I was graced with an excellent team at Oxford University Press Canada. Many thanks to Lisa Meschino, Roberta Osborne, Jodi Lewchuk, Nancy Reilly, Jessica Coffey, and Tara Tovell for all their work on behalf of this book. I'd also like to acknowledge the students in my Sociology of Gender classes at the University of Alberta, from whom I am slowly learning what teaching gender can be, at its best. I hope this book intrigues, entertains, and possibly enlightens its readers.

Introduction

Amy Kaler and Michael S. Kimmel

Every day there's another story about how women and men are different. They say we have different brain chemistries, different brain organization, and different hormones, different bodies and different selves. They say we have different ways of knowing, that we listen to different moral voices, and that we have different ways of speaking and hearing each other.

Some stories even hold that we come from different planets, women from Venus and men from Mars. In his best-selling series of books on this theme, pop psychologist John Gray informs us that not only do women and men communicate differently, 'but they think, feel, perceive, react, respond, love, need, and appreciate differently' (Gray, 1995: 5). It's a miracle of cosmic proportions that we ever understand one another!

Yet we're all here together in the same classes, eating in the same dining halls, walking on the same campuses, reading the same books, being subject to the same criteria for grading. When we're not at school, we live in the same houses, eat the same meals, surf the same internet, read the same magazines, and watch the same TV shows. How can we be so different and yet lead lives that are so similar??

This is just one of the enduring puzzles of gender. In the past three decades, the pioneering work of feminist scholars, both in traditional disciplines and in women's studies, has made us increasingly aware of how gender affects individual life experiences and how individuals collectively create gender. We know that gender is changeable, that some experiences are more strongly gendered than others, and that gender interacts with other forms of categorization, such as race, class, sexuality, and religion, to influence individual identities. Today, people are probably more conscious of gender as a social force than at any other time in history.

Three decades ago, social scientists would have listed only social class and race as the master statuses that defined and proscribed social life. When the groundbreaking British sociologist Ann Oakley was a PhD student in the mid-1970s and wanted to do her doctoral research on the unpaid work women do in their homes (also known as housework), her academic supervisor argued that such a study would not be considered a legitimate part of the social sciences. Sociology was not about women's trivial preoccupations! But today, thanks to the stubbornness of Oakley and other pioneering sociologists, gender can't be dismissed as a minor add-on to the real business of sociology. Although individual experiences of gender are diverse, there are two near-universal phenomena that define gender in almost every culture we have ever known. First: *Virtually every single society differentiates people on the basis of gender.* Why are women and men perceived as different in every known society? What are the differences that are perceived? Why is gender such an important way of differentiating who does what work, under what conditions, and gets what rewards (also known as the division of labour)? And, second: *Virtually every known society is also based on male domination.* Why are social, political, ideological, material, and economic resources divided unequally between men and women? Why do men end up with more money, leisure time, prestige, and possessions than women do, time and time again?

It's important to note that we are talking about broad social trends here. Not every individual man has more power than every individual woman. Other social categories, such as race, class, and religion, also influence the distribution of the good things in life. Nonetheless, when looking at societies at the collective level, men, as a group, almost always hold more power and resources, on average, than do women as a group. Of course, there are dramatic differences across societies regarding the ways in which men and women are thought to be different; the levels of gender inequality; and the amount of power (including violence) that is used to maintain systems of difference and domination. But the basic fact remains: *virtually every society known to us is founded upon assumptions of gender difference and the politics of gender inequality.*

Most of the arguments about gender difference begin, as will this book, with biology. Women and men *are* biologically different, after all. Our reproductive anatomies are different. Our brain structures differ, our brain chemistries differ. Our musculature is different. We have different levels of different hormones circulating through our different bodies. Surely, these add up to fundamental, intractable, and universal differences, and these differences provide the foundation for male domination, don't they? You can't argue with Mother Nature, can you?

In these models, biological 'sex'—by which we mean the chromosomal, chemical, anatomical apparatuses that make us either male or female— leads inevitably to 'gender', by which we mean the cultural and social meanings, experiences, and institutional structures that are defined as appropriate for those males and females. 'Sex' is male and female; 'gender' refers to cultural definitions of masculinity and femininity—the meanings of maleness or femaleness.

In the age-old question of whether nature or nurture defines our personalities, biological models of sex difference come down on the 'nature' side. Of course, most sensible people recognize that both nature *and* nurture are necessary for gender development. Our biological sex provides the raw material for our development—and all that evolution, different chromosomes, and hormones have to have some effect on who we are and who we become.

But biological sex varies very little from society to society, and yet experiences of gender vary enormously. And it has been the task of the social and behavioural sciences to explore the variations in gender. Biological universalism can't explain this diversity. This is the point at which the social and behavioural sciences—anthropology, history, psychology, sociology—have all had an important role to play in our understanding of gender.

What they suggest is that what it means to be a man or a woman will vary in four significant ways. First, the *meanings* of gender differences vary from one society to another. What it means to be a man or a woman among Aboriginal peoples in the Australian outback or in the Yukon territories is probably significantly different from what it means to be a man or a woman in Norway or Ireland. It has been the task of anthropologists to specify some of those differences, to explore the different meanings that gender has in different cultures. Some cultures, like our own, encourage men to be stoic and to prove their masculinity, and men in other cultures seem even more preoccupied with demonstrating sexual prowess than North American men seem to be. Other cultures prescribe a more relaxed definition of masculinity, based on civic participation, emotional responsiveness, and the collective provision for the community's needs. Some cultures encourage women to be decisive and competitive; others insist that women are naturally passive, helpless, and dependent.

Second, the experiences of being masculine or feminine vary within any one culture *over time*. The experience of being a man or a woman in seventeenth-century Quebec is probably very different from what it might mean there today. Dr Kimmel's own research has suggested that the meanings of manhood have changed dramatically from the founding of America in 1776 to the present (see Kimmel, 1996).

Third, the meaning of masculinity and femininity will change *over the life course* as any individual person grows. Growing up and growing older brings new challenges and new opportunities for individuals to experience life as gendered beings, from early childhood through adolescence, adulthood, midlife, and the senior years. Accepting the idea that individuals face different developmental tasks as they grow and develop, psychologists have examined the ways in which the meanings of masculinity and femininity change over the course of a person's life. The issues confronting a man about proving himself, feeling successful, and the social institutions in which he will attempt to enact those experiences will change, as will the meanings of femininity for prepubescent women, women in child-bearing years, and post-menopausal women, or for women entering the labour market or those retiring from it.

Finally, the meanings of gender will vary *among* different groups of women and men within any particular culture at any particular time. Simply put, not all Canadian men and women are the same. Our experiences are also structured by class, race, ethnicity, age, sexuality, and region of the country. Each of these axes modifies the others. When we focus on gender in this book, we don't assume that it is consistent in the face of all these other kinds of differences. Imagine, for example, an older, black, gay man in Montreal and a young, white, heterosexual farm boy in southern Saskatchewan. Wouldn't they have different definitions of masculinity? Or imagine a 22-year-old lesbian, Somali-Canadian in Toronto and a wealthy, white, Irish Catholic widow in Newfoundland. Wouldn't their experiences of being female be very different? One of the important elements of a sociological approach is to explore the differences *among* men and *among* women, since, as it turns out, these are often more decisive than the differences between women and men.

If gender varies across cultures, over historical time, over the life course, and among men and women within any one culture, this means we really cannot speak of masculinity or femininity as though they were constant, universal essences, common to all women and to all men. Rather, gender is an ever-changing assemblage of meanings, behaviours, opportunities and resources. It's more appropriate, and more realistic, to think of *masculinities* and *femininities*, rather than simple *masculinity* and *femininity* as though these words meant the same thing everywhere and all the time.

At the same time, we can't forget that all masculinities and femininities are not created equal. Some expressions of masculinity and femininity are more powerful and persuasive than others. In North American society, almost everyone can point

to models of idealized femininity and masculinity, standards to which individuals learn to compare themselves (and thereby find themselves wanting).

We also learn what is considered *unfeminine* or *unmasculine*. In fact, some sociologists and psychologists would argue that North Americans are less preoccupied with emulating the models of their own gender that are held up to them than they are with avoiding excessive resemblance to the other gender. Think of the horror with which small boys recoil from being called a 'sissy'. And while women may admire the androgynous style and range of gender expression available to women at the beginning of the twenty-first century, very few would actually embrace the label 'mannish'. Men, in particular, are often under pressure to make it clear—eternally, compulsively, decidedly—that they are not 'like' women.

For both women and men, this is the 'hegemonic' definition—the one that is most powerful in our society, although not without its critics and dissenters. The sociologist Erving Goffman once described this hegemonic definition of masculinity as follows:

> In an important sense there is only one complete unblushing male: a young, married, white, urban, northern, heterosexual, Protestant, father, of college education, fully employed, of good complexion, weight, and height, and a recent record in sports. . . . Any male who fails to qualify in any one of these ways is likely to view himself—during moments at least—as unworthy, incomplete, and inferior. (Goffman, 1963: 128)

Women also must contend with such an exaggerated ideal of femininity. The sociologist Raewyn Connell calls it 'emphasized femininity'. Emphasized femininity is organized around compliance with gender inequality, and is 'oriented to accommodating the interests and desires of men'. One sees emphasized femininity in 'the display of sociability rather than technical competence, fragility in mating scenes, compliance with men's desire for titillation and ego-stroking in office relationships, [and] acceptance of marriage and child care as a response to labour-market discrimination against women' (Connell, 1987: 183, 188, 187). Emphasized femininity exaggerates gender difference as a strategy of 'adaptation to men's power' stressing empathy and nurturance; 'real' womanhood is described as 'fascinating' and women are advised that they can wrap men around their fingers by knowing and playing by 'the rules'.

Parts 1 and 2 of this book recapitulate the nature/nurture tensions in sociological approaches to gender. Part 1, on biological differences and similarities presents some evidence of distinct and categorical biological differences, and a couple of critiques of that research from a neurobiologist and a psychologist respectively. Cross-cultural research by anthropologists offered a way to critique the claims of biological inevitability and universality lodged in those biological arguments. It falls to sociologists and anthropologists to explore the variations among different groups of women and men, and also to specify the ways in which some versions of masculinity or femininity become hegemonic, and are thus the models against which all other versions of gender are arrayed and measured. As illustrated in Part 2, sociologists today are concerned less with the fixed and limiting concept of 'sex roles', the term favoured in the mid-twentieth century, and more with understanding *gender relations*—the social and political dynamics that shape our conceptions of 'appropriate' sex roles. Thus, sociologists are interested not only in gendered individuals, and the ways in which we each acquire our gendered identities—but also in gendered institutions. By institutions here, we mean not buildings of stone or concrete, but recurrent patterns of interactions connected through shared agendas and goals, even when these goals may not be explicit or obvious. In this way, a baby shower may be considered a social institution (and a very gendered one, at that!), and so may the United Nations, the café where you get your morning coffee, or a AAA hockey team. Some institutions are extremely gendered, by which we mean that men's and women's experiences in these institutions are very different—just think about a traditional 'white wedding'—and that they strongly reinforce ideas about gender. Other institutions

may be less gendered—think about an organic chemistry class, for instance— in that gender is not a prominent feature of the institution, although gender may be present in subtle, unexpected ways.

Sociologists thus return us to the original framing questions—the near-universality of assumptions about gender difference and the near-universality of male domination over women. They argue that male domination is reproduced not only by socializing women and men differently, but also by placing them in organizations and institutions in which specifically gendered norms and values predominate and by which both women and men are then evaluated and judged. Gendered individuals do not inhabit gender-neutral social situations, they contend; both individual and institution bear the mark of gender.

In Parts 3 and 4, we explore institutions and individuals. We begin in Part 3 with the most basic unit of social life, the body itself, and demonstrate that bodies bear the signs of both physical sex and social gender. Through our bodies, we express some of the most intimate and important relationships in our lives, and Part 4 explores these gendered intimacies.

For most people, the primary social institution through which we learn gender is the family. In Part 5, we examine families as institutions that are both gendered *and* gendering, from which individuals go forth to engage with bigger, broader institutions. For most people, school provides the first encounter with the world beyond the family, and the process of learning (both the formal classroom subjects and the 'hidden curriculum' of the playgrounds, halls, and cafeterias) is often deeply gendered. This gendering is explored in Part 6, on schools.

After, or often during, formal education, most individuals work, whether for money in the paid workforce, or without pay in the tasks of raising children and running households. Part 7 examines both the work*place* and the work*force* as institutions structured by gender.

Family, school, and work—is that all there is in a gendered life? Most people would quickly point out the pervasive, even saturating, influence of media. Thanks to new technologies, words and images of gender, carrying explicit and implicit messages, are inescapable, and Part 8, on media, explores some of these representations of gender.

Despite the pervasive gendering influences of all these institutions, human beings are not passive recipients of ideas about gender who create and recreate inegalitarian social structures without thinking. Part 9, on gendered social movements explores some of the ways in which people have rethought and reworked gender, with varying degrees of success and with not a little controversy.

Finally, in Part 10, we examine the most blatant and poisonous manifestation of gender inequalities—gender violence. This type of violence is perpetrated by people who believe that some aspect of their gender (usually, but not always, some aspect of masculinity) legitimates their use of violence against others who appear to threaten their gendered world. In the future, the real measure of gender transformation will be the extent to which gender violence is eradicated, so that individuals' sex no longer determines their likelihood of perpetrating or experiencing violence.

Although this book adopts some of the conventions of thinking about gender in terms of differences between men and women, we hope that astute readers will see the profound similarities underlying the differences. As a statistician might put it, within-group variation consistently exceeds between-group variations. As someone more versed in pop culture might add, men aren't from Mars and women aren't from Venus—in the end, we are all from Earth.

References

Connell, R.W. 1987. *Gender and Power*. Stanford, CA: Stanford University Press.

Goffman, E. 1963. *Stigma*. Englewood Cliffs, NJ: Prentice-Hall.

Gray, J. 1995. *Men Are from Mars, Women Are from Venus*. New York: Harper Collins.

Kimmel, M. 1996. *Manhood in America: A Cultural History*. New York: The Free Press.

PART I

Anatomy and Destiny: Biological Arguments about Gender Difference

Many people believe that anatomy is destiny and that the constitution of our bodies determines our social and psychological disposition. In other words, they think that biological sex decides our gendered experiences. The idea that gender is part of sex is so deep-seated that many people are not even aware that they have conflated the two in their minds.

Biological theories offer the tidiest and easiest explanations for both gender difference and gender inequality. According to this way of thinking, the observable differences between males and females derive from different anatomical organization, which makes us different as men and women, and those anatomical differences are the origin of gender inequality. Biologists rely on three different sets of evidence. Evolutionists, such as sociobiologists and evolutionary psychologists, argue that sex differences derive from the differences in our reproductive anatomies, which lead to divergences in the sorts of behaviour that lend themselves to success in reproduction, often referred to as different reproductive 'strategies'. Females produce only one egg at a time, have a narrow window in which that egg may be fertilized, and must invest much energy and time in ensuring the survival of one baby. Thus, the theory goes, their 'natural' instincts have evolved toward high sexual selectivity and monogamy, to obtain the best genetic material for fertilizing their few precious eggs, and to capture men's resources and their ability to provide food, shelter, and protection. Males, by contrast, are naturally promiscuous, since they have no shortage of sperm, nor any reproductive 'windows' that must be utilized. They also are not burdened by the physical costs of carrying and bearing an infant. Thus, their reproductive success depends upon fertilizing as many eggs as possible without tying themselves to only one woman. Out of the many pregnancies that may result from this strategy, some are likely to survive and perpetuate the male's genes. A second source of evidence of biological difference focuses on some differences in brain function and brain chemistry. In the late nineteenth century, studies showed that men's brains were heavier, or more complex, than women's, and thus, women ought not to seek higher education or vote. (Similar studies also 'proved' that the brains of white people were heavier and more complex than those of black people.) Today, such studies are largely discredited, but studies of sex differences in the brain continue. We now read about how males and females rely more on different halves of their brains, or that they use the two halves differently, or that the two halves are differently connected.

Finally, some biologists focus on the ways in which hormonal differences determine the dramatically divergent paths that males and females take from puberty onwards, when the amounts and activities of those hormones increase dramatically. Testosterone causes aggression, and since males have far more testosterone than females, male aggression—and social, political, and economic dominance—is thus explained.

To the social scientist, though, this biological 'evidence' obscures as much as it reveals, telling us more about our own cultural need to find these differences than about the differences themselves. Biological explanations collapse all other sources of difference—race, ethnicity, and age—into one single dichotomous variable that exaggerates the differences between women and men, and also minimizes the similarities between them. 'Believing is seeing,' notes sociologist Judith Lorber in the title of her essay in this section, and a view of these differences as decisive is often used as a justification for gender inequality.

The readings in this section offer a cross-section of the main biological arguments. David M. Buss summarizes the evidence from evolutionary psychology that different reproductive strategies determine different psychological dispositions. Neurobiologist Robert Sapolsky suggests that the research on hormonal differences do not make a convincing case, while Judith Lorber challenges the assumptions of biological research, arguing that biology's inherent conservatism—justifying existing inequalities by reference to observed differences and ignoring observed similarities—is more than bad politics: it's also bad science. Fausto-Sterling presents perhaps the most audacious challenge to the idea that physical sex produces social gender; she argues that the very idea that there are two distinct and unambiguous human sexes is wrong.

CHAPTER 1

Psychological Sex Differences through Sexual Selection

David M. Buss

Evolutionary psychology predicts that males and females will be the same or similar in all those domains in which the sexes have faced the same or similar adaptive problems. Both sexes have sweat glands because both sexes have faced the adaptive problem of thermal regulation. Both sexes have similar (although not identical) taste preferences for fat, sugar, salt, and particular amino acids because both sexes have faced similar (although not identical) food consumption problems. Both sexes grow calluses when they experience repeated rubbing on their skin because both sexes have faced the adaptive problem of physical damage from environmental friction.

In other domains, men and women have faced substantially different adaptive problems throughout human evolutionary history. In the physical realm, for example, women have faced the problem of childbirth; men have not. Women, therefore, have evolved particular adaptations that are absent in men, such as a cervix that dilates to 10 centimetres just prior to giving birth, mechanisms for producing labour contractions, and the release of oxytocin in the bloodstream during childbirth.

Men and women have also faced different information-processing problems in some adaptive domains. Because fertilization occurs internally within the woman, for example, men have faced the adaptive problem of uncertain paternity in putative offspring. Men who failed to solve this problem risked investing resources in children who were not their own. All people descend from a long line of ancestral men whose adaptations (i.e., psychological mechanisms) led them to behave in ways that increased their likelihood of paternity and decreased the odds of investing in children who were putatively theirs but whose genetic fathers were other men. This does not imply, of course, that men were or are consciously aware of the adaptive problem of compromised paternity.

Women faced the problem of securing a reliable or replenishable supply of resources to carry them through pregnancy and lactation, especially when food resources were scarce (e.g., during droughts or harsh winters). All people are descendants of a long and unbroken line of women who successfully solved this adaptive challenge—for example, by preferring mates who showed the ability to accrue resources and the willingness to provide them for particular women. Those women who failed to solve this problem failed to survive, imperiled the survival chances of their children, and hence failed to continue their lineage.

Evolutionary psychologists predict that the sexes will differ in precisely those domains in which women and men have faced different sorts of adaptive problems. To an evolutionary psychologist, the likelihood that the sexes are psychologically identical in domains in which they have recurrently confronted different adaptive problems over the long expanse of human evolutionary history is essentially zero. The key question, therefore, is not whether men and women differ psychologically. Rather, the key questions about sex differences, from an evolutionary psychological perspective, are (1) In what domains have women and men faced different adaptive problems?; (2) What are the sex-differentiated psychological mechanisms of women and men that have evolved in response to these sex-differentiated adaptive problems?; and (3) Which social, cultural, and contextual inputs moderate the magnitude of expressed sex differences?

Sexual Selection Defines the Primary Domains in Which the Sexes Have Faced Different Adaptive Challenges

Although many who are not biologists equate evolution with natural selection or survival selection, Darwin (1871) sculpted what he believed to be a second theory of evolution—the theory of sexual selection. Sexual selection is the causal process of the evolution of characteristics on the basis of reproductive advantage, as opposed to survival advantage. Sexual selection occurs in two forms. First, members of one sex can successfully outcompete members of their own sex in a process of intrasexual competition. Whatever characteristics lead to success in these same-sex competitions—be they greater size, strength, cunning, or social skills—can evolve or increase in frequency by virtue of the reproductive advantage accrued by the winners through increased access to more numerous or more desirable mates.

Second, members of one sex can evolve preferences for desirable qualities in potential mates through the process of intersexual selection. If members of one sex exhibit some consensus about which qualities are desirable in the other sex, then members of the other sex who possess the desirable qualities will gain a preferential mating advantage. Hence, the desirable qualities—be they morphological features such as antlers or plumage or psychological features such as a lower threshold for risk-taking to acquire resources—can evolve by virtue of the reproductive advantage attained by those who are preferentially chosen for possessing the desirable qualities. Among humans, both causal processes—preferential mate choice and same-sex competition for access to mates—are prevalent between both sexes, and probably have been throughout human evolutionary history.

Hypotheses about Psychological Sex Differences Follow from Sexual Asymmetries in Mate Selection and Intrasexual Competition

Although a detailed analysis of psychological sex differences is well beyond the scope of this article, a few of the most obvious differences in adaptive problems include the following.

Paternity Uncertainty

Because fertilization occurs internally within women, men are always less than 100 per cent certain (again, no conscious awareness implied) that their putative children are genetically their own. Some cultures have phrases to describe this, such as 'Mama's baby, papa's maybe.' Women are always 100 per cent certain that the children they bear are their own.

Identifying Reproductively Valuable Women

Because women's ovulation is concealed and there is no evidence that men can detect when women ovulate, ancestral men had the difficult adaptive challenge of identifying which women were more fertile. Although ancestral women would also have faced the problem of identifying fertile men, the problem is considerably less severe both because most men remain fertile throughout their life span, whereas fertility is steeply age graded among women, and because women invest more

heavily in offspring, making them the more 'valuable' sex and more intensely competed for by men seeking sexual access. Thus, there is rarely a shortage of men willing to contribute the sperm necessary for fertilization, whereas from a man's perspective, there is a pervasive shortage of fertile women.

Gaining Sexual Access to Women

Because of the large asymmetry between men and women in their minimum obligatory parental investment—nine months gestation for women versus an act of sex for men—the direct reproductive benefits of gaining sexual access to a variety of mates would have been much higher for men than for women throughout human evolutionary history. Therefore, in social contexts that allowed some short-term mating or polygynous mating, men who succeeded in gaining sexual access to a variety of women—other things being equal—would have experienced greater reproductive success than men who failed to gain such access.

Identifying Men Who Are Able to Invest

Because of the tremendous burdens of a nine-month pregnancy and subsequent lactation, women who selected men who were able to invest resources in them and their offspring would have been at a tremendous advantage in survival and reproductive currencies compared to women who were indifferent to the investment capabilities of the men with whom they chose to mate.

Identifying Men Who Are Willing to Invest

Having resources is not enough. Copulating with a man who had resources but who displayed a hasty post-copulatory departure would have been detrimental to the woman, particularly if she became pregnant and faced raising a child without the aid and protection of an investing father. A man with excellent resource-accruing capacities might channel resources to another woman or pursue short-term sexual opportunities with a variety of women. A woman who had the ability to detect a man's willingness to invest in her and her children would have an adaptive advantage compared to women who were oblivious to a man's willingness or unwillingness to invest.

These are just a few of the adaptive problems that women and men have confronted differently or to differing degrees. Other examples of sex-linked adaptive problems include those of coalitional warfare, coalitional defense, hunting, gathering, combating sex-linked forms of reputational damage, embodying sex-linked prestige criteria, and attracting mates by fulfilling the differing desires of the other sex—domains that all have consequences for mating but are sufficiently wide-ranging to span a great deal of social psychology. It is in these domains that evolutionary psychologists anticipate the most pronounced sex differences—differences in solutions to sex-linked adaptive problems in the form of evolved psychological mechanisms.

Psychological Sex Differences Are Well Documented Empirically in the Domains Predicted by Theories Anchored in Sexual Selection

When Maccoby and Jacklin (1974) published their classic book on the psychology of sex differences, knowledge was spotty and methods for summarizing the literature were largely subjective and interpretive. Since that time, there has been a veritable explosion of empirical findings, along with quantitative meta-analytic procedures for evaluating them. Although new domains of sex differences continue to surface, such as the recently documented female advantage in spatial location memory, the outlines of where researchers find large, medium, small, and no sex differences are starting to emerge more clearly.

A few selected findings illustrate the heuristic power of evolutionary psychology. Cohen (1977) used the widely adopted d statistic as the index of magnitude of effect to propose a rule of thumb for evaluating effect sizes: 0.20 = 'small', 0.50 = 'medium', and 0.80 = 'large'. In *Sex, Power, Conflict: Feminist and Evolutionary Perspectives* (Buss and Malamuth, 1996), J.S Hyde has pointed out that sex differences in the intellectual and cognitive ability domains tend to be small. Women's verbal skills tend to be slightly higher than men's ($d = -0.11$). Sex differences in math also tend to be small ($d = 0.15$). Most tests of general cognitive ability, in short, reveal small sex differences.

The primary exception to the general trend of small sex differences in the cognitive abilities domain occurs with spatial rotation. This ability is essential for successful hunting, in which the trajectory and velocity of a spear must anticipate correctly the trajectory of an animal as each moves with different speeds through space and time. For spatial rotation ability, $d = 0.73$. Other sorts of skills involved in hunting also show large magnitudes of sex differences, such as throwing velocity ($d = 2.18$), throwing distance ($d = 1.98$), and throwing accuracy ($d = 0.96$; Ashmore, 1990). Skilled hunters, as good providers, are known to be sexually attractive to women in current and traditional tribal societies.

Large sex differences appear reliably for precisely the aspects of sexuality and mating predicted by evolutionary theories of sexual strategies. Oliver and Hyde (1993), for example, documented a large sex difference in attitudes toward casual sex ($d = 0.81$). Similar sex differences have been found with other measures of men's desire for casual sex partners, a psychological solution to the problem of seeking sexual access to a variety of partners. For example, men state that they would ideally like to have more than 18 sex partners in their lifetimes, whereas women state that they would desire only 4 or 5. In another study that has been replicated twice, 75 per cent of the men but 0 per cent of the women approached by an attractive stranger of the opposite sex consented to a request for sex.

Women tend to be more exacting than men, as predicted, in their standards for a short-term mate ($d = 0.79$). Women tend to place greater value on good financial prospects in a mate—a finding confirmed in a study of 10,047 individuals residing in thirty-seven cultures located on six continents and five islands from around the world (Buss, 1989). More so than men, women especially disdain qualities in a potential mate that signal an inability to accrue resources, such as lack of ambition ($d = 1.38$) and lack of education ($d = 1.06$). Women desire physical protection abilities more than men, both in short-term mating ($d = 0.94$) and in long-term mating ($d = 0.66$).

Men and women also differ in the weighting given to cues that trigger sexual jealousy. Buss, Larsen, Westen, and Semmelroth (1992) presented men and women with the following dilemma: 'What would upset or distress you more: (a) imagining your partner forming a deep emotional attachment to someone else or (b) imagining your partner enjoying passionate sexual intercourse with that other person?' (252). Men expressed greater distress about sexual than emotional infidelity, whereas women showed the opposite pattern. The difference between the sexes in which scenario was more distressing was 43 per cent ($d = 0.98$). These sex differences have been replicated by different investigators with physiological recording devices and have been replicated in other cultures.

These sex differences are precisely those predicted by evolutionary psychological theories based on sexual selection. They represent only a sampling from a larger body of supporting evidence. The sexes also differ substantially in a wide variety of other ways that are predicted by sexual selection theory, such as in thresholds for physical risk-taking, in frequency of perpetrating homicides, in thresholds for inferring sexual intent in others, in perceptions of the magnitude of upset that people experience as the victims of sexual aggression, and in the frequency of committing violent crimes of all sorts. As noted by Donald Brown (1991), 'It will be irresponsible to continue shunting these [findings] aside, fraud to deny that they exist' (156). Evolutionary psychology sheds light on why these differences exist.

Conclusions

Strong sex differences occur reliably in domains closely linked with sex and mating, precisely as predicted by psychological theories based on sexual selection. Within these domains, the psychological sex differences are patterned in a manner that maps precisely onto the adaptive problems men and women have faced over human evolutionary history. Indeed, in most cases, the evolutionary hypotheses about sex differences were generated a decade or more before the empirical tests were conducted and the sex differences discovered. These models thus have heuristic and predictive power.

The evolutionary psychology perspective also offers several insights into the broader discourse on sex differences. First, neither women nor men can be considered 'superior' or 'inferior' to the other, any more than a bird's wings can be considered superior or inferior to a fish's fins or a kangaroo's legs. Each sex possesses mechanisms designed to deal with its own adaptive challenges—some similar and some different—and so notions of superiority or inferiority are logically incoherent from the vantage point of evolutionary psychology. The meta-theory of evolutionary psychology is descriptive, not prescriptive—it carries no values in its teeth.

Second, contrary to common misconceptions about evolutionary psychology, finding that sex differences originated through a causal process of sexual selection does not imply that the differences are unchangeable or intractable. On the contrary, understanding their origins provides a powerful heuristic to the contexts in which the sex differences are most likely to be manifested (e.g., in the context of mate competition) and hence provides a guide to effective loci for intervention if change is judged to be desirable.

Third, although some worry that inquiries into the existence and evolutionary origins of sex differences will lead to justification for the status quo, it is hard to believe that attempts to change the status quo can be very effective if they are undertaken in ignorance of sex differences that actually exist. Knowledge is power, and attempts to intervene in the absence of knowledge may resemble a surgeon operating blindfolded—there may be more bloodshed than healing.

The perspective of evolutionary psychology jettisons the outmoded dualistic thinking inherent in much current discourse by eliminating the false dichotomy between biological and social. It offers a truly interactionist position that specifies the particular features of social context that are especially critical for processing by our evolved psychological mechanisms. No other theory of sex differences has been capable of predicting and explaining the large number of precise, detailed, patterned sex differences discovered by research guided by evolutionary psychology. Evolutionary psychology possesses the heuristic power to guide investigators to the particular domains in which the most pronounced sex differences, as well as similarities, will be found. People grappling with the existence and implications of psychological sex differences cannot afford to ignore their most likely evolutionary origins through sexual selection.

References

Brown, D. 1991. *Human Universals*. Philadelphia: Temple University Press.

Buss, D.M. 1989. 'Sex Differences in Human Mate Preferences: Evolutionary Hypotheses Tested in 37 Cultures', *Behavioral and Brain Sciences* 12: 1–49.

Buss, D.M., R. Larsen, D. Westen, and J. Semmelroth. 1992. 'Sex Differences in Jealousy: Evolution, Physiology, and Psychology', *Psychological Science* 3: 251–5.

Cohen, J. 1977. *Statistical Power Analysis for the Behavioral Sciences*. San Diego, CA: Academic Press.

Darwin, C. 1871. *The Descent of Man and Selection in Relation to Sex*. London: Murray.

Hyde, J.S. 1996. 'Where Are the Gender Differences? Where are the Gender Similarities?', in D.M. Buss and Malamuth, eds., *Sex, Power, Conflict: Feminist and Evolutionary Perspectives*. New York: Oxford University Press.

Maccoby, E.E., and C.N. Jacklin. 1974. *The Psychology of Sex Differences*. Stanford, CA: Stanford University Press.

Oliver, M.B., and J.S. Hyde. 1993. 'Gender Differences in Sexuality: A Meta-analysis', *Psychological Bulletin* 114: 29–51.

CHAPTER 2

Testosterone Rules

Robert M. Sapolsky

Face it, we all do it—we all believe in stereotypes about minorities. These stereotypes are typically pejorative and false, but every now and then they have a core of truth. I know, because I belong to a minority that lives up to its reputation. I have a genetic abnormality generally considered to be associated with high rates of certain socially abhorrent behaviours: I am male. Thanks to an array of genes that produce some hormone-synthesizing enzymes, my testes churn out a corrosive chemical and dump the stuff into my bloodstream, and this probably has behavioural consequences. We males account for less than 50 per cent of the population, yet we generate a huge proportion of the violence. Whether it is something as primal as having an axe fight in a rain forest clearing or as detached as using computer-guided aircraft to strafe a village, something as condemned as assaulting a cripple or as glorified as killing someone wearing the wrong uniform, if it is violent, we males excel at it.

Why should this be? We all think we know the answer: something to do with those genes being expressed down in the testes. A dozen millennia ago or so, an adventurous soul managed to lop off a surly bull's testicles, thus inventing behavioural endocrinology. It is unclear from the historical records whether the experiment resulted in grants and tenure, but it certainly generated an influential finding: that the testes do something or other to make males aggressive pains in the ass.

That something or other is synthesizing the infamous corrosive chemical, testosterone (or rather, a family of related androgen hormones that I'll call testosterone for the sake of simplicity, hoping the androgen specialists won't take it the wrong way). Testosterone bulks up muscle cells—including those in the larynx, giving rise to operatic basses. It makes hair sprout here and there, undermines the health of blood vessels, alters biochemical events in the liver too dizzying to contemplate, and has a profound impact, no doubt, on the workings of cells in big toes. And it seeps into the brain, where it influences behaviour in a way highly relevant to understanding aggression.

Genes are the hand behind the scene, directing testosterone's actions. They specify whether steroidal building blocks are turned into testosterone or estrogen, how much of each, and how quickly. They regulate how fast the liver breaks down circulating testosterone, thereby determining how long an androgenic signal remains in the bloodstream. They direct the synthesis of testosterone receptors—specialized proteins that catch hold of testosterone and allow it to have its characteristic effects on target cells. And genes specify how many such receptors the body has, and how sensitive they are. Insofar as testosterone alters brain function and produces aggression, and genes regulate how much testosterone is made and how effectively it works, this should be the archetypal case for studying how genes can control our behaviour. Instead, however, it's the archetypal case for learning how little genes actually do so.

Some pretty obvious evidence links testosterone with aggression. Males tend to have higher testosterone levels in their circulation than do females, and to be more aggressive. Times of life when males are swimming in testosterone—for example, after reaching puberty—correspond to when aggression peaks. Among many species, testes are mothballed most of the year, kicking into action and pouring out testosterone only during a very circumscribed mating season—precisely the time when male–male aggression soars.

Impressive though they seem, these data are only correlative—testosterone found on the scene, repeatedly, with no alibi when some aggression has occurred. The proof comes with the knife, the performance of what is euphemistically known as a subtraction experiment. Remove the source of testosterone in species after species, and levels of aggression typically plummet. Reinstate normal testosterone levels afterward with injections of synthetic testosterone, and aggression returns.

The subtraction and replacement paradigm represents pretty damning proof that this hormone, with its synthesis and efficacy under genetic control, is involved in aggression. 'Normal testosterone levels appear to be a prerequisite for normative levels of aggressive behaviour' is the sort of catchy, hum-able phrase the textbooks would use. That probably explains why you shouldn't mess with a bull moose during rutting season. But it's not why a lot of people want to understand this sliver of science. Does the action of testosterone tell us anything about individual differences in levels of aggression, anything about why some males—some human males—are exceptionally violent? Among an array of males, are the highest testosterone levels found in the most aggressive individuals?

Generate some extreme differences and that is precisely what you see. Castrate some of the well-paid study subjects, inject others with enough testosterone to quadruple the normal human levels, and the high-testosterone males are overwhelmingly likely to be the more aggressive ones. Obviously, extreme conditions don't tell us much about the real world, but studies of the normative variability in testosterone—in other words, seeing what everyone's natural levels are like without manipulating anything—also suggest that high levels of testosterone and high levels of aggression tend to go together. This would seem to seal the case that interindividual differences in levels of aggression among normal individuals are probably driven by differences in levels of testosterone. But that conclusion turns out to be wrong.

Here's why. Suppose you note a correlation between levels of aggression and levels of testosterone among normal males. It could be because (a) testosterone elevates aggression; (b) aggression elevates testosterone secretion; or (c) neither causes the other. There's a huge bias to assume option a, while b is the answer. Study after study has shown that if you examine testosterone levels when males are first placed together in the social group, testosterone levels predict nothing about who is going to be aggressive. The subsequent behavioural differences drive the hormonal changes, rather than the other way around.

Because of a strong bias among certain scientists, it has taken forever to convince them of this point. Suppose you're studying what behaviour and hormones have to do with each other. How do you study the behavioural part? You get yourself a notebook, a stopwatch, and a pair of binoculars. How do you measure the hormones and analyze the genes that regulate them? You need some gazillion-dollar machines; you muck around with radiation and chemicals, wear a lab coat, and maybe even goggles—the whole nine yards. Which toys would you rather get for Christmas? Which facet of science are you going to believe in more? The higher the technology, the more scientific the discipline. Hormones seem to many to be more substantive than behaviour, so when a correlation occurs, it must be because hormones regulate behaviour, not the other way around.

This is a classic case of what is often called physics envy, a disease that causes behavioural biologists to fear their discipline lacks the rigour of physiology, physiologists to wish for the techniques of biochemists, biochemists to covet the clarity of the answers revealed by molecular geneticists, all the way down until you get to the physicists who confer only with God. Recently, a zoologist friend had obtained blood samples from the carnivores he studies and wanted some hormones in the samples tested in my lab. Although inexperienced with the technique, he offered to help in any way possible. I felt hesitant asking him to do anything tedious, but since he had offered, I tentatively said, 'Well, if you don't mind some unspeakable drudgery, you could number about a thousand assay vials.' And this scientist, whose superb work has graced the most prestigious science journals in the world, cheerfully answered, 'That's okay. How often do I get to do real science, working with test tubes?'

Difficult though scientists with physics envy find it to believe, interindividual differences in testosterone levels don't predict subsequent differences in aggressive behaviour among individuals. Similarly, fluctuations in testosterone levels within one individual over time don't predict subsequent changes in the levels of aggression in that one individual—get a hiccup in testosterone secretion one afternoon and that's not when the guy goes postal.

Look at our confusing state: normal levels of testosterone are a prerequisite for normal levels of aggression. Yet if one male's genetic makeup predisposes him to higher levels of testosterone than the next guy, he isn't necessarily going to be more aggressive. Like clockwork, that statement makes the students suddenly start coming to office hours in a panic, asking whether they missed something in their lecture notes.

Yes, it's going to be on the final, and it's one of the more subtle points in endocrinology—what's referred to as a hormone having a 'permissive effect'. Remove someone's testes and, as noted, the frequency of aggressive behaviour is likely to plummet. Reinstate pre-castration levels of testosterone by injecting the hormone, and pre-castration levels of aggression typically return. Fair enough. Now, this time, castrate an individual and restore testosterone levels to only 20 per cent of normal. Amazingly, normal pre-castration levels of aggression come back. Castrate and now introduce twice the testosterone levels from before castration, and the same level of aggressive behaviour returns. You need some testosterone around for normal aggressive behaviour. Zero levels after castration, and down it usually goes; quadruple levels (the sort of range generated in weight lifters abusing anabolic steroids), and aggression typically increases. But anywhere from roughly 20 per cent of normal to twice normal and it's all the same. The brain can't distinguish among this wide range of basically normal values.

If you knew a great deal about the genetic makeup of a bunch of males, enough to understand how much testosterone they secreted into their bloodstream, you still couldn't predict levels of aggression among those individuals. Nevertheless, the subtraction and reinstatement data seem to indicate that, in a broad sort of way, testosterone causes aggressive behaviour. But that turns out not to be true either, and the implications of this are lost on most people the first 30 times they hear about it. Those implications are important, however—so important that it's worth saying 31 times.

Round up some male monkeys. Put them in a group together and give them plenty of time to sort out where they stand with each other—grudges, affiliative friendships. Give them enough time to form a dominance hierarchy, the sort of linear ranking in which number 3, for example, can pass his day throwing around his weight with numbers 4 and 5, ripping off their monkey chow, forcing them to relinquish the best spots to sit in, but numbers 1 and 2 still expect and receive from him the most obsequious brown-nosing.

Hierarchy in place, it's time to do your experiment. Take that third-ranking monkey and give him some testosterone. None of this within-the-normal-range stuff. Inject a ton of it, way higher than what you normally see in rhesus monkeys, give him enough testosterone to grow antlers and a beard on every neuron in his brain. And, no surprise, when you check the behavioural data, he will probably be participating in more aggressive interactions than before.

So even though small fluctuations in the levels of the hormone don't seem to matter much, testosterone still causes aggression, right? Wrong. Check out number 3 more closely. Is he raining aggressive terror on everyone in the group, frothing with indiscriminate violence? Not at all. He's still judiciously kowtowing to numbers 1 and 2 but has become a total bastard to numbers 4 and 5. Testosterone isn't causing aggression, it's exaggerating the aggression that's already there.

Another example, just to show we're serious. There's a part of your brain that probably has lots to do with aggression, a region called the amygdala. Sitting near it is the Grand Central Station of emotion-related activity in your brain, the hypothalamus. The amygdala communicates with the hypothalamus by way of a cable of neuronal connections called the stria terminalis. (No more jargon, I promise.) The amygdala influences aggression via that pathway, sending bursts of electrical excitation that ripple down the stria terminalis to the hypothalamus and put it in a pissy mood.

Once again, do your hormonal intervention: flood the area with testosterone. You can inject the hormone into the bloodstream, where it eventually makes its way to the amygdala. You can surgically microinject the stuff directly into the area. In a few years, you may even be able to construct animals

with extra copies of the genes that direct testosterone synthesis, producing extra hormone that way. Six of one, half a dozen of the other. The key thing is what doesn't happen next. Does testosterone make waves of electrical excitation surge down the stria terminalis? Does it turn on that pathway? Not at all. If, and only if, the amygdala is already sending an excited volley down the stria terminalis, testosterone increases the rate of such activity by shortening the resting time between bouts. It's not turning on the pathway, it's increasing the volume of signalling if it is already turned on. It's not causing aggression, it's exaggerating the preexisting pattern of it, exaggerating the response to environmental triggers of aggression.

In every generation, it is the duty of behavioural biologists to try to teach this critical point, one that seems a maddening cliché once you get it. You take that hoary old dichotomy between nature and nurture, between intrinsic factors and extrinsic ones, between genes and environment, and regardless of which behaviour and underlying biology you're studying, the dichotomy is a sham. No genes. No environment. Just the interaction between the two.

Do you want to know how important environment and experience are in understanding testosterone and aggression? Look back at how the effects of castration are discussed earlier. There were statements like 'Remove the source of testosterone in species after species and levels of aggression typically plummet.' Not 'Remove the source . . . and aggression always goes to zero.' On the average it declines, but rarely to zero, and not at all in some individuals. And the more social experience an individual had, being aggressive prior to castration, the more likely that behaviour persists 'sans cojones'. In the right context, social conditioning can more than make up for the complete absence of the hormone.

A case in point: the spotted hyena. These animals are fast becoming the darlings of endocrinologists, sociobiologists, gynecologists, and tabloid writers, because of their wild sex reversal system. Females are more muscular and more aggressive than males, and are socially dominant to them; rare traits in the mammalian world. And get this: females secrete more of certain testosterone-related hormones than the males do, producing muscles, aggression, and masculinized private parts that make it supremely difficult to tell the sex of a hyena. So high androgen levels would seem, again, to cause aggression and social dominance. But that's not the whole answer.

High in the hills above the University of California at Berkeley is the world's largest colony of spotted hyenas, massive bone-crunching beasts who fight each other for the chance to have their ears scratched by Laurence Frank, the zoologist who brought them over as infants from Kenya. Various scientists are studying their sex reversal system. The female hyenas are bigger and more muscular than the males and have the same weirdo genitals and elevated androgen levels as their female cousins back in the savanna. Everything is just as it is in the wild—except the social system. As those hyenas grew up, there was a very significant delay in the time it took for the females to begin socially dominating the males, even though the females were stoked on androgens. They had to grow up without the established social system to learn from.

When people first realize that genes have a great deal to do with behaviour—even subtle, complex, human behaviour—they are often struck with an initial evangelical enthusiasm, placing a convert's faith in the genetic components of the story. This enthusiasm is typically reductive—because of physics envy, because reductionism is so impressive, because it would be so nice if there were a single gene (or hormone or neurotransmitter or part of the brain) responsible for everything. But even if you completely understood how genes regulate all the important physical factors involved in aggression—testosterone synthesis and secretion, the brain's testosterone receptors, the amygdala neurons and their levels of transmitters, the favourite colour of the hypothalamus—you still wouldn't be able to predict levels of aggression accurately in a group of normal individuals.

This is no mere academic subject. We are a fine species with some potential, yet we are racked by sickening amounts of violence. Unless we are hermits, we feel the threat of it, often every day, and should our leaders push the button, we will all be lost in a final global violence. But as we try to understand this feature of our sociality, it is critical to remember the limits of the biology. Knowing the genome, the complete DNA sequence, of some suburban teenager is never going to tell us why that kid, in his after-school chess club, has developed a particularly aggressive style with his bishops. And it certainly isn't going to tell us much about the teenager in some inner city hellhole who has taken to mugging people. 'Testosterone equals aggression' is inadequate for those who would offer a simple biological solution to the violent male. And 'testosterone equals aggression' is certainly inadequate for those who would offer the simple excuse that boys will be boys. Violence is more complex than a single hormone, and it is supremely rare that any of our behaviours can be reduced to genetic destiny. This is science for the bleeding-heart liberal: the genetics of behaviour is usually meaningless outside the context of the social factors and environment in which it occurs.

CHAPTER 3

Believing Is Seeing: Biology as Ideology

Judith Lorber

Until the eighteenth century, Western philosophers and scientists thought that there was one sex and that women's internal genitalia were the inverse of men's external genitalia: the womb and vagina were the penis and scrotum turned inside out (Laqueur, 1990). Current Western thinking sees women and men as so different physically as to sometimes seem to be two species. The bodies, which have been mapped inside and out for hundreds of years, have not changed. What have changed are the justifications for gender inequality. When the social position of all human beings was believed to be set by natural law or was considered God-given, biology was irrelevant; women and men of different classes all had their assigned places. When scientists began to question the divine basis of social order and replaced faith with empirical knowledge, what they saw was that women were very different from men in that they had wombs and menstruated. Such anatomical differences destined them for an entirely different social life from men.

In actuality, the basic bodily material is the same for females and males, and except for procreative hormones and organs, female and male human beings have similar bodies (Naftolin and Butz, 1981). Furthermore, as has been known since the middle of the nineteenth century, male and female genitalia develop from the same fetal tissue, and so infants can be born with ambiguous genitalia (Money and Ehrhardt, 1972). When they are, biology is used quite arbitrarily in sex assignment. Suzanne Kessler (1990) interviewed six medical specialists in pediatric intersexuality and found that whether an infant with XY chromosomes and anomalous genitalia was categorized as a boy or a girl depended on the size of the penis—if a penis was very small, the child was categorized as a girl, and sex-change surgery was used to make an artificial vagina. In the late nineteenth century, the presence or absence of ovaries was the determining criterion of gender assignment for hermaphrodites because a woman who could not procreate was not a complete woman (Kessler, 1990: 20).

Yet in Western societies, we see two discrete sexes and two distinguishable genders because our society is built on two *classes* of people, 'women' and 'men'. Once the gender category is given, the attributes of the person are also gendered: Whatever a 'woman' is must be 'female'; whatever a 'man' is must be 'male'. Analyzing the social processes that construct the categories we call 'female and male', 'women and men', and 'homosexual and heterosexual' uncovers the ideology and power differentials congealed in these categories (Foucault, 1978). This article will use two familiar areas of

social life—sports and technological competence—to show how myriad physiological differences are transformed into similar-appearing, gendered social bodies. My perspective goes beyond accepted feminist views that gender is a cultural overlay that modifies physiological sex differences. That perspective assumes either that there are two fairly similar sexes distorted by social practices into two genders with purposefully different characteristics or that there are two sexes whose essential differences are rendered unequal by social practices. I am arguing that bodies differ in many ways physiologically, but they are completely transformed by social practices to fit into the salient categories of a society, the most pervasive of which are 'female' and 'male' and 'women' and 'men'.

Neither sex nor gender are pure categories. Combinations of incongruous genes, genitalia, and hormonal input are ignored in sex categorization, just as combinations of incongruous physiology, identity, sexuality, appearance, and behaviour are ignored in the social construction of gender statuses. Menstruation, lactation, and gestation do not demarcate women from men. Only some women are pregnant and then only some of the time; some women do not have a uterus or ovaries. Some women have stopped menstruating temporarily, others have reached menopause, and some have had hysterectomies. Some women breast-feed some of the time, but some men lactate (Jaggar, 1983: 165 fn). Menstruation, lactation, and gestation are individual experiences of womanhood (Levesque-Lopman, 1988), but not determinants of the social category 'woman', or even 'female'. Similarly, 'men are not always sperm-producers, and in fact, not all sperm producers are men. A male-to-female transsexual, prior to surgery, can be socially a woman, though still potentially (or actually) capable of spermatogenesis' (Kessler and McKenna, [1978] 1985: 2).

When gender assignment is contested in sports, where the categories of competitors are rigidly divided into women and men, chromosomes are now used to determine in which category the athlete is to compete. However, an anomaly common enough to be found in several women at every major international sports competition are XY chromosomes that have not produced male anatomy or physiology because of a genetic defect. Because these women are women in every way significant to the sports competition, the prestigious International Amateur Athletic Federation has urged that sex be determined by simple genital inspection (Kolata, 1992). Transsexuals would pass this test, but it took a lawsuit for Renée Richards, a male-to-female transsexual, to be able to play tournament tennis as a woman, despite his male sex chromosomes (Richards, 1983). Oddly, neither basis for gender categorization—chromosomes nor genitalia—has anything to do with sports prowess (Birrell and Cole, 1990).

In the Olympics, in cases of chromosomal ambiguity, women must undergo 'a battery of gynecological and physical exams to see if she is "female enough" to compete. Men are not tested' (Carlson, 1991: 26). The purpose is not to categorize women and men accurately, but to make sure men don't enter women's competitions, where, it is felt, they will have the advantage of size and strength. This practice sounds fair only because it is assumed that all men are similar in size and strength and different from all women. Yet, in Olympic boxing and wrestling matches, men are matched within weight classes. Some women might, similarly, successfully compete with some men in many sports. Women did not run in marathons until about 20 years ago. In 20 years of marathon competition, women have reduced their finish times by more than 90 minutes; they might catch up with men's running times in races of other lengths within the next 50 years because they are increasing their fastest speeds more rapidly than are men (Fausto-Sterling, 1985: 213–18).

The reliance on only two sex and gender categories in the biological and social sciences is as epistemologically spurious as the reliance on chromosomal or genital tests to group athletes. Most research designs do not investigate whether physical skills or physical abilities are really more or less common in women and men (Epstein, 1988). They start out with two social categories ('women', 'men'), assume they are biologically different ('female', 'male'), look for similarities among them and differences between them, and attribute what they have found for the social categories to sex differences (Gelman, Collman, and Maccoby, 1986).

These designs rarely question the categorization of their subjects into two and only two groups, even though they often find more significant within-group differences than between-group differences (Hyde, 1990). The social construction perspective on sex and gender suggests that instead of starting with the two presumed dichotomies in each category—female, male; woman, man—it might be more useful in gender studies to group patterns of behaviour and only then look for identifying markers of the people likely to enact such behaviours.

What Sports Illustrate

Competitive sports have become, for boys and men, as players and as spectators, a way of constructing a masculine identity, a legitimated outlet for violence and aggression, and an avenue for upward mobility (Dunning, 1986; Kemper, 1990, 167–206; Messner, 1992). For men in Western societies, physical competence is an important marker of masculinity (Fine, 1987; Majors, 1990; Glassner, 1992). In professional and collegiate sports, physiological differences are invoked to justify women's secondary status, despite the clear evidence that gender status overrides physiological capabilities. Assumptions about women's physiology have influenced rules of competition; subsequent sports performances then validate how women and men are treated in sports competitions.

Gymnastic equipment is geared to slim, wiry, prepubescent girls and not to mature women; conversely, men's gymnastic equipment is tailored for muscular, mature men, not slim, wiry, prepubescent boys. Boys could compete with girls, but are not allowed to; women gymnasts are left out entirely. Girl gymnasts are just that—little girls who will be disqualified as soon as they grow up (Vecsey, 1990). Men gymnasts have men's status. In women's basketball, the size of the ball and rules for handling the ball change the style of play to 'a slower, less intense, and less exciting modification of the "regular" or men's game' (Watson, 1987: 441). In the 1992 Winter Olympics, men figure skaters were required to complete three triple jumps in their required program; women figure skaters were forbidden to do more than one. These rules penalized artistic men skaters and athletic women skaters (Janofsky, 1992). For the most part, Western sports are built on physically trained men's bodies:

> Speed, size, and strength seem to be the essence of sports. Women *are* naturally inferior at 'sports' so conceived.
>
> But if women had been the historically dominant sex, our concept of sport would no doubt have evolved differently. Competitions emphasizing flexibility, balance, strength, timing, and small size might dominate Sunday afternoon television and offer salaries in six figures (English, 1982: 266, emphasis in original).

Organized sports are big businesses and, thus, who has access and at what level is a distributive or equity issue. The overall status of women and men athletes is an economic, political, and ideological issue that has less to do with individual physiological capabilities than with their cultural and social meaning and who defines and profits from them (Messner and Sabo, 1990; Slatton and Birrell, 1984). Twenty years after the passage of Title IX of the US Civil Rights Act, which forbade gender inequality in any school receiving federal funds, the goal for collegiate sports in the next five years is 60 per cent men, 40 per cent women in sports participation, scholarships, and funding (Moran, 1992).

How access and distribution of rewards (prestigious and financial) are justified is an ideological, even moral, issue (Birrell, 1988: 473–6, Hargreaves, 1982). One way is that men athletes are glorified and women athletes ignored in the mass media. Messner and his colleagues found that in 1989, in TV sports news in the United States, men's sports got 92 per cent of the coverage and women's sports 5 per cent, with the rest mixed or gender-neutral (Messner, Duncan, and Jensen, 1993). In 1990, in four of the top-selling newspapers in the United States, stories on men's sports outnumbered those on women's sports 23-to-1. Messner and his colleagues also found an implicit hierarchy in naming, with women athletes most likely to be called by first names, followed by black men athletes, and only white men athletes routinely referred to by their last names. Similarly,

women's collegiate sports teams are named or marked in ways that symbolically feminize and trivialize them—the men's team is called Tigers, the women's Kittens (Eitzen and Baca Zinn, 1989).

Assumptions about men's and women's bodies and their capacities are crafted in ways that make unequal access and distribution of rewards acceptable (Hudson, 1978; Messner, 1988). Media images of modern men athletes glorify their strength and power, even their violence (Hargreaves, 1986). Media images of modern women athletes tend to focus on feminine beauty and grace (so they are not really athletes) or on their thin, small, wiry, androgenous bodies (so they are not really women). In coverage of the Olympics,

> loving and detailed attention is paid to pixie-like gymnasts; special and extended coverage is given to graceful and dazzling figure skaters; the camera painstakingly records the fluid movements of swimmers and divers. And then, in a blinding flash of fragmented images, viewers see a few minutes of volleyball, basketball, speed skating, track and field, and alpine skiing, as television gives its nod to the mere existence of these events (Boutilier and SanGiovanni, 1983: 190).

Extraordinary feats by women athletes who were presented as mature adults might force sports organizers and audiences to rethink their stereotypes of women's capabilities, the way elves, mermaids, and ice queens do not. Sports, therefore, construct men's bodies to be powerful and women's bodies to be sexual. As Connell (1987: 85) says,

> The meanings in the bodily sense of masculinity concern, above all else, the superiority of men to women, and the exaltation of hegemonic masculinity over other groups of men which is essential for the domination of women.

In the late 1970s, as women entered more and more athletic competitions, supposedly good scientific studies showed that women who exercised intensely would cease menstruating because they would not have enough body fat to sustain ovulation

(Brozan, 1978). When one set of researchers did a year-long study that compared 66 women—21 who were training for a marathon, 22 who ran more than an hour a week, and 23 who did less than an hour of aerobic exercise a week—they discovered that only 20 per cent of the women in any of these groups had 'normal' menstrual cycles every month (Prior et al., 1990). The dangers of intensive training for women's fertility therefore were exaggerated as women began to compete successfully in arenas formerly closed to them.

Given the association of sports with masculinity in the United States, women athletes have to manage a contradictory status. One study of women college basketball players found that although they 'did athlete' on the court, 'pushing, shoving, fouling, hard running, fast breaks, defense, obscenities and sweat' (Watson, 1987: 441), they 'did woman' off the court, using the locker room as their staging area:

> While it typically took fifteen minutes to prepare for the game, it took approximately fifteen minutes after the game to shower and remove the sweat of an athlete, and it took another thirty minutes to dress, apply make-up and style hair. It did not seem to matter whether the players were going out into the public or getting on a van for a long ride home. Average dressing time and rituals did not change (Watson, 1987: 443).

Another way women manage these status dilemmas is to redefine the activity or its result as feminine or womanly (Mangan and Park, 1987). Thus women bodybuilders claim 'flex appeal is sex appeal' (Duff and Hong, 1984: 378).

Such a redefinition of women's physicality affirms the ideological subtext of sports that physical strength is men's prerogative and justifies men's physical and sexual domination of women (Hargreaves, 1986; Messner, 1992; Olson, 1990; Theberge, 1987; Willis, 1982). When women demonstrate physical strength, they are labelled unfeminine:

> It's threatening to one's takeability, one's rapeability, one's femininity, to be strong and physically self-possessed. To be able to resist rape, not to communicate rapeability with

one's body, to hold one's body for uses and meanings other than that can transform what *being a woman means* (MacKinnon, 1987: 122, emphasis in original).

Resistance to that transformation, ironically, was evident in the policies of American women physical education professionals throughout most of the twentieth century. They minimized exertion, maximized a feminine appearance and manner, and left organized sports competition to men (Birrell, 1988; Mangan and Park, 1987).

Dirty Little Secrets

As sports construct gendered bodies, technology constructs gendered skills. Meta-analyses of studies of gender differences in spatial and mathematical ability have found that men have a large advantage in ability to mentally rotate an image, a moderate advantage in a visual perception of horizontality and verticality and in mathematical performance, and a small advantage in ability to pick a figure out of a field (Hyde, 1990). It could be argued that these advantages explain why, within the short space of time that computers have become ubiquitous in offices, schools, and homes, work on them and with them has become gendered: men create, program, and market computers, make war and produce science and art with them; women microwire them in computer factories and enter data in computerized offices; boys play games, socialize, and commit crimes with computers; girls are rarely seen in computer clubs, camps, and classrooms. But women were hired as computer programmers in the 1940s because

> the work seemed to resemble simple clerical tasks. In fact, however, programming demanded complex skills in abstract logic, mathematics, electrical circuitry, and machinery, all of which . . . women used to perform in their work. Once programming was recognized as 'intellectually demanding', it became attractive to men (Donato, 1990: 170).

A woman mathematician and pioneer in data processing, Grace M. Hopper, was famous for her work on programming language (Perry and Greber, 1990: 86). By the 1960s, programming was split into more and less skilled specialties, and the entry of women into the computer field in the 1970s and 1980s was confined to the lower-paid specialties. At each stage, employers invoked women's and men's purportedly natural capabilities for the jobs for which they were hired (Cockburn, 1983, 1985; Zimmerman, 1983; Hartmann, Kraut, and Tilly, 1986; Hartmann, 1987; Wright et al., 1987; Donato, 1990; Kramer and Lehman, 1990).

It is the taken-for-grantedness of such everyday gendered behaviour that gives credence to the belief that the widespread differences in what women and men do must come from biology. To take one ordinarily unremarked scenario: In modern societies, if a man and woman who are a couple are in a car together, he is much more likely to take the wheel than she is, even if she is the more competent driver. Molly Haskell calls this taken-for-granted phenomenon 'the dirty little secret of marriage: the husband-lousy-driver syndrome' (1989: 26). Men drive cars whether they are good drivers or not because men and machines are a 'natural' combination (Scharff, 1991). But the ability to drive gives one mobility; it is a form of social power.

In the early days of the automobile, feminists co-opted the symbolism of mobility as emancipation: 'Donning goggles and dusters, wielding tire irons and tool kits, taking the wheel, they announced their intention to move beyond the bounds of women's place' (Scharff, 1991: 68). Driving enabled them to campaign for women's suffrage in parts of the United States not served by public transportation, and they effectively used motorcades and speaking from cars as campaign tactics (Scharff, 1991). Sandra Gilbert also notes that during the First World War, women's ability to drive was physically, mentally, and even sensually liberating:

> For nurses and ambulance drivers, women doctors and women messengers, the phenomenon of modern battle was very different from that experienced by entrenched combatants. Finally given a chance to take the wheel, these post-Victorian girls raced motorcars along foreign roads like adventurers exploring new

lands, while their brothers dug deeper into the mud of France. . . . Retrieving the wounded and the dead from deadly positions, these once-decorous daughters had at last been allowed to prove their valor, and they swooped over the wastelands of the war with the energetic love of Wagnerian Valkyries, their mobility alone transporting countless immobilized heroes to safe havens (1983: 438–9).

Not incidentally, women in the United States and England got the vote for their war efforts in the First World War.

Social Bodies and the Bathroom Problem

People of the same racial ethnic group and social class are roughly the same size and shape—but there are many varieties of bodies. People have different genitalia, different secondary sex characteristics, different contributions to procreation, different orgasmic experiences, different patterns of illness and aging. Each of us experiences our bodies differently, and these experiences change as we grow, age, sicken, and die. The bodies of pregnant and non-pregnant women, short and tall people, those with intact and functioning limbs and those whose bodies are physically challenged are all different. But the salient categories of a society group these attributes in ways that ride roughshod over individual experiences and more meaningful clusters of people.

I am not saying that physical differences between male and female bodies don't exist, but that these differences are socially meaningless until social practices transform them into social facts. West Point Military Academy's curriculum is designed to produce leaders, and physical competence is used as a significant measure of leadership ability (Yoder, 1989). When women were accepted as West Point cadets, it became clear that the tests of physical competence, such as rapidly scaling an eight-foot wall, had been constructed for male physiques—pulling oneself up and over using upper-body strength. Rather than devise tests of physical competence for women, West Point provided boosters that mostly women used—but that lost them test points—in the case of the wall, a platform. Finally, the women themselves figured out how to use their bodies successfully. Janice Yoder describes this situation:

> I was observing this obstacle one day, when a woman approached the wall in the old prescribed way, got her fingertips grip, and did an unusual thing: she walked her dangling legs up the wall until she was in a position where both her hands and feet were atop the wall. She then simply pulled up her sagging bottom and went over. She solved the problem by capitalizing on one of women's physical assets: lower-body strength (1989: 530).

In short, if West Point is going to measure leadership capability by physical strength, women's pelvises will do just as well as men's shoulders.

The social transformation of female and male physiology into a condition of inequality is well illustrated by the bathroom problem. Most buildings that have gender-segregated bathrooms have an equal number for women and for men. Where there are crowds, there are always long lines in front of women's bathrooms but rarely in front of men's bathrooms. The cultural, physiological, and demographic combinations of clothing, frequency of urination, menstruation, and childcare add up to generally greater bathroom use by women than men. Thus, although an equal number of bathrooms seems fair, equity would mean more women's bathrooms or allowing women to use men's bathrooms for a certain amount of time (Molotch, 1988).

The bathroom problem is the outcome of the way gendered bodies are differentially evaluated in Western cultures: men's social bodies are the measure of what is 'human'. Gray's *Anatomy*, in use for 100 years, well into the twentieth century, presented the human body as male. The female body was shown only where it differed from the male (Laqueur, 1990). Denise Riley says that if we envisage women's bodies, men's bodies, and human bodies 'as a triangle of identifications, then it is rarely an equilateral triangle in which both sexes are pitched at matching distances from

the apex of the human' (1988: 197). Catharine MacKinnon also contends that in Western society, universal 'humanness' is male because

> virtually every quality that distinguishes men from women is already affirmatively compensated in this society. Men's physiology defines most sports, their needs define auto and health insurance coverage, their socially defined biographies define workplace expectations and successful career patterns, their perspectives and concerns define quality in scholarship, their experiences and obsessions define merit, their objectification of life defines art, their military service defines citizenship, their presence defines family, their inability to get along with each other—their wars and rulerships—define history, their image defines god, and their genitals define sex. For each of their differences from women, what amounts to an affirmative action plan is in effect, otherwise known as the structure and values of American society (1987: 36).

The Paradox of Human Nature

Gendered people do not emerge from physiology or hormones but from the exigencies of the social order, mostly, from the need for a reliable division of the work of food production and the social (not physical) reproduction of new members. The moral imperatives of religion and cultural representations reinforce the boundary lines among genders and ensure that what is demanded, what is permitted, and what is tabooed for the people in each gender is well known and followed by most. Political power, control of scarce resources, and, if necessary, violence uphold the gendered social order in the face of resistance and rebellion. Most people, however, voluntarily go along with their society's prescriptions for those of their gender status because the norms and expectations get built into their sense of worth and identity as a certain kind of human being and because they believe their society's way is the natural way. These beliefs emerge from the imagery that pervades the way we think, the way we see and hear and speak, the way we fantasize, and the way we feel. There is no core or bedrock human nature below these endlessly looping processes of the social production of sex and gender, self and other, identity and psyche, each of which is a 'complex cultural construction' (Butler, 1990: 36). The paradox of 'human nature' is that it is always a manifestation of cultural meanings, social relationships, and power politics—'not biology, but culture, becomes destiny' (Butler, 1990: 8).

Feminist inquiry has long questioned the conventional categories of social science, but much of the current work in feminist sociology has not gone beyond adding the universal category 'women' to the universal category 'men'. Our current debates over the global assumptions of only two categories and the insistence that they must be nuanced to include race and class are steps in the direction I would like to see feminist research go, but race and class are also global categories (Spelman, 1988; Collins, 1990). Deconstructing sex, sexuality, and

gender reveals many possible categories embedded in the social experiences and social practices of what Dorothy Smith calls the 'everyday/everynight world' (1990). These emergent categories group some people together for comparison with other people without prior assumptions about who is like whom. Categories can be broken up and people regrouped differently into new categories for comparison. This process of discovering categories from similarities and differences in people's behaviour or responses can be more meaningful for feminist research than discovering similarities and differences between 'females' and 'males' or 'women' and 'men' because the social construction of the conventional sex and gender categories already assumes differences between them and similarities among them. When we rely only on the conventional categories of sex and gender, we end up finding what we looked for— we see what we believe, whether it is that 'females' and 'males' are essentially different or that 'women' and 'men' are essentially the same.

References

Birrell, S.J. 1988. 'Discourses on the Gender/Sport Relationship: From Women in Sport to Gender Relations', in K. Pandolf, ed., *Exercise and Sport Science Reviews*, Vol. 16. New York: Macmillan.

Birrell, S.J., and S.L. Cole. 1990. 'Double Fault: Renee Richards and the Construction and Naturalization of Difference', *Sociology of Sport Journal* 7: 1–21.

Boutilier, M.A., and L. SanGiovanni. 1983. *The Sporting Woman*. Champaign, IL: Human Kinetics.

Brozan, N. 1978. 'Training Linked to Disruption of Female Reproductive Cycle', *New York Times*, 17 April.

Butler, J. 1990. *Gender Trouble: Feminism and the Subversion of Identity*. New York and London: Routledge & Kegan Paul.

Carlson, A. 1991. 'When Is a Woman Not a Woman?', *Women's Sport and Fitness* (March): 24–9.

Cockburn, C. 1983. *Brothers: Male Dominance and Technological Change*. London: Pluto.

———. 1985. *Machinery of Dominance: Women, Men, and Technical Know-How*. London: Pluto.

Collins, P.H. 1990. *Black Feminist Thought: Knowledge, Consciousness, and the Politics of Empowerment*. Boston: Unwin Hyman.

Connell, R.W. 1987. *Gender and Power*. Stanford, CA: Stanford University Press.

Donato, K.M. 1990. 'Programming for Change? The Growing Demand for Women Systems Analysts', in B.F. Reskin and P.A Roos, eds., *Job Queues, Gender Queues: Explaining Women's Inroads into Male Occupations*. Philadelphia: Temple University Press.

Duff, R.W., and L.K. Hong. 1984. 'Self-images of Women Bodybuilders', *Sociology of Sport Journal* 2: 374–80.

Dunning, E. 1986. 'Sport as a Male Preserve: Notes on the Social Sources of Masculine Identity and Its Transformations', *Theory, Culture, and Society* 3: 79–90.

Eitzen, D.S., and M.B. Zinn. 1989. 'The De-athleticization of Women: The Naming and Gender Marking of Collegiate Sport Teams', *Sociology of Sport Journal* 6: 362–70.

English, J. 1982. 'Sex Equality in Sports', in M. Vetterling-Braggin, ed., *Femininity, Masculinity, and Androgyny*. Boston: Littlefield, Adams.

Epstein, C.F. 1988. *Deceptive Distinctions: Sex, Gender, and the Social Order*. New Haven, CT: Yale University Press.

Fausto-Sterling, A. 1985. *Myths of Gender: Biological Theories about Women and Men.* New York: Basic Books.

Fine, G.A. 1987. *With the Boys: Little League Baseball and Preadolescent Culture.* Chicago: University of Chicago Press.

Foucault, M. 1978. *The History of Sexuality: An Introduction.* R. Hurley, trans. New York: Pantheon.

Gelman, S.A., P. Collman, and E.E. Maccoby. 1986. 'Inferring Properties from Categories versus Inferring Categories from Properties: The Case of Gender', *Child Development* 57: 396–404.

Gilbert, S.M. 1983. 'Soldier's Heart: Literary Men, Literary Women, and the Great War', *Signs: Journal of Women in Culture and Society* 8: 422–50.

Glassner, B. 1992. 'Men and Muscles', in M.S. Kimmel and M.A. Messner, eds., *Men's Lives.* New York: Macmillan.

Hargreaves, J.A., ed. 1982. *Sport, Culture, and Ideology.* London: Routledge & Kegan Paul.

———. 1986. 'Where's the Virtue? Where's the Grace? A Discussion of the Social Production of Gender Relations in and through Sport', *Theory, Culture, and Society* 3: 109–21.

———, ed. 1987. *Computer Chips and Paper Clips: Technology and Women's Employment,* Vol. 2. Washington, DC: National Academy Press.

Hargreaves, J.A., R.E. Kraut, and L.A. Tilly, eds. 1986. *Computer Chips and Paper Clips: Technology and Women's Employment,* Vol. 1. Washington, DC: National Academy Press.

Haskell, M. 1989. 'Hers: He Drives Me Crazy', *New York Times Magazine* (24 September): 26, 28.

Hudson, J. 1978. 'Physical Parameters Used for Female Exclusion from Law Enforcement and Athletics', in C.A. Oglesby, ed., *Women and Sport: From Myth to Reality.* Philadelphia: Lea and Febiger.

Hyde, J.S. 1990. 'Meta-analysis and the Psychology of Gender Differences', *Signs: Journal of Women in Culture and Society* 16: 55–73.

Jaggar, A.M. 1983. *Feminist Politics and Human Nature.* Totowa, NJ: Rowman & Allanheld.

Janofsky, M. 1992. 'Yamaguchi Has the Delicate and Golden Touch', *New York Times,* 22 February.

Kemper, T.D. 1990. *Social Structure and Testosterone: Explorations of the Sociobiosocial Chain.* New Brunswick, NJ: Rutgers University Press.

Kessler, S.J. 1990. 'The Medical Construction of Gender: Case Management of Intersexed Infants', *Signs: Journal of Women in Culture and Society* 16: 3–26.

Kessler, S.J., and W. McKenna. [1978] 1985. *Gender: An Ethnomethodological Approach.* Chicago: University of Chicago Press.

Kolata, G. 1992. 'Track Federation Urges End to Gene Test for Femaleness', *New York Times,* 12 February.

Kramer, P.E., and S. Lehman. 1990. 'Mismeasuring Women: A Critique of Research on Computer Ability and Avoidance', *Signs: Journal of Women in Culture and Society* 16: 158–72.

Laqueur, T. 1990. *Making Sex: Body and Gender from the Greeks to Freud.* Cambridge, ma: Harvard University Press.

Levesque-Lopman, L. 1988. *Claiming Reality: Phenomenology and Women's Experience.* Totowa, NJ: Rowman & Littlefield.

MacKinnon, C. 1987. *Feminism Unmodified.* Cambridge,MA: Harvard University Press.

Majors, R. 1990. 'Cool Pose: Black Masculinity in Sports', in M.A. Messner and D.F. Sabo, eds., *Sport, Men, and the Gender Order: Critical Feminist Perspectives.* Champaign, IL: Human Kinetics.

Mangan, J.A., and R.J. Park. 1987. *From Fair Sex to Feminism: Sport and the Socialization of Women in the Industrial and Post-industrial Eras.* London: Frank Cass.

Messner, M.A. 1988. 'Sports and Male Domination: The Female Athlete as Contested Ideological Terrain', *Sociology of Sport Journal* 5: 197–211.

———. 1992. *Power at Play: Sports and the Problem of Masculinity.* Boston: Beacon Press.

Messner, M.A., M.C. Duncan, and K. Jensen. 1993. 'Separating the Men from the Girls: The Gendered Language of Television Sports', *Gender & Society* 7: 121–37.

Messner, M.A., and D.F. Sabo, eds. 1990. *Sport, Men, and the Gender Order: Critical Feminist Perspectives.* Champaign, IL: Human Kinetics.

Molotch, H. 1988. 'The Restroom and Equal Opportunity', *Sociological Forum* 3: 128–32.

Money, J., and A.A. Ehrhardt. 1972. *Man & Woman, Boy & Girl.* Baltimore, MD: Johns Hopkins University Press.

Moran, M. 1992. 'Title IX: A 20-year Search for Equity', *New York Times* (Sports Section), 21–23 June.

Naftolin, F., and E. Butz, eds. 1981. 'Sexual Dimorphism', *Science* 211: 1263–324.

Olson, W. 1990. 'Beyond Title IX: Toward an Agenda for Women and Sports in the 1990s', *Yale Journal of Law and Feminism* 3: 105–51.

Perry, R., and L. Greber. 1990. 'Women and Computers: An Introduction', *Signs: Journal of Women in Culture and Society* 16: 74–101.

Prior, J.C., Y.M. Yigna, M.T. Shechter, and A.E. Burgess. 1990. 'Spinal Bone Loss and Ovulatory Disturbances', *New England Journal of Medicine* 323: 1221–7.

Richards, R., with J. Ames. 1983. *Second Serve*. New York: Stein and Day.

Riley, D. 1988. *Am I That Name? Feminism and the Category of Women in History*. Minneapolis: University of Minnesota Press.

Scharff, V. 1991. *Taking the Wheel: Women and the Coming of the Motor Age*. New York: Free Press.

Slatton, B., and S. Birrel. 1984. 'The Politics of Women's Sport', *Arena Review* 8 (July).

Smith, D.E. 1990. *The Conceptual Practices of Power: A Feminist Sociology of Knowledge*. Toronto: University of Toronto Press.

Spelman, E. 1988. *Inessential Woman: Problems of Exclusion in Feminist Thought*. Boston: Beacon Press.

Theberge, N. 1987. 'Sport and Women's Empowerment', *Women Studies International Forum* 10: 387–93.

Vecsey, G. 1990. 'Cathy Rigby, Unlike Peter, Did Grow Up', *New York Times* (Sports Section), 19 December.

Watson, T. 1987. 'Women Athletes and Athletic Women: The Dilemmas and Contradictions of Managing Incongruent Identities', *Sociological Inquiry* 57: 431–6.

Willis, P. 1982. 'Women in Sport in Ideology', in J.A. Hargreaves, ed., *Sport, Culture, and Ideology*. London: Routledge & Kegan Paul.

Wright, B.D., M.M. Ferree, G.O. Mellow, L.H. Lewis, M-L.D. Samper, R. Asher, and K. Claspell, eds. 1987. *Women, Work, and Technology: Transformations*. Ann Arbor, MI: University of Michigan Press.

Yoder, J.D. 1989. 'Women at West Point: Lessons for Token Women in Male-dominated Occupations', in J. Freeman, ed., *Women: A Feminist Perspective*, 4th ed. Palo Alto, CA: Mayfield.

Zimmerman, J., ed. 1983. *The Technological Woman: Interfacing with Tomorrow*. New York: Praeger.

CHAPTER 4

The Five Sexes:
Why Male and Female Are Not Enough

Anne Fausto-Sterling

In 1843 Levi Suydam, a 23-year-old resident of Salisbury, Connecticut, asked the town board of selectmen to validate his right to vote as a Whig in a hotly contested local election. The request raised a flurry of objections from the opposition party, for reasons that must be rare in the annals of American democracy: it was said that Suydam was more female than male and thus (some 80 years before suffrage was extended to women) could not be allowed to cast a ballot. To settle the dispute a physician, one William James Barry, was brought in to examine Suydam. And, presumably upon encountering a phallus, the good doctor declared the prospective voter male. With Suydam safely in their column the Whigs won the election by a majority of one.

Barry's diagnosis, however, turned out to be somewhat premature. Within a few days he discovered that, phallus notwithstanding, Suydam menstruated regularly and had a vaginal opening. Both his/her physique and his/her mental predispositions were more complex than was first suspected. S/he had narrow shoulders and broad hips and felt occasional sexual yearnings for women. Suydam's 'feminine propensities, such as a fondness for gay colors, for pieces of calico, comparing and placing them together, and an aversion for bodily labor, and an inability to perform the same, were remarked by many,' Barry later wrote. It is not clear whether Suydam lost or retained the vote, or whether the election results were reversed.

Western culture is deeply committed to the idea that there are only two sexes. Even language refuses other possibilities; thus to write about Levi Suydam I have had to invent conventions—*s/he* and *his/her*—to denote someone who is clearly neither male nor female or who is perhaps both sexes at once. Legally, too, every adult is either man or woman, and the difference, of course, is not trivial. For Suydam it meant the franchise; today it means being available for, or exempt from, draft registration, as well as being subject, in various ways, to a number of laws governing marriage, the family, and human intimacy. In many parts of the United States, for instance, two people legally registered as men cannot have sexual relations without violating anti-sodomy statutes.

But if the state and the legal system have an interest in maintaining a two-party sexual system, they are in defiance of nature. For biologically speaking, there are many gradations running from female to male; and depending on how one calls the shots, one can argue that along that spectrum lie at least five sexes—and perhaps even more.

For some time medical investigators have recognized the concept of the intersexual body. But the standard medical literature uses the term *intersex* as a catch-all for three major subgroups with some mixture of male and female characteristics: the so-called true hermaphrodites, whom I call herms, who possess one testis and one ovary (the sperm-and egg-producing vessels, or gonads); the male pseudohermaphrodites (the 'merms'), who have testes and some aspects of the female genitalia but no ovaries; and the female pseudohermaphrodites (the 'ferms'), who have ovaries and some aspects of the male genitalia but lack testes. Each of those categories is in itself complex; the percentage of male and female characteristics, for instance, can vary enormously among members of the same subgroup. Moreover, the inner lives of the people in each subgroup—their special needs and their problems, attractions, and repulsions—have gone unexplored by science. But on the basis of what is known about them, I suggest that the

three intersexes, herm, merm, and ferm, deserve to be considered additional sexes each in its own right. Indeed, I would argue further that sex is a vast, infinitely malleable continuum that defies the constraints of even five categories.

Not surprisingly, it is extremely difficult to estimate the frequency of intersexuality, much less the frequency of each of the three additional sexes: it is not the sort of information one volunteers on a job application. The psychologist John Money of Johns Hopkins University, a specialist in the study of congenital sexual-organ defects, suggests intersexuals may constitute as many as 4 per cent of births. As I point out to my students at Brown University, in a student body of about 6,000, that fraction, if correct, implies there may be as many as 240 intersexuals on campus—surely enough to form a minority caucus of some kind.

In reality though, few such students would make it as far as Brown in sexually diverse form. Recent advances in physiology and surgical technology now enable physicians to catch most intersexuals at the moment of birth. Almost at once such infants are entered into a program of hormonal and surgical management so that they can slip quietly into society as 'normal' heterosexual males or females. I emphasize that the motive is in no way conspiratorial. The aims of the policy are genuinely humanitarian, reflecting the wish that people be able to 'fit in' both physically and psychologically. In the medical community, however, the assumptions behind that wish—that there be only two sexes, that heterosexuality alone is normal, that there is one true model of psychological health—have gone virtually unexamined.

The word *hermaphrodite* comes from the Greek names Hermes, variously known as the messenger of the gods, the patron of music, the controller of dreams, or the protector of livestock, and Aphrodite, the goddess of sexual love and beauty. According to Greek mythology, those two gods parented Hermaphroditus, who at age fifteen became half male and half female when his body fused with the body of a nymph he fell in love with. In some true hermaphrodites the testis and the ovary grow separately but bilaterally; in others they grow together within the same organ, forming an ovotestis. Not infrequently, at least one of the gonads functions quite well, producing either sperm cells or eggs, as well as functional levels of the sex hormones—androgens or estrogens. Although in theory it might be possible for a true hermaphrodite to become both father and mother to a child, in practice the appropriate ducts and tubes are not configured so that egg and sperm can meet.

In contrast with the true hermaphrodites, the pseudohermaphrodites possess two gonads of the same kind along with the usual male (XY) or female (XX) chromosomal makeup. But their external genitalia and secondary sex characteristics do not match their chromosomes. Thus merms have testes and XY chromosomes, yet they also have a vagina and a clitoris, and at puberty they often develop breasts. They do not menstruate, however. Ferms have ovaries, two X chromosomes and sometimes a uterus, but they also have at least partly masculine external genitalia. Without medical intervention they can develop beards, deep voices and adult-size penises.

Intersexuality itself is old news. Hermaphrodites, for instance, are often featured in stories about human origins. Early biblical scholars believed Adam began life as a hermaphrodite and later divided into two people—a male and a female—after falling from grace. According to Plato there once were three sexes—male, female, and hermaphrodite—but the third sex was lost with time.

Both the Talmud and the Tosefta, the Jewish books of law, list extensive regulations for people of mixed sex. The Tosefta expressly forbids hermaphrodites to inherit their fathers' estates (like daughters), to seclude themselves with women (like sons), or to shave (like men). When hermaphrodites menstruate they must be isolated from men (like women); they are disqualified from serving as witnesses or as priests (like women), but the laws of pederasty apply to them.

In Europe a pattern emerged by the end of the Middle Ages that, in a sense, has lasted to the present day: hermaphrodites were compelled to choose an established gender role and stick with it. The penalty for transgression was often death. Thus in the 1600s a Scottish hermaphrodite living as a woman was buried alive after impregnating his/her master's daughter.

For questions of inheritance, legitimacy, paternity, succession to title, and eligibility for certain professions to be determined, modern Anglo-Saxon legal systems require that newborns be registered as either male or female. In the United States today, state laws govern sex determination. Illinois permits adults to change the sex recorded on their birth certificates should a physician attest to having performed the appropriate surgery. The New York Academy of Medicine, on the other hand, has taken an opposite view. In spite of surgical alterations of the external genitalia, the academy argued in 1966, the chromosomal sex remains the same. By that measure, a person's wish to conceal his or her original sex cannot outweigh the public interest in protection against fraud.

During this century the medical community has completed what the legal world began—the complete erasure of any form of embodied sex that does not conform to a male–female, heterosexual pattern. Ironically, a more sophisticated knowledge of the complexity of sexual systems has led to the repression of such intricacy.

In 1937 the urologist Hugh H. Young of Johns Hopkins University published a volume titled *Genital Abnormalities, Hermaphroditism and Related Adrenal Diseases*. The book is remarkable for its erudition, scientific insight, and open-mindedness. In it Young drew together a wealth of carefully documented case histories to demonstrate and study the medical treatment of such 'accidents of birth'. Young did not pass judgment on the people he studied, nor did he attempt to coerce into treatment those intersexuals who rejected that option. And he showed unusual even-handedness in referring to those people who had had sexual experiences as both men and women as 'practising hermaphrodites'.

One of Young's more interesting cases was a hermaphrodite named Emma who had grown up as a female. Emma had both a penis-size clitoris and a vagina, which made it possible for him/her to have 'normal' heterosexual sex with both men and women. As a teenager Emma had had sex with a number of girls to whom s/he was deeply attracted; but at the age of nineteen s/he had married a man. Unfortunately, he had given Emma little sexual pleasure (though he had had no complaints), and so throughout that marriage and subsequent ones Emma had kept girlfriends on the side. With some frequency s/he had pleasurable sex with them. Young describes his subject as appearing 'to be quite content and even happy'. In conversation, Emma occasionally told him of his/her wish to be a man, a circumstance Young said would be relatively easy to bring about. But Emma's reply strikes a heroic blow for self-interest:

> Would you have to remove that vagina? I don't know about that because that's my meal ticket. If you did that, I would have to quit my husband and go to work, so I think I'll keep it and stay as I am. My husband supports me well, and even though I don't have any sexual pleasure with him, I do have lots with my girlfriends.

Yet even as Young was illuminating intersexuality with the light of scientific reason, he was beginning its suppression. For his book is also an extended treatise on the most modern surgical and hormonal methods of changing intersexuals into either males or females. Young may have differed from his successors in being less judgmental and controlling of the patients and their families, but he nonetheless supplied the foundation on which current intervention practices were built.

By 1969, when the English physicians Christopher J. Dewhurst and Ronald R. Gordon wrote *The Intersexual Disorders*, medical and surgical approaches to intersexuality had neared a state of rigid uniformity. It is hardly surprising that such a hardening of opinion took place in the era of the feminine mystique—of the post–Second World War flight to the suburbs and the strict division of family roles according to sex. That the medical consensus was not quite universal (or perhaps that it seemed poised to break apart again) can be gleaned from the near-hysterical tone of Dewhurst and Gordon's book, which contrasts markedly with the calm reason of Young's founding work. Consider their opening description of an intersexual newborn:

> One can only attempt to imagine the anguish of the parents. That a newborn should have a deformity . . . [affecting] so fundamental an issue as the very sex of the child . . . is a tragic event which immediately conjures up visions of a hopeless psychological misfit doomed to live always as a sexual freak in loneliness and frustration.

Dewhurst and Gordon warned that such a miserable fate would, indeed, be a baby's lot should the case be improperly managed; 'but fortunately,' they wrote, 'with correct management the outlook is infinitely better than the poor parents—emotionally stunned by the event—or indeed anyone without special knowledge could ever imagine.'

Scientific dogma has held fast to the assumption that without medical care hermaphrodites are doomed to a life of misery. Yet there are few empirical studies to back up that assumption, and some of the same research gathered to build a case for medical treatment contradicts it. Francis Benton, another of Young's practising hermaphrodites, 'had not worried over his condition, did not wish to be changed, and was enjoying life'. The same could be said of Emma, the opportunistic hausfrau. Even Dewhurst and Gordon, adamant about the psychological importance of treating intersexuals at the infant stage, acknowledged great success in 'changing the sex' of older patients. They reported on 20 cases of children reclassified into a different sex after the supposedly critical age of 18 months. They asserted that all the reclassifications were 'successful,' and they wondered then whether re-registration could be 'recommended more readily than [had] been suggested so far'.

The treatment of intersexuality in this century provides a clear example of what the French historian Michel Foucault has called biopower. The knowledge developed in biochemistry, embryology, endocrinology, psychology, and surgery has enabled physicians to control the very sex of the human body. The multiple contradictions in that kind of power call for some scrutiny. On the one hand, the medical 'management' of intersexuality certainly developed as part of an attempt to free people from perceived psychological pain (though whether the pain was the patient's, the parents', or the physician's is unclear). And if one accepts the assumption that in a sex-divided culture, people can realize their greatest potential for happiness and productivity only if they are sure they belong to one of only two acknowledged sexes, modern medicine has been extremely successful.

On the other hand, the same medical accomplishments can be read not as progress but as a mode of discipline. Hermaphrodites have unruly bodies. They do not fall naturally into a binary classification; only a surgical shoehorn can put them there. But why should we care if a 'woman', defined as one who has breasts, a vagina, a uterus and ovaries, and who menstruates, also has a clitoris large enough to penetrate the vagina of another woman? Why should we care if there are people whose biological equipment enables them to have sex 'naturally' with both men and women? The answers seem to lie in a cultural need to maintain clear distinctions between the sexes. Society mandates the control of intersexual bodies because they blur and bridge the great divide. Inasmuch as hermaphrodites literally embody both sexes, they challenge traditional beliefs about sexual difference: they possess the irritating ability to live sometimes as one sex and sometimes the other, and they raise the spectre of homosexuality.

But what if things were altogether different? Imagine a world in which the same knowledge that has enabled medicine to intervene in the management of intersexual patients has been placed at the service of multiple sexualities. Imagine that the sexes have multiplied beyond currently imaginable limits. It would have to be a world of shared powers. Patient and physician, parent and child, male and female, heterosexual and homosexual—all those oppositions and others would have to be dissolved as sources of division. A new ethic of medical treatment would arise, one that would permit ambiguity in a culture that had overcome sexual division. The central mission of medical treatment would be to preserve life. Thus hermaphrodites would be concerned primarily not about whether they can conform to society but about whether they might develop potentially life-threatening conditions—hernias, gonadal tumours, salt imbalances caused by adrenal malfunctions—that sometimes accompany hermaphroditic development. In my ideal world, medical intervention for intersexuals would take place only rarely before the age of reason; subsequent treatment would be a co-operative venture between physician, patient, and other advisers trained in issues of gender multiplicity.

I do not pretend that the transition to my utopia would be smooth. Sex, even the supposedly 'normal', heterosexual kind, continues to cause untold anxieties in Western society. And certainly a culture that has yet to come to grips—religiously and, in some states, legally—with the ancient and relatively uncomplicated reality of homosexual love will not readily embrace intersexuality. No doubt the most troublesome arena by far would be the rearing of children. Parents, at least since the Victorian era, have fretted, sometimes to the point of outright denial, over the fact that their children are sexual beings.

All that and more amply explains why intersexual children are generally squeezed into one of the two prevailing sexual categories. But what would be the psychological consequences of taking the alternative road—raising children as unabashed intersexuals? On the surface, that tack seems fraught with peril. What, for example, would happen to the intersexual child amid the unrelenting cruelty of the schoolyard? When the time came to shower in gym class, what horrors and humiliations would await the intersexual as his/her anatomy was displayed in all its nontraditional glory? In whose gym class would s/he register to begin with? What bathroom would s/he use? And how on earth would Mom and Dad help shepherd him/her through the minefield of puberty?

In the past 30 years those questions have been ignored, as the scientific community has, with remarkable unanimity, avoided contemplating the alternative route of unimpeded intersexuality. But modern investigators tend to overlook a substantial body of case histories, most of them compiled between 1930 and 1960, before surgical intervention became rampant. Almost without exception, those reports describe children who grew up knowing they were intersexual (though they did not advertise it) and adjusted to their unusual status. Some of the studies are richly detailed—described at the level of gym-class showering (which most intersexuals avoided without incident); in any event, there is not a psychotic or a suicide in the lot.

Still, the nuances of socialization among intersexuals cry out for more sophisticated analysis. Clearly, before my vision of sexual multiplicity can be realized, the first openly intersexual children and their parents will have to be brave pioneers who will bear the brunt of society's growing pains. But in the long view—though it could take generations to achieve—the prize might be a society in which sexuality is something to be celebrated for its subtleties and not something to be feared or ridiculed.

Postscript

For an account of developments that occurred in the decade after I wrote this article, please see my 10-year follow-up piece, `The Five Sexes, Revisted', which is available online at http://www. neiu.edu/~lsfuller/5sexesrevisited.htm.

QUESTIONS FOR CRITICAL THOUGHT

1. Imagine waking up tomorrow and reading in the newspaper that a team of scientists has proven conclusively, emphatically, and beyond all doubt that all gender differences are based in biology and that men and women are biologically 'programmed' to behave as they do. How might this change the way you think about your life?

2. Sapolsky argues that attributing male aggression to testosterone is a misleading oversimplification of a complex set of biological processes. Do you know of any other biological processes that have been subject to similar oversimplification?

3. Why has so much time, money, and effort been invested in trying to determine whether gender differences are attributable to biology? Why has this particular research area been so active and so controversial?

4. What do you think about Buss's argument that physical asymmetries between the sexes in reproductive capacities have produced major differences in gendered behaviour?

5. Do you believe that the differences between males and females have been exaggerated, as Lorber does? Or do you believe that these differences have not been sufficiently appreciated? Or are you not sure?

6. Fausto-Sterling imagines a utopian world in which intersexuality would be viewed not as a deviation from a rigid two-sex model, but as just one of the many variations in human bodies. How might this world be different from the one you live in now?

PART II

Cultural Constructions of Gender

I f gender is not just a gloss on physical sex differences, what is it? To say that gender differences and relations are cultural is to state the very obvious. However, no one has yet come up with an uncontested definition of what 'culture' is. Sociologists and anthropologists have wrestled over the term, defining it variously as, among other things, a learned system of assigning meanings to experiences; the collective concepts and ideas with which individuals interpret their world; and the sum total of behaviour patterns, values, ideas, and preferences that characterize a society. In decades past, anthropologists tended to focus on more on the intangible, conceptual aspects of culture, such as religious beliefs or kinship systems, while sociologists focused more on how power was exercised in very material ways, through studies of criminology and 'deviance' or through studying changes in forms of economic production. However, this distinction no longer holds, as both sociologists and anthropologists study the interaction of symbolic systems with the distribution of power.

Within gender studies, the central contribution of 'culture', regardless of how it is defined, is that masculinity and femininity are enacted in very different ways, in different times and places. There are some broad tendencies, to be sure—such as the disproportionate responsibility women bear for maintaining the health and well-being of family members, or the relatively greater sexual latitude accorded to men, but for every one of these generalizations, exceptions can be found.

Twenty anthologies the size of this one could be devoted to gender and culture, without even beginning to scratch the surface of the subject. The readings in this section are intended to give you some insight into how one might think about the ways in which culture creates gender, and vice versa.

We open with one of the classic statements on gender and culture. Candace West and Don Zimmerman's foundational article on gender as something that is enacted in everyday life clarifies and develops the concept of 'doing gender'. From this perspective, gender is not a way of dividing the human race into two groups, nor is it a quality possessed by individuals, objects, or situations. Instead, gender exists as interpersonal actions; an infinite set of interpersonal encounters through patterns and variations emerge, related to the gender of the actor.

Tabassum Ruby examines the symbolic meanings assigned to the *hijab*, the veil worn by some devout Muslim women. Wearing *hijab* is clearly a gendered behaviour, one of many rules and practices that mark out the difference between genders. However,

Ruby demonstrates that this powerful cultural symbol carries multiple meanings for the women who adopt it. Wearing *hijab* is undoubtedly doing femininity, but for the women who take it up, the gendered meanings of the veil are diverse and variable.

Shauna Pomerantz, Dawn Currie, and Deirdre Kelly take on a classic anthropological subject—the workings of a subculture existing within a larger society. Their study of female youth skater culture in Vancouver demonstrates the tension between what they define as 'emphasized femininity'—undoubtedly a carryover from the non-skater world—and a new subcultural way of doing femininity enacted by the Park Gang of skater girls.

The transgendered people studied by Patricia Gagne, Richard Tewksbury, and Deanne McGaughey have to do gender in a way that is much more deliberate and self-conscious than it is for most non-transgendered people. Their efforts to pass as members of their desired gender demonstrate how much work is involved in maintaining the cultural architecture of gender, and how difficult it is to 'cross the line' into the territory of the other gender.

In a twist on the 'doing gender' approach to studying daily life, the women interviewed by Nancy Theberge insist that they do not in fact do gender when they are on the ice, and that they are emphatically not creating a feminized version of hockey. By distancing themselves from the idea of 'women's hockey', these players may be unintentionally reinforcing a binary opposition of gendered sport, in which the 'feminized' variant is an inferior knock-off of the original. This is especially salient for hockey, which, Theberge argues, has come to symbolize the idealized form of Canadian sport (and of Canadian masculinity).

CHAPTER 5

Doing Gender

Candace West and Don H. Zimmerman

In the beginning, there was sex and there was gender. Those of us who taught courses in the area in the late 1960s and early 1970s were careful to distinguish one from the other. Sex, we told students, was what was ascribed by biology: anatomy, hormones, and physiology. Gender, we said, was an achieved status: that which is constructed through psychological, cultural, and social means. To introduce the difference between the two, we drew on singular case studies of hermaphrodites and anthropological investigations of 'strange and exotic tribes'.

Inevitably (and understandably), in the ensuing weeks of each term, our students became confused. Sex hardly seemed a 'given' in the context of research that illustrated the sometimes ambiguous and often conflicting criteria for its ascription. And gender seemed much less an 'achievement' in the context of the anthropological, psychological, and social imperatives we studied—the division of labour, the formation of gender identities, and the social subordination of women by men. Moreover, the received doctrine of gender socialization theories conveyed the strong message that while gender may be 'achieved', by about age five, it was certainly fixed, unvarying, and static—much like sex.

Since about 1975, the confusion has intensified and spread far beyond our individual classrooms. For one thing, we learned that the relationship between biological and cultural processes was far more complex—and reflexive—than we previously had supposed. For another, we discovered that certain structural arrangements, for example, between work and family, actually produce or enable some capacities, such as to mother, that we formerly associated with biology. In the midst of all this, the notion of gender as a recurring achievement somehow fell by the wayside.

Our purpose in this article is to propose an ethnomethodologically informed, and therefore distinctively sociological, understanding of gender as a routine, methodical, and recurring accomplishment. We contend that the 'doing' of gender is undertaken by women and men whose competence as members of society is hostage to its production. Doing gender involves a complex of socially guided perceptual, interactional, and micropolitical activities that cast particular pursuits as expressions of masculine and feminine 'natures'.

When we view gender as an accomplishment, an achieved property of situated conduct, our attention shifts from matters internal to the individual and focuses on interactional and, ultimately, institutional arenas. In one sense, of course, it is individuals who 'do' gender. But it is a situated doing, carried out in the virtual or real presence of others who are presumed to be oriented to its production. Rather than as a property of individuals, we conceive of gender as an emergent feature of social situations: both as an outcome of and a rationale for various social arrangements and as a means of legitimating one of the most fundamental divisions of society.

To advance our argument, we undertake a critical examination of what sociologists have meant by *gender*, including its treatment as a role enactment in the conventional sense and as a 'display' in Goffman's (1976) terminology. Both *gender role* and *gender display* focus on behavioural aspects of being a woman or a man (as opposed, for example, to biological differences between the two). However, we contend that the notion of gender as a role obscures the work that is involved in producing gender in everyday activities, while the notion of gender as a display relegates it to the periphery of interaction. We argue, instead, that participants in interaction organize their various and manifold activities to reflect or express gender, and they are disposed to perceive the behaviour of others in a similar light.

To elaborate our proposal, we suggest at the outset that important but often overlooked distinctions be observed among *sex, sex category*, and *gender*. *Sex* is a determination made through the application of socially agreed upon biological criteria for classifying persons as females or males. The criteria for classification can be genitalia at birth or chromosomal typing before birth, and they do not necessarily agree with one another. Placement in a *sex category* is achieved through application of the sex criteria, but in everyday life, categorization is established and sustained by the socially required identificatory displays that proclaim one's membership in one or the other category. In this sense, one's sex category presumes one's sex and stands as proxy for it in many situations, but sex and sex category can vary independently; that is, it is possible to claim membership in a sex category even when the sex criteria are lacking. *Gender*, in contrast, is the activity of managing situated conduct in light of normative conceptions of attitudes and activities appropriate for one's sex category. Gender activities emerge from and bolster claims to membership in a sex category.

We contend that recognition of the analytical independence of sex, sex category, and gender is essential for understanding the relationships among these elements and the interactional work involved in 'being' a gendered person in society. While our primary aim is theoretical, there will be occasion to discuss fruitful directions for empirical research following from the formulation of gender that we propose.

We begin with an assessment of the received meaning of gender, particularly in relation to the roots of this notion in presumed biological differences between women and men.

Perspectives on Sex and Gender

In Western societies, the accepted cultural perspective on gender views women and men as naturally and unequivocally defined categories of being, with distinctive psychological and behavioural propensities that can be predicted from their reproductive functions. Competent adult members of these societies see differences between the two as fundamental and enduring—differences seemingly supported by the division of labour into women's and men's work and an often elaborate differentiation of feminine and masculine attitudes and behaviours that are prominent features of social organization. Things are the way they are by virtue of the fact that men are men and women are women—a division perceived to be natural and rooted in biology, producing, in turn, profound psychological, behavioural, and social consequences. The structural arrangements of a society are presumed to be responsive to these differences.

Analyses of sex and gender in the social sciences, though less likely to accept uncritically the naive biological determinism of the view just presented, often retain a conception of sex-linked behaviours and traits as essential properties of individuals. The 'sex differences approach' is more commonly attributed to psychologists than to sociologists, but the survey researcher who determines the 'gender' of respondents on the basis of the sound of their voices over the telephone is also making trait-oriented assumptions. Reducing gender to a fixed set of psychological traits or to a unitary 'variable' precludes serious consideration of the ways it is used to structure distinct domains of social experience.

Taking a different tack, role theory has attended to the social construction of gender categories, called 'sex roles' or, more recently, 'gender roles' and has analyzed how these are learned and enacted. Beginning with Linton (1936) and continuing through the works of Parsons (Parsons, 1951; Parsons and Bales, 1955) and Komarovsky (1946, 1950), role theory has emphasized the social and dynamic aspect of role construction and enactment. But at the level of face-to-face interaction, the application of role theory to gender poses problems of its own. Roles are *situated* identities—assumed and relinquished as the situation demands—rather than *master identities*, such as the sex category, that cut across situations. Unlike most roles, such as 'nurse', 'doctor', and 'patient', or 'professor' and 'student', gender has no specific site or organizational context.

Moreover, many roles are already gender marked, so that special qualifiers—such as 'female doctor' or 'male nurse'—must be added to exceptions to the rule. Thorne (1980) observes that conceptualizing gender as a role makes it difficult to assess its influence on other roles and reduces its explanatory usefulness in discussions of power and inequality. Drawing on Rubin (1975), Thorne calls for a reconceptualization of women and men as distinct social groups, constituted in 'concrete, historically changing—and generally unequal—social relationships' (Thorne, 1980: 11).

We argue that gender is not a set of traits, nor a variable, nor a role, but the product of social doings of some sort. What then is the social doing of gender? It is more than the continuous creation of the meaning of gender through human actions. We claim that gender itself is constituted through interaction. To develop the implications of our claim, we turn to Goffman's (1976) account of 'gender display'. Our object here is to explore how gender might be exhibited or portrayed through interaction, and thus be seen as 'natural', while it is being produced as a socially organized achievement.

Gender Display

Goffman contends that when human beings interact with others in their environment, they assume that each possesses an 'essential nature'— a nature that can be discerned through the 'natural signs given off or expressed by them' (1976: 75). Femininity and masculinity are regarded as 'proto-types of essential expression—something that can be conveyed fleetingly in any social situation and yet something that strikes at the most basic charac-terization of the individual' (1976: 75). The means through which we provide such expressions are 'perfunctory, conventionalized acts' (1976: 69), which convey to others our regard for them, indi-cate our alignment in an encounter, and tenta-tively establish the terms of contact for that social situation. But they are also regarded as expressive behaviour, testimony to our 'essential natures'.

Goffman (1976) sees *displays* as highly con-ventionalized behaviours structured as two-part exchanges of the statement–reply type, in which the presence or absence of symmetry can establish deference or dominance. These rituals are viewed as distinct from but articulated with more con-sequential activities, such as performing tasks or engaging in discourse. Hence, we have what he terms the 'scheduling' of displays at junctures in activities, such as the beginning or end, to avoid interfering with the activities themselves. Goffman formulates *gender display* as follows:

> If gender be defined as the culturally estab-lished correlates of sex (whether in conse-quence of biology or learning), then gender display refers to conventionalized portrayals of these correlates (1976: 69).

These gendered expressions might reveal clues to the underlying, fundamental dimensions of the female and male, but they are, in Goffman's view, optional performances. Masculine courtesies may or may not be offered and, if offered, may or may not be declined (1976: 71). Moreover, human beings 'themselves employ the term "expression", and conduct themselves to fit their own notions of expressivity' (1976: 75). Gender depictions are less a consequence of our 'essential sexual natures' than interactional portrayals of what we would like to convey about sexual natures, using convention-alized gestures. Our human nature gives us the ability to learn to produce and recognize masculine and feminine gender displays—'a capacity [we]

have by virtue of being persons, not males and females' (1976: 76).

Upon first inspection, it would appear that Goffman's formulation offers an engaging socio-logical corrective to existing formulations of gender. In his view, gender is a socially scripted dramatization of the culture's *idealization* of femin-ine and masculine natures, played for an audience that is well schooled in the presentational idiom. To continue the metaphor, there are scheduled performances presented in special locations, and like plays, they constitute introductions to, or time out from, more serious activities.

There are fundamental equivocations in this perspective. By segregating gender display from the serious business of interaction, Goffman obscures the effects of gender on a wide range of human activities. Gender is not merely something that happens in the nooks and crannies of inter-action, fitted in here and there and not interfering with the serious business of life. While it is plaus-ible to contend that gender displays—construed as conventionalized expressions—are optional, it does not seem plausible to say that we have the option of being seen by others as female or male.

It is necessary to move beyond the notion of gender display to consider what is involved in doing gender as an ongoing activity embedded in every-day interaction. Toward this end, we return to the distinctions among sex, sex category, and gender introduced earlier.

Sex, Sex Category, and Gender

Garfinkel's (1967) case study of Agnes, a transsex-ual raised as a boy who adopted a female iden-tity at age 17 and underwent a sex reassignment operation several years later, demonstrates how gender is created through interaction and, at the same time, structures interaction. Agnes, whom Garfinkel characterized as a 'practical methodolo-gist', developed a number of procedures for passing as a 'normal, natural female' both prior to and after her surgery. She had the practical task of managing the fact that she possessed male genitalia and that she lacked the social resources a girl's biography would presumably provide in everyday interaction.

In short, she needed to display herself as a woman, simultaneously learning what it was to be a woman. Of necessity, this full-time pursuit took place at a time when most people's gender would be well-accredited and routinized. Agnes had to consciously contrive what the vast majority of women do without thinking. She was not 'faking' what 'real' women do naturally. She was obliged to analyze and figure out how to act within socially structured circumstances and conceptions of femininity that women born with appropriate biological credentials come to take for granted early on. As in the case of others who must 'pass', such as transvestites, Kabuki actors, or Dustin Hoffman's 'Tootsie', Agnes's case makes visible what culture has made invisible—the accomplishment of gender.

Garfinkel's (1967) discussion of Agnes does not explicitly separate three analytically distinct, although empirically overlapping, concepts—sex, sex category, and gender.

Sex

Agnes did not possess the socially agreed-upon biological criteria for classification as a member of the female sex. Still, Agnes regarded herself as a female, albeit a female with a penis, which a woman ought not to possess. The penis, she insisted, was a 'mistake' in need of remedy (Garfinkel, 1967). Like other competent members of our culture, Agnes honoured the notion that there are 'essential' biological criteria that unequivocally distinguish females from males. However, if we move away from the commonsense viewpoint, we discover that the reliability of these criteria is not beyond question. Moreover, other cultures have acknowledged the existence of 'cross-genders' and the possibility of more than two sexes.

More central to our argument is Kessler and McKenna's (1978) point that genitalia are conventionally hidden from public inspection in everyday life; yet we continue, through our social rounds, to 'observe' a world of two naturally, normally sexed persons. It is the *presumption* that essential criteria exist, and would or should be there if looked for, that provides the basis for sex categorization. Drawing on Garfinkel, Kessler and McKenna argue that 'female' and 'male' are cultural events—products of

what they term the 'gender attribution process'—rather than some collection of traits, behaviours, or even physical attributes. Illustratively, they cite the child who, viewing a picture of someone clad in a suit and a tie, contends, 'It's a man, because he has a pee-pee' (Kessler and McKenna, 1978: 154). Translation: 'He must have a pee-pee [an essential characteristic] because I see the *insignia* of a suit and tie.' Neither initial sex assignment (pronouncement at birth as a female or male) nor the actual existence of essential criteria for that assignment (possession of a clitoris and vagina or penis and testicles) has much—if anything—to do with the identification of sex category in everyday life. There, Kessler and McKenna note, we operate with a moral certainty of a world of two sexes. We do not think, 'Most persons with penises are men, but some may not be' or 'Most persons who dress as men have penises.' Rather, we take it for granted that sex and sex category are congruent—that knowing the latter, we can deduce the rest.

Sex Categorization

Agnes's claim to the categorical status of female, which she sustained by appropriate identificatory displays and other characteristics, could be *discredited* before her transsexual operation, if her possession of a penis became known, and after by her surgically constructed genitalia. In this regard, Agnes had to be continually alert to actual or potential threats to the security of her sex category. Her problem was not so much about living up to some prototype of essential femininity but preserving her categorization as female. This task was made easy for her by a very powerful resource, namely, the process of commonsense categorization in everyday life.

The categorization of members of society into indigenous categories such as 'girl' or 'boy', or 'woman' or 'man', operates in a distinctively social way. The act of categorization does not involve a positive test, in the sense of a well-defined set of criteria that must be explicitly satisfied prior to making an identification. Rather, the application of membership categories relies on an 'if–can' test in everyday interaction. This test stipulates that if people *can be seen* as members of relevant categories, *then categorize them that way*. That is, use the category that seems appropriate, except in the presence of discrepant information or obvious features that would rule out its use. This procedure is quite in keeping with the attitude of everyday life, which has us take appearances at face value unless we have special reason to doubt. It should be added that it is precisely when we have special reason to doubt that the issue of applying rigorous criteria arises, but it is rare, outside legal or bureaucratic contexts, to encounter insistence on positive tests.

Agnes's initial resource was the predisposition of those she encountered to take her appearance (her figure, clothing, hair style, and so on), as the undoubted appearance of a normal female. Her further resource was our cultural perspective on the properties of 'natural, normally sexed persons'. Garfinkel (1967) notes that in everyday life, we live in a world of two—and only two—sexes. This arrangement has a moral status, in that we include ourselves and others in it as 'essentially, originally, in the first place, always have been, always will be, once and for all, in the final analysis, either "male" or "female"' (Garfinkel, 1967: 122). Consider the following case:

> This issue reminds me of a visit I made to a computer store a couple of years ago. The person who answered my questions was truly a *salesperson*. I could not categorize him/her as a woman or a man. What did I look for? (1) Facial hair: She/he was smooth skinned, but some men have little or no facial hair. (This varies by race; Native Americans and Blacks often have none.) (2) Breasts: She/he was wearing a loose shirt that hung from his/her shoulders. And, as many women who suffered through a 1950s' adolescence know to their shame, women are often flat-chested. (3) Shoulders: His/hers were small and round for a man, broad for a woman. (4) Hands: Long and slender fingers, knuckles a bit large for a woman, small for a man. (5) Voice: Middle range, unexpressive for a woman, not at all the exaggerated tones some gay males affect. (6) His/her treatment of me: Gave off no signs that would let me know if I were of the same

or different sex as this person. There were not even any signs that he/she knew his/her sex would be difficult to categorize and I wondered about that even as I did my best to hide these questions so I would not embarrass him/her while we talked of computer paper. I left still not knowing the sex of my salesperson, and was disturbed by that unanswered question (child of my culture that I am) (Diane Margolis, personal communication).

What can this case tell us about situations such as Agnes's or the process of sex categorization in general? First, we infer from this description that the computer salesperson's identificatory display was ambiguous, since she or he was not dressed or adorned in an unequivocally female or male fashion. It is when such a display *fails* to provide grounds for categorization that factors such as facial hair or tone of voice are assessed to determine membership in a sex category. Second, beyond the fact that this incident could be recalled after 'a couple of years', the customer was not only 'disturbed' by the ambiguity of the salesperson's category but also assumed that to acknowledge this ambiguity would be embarrassing to the salesclerk. Not only do we want to know the sex category of those around us (to see it at a glance, perhaps), but we also presume that others are displaying it for us, in as decisive a fashion as they can.

Gender

Agnes attempted to be '120 per cent female' (Garfinkel, 1967: 129)—that is, unquestionably in all ways and at all times feminine. She thought she could protect herself from disclosure before and after surgical intervention by comporting herself in a feminine manner, but she also could have given herself away by overdoing her performance. Sex categorization and the accomplishment of gender are not the same. Agnes's categorization could be secure or suspect, but did not depend on whether or not she lived up to some ideal conception of femininity. Women can be seen as unfeminine, but that does not make them 'unfemale'. Agnes faced an ongoing task of being a woman—something beyond style of dress (an identificatory display) or allowing men to light her cigarette (a gender display). Her problem was to produce configurations of behaviour that would be seen by others as normative gender behaviour.

Agnes's strategy of 'secret apprenticeship', through which she learned expected feminine decorum by carefully attending to her fiancé's criticisms of other women, was one means of masking incompetencies and simultaneously acquiring the needed skills (Garfinkel, 1967). It was through her fiancé that Agnes learned that sunbathing on the lawn in front of her apartment was 'offensive' (because it put her on display to other men). She also learned from his critiques of other women that she should not insist on having things her way and that she should not offer her opinions or claim equality with men (Garfinkel, 1967: 147–8). (Like other women in our society, Agnes learned something about power in the course of her 'education'.)

Popular culture abounds with books and magazines that compile idealized depictions of relations between women and men. Those focused on the etiquette of dating or prevailing standards of feminine comportment are meant to be of practical help in these matters. However, the use of any such source *as a manual of procedure* requires the assumption that doing gender merely involves making use of discrete, well-defined bundles of behaviour that can simply be plugged into interactional situations to produce recognizable enactments of masculinity and femininity. The man 'does' being masculine by, for example, taking the woman's arm to guide her across a street, and she 'does' being feminine by consenting to be guided and not initiating such behaviour with a man.

Agnes could perhaps have used such sources as manuals, but, we contend, doing gender is not so easily regimented. Such sources may list and describe the sorts of behaviours that mark or display gender, but they are necessarily incomplete. And to be successful, marking or displaying gender must be finely fitted to situations and modified or transformed as the occasion demands. Doing gender consists of managing such occasions so that, whatever the particulars, the outcome is seen and seeable in context as gender-appropriate or, as the case may be, gender-*in*appropriate—that is, *accountable*.

Gender and Accountability

As Heritage (1984: 136–7) notes, members of society regularly engage in 'descriptive accountings of states of affairs to one another', and such accounts are both serious and consequential. These descriptions name, characterize, formulate, explain, excuse, excoriate, or merely take notice of some circumstance or activity and thus place it within some social framework (locating it relative to other activities, like and unlike).

Such descriptions are themselves accountable, and societal members orient to the fact that their activities are subject to comment. Actions are often designed with an eye to their accountability—that is, how they might look and how they might be characterized. The notion of accountability also encompasses those actions undertaken so that they are specifically unremarkable and thus not worthy of more than a passing remark, because they are seen to be in accord with culturally approved standards.

Heritage observes that the process of rendering something accountable is interactional in character:

> [This] permits actors to design their actions in relation to their circumstances so as to permit others, by methodically taking account of circumstances, to recognize the action for what it is (1984: 179).

The key word here is *circumstances*. One circumstance that attends virtually all actions is the sex category of the actor. As Garfinkel comments:

> [T]he work and socially structured occasions of sexual passing were obstinately unyielding to [Agnes's] attempts to routinize the grounds of daily activities. This obstinacy points to the *omnirelevance* of sexual status to affairs of daily life as an invariant but unnoticed background in the texture of relevances that compose the changing actual scenes of everyday life (1967: 118, emphasis added).

If sex category is omnirelevant (or even approaches being so), then a person engaged in virtually any activity may be held accountable for performance of that activity as a *woman* or a *man*, and their incumbency in one or the other sex category can be used to legitimate or discredit their other activities. Accordingly, virtually any activity can be assessed as to its womanly or manly nature. And note, to 'do' gender is not always to live up to normative conceptions of femininity or masculinity; it is to engage in behaviour *at the risk of gender assessment*. While it is individuals who do gender, the enterprise is fundamentally interactional and institutional in character, for accountability is a feature of social relationships and its idiom is drawn from the institutional arena in which those relationships are enacted. If this be the case, can we ever *not* do gender? Insofar as a society is partitioned by 'essential' differences between women and men and placement in a sex category is both relevant and enforced, doing gender is unavoidable.

Resources for Doing Gender

Doing gender means creating differences between girls and boys and women and men, differences that are not natural, essential, or biological. Once the differences have been constructed, they are used to reinforce the 'essentialness' of gender. In a delightful account of the 'arrangement between the sexes', Goffman (1977) observes the creation of a variety of institutionalized frameworks through which our 'natural, normal sexedness' can be enacted. The physical features of social setting provide one obvious resource for the expression of our 'essential' differences. For example, the sex segregation of North American public bathrooms distinguishes 'ladies' from 'gentlemen' in matters held to be fundamentally biological, even though both 'are somewhat similar in the question of waste products and their elimination' (Goffman, 1977: 315). These settings are furnished with dimorphic equipment (such as urinals for men or elaborate grooming facilities for women), even though both sexes may achieve the same ends through the same means (and apparently do so in the privacy of their own homes). To be stressed here is the fact that:

> The *functioning* of sex-differentiated organs is involved, but there is nothing in this functioning that biologically recommends segregation; that

arrangement is a totally cultural matter . . . toilet segregation is presented as a natural consequence of the difference between the sex-classes when in fact it is a means of honoring, if not producing, this difference (Goffman, 1977: 316).

Standardized social occasions also provide stages for evocations of the 'essential female and male natures'. Goffman cites organized sports as one such institutionalized framework for the expression of manliness. There, those qualities that ought 'properly' to be associated with masculinity, such as endurance, strength, and competitive spirit, are celebrated by all parties concerned—participants, who may be seen to demonstrate such traits, and spectators, who applaud their demonstrations from the safety of the sidelines (1977: 322).

Assortative mating practices among heterosexual couples afford still further means to create and maintain differences between women and men. For example, even though size, strength, and age tend to be normally distributed among females and males (with considerable overlap between them), selective pairing ensures couples in which boys and men are visibly bigger, stronger, and older (if not 'wiser') than the girls and women with whom they are paired. So, should situations emerge in which greater size, strength, or experience is called for, boys and men will be ever ready to display it and girls and women, to appreciate its display.

Gender may be routinely fashioned in a variety of situations that seem conventionally expressive to begin with, such as those that present 'helpless' women next to heavy objects or flat tires. But, as Goffman notes, heavy, messy, and precarious concerns can be constructed from *any* social situation, 'even though by standards set in other settings, this may involve something that is light, clean, and safe' (Goffman, 1977: 324). Given these resources, it is clear that any interactional situation sets the stage for depictions of 'essential' sexual natures. In sum, these situations 'do not so much allow for the expression of natural differences as for the production of that difference itself' (Goffman, 1977: 324).

Many situations are not clearly sex categorized to begin with, nor is what transpires within them obviously gender relevant. Yet any social encounter can be pressed into service in the interests of doing gender. Thus, Fishman's (1978) research on casual conversations found an asymmetrical 'division of labour' in talk between heterosexual intimates. Women had to ask more questions, fill more silences, and use more attention-getting beginnings in order to be heard. Her conclusions are particularly pertinent here:

> Since interactional work is related to what constitutes being a woman, with what a woman is, the idea that it is work is obscured. The work is not seen as what women do, but as part of what they are (Fishman, 1978: 405).

We would argue that it is precisely such labour that helps to constitute the essential nature of women as women in interactional contexts.

Individuals have many social identities that may be donned or shed, muted or made more salient, depending on the situation. One may be a friend, spouse, professional, citizen, and many other things to many different people—or, to the same person at different times. But we are always women or men—unless we shift into another sex category. What this means is that our identificatory displays will provide an ever-available resource for doing gender under an infinitely diverse set of circumstances.

Some occasions are organized to routinely display and celebrate behaviours that are conventionally linked to one or the other sex category. On such occasions, everyone knows his or her place in the interactional scheme of things. If an individual identified as a member of one sex category engages in behaviour usually associated with the other category, this routinization is challenged. Hughes (1945: 356) provides an illustration of such a dilemma:

> [A] young woman . . . became part of that virile profession, engineering. The designer of an airplane is expected to go up on the maiden flight of the first plane built according to the design. He [sic] then gives a dinner to the engineers and workmen who worked on the new plane. The dinner is naturally a stag party. The young woman in question designed

a plane. Her co-workers urged her not to take the risk—for which, presumably, men only are fit—of the maiden voyage. They were, in effect, asking her to be a lady instead of an engineer. She chose to be an engineer. She then gave the party and paid for it like a man. After food and the first round of toasts, she left like a lady.

On this occasion, parties reached an accommodation that allowed a woman to engage in presumptively masculine behaviours. However, we note that in the end, this compromise permitted demonstration of her 'essential' femininity, through accountably 'ladylike' behaviour.

Hughes (1945: 357) suggests that such contradictions may be countered by managing interactions on a very narrow basis—for example, 'keeping the relationship formal and specific'. But the heart of the matter is that even—perhaps, especially—if the relationship is a formal one, gender is still something one is accountable for. Thus a woman physician (notice the special qualifier in her case) may be accorded respect for her skill and even addressed by an appropriate title. Nonetheless, she is subject to evaluation in terms of normative conceptions of appropriate attitudes and activities for her sex category and under pressure to prove that she is an 'essentially' feminine being, despite appearances to the contrary. Her sex category is used to discredit her participation in important clinical activities, while her involvement in medicine is used to discredit her commitment to her responsibilities as a wife and mother. Simultaneously, her exclusion from the physician colleague community is maintained and her accountability *as a woman* is ensured.

In this context, 'role conflict' can be viewed as a dynamic aspect of our current 'arrangement between the sexes' (Goffman, 1977), an arrangement that provides for occasions on which persons of a particular sex category can 'see' quite clearly that they are out of place and that if they were not there, their current troubles would not exist. What is at stake is, from the standpoint of interaction, the management of our 'essential' natures, and from the standpoint of the individual, the continuing accomplishment of gender. If, as we have argued, sex category is omnirelevant, then any occasion, conflicted or not, offers the resources for doing gender.

We have sought to show that sex category and gender are managed properties of conduct that are contrived with respect to the fact that others will judge and respond to us in particular ways. We have claimed that a person's gender is not simply an aspect of what one is, but, more fundamentally, it is something that one *does*, and does recurrently, in interaction with others.

What are the consequences of this theoretical formulation? If, for example, individuals strive to achieve gender in encounters with others, how does a culture instill the need to achieve it? What is the relationship between the production of gender at the level of interaction and such institutional arrangements as the division of labour in society? And, perhaps most important, how does doing gender contribute to the subordination of women by men?

Research Agendas

To bring the social production of gender under empirical scrutiny, we might begin at the beginning, with a reconsideration of the process through which societal members acquire the requisite categorical apparatus and other skills to become gendered human beings.

Recruitment to Gender Identities

The conventional approach to the process of becoming girls and boys has been sex-role socialization. In recent years, recurring problems arising from this approach have been linked to inadequacies inherent in role theory *per se*—its emphasis on 'consensus, stability and continuity' (Stacey and Thorne, 1985: 307), its ahistorical and depoliticizing focus (Thorne, 1980: 9; Stacey and Thorne, 1985: 307), and the fact that its 'social' dimension relies on 'a general assumption that people choose to maintain existing customs' (Connell, 1985: 263).

In contrast, Cahill (1982, 1986a, 1986b) analyzes the experiences of preschool children using a social model of recruitment into normally gendered identities. Cahill argues that

categorization practices are fundamental to learning and displaying feminine and masculine behaviour. Initially, he observes, children are primarily concerned with distinguishing between themselves and others on the basis of social competence. Categorically, their concern resolves itself into the opposition of 'girl/boy' classification versus 'baby' classification (the latter designating children whose social behaviour is problematic and who must be closely supervised). It is children's concern with being seen as socially competent that evokes their initial claims to gender identities:

> During the exploratory stage of children's socialization . . . they learn that only two social identities are routinely available to them, the identity of 'baby', or, depending on the configuration of their external genitalia, either 'big boy' or 'big girl'. Moreover, others subtly inform them that the identity of 'baby' is a discrediting one. When, for example, children engage in disapproved behavior, they are often told 'You're a baby' or 'Be a big boy.' In effect, these typical verbal responses to young children's behavior convey to them that they must behaviorally choose between the discrediting identity of 'baby' and their anatomically determined sex identity (Cahill, 1986a: 175).

Subsequently, little boys appropriate the gender ideal of 'efficaciousness'—that is, being able to affect the physical and social environment through the exercise of physical strength or appropriate skills. In contrast, little girls learn to value 'appearance'—that is, managing themselves as ornamental objects. Both classes of children learn that the recognition and use of sex categorization in interaction is not optional, but mandatory.

Being a 'girl' or a 'boy' then, is not only being more competent than a 'baby', but also being competently female or male—that is, learning to produce behavioural displays of one's 'essential' female or male identity. In this respect, the task of four- to five-year-old children is very similar to Agnes's:

> For example, the following interaction occurred on a preschool playground. A 55-month-old

boy (D) was attempting to unfasten the clasp of a necklace when a preschool aide walked over to him.

A: Do you want to put that on?
D: No. It's for girls.
A: You don't have to be a girl to wear things around your neck. Kings wear things around their neck. You could pretend that you're a king.
D: I'm not a king. I'm a boy (Cahill, 1986a: 176).

As Cahill notes in this example, although D may have been unclear as to the sex status of a king's identity, he was obviously aware that necklaces are used to announce the identity 'girl'. Having claimed the identity 'boy' and having developed a behavioural commitment to it, he was leery of any display that might furnish grounds for questioning his claim.

In this way, new members of society come to be involved in a *self-regulating process* as they begin to monitor their own and others' conduct with regard to its gender implications. The 'recruitment' process involves not only the appropriation of gender ideals (by the valuation of those ideals as proper ways of being and behaving) but also *gender identities* that are important to individuals and that they strive to maintain. Thus gender differences, or the sociocultural shaping of 'essential female and male natures', achieve the status of objective facts. They are rendered normal, natural features of persons and provide the tacit rationale for differing fates of women and men within the social order.

Additional studies of children's play activities as routine occasions for the expression of gender-appropriate behaviour can yield new insights into how our 'essential natures' are constructed. In particular, the transition from what Cahill (1986a) terms 'apprentice participation' in the sex-segregated worlds that are common among elementary school children to 'bona fide participation' in the heterosocial world so frightening to adolescents is likely to be a keystone in our understanding of the recruitment process.

Gender and the Division of Labour

Whenever people face issues of *allocation*—who is to do what, get what, plan or execute action, direct

or be directed, incumbency in significant social categories such as 'female' and 'male' seems to become pointedly relevant. How such issues are resolved conditions the exhibition, dramatization, or celebration of one's 'essential nature' as a woman or man.

Berk (1985) offers elegant demonstration of this point in her investigation of the allocation of household labour and the attitudes of married couples toward the division of household tasks. Berk found little variation in either the actual distribution of tasks or perceptions of equity in regard to that distribution. Wives, even when employed outside the home, do the vast majority of household and childcare tasks. Moreover, both wives and husbands tend to perceive this as a 'fair' arrangement. Noting the failure of conventional sociological and economic theories to explain this seeming contradiction, Berk contends that something more complex is involved than rational arrangements for the production of household goods and services:

> Hardly a question simply of who has more time, or whose time is worth more, who has more skill or more power, it is clear that a complicated relationship between the structure of work imperatives and the structure of normative expectations attached to work as *gendered* determines the ultimate allocation of members' time to work and home (Berk, 1985: 195–6).

She notes, for example, that the most important factor influencing wives' contribution of labour is the total amount of work demanded or expected by the household; such demands had no bearing on husbands' contributions. Wives reported various rationales (their own and their husbands') that justified their level of contribution and, as a general matter, underscored the presumption that wives are essentially responsible for household production.

Berk contends that it is difficult to see how people 'could rationally establish the arrangements that they do solely for the production of household goods and services' (1985: 201)—much less, how people could consider them 'fair'. She argues that our current arrangements for the domestic division of labour support *two* production processes: household goods and services (meals, clean children, and so on) and, at the same time, gender. As she puts it:

> Simultaneously, members 'do' gender, as they 'do' housework and child care, and what [has] been called the division of labor provides for the joint production of household labor and gender; it is the mechanism by which both the material and symbolic products of the household are realized (1985: 201).

It is not simply that household labour is designated as 'women's work', but that for a woman to engage in it and a man not to engage in it is to draw on and exhibit the 'essential nature' of each. What is produced and reproduced is not merely the activity and artifact of domestic life, but the material embodiment of wifely and husbandly roles, and derivatively, of womanly and manly conduct. What are also frequently produced and reproduced are the dominant and subordinate statuses of the sex categories.

How does gender get done in work settings outside the home, where dominance and subordination are themes of overarching importance? Hochschild's (1983) analysis of the work of flight attendants offers some promising insights. She found that the occupation of flight attendant consisted of something altogether different for women than for men:

> As the company's main shock absorbers against 'mishandled' passengers, their own feelings are more frequently subjected to rough treatment. In addition, a day's exposure to people who resist authority in a woman is a different experience than it is for a man. . . . In this respect, it is a disadvantage to be a woman. And in this case, they are not simply women in the biological sense. They are also a highly visible distillation of middle-class American notions of femininity. They symbolize Woman. Insofar as the category 'female' is mentally associated with having less status and authority, female flight attendants are more readily classified as 'really' females than other females are (1983: 175).

In performing what Hochschild terms the 'emotional labor' necessary to maintain airline profits, women flight attendants simultaneously produce enactments of their 'essential' femininity.

Sex and Sexuality

What is the relationship between doing gender and a culture's prescription of 'obligatory heterosexuality'? As Frye (1983: 22) observes, the monitoring of sexual feelings in relation to other appropriately sexed persons requires the ready recognition of such persons 'before one can allow one's heart to beat or one's blood to flow in erotic enjoyment of that person'. The appearance of heterosexuality is produced through emphatic and unambiguous indicators of one's sex, layered on in ever more conclusive fashion (Frye, 1983: 24). Thus, lesbians and gay men concerned with passing as heterosexuals can rely on these indicators for camouflage; in contrast, those who would avoid the assumption of heterosexuality may foster ambiguous indicators of their categorical status through their dress, behaviours, and style. But 'ambiguous' sex indicators are sex indicators nonetheless. If one wishes to be recognized as a lesbian (or heterosexual woman), one must first establish a categorical status as female. Even as popular images portray lesbians as 'females who are not feminine' (Frye, 1983: 129), the accountability of persons for their 'normal, natural sexedness' is preserved.

Nor is accountability threatened by the existence of 'sex-change operations'—presumably, the most radical challenge to our cultural perspective on sex and gender. Although no one coerces transsexuals into hormone therapy, electrolysis, or surgery, the alternatives available to them are undeniably constrained:

> When the transsexual experts maintain that they use transsexual procedures only with people who ask for them, and who prove that they can 'pass', they obscure the social reality. Given patriarchy's prescription that one must be *either* masculine or feminine, free choice is conditioned (Raymond, 1979: 135, emphasis added).

The physical reconstruction of sex criteria pays ultimate tribute to the 'essentialness' of our sexual natures—as women *or* as men.

Gender, Power, and Social Change

Let us return to the question: Can we avoid doing gender? Earlier, we proposed that insofar as sex category is used as a fundamental criterion for differentiation, doing gender is unavoidable. It is unavoidable because of the social consequences of sex category membership: the allocation of power and resources not only in the domestic, economic, and political domains but also in the broad arena of interpersonal relations. In virtually any situation, one's sex category can be relevant, and one's performance as an incumbent of that category (i.e., gender) can be subjected to evaluation. Maintaining such pervasive and faithful assignment of lifetime status requires legitimation.

But doing gender also renders the social arrangements based on sex category accountable as normal and natural—that is, legitimate—ways of organizing social life. Differences between women and men that are created by this process can then be portrayed as fundamental and enduring dispositions. In this light, the institutional arrangements of a society can be seen as responsive to the differences—the social order being merely an accommodation to the natural order. Thus if, in doing gender, men are also doing dominance and women are doing deference, the resultant social order, which supposedly reflects 'natural differences', is a powerful reinforcer and legitimator of hierarchical arrangements. Frye observes:

> For efficient subordination, what's wanted is that the structure not appear to be a cultural artifact kept in place by human decision or custom, but that it appear *natural*—that it appear to be quite a direct consequence of facts about the beast which are beyond the scope of human manipulation. . . . That we are trained to behave so differently as women and men, and to behave so differently toward women and men, itself contributes mightily to the appearance of extreme dimorphism, but also, the *ways* we act as women and men, and the *ways* we act toward women and men, mold our bodies and our minds to the shape of subordination and dominance. We do become what we practice being (Frye, 1983: 34).

If we do gender appropriately, we simultaneously sustain, reproduce, and render legitimate the institutional arrangements that are based on sex category. If we fail to do gender appropriately, we as individuals—not the institutional arrangements—may be called to account (for our character, motives, and predispositions).

Social movements such as feminism can provide the ideology and impetus to question existing arrangements, and the social support for individuals to explore alternatives to them. Legislative changes, such as those proposed by the Equal Rights Amendment, can also weaken the accountability of conduct to sex category, thereby affording the possibility of more widespread loosening of accountability in general. To be sure, equality under the law does not guarantee equality in other arenas. As Lorber (1986: 577) points out, assurance of 'scrupulous equality of categories of people considered essentially different needs constant monitoring'. What such proposed changes can do is provide the warrant for asking why, if we wish to treat women and men as equals, there needs to be two sex categories at all.

The sex category/gender relationship links the institutional and interactional levels, a coupling that legitimates social arrangements based on sex category and reproduces their asymmetry in face-to-face interaction. Doing gender furnishes the interactional scaffolding of social structure, along with a built-in mechanism of social control. In appreciating the institutional forces that maintain distinctions between women and men, we must not lose sight of the interactional validation of those distinctions that confers upon them their sense of 'naturalness' and 'rightness'.

Social change, then, must be pursued both at the institutional and cultural level of sex category and at the interactional level of gender. Such a conclusion is hardly novel. Nevertheless, we suggest that it is important to recognize that the analytical distinction between institutional and interactional spheres does not pose an either/or choice when it comes to the question of effecting social change. Reconceptualizing gender, not as a simple property of individuals, but as an integral dynamic of social orders implies a new perspective on the entire network of gender relations:

[T]he social subordination of women, and the cultural practices which help sustain it; the politics of sexual object choice, and particularly the oppression of homosexual people; the sexual division of labor, the formation of character and motive, so far as they are organized as femininity and masculinity; the role of the body in social relations, especially the politics of childbirth; and the nature of strategies of sexual liberation movements (Connell, 1985: 261).

Gender is a powerful ideological device, which produces, reproduces, and legitimates the choices and limits that are predicated on sex category. An understanding of how gender is produced in social situations will afford clarification of the interactional scaffolding of social structure and the social control processes that sustain it.

References

Berk, S.F. 1985. *The Gender Factory: The Apportionment of Work in American Households*. New York: Plenum.

Cahill, S.E. 1982. 'Becoming Boys and Girls'. PhD dissertation, Department of Sociology, University of California, Santa Barbara.

——. 1986a. 'Childhood Socialization as Recruitment Process: Some Lessons from the Study of Gender Development', in P. Adler and P. Adler, eds., *Sociological Studies of Child Development*, pp. 163–86. Greenwich, CT: JAI Press.

——. 1986b. 'Language Practices and Self-Definition: The Case of Gender Identity Acquisition', *The Sociological Quarterly* 27: 295–311.

Connell, R.W. 1985. 'Theorizing Gender', Sociology 19: 260–72. Fishman, P. 1978. 'Interaction: The Work Women Do', *Social Problems* 25: 397–406.

Frye, M. 1983. *The Politics of Reality: Essays in Feminist Theory*. Trumansburg, NY: The Crossing Press.

Garfinkel, H. 1967. *Studies in Ethnomethodology*. Englewood Cliffs, NJ: Prentice-Hall.

Goffman, E. 1976. 'Gender Display', *Studies in the Anthropology of Visual Communication* 3: 69–77.

——. 1977. 'The Arrangement Between the Sexes', *Theory and Society* 4: 301–31.

Heritage, J. 1984. *Garfinkel and Ethnomethodology*. Cambridge, UK: Polity Press.

Hochschild, A.R. 1983. *The Managed Heart. Commercialization of Human Feeling*. Berkeley: University of California Press.

Hughes, E.C. 1945. 'Dilemmas and Contradictions of Status', *American Journal of Sociology* 50: 353–59.

Kessler, S.J., and W. McKenna. 1978. *Gender: An Ethnomethodological Approach*. New York: Wiley.

Komarovsky, M. 1946. 'Cultural Contradictions and Sex Roles', *American Journal of Sociology* 52: 184–9.

——. 1950. 'Functional Analysis of Sex Roles', *American Sociological Review* 15: 508–16.

Linton, R. 1936. *The Study of Man*. New York: Appleton-Century.

Lorber, J. 1986. 'Dismantling Noah's Ark', *Sex Roles* 14: 567–80.

Parsons, T. 1951. *The Social System*. New York: Free Press. Parsons, T., and R.F. Bales. 1955. *Family, Socialization and Interaction Process*. New York: Free Press.

Raymond, J.G. 1979. *The Transsexual Empire*. Boston: Beacon.

Rossi, A. 1984. 'Gender and Parenthood', *American Sociological Review* 49: 1–19.

Rubin, G. 1975. 'The Traffic in Women: Notes on the "Political Economy" of Sex', in R. Reiter, ed., *Toward an Anthropology of Women*, pp. 157–210. New York: Monthly Review Press.

Stacey, J., and B. Thorne. 1985. 'The Missing Feminist Revolution in Sociology', *Social Problems* 32: 301–16.

Thorne, B. 1980. 'Gender . . . How Is It Best Conceptualized?' Unpublished manuscript.

CHAPTER 6

Listening to the Voices of *Hijab*

Tabassum F. Ruby

With the increasing number of *muhajibah*[1] around the globe, the issue of the *hijab* has become a topic of debate among Muslim and non-Muslim scholars. Researchers such as Nasser (1999) have pointed out that the 'new *hijab* phenomenon' initially began two decades ago in countries such as Egypt, and Muslim women around the globe have since embraced the practice. In Canada, the *hijab* is often seen as a symbol of Muslim women's oppression and a restriction to their mobility, particularly in the media.[2] Many Muslim women, however, claim that the *hijab* empowers them in numerous ways: making their identities[3] distinct; taking control of their bodies; and giving them a sense of belonging to a wider Muslim world. Thus, the discussion on the *hijab* is contentious, revealing the complexity of the issue.

The intricacy of the issue of *hijab*, nonetheless, is not limited to whether the *hijab* oppresses a Muslim woman or liberates her. Most often, the Muslim community and the dominant culture recognize the *hijab* as clothing that is used to cover the female body (i.e., a headscarf and/or long coat). This research, however, indicates that immigrant Muslim women[4] perceive the *hijab* in a variety of ways and associate it with diverse meanings that range from covering of the head to modest behaviour. As a result, the participants often negotiate their places in the larger community, as well as in the Muslim community, because they feel pressure whether wearing or not wearing the *hijab*.

Methodology and Sampling

There is a small population of immigrant Muslim women in Saskatoon (the geographical location of my research), and most of them know each other. I have personal contact with many of these Muslim women, and through the use of the 'snowball technique', I was able to identify participants. The 'snowball' or 'chain' method occurs when 'sampling identifies cases of interest from people who know other people with relevant cases' (Bradshaw and Straford, 2000: 44). In recruiting the sample, the Islamic Association of Saskatchewan played a particularly important role. Along with Friday prayers, weekly gatherings in the mosque facilitated meetings with diverse groups of women and provided opportunities to talk with them about my research project.[5]

Using focus groups, I interviewed 14 women who came from 12 different countries. I conducted three interview sessions and divided my participants into two groups of five based on whether or not they wore a headscarf. I conducted one interview session with participants who did not wear a headscarf and one with those who did. Each interview session was 90 minutes long. My third group consisted of a mix of participants, some of whom wore the headscarf and some who did not. The session with the mixed group, which had four participants, lasted 110 minutes. With the participants' permission, the interviews were audiotaped.

In order to protect the anonymity of my participants, personal details such as place of birth, age, and occupation cannot be fully described here, but general characteristics are as follows. The participants' countries of origin include Afghanistan, Bangladesh, Brunei, Burma, Egypt, Guyana, India, Iran, Jordan, Kuwait, Pakistan, and Turkey. The women's ages range from just under 20 to 60. The participants' occupations vary from physician to accountant, writer to insurance officer, and students. Their immigrant experiences range from arrival in Canada within the last few years to immigration more than two decades ago. Some informants have lived in other cities such as Toronto and Edmonton; others have resided in Saskatoon since they emigrated. Six participants did not wear the *hijab*, and eight were *muhajibah*. As the overall number of participants is quite small, the results of this study may best serve as a 'case study'.

Before illustrating the participants' views about the *hijab*, I would like to outline some of the basic concepts of the *hijab* in the Muslim context, because many participants referred to them. The Qur'anic verses that are traditionally cited to describe women's dress code are as follows:

> And say to the believing women that they should lower their gaze and guard their modesty; that they should not display their beauty and ornaments except what (must ordinarily) appear thereof; that they should draw their veils over their bosoms and not display their beauty. . . . And that they should not strike their feet in order to draw attention to their hidden ornaments (24:31).
>
> O Prophet! Tell thy wives and daughters, and the believing women, that they should cast their outer garments over their persons (when abroad): this is most convenient, that they should be known (as such) and not molested. And God is oft forgiving, most merciful (33:59).

The scholars' explanation that women should cover their bodies is not only based on the interpretation of the cited verses, but also on *hadith*[6] literature. However, many *hadiths* that are often cited as justification for women's covering have been challenged, with researchers arguing that these *hadiths* are not authentic[7] (*sahih*'). Ibe-al-Jawzi (d. 1201), as cited in Roald (2001), argues that women should stay at home and, if they need to go out, should wear the *hijab* because they can cause *fitnah* (temptation).[8] Ibe-al-Jawzi bases his argument on a *hadith* that reads: the Prophet says that 'the best mosque for woman is her home.' Contrary to Ibe-al-Jawzi, however, Al-Ghazzali (1989) argues that there are many *hadiths* that provide evidence that women used to pray at the mosque during the Prophet's time and that those *hadiths* are stronger than the one cited (Roald, 2001).

Khaled (2001) argues that the debate on the *hijab* among classical and contemporary scholars is fundamentally rooted in the previously mentioned idea of *fitnah*[9] (temptation). He states that the Qur'an uses the word *fitnah* for non-sexual temptations, such as 'money and severe trials and tribulations' (Khaled, 2001: 233). Nonetheless, scholars often associate the notion of *fitnah* with women's sexuality, which is signalled, in part, by an uncovered appearance in public. Khaled writes that women are prohibited from attending mosques or driving cars, and that 'every item and colour of clothing is analyzed under the doctrine of *fitnah*' (Khaled, 2001: 235). He argues, however, that these restrictions are misplaced, and that *fitnah* reflects men's fantasies of uncontrollable lust, which they have associated with women's sexuality.

Khaled further argues that the injunction that women need to cover their bodies to avoid bringing on *fitnah* is not in harmony with Islam's message; the Qur'an does not use the word to imply women's temptation, and does not view women's bodies as *fitnah*. Moreover, Islam requires lowering of the gaze and guarding modesty for both men and women; thus, a covered female body will not lead to a modest society (the essence of the *hijab*) until men behave in a similar manner.

What Is the *Hijab*? The Discussion among the Participants

That is a question that I ask myself (Almas).[10]

The extent to which Muslim women should cover their bodies is not only a controversial issue among scholars, but also emerged as a contentious matter among the participants in this study, where the meanings of the *hijab* are interpreted in a variety of ways. The *hijab,* in the form of physical garments, signifies headscarves (as worn by some of the women interviewed), but also modest clothing that does not include the covering of the head. Equally important, the *hijab* in this research also refers to modest behaviour.

Some participants indicated that although the Qur'an requires head covering, 'the instructions are not clear, and people have diverse views about the *hijab*.' Scholars such as Asad (1980) have pointed out that there are sound reasons for not stating precise rules regarding the covering of women's bodies. He argues that human circumstances vary over time, and that the verses are moral guidelines that could be observed against the ever-changing background of time and social environment. Similarly, Dilshad', one of the participants, recognized the purpose of the vague regulations of Islam, and stated that the religion accommodates people's cultural differences. She remarked:

> Islam defines certain [rules] very strictly, because you have to follow them throughout your life. Even till the end of the world . . . these rules will remain the same. But some things are [a] little flexible, because you have to adjust with time, culture, and country.

The idea of the *hijab* with reference to head-scarves or covering of the body, however, is only one element of the *hijab*. Most participants reported that physical articles such as clothing would not serve the purpose of the *hijab* unless women believe in the practice. Islam requires lowering the gaze, avoiding seeing what is forbidden, and not inviting the male gaze. For these reasons, many participants mentioned that whether a woman wears a headscarf or not, modest behaviour is a fundamental aspect of the *hijab*. Raheelah, for example, remarked that the *hijab* is not limited to head covering; conducting life unpretentiously is also significant in fulfilling the requirements of the *hijab*. 'To me,' she stated, 'the *hijab* is not just covering of your head . . . it is your life, your portrayal of yourself as a person. As long as you dress decently, and you do not draw attention to yourself, that to me is the *hijab*.' Raheelah does not wear a headscarf, but her concept of the *hijab* dictates modesty of dress, such as not wearing miniskirts or tight dresses that could be seen as bringing attention to oneself. She also believes that moral behaviour is part of the *hijab*. This indicates that she sees the *hijab* not as a material garment, but as an ethical belief. Raheelah then, while not wearing the headscarf, feels that she is maintaining the boundaries of the *hijab*.

Why or Why Not Wear the *Hijab*?

It keeps the society pure in many, many ways (Dilshad').

Following the discussion of the concept of the *hijab*, some participants mentioned the rationale of the Qur'an in requiring the *hijab*. For example, Farza'nah' argues that the *hijab*[11] sets a boundary between men and women that helps them avoid premarital relationships, which are not permissible in Islam. She commented that a woman's beauty needs to be concealed, because beauty brings a 'lot of other things . . . freedom, the kind that we see here'. Farza'nah' identifies the *hijab* as a means of minimizing easy interaction between men and women, which in turn promotes chastity. However, according to Farza'nah's views, chastity is not restricted to women's behaviour, but it is extended to society, where women's modesty grants chaste society.

Contrary to Farza'nah's opinion, Dilshad' did not think that women's bodies should be covered simply because they are eye-catching. She believes that the *hijab* is a tool that diminishes sexual appeal and, as a result, promotes a virtuous public domain. She stated that women need to wear the *hijab* because 'it keeps the society pure in many, many ways.' Despite the seeming differences about the attractiveness of women's bodies, both Farza'nah' and Dilshad' linked the *hijab* with women's sexuality. Underlying their views is a concept of women's bodies as either tempting (their beauty will seduce men) or polluting (their immodest behaviour can corrupt society). The status of women's bodies, in turn, is seen as a sign of the moral status of the nation, because women are perceived as the cultural carriers of their society (Yuval-Davis, 1994). Thus, a chaste, moral, or pure society is dependent upon the condition of women's bodies according to Farza'nah' and Dilshad'.

Farza'nah's and Dilshad's reasoning also indicates that because they see women's bodies as *fitna*, their views contradict the Qur'an as discussed earlier. In verse 33:59, already mentioned, the Qur'an states that women should cover themselves so as not to be 'molested'. The context of the verse indicates that at the time this verse was revealed, men treated slave women very disrespectfully, and there were incidents in Medina[12] when the men assaulted Muslim women. The offenders' excuse was that they did not know that these were Muslim women. In order to protect Muslim women, it was stated that they should dress modestly so that they could be recognized. Implied in the Qur'an is the idea that men are the aggressors and women the victims, whereas according to these participants, women are the actors and men the victims (Roald, 2001). Thus, as Roald (2001) points out, many Muslims have turned the Qur'anic view around to suggest that women are responsible for a corrupted and unchaste society.

While some women wear the *hijab* because they feel responsible for a moral society, others wear it because it offers them respect, dignity, and protection. Almas, for example, is just under 20 and away from her country of origin, as well as her family, for the first time. She reported that because she is living by herself, the *hijab* has become a security measure, that men are respectful towards *muhajibah* and do not treat them like sexual objects. She remarked that 'to me now it's like protection . . . I wear the *hijab* and people do not treat you the way they treat other girls here. They are more respectful.' Although she had difficulty explaining why men respect *muhajibah*, for Almas the *hijab*, as it desexualizes her body, is a device for earning respect and ensuring her safety from potential male viewers. Many studies, such as Read and Bartkowski (2000) have found that many women wear the *hijab* because they think men will respect them. These researchers did not discuss why men respect *muhajibah*, and it was difficult for me to speculate about the reason(s). Nonetheless, Almas's remarks indicate that she feels that the *hijab* gives her the status of a respectable person, which shows that the *hijab* has a significant impact on its wearer regarding her social relationships and her perception of her 'self'.

Since people often recognize the *hijab*[13] as a religious sign that offers its wearers respect and dignity, many Muslims look negatively upon women who do not wear it, and non-wearers often feel community pressure to conform. Despite the dominant view that the *hijab* is a symbol of religious commitment, non-wearers of headscarves[14] argue that a woman

not wearing a headscarf still could be a dedicated *muslimah*.[15] Bilqis', for instance, remarked:

> Within the Muslim community, if you are not wearing the *hijab*, then you know you are not Muslim or you are not Muslim enough, when . . . it's a totally personal choice, you know. My relationship as a Muslim and my spiritual development is between me and God, and that's it.

The participants who did not wear headscarves perceived the *hijab* as a cultural dress code rather than as a religious symbol. These women indicated that wearing the *hijab* is a new cultural phenomenon, locally and globally, and that it does not have a religious connotation. Ati'yah, for example, remarked, 'I think it's more like a culture that is the way they are raised there ["back home"]. . . . I do not think it is taken as a religion when they started.' According to Ati'yah, women are taught traditionally to cover their bodies with the *hijab*, and they do not wear it because of religious requirement.

Although non-wearers of the headscarves ascribed different reasons for wearing the *hijab* from those who did wear it, both group categories felt that the *hijab* was a way of demonstrating the difference between Muslim and Western values. Mali'hah, for instance, commented that morality is declining in Canadian society, and wearing the *hijab* shows people that its wearers do not subscribe to immoral values; also, she added, *muhajibah* are afraid, because they do not have control over these undesired values.

The *Hijab* as an Identity Symbol

> In the global context, if I see a woman in the *hijab* I know she is a Muslim and it creates a sense of community in that respect, which is a nice feeling, I think (Bilqis').

The reasons for wearing it can be diverse, but the *hijab* has become a very powerful, pervasive symbol of Muslim women's identity, particularly in the West. Ibrahim (1999) states that it is a growing feeling on the part of Muslim women that they no longer wish to identify with the West, and that reaffirmation of their identities as Muslims requires the kind of visible sign that the adoption of traditional clothing implies. For these women, the issue is not that they have to dress traditionally, but that they choose to embrace the *hijab* as a marker of their Muslim identities.

Similarly, many participants who wear the *hijab*[16] claimed that it was a mark of their Muslim identities, ensuring that people immediately recognize them as Muslim women. Sima, for example, who wears a headscarf, commented that her distinct clothing symbolizes Muslim identities, and that the *hijab* makes her visible in a non-Muslim society. Being visible as a Muslim, however, also means encountering the negative stereotypes that are linked with Muslims, and Sima is aware of that. She remarked:

> Nothing else tells them that I am a Muslim, just my *hijab*. And . . . if they have the idea, oh, Muslims are terrorists, they might look at me like [that], and if they have the idea that, oh, Muslims are good people, they might look at me [with] respect. But still it gives me . . . identity.

Nasser (1999: 409) writes that adoption of the *hijab* 'conveys a public message/statement, both about the wearer and about the relationship between the wearer and potential viewers'. Accordingly, Sima's response shows that she recognizes her *hijab* as a public statement. However, whether she would be identified as a 'terrorist' or a 'good' person in Canada is a secondary consideration for her. The significant element to her is that she will be known as a Muslim in a non-Muslim country. Sima thus uses her *hijab* as a tool for declaring her Muslim identities.

The concept of the *hijab* is not limited to personal identity; it has also become the symbol of the Muslim *ummah*, or community. An immigrant Muslim woman's attempt to identify herself as a Muslim by wearing a headscarf is an acknowledgment of general support for the attitudes, values, and beliefs of Islam and her culture that links her to the broader community of believers (Daly, 1999; Read and Bartkowski, 2000). Some participants in this study also saw the *hijab* as representative of the Muslim community, and argued that the *hijab*

helped them to stay away from un-Islamic practices. Farza'nah' stated that the practice of the *hijab* defined boundaries for her, and that she would not do anything that could portray the religion negatively:

> The *hijab* limits me from doing certain things. When I have the *hijab* on . . . as a Muslim woman, I consider myself basically representative of the whole Muslim community. So, I do not go to bars with my *hijab* on. I do not go to strip clubs with my *hijab* on because I know [that] by wearing the *hijab*, I am not representing only myself . . . it's the whole Muslim community, basically.

The *hijab* not only links the wearers with a larger community, but it is also a symbol of rites of passage. In Iran, reported Pervin', when a young woman begins to wear the *hijab*, the family celebrates it. It is a 'memorable' event and 'part of the life of a girl as a graduation party'. According to Sima,[17] it signifies that a young woman is now a responsible person, and family and friends rejoice in her honour. In this cultural context, the *hijab* appears as a sign of adulthood and offers the wearer prestige and appreciation from friends and family members.

The participants in this study who have maintained the practice of wearing headscarves in Canada indicated that they are stricter in the use of their *hijab* in Canada than are those 'back home'. Shaffir (1978) states that usually people become more loyal to their traditions and customs if their identities are threatened by the larger society:

> A feature common to groups that perceive the outside world as a threat is the belief that they must resist the assimilative influence of the larger society. . . . [This helps the] group members to feel more committed and increases their awareness of their separate identity (Shaffir, 1978: 41).

Confirming Shaffir's observations, a number of informants in this study reported that they have embraced the *hijab* in Canada more enthusiastically than have people in their country of origin. Pervin', for instance, stated, 'I find that our *hijab* here is better than people are wearing in Iran . . . and I think the reason is [that] . . . somehow we need more to do this here than there.' The *hijab* helps Pervin' keep her distinct identities in a non-Muslim country, and it appears as a sign of resistance to the assimilative influence of the larger society.

In comparing the practice of wearing the *hijab* in Canada to its usage 'back home', the wearers of headscarves are crafting their Muslim identities not only in relation to the dominant values of their residing country, but also to the values of their country of origin. Many informants held a static view of their places of birth, and on their occasional visits they were surprised that the societies had changed. They argued that there is now a tendency 'back home' for women to dress in tight clothes and not to wear 'proper' *hijab*. The contrast of two different places allows these informants to notice differences in the *hijab*, and 'improper' *hijab* emerges as a symbol of the loss of Islamic values. Thus, the *hijab* for these participants stands as a guardian of Muslim standards, and they thought that 'back home' people were careless in not maintaining it.

The *Hijab*, Body, and Gaze

The study of dress as situated practice requires moving between, on the one hand, the discursive and representational aspects of dress, and the way the body/dress is caught up in relations of power, and on the other, the embodied experience of dress and the use of dress as a means by which individuals orientate themselves to the social world (Entwistle, 2000: 39).

Many prominent scholars, such as El Saadawi (1980) and Mernissi (1987, 1991) have situated the practice of veiling as an act of controlling women, both physically and psychologically. These writers argue that veiling represents, and is a result of, oppressive social hierarchies and male domination (Read and Bartkowski, 2000; Roald, 2001); therefore, it should be condemned. Mernissi (1991), for instance, states 'all debates on democracy get tied up in the woman question and that piece of cloth

[the *hijab*] that opponents of human rights today claim to be the very essence of Muslim identity' (188). Mernissi views the *hijab* as a hindrance to accessing human rights and, consequently, inherently oppressive. Equally important, she denies the lived experiences of many of those women who recognize the *hijab* as a positive experience that empowers them and grants them Muslim identities.

For the wearers of the headscarves in this study, the *hijab* is a tool that confers power and, contrary to the above writers' opinions, helps many of them to take control of their bodies. Many of the participants seem to be utilizing the *hijab* to set boundaries between themselves and the outside world. Di'ba, for example, commented that she likes keeping her curtains closed when she has the lights on, because otherwise people walking down the street can see her. One of Di'ba's friends, however, finds her precautions odd, and argues that Islam is not that strict, that she can relax without the *hijab* while she is in her home. For Di'ba, putting a barrier between herself and potential viewers is not due to Islamic restrictions; rather, she wants to create a space where she feels free from the male gaze. Di'ba reported her friend's reaction:

What's the big deal? Like, you are in your house. . . . Allah is not going to punish you for what you are doing in your own house, you know. And I am, like, but it is not about being punished . . . I do not know how Allah is going to view this, but I do not want people, like [some] guy, [looking in]. . . that's the thing.

Secor (2002) writes that veiling, as a form of dress, is a spatial practice embedded in relations of power and resistance. Accordingly, extending the idea of the *hijab* from headscarf to the creation of 'safe' space, Di'ba uses her curtains to assert power and resistance, her freedom from the undesired gaze.

The notion that the *hijab* liberates women from the male gaze and helps them to be in charge of their own bodies is a very prominent claim by those Muslim women who wear it. They argue that the *hijab* is not a mark of oppression; rather, it is a sign of liberation that protects them from a sexist society. The *hijab* allows Muslim women physical mobility because they feel free from the male gaze. Consequently, they move in the public sphere more comfortably (Hoodfar, 1993; Odeh, 1993; Khan, 1995). Noreen's story of being released from the gaze by wearing the *hijab* is particularly significant, because she suffered heavily from the 'inspecting gaze'. Noreen was 18 years old when she got married and came to Canada. When her husband did not let her wear the *hijab*, she reports, 'it got [her] into real trouble.' She and her husband ran a store where she often worked by herself. After being harassed in her workplace by some non-Muslim men, her husband consented to allowing her to wear the *hijab*.

From the conversation in other parts of my interview with Noreen about her experience of harassment, she was not only the victim of harassment, but her response to the harassers was also inspected by her husband. The behaviour of Noreen's spouse indicates that he blamed the victim, as if Noreen were responsible for the harassment. The *hijab*, however, elevated her position from the 'observed' to the 'observer', as she felt free from the male gaze. This granted Noreen the protection that otherwise might not have been possible for her.

Contrary to the opinions of those women who perceive the *hijab* as protection, the non-wearers of the headscarves argued that the *hijab* is not an appropriate dress in Canada. These participants stated that while the basic purpose of the *hijab* is not to draw attention to oneself, in Canada, where it is not customary dress, people often scrutinize women who wear the *hijab*. Citing the example of her daughters who wear the *hijab*, Ati'yah reported that whenever she goes out with her daughters, she notices that people stare at them, which 'is the opposite of what the *hijab* is supposed to be'. Ati'yah's observation indicates that the *hijab* is a marker of difference in Canada, as people find it 'strange'. Equally important, since it draws attention to the wearer, Ati'yah sees it as contrary to the teachings of the Qur'an.

While some women in this study retain their distinct Muslim identities by wearing the *hijab*, Ati'yah, in order to be more anonymous in mainstream society, did not wear the *hijab*. Both wearers and non-wearers are crafting their identities and

negotiating a place as Muslim women immigrants in a Western society.

As noted earlier, the sample of this study is very small and the results cannot be generalized to the larger population of Muslim women in Saskatoon. Nonetheless, the results indicate that the reasons for wearing or not wearing the *hijab* are varied and complex, and cannot be reduced simply to religious or cultural reasons.

Western Perception of the *Hijab*

Veiling—to Western eyes, the most visible marker of the differentness and inferiority of Islamic societies—became the symbol now of both the oppression of women (or, in the language of the day, Islam's degradation of women) and the backwardness of Islam, and it became the open target of colonial attack and the spearhead of the assault on Muslim societies (Ahmed, 1992: 152).

The formation of identities is not only restricted to the ways in which we relate and present ourselves to others; it also depends on how others perceive us. One avenue for understanding the ways in which a society views different people or cultures is to study media representations, because the media often play a powerful role in suggesting and shaping national and personal identities. Studies such as Bullock and Jafri (2000), Jafri (1998), and Kutty (1997) show that mainstream North American media have consistently portrayed an image of 'the Muslim woman' as an oppressed and passive *hijab* wearer. Bullock and Jafri (2000) argue that Muslim women are presented by the media as 'others', members of a religion that does not promote 'Canadian' values but, rather, anti-Canadian values such as indiscriminate violence and gender oppression.

In mainstream society, the negative stereotypes of Muslim women have become more visible since the attacks in New York on 11 September 2001, and the *hijab* has become a sign of a 'terrorist' woman. There are a number of incidents in Canada where *muhajibah* were harassed after September 11,[18] and some participants mentioned that they also had encountered racist harassment. Pervin', for instance, who has also experienced racism in Canada, reported that someone has since called her a 'terrorist', and she inferred that it was because she wore the *hijab*. 'Some guy said "Terrorist", because I wear the *hijab*', she remarked. 'Some people stare at me. They think that if you have the *hijab*, you are a "terrorist" . . . really, some of them think so.' Pervin's experience reveals the powerful and negative stereotypes that have linked the *hijab*—the sign of Muslim identity—with terrorism, resulting in verbal, racial, and ethnic assaults like the one cited above. These racist incidents demonstrate that Muslim women (and men) are often seen as 'other' in Canadian society and, despite claims that it is a multicultural country, many Muslims face difficulties living in Canada.

The participants not only mentioned the negative stereotype of the *hijab*, but they also recognized that many Western-style clothes could be construed as oppressive. Bilqis', for example, remarked that many North American women wear short dresses and expose their bodies, but this is not perceived as an act of oppression in Canada, whereas covering the body is interpreted as a sign of subjugation. She commented:

> Western women, when they see a Muslim woman in the *hijab*, they think, ah, oppression. But you know, ten-inch heels and a mini-skirt is not seen as oppressive. To me it is more oppressive than a putting a scarf on your head.

Wolf (1991) has demonstrated that the 'beauty myth' has often resulted in the objectification of women, and the expenditure of large amounts of money to achieve the ideal body. Wolf (1991: 13) writes that there is no justification for the beauty myth: 'What it is doing to women today is a result of nothing more exalted than the need of today's power structure, economy, and culture to mount a counteroffensive against women.' Similarly, Bilqis' argues that the Western style of wearing scanty outfits is a form of women's oppression.

Conclusion

This article discussed the concept of the *hijab* and its meanings to immigrant Muslim women.

Wearing the *hijab* in the last two decades has become a popular phenomenon, locally and globally; however, to what extent Muslim women need to cover is a debatable question among scholars as well as among the participants. The idea of the *hijab* ranges from wearing headscarves to demonstrating modest behaviour, depending on one's understanding of religious precepts. The participants described the *hijab* in a variety of ways; some linked it with the moral Muslim society and others thought that it was a sign of opposing immoral values. For those informants who wear the *hijab*, it is a religious obligation. The non-wearers of the headscarves view it as a cultural symbol. The *hijab* as a mark of identity is a persistent theme and the *muhajibah* use the *hijab* to assert agency, which in turn confers status and dignity to its wearers. At the same time, however, the *hijab* disempowers non-wearers because the Muslim community does not perceive them as 'good' *muslimah*.

While the *hijab* holds multiple meanings for Muslim women, mainstream North American society's perception of the *hijab* is usually negative, and the practice is often presented in the Canadian media without proper cultural and historical reference. Unlike the participants' views, the depiction of the *hijab* in Canada suggests that there is only one form of the *hijab*—that is, as a symbol of the oppression of Muslim women. Canadian attitudes towards the *hijab* suggest that Westerners 'know the Orient better than the Orient can know itself' (Khan, 1995: 149).

In some situations the *hijab* may indeed be imposed on Muslim women, but in this study many of the participants chose to wear it. Living in Canada, where the connotation of the *hijab* is often negative, has a strong impact on those immigrant Muslim women who wear it, as they consequently face negative stereotypes of Muslim women such as being labelled 'terrorists'. In spite of these racist acts, the *muhajibah* wear the *hijab* as a sign of their Muslim identities and in opposition to 'immodest' Western values. Those who do not identify with the visible marker recognize that the *hijab* is not an acceptable dress code in Canada. In fact, their refusal to wear the *hijab* could be read as a symbol of assimilation, but in not drawing attention to themselves and by wearing modest clothes (without the headscarf) these women, nonetheless, maintain the practice of the *hijab*. Thus, the non-wearers of the headscarves may not confront the racism that wearing the *hijab* can prompt; however, they usually encounter criticism within the Muslim community. The *hijab*, therefore, in the form of Muslim woman's clothing, emerges as a device to negotiate spaces within the Muslim community, as well as in the dominant western culture.

Notes

1. A woman who wears a *hijab*, such as a head-scarf, is called *muhajibah*.
2. Media is defined here as any form of written text (i.e., books, magazines, journal articles, reports or articles in newspapers) and audio or visual productions (i.e., radio, television shows, and documentary films).
3. The use of the word 'identities' in plural form is more appropriate here because a person's identity is multi-faceted. For instance, a Muslim woman living in Saskatoon is not only viewed as a woman, but also as a woman of colour, an immigrant, and a member of an ethnic, as well as a religious, group.
4. The term refers here to any Muslim woman born outside Canada, but currently is residing in Canada with any kind of official documents, such as a Canadian passport or student visa.
5. Please note that men's and women's gatherings are held separately in the mosque.
6. A collection of the Prophet's sayings and actions is called *hadiths*.
7. There is a science of knowledge that studies the authenticity of *hadiths*.
8. I will discuss this issue below. The idea of *fitnah* is also found in the Judeo-Christian veiling tradition, where it was thought that an uncovered female head aroused sexual desire in men (Bronner, 1993; D'Angelo, 1995).
9. Please note that he discusses the *hadith* literature in reference to the *fitnah*, and argues that they are not authentic *hadiths*.
10. Please note that all participants have been given pseudonyms.
11. The *hijab* here signifies a headscarf.
12. Geographical location where the Prophet was residing.
13. Here the *hijab* is identified by the form of head-scarf and/or long coat.
14. I used the word headscarf here to make a distinction between those whose concept of the *hijab* includes the physical article, such as a headscarf, and those who view the *hijab* as modest clothing (without the head covering) and modest behaviour.
15. *Muslimah* is the feminine for a Muslim woman.
16. The *hijab* here particularly refers to the material article; nonetheless, modest behaviour is not excluded.
17. As stated earlier, please note that as I conducted focus groups, the participants talked among themselves and commented on each other's views.
18. See for instance, *The Globe and Mail* (15 October 2001), and Jain (2001).

References

Al-Ghazzali, M. 1989. *as-sunna an-anbawiya bayna ahl al-fiqh wa ahl al-hadith*. Cairo: Dar ash-Shuruq.

Asad, M., trans. 1980. . Gibraltar: Dar Al-Andalus.

Bradshaw, M., and E. Straford. 2000. 'Qualitative Research Design and Rigour', in Iain Hay, ed., *Qualitative Research Methods in Human Geography*, pp. 37–49. South Melbourne: Oxford University Press.

Bronner, L.L. 1993. 'From Veil to Wig: Jewish Women's Hair Covering', *Judaism* 42, 4: 465–77.

Bullock, K., and J. Jafri. 2000. 'Media (Mis) Representations: Muslim Women in the Canadian Nation', *Canadian Woman Studies* 20, 2 (Summer): 35–40.

Daly, C.M. 1999. 'The Paarda' Expression of Hejaab among Afghan Women in a non-Muslim community', in L. Arthur, ed., *Religion, Dress and the Body*, pp. 147–61. Oxford: Berg.

D'Angelo, R.M. 1995. 'Veils, Virgins, and the Tongues of Men and Angels: Women's Heads in Early Christianity', in H. Eilberg-Schwartz and W. Doniger, eds., *Off with Her Head! The Denial of Women's Identity in Myth, Religion, and Culture*, pp. 131–64. Berkeley, CA: University of California Press.

El Saadawi, N. 1980. *The Hidden Face of Eve: Women in the Arab World*, Hetata, trans. London: ZED Press.

Entwistle, J. 2000. *The Fashioned Body: Fashion, Dress, and Modern Social Theory*. Cambridge: Polity Press; Malden, MA: Blackwell.

Hoodfar, H. 1993. 'The Veil in Their Minds and on our Heads: The Persistence of Colonial Images of Muslim Women', *Resources for Feminist Research* 22, 3/4: 5–18.

Ibrahim, B.S. 1999. *Women in Islam: Hijab*. Aalim: Islamic Research Foundation (IRF).

Jafri, G.J. 1998. 'The Portrayal of Muslim Women in Canadian Mainstream Media: A Community-based Analysis'. Online Afghan Women's Organization. Project report. Available at www.fmw.org/political_activities.htm.

Khaled, A. 2001. *Speaking in God's Name: Islamic Law, Authority and Women*. Oxford: Oneworld.

Khan, S. 1995. 'The Veil as a Site of Struggle: The Hejab in Quebec', *Canadian Woman Studies* 15, 2/3: 146–52.

Kutty, S. 1997. 'Speaking for Her: The Representation of the Muslim Woman in Popular Culture'. Canadian Muslim Civil Liberties Association. Pamphlet.

Mernissi, F. 1987. *Beyond the Veil: Male–Female Dynamics in Modern Muslim Society*. London: Al Sagi Books.

——. 1991. *Women and Islam: A Historical and Theological Enquiry*, M.J. Lakeland, trans. Oxford: B. Blackwell. Basil.

Nasser, M. 1999. 'The New Veiling Phenomenon—Is It an Anorexic Equivalent? A Polemic', *Journal of Community & Applied Social Psychology* 9: 407–12.

Odeh, L.A. 1993. 'Post-colonial Feminism and the Veil: Thinking the Difference', *Feminist Review* 43 (Spring): 26–37.

Read, G., and P.J. Bartkowski. 2000. 'To Veil or Not to Veil? A Case Study of Identity Negotiation among Muslim Women in Austin, Texas', *Gender and Society* 14, 3 (June): 395–417.

Roald, S.A. 2001. *Women in Islam: The Western Experience*. London: Routledge.

Shaffir, W. 1978. 'Canada: Witnessing as Identity Consolidation: The Case of the Lubavitcher Chassidim', in H. Mol, ed., *Identity and Religion: International, Cross-cultural Approaches*, pp. 39–57. Beverly Hills, CA: Sage Publications.

Wolf, N. 1991. *The Beauty Myth*. Toronto: Vintage Books.

Yusuf, A.A., trans. 1946. *The Holy Qur'an*. Durban: Islamic Propagation Center International.

Yuval-Davis, N. 1994. 'Identity Politics and Women's Ethnicity', in V. Moghadam, ed., *Identity Politics and Women: Cultural Reassertions and Feminism in International Perspective*, pp. 408–24. Boulder, CO: Westview Press.

CHAPTER 7

Sk8ter Girls: Skateboarders, Girlhood, and Feminism in Motion

Shauna Pomerantz, Dawn H. Currie, and Deirdre M. Kelly

Labelled 'post-feminist' by some of the academic and popular press, teenage girls have often been accused of letting feminism down (Douglas, 1994; Pipher, 1994; Summers, 1994; Abraham, 1997; Curthoys, 1997; Gamer, 1997; Bellafante, 1998; Rapping, 2000; Preston, 2001).[1] Younger generations are frequently charged with enjoying all the freedoms won for them by the women's movement without engaging in the struggle themselves. Teenage girls are repeatedly labelled post-feminist as a way of suggesting that they are not carrying on the traditions of the women's movement and have in some sense failed second-wave feminism in its legacy of collective political action and social change.

In the wake of post-feminist discourses, we wonder if today's girls really have let feminism down or if they have simply been ignored. There is little emphasis on the lives of 'regular' girls and their practical experiences of the social world. Where are the 'everyday' girls who do 'everyday' things? When we talk to girls about everyday things, we may begin to hear all the ways in which girls are quietly but powerfully changing the face of girlhood through localized and specific gender struggles.

In her study of bedroom culture in the new millennium, Anita Harris (2001) suggests that girls have developed 'new forms of political expression' (128) that take place in new spaces. Harris explores how girls 'express their politics when the prevailing view is that they have no politics to speak of at all' (139). Focusing on 'gurl' websites, alternative music spheres, and underground zines, she demonstrates 'that young women are passionately engaged in social change agendas, but that these occur in marginal, virtual or underground places' (139). It is here, at the margins of space and place, where girls may be 'doing' feminism. Furthermore, girls may be pushing feminism in exciting and diverse directions, away from the usual possibilities that currently receive post-feminist attention. What follows is one such example that was an 'incidental' find in a larger study on alternative girlhoods.[2] While interviewing girls within the frame of new subjectivities, we happened upon a group of eight (girl) skateboarders, whom we call the 'Park Gang'. Becoming girl skateboarders meant that the Park Gang had to challenge the skater boys who dominated the park. They also consciously stood in resistance to what Connell (1987) calls 'emphasized femininity.'[3]

Emphasized femininity is a kind of traditional femininity based on subordination to men and boys. In order to resist emphasized femininity, the Park Gang engaged in a transgressively feminine bodily comportment that is not common for girls. As becoming a girl skater in today's North American context often necessitates engaging in these discursive and embodied struggles, the subject position of 'skater girl' is a social category that holds the possibility for a feminist politics. Subject positions contribute to subjectivity or how we understand ourselves in relation to the world.

Subjectivity 'is produced in a whole range of discursive practices—economic, social, and political—the meanings of which are a constant site of struggle over power' (Weedon, 1987: 21). By occupying the subject position of skater, the Park Gang worked towards a subjectivity that indicated a feminist politics through resistance to the male-dominated space of the park and the emphasized femininity of the girls who hung around the skater boys. By 'doing' skateboarding, the Park Gang worked to resist the traditional femininity modelled by other girls at the park—the girls 'who just watched'. Thus, skateboarding became a subject position fraught with gendered struggles that highlighted the discursive and embodied construction of girlhood.

Legitimation at the Skate Park: Skateboarding as a Discursive Resignification of Girlhood

> Most skaters are young teenage boys who think they are kings and the world sits below them. Trying to tell them that women should be able to skate without being harassed may be an impossible task, but it must be done (Jigsaw Youth, 2002).

Skate parks are generally awash in a grey, graffiti-ridden concrete that is the necessary landscape for practising tricks. Vancouver has several good places for skateboarding, but most are burdened with a reputation for drugs and vandalism. The largest indoor park in the city was recently shut down for its high level of drug trafficking and defacement of property. Underground skaters who detest anything remotely mainstream avoid the parks, confining their practice to the streets, the parking lots of local establishments, and the (now monitored by security) area surrounding the art gallery downtown. For those skaters who do not mind mainstream skateboarding, the parks are the best place to practice, learn tricks, and participate in skate culture. But no matter which skate park or street location you choose to frequent, one thing is abundantly clear—there are very few girl skateboarders.

As Sandy, a self-proclaimed skateboarding 'coach' for her friends, announced in no uncertain terms, 'Like, a lot of girls don't skateboard!'[4] Skateboarding is not a common activity for girls and finding a girl on a skateboard is rare. Despite the recent media frenzy around teen pop singer Avril Lavigne, who has been dubbed a 'skate punk' for her style and loose connections to skateboarding, girls are often relegated to the sidelines while the boys 'do their thing'. Further evidence can be found by visiting skate parks, where girls hang off the railing as watchers, fans, and girlfriends. Evidence of this can also be found on numerous Internet skater zines dedicated to girls.[5] One girl skater writes, 'Every time I venture out to skate, either alone or with friends, I am in some way harassed, threatened, or opposition to my skating is voiced in some manner' (Jigsaw Youth, 2002). And there is this testimonial of frustration by Morgan:

> Once upon a time, I was a lonely girl skater in a big city. I went to the indoor park a few times a week, but there were never any other girls there and the guys seemed to want little to do with the girl in the corner teaching herself kickturns. As much as I loved skating, it was necessary to give myself a serious pep talk to get motivated to go back to the park each day (Frontside Betty, 2002).

These accounts of life at the skate park indicate the gendered nature of skater culture, where girls have to work much harder and overcome many more obstacles than boys to gain legitimate skater status. The subordination and delegitimation of girls to boys is a common theme in youth subcultures. Paul Willis (1981) represents girls in working class 'lad' culture as sexual objects for the more powerful boys. In Dick Hebdige's (1979) analysis of punk culture, girls are represented as accoutrement and secondary figures. McRobbie and Garber (1997 [1976]) first pointed out that youth cultural studies theorists saw girls as backdrop characters in male-dominated subcultures, whose lives revolved around finding a boyfriend, looking attractive, and being promiscuous. But in their own analysis of girls in male subcultures, they concluded that

traditional sex roles were also dominant in biker culture, mod culture, and hippy culture. Girls were given very little status and almost no legitimation. In skater culture, girls are assigned a similar kind of derogatory positioning. Yet despite the sexism of the skate park and of skateboarding in general, there are still some girls who choose to take up the label of 'skater'.

The members of the Park Gang were 14 and 15 years old at the time of the study—born in the decade defined by a backlash against second-wave feminism (Faludi, 1991). They all lived in an area of Vancouver known for its family orientation, professional demographic, and urban chic. Four were Canadian-born Chinese girls, two were white, one was a Canadian-born Latina, and one was half First Nations, half white. This racial mix is representative of the city of Vancouver itself, which is ethnically and racially highly diverse. With the exception of one girl, who attended a Catholic school, the girls all attended a large urban high school known for its Asian population and academic achievement. Skateboarding was a passion for four of the girls; two of the girls called themselves 'coaches' in the sense that they skated but preferred to 'just help'; and two of the girls were skaters by association, meaning that they were involved in skate culture, music, and style—like all of the Park Gang—but without the desire to actually skate.[6] They all hung out at a skate park that would be considered amateurish compared to the larger and more daunting parks downtown. This particular park was connected to a community centre in an affluent neighbourhood. It was relatively clean and safe.

Members of the Park Gang were relatively new skaters when we met them. They came to the sport through older brothers or boys at school. Grover noted that she got started because a friend did not want to learn alone:

> There are not too many girl skateboarders so it is kind of better—she felt more comfortable if there was, like, you know, another person that, you know, could be with her. And so she asked if I wanted to try it, so I said sure, and, um, her brothers started teaching us and I found it

was something that, it was a lot of fun, so I just stayed with it, so I'm still learning.

When more of the Park Gang decided to try skateboarding, they ventured into the skate park with their boards for the first time, hoping to gain acceptance and practice. But the park proved to be a location of struggle that was dominated by skater boys, who put the girls under surveillance. The skater boys were always asking members of the Park Gang to show them what they could do and Zoey spoke of the constant questioning of the girls' abilities. They often asked her, 'Why don't you skate more?' She admitted that, 'sometimes we don't want to skate around them 'cause, like, they do really good stuff and we're just kind of learning.'

The Park Gang quickly realized that being the only girl skaters at the park singled them out for some harassment. To the skater boys who dominated the park and acted as its gatekeepers, the park was their space—a space that left very little room for girls, unless they were occupying the traditionally feminine subject positions of watcher, fan, or girlfriend. Gracie theorized that girls skate less than boys due to this kind of territorial attitude: 'Some [girls] are kind of, like, scared, because, um, of what people might think of them.' When asked what she meant, Gracie noted that the lack of girls who skated at the park might make the boys question girls' right to belong. Onyx added that the skater boys viewed the Park Gang as 'invading their space'. Grover felt that the Park Gang threatened the skater boys 'just because, you know, girls are doing their sport.' She went on to explain the attitudes of some of the boys at the park.

Sometimes, they'll be kind of, like, rude, like, I don't know if it's on purpose, but they just, you know, have this kind of attitude. . . . I guess they think they're so good and one of them or two of them—I'm not sure if all of them are, like, sponsored by skateboarding companies—so they always feel, like, you know, they're kind of superior and so, you know, we're only a year younger, so it's kind of, like, we're obviously not as good as them, but they kind of forget that they had to start

somewhere too, so, and it would be harder for us because we're girls.

The territory of the park became a contested space. The boys saw it as theirs. The girls wanted access. Grover, Gracie, and Onyx understood that the boys were threatened by their presence, but wished the boys could appreciate how hard it was for girls to get started. They wanted the boys to see them as equals who deserved the same kind of camaraderie that they gave each other. But instead, the boys saw them as interlopers with little legitimate claim to the space. Some of the boys accused some of the Park Gang of being 'posers'. Often, girls who try to gain skater status are seen as posers. A poser wears the right clothes, such as wide sneakers with fat laces, brand-name pants and hoodies, and, of course, carries a skateboard. But posers do not really skate. Although boys can be posers too, girls who attempt access to the label 'skater' are singled out for this derogatory title. It is assumed that girls hang around the skate park as a way to meet skater boys, to flirt.

When this accusation was levelled at some of the Park Gang, they immediately took action to prove the skater boys wrong. Zoey recounted the story.

There's this one time where a couple of the guys thought we were just—they said it out loud that we're just there for the guys and we're like, 'No!' And they're like, 'But you're here all the time, like almost every day, skateboarding, and so are we.' So we did this whole thing where we didn't come there for quite a while just to show them; and then we came back and they stopped bugging us about it.

The girls involved in the park boycott practised at an elementary school for two weeks and went to the park only when they knew the boys would not be around. When asked what they had gained by boycotting the park, Zoey responded, 'That we're not there just for the guys and we're not there to watch them and be around them.' Suddenly, the girls received more respect and experienced less harassment from the skater boys. Zoey noted a distinct change in their attitude. 'I guess to some level, they treated us like an equal to them, kind of.' Instead of placing the girls under surveillance, the skater boys watched the Park Gang in order to see 'how they were doing'. They suddenly became curious about the girls' progress. When asked if they thought they had successfully changed the opinions of the skater boys, Zoey enthusiastically replied, 'Well, yes!'

Before the boycott, the skater girls were thought of in a very specific way: as posers, flirts, or interlopers. But through the boycott, the girls believed they altered how the boys thought of them and, more significantly, how they thought of themselves. In their efforts to change the meaning of 'skater', the Park Gang acknowledged how they had been subordinated at the park and successfully resignified the commonly accepted process of belonging. They carved out a space for girls where none used to exist. In this way, the Park Gang legitimated the subject position of 'skater' for girls at the park and expanded the possibilities for subjectivity within girlhood. As Pete pointed out, 'lots of girls have actually started [skating] because my group started and then they kind of feel in power. I think they kind of feel empowered that they can start now, that it's okay for girls to skate.' This discursive resignification of girlhood through the skater label enacted a feminist politics that worked to reshape gender categories in a male-dominated locale. As a result of their purposeful positioning as skaters, the Park Gang also worked toward an embodied resignification of girlhood that challenged not just the skater boys, but the traditional femininity of other girls at the park.

Kickflipping Femininity: Skateboarding as an Embodied Resignification of Girlhood

First of all don't play dumb. If you are going to skate, skate!!! Who cares what the guys think. And please don't hang out at the skate park with your skateboard just to pick up guys. Cause it ain't working! Just be yourself and you will go a lot farther (Whitney, 2001).

The skate park was a hangout for all different kinds of youth, many of whom did not skate, but instead chose to sit on the benches, picnic tables, and steps that surrounded the concrete area designated for skaters. It was a place where girls and boys could gather to socialize. Some of the girls were well known as the 'popular' girls at school. They had boyfriends, money to spend on the 'right' clothes, and a nickname ascribed to them by the Park Gang based on the fact that they often wore buns in their hair—'Bun Girls'. The Park Gang saw Bun Girls as representative of a certain kind of girl that they did not respect. Pete explained that the Bun Girls were annoying people who lived by an image 'that kind of pisses me off'. When asked to explain, Pete painted this picture: 'Skinny, the whole thing, the whole skinniness, having, being skinny, thin, pretty, makeup, umm, lots of money, shoes, be spoiled and then kind of living their life for a guy. That kind of annoys me too!' She went on to say: 'I notice that they [Bun Girls], like, all dress, like, they have, they have to have some sort of motivation to dress up like that and I think it's to be popular, to kind of, um, get guys. And so, I don't like that. I think it's just totally wrong to live your life like that!'

The Park Gang continuously described the Bun Girls as trendy, boy crazy, and clueless. Their 'ditzy' reputation stemmed from the fact that they spent much of their energy worrying about clothes, looks, and boyfriends. Bun Girls wore tight, low-cut tank tops and tight, low-cut jeans from expensive, brand-name stores. Their appearance was coiffed, polished, and en vogue. The Bun Girls had a power that was based on bodily display, sexiness, and a perceived maturity or sophistication. While some of the skater boys responded to the Bun Girls' sexuality, the Park Gang generally tried to resist enacting this kind of power, seeing it as 'fake' and built around a passive bid for attention from the boys.[7] Gracie noted that Bun Girls often played 'dumb' and 'tough' when they did not mean it at all. Sandy explained this fake attitude: 'Yeah, like, [the Bun Girls are like] 'Oh, I don't care about that!' when really they would care or they're just hiding it. Like, as if people are putting up, like, a façade!'

Members of the Park Gang often actively worked to resist Bun Girl femininity. Instead of caring about what others thought of them, the Park Gang saw themselves as individuals with unique personalities who took pride in being different, fun, and alternative. A Bun Girl was seen to be a carbon copy without any sort of defining characteristics, except, as Grover put it 'caring what other people think'. For members of the Park Gang, this kind of self-conscious behaviour was all too typical and gave girls a bad name. Zoey put it like this: 'Yeah, because, you know, the whole thing, like, where a lot of girls want to be sexy? That is totally the opposite of us. We don't. We don't and we kind of don't really like those kind of girls that do, because it's for popularity and stuff like that.'

The Bun Girls were 'watchers' at the park who used their inability to skate as a way to meet skater boys. As Zoey described them: 'They're [Bun Girls] always, like, they get on the board and ask for, like, the guys to hold their hand and pull them and they start screaming, you know, acting weird.' When asked what members of the Park Gang did when they saw the Bun Girls acting this way, Zoey replied, 'We just roll our eyes and walk away.' Bun Girl femininity was giggly, ditzy, and purposefully subordinate to boys. It was based on physical appearance, money, clothing, and inactivity. Creating a distance between the Bun Girls and themselves was as important to the Park Gang as gaining the respect of the skater boys. By purposefully juxtaposing themselves to the Bun Girls, members of the Park Gang demonstrated an embodied resistance to a dominant form of femininity that they saw as detrimental to girlhood itself. For example, in order to differentiate themselves from Bun Girl femininity, the Park Gang dressed casually and comfortably. They avoided wearing makeup and did not engage in sexual display through style. They also worked to speak their minds and did not pretend to be 'ditzy' or in need of skater boy assistance on their boards. But the real distinction between Bun Girl femininity and the embodied resistance of the Park Gang was the difference between 'watcher' and 'doer' at the skate park. As 'doers', or girls who actually skated, the Park Gang engaged in the embodied resignification of Bun Girl femininity through a distinct bodily comportment.

Skateboarding is a sport that demands physicality and bravery. To skate is to know how to fall and how to attempt many complicated and risky tricks.

Even the most basic trick, the ollie, where a skater jumps in the air with her board attached to her feet and then lands smoothly on it again, runs the risk of injury. Ollies, kickflips, grinding, and carving are all skater tricks that must be performed fearlessly and with the full knowledge that falling is likely (especially for the Park Gang, who were new to tricks and only just attempting them for the first time). This kind of physical audacity is not generally associated with being a girl. As Iris Marion Young (1989) suggests, typical motility and spatiality for girls can be timid, uncertain, and hesitant, as girls are not brought up to have the same kind of confidence and freedom in their movements as boys. Young sees femininity as based on a particular bodily comportment that is restrictive of big movement and risk-taking. Girls are not often seen to be capable of achieving physical acts that require strength and power or handling the pain that such physical acts can incur. Willingly inviting pain is seen to be boys' territory. Boys are ascribed the kind of confidence and craziness needed to carry skater tricks through to completion. Girls are not. Members of the Park Gang were aware of this gendered notion of motility and bodily comportment. When asked why girls did not skate as much as boys, Onyx noted that girls might see skateboarding as 'a guy thing to do. It is our thing to sit around and chit chat and gossip and stuff and watch them skateboard.' Grover added, 'Yeah, and some girls are kind of, like, scared.' But Onyx retorted that she and her friends did not 'think like that. We wanted to try it.' Emily, too, reasoned that girls 'don't want to continuously fall', and realized that skater boys are much less worried: 'Like, guys there, they fall and they keep falling, but it's amazing, but they always get back up and, like, try the same thing again. It's quite amazing.'

By 'doing' skateboarding, members of the Park Gang engaged in a transgressive bodily comportment for girls. They were willing to straddle their boards with a wide stance; dangle their arms freely by their sides; and spread eagle for balance. They knowingly made spectacles out of themselves, courting the gaze of the skater boys and the Bun Girls. While some members of the Park Gang were not keen to 'wipe out', others, like Zoey, lovingly recounted their experiences of falling: 'like, the first time I wiped out, I was just, like, "Whoa!" I fell really hard. I was, like, "Aahh!" kind of. And then I just wanted to do it again, because it was like, "Wow!" The adrenaline rush some of the Park Gang felt came from knowing they were engaged in an activity that most girls (and boys) did not have the guts to try. As Amanda suggested, most boys at the park were more 'risk taking' than girls. 'They don't care if they, like, get bruises and stuff. They'll be, like, "Yeah! Cuts!" And then girls will be, like, "Oh no!"' But some members of the Park Gang willingly accepted the risks involved in skateboarding as a way of setting themselves apart

from Bun Girl femininity. Not only could they become skaters who challenged the skater boys at the park, but the Park Gang also realized that they could challenge forms of femininity with which they disagreed. The Park Gang's purposeful positioning as skaters once again worked to push the boundaries of girlhood in productive directions.

Acknowledgments

We would like to thank the Social Sciences and Humanities Research Council of Canada for providing support for this research.

Notes

1. Susan Bolotin (1982) originally introduced the term 'post-feminist' in the *New York Times Magazine*. Her article, entitled 'Voices from the Post-Feminist Generation', was a firsthand look at young women and their disinterest in feminism. Susan Faludi (1991) characterizes the emergence of post-feminism in the media as an example of feminist backlash that gives young women the 'false impression that equality has been achieved and encourages young women to pursue their individual freedoms at the expense of a collective female identity' (13). Similarly, Budgeon and Currie (1995: 184) see the post-feminist discourse in the media as an endorsement of a 'women-centred individualism' that 'assumes rather than questions equal opportunity for women'.

2. The larger study, entitled *Girl Power*, was a three-year research project carried out in Vancouver, Canada from 2000–2003. Shauna Pomerantz conducted the skater girl interviews over this period, interviewing each girl twice in various pairings. Pairings for the first set of interviews were not always the same for the second set.

3. For a detailed discussion of 'emphasized femininity' and its relation to skater girlhood, see Kelly, Pomerantz, and Currie (in press).

4. All names are pseudonyms chosen by the girls in the study.

5. Examples of online skater girl zines include: frontsidebetty.com, withitgirl.com, sk8rgirl.com, girlskateboarding.com, girlsskatebetter.com, and gurlzonboards.com.

6. Although skate culture has been continuously redefined since its original incarnation in 1970s Californian surf culture, many elements remain the same today—a dedication to punk rock (now splintered into pop punk, old school punk, hardcore, and Goth), a love of baggy clothes, a close connection to marijuana and 'partying', and a slacker reputation (think Bart Simpson). In contemporary North American society, skateboarding has been taken up by mainstream marketing machines, such as Nike and Adidas and sold back to its constituents as a skater image, composed of expensive sneakers, brand name clothes, and flashy accoutrement. While the Park Gang liked pop punk bands, such as Linkin Park, Sum 41, and Green Day, they did not buy expensive skater clothes from the numerous skate shops in Vancouver's trendiest neighbourhoods, opting instead for an alternative second-hand look. Grover, for instance, wore men's dress shirts and black gloves with the fingers cut off. The Park Gang also did not smoke marijuana or 'party' and considered themselves to be 'good' girls who listened to their parents. They saw skate culture as 'fun', 'crazy', and 'alternative', but had no wish to be lumped in with other skaters, who broke the law, drank, did drugs, or slacked off in school.

7. It should be noted, though, that Onyx—a very pretty member of the Park Gang—was aware of the attention she garnered through her looks and was just beginning to notice the power she held.

References

Abraham, Y. 1997. 'Lipstick Liberation', *Worcester Phoenix*, 30 May–6 June. Available at www.worcesterphoenix.com/archive/features/97/05/30LIPSTICK% 5LIBERATION.html (renewed 24 September 2004).

Bellafante, G. 1998. 'Feminism: It's All About Me!', *Time* [online], 29 March 2000. Available at www.time.com/time/magazine/1998/ dom/980629/cover2.html.

Bolotin, S. 1982. 'Voices from the Poor Feminist Generation', *New York Times Magazine* (13 October): 28–31.

Budgeon, S., and D.H. Currie. 1995. 'From Feminism to Postfeminism: Women's Liberation in Fashion Magazines', *Women's Studies International Forum* 18, 2: 173–86.

Connell, R.W. 1987. *Gender and Power*. Stanford, CT: Stanford University Press.

Curthoys, J. 1997. *Feminist Amnesia: The Wake of Women's Liberation*. London: Routledge.

Douglas, S.J. 1994. *Where the Girls Are: Growing Up Female with the Mass Media*. New York: Times Books.

Faludi, S. 1991. *Backlash: The Undeclared War against American Women*. New York: Crown Publishers.

Frontside Betty. 2002. 'About Frontside Betty'. Available at www.frontsidebetty.com/about/index.html (accessed 23 March 2002).

Garner, H. 1997. *The First Stone*. Sydney: Picador.

Harris, A. 2001. 'Revisiting Bedroom Culture: New Spaces for Young Women's Politics', *Hectate* 27, 1: 128–39.

Hebdige, D. 1979. *Subculture: The Meaning of Style*. London: Methuen.

Jigsaw Youth. 2002. 'Women in Skateboarding'. Available at http://gurlpages.com/unitedgirlfront/skate.html.

McRobbie, A., and J. Garber. 1997 [1976]. 'Girls and Subcultures', in K. Gelder and S. Thornton, eds., *The Subcultures Reader*, pp. 112–20. London: Routledge.

Pipher, M. 1994. *Reviving Ophelia: Saving the Selves of Adolescent Girls*. New York: Putnam.

Preston, C.B. 2001. 'Baby Spice: Lost Between Feminine and Feminist', *Journal of Gender, Social Policy & the Law* 9, 3: 541–619.

Rapping, E. 2000. 'You've Come Which Way, Baby? The Road that Leads from June Cleaver to Ally McBeal Looks A Lot Like a U-turn', *Women's Review of Books* 17, 10/11: 20–3.

Stacey, J. 1990. 'Sexism by a Subtler Name? Post-structural Conditions and Postfeminist Consciousness in Silicon Valley', in K.V. Hansen, and I.J. Philipson, eds., *Women, Class, and the Feminist Imagination: A Socialist Feminist Reader*, pp. 338– 56. Philadelphia, PA: Temple University Press.

Summers, A. 1994. *Damned Whores and God's Police*. Harmondsworth: Penguin.

Weedon, C. 1987. *Feminist Practice and Poststructuralist Theory*. Oxford, UK: Blackwell.

Whitney, A. 2001. 'Guys vs. Girls'. Available at www.realskate.com/girlsvsguys.htm (accessed 16 June 2002).

Willis, P.E. 1981. *Learning to Labor: How Working Class Kids Get Working Class Jobs*. New York: Columbia University Press.

Young, I.M. 1989. 'Throwing Like a Girl: A Phenomenology of Feminine Body Comportment, Motility, and Spatiality', in J. Allen and I.M. Young, eds., *The Thinking Muse: Feminism and Modern French Philosophy*, pp. 51–70. Bloomington: Indiana University Press.

CHAPTER 8

Coming Out and Crossing Over: Identity Formation and Proclamation in a Transgender Community

Patricia Gagné, Richard Tewksbury, and Deanna McGaughey

Much of the social scientific focus on transgendered individuals has derived from an interest in understanding 'deviation' from the 'normal' and 'natural' two-sex system (see Herdt, 1994). With the exception of Weinberg, Williams, and Pryor's (1994) research on transsexual bisexuals and treatises written by transgendered individuals (Morris 1974; Bornstein 1994; Rothblatt, 1995), the literature on transgenderism has focused primarily on issues of sex and gender. Within this literature, there has been little examination of sexuality (but see Herdt, 1994) and a virtual absence of research on the coming-out experiences of transgendered individuals.

In this article, we examine the coming-out experiences of a non-random sample of individuals who were members of the transgender community at the time we solicited volunteers for our project. Transgenderism refers to 'the lives and experiences of diverse groups of people who live outside normative sex/gender relations' (Namaste, 1994: 228). Persons who enact alternative gender presentations or who have internalized alternative gender identities are referred to as 'transgenderists' (Tewksbury and Gagné, 1996). When looking at the experiences of transgenderists, identity management concerns are at least as complex as those of bisexuals, gay men, and lesbians, if not more so. While there are some similarities between the coming-out processes of transgenderists and gay men, lesbians, and bisexuals, there are also salient differences. First, since around the end of the nineteenth century, homosexuality has been defined as an identity (D'Emilio, 1983; Foucault, [1978] 1990). As that identity and the communities and institutions built around it have become more visible, lesbians and gay men, and more recently bisexuals, have had

opportunities to find similar others. Thus, feelings of 'difference' are more easily identified, labelled, and accepted than they were before homosexuality defined 'who' the person was. While gay men, lesbians, and bisexuals have challenged the medical definition of homosexuality as a mental illness, they have, for the most part, adhered to the notion that sexuality is an important component in defining who the person is (D'Emilio, 1983; Adam, 1995). Challenges to this trend are only now emerging within queer communities and queer theory (Epstein, 1994; Namaste, 1994; Seidman, 1994, 1996; Stein and Plummer, 1994).

Although barriers to self-awareness and acceptance are declining, transgenderists continue to grapple with many of the issues that confronted sexual minorities in the United States prior to the 1970s. Most masculine-to-feminine transgenderists conform to traditional beliefs about sex and gender, whereas a minority attempt to step outside the gender binary by defining themselves in non-gendered or multiply gendered ways (Raymond, 1994). For example, within the transgender community, the declassification of transsexualism as a psychiatric diagnosis has been hotly debated, with those seeking to challenge medical definitions arguing that it should be removed from the *Diagnostic and Statistical Manual of Mental Disorders* (*DSM-IV*) and those still seeking access to hormones and sex reassignment surgery (SRS) arguing that being diagnosed transsexual is the only way they may become the women they truly are. In other words, they must 'confess' their transsexualism in ways that adhere to medical models in order to proceed from one sex to the other. Similarly, most transsexuals adhere to beliefs that their desires to live as women were the result of biological 'mistakes' that left them as feminine persons in male bodies (Stoller, 1971; Pauly, 1990). Rather than choosing to live as feminine males, they opt to cross over to full-time womanhood. Similarly, most cross-dressers look on their sartorial transitions as opportunities to express their feminine selves (Talamini, 1981; Wood-house, 1989). They deem feminine behaviour in masculine attire to be highly inappropriate.

While transgenderism is an issue of sex and gender, it does entail aspects of sexual *reorientation*. Thus, sexually active transgenderists must recognize, tolerate, and learn to accept an alternative gender identity; develop a repertoire of coping strategies to manage public presentations of gender; and, in some cases, manage the actual transformation of permanent identity and anatomy. Whether gender transformations are temporary or permanent, the sense that one really is the sex associated with the gender portrayed involves a reexamination of sexual identity. For example, some anatomically male transsexuals and cross-dressers, in the process of establishing a feminine self, engage in sexual activity with other anatomical male persons. While the observers may morphologically define the experience as *homosexual* or *same sexed*, the social women experiencing the interaction tend to define it as *heterosexual*. Such activity is highly valued as a way of exploring femininity. For transgenderists, the discovery of a sexual identity, or a sense of who the individual is as a sexual person, frequently occurs within a sex/gender system. That does not address sexual issues among those whose sex and gender do not fit within the binary system. Furthermore, those who do have SRS must sexually 'come out' to themselves and others by reexamining their sexual preferences and orientations. As gender and/or sex changes, the subjective and social meanings of sexual interactions are also transformed. While gay men, lesbians, and bisexuals must come out sexually, their experiences are not confounded by alterations in gender and genital makeup.

Research on the coming-out processes and experiences of transgenderists provides an opportunity to examine the management of the transformation of three aspects of socially normative expectations,

rather than just one. Whereas lesbians, gay men, and bisexuals are able to carefully control information dissemination, transgenderists must manage both their actual and virtual social identities (Goffman, 1963) on three dimensions. Lesbians, gay men, and bisexuals can selectively come out, whereas transgenderists, because of changes in gender or biological appearance, are often forced out of the closet, creating awkward—or even dangerous—situations. Transgenderists provide an opportunity to examine the private and public dimensions of achieving a new gender through interaction with others and the emergence and management of alternative sex, gender, and sexual identities.

Method

We completed 65 semi-structured, in-depth, tape-recorded interviews with masculine-to-feminine individuals from several points along the transgender spectrum (see Tewksbury and Gagné, 1996). *Transgenderism* is an umbrella term that encompasses a variety of identities—including transsexual; fetish and non-fetishistic cross-dresser; drag queen, and other terms—as devised by individuals who live outside the dominant gender system. In this study, we have categorized individuals on the basis of the identity they proclaimed to us. All volunteers in our sample were members of the transgender communities through which we recruited volunteers for our study. The majority in our sample had refined their self-identifications in the process of coming out.

Included in our sample are individuals who self-identify as pre- (n = 27), post- (n = 10), and non-operative (n = 4) transsexual. Transsexuals are people who believe themselves to be female and who wish to, or do, live full-time as women. Preoperative transsexuals are those who desire to have, but have not yet had, SRS. Post-operative transsexuals are those who have had SRS. Non-operative transsexuals are those who live full-time or nearly full-time as women but who do not wish to have SRS. Some have availed themselves of other medical and cosmetic procedures—including female hormones, breast implants, and electrolysis, whereas others alter their gender presentations without bodily alteration. During childhood (before age 10), about one-third (*n* = 16) felt a strong desire to become a girl or believed themselves to be female. The remainder began to recognize a desire to be female during adolescence (*n* = 15) or adulthood (*n* = 10). They self-identified as heterosexual, bisexual, lesbian, and asexual. Although our sample included many male individuals who had had sexual relationships or encounters with other male persons, no one in our sample self-identified as gay at the time of the interview or at any time during their lives.

A small number of persons (*n* = 5) who cross-dressed and had no desire for SRS referred to themselves in more politically oriented terms. While there are subtle differences in politics, all five of these people have used transgenderism to challenge binary assumptions about sex, gender, and sexuality. Their intent is not to 'pass' as women but to challenge the idea that gender is a 'natural' expression of sex and sexuality. This group of five includes one 'radical transgenderist'—an anatomical, heterosexual male person with a masculine gender identity, who uses cross-dressing as a means to express feminine aspects of self and to challenge traditional binary conceptualizations of sex, gender, and sexuality. It also includes one 'ambigenderist', an individual who lives alternatively as a man and a woman, and who believes that categories of sexual orientation do not exist and that sexuality is a spectrum. Depending on how he or she feels, he or she frequently went out 'in between'—as neither a man nor a woman (with long hair, makeup, high heels, tight pants, and a two-day growth of beard). In addition, this group includes three people who self-identified as a 'third gender'. These three individuals believed that all people have both masculine and feminine attributes. Their desire was to develop and be able to publicly present both aspects of self and to live as a combination of both genders. Like the ambigenderist, they resisted categorizing themselves according to sexual identity. In our discussions of the transgendered people in our sample, we have self-consciously adhered to the self-identifications used by our volunteers, with the exception of the final group of five. For purposes of clarity, we refer to this group as gender radicals. We have taken the liberty of doing this because all of them emphasized their desire to eliminate the existing system of gender, rather than just their own gender.

Our research was conducted over a one-year period, spanning 1994 and 1995. Early in the research process, we made a conscious decision to include all full-time or nearly full-time transgenderists who volunteered. We solicited volunteers through 14 transgender support groups, transgender online services, and by responding to personal ads in a national transgender publication. People in every region of the contiguous 48 states volunteered for interviews, making our research national in scope. Participants resided in large urban areas, small towns, suburbs, and rural areas. Our sample includes 4 African Americans, 2 Asians, 1 Hispanic, and 58 Caucasians. Participants ranged in age from 24 to 68 years, with a mean age of 44. Occupationally, they were diverse with jobs ranging from doctors, airline pilots, computer systems analysts, engineers, college professors, schoolteachers, enlisted members of the military, police officers, welders, mechanics, food service and clerical workers, and janitors. Although our sample was occupationally diverse, the majority was well educated and had long employment histories in the skilled trades and professions. Most members of our sample were either employed or voluntarily unemployed (i.e., retired or student) at the time we talked with them. Nonetheless, one post-operative and eight preoperative transsexuals were unemployed, and the majority of those who lived full-time as the gender into which they were not assigned at birth were vastly underemployed.[1]

Respondents were guided through several areas of inquiry, including their earliest transgender experiences or feelings; being discovered cross-dressed; acquiring girls' or women's clothing, makeup, and wigs; learning about and refining a feminine appearance or persona; participating in transgender support groups or online communities; finding therapists and surgeons and experiences with the medical community; identifying and labelling emotions, feelings, behaviours, and identity; telling others; transformations or stability in sexual fantasy, behaviour, and identity; and political and gender attitudes. Interviews ranged from 45 minutes to eight hours in length, averaging about three hours.

Early Transgendered Experiences

Examination of the earliest recollections that transgendered individuals have of feeling that either their sex or gender was 'wrong' or did not 'fit' for them are useful in providing insight into the earliest manifestations that become alternative identities. Many recollections of childhood may, in fact, be reconstructed biographies. Nonetheless, these are materials from which individuals mold current identities and, therefore are valid and significant.[2] This is the process in which the collective creation of biographical stories brings phenomenologically real 'true selves' into being (Mason-Schrock, 1996).

Gender constancy—a sense that a person's gender is a permanent aspect of self—is acquired between the ages of three and five years (Kohlberg, 1966; Kohlberg and Ulian, 1974). In our sample, 16 transsexuals recalled wanting to be girls or knowing that they really were girls during early childhood. For all but one of the remainder, feelings of being or wanting to be a woman emerged during adolescence or adulthood. Among cross-dressers, all reported knowing they were boys in early childhood and throughout adolescence, but four said they remembered wishing they could be girls during early childhood, and two reported knowing they were male but wishing they could become female during adolescence. Fetishistic cross-dressers and gender radicals did not report feeling they were or wanting to become women. Feminine behaviours and feelings of being or wanting to be girls created confusion for young children and adolescents, particularly when they received messages that they could not be or act that way.

For transsexuals and cross-dressers, one way of making sense of the incongruity between sex and gender was to explore whether a feminine boy might actually be able to become a girl. For example, one cross-dresser explained that at about the age of five, 'I remember . . . asking my mother out in the backyard, "Am I always going to be a boy? Could I change and be a girl someday?"' Such

questions are undoubtedly common among young children. For most children, clothing and other expressions of gender are signifiers of maleness or femaleness. Cross-dressers explained that they were satisfied with explanations that they could not change their anatomy and become female but that they continued to want to temporarily 'become' girls by wearing feminine clothing, makeup, and wigs. As adults, all but four cross-dressers (who were exploring the possibility they might be transsexual) reported knowing they were male and being happy with their sex and gender identity. Throughout their lives, they were able to conceal their transgenderism much more easily than were transsexuals, who felt compelled to act and be feminine at all times.

Among transsexuals, confusion over gender, desires to be female, or feelings of being female were commonly reported in childhood and over the life course. Many of the transsexuals in our sample thought they really were girls (in the dominant cultural sense) until they began to receive messages to the contrary. For example, one postoperative transsexual explained her earliest understanding of gender and the way in which it started to be corrected. She said,

> I was probably three or four years old. . . . I remember playing with paper dolls and Barbie dolls and stuff with my sisters and wearing their clothes. I didn't even know I wasn't a girl until [at school] I was told it was time to line up for a restroom break.

Differentiating themselves from girls did not come easily for these 16 transsexuals. Socializing messages might be gentle and subtle, as the ones above, or more laden with overt hostility and anger. For example, another preoperative transsexual explained,

> I can remember begging my mother to let me wear her clothes. . . . I kicked and screamed. . . . Another time she was ironing and I wanted my own ironing board and iron and be just like mommy. This time she got really angry and I guess I was becoming

aware of the fact that I wasn't ever going to be a little girl, that it was socially unacceptable . . . because she said, 'You want to be a little girl? Well, we'll put you in a little dress and tie your hair up in ribbons.' . . . She became aggressive about it and at that point I understood that it was socially unacceptable.

In early childhood, cross-dressing and cross-gender behaviour appear to have been tolerated. However, as children advanced beyond the 'toddler' stage, they were pressured by adults and other children to recognize and adhere to traditional conceptualizations of gender and conform to masculine stereotypes. Pressures to conform to the gender binary were often based on homophobic assumptions about gender 'deviants'. For example, a non-operative transsexual said,

Around the time I was 9 or 10 years old, there was one boy in the neighborhood . . . [who] was never allowed to spend the night at my house. . . . All he would tell me is, 'My dad won't let me.' One afternoon I approached his dad about it. . . . This man turned an incredible red-purple color and shaking and pointing a finger in my face [said], 'Because you're a fucking queer!' I didn't know what those words meant, but it was clear from his body language that whatever those words were tied to was not ok.

The pressure to adhere to the masculine stereotype was strong, and many in our sample tried to conform. Cross-dressers hid their dressing, segmenting it off from the rest of their lives. Among transsexuals, such segmentation of the feminine aspect of self was more difficult. The majority felt more comfortable playing with girls, participating in 'girls' activities, and expressing and presenting themselves in more feminine ways. For those whose transgender feelings and behaviours began in early childhood, pressures to 'fit' into the masculine stereotype and 'act' like boys created confusion about identity, an internalized sense of deviance, and frequently strong self-loathing. For example, a preoperative transsexual said, 'I didn't

know it was transsexual. I just didn't feel like a male. Everyone was telling me I was and I felt I had to act that way. . . . I felt it was something very, very wrong.'

After an initial period of confusion about sex and gender, most children recognized that cross-dressing and feminine behaviour were deviant and, therefore, they tried to repress it and keep it secret. This suggests that as children begin to understand the binary gender system, they become ashamed of feminine or transgendered feelings, learn to hide their behaviours, and become confused about who they are and how they fit into the world. Many in our sample talked about becoming addicted to alcohol or drugs later in life, in an effort to numb the emotional pain they experienced and to repress the 'true self', which did not fit and, therefore, needed to be repressed. Throughout adolescence and adulthood, most went through periods of 'purging', when they would stop engaging in transgendered behaviour and throw out feminine clothing, makeup, and wigs. Despite the stigma attached to transgenderism, however, the need to 'be themselves' was strong. Even as they tried to stop, and as their feminine attributes were criticized and sanctioned, they found it impossible to stop and learned to become more and more secretive. For example, a preoperative transsexual explained,

I was being beat up, called sissy. . . . I didn't feel normal. I felt like, 'Why are you doing this? This isn't right. You're a boy.' But I couldn't stop. The curiosity kept drawing me to it and I kept doing it. I felt guilty and I always thought after I . . . took the clothes off, 'I'm not going to do this anymore. This is silly.' A few days later . . . I was back doing it again.

Coming Out to One's Self

For many transgendered individuals, coming to terms with identity is driven by three factors: (1) events that inform them that to feel as they do is 'wrong' (2) finding that there are names for their feelings, and (3) learning that there are others who have had similar experiences. The search for authenticity is a motivating factor in the desire to resolve identity (Gecas, 1991). Because of the centrality of community in the formation and legitimation of identity (see Taylor and Whittier, 1992), the efforts of transgenderists to find and express a 'true self' are mitigated by their contacts with the transgendered world, just as they are affected by the dominant culture. To 'confess' gender (or transgenderism), one must communicate in an established idiom or risk the desired authenticity. While new identities are emergent, they are created within the constraints of current understandings. Furthermore, because of dominant beliefs that incongruity between assumed sex and presented gender is indicative of homosexuality, and that such is deviant, as transgenderists mix or replace masculinity with femininity on either a temporary or permanent basis, they frequently wonder what this implies about their sexuality.

When individuals fail to adhere to the gender binary, they are often told they are wrong or bad, so they tend to initially think of themselves as sick or deviant. Until they find similar others who have rejected stigma, self-blame and the internalization of deviance are common. As the transgenderists in our sample became aware that there were others in the world like them, they experienced a sense of self-recognition, and most quickly aligned themselves with new potential identities. The refinement and adoption of relatively stable identities occurred within the possibilities offered by the transgender subculture, which has been heavily influenced by medical models of transgenderism.

Most transsexuals and a minority of the cross-dressers in our sample reported being labelled 'sissies' by parents, siblings, and schoolmates. Those labelled 'sissy' or 'girl-like' experienced extreme stigmatization, isolation, and at times abuse. Derogative comments from family members seemed to affect the self-esteem and self-concept more than insults from peers or other non-relatives. One non-operative transsexual married to a woman recounted how her parents and friends pressured her to be more masculine. She said,

> The kids in the neighborhood that I wanted to be friends with . . . were the girls. . . . I wanted my own doll and remember the boys in the neighborhood seemed to have a real

problem with that. . . . In that same time period, my dad came into my bedroom one night and he took all the dolls out of my bed. He said I could keep the animals but the dolls had to go because, 'You're a little boy and little boys don't sleep with dolls.'

Even with such social sanctions, the feelings persisted. Among transsexuals and a minority of cross-dressers, to be doing what girls were doing felt comfortable and natural. For many, playing with boys was stressful, anxiety provoking, and often induced feelings of failure and low self-esteem. Consequently, many transgenderists found ways to separate themselves from those who reinforced the feeling of difference and deviance, staying to themselves as much as possible.

Just as children tried to conceal transgenderism or conform to the expectations of family and other socializing agents, adults were likely to engage in similar coping strategies until they began to accept themselves as transgenderists. Transsexuals tended to react to negative messages by being hypermasculine. As adults, many in our sample went into physically strenuous or high-risk occupations where they could prove their masculinity. [One participant] said, 'I would avoid doing anything that someone might see as being a remotely feminine kind of thing. I wouldn't even help my ex-[wife] plant a flower garden.' Out of our entire sample, 18 had served in the military. Most said they hoped the experience would make men out of them. Although an extreme example of this sentiment, another preoperative transsexual explained,

> I knew there was something wrong with me and I wanted to do whatever I could to make a real man out of myself. So I joined the army. Voluntarily went to Vietnam. Voluntarily carried a machine gun in the jungle. I was a paratrooper. I was a Green Beret. I did everything I could do in that three-year period to make a man out of myself.

Cross-dressers were less likely to react in hypermasculine ways, primarily because they kept their feminine side hidden.

Throughout childhood, adolescence, and early to mid-adulthood most transgenderists in our study experienced shame and confusion for not being 'right'. They lived in a social region for which there was no idiom. Because they were sanctioned for feminine attributes and behaviour, they learned that there was no place for feminine boys or men in society. Feeling more comfortable with girls, they began to understand gender and sex within the social options presented to them. The socially constructed aspects of reality were so strong that believing they were born with the wrong genitals seemed more plausible than violating the gender binary. Even in adulthood, transsexuals frequently made efforts to conceal their genitals, even from themselves, by tucking them between the legs or taping them up. While relatively uncommon in our sample (during adulthood, $n = 2$), when transsexuals were unaware of available medical options or were unable to afford SRS, they attempted self-castration. These efforts indicate the degree to which gender is signified by genitalia.

It was common in our sample for transgenderists to experience sexual attractions to other men, to have sexual fantasies about men, or both. At the same time, they experienced social sanctions and pressures to conform to dominant conceptualizations of gender. While they worried they might be gay, they began to experience and explore sexuality within the binary system and its ancillary compulsory heterosexuality (Rich, 1989). As a 36-year-old bisexual cross-dresser explained, 'You're getting all kinds of messages that men are men and women are women. Sissy boys and fags. The adolescent years are really, really hard on homosexuals and anything not mainstream sexually.' Within our sample, adolescent male persons and adult men in the early stages of identity formation were frequently confused about the implications feminine behaviour had for their sexuality. As men, they knew sex with male individuals was unacceptable; but as women, it was a source of validation. Most reacted by repressing attractions to men, at least until they began to go out in public as women, when sexual interactions with men were indicative of passage into social womanhood.

None of the people in our sample adopted a gay identity, even temporarily, although sexual experimentation with male persons was a common aspect of the coming-out experience. Because of an understanding that transgenderism, homosexuality, and femininity were wrong, all but two transgenderists made efforts to conceal, to purge, to deny, and to cure themselves in order to avoid acceptance of their transgenderism.

Most commonly, the triggering event for acceptance of an identity came when, either accidentally or intentionally, the individual encountered others who served as symbols for available identities. However, role models who challenged binary conceptualizations of gender were largely unavailable because 'there is no place for a person who is neither a woman or a man' (Lorber, 1994: 96), finding role models and formulating an identity outside the gender binary is virtually impossible. Thus, alternative identities were restricted to those available within the gender binary, usually found among those who had crossed *from* one gender *to* the only other one known to be legitimately available.

Learning of the availability of transsexualism and seeing such women on television and reading about them in newspapers and magazines provided opportunities to know that there were alternative identities available. One newly post-operative transsexual looked back on her late teens as generally unhappy and confusing but says that she made a major discovery about both herself and society when

> I was in high school and I started to hear about Renee Richards. I graduated high school in '72, so she was just coming out when I was just starting high school. At that time, I still thought that I was alone in the world. . . . When I started to hear about Renee Richards, then I said, 'Maybe there is somebody else, but this is the only other person that knows where I'm coming from.'

Finding others who felt as they did helped to alleviate, but not remove, the sense of isolation experienced by transgendered individuals. Nonetheless, through such initial exposures, many individuals learned that there were alternatives to living in confusion and shame, if one was willing to transform (either temporarily or permanently) to the other gender. Simply learning that SRS was possible led some to reconfigure their identities and reassess their place in the world.

In today's information age, online computer services appear to be emerging as a primary location for finding both virtual and real mentors. It was common for transgenderists who deciphered and accepted their identities in the 1990s to have done so with the assistance of online bulletin boards and personal conversations with already-identifying transgenderists. Here, in the privacy of one's home or work area, contacts could be made that allowed both experimentation with identities and informational inquiries that did not jeopardize existing identities or social, occupational, and familial relationships. In addition, online services allowed individuals to access information beyond that concerning the strictly erotic aspects of cross-dressing. For some transgenderists, this was a critical factor, as tabloid media and sensationalist reports have created a common misperception of cross-dressing as primarily an erotic activity. A self-identified radical transgenderist credits his subscription to one online service with helping him understand that cross-dressing need not be sexually charged. He said, 'It wasn't until I got a hold of [online service] that I got exposed to aspects other than the erotic aspects, which are all over the place.'

For some, the occasion of encountering both real and reported transgenderists served only to raise more issues to be resolved. For example, one cross-dresser recalled finding fetishistic cross-dressers and transexuals in cyberspace. He related, 'Although there were similarities, there were also some grave differences, primarily in the fact that I felt more romantic interest. I didn't feel I was a heterosexual female trapped in a male body. I liked my male body.' Still, finding others even tangentially similar provided a forum in which to discover options and explore alternative identities. Thus, while we 'do' gender in interaction with others, it appears that the emergence of transgender identity and alternatives to the gender binary are dependent on others who will recognize one as an authentic social actor (West and Zimmerman, 1987).

Coming Out to Others

Accepting an identity for one's self was one thing; proclaiming and working to get others to accept it was quite different. Going public with a transgendered identity could be an intimidating experience, to say the least. The degree to which transgenderists were intimidated about revealing their transgenderism may be heard in the words of a 10-month, post-operative transsexual, who said,

> For somebody who's been a freak, a hippie, and a marijuana dealer, . . . and a flamboyant dresser, and somebody who refuses to get a conventional job and all this, somebody who's not been afraid of public opinion, it's, I think, notable that the gender area of my life and the social expectations were the one area I was afraid of public opinion.

Intimidation came from two fronts: (1) fears about how one would be treated by others and (2) anxieties about how others would cope with what was certainly seen by many as 'non-traditional' behaviour. Fear of the responses one will receive is to be expected. With the close cultural association drawn between transgenderism and homosexuality (Altman, 1982; Talamini, 1982; Bullough and Bullough, 1993), fears of violent and isolating homophobic reactions seem warranted.[3] In addition, as people become involved in significant relationships with others, many expressed concerns about how the news that they were transgendered would affect those close to them. These concerns typically centred on one's family, both nuclear and extended.

According to the accounts of those who have proclaimed their transgender identities to significant others, the fears about negative reactions were largely exaggerated, but not altogether unwarranted. Less than one-fourth of all persons interviewed for this project reported that their first experience of coming out to someone else lead to a negative reaction. This was related to several factors. First, transgenderists had exaggerated fears about the reactions of most significant others. Second, most individuals were actually successful at controlling knowledge of their transgenderism.

They consciously selected individuals to come out to those who were, in fact, sympathetic to the alternative identity. Who would be accepting was ascertained through discussions of various potentially volatile issues. In that way, transgenderists learned if there was a need for caution or preparatory education of the recipient. Those who received negative reactions to their proclamations were least likely to have gathered information or to have laid the necessary groundwork. Instead, they simply announced the new identity. For example, a preoperative transsexual decided to tell an 18-year-old daughter, who did not even know that her father had been cross-dressing, when the daughter moved back home. She said,

> After a week or two there, it seemed inappropriate not to tell my daughter. The girl lives in the house. For crying out loud, she's 18 years old. So I told her and I didn't really build up to it or anything. . . . She was always in the bathroom, doing hair and makeup and stuff. I stopped in to chat. I suppose it was like a bomb or something like that. 'By the way . . . I'm going to have a sex change.' She turned into an ice cube.

Although the experience of telling one's first 'other' was not necessarily a negative experience, fears remained, and careful, often painful, decisions were made regarding with whom to share an emergent identity. Interestingly, two factors stand out about these early disclosures. First, they were usually done only out of a sense of responsibility, when someone was perceived as 'needing to know'. Second, the individuals with whom this information was shared were almost always female, most often a significant other. This was true among all groups of transgenderists in our sample.

While some elected to share with their mothers, there was a characteristic tendency for most to report that it was extremely difficult to share their new identity with their parents. For some, this was more easily accomplished when the interaction with one's parents was not face-to-face or when the situation could be escaped quickly. Despite the urge to deliver the news and run, those who came out to others face-to-face, who had provided (or

offered to provide) information about transgenderism, and gave others time and space to cope with the information were most likely to receive tolerant, accepting, or supportive reactions. Still, much of the reaction to being told was dependent on the values of the recipient of the news, as well as the relationship itself. For example, a two-year post-operative transsexual who had been living with her male partner prior to having surgery recalled telling her mother about her decision to have SRS. She said, 'I told her, "Mom, I'm transsexual and I'm going to have SRS." My mom's response was, "Oh, thank God! I can deal with this." She thought I was going to tell her [my partner] and I were HIV positive.'

The arena where transgenderists (usually transsexuals) were least likely to receive positive reactions was at work. Although there were a few people who were permitted to transition on the job, it was more common for transsexuals to be fired, demoted, pressured to quit, and harassed by other workers. Some found employment in unskilled, low-wage jobs, such as janitors or in fast-food restaurants; others worked for temporary agencies. A few in our sample went back to college, transitioning as students. The loss of identity and the structure of one's daily routine that comes with a career was more difficult for transsexuals to cope with than the actual loss of income. After accepting a severance package in exchange for her silence about her job termination, one post-operative transsexual wrote to the first author, 'I have spent my entire life becoming the best [job title] I could be. Today I sold myself for 50 pieces of silver.' Frequently, the loss of professional identity and income came at the same time that relationships with old friends and family members were being risked and sometimes lost.

Early excursions into the public domain were commonly as frightening as coming out to significant others or on the job. While going out and passing in public may be thought to be different from coming out, it is important to recognize that for the majority of transgenderists, the goal is to be perceived and accepted as a woman, not a transgenderist. Telling others about their transgenderism is done primarily to lay the groundwork for greater expression, acceptance, and legitimation of a feminine identity, and this was accomplished in public and in private interactions. Although there was variation between going out in public or telling a significant other first, every person in our sample felt a need to expand their spheres of interaction with others. While control over access to information about the transgendered identity remained important, this became less salient as the need to interact with others publicly increased. Because of the fear of the danger inherent in negative public reactions, most transgenderists carefully planned and carried out their initial public excursions in limited-access locations.

When transgenderists began to go out in public, they did so because of a need to receive reactions from others to legitimate identity. While some have undoubtedly been driven back into the closet by their initial forays into public places, in our sample, such excursions served to increase commitment to the emergent identity. Selection of safe places for public ventures meant that transgenderists looked for locations where they could make quick and easy entrances and exits and where they are unlikely to encounter disapproving others. Transgenderists most commonly reported that their first ventures were to gay community events or locations, simply driving in their cars, or going to known meeting places for transgenderists. The most common site for first ventures was gay bars. Here, among other marginalized community members, individuals could try out their new identities. Despite a strong desire to avoid being perceived as homosexual, gay bars were defined as safe havens (Levine, Shaiova, and Mihailovic, 1975). For example, a preoperative transsexual, who had been living as a woman full-time for seven months, related that 'while I was working on coming out full-time, I needed a safe place to go while I practised. The bar was it. I know the drag queens might not like that. It was still a safe place for me though.'

Typically, successful ventures provided the impetus and courage for transgenderists to move forward and present themselves face-to-face with others; however, these steps were taken slowly and carefully. Movement was usually into either a gay bar or a gathering of other transgenderists. For example, a preoperative transsexual who is fully out only to one family member and acquaintances in the transgender community, explained her first time out in public as follows:

> About 10 years ago. . . . I was out very late one night, got in my car, drove downtown to the north side of the city which is known for its gays, lesbians, and an occasional transvestite. Walked to what I thought was a bar where transvestites hung out and sat down, had a couple of drinks, couple cigarettes. . . . I did things like get dressed and drove around. I'd go for a short walk around the block or something. I didn't think I was good enough yet to go out in daylight and try to pull it off as a woman.

In gay bars and neighbourhoods, transgenderists were most likely to be interpreted as marginal members of the queer subculture. Such settings provide a place where one who is 'neither woman nor man' (Lorber, 1994: 96) is most likely to find a social place that does not disturb the social order.

For others, the impetus to appear in public for the first time surfaced when opportunities arose to meet other transgenderists in the context of a support group. Support groups were one location where the most important identity tests occurred, when the individual encountered other transgenderists. As they entered such groups, transgenderists commonly reported a feeling of total acceptance and freedom to be themselves, often for the first time in their lives. If these supposedly similar others were willing to accept the individual, and the individual felt safe in the group, this communicated that she or he truly was transgendered. The value of support groups, online services, organizations, and publications becomes most clear in this context.

Support groups can be very important in facilitating identity exploration and the arrival at a 'final' identity, but they could also induce anxiety, confusion, and fright in individual transgenderists. While they may have already confronted their 'difference' in their own minds and with others in their lives, to come face-to-face with 'the real thing' could be intimidating. For those who were courageous enough to take such steps, support groups almost always functioned as they were intended: they provided support for a stigmatized identity. Nonetheless, such acceptance was provided within a narrow range of social options that were based on acceptance of a binary system of sex and gender. Transsexualism was commonly explained by biological theories, and those who had completed the transition process gave insight on how to gain access to medical procedures to those in earlier stages. Among cross-dressers, 'dressing' was encouraged as an acceptable way for men to express the feminine self. All transgenderists were encouraged to perfect their ability to pass during informal interactions and copious seminars on style, makeup, feminine body language, and the feminine voice and diction.

Resolution of Identity

After a lifetime of being stigmatized and feeling as if they did not fit, the transgenderists in our sample engaged in a long process of identity exploration. The majority in our sample explained that they had arrived at a 'true' identity, with which they felt they could 'be themselves'. Only a minority of men who cross-dressed, but were exploring transsexualism, had not yet resolved their identities. In their efforts to resolve and establish an identity that was comfortable, the individuals in our sample shared diverse goals and visions for themselves and the community. Transsexuals sought to 'completely' transform and live convincingly as their true (female) selves. Cross-dressers sought only to have opportunities to temporarily vary their public identity presentations, express their femininity, and be recognized and treated as women. Only the gender radicals in our sample wished to live and be recognized as transgendered. Significant differences appeared among specific transgender identities. Among most transsexuals and cross-dressers, there was an overwhelming desire that femininity and treatment as a woman were achieved. For a minority, as experience and confidence were gained, passing was a desirable, but no longer essential, aspect of going out in public. These people tended to recognize that physical stature, including height and musculature, made

it difficult, if not impossible, for them to pass. Among gender radicals, concerns with presenting a convincing appearance as a woman were secondary, if at all important for them. The goal was to challenge dominant conceptualizations of gender and create new possibilities.

Among transsexuals, because of the internalized identity as women, it was most common to find an aspiration to be seen and identified by others as real women. When discussing this feeling, transsexuals expressed a need to 'pass' in their daily interactions. This desire was paramount for such individuals and taken as a symbolic testament of final arrival at their desired self and socially constructed identity. One divorced, preoperative transsexual summarized this sentiment well when she commented, '[Passing] to me is the most important aspect of the whole thing. If you can't do that, I don't see the point of living this way.' Enduring the internal and social struggles encountered in the process of recognizing and accepting a new identity and introducing oneself to the outside world was valued only if there could be a non-stigmatizing, 'normal' resolution to the process. Transsexuals did not wish to challenge the gender binary, although most perceived their transitions as very radical actions. Rather, their goal was to 'become' the women they 'truly are' and to pass from being their masculine selves into full womanhood. Often, after learning to pass and completing the transformation process, transsexuals dropped out of the transgender community and assumed their place as women in society.

Within the transgender community, a desire to pass and blend into society sometimes introduced tensions and additional levels of hierarchy and structure. Those who sought to pass, and believed they had the ability to do so, sometimes believed that varying statuses of achievement (passing ability) were important. Some passable transgenderists, therefore, viewed those who could not pass as liabilities. One transsexual showed her aptitude for clear expression when she explained her withdrawal from a local support group because, 'I didn't feel the group gave me anything. I was too far ahead of them. . . . We're still friends, but I won't walk down the street with them.'

Although most transgenderists were concerned with passing as well as possible, there is an emergent group within the community that seeks a free expression of gender, outside of the binary system. For example, the ambigenderist in our sample explained that she had moved beyond such concerns, focusing on her own welfare and identity, not the perceptions of others.

> At one time, [passing] was important. I don't care anymore. A lot of times I'll go out in a dress . . . no makeup on. I'm not trying to pass and I know I'm not going to pass. I am who I am. . . . It is political, everything's political. A social statement about who I am and I'm going to express myself.

For both those who were and were not seeking to pass when in public, the most common, overwhelming desire was to simply be accepted. This was difficult unless they could find ways to fit within the binary and symbolically communicate identity within the idiomatic system of gender expression. To 'blend in' to society as a woman was something most transgenderists, especially transsexuals, saw as an ultimate goal. The ultimate resolution was an identity that was not wrapped in the language of transgenderism. To be known as simply just another person was desirable.

Despite one's own aspirations for individual identity and ability to blend socially, there was a sense of community among the vast majority of transgenderists that facilitated a desire to work with others and to contribute to the developmental processes of other community members.

This attempt to contribute to the development of others in the community came in both implicit and explicit forms. For some, this could be accomplished simply by being visible to other community members. More often, such forms of encouragement and assistance were much more direct and overt. For example, a gender radical, who is an active member of a local support group, editor of a local transgender community newsletter, and who conducts research on the structure of the transgender community, merged the implicit and explicit. This person explained,

I feel the best thing I can do to create change is just to thrive, to be myself, to present myself in a way that I am comfortable with. The hell with everything else. We need to be more open. We need to be more proud of who we are as opposed to being more ashamed. I think our movement could be much stronger. . . . I want people to start questioning things even though they may look at me oddly. People always say that I am sick or insane. Maybe one person may start to look at things differently. If other people start seeing that, we can act normally in the open with people knowing about you and that they don't have to be frightened.

Conclusion

Gender is so pervasive that it is taken for granted and often completely overlooked, until the norms of gender presentation, interaction, or organization are inadvertently violated or deliberately challenged (Lorber, 1994). Gender receives constant surveillance and is continually policed through social interactions that socialize new and existing members of society and sanction those who violate the rules (see Gagné and Tewksbury, 1996). At the organizational level, individuals are categorized and assigned meaning and roles on the basis of gender. This is based on the erroneous assumption that gender will be congruent with sex. In organizational settings, sleeping arrangements are often based on sex/gender (as in dormitory arrangements) and bathrooms and locker rooms are segregated by sex/gender (see Rothblatt, 1995). Where individuals' gender does not 'match' their sex, there is little organizational space in which they can exist. At the institutional level (in the military, economic, religious, legal, political, and medical realms), individuals' roles, rights, and responsibilities are determined by gender, under the assumption that gender is indicative of sex (or sexuality) and that labour must continue to be divided on that basis. In everyday life, gender is achieved and reinforced through interactions, where its idiom is derived from, and either legitimated or stigmatized by, the very superstructure and infrastructure in which it exists (West and Fenstermaker, 1995).

Individuals who attempt to challenge the binary conceptualization of sex and gender, by living androgynously between genders, are likely to be ridiculed and stigmatized (see Gagné and Tewksbury, 1996). Those who attempt to live outside of the sex/gender binary, for example, by publicly confessing that they are male persons with (or who would like to have) breasts or vaginas, are also likely to be ostracized. Those who are willingly or unwittingly unconvincing in their gender presentations and interactions are subject to greater levels of emotional and physical abuse than are those who are able to pass. It is those who are publicly perceived as 'not women/ not men' who pose the greatest challenge to the binary system. Nonetheless, the goal of most is to be perceived as a woman and treated like a lady. Those who pass are perceived as women, and any challenge they might have posed to the gender system goes unnoticed.

As we have shown, the recognition, exploration, establishment, and final resolution of an identity outside cultural understandings is a difficult, complex, and for some, impossible process. Despite the policing of gender that was experienced by the transgenderists in our sample, the need to express a 'true self' was an overwhelming urge that could not be denied. Although many tried to hide their femininity through hypermasculine activity or self-isolation, and most tried to deny transgendered feelings and urges, all eventually found the urge to 'be themselves' overwhelmingly undeniable. Among our sample, others' reactions to them playing with girls, engaging in 'girls' activities, cross-dressing, wearing makeup, and other expressions of a feminine self caused confusion, anxiety, and a deep sense of shame. Only when they discovered that there were others like them were they able to begin to make sense of what they were experiencing and who they were. Entering into a community of supportive others allowed for an exploration and resolution of identity. Our data suggest that gender is not a natural and inevitable outgrowth of sex. Those who are not comfortable expressing gender that is congruent with genital configuration experience an overwhelming urge to express gender in alternative ways. Nonetheless, the vast majority stay within the gender binary as masculine men and feminine women. The tendency to stay within the binary gender system is so strong that as Hausman (1993) has asserted, gender determines sex, rather than the reverse. Given the limited range of identities available to them, it is interesting, but not surprising, that the overwhelming majority of transgendered individuals adhere to traditional conceptualizations of sex and gender.

Notes

1. We recognize that there is a transgender community within the impoverished class, but we were unable to solicit volunteers from that segment of the population through the routes we used.

2. This view, however, is disputed by others who believe that retrospective biography construction is actually a search for ways 'to fashion this information into a story that leads inexorably to the identity' that is being constructed (Mason-Schrock, 1996: 176–7).

3. A substantial minority of our sample talked about experiencing intimidation, harassment, and violence in public places. It was not uncommon for those learning to 'pass' to be called 'faggot' or other homophobic epithets. One very tall, muscular cross-dresser told us about having her wig pulled off and being physically assaulted.

References

Adam, B. 1995. *The Rise of a Gay and Lesbian Movement*, rev. ed. New York: Twayne.

Altman, D. 1982. *The Homosexualization of America*. Boston: Beacon.

Bornstein, K. 1994. *Gender Outlaw. On Men, Women, and the Rest of Us*. New York: Random House.

Bullough, V.L., and B. Bullough. 1993. *Cross Dressing, Sex, and Gender*. Philadelphia: University of Pennsylvania Press.

D'Emilio, J. 1983. *Sexual Politics, Sexual Communities: The Making of a Homosexual Minority in the United States, 1940–1970*. Chicago: University of Chicago Press.

Epstein, S. 1994. 'A Queer Encounter: Sociology and the Study of Sexuality', *Sociological Theory* 12: 188–202.

Foucault, M. [1978] 1990. *The History of Sexuality: An Introduction*. Vol. 1, R. Hurley, trans. New York: Vintage.

Gagné, P., and R. Tewksbury. 1996. 'No "Man's" Land: Transgenderism and the Stigma of the Feminine Man', in M. Texler Segal and V. Demos, eds., *Advances in Gender Research*. Vol. 1. Greenwich, CT: jai Press.

Gecas, V. 1991. 'The Self-Consent as a Basis for a Theory of Motitvation', in J.A. Howard and P.L. Callero, eds., *The Self–Society Dynamic*. Cambridge, UK: Cambridge University Press.

Goffman, E. 1963. *Stigma: Notes on the Management of a Spoiled Identity*. Englewood Cliffs, NJ: Prentice-Hall.

Hausman, B.L. 1993. 'Demanding Subjectivity: Transsexualism, Medicine and the Technologies of Gender', *Journal of the History of Sexuality* 3: 270–302.

Herdt, G. 1994. 'Introduction: Third Sexes and Third Genders', in G. Herdt, ed., *Third Sex, Third Gender: Beyond Sexual Dimorphism in Culture and History*. New York: Zone Books.

Kohlberg, L. 1966. 'A Cognitive-Developmental Analysis of Children's Sex-role Concepts and Attitudes', in E.E. Maccoby, ed., *The Development of Sex Differences*. Stanford, CA: Stanford University Press.

Kohlberg, L., and D.Z. Ulian. 1974. 'Stages in the Development of Psychosexual Concepts and Attitudes', in R.C. Friedman, R.M. Richard, and R.L. Vande Wiele, eds., *Sex Differences in Behavior*. New York: Wiley.

Laqueur, T. 1990. *Making Sex: Body and Gender from the Greeks to Freud*. Cambridge, ma: Harvard University Press.

Levine, E.M., C.H. Shaiova, and M. Mihailovic. 1975. 'Male to Female: The Role Transformation of Transexuals', *Archives of Sexual Behavior* 5: 173–85.

Lorber, J. 1994. *Paradoxes of Gender*. New Haven, CT: Yale University Press.

Mason-Schrock, D. 1996. 'Transsexuals' Narrative Construction of the "true self"', *Social Psychology Quarterly* 59: 176–92.

Morris, J. 1974. *Conundrum*. Faber & Faber.

Namaste, K. 1994. 'The Politics of Inside/Out: Queer Theory, Poststructuralism, and a Sociological Approach to Sexuality', *Sociological Theory* 12: 220–31.

Pauly, I.B. 1990. 'Gender Identity Disorders: Evaluation and Treatment', *Journal of Sex Education & Therapy* 16: 2–24.

Raymond, J.G. 1994. *The Transsexual Empire: The Making of the She-male*. New York: Teachers College Press.

Rich, A. 1989. 'Compulsory Heterosexuality and Lesbian Existence', in L. Richardson and V. Taylor, eds., *Feminist Frontiers II: Rethinking Sex, Gender, and Society*. New York: Random House.

Rothblatt, M. 1995. *The Apartheid of Sex: A Manifesto on the Freedom of Gender*. New York: Crown.

Seidman, S. 1994. 'Symposium: Queer Theory/ Sociology: A Dialogue', *Sociological Theory* 12: 166–77.

———, ed. 1996. *Queer Theory/Sociology*. Cambridge, MA: Blackwell.

Stein, A., and K. Plummer. 1994. 'I can't even think straight': Queer Theory and the Missing Sexual Revolution in Sociology', *Sociological Theory* 12: 1778–87.

Stoller, R.J. 1971. 'The Term "Transvestism"', *Archives of General Psychiatry* 24: 230–7.

Stone, G.P. 1975. 'Appearance and the Self', in D. Brissett and C. Edgley, eds., *Life as Theatre: A Dramaturgical Sourcebook*. Chicago: Aldine.

Talamini, J.T. 1981. 'Transvestism: Expression of a SecondSelf', *Free Inquiry in Creative Sociology* 9: 72–4.

———. 1982. *Boys Will Be Girls: The Hidden World of the Heterosexual Male Transvestite*. Lanham, MD: University Press of America.

Taylor, V., and N. Whittier. 1992. 'Collective Identity and Social Movement Communities: Lesbian Feminist Mobilization', in A.D. Morris and C. McClurg Mueller, eds., *Frontiers in Social Movement Theory*. New Haven, CT: Yale University Press.

Tewksbury, R., and P. Gagné. 1996. 'Transgenderists: Products of Non-normative Intersections of Sex, Gender, and Sexuality', *Journal of Men's Studies* 5: 105–29.

Weinberg, R.S. 1978. 'On "Doing" and "Being" Gay: Sexual Behavior and Homosexual Male Self-identity', *Journal of Homosexuality* 4: 563–78.

West, C., and D.H. Zimmerman. 1987. 'Doing Gender', *Gender & Society* 1: 125–51.

West, C., and S. Fenstermaker. 1995. 'Doing Difference', *Gender & Society* 9: 8–37.

Woodhouse, A. 1989. *Fantastic Women: Sex, Gender and Transvestism*. New Brunswick, NJ: Rutgers University Press.

CHAPTER 9

'It's Part of the Game': Physicality and the Production of Gender in Women's Hockey

Nancy Theberge

Perhaps as much as any social setting in the contemporary period, the world of sport is seeing considerable change regarding the condition of women and gender relations. To be sure, professional sport remains largely a male preserve in which the majority of opportunities and rewards go to men. In other contexts, including school and university sport and international competitions, including most notably the Olympics, opportunities for women are expanding, performances are improving, and public interest is rising. These developments pose a challenge to ideologies of gender and to the historical association between gender, physicality, and power.

A particularly significant challenge to gender ideologies is the increased involvement of women in sports that Bryson (1990: 174) calls 'flag carriers' of masculinity. These are sports that 'quintessentially promote hegemonic masculinity and to which a majority of people are regularly exposed' (Bryson, 1990: 174). Writing from an Australian setting, Bryson cites as examples cricket and football (i.e., soccer). In the North American context, the best examples are football and ice hockey. In these sports, which celebrate force and toughness and involve direct confrontation between competitors, it is 'dominate or lose' (Whitson, 1994: 359).

This article provides an analysis of challenges to hegemonic masculinity posed by women's participation in the 'flag carrier' sport of ice hockey. Data are taken from fieldwork and interviews with players and coaches participating at the highest

levels of the sports in Canada. The analysis begins with a discussion of the satisfaction players derive from the physicality of sport. This is followed by a detailed examination of the material and ideological conditions that structure the experience of physicality. A key determinant of the practice of women's hockey is rules that limit—but by no means eliminate—body contact. Debates about the place of contact in women's hockey and its relationship to injury occur within a framework in which men's sport is positioned as the 'real' thing. The conclusion contrasts the transformative potential of sports organized within the dominant model of masculine sport with possibilities presented by activities organized outside the framework of institutionalized sport.

Data and Methodology

Women's hockey is now experiencing a period of growth and development, with the most notable event in this regard being its inclusion in the Olympic program for the 1998 games in Nagano, Japan. The first World Championships were held in 1990, with subsequent events in 1992 and 1994. Canada has won all three of these competitions.

In Canada, the sport is growing; the number of female players registered with the Canadian Hockey Association increased from 8,146 in 1990–1 to 19,050 in 1994–5. These figures do not include girls playing on boys' teams, for which there are no reliable statistics (Etue and Williams,

1996). While school and university programs are expanding, the sport is primarily organized in clubs that are affiliated with provincial associations, which in turn are affiliated with the national governing body, the Canadian Hockey Association.

The analysis presented here is part of a broader study of women's ice hockey in Canada. The primary focus of the research is a team I call the Blades, which plays in a league located in a large Canadian metropolitan area. The league in which the Blades play is generally considered to be the strongest in the country. As an indication of this strength, several players from the Blades and from other teams in its league were members of one or more Canadian national teams that won World Championships in 1990, 1992, and 1994.

The research began when I attended the Annual General Meeting of the Provincial Women's Hockey Association in May 1992, where I met a woman who plays on the Blades and also operates a girls' hockey camp. In July I spent several days at the camp, where I met the Blades coach and told him of my interest in doing research in women's hockey. He was supportive, and in November, shortly after the start of the season, I attended a practice during which the coach introduced me to the team. I then met with the players in the coach's absence, explained my interests, and asked for permission to spend time with the team for the purpose of doing research.

Following this meeting, I began to attend games, practices, and other events such as the annual Christmas party. The fieldwork continued from November 1992 until the completion of the season in April 1993 and through the following season, from October 1993 until April 1994. I had complete access to team activities, including access to the team change room where I spent time with the players before and after games and practices. I also accompanied the team to out-of-town tournaments, including the provincial and national championships. Following each game, practice, or other events, I wrote field notes. The field notes cover a range of issues concerned with the practice and organization of the sport, team activities, and team dynamics.

To provide some perspective on experiences of players from elsewhere in the sport, I interviewed

an additional eight players from three provinces, all of whom played at an elite level. I also interviewed eleven coaches from three provinces, all of whom also have experience at the highest levels of women's hockey. These additional interviews, conducted between 1993 and 1995, focused on the practice of the sport and the organization of women's hockey in Canada. All of the interviews were tape-recorded and transcribed.

There is no professional women's hockey in Canada, and the women who are the subject of this research have 'day jobs' or are students. Their involvement in hockey is nonetheless of a very high calibre, and they are committed athletes. For the purpose of the analysis provided here, it is important to note that the data are taken from athletes who participate at the highest level of the sport.

Playing the Game: The Construction of Women's Hockey

The rules of play in men's and women's ice hockey are substantially the same, with one major difference: the rules on women's hockey prohibit intentional body checking—that is, intentional efforts to hit, or 'take out', an opposing player. To be sure, there is still considerable use of the body and body contact in women's hockey, both intentional and unintentional. To watch a game is to see players constantly try to outmanoeuvre and outmuscle one another. At the same time, women's games are noticeably different from the full-contact game played at the higher levels of the men's sport.

Interviews with players and coaches reveal a variety of views about the elimination of body checking from women's hockey. Respondents generally agree this results in a game in which speed, strategy, and playing skills are featured more prominently than in a full-contact game, which emphasizes power and force. Beyond this point of agreement, however, lies greater debate about the construction of women's hockey, with contrasting assessments of the relation of women's and men's hockey.

Until the late 1980s, the rules regarding body contact in women's hockey varied across Canada. The sample of women interviewed for this research includes a number who have played both full contact and the current game, which prohibits body checking. These players see advantages to both versions. While most acknowledge the attraction of the game that favours speed and playmaking, a number of these same players also express a sense of pleasure and accomplishment in playing the full-contact game and in receiving and taking a body check well. In interviews, these women describe body checking as 'part of the game', 'the way it should be', and 'part of the fun'. In this view, body checking is a skill, one among a repertoire of abilities that players can master. The following statement by a player is a representative account:

> It's a certain aggressiveness. You're putting your strength against, your technique against. It's still a technique. It's not somebody, to me it's not go and kill that person, they hurt me, I'm going to get them back. It's nothing like that. It's a technique that you've learned and you can complete, and maybe you can complete it better than they can. You can prove your flexibility and your stamina, your stability on the ice.

Other players support the limitations on contact. One woman, who has never played the full-contact game, said:

> I prefer it without. Maybe just because I've always played without. You know the women's game being a bit different from the men's game, it may actually be better without it. I like to think of it as more of a finesse game. And I don't know if body contact has any part in it, really if it would enhance it in any way. I mean I think maybe the reason for having the body contact in the men's game is possibly just to make it more exciting to watch. I don't know. It's hard to say when you haven't really played that much.

Coaches also express a range of views. Some indicate that the women's game, as it is played today, is ideal—it is physical, sometimes very physical, and 'just right' in this regard. Some see the inclusion of body checking as the 'wedge' that leads to the unacceptably rough play that characterizes men's hockey. One coach offered the following comments:

> I ask myself sometimes, 'Would body contact be a good thing?' It could be good if they stay within the limits, which seems very hard to do. And if the guys didn't do it, we're not smarter than the guys. . . . Women's hockey, if you were allowed body contact, to me, we'll end up as guys' hockey with slashing and cross checking. In my head, it's hard to believe it won't happen.

Other coaches have reservations about, or actively disagree with, the current formulation. Like some players, these coaches say checking is 'part of the game' and a skill that can be—and should be—taught and used effectively. The argument that body checking is responsible for the violence that plagues the men's game is also disputed. Several respondents noted that women's hockey already has severe penalties—usually suspension for several games—that limit the incidence of dirty play. So long as these sanctions are in place, it is argued, introducing body checking will not lead to an increased incidence of other, undesirable features of men's hockey.

A number of players recognized the dilemma of playing an alternative version of the sport. The player quoted above on the technique of body checking had extensive experience playing boys' hockey before moving to women's hockey in late adolescence. She commented on the women's game:

> It is a different game and there are different rules. . . . I think a lot of women think it's better. But I prefer the game where you're allowed contact. I grew up playing that game. I just think it's different and why make it different . . . I want to be able to say I play hockey and [people] understand it's the same hockey. But now I have to say I play girls' hockey. It's not the same game as boys' hockey. . . . They're changing the game.

Another player, whose only experience is in women's hockey, offered further commentary. She described her reaction to a seminar she attended during which an official from the Canadian Hockey Association emphasized the uniqueness of the game:

> When you're playing a sport, you don't go out there saying, 'Ok, I'm a woman. Ok, I have to play like one.' You go out there and you play aggressive, you play your game and that's that, whereas people are trying, I think, to give the image that it's just an all-skill game and it's a woman's game kind of thing. Basically they were saying that you know women don't compare to men. Which is true, when you get to the older ages. I mean there's no NHL calibre women in the game right now and that's fine. Strength factor and everything, I mean people are going to know that no matter what. But you don't have to go around saying that this is a woman's sport, there's no contact, it's totally skill, and make it sound like it's a nothing sport either. I think that's part of the reason why women's hockey went nowhere for so many years.

A third player, who played women's hockey when body checking was allowed, also expressed cynicism about efforts to de-emphasize the physical aspects and to promote women's hockey on the basis of its difference from the men's game. This player explicitly acknowledged a connection between the rules of play in women's hockey and concerns about its image:

> It doesn't make any sense to me. If they want to say, I don't know, the words feminine, I don't like those types of terms, masculine, feminine, all that crap. If they want to do it [promote women's hockey], that's not the way to do it, for my view. Hitting doesn't make you any more of a boy than non-hitting. I just don't know what they are trying to do.

The relationship between the risk of injury and the place of body checking is one of the contested features of the debate about the construction of women's hockey. Some coaches and players believe that a main reason for eliminating body checking

is to reduce the risk of injury. Others dispute this association and believe that eliminating body checking has actually increased the risk of injury.[1] The explanation is that without checking, there is more illegal contact and stick work. One player who said, 'I think I've had more injuries with the no intentional body checking rule in,' explained the effect of the rule on the practice of the game:

> I think because [with no body checking] I'm not expecting some of the hits that I'm getting because some people don't play within the rules. And if they can hit you or hurt you and hit you and put you into the boards or whatever when you're not expecting it, which usually I don't because I think, no, we play within the rules, they don't want to get a penalty, they don't want to hurt me. You know I'm nice person [she laughs]. So I don't expect it.

Another player offered further explanation:

> I think most of the players at first liked the idea of no checking, no intentional body checking. Some of them I think have come around and said, 'Hey, yeah, less stick work.' So okay, say you get frustrated out there and you hit somebody clean and you know it's coming, like if you know it's coming you're not going to get hurt. That's the way I always feel. If . . . there's body checking I know I'm going to get hurt. Fine. I know how to go into the boards a little differently. . . . So with that in mind, yeah, I prefer the body checking, myself. It's the game.

When asked why players seem to see an inevitable trade-off between checking and illegal stick work, she explained:

> Well because you've got to slow them down somehow. You've got to get in front of them somehow and usually if you can't hit them or at least take a piece of them, that's the only thing left. And that's your stick to slow them down. Myself—unless you can outskate them. Well, that's not me.

This player's comments speak to the view that checking is part of the repertoire of a hockey player's skills. When it is not available, players resort to other tactics to accomplish their task. These tactics include illegal and sometimes dangerous practices.

Other players who spoke of the risks of body checking attributed these risks to the fact that players are not taught to receive and take checks.

One player said that when there was body checking:

> It wasn't clean at all. Girls aren't taught how to hit. 'Cause you don't hit all the way up. Then all of a sudden you get to senior A and there's contact. No one knows how to hit; sticks are up, hands are up.

A second player provided a similar analysis. When asked about playing the game when there was body checking, she said:

> Well to be honest with you checking was fine but I believe that the women weren't taught properly how to check. And there was a lot of injuries, like I was pretty scared of a few people out there just because I know, they were going to hit you like this [demonstrates], with their fists up or whatever. If checking had been taught, you know properly at a young age, just like the boys, they learn checking at a young age up, then maybe it wouldn't be so bad. Like you know, to take a hit on the boards is fine. It's just, I don't think women know how to check properly.

Conclusion: Women's Hockey and the Challenge to Masculine Hegemony

This discussion has focused on two aspects of the debate around physicality in women's hockey: the risk of injury and the appeal of a full-contact version of the sport versus one that prohibits body checking but is nonetheless very physical. Debate over these issues occurs within a material and ideological context that conditions the practice of the sport.

Suggestions that a 'problem' with body checking is that girls are not taught this skill complement the observation that eliminating checking improves the game by making it easier to officiate. Both imply that the 'problem' with checking is not the practice, per se, but limitations in the organization of the sport regarding training and skill development of athletes and officials.

Some respondents likened their support for the inclusion of body checking in women's hockey to the professionalization of the sport. When asked about reasons for the prohibition of body checking, a coach and a player both responded, 'These people [we] aren't being paid to play' and 'They [we] have to get up and go to work the next day.' Another coach who endorsed the inclusion of body checking went on to note that it would only be feasible if the game were organized professionally and women could earn a living by their efforts. In effect, he was arguing for a structure that offers material rewards to athletes commensurate with their own investment and commitment.

Gender equality has received increased attention in many sports, including hockey, in recent years (Williams, 1995). Calls for better training of players, coaches, and officials, and improved material conditions, including medical support, are an important aspect of the struggle within women's hockey to gain legitimation. At the same time, this struggle heightens the significance of the debate around the construction of the sport. As women players become bigger, stronger, and more skilled and as the practices of the game become more intense and physical, the question 'How should women play hockey?' raises the ideological stakes.

Women's hockey is played in a cultural context in which men's sport is hegemonic. This view that body checking is an integral 'part of the game' is emblematic of hockey as it has historically been conceptualized, practised, and epitomized by the National Hockey League. Debates about what version of the game is most appealing, and the relation between physicality and the incidence of dirty play, occur in a context in which this version has been positioned as the 'real' game and the model against which others have been compared and evaluated (Theberge, 1995).

The dominance of the 'NHL model' of hockey is under challenge today, not only from women's hockey, but also from within boys' hockey, about which parents and officials have expressed concern. Targets of criticism in boys' hockey are the style of play, which emphasizes intimidation and domination, and the competitive and elitist system that eliminates boys by early adolescence, boys who are unable to perform by these standards. In response to these concerns, some provincial and local hockey associations have implemented programs that prohibit body checking, reduce the emphasis on winning, and stress the enjoyment of participation (Gruneau and Whitson, 1993). Other alternatives to the dominant model are recreational men's leagues that prohibit body checking in the interests of safety and make the game more attractive to participants. As Gruneau and Whitson (1993: 162) note, however, 'NHL-style customs and values remain those ones that really "count" in the subculture of Canadian hockey.'

The dominance of men's hockey provides the background for much of the debate over the construction of the women's game. Against this background, to argue that women's hockey need not be the same as men's is to position the women's game as not only different from but inferior to the 'real' game. Alternatively, to argue women should play the same game as men is to capitulate to the violence and other problems that plague men's hockey. Within the confines of a debate structured by the model of the 'NHL style' of play, the challenge posed by women's hockey to dominant views of how the game should be played is severely diminished.

As noted, some of the players and coaches interviewed for this research dispute the contention that playing by the same rules as men will inevitably lead to the reproduction of the problems in the men's hockey. They argue that women's hockey can be constructed, and the rules enforced, in a way that eliminates the violence and other unacceptable features of the men's game while including full body contact. Some contest the view that body checking increases the rate of injury. These views are significant because they suggest that debate about the construction of the women's game should not be contained by the practices and experiences of men's hockey. These arguments, however, are rarely part of the public discussion of women's hockey.

The prohibition of body checking is central to a strategy to promote women's hockey by emphasizing its differences from the men's game.[2] While the game clearly is different from men's hockey in the absence of body checking, evidence of troubling similarities is provided in the discussion of pain and injury in women's hockey. A growing body of literature examines the violence inflicted on athletic bodies through the routinization of pain and injury in sport. Initial interest in this issue focused on male athletes (Messner, 1990; Curry, 1993; Young 1993; Young, White, and McTeer, 1994). More recent work has extended the discussion to women. Young and White (1995) examined experiences of pain and injury among a sample of elite women athletes who had incurred a variety of injuries, including broken bones, separated shoulders, dislocated knee caps, and herniated disks. These athletes normalized the presence of pain in their lives, through strategies of denial and 'disrespect' or indignation toward painful injuries. Citing comparisons with earlier work they conducted with male athletes, Young and White (1995: 51) identify similarities in the acceptance of physical danger and injury and conclude that 'if difference exists between the way male and female athletes in our projects appear to understand pain and injury, it is only a matter of degree.' In a study of university students, Nixon (1996) found higher pain thresholds among athletes than non-athletes and no significant gender differences in their acceptance of pain.

Injury and pain were routine features of the lives of the hockey players examined here. For these athletes, overcoming injury and pain is a measure of both ability and commitment. Like the athletes Young and White (1995) studied, the hockey players in this study showed little critical awareness of the physical dangers of their sport participation. In interviews, players were asked to comment on the element of risk in women's hockey. Most denied that it was risky, often following this assessment with rationalizations about the presence of danger in everyday life—for example, the possibility of being hit by a car while crossing a street. The increasing evidence that women athletes readily accept violence inflicted on their bodies in competitive sport suggests an incorporation of, rather than resistance to, the dominant model of men's sport.

Testimony provided at the outset of this discussion indicates the satisfaction and sense of accomplishment women hockey players derive from their sport participation. These sentiments are directly tied to the physicality of sport and the possibility for the exercise of skill and force in athletic competition. A number of writers (MacKinnon, 1987; Theberge, 1987; Whitson, 1994) have identified these features as the basis of sport's potential to challenge traditional ideologies of gender and empower women. While women hockey players experience empowerment from their sport participation, the challenge to masculine hegemony posed by the sport is diminished in two key ways.

The transformative possibilities of women's sport are seriously compromised by the uncritical adoption of a 'sport ethic' (Hughes and Coakley, 1991) that celebrates toughness in the face of physical violence. One of the troubling ironies of improved material resources in women's hockey is that players now have greater affinities with a system that normalizes injury and pain.

Ideologically, the challenge to masculine hegemony is weakened by the location of the debate about the practice of women's hockey within a framework that positions men's hockey as the 'real' game. While women's hockey provides clear and compelling refutation of the myth of female frailty, the potential of the sport to challenge traditional ideologies of gender is diminished by its construction as a milder version of the sport that 'really counts'.

The analysis presented here suggests the complexities inherent in women's involvement in 'flag carrier' sports such as ice hockey. Drawing from Connell's (1983) observation that every sport involves a balance between force and skill, Whitson (1994) suggests that the more force is decisive, the more a physically dominating hegemonic masculinity can be celebrated and the more likely it is that the culture of sport will be part of the defence of the existing gender order. Whitson acknowledges that sports such as hockey and football do allow for empowerment in the absence of

domination and cites testimony from former NHL player Eric Nesterenko (in Terkel, 1974) on the pleasure of performing the skills required in ice hockey. This pleasure, however, was never allowed to be the central purpose of participation and usually was subordinated by the quest for victory, a quest that demanded an emphasis on force and domination. This quest, Whitson argues, becomes the norm in organized male sport at an early age.

Possibilities for challenge to masculine hegemony do exist within the context of team sports. An example is provided in Birrell and Richter's (1987) account of a women's recreational softball league. The women Birrell and Richter interviewed consciously rejected the view that the dominant model of sport, which many referred to as the 'male model', is the only 'real' version. Informed by this belief, they rejected an excessive emphasis on winning and domination and an ethic of endangerment that values performance over safety. Instead, they actively worked to construct and practice their own vision of sport, which emphasized the pleasure and satisfaction of participation and the development of physical skills in a supportive context.

In an analysis of the historical significance of sport for the politics of gender relations, Messner (1988) argues women's increasing athleticism represents a genuine quest for equality. This quest, however, is marked by contradictions and ambiguities over the socially constructed meanings of sport and gender. Messner concludes that in the contemporary period the woman athlete is 'contested ideological terrain'.

The cultural struggle in women's hockey is conditioned by its relation to the dominant male model. Unlike the recreational softball community studied by Birrell and Richter (1987), in which participants consciously challenged the 'male model', the struggle within elite-level women's hockey occurs largely within a value system regulated by this model. While women's hockey provides participants with pleasure and a sense of personal empowerment, it does so in a context that reproduces the problems of institutionalized sport. A more fully transformative vision of hockey would offer empowerment in a setting that rejects violence and the normalization of injury in favour of an ethic of care.

Notes

1. Interviews with women who played full contact hockey during the 1980s reveal that part of the collective memory of the league in which the Blades compete is stories of particular hits and players who had an especially forceful game. While these stories are an important part of the history of the sport, there are no data to test the relationship between playing full-contact hockey and rates of injury. Some believe that to the extent body checking increases injuries, this is 'limited' to serious injuries such as broken bones.

2. The main challenge to the prohibition against body checking comes not domestically but within the International Ice Hockey Federation, in which some countries argue for the inclusion of body checking in international women's hockey. Proponents of the rule change generally are from countries where development lags behind that in Canada and the United States, the dominant countries in the sport. Because the inclusion of body checking is generally agreed to slow the game down and reduce the advantage of superior playing skills, body checking is thought to offer an advantage to weaker teams. (My thanks to Elizabeth Etue for information on this issue.) It should be noted that it is unlikely that Canadian support for prohibiting body checking arises out of a concern for a loss of competitive dominance should the rules be changed. The first World Championships in 1990 were played with body checking. Canada won this tournament, as well as subsequent tournaments in 1992 and 1994 played without body checking.

References

Birrell, S., and D. Richter. 1987. 'Is a Diamond Forever? Feminist Transformations of Sport', *Women's Studies International Forum* 10: 395–409.

Bryson, L. 1990. 'Challenges to Male Hegemony in Sport', in M. Messner and D. Sabo, eds., *Sport, Men and the Gender Order*. Champaign, IL: Human Kinetics.

Connell, R.W. 1983. 'Men's Bodies', in R.W. Connell, ed., *Which Way Is Up?* Sydney: Allen & Unwin.

Curry, T. 1993. 'A Little Pain Never Hurt Anyone: Athletic Career Socialization and the Normalization of Sport Injury', *Symbolic Interaction* 16: 273–90.

Etue, E., and M. Williams. 1996. *On the Edge: Women Making Hockey History*. Toronto: Second Story.

Gruneau, R., and D. Whitson. 1993. *Hockey Night in Canada*. Toronto: Garamond.

Hughes, R., and J. Coackley. 1991. 'Positive Deviance among Athletes: The Implications of Over-conformity to the Sport Ethic', *Sociology of Sport Journal* 8: 307–25.

MacKinnon, C. 1987. 'Women, Self-possession, and Sport', in C. MacKinnon, ed., *Feminism Unmodified*. Cambridge, MA: Harvard University Press.

Messner, M. 1988. 'Sports as Male Domination: The Female Athlete as Contested Ideological Terrain', *Sociology of Sport Journal* 5: 197–211.

———. 1990. 'When Bodies are Weapons: Masculinity and Violence in Sport', *International Review for the Sociology of Sport* 25: 203–18.

Nixon, H. 1996. 'The Relationship of Friendship Networks, Sports Experiences, and Gender to Expressed Pain Thresholds', *Sociology of Sport Journal* 13: 78–86.

Terkel, S. 1974. *Working*. New York: Avon Books.

Theberge, N. 1987. 'Sport and Women's Empowerment', *Women's Studies International Forum* 10: 387–93.

———. 1995. 'Sport, Caractere Physicque et Differenciation Sexuelle', *Sociologie et Societés* 27: 105–16.

Whitson, D. 1994. 'The Embodiment of Gender: Discipline, Domination, and Empowerment', in S. Birrell and C. Cole, eds., *Women, Sport, and Culture*. Champaign, IL: Human Kinetics.

Williams, M. 1995. 'Women's Hockey: Heating Up the Equity Debate', *Canadian Woman Studies* 15: 78–81.

Young K. 1993. 'Violence, Risk, and Liability in Male Sports Culture', *Sociology of Sport Journal* 10: 373–97.

Young, K., and P. White. 1995. 'Sport, Physical Danger, and Injury: The Experiences of Elite Women Athletes', *Journal of Sport and Social Issues* 19: 45–61.

Young, K., P. White, and W. McTeer. 1994. 'Body Talk: Male Athletes Reflect on Sport, Injury, and Pain', *Sociology of Sport Journal* 11: 175–94.

QUESTIONS FOR CRITICAL THOUGHT

1 Ruby describes the *hijab* as an article of clothing which has a wide variety of meanings for the women who wear it. What other examples of clothing or other items which carry multiple gendered meanings can you think of?

2. Have you taken part in a youth subculture such as the 'Sk8r' world described by Pomerantz and Currie? If so, how was gender enacted in these subcultures?

3. What does a transgendered person have to do to 'pass' in a society that is based on the assumption that there are two and only two genders? Could you successfully 'pass' as a member of a different gender?

4. Is it possible to live in the world without 'doing gender'? Or perhaps more accurately, is it possible to live in the world without being interpreted by others as a gendered person?

5. Theberge's hockey players are divided as to whether there are (or should be) distinctive 'masculine' and 'feminine' ways to play hockey. Can you think of other activities or behaviours which have identifiable 'masculine' and 'feminine' forms?

PART III

The Gendered Body

Perhaps nothing is more deceptive than the 'naturalness' of our bodies. We experience what happens to our bodies, and what happens *in* our bodies, as utterly natural, physical phenomena.

Yet to the social scientist, nothing could be farther from the truth. Our bodies are both shaped and interpreted in entirely gendered ways. How our bodies look, what our bodies feel, and what we think about how our bodies look and feel, are filtered through cultural lenses that makes some kinds of bodies seem desirable and other kinds seem unacceptable. However, these lenses are not 'natural' or universal. Cultural standards of health, beauty, musculature, and aesthetics are constantly changing. Take, for example, women's notions of beauty. Fortunes are made by companies that purvey the beauty myth—as feminist writer Naomi Wolf called it—and remind women that they do not measure up to these cultural standards, and then provide products that will help them try. By such logic, women who experience eating disorders are not deviant non-conformists, but rather over-conformists to unrealizable norms of femininity. Feminist philosopher Susan Bordo's essay reminds us of the ways in which the types of female bodies valorized in contemporary North American society articulate with particular forms of femininity.

While many people feel pressured to consume body-enhancing products, for a minority, their bodies are themselves the products. For example, the figure skaters described by Karen McGarry are used to 'sell' excitement, beauty, and Canadian pride. In order to do this, their bodies must be easily readable as both gender-normative and hetero-normative. The skaters and other entrepreneurs of the body experience an intensified form of the same pressures that 'ordinary' men and women confront.

However, 'ordinary' men and women are not merely passive templates, uncritically receiving and accepting cultural messages about 'good' and 'bad' bodies. Pamela Wakewich's work shows how people can, and do, create their own ideas about what it means to have a 'good' body, ideas that have more to do with health and well-being than with unrealizable standards of beauty.

CHAPTER 10

The Body and the Reproduction of Femininity[1]

Susan Bordo

Reconstructing Feminist Discourse on the Body

The body—what we eat, how we dress, and the daily rituals to which we attend—is a medium of culture. The body, as anthropologist Mary Douglas has argued, is a powerful symbolic form, a surface on which the central rules, hierarchies, and even metaphysical commitments of a culture are inscribed and thus reinforced through the concrete language of the body (Douglas, 1966, 1982). The body may also operate as a metaphor for culture. From quarters as diverse as Plato and Hobbes to French feminist Luce Irigaray, an imagination of body morphology has provided a blueprint for diagnosis and/or vision of social and political life.

The body is not only a text of culture. It is also, as anthropologist Pierre Bourdieu and philosopher Michel Foucault (among others) have argued, a practical, direct locus of social control. Banally, through table manners and toilet habits, through seemingly trivial routines, rules, and practices, culture is 'made body', as Bourdieu puts it—converted into automatic, habitual activity. As such, it is put 'beyond the grasp of consciousness . . . [untouchable] by voluntary, deliberate transformations' (Bourdieu, 1977: 94). Our conscious politics, social commitments, and strivings for change may be undermined and betrayed by the life of our bodies—not the craving, instinctual body imagined by Plato, Augustine, and Freud, but what Foucault calls the 'docile body', regulated by the norms of cultural life.[2]

Throughout his later 'genealogical' works (*Discipline and Punish, The History of Sexuality*), Foucault constantly reminds us of the primacy of practice over belief. Not chiefly through ideology, but through the organization and regulation of the time, space, and movements of our daily lives, our bodies are trained, shaped, and impressed with the stamp of prevailing historical forms of selfhood, desire, masculinity, and femininity. Such an emphasis casts a dark and disquieting shadow across the contemporary scene. Women, as study after study shows, are spending more time on the management and discipline of our bodies than we have in a long, long time. In a decade marked by a reopening of the public arena to women, the intensification of such regimens appears diversionary and subverting. Through the pursuit of an ever-changing, homogenizing, elusive ideal of femininity—a pursuit without a terminus, requiring that women constantly attend to minute and often whimsical changes in fashion—female bodies become docile bodies—bodies whose forces and energies are habituated to external regulation, subjection, transformation, and 'improvement'. Through the exacting and normalizing disciplines of diet, makeup, and dress—central organizing principles of time and space in the day of many women—we are rendered less socially oriented and more centripetally focused on self-modification. Through these disciplines, we continue to memorize on our bodies, the feel and conviction of lack, of insufficiency, of never being good enough. At the farthest extremes, the practices of femininity may lead us to utter demoralization, debilitation, and death.

Viewed historically, the discipline and normalization of the female body—perhaps the only gender oppression that exercises itself, although to different degrees and in different forms, across age, race, class, and sexual orientation—has to be acknowledged as an amazingly durable and flexible strategy of social control. In our own era, it is difficult to avoid the recognition that the contemporary preoccupation with appearance, which still affects women far more powerfully than men, even in our narcissistic and visually-oriented culture, may function as a backlash phenomenon, reasserting existing gender configurations against any attempts to shift or transform power relations.[3] Surely we are in the throes of this backlash today. In newspapers and magazines we daily encounter stories that promote traditional gender relations and prey on anxieties about change: stories about latch-key children, abuse in daycare centres, the 'new woman's' troubles with men, her lack of marriageability, and so on. A dominant visual theme in teenage magazines involves women hiding in the shadows of men, seeking solace in their arms, willingly contracting the space they occupy. The last, of course, also describes our contemporary aesthetic ideal for women, an ideal whose obsessive pursuit has become the central torment of many women's lives. In such an era we desperately need an effective political discourse about the female body, a discourse adequate to an analysis of the insidious, and often paradoxical, pathways of modern social control.

Developing such a discourse requires reconstructing the feminist paradigm of the late 1960s and early 1970s, with its political categories of oppressors and oppressed, villains and victims. Here I believe that a feminist appropriation of some of Foucault's later concepts can prove useful. Following Foucault, we must first abandon the idea of power as something possessed by one group and levelled against another; we must instead think of the network of practices, institutions, and technologies that sustain positions of dominance and subordination in a particular domain.

Second, we need an analytics adequate to describe a power whose central mechanisms are not repressive, but *constitutive*: 'a power bent on generating forces, making them grow, and ordering them, rather than one dedicated to impeding them, making them submit, or destroying them.' Particularly in the realm of femininity, where so much depends on the seemingly willing acceptance of various norms and practices, we need an analysis of power 'from below', as Foucault puts it; for example, of the mechanisms that shape and proliferate—rather than repress—desire, generate

and focus our energies, construct our conceptions of normalcy and deviance (Foucault, 1980).

And, third, we need a discourse that will enable us to account for the subversion of potential rebellion, a discourse that, while insisting on the necessity of objective analysis of power relations, social hierarchy, political backlash, and so forth, will nonetheless allow us to confront the mechanisms by which the subject, at times, becomes enmeshed in collusion with forces that sustain her own oppression.

This essay will not attempt to produce a general theory along these lines. Rather, my focus will be the analysis of one particular arena where the interplay of these dynamics is striking and perhaps exemplary. It is a limited and unusual arena—that of a group of gender-related and historically localized disorders: hysteria, agoraphobia, and anorexia nervosa.[4] I recognize that these disorders have also historically been class-and race-biased, largely (although not exclusively) occurring among white middle- and upper-middle-class women. Nonetheless, anorexia, hysteria, and agoraphobia may provide a paradigm of one way in which potential resistance is not merely undercut but *utilized* in the maintenance and reproduction of existing power relations.[5]

The central mechanism I will describe involves a transformation (or, if you wish, duality) of meaning, through which conditions that are objectively (and, on one level, experientially) constraining, enslaving, and even murderous, come to be experienced as liberating, transforming, and life-giving. I offer this analysis, although limited to a specific domain, as an example of how various contemporary critical discourses may be joined to yield an understanding of the subtle and often unwitting role played by our bodies in the symbolization and reproduction of gender.

The Body as a Text of Femininity

The continuum between female disorder and 'normal' feminine practice is sharply revealed through a close reading of those disorders to which women have been particularly vulnerable. These, of course, have varied historically: neurasthenia and hysteria in the second half of the nineteenth century; agoraphobia and, most dramatically, anorexia nervosa and bulimia in the second half of the twentieth century. This is not to say that anorectics did not exist in the nineteenth century—many cases were described, usually in the context of diagnoses of hysteria (Showalter, 1985: 128–9)—or that women no longer suffer from classical hysterical symptoms in the twentieth century. But the taking up of eating disorders on a mass scale is as unique to the culture of the 1980s as the epidemic of hysteria was to the Victorian era.[6]

The symptomatology of these disorders reveals itself as textuality. Loss of mobility, loss of voice, inability to leave the home, feeding others while starving oneself, taking up space, and whittling down the space one's body takes up—all have symbolic meaning, all have political meaning under the varying rules governing the historical construction of gender. Working within this framework, we see that whether we look at hysteria, agoraphobia, or anorexia, we find the body of the sufferer deeply inscribed with an ideological construction of femininity emblematic of the period in question. The construction, of course, is always homogenizing and normalizing, erasing racial, class, and other differences and insisting that all women aspire to a coercive, standardized ideal. Strikingly, in these disorders, the construction of femininity is written in disturbingly concrete, hyperbolic terms: exaggerated, extremely literal, at times virtually caricatured presentations of the ruling feminine mystique. The bodies of disordered women in this way offer themselves as an aggressively graphic text for the interpreter—a text that insists, actually demands, that it be read as a cultural statement, a statement about gender.

Both nineteenth-century male physicians and twentieth-century feminist critics have seen, in the symptoms of neurasthenia and hysteria (syndromes that became increasingly less differentiated as the century wore on), an exaggeration of stereotypically feminine traits. The nineteenth-century 'lady' was idealized in terms of delicacy and dreaminess, sexual passivity, and a charmingly labile and capricious emotionality (Vicinus, 1972, x–xi). Such notions were formalized and scientized in the work of male theorists from Acton and Krafft-Ebing to Freud, who described 'normal', mature femininity in such terms.[7] In this context, the dissociations, the drifting

and fogging of perception, the nervous tremors and faints, the anesthesias, and the extreme mutability of symptomatology associated with nineteenth-century female disorders can be seen to be concretizations of the feminine mystique of the period, produced according to rules that governed the prevailing construction of femininity. Doctors described what came to be known as the hysterical personality as 'impressionable, suggestible, and narcissistic; highly labile, their moods changing suddenly, dramatically, and seemingly for inconsequential reasons . . . egocentric in the extreme . . . essentially asexual and not uncommonly frigid' (Smith-Rosenberg, 1985: 203)—all characteristics normative of femininity in this era. As Elaine Showalter points out, the term hysterical itself became almost interchangeable with the term *feminine* in the literature of the period (Showalter, 1985: 129).

The hysteric's embodiment of the feminine mystique of her era, however, seems subtle and ineffable compared to the ingenious literalism of agoraphobia and anorexia. In the context of our culture this literalism makes sense. With the advent of movies and television, the rules for femininity have come to be culturally transmitted more and more through standardized visual images. As a result, femininity itself has come to be largely a matter of constructing, in the manner described by Erving Goffman, the appropriate surface presentation of the self (Goffman, 1959). We are no longer given verbal descriptions or exemplars of what a lady is or of what femininity consists. Rather, we learn the rules directly through bodily discourse: through images that tell us what clothes, body shape, facial expression, movements, and behaviour are required.

In agoraphobia and, even more dramatically, in anorexia, the disorder presents itself as a virtual, though tragic, parody of twentieth-century constructions of femininity. The 1950s and early 1960s, when agoraphobia first began to escalate among women, was a period of reassertion of domesticity and dependency as the feminine ideal. Career woman became a dirty word, much more so than it had been during the war, when the economy depended on women's willingness to do 'men's work'. The reigning ideology of femininity, so well described by Betty Friedan and perfectly captured in the movies and television shows of the era, was child-like, non-assertive, helpless without a man, 'content in a world of bedroom and kitchen, sex, babies and home' (Friedan, 1962: 36).[8] The housebound agoraphobic lives this construction of femininity literally. 'You want me in this home? You'll have me in this home—with a vengeance!' The point, upon which many therapists have commented, does not need belabouring. Agoraphobia, as I.G. Fodor has put it, seems 'the logical—albeit extreme—extension of the cultural sex-role stereotype for women' in this era (Fodor, 1974: 119; see also Brehony, 1983).

The emaciated body of the anorectic, of course, immediately presents itself as a caricature of the contemporary ideal of hyper-slenderness for women, an ideal that, despite the game resistance of racial and ethnic difference, has become the norm for women today. But slenderness is only the tip of the iceberg, for slenderness itself requires interpretation. 'C'est le sens qui fait vendre', said Barthes, speaking of clothing styles—it is meaning that makes the sale (Culler, 1983: 74). So, too, it is meaning that makes the body admirable. To the degree that anorexia may be said to be 'about' slenderness, it is about slenderness as a citadel of contemporary and historical meaning, not as an empty fashion ideal. As such, the interpretation of slenderness yields multiple readings, some related to gender, some not. For the purposes of this essay I will offer an abbreviated, gender-focused reading. But I must stress that this reading illuminates only partially, and that many other currents not discussed here—economic, psychosocial, and historical, as well as ethnic and class dimensions—figure prominently.[9]

We begin with the painfully literal inscription, on the anorectic's body, of the rules governing the construction of contemporary femininity. That construction is a double bind that legislates contradictory ideals and directives. On the one hand, our culture still widely advertises domestic conceptions of femininity, the ideological moorings for a rigorously dualistic sexual division of labour that casts woman as chief emotional and physical nurturer. The rules for this construction of femininity (and I speak here in a language both symbolic and literal) require that women learn to feed others, not the

self, and to construe any desires for self-nurturance and self-feeding as greedy and excessive.[10] Thus, women must develop a totally other-oriented emotional economy. In this economy, the control of female appetite for food is merely the most concrete expression of the general rule governing the construction of femininity: that female hunger—for public power, for independence, for sexual gratification—be contained, and the public space that women be allowed to take up be circumscribed, limited. Figure 10.1, which appeared in a women's magazine fashion spread, dramatically illustrates the degree to which slenderness, set off against the resurgent muscularity and bulk of the current male body-ideal, carries connotations of fragility and lack of power in the face of a decisive male occupation of social space. On the body of the anorexic woman such rules are grimly and deeply etched.

On the other hand, even as young women today continue to be taught traditionally 'feminine' virtues, to the degree that the professional arena is open to them, they must also learn to embody the

Figure 10.1

'masculine' language and values of that arena—self-control, determination, cool, emotional discipline, mastery, and so on. Female bodies now speak symbolically of this necessity in their slender spare shape and the currently fashionable men's-wear look. (A contemporary clothing line's clever mirror-image logo, shown in Figure 10.2, offers women's fashions for the 'New Man', with the model posed to suggest phallic confidence combined with female allure.) Our bodies, too, as we trudge to the gym every day and fiercely resist both our hungers and our desire to soothe ourselves, are becoming more and more practised at the 'male' virtues of control and self-mastery. Figure 10.3 illustrates this contemporary equation of physical discipline with becoming the 'captain' of one's soul. The anorectic pursues these virtues with single-minded, unswerving dedication. 'Energy, discipline, my own power will keep me going,' says ex-anorectic Aimee Liu, recreating her anorexic days. 'I need nothing and no one else. . . . I will be master of my own body, if nothing else, I vow' (Lie, 1979: 123).

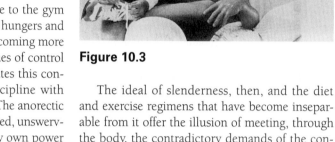

Figure 10.3

The ideal of slenderness, then, and the diet and exercise regimens that have become inseparable from it offer the illusion of meeting, through the body, the contradictory demands of the contemporary ideology of femininity. Popular images reflect this dual demand. In a single issue of *Complete Woman* magazine, two articles appear, one on 'Feminine Intuition', the other asking, 'Are You the New Macho Woman?' In *Vision Quest*, the young male hero falls in love with the heroine, as he says, because 'she has all the best things I like in girls and all the best things I like in guys,' that is, she's tough and cool, but warm and alluring. In the enormously popular *Aliens*, the heroine's personality has been deliberately constructed, with near-comic book explicitness, to embody traditional nurturant femininity alongside breathtaking macho prowess and control; Sigourney Weaver, the actress who portrays her, has called the character 'Rambolina'.

In the pursuit of slenderness and the denial of appetite, the traditional construction of femininity intersects with the new requirement for women to embody the 'masculine' values of the public arena. The anorectic, as I have argued, embodies this intersection, this double bind, in a particularly painful and graphic way.[11] I mean *double bind* quite literally here. 'Masculinity' and 'femininity', at least since the nineteenth century and arguably before, have been constructed through a process of mutual exclusion. One cannot simply add the historically feminine virtues to the historically masculine ones to yield a New Woman, a New Man, a new ethics,

Figure 10.2

or a new culture. Even on the screen or on television, embodied in created characters like the *Aliens* heroine, the result is a parody. Unfortunately, in this image-bedazzled culture, we find it increasingly difficult to discriminate between parodies and possibilities for the self. Explored as a possibility for the self, the 'androgynous' ideal ultimately exposes its internal contradiction and becomes a war that tears the subject in two—a war explicitly thematized, by many anorectics, as a battle between male and female sides of the self.

Protest and Retreat in the Same Gesture

In hysteria, agoraphobia, and anorexia, then, the woman's body may be viewed as a surface on which conventional constructions of femininity are exposed starkly to view, through their inscription in extreme or hyperliteral form. They are written, of course, in languages of horrible suffering. It is as though these bodies are speaking to us of the pathology and violence that lurks just around the corner, waiting at the horizon of 'normal' femininity. It is no wonder that a steady motif in the feminist literature on female disorder is that of pathology as embodied *protest*—unconscious, inchoate, and counterproductive protest without an effective language, voice, or politics, but protest nonetheless.

American and French feminists alike have heard the hysteric speaking a language of protest, even or perhaps especially when she was mute. Dianne Hunter interprets Anna O.'s aphasia, which manifested itself in an inability to speak her native German, as a rebellion against the linguistic and cultural rules of the father and a return to the 'mother-tongue': the semiotic babble of infancy, the language of the body. For Hunter, and for a number of other feminists working with Lacanian categories, the return to the semiotic level is both regressive and, as Hunter puts it, an 'expressive' communication 'addressed to patriarchal thought', 'a self-repudiating form of feminine discourse in which the body signifies what social conditions make it impossible to state linguistically' (Hunter, 1985: 114). 'The hysterics are accusing; they are pointing,' writes Catherine

Clément in *The Newly Born Woman*; they make a 'mockery of culture' (Clément and Cixous, 1986: 42). In the same volume, Hélène Cixous speaks of 'those wonderful hysterics, who subjected Freud to so many voluptuous moments too shameful to mention, bombarding his mosaic statute/law of Moses with their carnal, passionate body-words, haunting him with their inaudible thundering denunciations.' For Cixous, Dora, who so frustrated Freud, is 'the core example of the protesting force in women' (Clément and Cixous, 1986: 95). The literature of protest includes functional as well as symbolic approaches.

Robert Seidenberg and Karen DeCrow, for example, describe agoraphobia as a 'strike' against 'the renunciations usually demanded of women' and the expectations of housewifely functions such as shopping, driving the children to school, accompanying their husband to social events (1983: 31). Carroll Smith-Rosenberg presents a similar analysis of hysteria, arguing that by preventing the woman from functioning in the wifely role of caretaker of others, of 'ministering angel' to husband and children, hysteria 'became one way in which conventional women could express—in most cases unconsciously—dissatisfaction with one or several aspects of their lives' (1985: 208). A number of feminist writers, among whom Susie Orbach is the most articulate and forceful, have interpreted anorexia as a species of unconscious feminist protest. The anorectic is engaged in a 'hunger strike', as Orbach calls it, stressing that this is a political discourse, in which the action of food refusal and dramatic transformation of body size 'expresses with [the] body what [the anorectic] is unable to tell us with words'—her indictment of a culture that disdains and suppresses female hunger, makes women ashamed of their appetites and needs, and demands that women constantly work on the transformation of their body (Orbach, 1985).[12]

The anorectic, of course, is unaware that she is making a political statement. She may, indeed, be hostile to feminism and any other critical perspectives that she views as disputing her own autonomy and control or questioning the cultural ideals around which her life is organized. Through embodied rather than deliberate demonstration she exposes and indicts those ideals, precisely by pursuing them to the point at which their destructive potential is revealed for all to see.

The same gesture that expresses protest, moreover, can also signal retreat; this, indeed, may be part of the symptom's attraction. Kim Chernin, for example, argues that the debilitating anorexic fixation, by halting or mitigating personal development, assuages this generation's guilt and separation anxiety over the prospect of surpassing our mothers, of living less circumscribed, freer lives (Chernin, 1985). Agoraphobia, too, which often develops shortly after marriage, clearly functions in many cases as a way to cement dependency and attachment in the face of unacceptable stirrings of dissatisfaction and restlessness.

Although we may talk meaningfully of protest, then, I want to emphasize the counterproductive, tragically self-defeating (indeed, self-deconstructing) nature of that protest. Functionally, the symptoms of these disorders isolate, weaken, and undermine the sufferers; at the same time they turn the life of the body into an all-absorbing fetish, beside which all other objects of attention pale into unreality. On the symbolic level, too, the protest collapses into its opposite and proclaims the utter capitulation of the subject to the contracted female world. The muteness of hysterics and their return to the level of pure, primary bodily expressivity have been interpreted, as we have seen, as rejecting the symbolic order of the patriarchy and recovering a lost world of semiotic, maternal value. But at the same time, of course, muteness is the condition of the silent, uncomplaining woman—an ideal of patriarchal culture. Protesting the stifling of the female voice through one's own voicelessness—that is, employing the language of femininity to protest the conditions of the female world—will always involve ambiguities of this sort. Perhaps this is why symptoms crystallized from the language of femininity are so perfectly suited to express the dilemmas of middle-class and upper-middle-class women living in periods poised on the edge of gender change, women who have the social and material resources to carry the traditional construction of femininity to symbolic excess but who also confront the anxieties of new possibilities. The late nineteenth century,

the post–Second World War period, and the late twentieth century are all periods in which gender becomes an issue to be discussed and in which discourse proliferates about 'the Woman Question', 'the New Woman', 'What Women Want', 'What Femininity Is'.

Collusion, Resistance, and the Body

The pathologies of female protest function, paradoxically, as if in collusion with the cultural conditions that produce them, reproducing rather than transforming precisely that which is being protested. In this connection, the fact that hysteria and anorexia have peaked during historical periods of cultural backlash against attempts at reorganization and redefinition of male and female roles is significant. Female pathology reveals itself here as an extremely interesting social formation through which one source of potential for resistance and rebellion is pressed into the service of maintaining the established order.

In our attempt to explain this formation, objective accounts of power relations fail us. For whatever the objective social conditions are that create a pathology, the symptoms themselves must still be produced (however unconsciously or inadvertently) by the subject. That is, the individual must invest the body with meanings of various sorts. Only by examining this productive process on the part of the subject can we, as Mark Poster has put it, 'illuminate the mechanisms of domination in the processes through which meaning is produced in everyday life'; that is, only then can we see how the desires and dreams of the subject become implicated in the matrix of power relations (Poster, 1984: 28).

Here, examining the context in which the anorexic syndrome is produced may be illuminating. Anorexia will erupt, typically, in the course of what begins as a fairly moderate diet regime, undertaken because someone—often the father—has made a casual critical remark. Anorexia *begins in*, emerges out of, what is, in our time, conventional feminine practice. In the course of that practice, for any number of individual reasons, the practice is pushed a little beyond the parameters of moderate dieting. The young woman discovers what it feels like to crave and want and need and yet, through the exercise of her own will, to triumph over that need. In the process, a new realm of meanings is discovered, a range of values and possibilities that Western culture has traditionally coded as 'male' and rarely made available to women: an ethic and aesthetic of self-mastery and self-transcendence, expertise, and power over others through the example of superior will and control. The experience is intoxicating and habit-forming.

At school the anorectic discovers that her steadily shrinking body is admired, not so much as an aesthetic or sexual object, but for the strength of will and self-control it projects. At home she discovers, in the inevitable battles her parents fight to get her to eat, that her actions have enormous power over the lives of those around her. As her body begins to lose its traditional feminine curves, its breasts and hips and rounded stomach, it begins to feel and look more like a spare, lanky male body, and she begins to feel untouchable, out of reach of hurt, 'invulnerable, clean and hard as the bones etched into my silhouette', as one student described it in her journal. She despises, in particular, all those parts of her body that continue to mark her as female. 'If only I could eliminate [my breasts],' says Liu, 'cut them off if need be' (1979: 99). For her, as for many anorectics, the breasts represent a bovine, unconscious, vulnerable side of the self. Liu's body symbolism is thoroughly continuous with dominant cultural associations. Brett Silverstein's studies on the 'Possible Causes of the Thin Standard of Bodily Attractiveness for Women' (1986) testify empirically to what is obvious from every comedy routine involving a dramatically shapely woman: namely, our cultural association of curvaceousness with incompetence. The anorectic is also quite aware, of course, of the social and sexual vulnerability involved in having a female body; many, in fact, were sexually abused as children.

Through her anorexia, by contrast, she has unexpectedly discovered an entry into the privileged male world, a way to become what is valued in our culture, a way to become safe, to rise above it all—for her, they are the same thing. She has discovered this, paradoxically, by pursuing conventional feminine behaviour—in this case, the discipline of perfecting the body as an object—to excess. At this point of excess, the conventionally feminine deconstructs, we might say, into its opposite and opens onto those values our culture has coded as male. No wonder anorexia is experienced as liberating and that the anorectic will fight family, friends, and therapists in an effort to hold onto it—fight them to the death, if need be. The anorectic's experience of power is, of course, deeply and dangerously illusory. To reshape one's body into a male body is not to put on male power and privilege. To *feel* autonomous and free while harnessing body and soul to an obsessive body-practice is to serve, not transform, a social order that limits female possibilities. And, of course, for the female to become male is only for her to locate herself on the other side of a disfiguring opposition. The new 'power look' of female bodybuilding, which encourages women to develop the same hulk-like, triangular shape that has been the norm for male body-builders, is no less determined by a hierarchical, dualistic construction of gender than was the conventionally 'feminine' norm that tyrannized female body-builders such as Bev Francis for years.

Although the specific cultural practices and meanings are different, similar mechanisms, I suspect, are at work in hysteria and agoraphobia. In these cases too, the language of femininity, when pushed to excess—when shouted and asserted, when disruptive and demanding—deconstructs into its opposite and makes available to the woman an illusory experience of power previously forbidden to her by virtue of her gender. In the case of nineteenth-century femininity, the forbidden experience may have been the bursting of fetters—particularly moral and emotional fetters. John Conolly, the asylum reformer, recommended institutionalization for women who 'want that restraint over the passions without which the female character is lost' (Showalter, 1985: 48). Hysterics often infuriated male doctors by their lack of precisely this quality. S. Weir Mitchell described these patients as 'the despair of physicians', whose 'despotic selfishness wrecks the constitution of nurses and devoted relatives, and in unconscious or half-conscious self-indulgence destroys the comfort of everyone around them' (Smith-Rosenberg, 1985:

207). It must have given the Victorian patient some illicit pleasure to be viewed as capable of such disruption of the staid nineteenth-century household. A similar form of power, I believe, is part of the experience of agoraphobia.

This does not mean that the primary reality of these disorders is not one of pain and entrapment. Anorexia, too, clearly contains a dimension of physical addiction to the biochemical effects of starvation. But whatever the physiology involved, the ways in which the subject understands and thematizes her experience cannot be reduced to a mechanical process. The anorectic's ability to live with minimal food intake allows her to feel powerful and worthy of admiration in a 'world', as Susie Orbach describes it, 'from which at the most profound level [she] feels excluded' and unvalued (1985: 103). The literature on both anorexia and hysteria is strewn with battles of will between the sufferer and those trying to 'cure' her; the latter, as Orbach points out, very rarely understand that the psychic values she is fighting for are often more important to the woman than life itself.

Textuality, Praxis, and the Body

The 'solutions' offered by anorexia, hysteria, and agoraphobia, I have suggested, develop out of the practice of femininity itself, the pursuit of which is still presented as the chief route to acceptance and success for women in our culture. Too aggressively pursued, that practice leads to its own undoing, in one sense. For if femininity is, as Susan Brownmiller has said, at its core a 'tradition of imposed limitations' (1984: 14), then an unwillingness to limit oneself, even in the pursuit of femininity, breaks the rules. But, of course, in another sense the rules remain fully in place. The sufferer becomes wedded to an obsessive practice, unable to make any effective change in her life. She remains, as Toril Moi has put it, 'gagged and chained to [the] feminine role', a reproducer of the docile body of femininity (1985: 192).

This tension between the psychological meaning of a disorder, which may enact fantasies of rebellion and embody a language of protest, and the practical life of the disordered body, which may utterly defeat rebellion and subvert protest, may be obscured by too exclusive a focus on the symbolic dimension and insufficient attention to praxis. As we have seen in the case of some Lacanian feminist readings of hysteria, the result of this can be a one-sided interpretation that romanticizes the hysteric's symbolic subversion of the phallocentric order while confined to her bed. This is not to say that confinement in bed has a transparent, univocal meaning—in powerlessness, debilitation, dependency, and so forth. The 'practical' body is no brute biological or material entity. It, too, is a culturally mediated form; its activities are subject to interpretation and description. The shift to the practical dimension is not a turn to biology or nature, but to another 'register', as Foucault puts it, of the cultural body, the register of the 'useful body' rather than the 'intelligible body' (Foucault, 1979: 136). The distinction can prove useful, I believe, to feminist discourse.

The intelligible body includes our scientific, philosophic, and aesthetic representations of the body—our cultural *conceptions* of the body, norms of beauty, models of health, and so forth. But the same representations may also be seen as forming a set of practical rules and regulations through which the living body is 'trained, shaped, obeys, responds', becoming, in short, a socially adapted and 'useful body' (Foucault, 1979: 136). Consider this particularly clear and appropriate example: the nineteenth-century hourglass figure, emphasizing breasts and hips against a wasp waist, was an intelligible *symbolic* form, representing a domestic, sexualized ideal of femininity. The sharp cultural contrast between the female and the male form, made possible by the use of corsets and bustles, reflected, in symbolic terms, the dualistic division of social and economic life into clearly defined male and female spheres. At the same time, to achieve the specified look, a particular feminine *praxis* was required—straitlacing, minimal eating, and reduced mobility—rendering the female body unfit to perform activities outside its designated sphere. This, in Foucauldian terms, would be the 'useful body' corresponding to the aesthetic norm.

The intelligible body and the useful body are two arenas of the same discourse; they often mirror and support each other, as in the above illustration. Another example can be found in the seventeenth-century philosophic conception of the body as a machine, mirroring an increasingly more automated productive machinery of labour. But the two bodies may also contradict and mock each other. A range of contemporary representations and images, as noted earlier, have coded the transcendence of female appetite and its public display in the slenderness ideal in terms of power, will, mastery, and the possibilities of success in the professional arena. These associations are carried visually by the slender superwomen of prime-time television and popular movies and promoted explicitly in advertisements and articles appearing routinely in women's fashion magazines, diet books, and weight-training publications. Yet the thousands of slender girls and women who strive to embody these images and who in that service suffer from eating disorders, exercise compulsions, and continual self-scrutiny and self-castigation are anything *but* the 'masters' of their lives.

Exposure and productive cultural analysis of such contradictory and mystifying relations between image and practice are possible only if the analysis includes attention to and interpretation of the 'useful' or, as I prefer to call it, the practical body. Such attention, although often in inchoate and theoretically unsophisticated form, was central to the beginnings of the contemporary feminist movement. In the late 1960s and early 1970s the objectification of the female body was a serious political issue. All the cultural paraphernalia of femininity, of learning to please visually and sexually through the practices of the body—media imagery, beauty pageants, high heels, girdles, makeup, simulated orgasm—were seen as crucial in maintaining gender domination.

Disquietingly, for the feminists of the present decade, such focus on the politics of feminine praxis, although still maintained in the work of individual feminists, is no longer a centerpiece of feminist cultural critique.[13] On the popular front, we find *Ms* magazine presenting issues on fitness and 'style', the rhetoric reconstructed for the 1980s to pitch 'self-expression' and 'power'. Although feminist theory surely has the tools, it

has not provided a critical discourse to dismantle and demystify this rhetoric. The work of French feminists has provided a powerful framework for understanding the inscription of phallocentric, dualistic culture on gendered bodies, but it has offered very little in the way of concrete analyses of the female body as a locus of practical cultural control. Among feminist theorists in this country, the study of cultural representations of the female body has flourished, and it has often been brilliantly illuminating and instrumental to a feminist rereading of culture.[14] But the study of cultural representations alone, divorced from consideration of their relation to the practical lives of bodies, can obscure and mislead.

Here, Helena Mitchie's significantly titled *The Flesh Made Word* offers a striking example. Examining nineteenth-century representations of women, appetite, and eating, Mitchie draws fascinating and astute metaphorical connections between female eating and female sexuality. Female hunger, she argues, and I agree, 'figures unspeakable desires for sexuality and power' (1987: 13). The Victorian novel's 'representational taboo' against depicting women eating (an activity, apparently, that only 'happens offstage', as Mitchie puts it) thus functions as a 'code' for the suppression of female sexuality, as does the general cultural requirement, exhibited in etiquette and sex manuals of the day, that the well-bred woman eat little and delicately. The same coding is drawn on, Mitchie argues, in contemporary feminist 'inversions' of Victorian values, inversions that celebrate female sexuality and power through images exulting in female eating and female hunger, depicting it explicitly, lushly, and joyfully.

Despite the fact that Mitchie's analysis centres on issues concerning women's hunger, food, and eating practices, she makes no mention of the grave eating disorders that surfaced in the late nineteenth century and that are ravaging the lives of young women today. The practical arena of women dieting, fasting, straitlacing, and so forth is, to a certain extent, implicit in her examination of Victorian gender ideology. But when Mitchie turns, at the end of her study, to consider contemporary feminist literature celebrating female eating and female hunger, the absence of even a passing glance at how women are *actually* managing their hungers today leaves her analysis adrift, lacking any concrete social moorings. Mitchie's sole focus is on the inevitable failure of feminist literature to escape 'phallic representational codes' (1987: 149). But the feminist celebration of the female body did not merely deconstruct on the written page or canvas. Largely located in the feminist counterculture of the 1970s, it has been culturally displaced by a very different contemporary reality. Its celebration of female flesh now presents itself in jarring dissonance with the fact that women, feminists included, are starving themselves to death in our culture.

This is not to deny the benefits of diet, exercise, and other forms of body management. Rather, I view our bodies as a site of struggle, where we must work to keep our daily practices in the service of resistance to gender domination, not in the service of docility and gender normalization. This work requires, I believe, a determinedly skeptical attitude toward the routes of seeming liberation and pleasure offered by our culture. It also demands an awareness of the often contradictory relations between image and practice, between rhetoric and reality. Popular representations, as we have seen, may forcefully employ the rhetoric and symbolism of empowerment, personal freedom, 'having it all'. Yet female bodies, pursuing these ideals, may find themselves as distracted, depressed, and physically ill as female bodies in the nineteenth century were made when pursuing a feminine ideal of dependency, domesticity, and delicacy. The recognition and analysis of such contradictions, and of all the other collusions, subversions, and enticements through which culture enjoins the aid of our bodies in the reproduction of gender, require that we restore a concern for female praxis to its formerly central place in feminist politics.

Notes

1. Early versions of this essay, under various titles, were delivered at the philosophy department of the State University of New York at Stony Brook, the University of Massachusetts conference on Histories of Sexuality, and the twenty-first annual conference for the Society of Phenomenology and Existential Philosophy. I thank all those who commented and provided encouragement on those occasions. The essay was revised and originally published in Alison Jaggar and Susan Bordo, eds., *Gender/Body/ Knowledge: Feminist Reconstructions of Being and Knowing* (New Brunswick: Rutgers University Press, 1989).

2. On docility, see Michel Foucault, *Discipline and Punish* (New York: Vintage, 1979), 135–69. For a Foucauldian analysis of feminine practice, see Sandra Bartky, 'Foucault, Femininity, and the Modernization of Patriarchal Power', in her *Femininity and Domination* (New York: Routledge, 1990); see also Susan Brownmiller, *Femininity* (New York: Ballantine, 1984).

3. During the late 1970s and 1980s, male concern over appearance undeniably increased. Study after study confirms, however, that there is still a large gender gap in this area. Research conducted at the University of Pennsylvania in 1985 found men to be generally satisfied with their appearance, often, in fact, 'distorting their perceptions [of themselves] in a positive, self-aggrandizing way' ('Dislike of Own Bodies Found Common Among Women', *New York Times*, 19 March 1985: C1). Women, however, were found to exhibit extreme negative assessments and distortions of body perception. Other studies have suggested that women are judged more harshly than men when they deviate from dominant social standards of attractiveness. Thomas Cash et al., in 'The Great American Shape-Up', *Psychology Today* (April 1986): 34, report that although the situation for men has changed, the situation for women has more than proportionally worsened. Citing results from 30,000 responses to a 1985 survey of perceptions of body image and comparing similar responses to a 1972 questionnaire, they report that the 1985 respondents were considerably more dissatisfied with their bodies than the 1972 respondents, and they note a marked intensification of concern among men. Among the 1985 group, the group most dissatisfied of all with their appearance, however, were teenage

women. Women today constitute by far the largest number of consumers of diet products, attenders of spas and diet centers, and subjects of intestinal by-pass and other fat-reduction operations.

4. On the gendered and historical nature of these disorders: the number of female to male hysterics has been estimated at anywhere from 2:1 to 4:1, and as many as 80 per cent of all agoraphobics are female (Annette Brodsky and Rachel Hare-Mustin, *Women and Psychotherapy* [New York: Guilford Press, 1980], 116, 122). Although more cases of male eating disorders have been reported in the late eighties and early nineties, it is estimated that close to 90 per cent of all anorectics are female (Paul Garfinkel and David Garner, *Anorexia Nervosa: A Multidimensional Perspective* [New York: Brunner/Mazel, 1982], 112–13). For a sophisticated account of female psychopathology, with particular attention to nineteenth-century disorders but, unfortunately, little mention of agoraphobia or eating disorders, see Elaine Showalter, *The Female Malady: Women, Madness and English Culture, 1830–1980* (New York: Pantheon, 1985). For a discussion of social and gender issues in agoraphobia, see Robert Seidenberg and Karen DeCrow, *Women Who Marry Houses: Panic and Protest in Agoraphobia* (New York: McGraw-Hill, 1983). On the history of anorexia nervosa, see Joan Jacobs Brumberg, *Fasting Girls: The Emergence of Anorexia Nervosa as a Modern Disease* (Cambridge: Harvard University Press, 1988).

5. In constructing such a paradigm I do not pretend to do justice to any of these disorders in its individual complexity. My aim is to chart some points of intersection, to describe some similar patterns, as they emerge through a particular reading of the phenomenon—a political reading, if you will.

6. On the epidemic of hysteria and neurasthenia, see Showalter, *The Female Malady;* Carroll Smith-Rosenberg, 'The Hysterical Woman: Sex Roles and Role Conflict in Nineteenth-Century America', in her *Disorderly Conduct: Visions of Gender in Victorian America* (Oxford: Oxford University Press, 1985).

7. See Carol Nadelson and Malkah Notman, *The Female Patient* (New York: Plenum, 1982), 5; E.M. Sigsworth and T.J. Wyke, 'A Study of Victorian Prostitution and Venereal Disease', in

Vicinus, *Suffer and Be Still*, 82. For more general discussions, see Peter Gay, *The Bourgeois Experience: Victoria to Freud*. Vol. 1: *Education of the Senses* (New York: Oxford University Press, 1984), esp. 109–68; Showalter, *The Female Malady*, esp. 121–44. The delicate lady, an ideal that had very strong class connotations (as does slenderness today), is not the only conception of femininity to be found in Victorian cultures. But it was arguably the single most powerful ideological representation of femininity in that era, affecting women of all classes, including those without the material means to realize the ideal fully. See Helena Mitchie, *The Flesh Made Word* (New York: Oxford, 1987), for discussions of the control of female appetite and Victorian constructions of femininity.

8. Betty Friedan, *The Feminine Mystique* (New York: Dell, 1962), 36. The theme song of one such show ran, in part, 'I married Joan . . . What a girl . . . what a whirl . . . what a life! I married Joan . . . What a mind . . . love is blind . . . what a wife!'

9. For other interpretive perspectives on the slenderness ideal, see 'Reading the Slender Body' in this volume; Kim Chernin, *The Obsession: Reflections on the Tyranny of Slenderness* (New York: Harper and Row, 1981); Susie Orbach, *Hunger Strike: The Anorectic's Struggle as a Metaphor for Our Age* (New York: W.W. Norton, 1985).

10. See 'Hunger as Ideology', in this volume, for a discussion of how this construction of femininity is reproduced in contemporary commercials and advertisements concerning food, eating, and cooking.

11. Striking, in connection with this, is Catherine Steiner-Adair's 1984 study of high-school women, which reveals a dramatic association between problems with food and body image and emulation of the cool, professionally 'together' and gorgeous superwoman. On the basis of a series of interviews, the high schoolers were classified into two groups: one expressed skepticism over the superwoman ideal, the other thoroughly aspired to it. Later administrations of diagnostic tests revealed that 94 per cent of the pro-superwoman group fell into the eating-disordered range of the scale. Of the other group, 100 per cent fell into the non-eating-disordered range. Media images notwithstanding, young

women today appear to sense, either consciously or through their bodies, the impossibility of simultaneously meeting the demands of two spheres whose values have been historically defined in utter opposition to each other.

12. When we look into the many autobiographies and case studies of hysterics, anorectics, and agoraphobics, we find that these are indeed the sorts of women one might expect to be frustrated by the constraints of a specified female role. Sigmund Freud and Joseph Breuer, in *Studies on Hysteria* (New York: Avon, 1966), and Freud, in the later *Dora: An Analysis of a Case of Hysteria* (New York: Macmillan, 1963), constantly remark on the ambitiousness, independence, intellectual ability, and creative strivings of their patients. We know, moreover, that many women who later became leading social activists and feminists of the nineteenth century were among those who fell ill with hysteria and neurasthenia. It has become a virtual cliché that the typical anorectic is a perfectionist, driven to excel in all areas of her life. Though less prominently, a similar theme runs throughout the literature on agoraphobia. One must keep in mind that in drawing on case studies, one is relying on the perceptions of other acculturated individuals. One suspects, for example, that the popular portrait of the anorectic as a relentless over-achiever may be coloured by the lingering or perhaps resurgent Victorianism of our culture's attitudes toward ambitious women. One does not escape this hermeneutic problem by turning to autobiography. But in autobiography one is at least dealing with social constructions and attitudes that animate the subject's own psychic reality. In this regard the autobiographical literature on anorexia, drawn on in a variety of places in this volume, is strikingly full of anxiety about the domestic world and other themes that suggest deep rebellion against traditional notions of femininity.

13. A focus on the politics of sexualization and objectification remains central to the anti-pornography movement (e.g., in the work of Andrea Dworkin, Catherine MacKinnon). Feminists exploring the politics of appearance include Sandra Bartky, Susan Brownmiller, Wendy Chapkis, Kim Chernin, and Susie Orbach. And a developing feminist interest in the work of Michel Foucault has begun to produce a poststructuralist feminism oriented toward practice; see, for example, Irene Diamond and Lee Quinby, *Feminism and Foucault: Reflections on Resistance* (Boston: Northeastern University Press, 1988).

14. See, for example, Susan Suleiman, ed., *The Female Body in Western Culture* (Cambridge:Harvard University Press, 1986).

References

Bourdieu, P. 1977. *Outline of a Theory of Practice*. Cambridge: Cambridge University Press.

Brehony, K. 1983. 'Women and Agoraphobia', in V. Franks and E. Rothblum, eds., *The Stereotyping of Women*. New York: Springer.

Brownmiller, S. 1984. *Femininity*. New York: Ballantine.

Chernin, K. 1985. *The Hungry Self: Women, Eating, and Identity*. New York: Harper and Row.

Clément, C., and Cixous, H. 1986. *The Newly Born Woman*, B. Wing, trans. Minneapolis: University of Minnesota Press.

Culler, J. 1983. *Roland Barthes*. New York: Oxford University Press.

Douglas, M. 1966. *Purity and Danger*. London: Routledge and Kegan Paul.

——. 1982. *Natural Symbols*. New York: Pantheon.

Fodor, I.G. 1974. 'The Phobic Syndrome in Women', in V. Franks and V. Burtle, eds., *Women in Therapy*. New York: Brunner/Mazel.

Foucault, M. 1979. *Discipline and Punish*. New York: Vintage.

——. 1980. *The History of Sexuality*. Volume 1: *An Introduction*. New York: Vintage.

Friedan, B. 1962. *The Feminine Mystique*. New York: Dell.

Goffman, E. 1959. *The Presentation of the Self in Everyday Life*. Garden City, NJ: Anchor Doubleday.

Hunter, D. 1985. 'Hysteria, Psychoanalysis and Feminism', in S. Garner, C. Kahane, and M. Sprenger, eds., *The (M)Other Tongue*. Ithaca, NY: Cornell University Press.

Liu, A. 1979. *Solitaire*. New York: Harper and Row.

Mitchie, H. 1987. *The Flesh Made Word*. New York: Oxford University Press.

Moi, T. 1985. 'Representations of Patriarchy: Sex and Epistemology in Freud's Dora', in C. Bernheimer and C. Kahane, eds., *In Dora's Case:*

Freud—Hysteria—Feminism. New York: Columbia University Press.

Orbach, S. 1985. *Hunger Strike: The Anorectic's Struggle as a Metaphor for Our Age.* New York: W.W. Norton.

Poster, M. 1984. *Foucault, Marxism, and History.* Cambridge: Polity Press.

Showalter, E. 1985. *The Female Malady: Women, Madness and English Culture, 1830–1980.* New York: Pantheon.

Siedenberg, R., and K. DeCrow. 1983. *Women Who Marry Houses: Panic and Protest in Agoraphobia.* New York: McGraw-Hill.

Silverstein, B. 1986. 'Possible Causes of the Thin Standard of Bodily Attractiveness for Women', *International Journal of Eating Disorders* 5: 907–16.

Smith-Rosenberg, C. 1985. 'The Hysterical Woman: Sex Roles and Role Conflict in Nineteenth-Century America', in C. Smith-Rosenberg, *Disorderly Conduct: Visions of Gender in Victorian America.* Oxford: Oxford University Press.

Vicinus, M. 1972. 'Introduction: The Perfect Victorian Lady', in M. Vicinus, *Suffer and Be Still: Women in the Victorian Age*, pp. x–xi. Bloomington: Indiana University Press.

CHAPTER 11

Mass Media and Gender Identity in High Performance Canadian Figure Skating

Karen McGarry

Introduction

This paper is based upon qualitative, anthropological fieldwork conducted between 2000 and 2002 among Canadian journalists, high performance (i.e., National, World, and Olympic level) figure skaters, coaches, sponsors, and others involved in the production of mediated representations of figure skating for mainstream Canadian television networks and other print media. With the permission of various organizations, I conducted participant observation and field work in skating arenas and in the media centres of major competitions to understand the role of figure skating in shaping a sense of Canadian national identity. As standard practice in anthropology, the names of those interviewed are withheld to protect their anonymity. The goal of this paper is to highlight the role of the media in promoting particular gendered images of figure skaters for public consumption, thereby drawing attention to two issues: (1) the socially constructed nature of various representations of men and women in the sport, and; (2) the ways in which particular gendered images of sports figures are promoted in the interests of nationalism.

Figure Skating, the Media, and Canadian Culture

Figure skating is viewed by many Canadians as an integral part of Canadian culture. Records of ice-skating date back to at least the 1700s, and figure skating, along with hockey, receives prime-time television coverage on major Canadian television networks. Figure skating, in fact, is ranked second only to hockey in terms of television spectatorship, government funding, and corporate sponsorship (Skate Canada, 2002). Its popularity among fans is heightened by the fact that since the 1940s, Canadians have won more than 500 international medals, making it one of the nation's most competitively successful amateur sports. Skaters such as Elvis Stojko, Kurt Browning, Elizabeth Manley, Barbara Ann Scott, Toller Cranston, Jamie Salé and David Pelletier, to name a few, have become household names and national icons in Canada.

Given figure skating's high spectatorship levels, it is not surprising that Skate Canada, the sport's amateur governing body, and CTV, Canada's self-declared 'official figure skating network' have opportunistically marketed figure skating as a distinctly 'Canadian' sport and a sport of national significance:

> Figure Skating is a sport of national significance to Canadians and is part of our heritage. Canadians have excelled in figure skating, achieving international success and celebrity status (Skate Canada Fact Sheet, 2002).

> It's part of our Canadian heritage. That's why CTV—'Canada's Figure Skating Network'—is committed to bringing you the best figure skating in the world. CTV has been partnered with the sport since 1961, and makes figure skating its core sports property (CTV website, 16 July 2001).

For Skate Canada and its top skaters, sponsorships are relatively easy to obtain (in comparison with other amateur sports). In fact, Skate Canada has become a primarily self-sustaining organization over the years, thanks mainly to lucrative sponsorship opportunities. While the organization continues to receive government funding, this represents a small portion (7 per cent) of its annual operating budget (Skate Canada, 2002). This means that the task of promoting a sense of national identity among Canadians has, in the case of figure skating, moved increasingly into the hands of non-state actors, and particularly the mass media and its sponsors and advertisers. Throughout my research, I learned that there exist powerful alliances of interest between skating sponsors and various Canadian media outlets, both of which have a vested economic interest in promoting various national representations that appeal to entertainment spectacles. These alliances, in turn, indirectly influence the gendered representations upheld for Canadian audiences. For example, at one event, I talked with a television sports network executive from a major

media outlet. Very excited to be there, she had this to say about her company's agreement with Skate Canada:

> *Executive:* When they [Skate Canada] approached us, we were excited to be a part of it all. We were looking for the best sports ambassadors for Canada to support. What's better than figure skating? They're good, clean-cut kids. We're proud too of our association with skating and our advertisers have really supported Elvis Stojko over the years.
> *Karen:* What was it about Elvis that makes him appealing?
> *Executive:* He's successful and a champion. And he's such a strong, masculine presence.

Top skaters recognize the importance of their sport to the country, and they rarely doubt that their image will not be promoted favourably. Their bodies have become commodified to the point where, as one skater confidently told me, 'I'm not trying to be arrogant here, but they [the network] would have my people [his sponsors] down their throats if I got criticized. I'm worth a lot to them.' In many ways then, figure skating represents an opportunity for understanding how the Canadian media and television, in conjunction with advertisers, influence the production of gendered, commodified identities on ice, and in doing so, produce highly specific gendered bodily representations of the nation.

Gender and Figure Skating

The gendered categories of 'masculinity' and 'femininity' are socially constructed concepts and societal ideals about an appropriate masculine or feminine behaviour vary spatially, from culture to culture, and temporally, depending upon various socio-historical circumstances (e.g., Butler, 1990). In other words, what is considered 'socially appropriate' behaviour for a female or male (today) is not the same as a century ago. Given the lucrative sponsorship potential of the sport, it is not surprising that the Canadian mainstream media and its sponsors and advertisers have sought to endorse 'clean cut', mainstream, heterosexual images of masculinity and femininity for public consumption.

While figure skating is rumoured to have the highest proportion of homosexual men of any amateur competitive sport (Pronger, 1999), it is ironically a sport in which men must exhibit the most blatantly heterosexual signs to be successful and to receive commercial endorsements. Since the late 1980s, Skate Canada, the media, and its sponsors have made a concerted effort to de-emphasize figure skating's balletic heritage, a tradition that was strengthened in the 1970s by skaters such as Canadian Olympian Toller Cranston, an openly homosexual competitor who introduced flamboyant costumes, cosmetics, ballet, and choreography into men's skating. Male homosexuality, it seems, is considered a financial liability to the sport. In 1998, for example, the two-time Olympic silver medallist, Brian Orser, was 'outed' in the media during a palimony lawsuit. Orser was devastated by the media exposure and claimed that such allegations of homosexuality would threaten his economic livelihood. Similarly, at the 2001 World Championships in Vancouver when a well-known male Canadian skater was contacted by a gay magazine about the possibility of doing a feature story on him, he was told by Skate Canada that he must decline the request. As one coach said to me, 'that is not the sort of picture that Skate Canada wants to paint for the country, especially in an international forum.' Every effort is made to construct such skaters as heterosexual.

The heterosexual masculine images of World Champion skaters like Kurt Browning and Elvis Stojko were endorsed enthusiastically in the media throughout the 1990s, a point also noted by Adams (1997). Usually skating to rock and roll music, or adopting the traditionally masculine personas of characters like ninjas, Scottish warriors, or karate experts, Stojko was constructed in the media as 'Canada's Terminator'. At one competition I attended, I watched Stojko warm up backstage with balletic exercises, but the camera technician, who was instructed to film Stojko's pre-competitive routine, waited until he decided to jog to film him. As he said to me, 'Elvis is such a macho guy; we want to show that side of him.' By emphasizing male skaters'

athletic abilities in media portrayals, links are made between the supposed 'strength' of the male figure skating body, and the 'strength' of the nation. As one sponsor said to me, 'We want to promote strong images of our male skaters to show the Americans and other nations that we are an important force to contend with.' The bottom line is that images of male heterosexuality sell to a broader, and hence more lucrative, spectator demographic.

Similar sorts of gender expectations and pressures exist for Canada's female skaters. Women are expected to emulate a soft, delicate femininity reminiscent of, as one coach told me, 'an Audrey Hepburn or Grace Kelly era'. The competitive future of female skaters who fail to project such images may, in some cases, be threatened. One female skater I spoke with, for example, told me that, subsequent to a competition, she was informed by a judge that her earring (she had three piercings in each ear), her nose ring, and her weight, were 'unfeminine' and that she might fare better in the future should she comport herself 'more accordingly and ladylike'. She also suggested that the skater should lose five pounds, as this would make her more attractive to the media.

Clearly then, the gendered images performed in figure skating are culturally constructed images, oftentimes produced in conjunction with the media. Some skaters I spoke with, for instance, informed me that they consult their agents and media organizations for input before deciding upon their annual costume and program themes.

Social Implications/Conclusion

The gendered images favoured in figure skating are important to discuss here because they have a variety of negative consequences for the sport. First, the persistence of idealized representations of gender can lead to the onset of debilitating emotional and physical disabilities among skaters. For women in particular, figure skating is notorious for the existence of eating disorders and a variety of other physical and psychological ailments (e.g., Ryan, 1995; Davis, 1997) as a result of the desire to achieve an 'idealized femininity'. The narrow range of opportunities for gendered identities also hampers the individual creative talents and artistic abilities of skaters, coaches, and choreographers, many of whom feel limited in the range of options available. Also, it is somewhat surprising, in the supposedly tolerant, multicultural, and inclusive environment of a nation like Canada, that such a rigid and narrow definition of gendered identities is accepted and promoted (oftentimes unconsciously) for public consumption. Clearly, this is a growing concern within the sport due to the increasing power and hegemony of the mainstream media and its powerful position in shaping modern identities. As nation-states gradually begin to lose control over the production of national identities in increasingly globalized contexts, non-state entities like the mass media are taking over or supplanting the state's role in nation-building. As this article has suggested, this has important connotations for the future of increasingly mediated sports like figure skating, where the bodies of skaters are heavily commodified and mainstream representations of national bodies dominate.

References

Adams, M. 1997. 'To be an Ordinary Hero: Male Figure Skaters and the Ideology of Gender', *Avante* 3, 3: 93–110.

Butler, J. 1990. *Gender Trouble: Feminism and the Subversion of Identity*. New York: Routledge.

CTV. 2001. *CTV and Figure Skating*. Available at *www.ctv.ca/sport* (accessed 16 July 2001).

Davis, C. 1997. 'Eating Disorders and Hyperactivity: A Psycho-biological Perspective', *Canadian Journal of Psychiatry* 42: 168–75.

Pronger, B. 1999. *The Arena of Masculinity: Sport, Homosexuality, and the Meaning of Sex*. New York: St Martin's Press.

Ryan, J. 1995. *Little Girls in Pretty Boxes: The Making and Breaking of Elite Gymnasts and Figure Skaters*. New York: Doubleday.

Skate Canada. 2002. *Skate Canada Fact Sheet*. Ottawa: Skate Canada.

CHAPTER 12

Contours of Everyday Life: Women's Reflections on Embodiment and Health over Time

Pamela Wakewich

Written on the body is a secret code only visible in certain lights; the accumulations of a lifetime gather there. In places the palimpsest is so heavily worked that the letters feels like Braille. I keep my body rolled up away from prying eyes. Never unfold too much, tell the whole story.

—Jeanette Winterson, *Written on the Body*

People have to inhabit their bodies, and their physical identity is part of themselves. Particularly as they grow older, they have a need to account for this identity, to draw together all that they have experienced. This body is their inheritance, it is the result of the events of their life, and it is their constraint.

—Mildred Blaxter, 'The Causes of Disease: Women Talking'

While efforts to incorporate the body into social theory have become prolific in the past decade, it is only recently that writers have begun to explore the ways in which people actively constitute and experience the body in everyday life.[1] Analysts have tended to focus upon representations of the female body in the professional discourses of medicine and science or the popular discourses of media and advertising, and to presume a direct link between these representations and women's experiences of the body.[2] Even where authors seek to present alternative frameworks, their analysis generally remain framed by the scientific and bio-medical categories and language that they wish to challenge. Body and identity are presented as static notions with the presumption that they remain fixed and homogeneous through time and place.

A similar limitation is evident in much con-temporary feminist literature that addresses the relationship between media and women's body image dissatisfaction. Largely influenced by writers like Foucault, analysts have carefully documented the ways in which media and advertising serve to promote and normalize disciplinary practices of the female body towards the achievement of unhealthy ideals. Susan Bordo's much cited essay 'Reading the Slender Body' brilliantly deconstructs the patholo-gized, individuated image that both medicine and media present us with—the woman who 'succeeds' in achieving these ideals only to damage her own health and perhaps risk her life in the process. Bordo's analysis clearly shows the importance of see-ing the 'everyday-ness' of these disciplinary practices and how they inscribe on the surface (and increas-ingly the interior) of women's bodies the 'bulimic personality' of contemporary American capitalist society. This society requires, at one and the same time, unrestrained consumption to achieve health and happiness and intense repression of desire and body boundaries to meet narrowly prescribed moral and cultural standards (Bordo, 1990).

Yet Bordo's analysis, along with those of many others who address this topic, leaves us with little, if any, indication of how women 'read' and respond to—or perhaps even resist—these dominant ideals. We get little sense of the extent to which these dominant ideals may or may not be significant or predominant in women's identity construction and how this may shift over time and in different social contexts, as well as in relation to other aspects of the multiple-subject positions women hold (such as class, ethnicity, age, sexuality, regional identity, and so on).

Studying Health and Body Perceptions in Northwestern Ontario

These concerns were the points of departure for a research project that I conducted in northwestern Ontario between 1996 and 1999. Comparing the experiences of white working-class and middle-class women and men, I explored how ideas about health and the body are shaped and reshaped over time, as well as how identities of gender, class, sex-uality, culture, region (in this case 'northern-ness') are constituted within and through discourses on health and the body.[3] The decision to interview both women and men was in part motivated by my desire to 'de-problematize' the female body, a problem that is evident in many current medico-scientific and feminist analyses.

In conducting this research, I used techniques of feminist oral history to elicit what Barbara Duden calls 'bio-logies', or body stories, in order to bring into view the everyday processes and social relations through which ideas about health and the body are constituted and experienced.[4]

My research was carried out in the city of Thunder Bay, in northwestern Ontario, a commun-ity whose own identity is in many ways negoti-ated and liminal.[5] By 'liminal', I mean it is at once northern (officially considered part of the provin-cial north), and yet not northern (being located only 50 kilometres from the American border). It is urban (having a population of some 120,000), and yet rural (being physically isolated from other large centres by at least a full day's drive in either direc-tion). It is an important regional business and ser-vice centre, and yet, residents feel largely ignored and insignificant in provincial terms. Its population is culturally diverse, comprising a mix of various Northern and Eastern European roots, a significant First Nations population as well as recent migrants from Latin America and South East Asia, and yet conformity of style, speech, and even behaviour is valued and remarked upon. As several of the women interviewed noted, straying too far from the accepted norms of dress and appearance may meet with social sanctions such as public commentary or ridicule. Although the primary resource industries (such as the paper mills and grain elevators) are no longer as significant to the local economy as they once were, and even though women make up an increasingly large share of the city's labour force, the city maintains an image in the eyes of both residents and outsiders of being a 'lunch-bucket' or 'workingman's' town (Dunk, 1991).

Interviews were conducted with 40 women and men between the ages of 30 and 65. In choosing this age range, I anticipated that participants would be old enough to have a 'history' of body experiences to reflect upon, and yet young enough to not be preoccupied with significant gerontological concerns. To address the dimension of social class, equal numbers of working-class and middle-class women and men were included. As Robert Crawford's research on working-class notions of health and white middle-class discourses on AIDS has suggested (Crawford, 1994), attentiveness to class enables a comparison of both gender and class discourses on the language and representation of health and the body, and the extent to which they are invoked in the constitution of identity. For working-class women, I expected that there might not be a distinctly positive association between the nature of work and body image. The exigencies of work, family, and limited income experienced by working-class women might be seen as antithetical to the possibility of 'cultivating' the ideal female body promoted by popular cultural representations. My interest here was to examine whether working-class women define their health and body experiences in relation to the middle-class norms represented in popular culture and medico-scientific discourse on the 'healthy' body, or whether alternative identities are constructed.

The 20 women interviewed ranged in age from 33 to 53, with a median age of 43. Sixteen of the women were currently married, one was living common-law, another was single, and two were

divorced. All but five of the women had children or dependents living at home. Some of these children were in their late teens and early twenties; however, the women still thought of them as dependents financially, emotionally and in terms of household labour. The working-class women's occupations included clerical work, grocery clerk, letter carrier, homemaker, babysitter, kitchen worker, union representative, and diploma nurses. The middle-class women's occupations included nurse administrators, lawyer, teacher, university professor, homemaker, small business owner/ workers and office administrator. Four of the women combined part-time work with primary childcare responsibilities, while the remainder were employed full-time, and most reported some additional responsibility for children or dependents. Nine of the women had more than one paid occupation—either a combination of part-time jobs, or a full-time job and a part-time job (such as union representative).

In broad terms, the interviews focused on the participants' past and current perceptions of health and embodiment with particular attention to the ways in which these have changed or remained stable through the course of their lives. Interviews explored the role of body image in the women's perceptions of health and well-being, construction of self and 'other', and the significance attributed to popular culture, family socialization, employment, medical interactions, and other aspects of the social environment in shaping ideas about health and the body.

The interview schedule focused on four main themes: (1) background information on family, education, employment, and social class; (2) definitions of health; (3) gender, work, family, leisure, and their relationship to health and identity; and (4) ideas about body and body image, and their relationship to gender, work, family, health, and identity.

Defining Health and Healthiness

For the majority of the women interviewed, ideas about health and body image are intimately inter-linked and have changed over their lives. For many, ideas about health and healthiness have evolved from a more conventional biomedical notion of health as the absence of disease (adhered to at an earlier age), to the assessment of well-being in more environmental or holistic terms. The women's notions of health discuss levels of physical energy, comfort in carrying out and balancing multiple roles, satisfaction with quality of work and family relations, and concerns about time for self and leisure.

When asked whether her idea of what it is to be healthy had always been the same, Carol, a 4-year-old university professor, responded this way: 'No. I'd say now, getting older that . . . there is no doubt that my sense of health is becoming much less separate from how I look, and much more to do with how I feel.' Laura, a 43-year-old nurse administrator and part-time graduate student, said, 'Probably as I have grown older my expectations for being healthy have actually increased rather than decreased. . . . To me now, being healthy does not just mean being free of disease or not on any medication, but being in the best state I can be in, mentally and physically.' Janet, also 43 and a teaching administrator, agreed that her notions of health had changed over time. As she notes: 'I used to think before that you had to be like five foot five, 120 pounds [and] go to the gym every day. That was my image of what it was to be healthy. I think now it's more like how you feel on the inside. Mentally, as well as physically. The two kind of go together.' Similarly, Debbie, a 44-year-old clerical worker, responded, 'I don't think that I thought about stress when I was [younger]. I don't think that I thought about assessing my health I that way. It is different now.'

The women generally evaluated their health in terms of coping with multiple roles and the quality of family relations.[6] In contrast to many of the men who discussed the importance of physical endurance and a perceived sense of strength when evaluating their appearance, and several expressed a sentiment of being 'overweight' even though they generally felt healthy.

Behaviours associated with staying healthy had also changed over the course of the women's lives. Many indicated that they did little consciously to stay healthy when they were younger, but now were much more conscientious about eating well, getting regular exercise, and rest. For most, time

was the more important constraint to achieving optimal health. They cited the difficulties of finding time for themselves (for leisure or exercise) while juggling multiple work and family roles.

Reflecting on her past and present health practices in response to my question 'Do you consider yourself a healthy person?' Mildred, a 49-year-old co-owner/worker in a small family business, replied:

Sigh . . . well, I would like to think I was. There certainly was a time when I had a lot more time to spend on getting myself that way, [such as] all the time [we were] raising the children and everything. I still make all our own bread and pastries, cookies and those things. I think that counts. I buy meat from the farmer that I know doesn't use steroids or penicillin. We raise our own chickens, eggs and stuff like that. I try working at it. I try to get exercise. Years ago I got tons more than I do now. I would have to say the working thing has just cramped my style considerably. I'm overweight, of course, and I don't get as much exercise as I should. Years ago when I was home I would walk for three hours a day. I love walking. I love being outside. I also feel at times, I've narrowed it down, I know what it is—it is nature deprivation. I feel nature deprivation if I don't get outside enough—you know, the less you do [exercise], the less you can do it. You get home and you're tired. You don't feel like going out.

I asked Mildred, 'When would you say you used to do more? Was it when your kids were younger?' and she replied:

Yeah. And I babysat, and I was at home. We had the business out of the house for a while too. When we started doing it [establishing the business], the transitional period, I could just be out more. It was easier to do it. . . . If I could afford somebody full time [to help with the business], I would be out of there in a flash. I would be home feeding the chickens and raising the pigs and things like that. Because that's what I enjoy doing.

Several of the women indicated that they didn't have a sense of entitlement of 'time off'. Women with younger children generally built their own leisure pursuits around activities that could include their children. Terri, a professional who had been very athletic in her youth, expressed frustration at trying to get a 'workout' for herself while doing activities with her children. Having recognized that the desires to spend time with her children and to exercise for herself were working at cross-purposes, she temporarily 'resolved' the issue by putting her own needs on hold until the children were older.

Class differences were also apparent in the women's definitions of health over the life course. Many middle-class women identified with current 'healthiest' discourses that emphasize health as an individual phenomenon, and blamed themselves for failing to live up to the ideals of dietary and exercise regimes promoted in public health rhetoric. Ironically, even those who were professionals identified structural elements such as the exigencies of the double-work day and an unequal division of labour in the home as the major impediments to self-care. Working-class women tended to evaluate and discuss their own health in relational, rather than individual, terms. They assessed their own health in terms of their self-sufficiency and their ability to serve others (their family members, for example).

In general, the women were attentive to, and aware of, body image issues through the course of their lives, yet the importance and meanings attributed to them had changed significantly for most.[7] Many had previously dieted and monitored their weight carefully as adolescents and in their early twenties, yet most had abandoned these practices, either due to a sense of frustration with their lack of success, or emptily as a form of resistance to what they perceived as inappropriate medicalization and monitoring of their bodies by parents, doctors, partners and others.

Laura, a 50-year-old clothing store owner and mother of two grown children, described how her ideas of body image and being healthy have changed over time in this way:

I guess I was, as a baby boomer, probably on the leading edge of anorexia and bulimia and all that kind of stuff. I never had bulimia, but I'm sure I was one of the first anorexics [and this] was never diagnosed. Just from trying to starve yourself because society said you should be a thin person. If you weren't [thin] you felt you should be, so you tried anything to get there. That has changed for me drastically. I'm not unhealthy and I'm certain my body image is no longer an issue [for me]. If somebody doesn't like me because I am heavy that's their problem, not mine.

When I asked Laura whether there was something specific that changed her notion of health, she said:

I think it was just finding out just after having my son that I couldn't starve myself every day. And why the heck should I have to—to be somebody else's image of what I should be? As long as I'm a good mother and a good person. Being in the [business of running a clothing store for large women] has certainly helped that too . . . if you're clean and your makeup's on and your clothes are nice and you keep yourself looking good, that's what people see.

Most of the women talked about having multiple body images. They emphasized the fluidity and contextualness of their own perceptions. Body image was different at home and in public spaces, in the company of friends and with strangers, at times of healthiness and during illness episodes, and often between work and leisure. Karen, a 33-year-old health administrator, described body image in the following way: 'It's how you perceive yourself. How I perceive myself is not just my physical being. It's whether I am confident in a certain situation of feeling secure. It does change if you are in a situation that you don't feel as confident [in].'

Debbie pointed out that her consciousness of body image is affected by whether she is in the company of women or of men. She states: 'I think I am more aware of what I look like and how I am perceived when I am with a bunch of women. Men are, even though you like to think men are fussy—they aren't fussy, they don't care. Women are much more critical. I think I worry about it more when I am with a bunch of women.' Marg, a 45-year-old office administrator similarly observed: 'I think it's different in different settings. . . . Okay, for instance when I'm dressed nicer and I look good. When I'm dressed in sloppy clothes around the house . . . I don't feel too powerful.'

For many of the women, different body images were also related to the quality of relationships with their partners or their peer group. Rita, a 43year-old small business owner who had divorced and remarried, described a very different sense of body image with her new partner whom she described as 'comfortable with me as I am'. Laura indicated that comfort with her body shifts in relation to contact with a group of female friends who are extremely physically active and concerned about appearance. Louise, a 38-year-old home-maker with three school-age children, described herself as a 'borderline' anorexic in adolescence, but had overcome this during her early twenties. She found the weigh-in and fundus[8] measurement during routine pregnancy checkups very anxiety-provoking; it created for her a negative shift in body image that has taken many years to resolve.

The women's notions of body image were fluid and changing over time. Often defined as body shape or physical appearance in adolescence, for some, body image expanded to a larger sense of 'presentation of self' (Goffman, 1959) as they aged. For professional and business women this incorporated not only appearance and styles of dress—or 'dressing for success' as many described it—but also a sense of self-confidence, a feeling of accomplishment or skill in their field of work, and an improved sense of healthiness over time. For many of the working-class women, being successfully relied upon by others and being seen as coping, were important aspects of the assessment of body image. Some of their responses expressed a kind of idealization of a 'northern' (almost akin to pioneer) women for whom strength and endurance were key dimensions of a positive body image.

Consciousness of the body was also described as situational and, again, varied along class and gender lines. Many of the women indicated that they were not conscious of their bodies on an ongoing basis. A few women who were particularly concerned about weight described their bodies as constraints (as the opening quote from Blaxter suggests), which they had difficulty transcending. However, most others indicated that body consciousness was situational, brought on by a particularly serious or sudden illness episode, by concerns about what to wear to a particular social event (for example, a class reunion or family gathering), by travelling to a large urban centre like Toronto where consciousness and monitoring of appearance seems more evident, or by shopping for clothing—especially the painful annual new bathing suit ritual. For many of the women, body consciousness and anxiety were also heightened by medical concerns encounters (even routine checkups) that frequently raised concerns about unhealthy weight, independent of a women's own assessment of her state of healthiness.

Media and Other Representations of the Female Body and Health

Responses to predominant media images of the idealized female body had also changed in the women's reflections. They differed on opinions about the extent to which ideals of slenderness and feminine beauty were more predominant or widely circulated today than when they were younger. Many remembered routinely reading or 'studying' the teen magazines of their youth, such as Seventeen, often with a sense of regret that the products and fashions advertised were not readily available in the North. While many continue to be avid magazine readers, the choice of magazines has changed from teen magazines to ones such as Canadian Living or Woman's Day, and the appeal cited was as much the recipes and advice columns as the clothing and fashion images.

When asked how they respond to or whether they 'see' themselves in the images of women presented in these magazines, most indicated a strong sense that the images were largely unreal and sometimes almost amusing in their absurdity. A few noted an increased representation of 'real' or average women in the magazines in recent years. They found this trend appealing and felt they paid much more attention to these ads or pictures because they could get a sense of how clothes might really look on them.

Medical information and advice columns in the magazines were frequently read by the women and taken much more seriously than fashion layouts. Many of the women found these columns to be an important source of personal and family health information and said they discussed them with friends. But even this information could be dismissed or resisted if the women didn't feel that it matched their own perspective.

Body and body image were seldom discussed in individual terms, but rather almost always constituted in relational terms. Constructing the self was done in relation to a constructed 'other'. Thus, norms or expectations of femininity were contrasted with norms of masculinity (and vice versa); middle-class concerns about presentation of self and success were presented as opposite to stereotypes of a working class lack of care or lack of discipline; and working-class concerns about the lack of time and money to pursue idealized health and body images were construed in relation to the presumption of generic middle-class investment in, and resources available to, achieve those ideals.

Contemporary senses of health and body image were referential to past notions and ideals and often made efforts to present an integrated or coherent history of embodiment. In some instances, where particularly troubling experiences of violence—such as sexual abuse or social stigma—were part of a woman's past, her efforts at providing an integrated narrative were contradictory or incomplete. The strong resonances of past experiences showed through the narrative surface, giving a texture much like the 'palimpsest' that Winterson's opening quote to this chapter so eloquently describes.

These observations suggest that women's ideas about body and body image are fluid and contextual. They are shaped and re-shaped over time and placed in relation to other aspects of identity and subjectivity. Ideas about the body are interlinked with notions of health and well-being and evolve in relation to both individual and collective experiences. Science, medicine, and media may play an important role in shaping and normalizing our ideals and behaviours—particularly in our younger years—but they are often ignored or actively resisted when the images they present us with fail to match our own evolving sense of health or well-being. Thus the analysis and incorporation of body and embodiment in social theory and feminist research must attend to the fluidity and contextualness of women's experiences, and explore their constitution and reconstitution in specific times and places with particular attention to the quality and nature of the social relations in which they are shaped.

Notes

1. See, for example, Kathy Davis, ed., *Embodied Practices: Feminist Perspectives on the Body* (London: Sage, 1997); Frigga Haug, ed., *Female Sexualization* (London: Verso, 1987); Nicole Sault, ed., *Many Mirrors: Body Image and Social Relations* (New Brunswick, NJ: Rutgers University Press, 1994); and Sue Scott and David Morgan, ed., *Body Matters* (London: The Falmer Press, 1993).

2. See Diane Barthel, *Putting on Appearance* (Philadelphia: Temple University Press, 1988); Susan Bordo, 'Reading the Slender Body', in Mary Jacobus and Evelyn Fox Keller, eds., *Body/Politics: Women and the Discourses of Science* (London: Routledge, 1990), 83–112; and Susie Orbach, *Hunger Strike: The Anorectic's Struggle as a Metaphor for Our Age* (New York: W.W. Northon, 1986).

3. This paper is drawn from portions of my PhD dissertation, 'Contours of Everyday Life: Reflections on Health and Embodiment over the Life Course' (University of Warwick, UK, 2000). To study the ways in which ideas about health and embodiment change over the life course, I conducted in-depth interviews with 40 working- and middle-class women and men in northwestern Ontario. Interviewing both women and men allowed a close comparison of the similarities and differences of women and men's experiences of health and embodiment, and the extent to which these were a potential source of gender consciousness.

All but two of the respondents were 'white'. I use the term 'white' here as a social construct following Richard Dyer, *White* (London: Rout-ledge, 1997) and Ruth Frankenberg, *White Women, Race Matters: The Social Construction of Whiteness* (Minneapolis: University of Minnesota Press, 1993). While the research sample reflects the ethnic diversity of the region, as other analysts have noted, the primary distinction recognized by local residents is that between First Nations, or Aboriginal Peoples, and 'whites'. See, for example, Thomas Dunk, *It's a Working Man's Town: Male Working-Class Culture in Northwestern Ontario* (Montreal: McGill-Queen's University Press, 1991). The dissertation includes an analysis of the terrain and interpretations of 'whiteness' as it is both visible and invisible in the participants' narratives of 'healthy selves' and 'unhealthy others'.

4. Barbara Duden, *The Woman Beneath the Skin*, uses the concept of 'bio-logies' or body stories to describe the changing understandings and representations of the body evident in the narratives given to eighteenth-century German physician Johannes Storch by his clients over the course of his professional relationship with them.

5. Liminality is valued by postmodern researchers because studying liminal or 'in-between' categories highlights the ways in which differences are marked by people and given 'presence' or value within a particular culture or subculture. See Sonya Andermahr, Terry Lovell, and Carol Wolkowitz, *A Concise Glossary of Feminist Theory* (London: Arnold, 1997) for a discussion of the use of liminality in postmodern research.

6. A similar point is raised by Nickie Charles and Vivienne Walters in their analysis of age and gender in South Wales' women's accounts of health. They point out, 'Women's accounts demonstrate that their experiences and explanations of health, while showing certain commonalities, vary with age and stage in the life cycle and are shaped by wider structural changes in employment patterns and gendered divisions of labour. Thus structural and cultural changes shape the discourses that women call upon when talking about health and illness. . . .' 'Age and Gender in Women's Accounts of Their Health: Interviews with Women in South Wales', *Sociology of Health and Illness* 20 (1998): 348.

7. By contrast, many of the men found it much harder to reflect on 'body' history and required more prompting to make connections between a sense of embodiment and specific activities or instances of their youth. Most often, they talked about embodiment in terms of success or endurance in sporting activities, the ability to do physical labour (especially for working-class men) or in relation to illness of self or appearance norms. Those who did were primarily middle-class men who discussed presentation of self in terms of their leadership image at work and their embodiment of corporate imagery.

8. The fundus is the top of the uterus. Its changing position is measured throughout the pregnancy to assess the growth and position of the baby.

References

Blaxter, M. 1983. 'The Causes of Disease: Women Talking', *Social Science and Medicine* 17: 69.

Bordo, S. 1990. 'Reading the Slender Body', in M. Jacobus and E. Fox Keller, eds., *Body/Politics: Women and the Discourses of Science*, pp. 83–112. London: Routledge.

Charles, N., and V. Walters. 1998. 'Age and Gender in Women's Accounts of Their Health: Interviews with Women in South Wales', *Sociology of Health and Illness* 20: 348.

Crawford, R. 1994. 'The Boundaries of the Self and the Unhealthy Other: Reflections on Health, Culture and AIDS', *Social Science and Medicine* 38: 1347–65.

Dunk, T. 1991. *It's a Working Man's Town: Male Working-Class Culture in Northwestern Ontario*. Montreal: McGill-Queen's University Press.

Goffman, E. 1959. *The Presentation of Self in Everyday Life*. Garden City, NY: Doubleday.

Winterson, J. 1994. *Written on the Body*. New York: Vintage Books.

QUESTIONS FOR CRITICAL THOUGHT

1. Bordo emphasizes the impact of media on the body image of young women, while the women Wakewich interviewed do not appear to base their own body image on what they see in media. How influential are the representations of male and female bodies we see in magazines, on TV, and on the Internet? What other forces influence how people think about their bodies?

2. How much do you depend on the appearances of bodies to shape your interactions with other people? Do you react differently to different kinds of bodies?

3. Do you think there is one dominant or hegemonic ideal of beauty for women today? What about for men?

4. What does it mean to be healthy for a woman? For a man? Are there gendered barriers to keeping bodies healthy?

5. McGarry describes a group of people who function as 'public bodies'—whose physical appearance is made available as a product to be consumed by the public. Think of other 'public bodies'. Do all 'public bodies' share any common traits?

PART IV

Gendered Intimacies

Nowhere are the differences between women and men more emphasized than in our intimate lives: our experiences of love, friendship, and sexuality. It is our intimate relationships that give rise to the cliché that men and women are truly from different planets.

But gender is not necessarily destiny when it comes to intimacy. In heterosexual relationships, we find a mixed pattern of convergence and divergence between men and women in terms of the way they experience love and sex. As Lily Tsui and Elena Nicoladis demonstrate in their study of first intercourse experiences among Canadian university students, men and women have much more similar experiences of first intercourse than the men-are-from-Mars-women-are-from-Venus model of gender difference might lead us to expect.

Melanie Beres develops this theme further, suggesting that men and women use very similar presumptions and discourses to shape their experience of heterosexual casual sex—although, as Beres argues, these discourses tend to position men as active sexual pursuers and women as more passive participants in sexual activities. Nonetheless, some women manage to find ways to meet their own sexual desires, even without overtly challenging dominant ways of thinking about sex.

Nick Mulé takes on the question of 'public intimacies', and the ways in which governments shape the way men and women experience sexuality, love, and relationships. Canada was one of the first countries in the world to legally recognize marriages between two people of the same sex, which most gender theorists have hailed as a major milestone. Mule, however, provocatively suggests that the legalization of same-sex marriage is merely a reform of the traditional institution of marriage, and not a transformation.

CHAPTER 13

Losing It: Similarities and Differences in First Intercourse Experiences of Men and Women[1]

Lily Tsui and Elena Nicoladis

Introduction

Historically, a woman's virginity was crucial to marriage in terms of both honour and value; women who were found not to be virgins on their wedding night (often determined by the presence of blood at first intercourse) were seen as worthless in many cultures. In contrast, 'proof' of male virginity is unavailable physically and less important culturally. Such differences in how virginity has been perceived in society have created an environment in which men and women may have different perceptions of first intercourse and its meanings.

Quantitative studies have demonstrated gender differences in both attitudes toward and actual experience of first intercourse. For example, Carpenter (2001) found that women were twice as likely as men to think of their virginity as a gift to a future partner (61 per cent versus 36 per cent), while men were three times more likely than women to view their virginity as a stigma (57 per cent versus 21 per cent). Darling, Davidson, and Passarello (1992) found that a greater percentage of men than women perceived their first intercourse to be physiologically satisfying (81 per cent versus 28 per cent) and psychologically satisfying (67 per cent versus 28 per cent).

Qualitative studies based on feminist analyses of power differences between men and women have suggested possible explanations for such findings. For example, young adults' accounts of first sexual intercourse reveal that men gain an affirmation of manhood through first intercourse. It is thus primarily a young man's moment that marks his 'coming of age' or his entry into manhood (Holland, Ramazanoglu, Sharpe, and Thomson, 2000). However, the dependence on women for this validation of men has taken on multiple social meanings, many of which are viewed by feminist thinkers as embedded in a patriarchal culture.

Holland et al. (2000) found that young men's accounts of first intercourse were mostly concerned with their own performance, orgasm, and sense of having reached a landmark. Their partners' pleasure or orgasm was seen as 'icing on the cake'. The problem with young men having this construction of first intercourse is that it leaves young women to cope with first intercourse experiences that may fail to meet their own expectations to affirm feelings of love and romance (Holland et al., 2000). In this view, sex differences in first intercourse experiences have their basis in different perceptions of its meaning and in constructions of sexuality.

Burr (2001) argues that the contemporary construction of men's sexuality as 'active, dynamic, powerful, and, potentially uncontrollable', also portrays women's sexuality as essentially passive. In this construction, sex for women is not about active participation but about something that is received (Darling et al., 1992). Women may thus be seen as dependent on men for introducing them to the physical pleasure aspects of sexual activities because conventional femininity demands that a woman appear to be sexually unknowing, to desire not just sex but a relationship, to let sex 'happen' without requesting it, to trust, to love, and to make men happy (Holland et al., 2000). Traditional dating scenarios reinforced this perspective in that the woman was expected to wait for the man to ask her out and the man was expected to handle details of cost, transportation, and activity (Allgeier and Royster, 1991).

Social discourses around sexuality, and particularly female sexuality, reflect and influence personal and educational perspectives on first intercourse. Fine (1997) identifies three such discourses. The first discourse, sexuality as violence, instills fear of sex by focusing on abuse, incest, and other negative outcomes of sexual activity. The second discourse, sexuality as victimization, identifies females as subject to the pressuring tendencies of male sexuality and focuses attention on the risk of women 'being used' or coerced and thus on ways to avoid the physical, social, and emotional risks of sexual intimacy. Messages related to unintended pregnancy and sexually transmitted infections (STIs) may reinforce notions of risk and are used by some to pressure for classroom priority on strategies to avoid sex, 'saying no', and 'abstinence only' approaches to sexuality education. In this context, Fine's third discourse, sexuality as individual morality, would value women's choice about sexuality as long as the choice is premarital abstinence. Such discourses, Fine suggests, lead to a construction of sexuality where the male is in search of desire and the female is in search of protection. Largely absent from public sexual education is a fourth discourse, sexuality as desire. Fine notes that

> The naming of desire, pleasure, or sexual entitlement, particularly for females, barely exists in the formal agenda of public schooling on sexuality . . . a genuine discourse of desire would invite adolescents to explore what feels good and bad, desirable and undesirable, grounded in experiences, needs, and limits (Fine, 1997).

The Present Study

Given the questions implicit in these background observations, the present study sought to identify university students' perspectives on various aspects of their first experience of consensual heterosexual sexual intercourse. The questionnaire designed for this purpose dealt with precursors to, experience of, and subsequent feelings about first intercourse. Students who had not had intercourse answered selected questions based on their expectations.

Apart from the anticipation arising from the literature review that men's and women's experiences would differ and that men's would be more positive, we refrained from making more specific hypotheses. This reticence was due to our perception that the literature had given a clearer picture of what to ask than what to expect. We consider the study to be a descriptive and exploratory step in determining if and how women's and men's experiences of first intercourse differ and to what extent the findings reflect the various constructions of sexuality portrayed in the literature.

Method

Questionnaire

Respondents who had experienced first intercourse answered questions about the context of their first intercourse, preparations prior to intercourse, actual circumstances of first intercourse, and feelings afterward. Those who had not experienced consensual first intercourse were asked about their expectations of first intercourse including preparation, anticipation of pain, orgasm, etc. The questionnaire is presented in Appendix A.

Definitions

This study defined first intercourse as the first time the person had consensual heterosexual intercourse. The four participants whose first experience of sexual intercourse happened in the context of a sexual assault therefore did not provide answers about their first intercourse based on this experience but rather on their first consensual experience, if that had occurred. If they had not had consensual intercourse, their responses were based on their expectations regarding first intercourse, as were those of others who had not had consensual intercourse.

Participants

Among the 358 introductory psychology undergraduate students who participated (114 men, 244 women), the mean age was 19.4 years ($SD = 2.32$, range 17–38). Participants who had not had intercourse were slightly but significantly younger on average than those who had (19.0 versus 19.73 years respectively) $t(356) = 2.99$; $p = .002$. Most participants were born in Canada (79 per cent). Grouping of free-response items on cultural background yielded six categories: 'Canadian' (30 per cent); 'European' (39 per cent); 'Asian' (18 per cent);

'Middle Eastern' (4 per cent); and 'Other' (10 per cent). Religious affiliation grouped into five categories: 'Christian (not Catholic)' (33 per cent); 'Catholic' (31 per cent); 'Hindu/Sikh/Muslim' (9 per cent); 'Buddhist/Taoist' (3 per cent); and 'No religious affiliation' (25 per cent).

Based on the definition of first intercourse as the first experience of consensual sexual intercourse, 55.6 per cent (n = 199) of the sample had experienced first intercourse and 44.4 per cent (n = 159) had not. Men and women did not differ in this respect (44.7 per cent of men and 44.3 per cent of women had not had first intercourse).

Results

Contextual Variables of First Intercourse

Age at first intercourse
All but one participant could recall their age at first intercourse. Mean age for first intercourse was 17.13 years ($SD = 1.65$; range 13–28) with no significant difference between the sexes (17.04 for women and 17.31 for men; see Table 13.1 for all age-related data).

Partner's age at participant's first intercourse
On average, women had first intercourse with partners who were significantly older than they were (mean of 17.04 years for women and 18.41 years for their partners) ($t(132) = -6.01$, $p < .001$, $d = -1.38$) whereas mean age at first intercourse for men (17.31 years) did not differ from that of their partners (17.6 years; see Table 13.1).

Relationship to partner at time of first intercourse
The great majority of both women and men (84 per cent overall) said they were in a couple/romantic relationship with their first intercourse partner while 16 per cent were not in a romantic relationship. There was no significant sex difference in relationship status at first intercourse (see Table 13.1).

Duration of relationship with partner prior to first intercourse
Among the 84 per cent of participants who were in a relationship at the time of first intercourse, mean relationship duration was 7.4 months ($SD = 7.29$ months, range = less than one month to 36 months) with men approaching a significantly greater

Table 13.1 Mean age and relationship status of participants and their partners at time of participants' first intercourse

	Men	Women
Age of Participant and Partner at First Intercourse		
Participant's Age	17.31	17.04*
Partner's Age	17.6	28.41*
Relationship Status with First Intercourse Partner		
Couple	83%	85%
Other Relationship	17%	15%
Length of Relationship and Time Known		
Mean Length of Relationship	5.74 months** (SD = 5.46)	8.14 months** (SD = 7.89)
Time Known Regardless of Relationship	26 months ns	34 months ns

* Difference for women and partners significant p < .001; n: men (63), partners (60); women (135), partners (130)
** Difference approaches significance at p = 0.51

likelihood of having shorter duration than women (5.74 months for men, 8.14 months for women) ($t(163) = 1.97$, p = .051, d = −2.40). On average, all participants had known their partner for 31 months (SD = 39.5; range was less than one month to 2 years) with no significant difference between the sexes in this respect (see Table 13.1).

Intercourse experience of participant's first partner
Just over half of the participants reported that they were the first person with whom their partner had intercourse (52.3 per cent). The sexes did not differ in this respect.

Perceptions of being in love at first intercourse and in hindsight
Women were significantly more likely than men to report that they were in love with their partner at the time of first intercourse (63 per cent and 43

per cent respectively) = 7.78 , p = .02). This difference was not present in hindsight (47 per cent and 41 per cent respectively) with men appearing to move from 'unsure' to 'no' and women from 'yes' to 'no' (see Table 13.2).

Decision to have intercourse
Participants were asked whether the decision to have first intercourse was mutual or whether one partner took the lead. While 57 per cent of men and 61 per cent of women said the decision was mutual, Chi-squared analysis showed a significant effect of gender on the decision to have first intercourse (see Table 13.3). In cases where women did not report a mutual decision, 79 per cent assigned the initiative to their partner and 21 per cent to themselves; for men, 42 per cent assigned the initiative to their partners, and 42 per cent to themselves (calculated from data in Table 13.3). Since these students were not reporting on first intercourse with other

Table 13.2 Participants' perception of being in love at time of first intercourse and in retrospect

	'In Love' at time of first intercourse? (%)		'In Love' in hindsight? (%)	
	Men (n = 63)	Women (n = 136)	Men (n = 63)	Women (n = 136)
Yes	43	63	41	47
No	35	25	48	42
Not sure	22	12	11	11
χ^2(2, N = 199)	7.78*	ns		

* p = .02
ns indicates not significant

Table 13.3 Participant perceptions of their and their partners' role in decision to have first intercourse

Participants	Mutual Decision	Male Partner Suggested	Female Partner Suggested
Men (n = 63)	57%	25%	18%
Women (n = 136)	61%	31%	8%
χ^2(2, N = 199)		12.53, p = .002*	

* When the decision was not identified as mutual, men were significantly more likely to have been the ones who suggested intercourse.

respondents, it is not possible to determine whether these sex differences in perception of who initiated would also be seen within couples.

Discussions prior to first intercourse
Among the six pre-intercourse discussion items listed in Table 13.4, participants were most likely to have discussed having sexual intercourse and condom use (63–73 per cent), somewhat less likely to have discussed other methods of birth control (48–58 per cent) and most unlikely to have discussed sexually transmitted infections, possible outcomes of pregnancy, and emotional implications of intercourse for them (32–40 per

cent). The sexes did not differ significantly on any of these items (see Table 13.4).

Circumstances associated with first intercourse
Nine items in Table 13.4 assessed different aspects of the participants' actual first intercourse experience. Although less than half of respondents indicated that first intercourse had occurred when they expected it to (41 per cent of males, 46 per cent of females), condom use at first intercourse was common (75–80 per cent). Alcohol use by self or partner was less common (14–21 per cent) and drug use by self or partner was rare (0–2 per cent). The sexes did not differ on any of these items (see Table 13.4).

Table 13.4 Participants 'yes' responses to questions about prior discussion, circumstances of, and follow-up to first intercourse (%)

	Men (n = 63)	Women (n = 136)	χ^2 (1, 199)
Pre-Intercourse Discussion			
Having intercourse	76	74	ns
Condom use	63	73	ns
Other methods of birth control	58	48	ns
Sexually transmitted infection	33	32	ns
Outcomes if pregnancy were to occur	33	37	ns
Emotional implications	33	40	ns
Circumstances Associated with First Intercourse			
Did intercourse occur when expected?	41	46	ns
Was a condom used?	75	80	ns
Were you drinking?	19	21	ns
Was your partner drinking?	14	18	ns
Were you using any drugs?	0	0	ns
Was your partner using any drugs?	2	2	ns
Was first intercourse painful?	5	52	41.49*
Did you have an orgasm?	76	12	81.91*
Did your partner have an orgasm?	32	73	30.18*
Feelings/Outcomes Subsequent to First Intercourse			
Physical satisfaction	62	35	12.39*
Emotional satisfaction	56	54	ns
Sex again with same partner?	87	89	ns
Stayed a couple or became a couple after?	83	86	ns
Pregnancy occur?	0	0	–

*p < .001
ns indicates not significant

Women were much more likely than men to report pain at first intercourse (52 per cent versus 5 per cent), much less likely than men to report orgasm at first intercourse (12 per cent versus 76 per cent), and more likely to report partner orgasm than were men (73 per cent versus 32 per cent). Each of these differences was statistically significant (see Table 13.4). We did not ask about prior orgasm history of women in our sample but note that our female participants appear less likely to have had orgasm at first intercourse (12 per cent) than was reported by our male respondents of their first intercourse partners (32 per cent; see Table 13.4).

Feelings and outcomes after first intercourse
Men were significantly more likely than women to report feeling physically satisfied after first intercourse (62 per cent versus 35 per cent). However, the sexes did not differ on reports of emotional satisfaction (56 per cent and 54 per cent), having had sex again with the same partner (87 per cent and 89 per cent), or staying as or becoming a couple after first intercourse (83 per cent and 86 per cent). None of the respondents reported pregnancy as a consequence of first intercourse. Men and women were similar in the extent to which they reported no regrets about first intercourse (76 per cent and 72 per cent) and in their perception that they had first intercourse at 'the right age' (63 per cent and 65 per cent; see Table 13.4).

Overall assessment of first intercourse experience
Participants were asked to give an overall 'rating' of their first intercourse experience based on six options (see Table 13.5). There was no statistically significant sex difference in these overall assessments with 72 per cent of men and 61 per cent of women rating the experience as either perfect, very good, or good in contrast to the 11 per cent and 13 per cent respectively who recalled their first intercourse as either 'bad' or 'very bad'.

Slightly less than one quarter of all respondents chose the 'neither good nor bad' option.

Expectations of first intercourse among participants who had not had intercourse
Participants who had not had intercourse (n = 159) answered 9 items from Table 13.4 based on their expectations of first intercourse. There responses are reported in the first two columns of Table 13.6. Students who had not had intercourse did not generally consider it important that their first intercourse partner would also have not had intercourse (36 per cent of men and 29 per cent of women said yes). We did not ask about current relationship status and thus cannot determine how many students in this subsample might, at the time of the study, have been in a relationship with an eventual first intercourse partner.

With respect to their expectations of discussion of particular topics prior to first intercourse, the sexes in this non-intercourse group differed significantly in their expectations about discussing methods of birth control other than condoms $X^2(2, N = 156) = 10.65$, p = .005. Women were more likely than men to expect such discussion (77 per cent versus 53 per cent respectively; see Table 13.6) and men more often unsure (41 per cent versus 17 per cent respectively). Men and women who had not had intercourse also differed significantly in their

Table 13.5 Participants' overall ratings of their first intercourse experience (%)

Response	Men (n = 63)	Women (n = 136)	total
Perfect, wouldn't change a thing	14	19	18
Very good	29	19	22
Good	29	23	25
Neither good or bad	18	26	23
Bad	8	10	10
Very bad	3	3	3

Table 13.6 Expectations of first intercourse among students who had not had intercourse and a comparison with those who had

Responses	First Intercourse Expectations (students who had not had intercourse)		Reported First Intercourse Experiences (students who had had intercourse)	
	Men (n = 51)	Women (n = 108)	Men (n = 63)	Women (n = 136)
Partners not having had intercourse before is important?	36	29		
Pre-Intercourse Discussion				
Discuss having intercourse	60	66	76	74
Discuss condom use	70	83	63	73
Discuss other methods of birth control	53	77	58	48
Discuss STIs	36	57	33	32
Discuss pregnancy	55	53	33	37
Discuss emotional implications	33	44	33	40
Physical Expectations				
Pain at first intercourse	4	34	5	52
Personal experience of orgasm	58	11	76	12
Partner's experience of orgasm	22	28	32	73

expectations about prior discussion of STIs, $X^2(2, N = 157) = 8.17$, $p = .017$ (57 per cent of women expected such discussion versus 36 per cent of men; 36 per cent of women and 46 per cent of men were unsure or did not know).

The sexes also differed in their expectation of pain at first intercourse, $X^2(2, N = 157) = 69.01$, $p < .001$, with a smaller percentage of men (4 per cent) than women (34 per cent) expecting to experience pain. Men and women also differed in expectations about their own and their future partner's likelihood of having orgasm at first intercourse, $X^2(2, N = 156) = 39.44$, $p < .001$, and $X^2(2, N = 156) = 7.80$, $p = .020$ respectively.

Comparison of expectations of participants who had not had intercourse with actual experiences of those who had first intercourse
Table 13.6 also provides an opportunity to compare the first intercourse expectations of the participants who had not had intercourse with the

first intercourse experiences of those who had. A comparison of the experiences of the latter with the expectations of the former invites speculation about the extent to which expectations may or may not match experience. For example, women who had not had intercourse appeared more likely to expect pre-intercourse discussion of birth control methods other than condoms (77 per cent) than was actually experienced by women who had first intercourse (48 per cent). The expected sex difference on this item experienced by those who had intercourse was in the reverse direction to that expected by those who had not. In the relation to the pre-intercourse discussion items as a whole, the trend appears to be for women who have not had intercourse to have higher expectations for such discussion than occurred in practice for those who had. Women's expectation of their own orgasm at first intercourse (11 per cent) matched that of women who had intercourse (12 per cent) but women's expectation of their partner's orgasm

(28 per cent) was lower than that reported about their partners by women who had had intercourse (73 per cent; see Table 13.6).

Discussion

In contrast to other studies that highlighted differences between the sexes in their experience of first intercourse (Darling et al., 1992; Cohen and Shotland, 1996; Guggino, 1997; Holland et al., 2000; Carpenter, 2001), the present findings indicate that, with some exceptions, women's and men's reports of the experience were quite similar. The average age at first intercourse was the same for both sexes. Men and women were equally likely to have had first intercourse within the context of a romantic relationship, to have known their first intercourse partner for the same average length of time, and to have had a first partner who had previous intercourse experience. Women were as likely as men to report activities indicating that they had discussed preparations for and other aspects of first intercourse. In a majority of cases, the decision to have first intercourse was a mutual one. On average, men and women gave similar responses to questions about condom use (usually), alcohol use (seldom), drug use (almost never) and whether first intercourse was expected. The finding that 75 per cent of men and 80 per cent of women reported condom use at first intercourse is consistent with the relatively high levels of protection against unintended pregnancy and STI at first intercourse reported in other recent Canadian studies of young adults (e.g., Hampton, Smith, Jeffrey, and McWatters, 2001). In addition, the sexes did not differ significantly in their evaluation of their feelings and follow-up to first intercourse in relation to emotional satisfaction, subsequent intercourse with first partner, regret, timing, and overall rating.

The women and men in our study who had not had intercourse were also similar to each other on such items as whether it was important that their first partner had also not previously had intercourse (about one-third said yes) and on their expectation of discussion in advance of condom use (high) and possible outcomes if unintended pregnancy were to occur (slightly over half).

The degree of gender similarity in this sample of university students may not represent accurately what is going on in the general population. However, it is also possible that this sample reflects a shift in the sexual practice of young people towards more equally balanced engagement in discussions and decisions related to sexual activity in general and first intercourse in particular. Since the limited research that has been done on first intercourse experience is from the United States, it has been tempting to assume that the Canadian population is similar. However, strongly conservative political and religious influences in the US may reflect an environment that has been more hostile than Canada to premarital sexual activity and hence to the education that would support more informed, and perhaps egalitarian, decision making and experiences surrounding first intercourse.

Some of our findings do suggest gender differences in which men appear to have greater influence on sexual interactions in heterosexual relationships, at least when it comes to first intercourse. The greater age differences between women and their first intercourse partners could result in men having more power and control in the sexual relationship. On the other hand this could simply be a reflection of our society's tendency for younger women to be drawn to older partners and vice versa. The fact that men had known their first intercourse partners for a shorter period of time than women is consistent with Cohen and Shotland's (1996) report that men consider sexual intercourse acceptable earlier in a dating relationship than do women. Among the approximately 40 per cent of women and men in our study who said first intercourse had not been a 'mutual decision', women were significantly more likely to say that their partner had suggested intercourse than were men. This fits with the traditional dating scenario in which men are more likely to take initiative with the sexual aspects of romantic relationships. However, our questions did not explore what these students meant by their partner 'taking the initiative' nor did they explore other aspects of relationship dynamics.

On average, women were more likely than men to believe that they were in love at first intercourse (men were more likely to be unsure). These views converged, in retrospect, with both sexes being equally likely to believe that they were not in love. The greater tendency for women to believe they were in love at first intercourse may reflect greater internalization by women than men of the feeling that sex is about love. There may be a parallel here in the finding of Quackenbush, Strassberg, and Tumer (1995) that the inclusion of romance in erotica can serve as a relationship buffer that make erotic material more acceptable to women. Similarly, the belief that they are 'in love' might be viewed as the relationship buffer necessary for some women to justify first intercourse.

We think these findings have important implications for sexual health education although we are also aware that the study has a number of limitations that invite cautious interpretation of the results. The study was conducted on a convenience sample of introductory psychology students and cannot be generalized to other populations, including students who did not go to university or who left school early. The questionnaire was designed for this study and has not been validated. Participants were only asked about consensual first intercourse and not about other sexual activities such as oral sex. Thus, the study cannot shed light on participants' prior sexual behaviour or on the attitudes that may have shaped their perceptions of their first intercourse experience. That being said, socially constructed gender differences appear to permeate all levels of society and to that extent the findings may well have useful applications for educators and health professionals.

Note

1. We would like to thank Jenn Mitchell, Kim Scott, and Hanna Wajda for their assistance in conducting this study. This research is partially supported by SSHRC funding to the second author.

References

Allgeir, E.R., and B.J.T. Royster. 1991. 'New Approaches to Dating and Sexuality', in E. Grauerholz and M.A. Koralewski, eds, *Sexual Coercion: A Sourcebook On Its Nature, Causes, and Prevention*, pp. 133–47. Lexington, MA: Lexington Books.

Burr, J. 2001. 'Women Have It. Men Want It. What Is It? Constructions of Sexuality in Rape Discourse', *Psychology, Evolution, & Gender* 3: 103–7.

Carpenter, L.M. 2001. 'The Ambiguity of "having sex": The Subjective Experience of Virginity Loss in the United States', *The Journal of Sex Research* 38: 127–39.

Cohen, L.L., and R.L. Shotland. 1996. 'Timing of First Sexual Intercourse in a Relationship: Expectations, Experiences, and Perceptions of Others', *The Journal of Sex Research* 33: 291–9.

Darling, C.A., J.K. Davidson, and L.C. Passarello. 1992. 'The Mystique of First Intercourse among College Youth: The Role of Partners, Contraceptive Practices, and Psychological Reactions', *Journal of Youth and Adolescence* 21: 97–117.

Fine, M. 1997. 'Sexuality, Schooling, and Adolescent Females: The Missing Discourse of Desire', in M.M. Gergen and S.N. Davis, eds., *Toward a New Psychology of Gender*, pp. 375–402. New York, NY: Routledge.

Guggino, J.M., and J.J., Jr., Ponzetti. 1997. 'Gender Differences in Affective Reactions to First Coitus', *Journal of Adolescence* 20: 189–200.

Hampton, M.R, P. Smith, B. Jeffery, and B. McWatters. 2001. 'Sexual Experience, Contraception, and STI Prevention among High School Students: Results from a Canadian Urban Centre', *The Canadian Journal of Human Sexuality* 10: 111–26.

Holland, J., C. Ramazanoglu, S. Sharpe, and R. Thomson. 2000. 'Deconstructing Virginity— Young People's Accounts of First Sex', *Sexual and Relationship Therapy* 15: 221–32.

Quackenbush, D.M., D.S. Strassberg, and C.W. Turner. 1995. 'Gender Effects of Romantic Themes in Erotica', *Archives of Sexual Behavior* 24: 21–35.

Appendix A: Survey items and response categories

Questions	Response Categories

Relationship to Partner

Were you a couple at the time? — Yes / Now

Did you consider yourself to be 'in love' with this person at the time when you had intercourse? — Yes / No / Not Sure

Looking back, do you think you were actually 'in love' with this person when you had intercourse, regardless of your answer to the last question? — Yes / No / Not Sure

How long had you known this person in total, regardless of changes in your relationship to this person? — ____ months and ____ years

Were you the first person with whom your partner has had intercourse? — Yes / No

What is your relationship to this person now? — Partner or Spouse / Friend / Acquaintance / No relationship / Other

Preparations Prior to Intercourse

Did you and your partner talk about having intercourse beforehand? — Yes / No / Not Sure

Did you and your partner discuss condom use before having first intercourse? — Yes / No / Not Sure

Did you and your partner discuss other methods of birth control before having first intercourse? — Yes / No / Not Sure

Did you and your partner discuss STIs before having first intercourse? — Yes / No / Not Sure

Did you and your partner discuss what to do if you / your partner became pregnant before having first intercourse? — Yes / No / Not Sure

Did you and your partner discuss the emotional implications of having intercourse before having first intercourse? — Yes / No / Not Sure

Do you think that you and your partner decided to have intercourse together, or did one of you take the lead? — Decided together / You took the initiative / Partner took the initiative

Circumstances of First Intercourse

Did first intercourse occur when you expected it to? — Yes / No / Not Sure

Where did you have intercourse for the first time? — Your home / Partner's home / Hotel or motel / Vehicle / Other

Did you / your partner use a condom? — Yes / No

Did you / your partner use any other form of contraceptive? — Yes / No

At the time you had intercourse, was there alcohol in your system? — Yes / No / Don't remember or know

Was there alcohol in your partner's system? — Yes / No / Don't remember or know

Were you on any drugs? — Yes / No / Don't remember or know

Was your partner on any drugs? — Yes / No / Don't remember or know

Did you find your first intercourse experience to be physically painful in any way? — Yes / No / Not Sure

Did you achieve orgasm? — Yes / Not / Not Sure / Don't Remember

Did your partner achieve orgasm? — Yes / Not / Not Sure / Don't Remember

Feelings / Outcomes Subsequent to First Intercourse

Did you feel physically satisfied with your first intercourse experience?   Yes / No / Not Sure

Did you feel emotionally satisfied with your first intercourse experience?   Yes / No / Not Sure

Did you and this particular partner ever have sex again?   Yes / No / Don't Remember

Did you and this partner stay together as a couple, or, if you were not
a couple at the time you had intercourse, did you and this partner
become a couple?   Yes / No

Do you regret having shared your first intercourse experience with this person?   Yes / No / Don't
Remember

Looking back, what do you think
about the timing of your first
intercourse experience?   I was about the right age / I was too young / I was too old / Not Sure

Did you or your partner become pregnant as a result of
your first intercourse experience?   Yes / No / I don't know

Did you or your partner get an STI as a result
of your first intercourse experience?   Yes, I caught something from him or her /
Yes, s / he caught something from me / No / Not Sure

Overall, how would you rate your first
intercourse experience?   Perfect, wouldn't change a thing / Very Good / Good /
Neither Good or Bad / Bad / Very Bad

Expectations About First Intercourse by Respondents who had not had Intercourse

Will it be important to you that the person with whom
you have intercourse for the first time is also having
intercourse for the first time?   Yes / Maybe / No / Don't Know

Do you think you and your future partner will talk about
having intercourse beforehand?   Yes / Maybe / No / Don't Know

Do you think you and your future partner will discuss
condom use before having first intercourse?   Yes / Maybe / No / Don't Know

Do you think you and your future partner will discuss other
methods of birth control before having first intercourse?   Yes / Maybe / No / Don't Know

Do you think you and your future partner will discuss STIs
before having first intercourse?   Yes / Maybe / No / Don't Know

Do you think you and your future partner will discuss what to do
if you / your partner became pregnant after having first intercourse?   Yes / Maybe / No / Don't Know

Do you think you and your future partner will discuss the emotional
implications of having first intercourse before having first intercourse?   Yes / Maybe / No / Don't Know

Do you think your first intercourse experience will be physically
painful in any way?   Yes / Maybe / No / Don't Know

Do you think you will achieve orgasm at first intercourse?   Yes / Maybe / No / Don't Know

Do you think your future partner will achieve orgasm at first intercourse?   Yes / Maybe / No / Don't Know

CHAPTER 14

'It Just Happens': Negotiating Casual Heterosexual Sex

Melanie Beres

In the summer of 2005, Melanie Beres spent several months in Jasper, Alberta, interviewing young people who had come to Jasper for seasonal work in the tourist industry. Her intent was to understand the negotiating of sexual consent in short-term heterosexual encounters ('hooking up' or 'one night stands'). Beres chose Jasper because of the dense population of transients and seasonal workers. The youth culture that grew up around this population perceived recreational sex as a common activity. In this chapter, Beres discusses the different ways in which men and women in Jasper talk about casual sex, and how they depict the process of consenting to a sexual encounter.

I begin this chapter by highlighting ways that the negotiation of casual sex in Jasper is dominated by discourses that privilege male sexual desire. I discuss the three discourses of heterosexuality as outlined by Hollway (1984) and I argue for a fourth discourse within casual sex; I label it the 'it just happens' discourse. Through this discourse, casual sex is constructed as something that 'just happens' and is beyond the control of the partners. I end with an analysis of the ways that women find spaces of power and agency within these discourses. Women do this by placing limits on casual sex, disrupting the 'coital imperative', and taking the typically 'male' position within the discourse and actively seeking casual sex.

The (Male) Models of Heterosexual Casual Sex in Jasper

'It Just Happens' Discourse

When I approached young adults in Jasper (YAJs) and told them about my study I explained that I was interested in learning about how casual sex happens in Jasper, and how partners communicate their willingness to participate in casual sex. I began interviews by asking them about their lives in Jasper and about their past dating and sexual experiences. At some point during the interview I inevitably asked

some version of the question 'How does casual sex happen?' or 'How do two people come to the understanding that they are going to have sex?'. At this point many of the participants stopped and stared at me with perplexed looks on their faces. I interpreted their reactions as saying 'Have you never had sex?'. The presumption seemed to be that if I had sex at some point, then I would have known how it happened. The answer would have been obvious. The answer (of course) is that 'it just happens'. Almost all of the women and a few of the men responded with some version of this statement.

Samantha: So you're like kind of like making eye contact, smiling at each other, and then all of a sudden we're like standing by each other talking. And just like . . . I don't know how it happened but we like; all of a sudden we were . . . (laughs) . . . we were just like talking and we were talking about that and like he started kissing me and we went back to my house. And it wasn't even a question of 'would you like to come to my house?'. You know what I mean? It was just like that. That's what happened. (laughs) And then in the middle of it, it was just like, oh my God!

Anne: He, he just kissed me. Like he just, we were holding hands and dancing then he kissed me and I kissed him back and then it just . . . Yeah, we were hugging and kissing. I was, it was not . . . I don't know, it just happened.

James: That's a really interesting question, because you don't really, I don't really analyze how it happens really, it just kind of happens.

This discourse of 'it just happens' reflects a sense that there is a force greater than and external to the two people involved in casual sex that is ultimately responsible for instigating sex. By using this discourse it seems more acceptable for women (and men?) to engage in casual sex. By saying that it 'just happens' women are relinquishing responsibility for engaging in casual sex. Anne expresses this sense by saying that she 'felt a little less of a slut if it wasn't something I really intended on doing, it just happened.' Anne's comment also highlights her negotiation of the good girl/bad girl dichotomy. In order to maintain her 'good girl' image of herself, it is only acceptable to engage in casual sex that is 'accidental'. By adopting this discourse, women are relinquishing themselves and their male partners of responsibility. It suggests that men are just as susceptible to this force as women. There is no recognition that their male partner may have orchestrated the casual sex in any way. Gwen provides a particularly poignant example.

Yeah. And then so, yeah, and then he just kept talking. Like we didn't dance or anything. We just sat by the bar and talked for like two hours and he just kept feeding me drinks. (laughs) But he was just drinking just as much as I was so it wasn't that big of a deal. So every time I'd get a drink, he would get a drink. And um . . . yeah, and then . . . And then I went to the washroom and then when I came out, he

wasn't there. It was like okay, I'm just going to go home. And then I was walking outside and he like got a cab and stuff. And he was like do you need a ride? Like I'll give you a cab and I'll give you a ride home. And then like sure, whatever. It was raining. It was ugly out. And then um . . . his friend was with him too and he said well why don't you just come over for a couple of beer? And I was like okay, I don't have to work until 3:30 the next day. I can do that. And um . . . so I went over. We had some beer. And then I was like okay, I'm going to go home. And he was like well no, let's just talk for a bit. And I was like okay, and then one thing led to another . . .

The way that Gwen tells the story, she sees it as a series of events that took place, finishing with 'and one thing led to another'. She does not see the man's behaviour as orchestrating her going home with him for casual sex. She dismisses his buying her lots of drinks, because he too is drinking. She does not think anything of him arranging a cab for her, or asking her home. She does not say anything to imply that his actions may have been planned—that he may be buying her alcohol to get her drunk so she would be more likely to go home with him. She ends the story with 'and one thing led to another' implying that neither one of them was in control of what was happening.

Most participants, especially women, expressed a sense that one thing led to another, rather than expressing an intent or interest in engaging in casual sex. James is one of the few men who also express this sense of 'it just happens'.

It's just something that happens, and you don't really know how it happened, but it happened. And ah, I've never had an experience where it's happened and then she's been like 'I really didn't want that to happen' which I'm very thankful for. But you know, you go to an after party or something, right like you're already just hardcore making out on the dance floor lets say, right and you're doing dry humping and bumping and grinding and hanging off each other as you leave the bar. You get to the guy's party house or wherever you're at right, you're sitting around. The next thing you know, nobody's in the room and you're lying on each other and one thing leads to another. Right like, that's really the only way to put it, you start making out that leads to nakedness that leads to sex.

James was thankful that no woman has ever told him afterwards that she did not want to have sex. He said this as though he cannot control the situation or outcome—as though he has no access to the woman's comfort levels, interests, or desires. If sex can just happen, and he has no control over what happens, he then has no control over any potential consequences of the interaction. This use of the 'it just happens' discourse assumes that they are not responsible for negotiating casual sex. This results in a failure for men to take responsibility for their actions and the potential for these actions to create harm.

Agnes, among others, connected the 'it just happens' discourse with alcohol. 'Alcohol is a huge key, like huge, and it really makes you, it really limits you, your ability to make good, clear, conscious decisions.' I spoke with only one person who said that most often his casual sex hookups occur in the absence of alcohol, often with people he meets in coffee shops or on the street. All other participants mentioned that alcohol plays an important part in their casual sex experiences. When I asked Susan how casual sex happens, alcohol was the first thing she mentioned.

Go to the bar. Start buying other people drinks and start drinking yourself. It's really really . . . it's all related to alcohol, I think. And for a lot of other people drugs, but I don't see that side of it because I've never been a part of that side of it. Um, but yeah, well it depends, well as a girl if that's what you're looking for when you come to Jasper. You dress really skanky and you get out on the dance floor and you drink lots. And there's gonna be a guy there. Guaranteed.

Many others mentioned being drunk as a necessary component of casual sex.

Teresa: Yeah, we were, we were both pretty drunk. We were outside having a cigarette and I leaned over and kissed him. I was like, come on, you can sleep at my place tonight. So we walked home. I lived like not even a block away from the bar that we both worked at. And, and um . . . got inside . . . I put on a tee shirt and a pair of boxers. He was in his shorts. He was in there and apparently I had my own shirt off and both of our own shorts off within about half an hour and it was completely not an issue and it doesn't surprise me whatsoever cause he was very, very attractive.

While a few men commented that moderating the amount of alcohol was important when they are interested in casual sex, no women expressed similar sentiments. Women did not limit alcohol when they engaged in casual sex, and were much less likely to be able to maintain a level of control during the interaction. The alcohol can then be used as an excuse for how or why sex 'just happened'. The discourse of 'it just happens' creates a version of casual sex where the illusion is that neither partner is responsible. By positioning themselves within this discourse women can then feel like 'good girls' who do not actively seek sex; they are 'not slutty'. Women are also taking responsibility off their male partners. Men are not viewed as controlling sex, or as orchestrating the interaction. The sex just happened; the men were not in control over what took place any more than the women.

Male Sexual Drive Discourse

While most women and a few men began talking about casual sex through the 'it just happens' discourse, this was not the only way that hookups were conceptualized.

Many men said they went out to parties or bars with an intention of hooking up, and they pay particular attention to what types of things women may want in men, or particular things to do to get women interested in them. For these men, casual sex does not just happen; it is something that they have to work for, and something they practice. Robert, a bouncer in one of the local bars said that he often sees men going from one group of women to another until they find someone willing to talk with them. Don said that he approaches a lot of women when he's looking for sex and that he knows he will get turned down frequently.

This fits in with what Hollway (1984) describes as the male sexual drive discourse in which men's sex drive is insatiable and that women's role in sexual activity is to be passive and go along with men's desires. Within this discourse men are sexual subjects acting in ways to fulfill their desire for sex. Through this discourse men also secure their masculinity, by reinforcing their ever-present sex drive. Conversely, women are positioned as sexual objects, necessary for men to satiate their desire for sex without any desires of their own. Men reported many strategies that they used in order to find a sexual partner. For instance, some men said that they will often approach many women, with the idea that the more women they approach, the greater the likelihood that they will find one who will have sex with them.

Even once men were in conversation, or dancing with a particular woman, it was important for them to continue to monitor women's behaviours in ways that would increase the chance of 'getting laid'. For instance, it was important that women should feel as though the situation was not threatening, and to feel comfortable and cared for.

> Don: You just give her a sense of security like, making them the focal point, and just looking out for them like, just simple sayings like, like obviously getting the door for them, like putting on their jacket but like actually pulling their hair back so it doesn't go under their jacket, like little things like that, and just looking out for them, even if it's just like creating some space for them, like in a crowded club or something like that just little things like that seemed to go a long way . . . you have to really play it by ear because it can be overdone . . . you have to give her her space and be relaxed then

the same time just be conscientious and make her feel comfortable, you know offer them like something to drink, right. I'm not saying offering them a shot or something like that, but like can I get you a drink, would you like my jacket, are you cold, and something like that.

Don is very deliberate in his approach with women; he sees himself in pursuit of sex and sees it as challenging to get women to have sex with him. He is quite aware of his actions and how they may help him reach his goal. While on the surface he seems concerned about women's comfort level, this is a means to an end, a way to get women to go to bed with him.

Don took up the male sexual drive discourse throughout his interview. When I first met him, he had just recently moved to Jasper, and had a girlfriend still living in their hometown. During the interview Don said that it was 'inevitable' that he would have casual sex during his time in Jasper. He seemed to believe that his sex drive was insatiable and it would be futile to resist his desire for casual sex. Don articulated his approach to women quite clearly and it was obvious that he thought carefully about how to approach women to get what he wants. He made references to the importance of 'knowing how to court a woman properly' and 'knowing your arts well'. By these he meant that it is important for men to know the right away to approach women and talk to them, to make them feel comfortable, and to build a sense of trust.

In order to satiate his 'natural' sexual desires, Don learned and implemented specific strategies that enabled him to have casual sex. In this version of the male sexual drive discourse Don positioned himself in a way that relinquishes both partners from responsibility. Here, Don accepts that he is responsible for learning how to quench his ever-present desire. His drive is 'natural' and thus it is 'inevitable' that he must have casual sex throughout the summer; however, by becoming skilled at the 'arts' of 'courting' he increases the likelihood and frequency that he will be able to satisfy these desires.

He talked in detail about monitoring women's behaviour to gauge their comfort level and willingness to have sex. In particular, a woman's breathing was very important.

> It is all about the girl's breathing, and that's like, a lot of guys don't realize that, but that's like, that's your like light signal that's your red, yellow, green, right there it's her breathing and just playing that off and so you just gradually sort of progress things forward to taking off clothes.

For Don, it was important that he maintain control over the situation and over casual sex. He talked positively about situations where women initiated casual sex, as long as the woman was not too direct.

> The odd time that I get approached by a girl it works, like it's nice to see a girl of confidence and stuff like that but you can't be too direct because then it's just too easy, it kills it, like you know unless I was just slumming it you know, and going for raunchy sex.

Several other men talked in similar ways about women who are actively seeking sex.

Colin: If they come on too strong, then you can kind of tell that they're kinda skanky. But if they come on sort of in a shy manner, then, then it's a good thing. Good cause it gives you room to open them up. You know what I mean? Like you've got to make them feel comfortable obviously or else it's just going to be stupid and suck. . . . If they're really aggressive, it's just like no; I don't want to do this. Cause it's not really giving you a challenge. Cause if they're really aggressive, it's just like well okay, I'll just take my shorts off and let's go.

Thus, the chase becomes a 'natural' part of casual sex, and courtship and seduction becomes the property of men.

A key component to the male sexual drive discourse is that men maintain control of the sexual experience. Overly sexually aggressive women threaten this control, men find this intimidating, and the women are then labelled 'slutty'.

Women were far less likely to articulate ways that casual sex happens. Even in cases where the women were interested in particular men, women waited for men to initiate contact.

Samantha: It's usually the guy who makes the first move I guess, towards me if they can see I'm attracted to them or whatever.

Even when women initiate sex, they still take up the male sexual drive discourse by assuming that the men will be willing to engage in sex.

Agnes: And I think it's more the girl to . . . be the one that decides whether or not it's going to happen because from my experiences, there's not very many times when a guy won't have sex. In fact, more often than not, that's all they're in it for is and not like looking for a relationship or just somebody to snuggle with.

Men also articulated this aspect of the male sexual drive discourse. When I asked men how they indicated their willingness for sex to their partners, many responded by saying that they do not have to demonstrate willingness.

Colin: I just like I'm, I'm a guy. I'm ready, willing and able anywhere anytime.

Gary: I think it's probably pretty rare that the guy says stop. I mean, I don't know with other guys for sure but . . . from, from what I know, then I say that the guy's not going to say stop. Unless there's something else like he has a girlfriend or something like that.

This male sexual drive discourse was the discourse most frequently referred to by both women and men as they talked about casual sex. The male sexual drive discourse is different from the 'it just happens' discourse in that both men and women who take up this discourse recognize that men actively pursue casual sex. This is viewed as the 'normal' and 'natural' way to engage in casual sex. It remained unquestioned by all but one female participant.

> Stacy: It's, it's so unfair that it's really assumed in our society that it's the guy's job to [initiate sex]. You know what I mean. It's the guy's job to invite the girl out on a date. It's the guy's job to initiate this. It's the guy's job to initiate that. Yeah, it's the guy's job to initiate sex. It's the guy's job to do everything. The girl's kind of the passive like you know? Passive partner who goes along with everything or doesn't. But is always like you know, things happen to her, she doesn't, you know what I mean? . . . Like don't treat me like some idiot! Like some damsel in fucking distress. So I think that that goes a long way into the bedroom too where like I don't expect him, you know what I mean? Like I'm willing to go out on a limb and face rejection, you know what I mean?

Have/Hold Discourse

While the male sexual drive discourse was the most frequently taken up, other discourses described by Hollway (1984) were alluded to by participants. Many women and a few men took up the have/hold discourse, which Hollway describes as the belief that sex comes with a committed and ongoing relationship. In this discourse women are positioned as the sexual subjects who were trying to establish a committed relationship with a man. Men are positioned as the objects of this discourse. Thus, the have/hold discourse works with the male sexual drive discourse; men are attempting to satiate their sexual desires, and women participate in sex to build and maintain a committed relationship.

It was surprising to see this discourse taken up when women and men were talking about casual sex. Although both women and men were aware

that many casual sex experiences do not lead to lasting and committed relationships, some women reported that one reason they engage in casual sex is because they may be interested in a relationship. Samantha and Agnes both said that some of the partners they chose were people they were interested in developing a relationship with. Most of these casual sex experiences did not lead to a relationship. Agnes said that she learnt that if she wanted a relationship that she should not sleep with a man the first night they are together because she found that after she slept with a man on the first 'date', he would no longer speak to her.

> We ended up sleeping together and woke up the next morning, and we slept together again and then he like, never talked to me after that. And we were supposed to hang out on New Year's Eve together, cuz it was like two nights after that and umm, I phoned him on New Year's Eve, and asked him what he was doing, and he was like 'oh I think I'm just going to stay home'. He totally blew me off.

As a result, Agnes made a rule for herself and lets men know that she will not have sex with them right away. She will, though, have sex with them on the second date. By staying around for a second night, they demonstrated a certain level of interest or commitment. Unfortunately, she found that waiting until the second night they were together did not change the end result.

> I ended up hooking up with this friend of mine, but now I like have this thing where I won't sleep with guys on the first date, just because I don't like the feeling of being used the next day and for me that's a really big thing, and so, but this guy . . . we hooked up one night and then, I wouldn't sleep with him, so the next night, he ended up spending the night and I slept with him and then he never talked to me again. And so now, like even that little theory of mine, is totally like . . . blown out the window.

Agnes told stories about hooking up with people for casual sex, and said 'I'm totally, like, fine to have casual sex with people, but like if they're under one impression and I'm under another and it's not the same then that kind of makes me mad.' In Agnes's version of this discourse, she is looking for more than just one night of sex. This commitment does not have to be in the form of an exclusive and romantic relationship. It could also be a casual affair that lasts several weeks.

Agnes is not the only woman who spoke of similar ideas. Jane recounts a story where she met a man she was interested in. At first she thinks he is a real 'gentleman' because he does not try to sleep with her the first night they are together. They did, however, have sex the second night they were together. Afterwards she was angry because he is no longer speaking to her. She called him a 'really big slut' and a liar. She sees his actions as being dishonest because, for her, having sex with someone is a sign that there is at least some interest and some commitment.

Even for some women who actively sought out one-night-stands, their subject position was at least partially constructed through the have/ hold discourse. After seeking out casual sex with a particular man Anne turned off her answering machine and purposely spent a lot of time out of the house for the following few days. She did not want to know if he had called or not.

> So it was not like I was expecting anything out of it, but I still, I do have like, like, I had like little fantasies about him, like staying or something like that, or like us continuing the relationship, so there must be, and I went into it totally like chasing him. I just wanted to have, to basically have casual sex, but I still have the future flashes.

Anne has purposely tried to disregard and shed the have/hold discourse and went out looking for a one-night-stand. Yet she still finds that she has what she calls 'future flashes' and that she fantasizes about a possible future with the man. She also mentioned a few times that she saw no reason why they could not be friends, or at least talk with one another after having casual sex.

I had one one-night-stand . . . and I just, I thought, like okay, well, you have sex with someone, and to me it doesn't matter, like sex . . . ok, I never felt like a slut when I do it, so I don't see other people . . . like I can never imagine other people thinking of me as a slut, but like, so I thought that we could just hang out with these guys afterwards and be friends, but it's weird, like once you've done the act, it's, there's like very like a lack of interest. . . . How are you supposed to meet anybody in this stupid town to hang out with, you know what I mean?

Here Anne takes up a different form of the have/ hold discourse. She is not concerned with creating or maintaining a sexual or romantic relationship. However, she expects that she should be able to maintain a friendly relationship with men with whom she has had sex. She views the men as potential people to hang out with and party with, people who can be part of her larger social network. She resents that most often after she has sex with them, she is excluded from their social network.

Men do not take up this discourse as it relates to casual sex. Almost all the men expected not to engage in any sort of relationship with someone after they had sex, unless there was a relationship established before they had sex. A few men mentioned that they would delay having sex with a woman if they wanted to have a relationship with her.

> Colin: Well if you have a connection with this person and you're super attracted to them and you can see yourself being with them, then you won't fuck them the first date. Like if you really want a relationship with them, you're not going to spoil it by screwing them.

> Don: Like a really good one is going home to smoke pot or to do blow but like I've cut blow out of my life, that was like a high school thing. But like blow's really good because it shows that you really wanna talk to them because when you do a lot of blow your dick is like a limp

spaghetti, and it's just like useless for sex and so shows that you care about conversation and bullshit like that.

For men, the have/hold discourse comes into play only when they want to develop a relationship with a woman, whereas for women, they often take it up whenever they are engaging in casual sex.

This discourse operates along with the male sexual drive discourse to enable casual sex among YAJs. Men engage in casual sex because of their 'natural' and insatiable drive for sexual gratification. Conversely, women participate in casual sex with the hope of developing a lasting and committed relationship.

Sexual Permissiveness Discourse

Both men and women deployed the sexual permissiveness discourse, according to which casual sexual activity is considered normal and expected. Many of the men and women I spoke with were surprised at how many women in Jasper initiate and seek out casual sex. Robert said, 'When I lived in [another province], it was the guys. But like here, it's anybody who's you know, guys or girls making the first move for sure.'

There was a sense that in Jasper it is a lot more acceptable for women to want casual sex, compared to other places.

> *Agnes*: When I was in high school, somebody who like had casual sex and slept with a lot of people was called a slut. But I seldom ever hear that term. And I don't know if people have just grown up to realize that yeah, casual sex is something that you do when you get older. Like you know, just cause you sleep with a couple of people doesn't make you a bad person or a slut for it. And I don't see that [in Jasper] at all.

Casual sex for women is accepted, rather than stigmatized, in Jasper (although if they are 'too' assertive or aggressive they risk being labelled a slut). Without this discourse, and the feeling that it is acceptable for women to have casual sex, it would be much more difficult for men to find willing partners. This discourse, which on the surface seems to support women's sexual desires, is necessary for men to engage in a lot of casual sex. This discourse can also obscure sexual double standards. It appears as though it is acceptable for both women and men to engage in casual sex. However, this is only acceptable if they are engaging in a 'masculine' version of casual sex and if women are adhering to normative constructions of femininity created through the male sexual drive discourse.

Women's Sexual Agency

The discourses discussed above create depictions of casual sex that benefit male sexual desires and needs and are subject to male initiation. However, within these discourses women carve out spaces to exercise agency over their own sexuality and engage in heterosexual casual sex. Women create different degrees of agency during their casual sex experiences. First, women take advantage of the perception that more men are interested in casual sex than women, and therefore women have more choice about with whom they have sex. Second, women exercise agency by interrupting sexual activity before they engage in casual sex. Third, they actively seek out and orchestrate casual sex to satisfy their own sexual desires.

Women exercise agency by taking advantage of the perception that there are a lot more men seeking casual sex than there are women, creating a situation where women have a lot of choice regarding with whom they go home.

> *Teresa*: There's so many men looking for sex that, you know, women really have their pick and choose of the litter. If they're just looking for a one-night-stand [the men I've talked to] said that you really have to stick out like a sore thumb or like be right there.

Men and women sometimes argue that women have more power than men when it comes to casual sex, because they have the power of choice. Jane says that 'girls have a lot of power in whether they go home with a man or not. Guys just kind of take their chance and hope they get lucky.' If women are looking for casual sex, it is much easier for them to find someone with whom to go home. In a sense they are taking advantage of the male sexual drive discourse and using it to their advantage to have casual sex when they desire it.

Additionally, women exercise agency within and around the male sexual drive discourse by placing limits on the sexual activity—getting what they want out of it and stopping the interaction when they are satisfied. Agnes says that 'I think too because the girl ultimately usually decides on . . . if there's going to be sex or not.' Thus, while casual sex operates on the presumption of a male model of sexuality, women and men perceive that women act as the 'gatekeepers' and determine whether or not casual sex will happen.

Men, as well as women, reported that women often act as limit-setters. Tim mentioned that sometimes women will be totally 'into making out', but they will not let him take off their pants. He reads this as an indication that they are menstruating; he suggests that many women get particularly 'horny' while they are menstruating. Regardless of whether or not these women are menstruating, taking up this strategy, or going along with his suggestion that they are menstruating gives them a chance to engage in casual sexual activity that does not lead to penetration. James mentioned similar strategies used by a few women.

Like, you'll be with the girl and you'll be making out and she'll stop and be like, you know, 'I really like you but I don't wanna go all the way because of this reason.' Right, like, there are still virgins out there, believe it or not, who are like, saving themselves for marriage, it's a really romantic concept that I really still enjoy, but you . . . it's a rarity I'll say . . . but they'll still have tonnes and tonnes of fun, but they just won't go all the way.

By being up front and telling men their limits, these women are opening up possibilities for casual sexual activity that do not include penetration. James mentioned that often they would engage in oral sex or genital touching. When men mentioned these strategies, they did not mind that the women were placing limits on sexual activity. James mentioned later on that 'realistically again, you know, a lot of them are tourists they're not gonna be around the next day, so you have bad luck that night you always go out a couple nights later and maybe your luck's changed.' If one woman is not willing to participate fully in a male model of casual sex that includes sexual penetration, then another one will be later on.

Thus, these women are able to negotiate the 'coital imperative' (Jackson, 1984) of heterosexual sex by placing boundaries and limits around the sexual activity. This way, women are able to indirectly satisfy their own sexual desires while operating within normative heterosexual discourses. They do this without completely rejecting the coital imperative. By saying that they want to wait until marriage to have sex or that they are having their period, they imply that they would otherwise be willing to engage in intercourse and are recognizing the central role that intercourse plays in heterosexual relations.

While the women I interviewed did not talk about strategies that included claiming they were menstruating or that they wanted to remain virgins, many of them mentioned setting limits as a way to ensure control over their casual sex.

Agnes: I just don't let it happen. I say no, like when they try to go that direction, I'm like 'no, I don't sleep with guys on the first date.'

Many women have a sense that they are in control of placing limits on sexual activity. Of course they do have to be careful about how they approach setting these limits.

Laurie: Well I guess, I would just, I don't know, I guess I would try to keep it kind of light and stuff, cause I don't want to piss them off right? Some guys could be weird and psycho (laughs) and so, I don't know I'd probably try to keep it light, put clothes on or whatever if I took my clothes off, and be like, 'oh, can you go?' or 'I'm gonna go home' or whatever.

While women exercised agency by setting limits and interrupting sexual activity prior to penetration, the reaction of the men they were with varied. In the examples discussed above, the women's excuses were considered 'legitimate' by the men. However, if a man did not consider the excuses 'legitimate' he often became frustrated and women were labeled 'teases'. These consequences acted as constraints and the men attempted to limit women's access to these strategies to create their own agency.

While many women set sexual limits, others reported orchestrating their own casual sex experiences focused on their own pleasure. Anne's story is a good example of this type of agency and of the tension between a male-oriented discursive construction of heterosexual casual sex and women's space for agency within that discourse. Anne carefully sought out and chose a man to have casual sex with.

> He's not young young, he's 19, but like I haven't been with a 19-year-old guy since I was 17, so it was really weird, but um it's so sad but it seems to safer to me, to go for someone who wasn't like, living in Jasper for so long, than for someone new and innocent, it sounds so dirty! (laughs) . . . but it's that attitude. Like he was a really good-looking boy, but he probably didn't know how good-looking quite yet you know what I mean . . . and I knew when I met him that he was like, how old he was and I knew he was leaving in August.

Anne carefully chose a man whose social position enabled her more control over the situation. She liked the idea that Jack was young and new to Jasper. To her, this meant that he was likely not very experienced and that he had not yet developed an attitude like many other men she met in Jasper. This gave her greater control over the situation. She went out with Jack and a few friends one night to go partying. Both of them got quite drunk, but the whole night she was focused on getting him to go home with her. At one point

they tried to go to a different bar, but Jack was so drunk that the bouncers would not let him in; he said that he would just go home.

> I was like, no, the whole point of going out with you guys is because of you, you can't go home, so, but I didn't say that, I'm like oh no no no, we can't leave one person out that's so wrong. And I asked the bouncer if we take him to the park and he sobers up can we come back in an hour, and they said as long as he can walk straight or something like that then we'll let him in. So that, so we ended up doing that.

Anne ensured that Jack would stay with the rest of the group until the end of the night so she could take him home with her. They did end up back at that bar. Anne and Jack were dancing and kissing on the dance floor. One of Jack's friends was leaving the bar and came up and shook Jack's hand to congratulate him on successfully picking up Anne.

> Like when the guy shook the guy's hand and like I don't care cause like, congratulations to me too, you know mean, that was my goal for the night, to go home with him. So like, and then we did, and he is so much fun.

Anne felt that she too should be congratulated; she was taking up the typically male role in casual sex. She took up the active role seeking sex, and he took on the more passive role by going along with it. When they did end up back at her place she was concerned about him, and his willingness to participate in sex.

> I know I wanted to have sex, like that was something that was going to happen for me. But I did ask him because I kinda felt . . . just because I was so forward with it all the time, I just wanted to make sure he was along for the, like was there as well. . . . Cause yeah, cause a lot of times I probably haven't been with the guy, and it just happened anyways, you just kind of follow along with the progression of things. . . . Like I asked him before we had sex, are you sure you're okay with this? And

he was like, yeah! Like what the fuck, like why are you asking that question?

She knew that she was not always really into the casual sex that took place previously, and she did not like the feeling that gave her. Therefore, she made a point of ensuring that Jack was a willing participant. Jack almost took offence to her question. Her question subverts the male sexual drive discourse by questioning his desire. He took this as also questioning his masculinity as framed within the male sexual drive discourse.

Throughout the sexual activity, Anne ensured that her desires would be met.

> I don't mind like, like helping myself get off when I'm having sex cause some guys are good at it, some guys know how to do it and you don't have to worry about it, but some guys are totally clueless, especially, maybe not so experienced guys and so I don't have an issue at all with for me it's for me and I know that I don't have a problem with I want to do this I want to do that. . . . Like when I was with Jack I did say it. I have no problem saying certain things like, like just stuff like getting on top, different positions and like can you move over here can you move over there.

Anne had no problem taking control over her sexual pleasure. During casual sex, she will pleasure herself if she is not getting what she wants from sex. She is also comfortable enough to ask for what she wants, a switch in position, or for Jack to shift to a different position. Anne uses her sense of agency to get what she wants; at the same time she recognizes that the model of casual sex is a male model and so she has learned how to temporarily manipulate the model to fit her desires.

> Like guys are assholes, I had no idea, no one told me, and it's not that I'm not angry at them, because I just see it, as that's the way they are, you just have to know that. I think girls should be given that knowledge, so that and then they can make their own decisions and what they want. If they want to participate

in it or not, because sometimes I do, sometimes I'm like, I want to, and I'm up for it but you have to be really aware of what you're getting into, because you can get really hurt like otherwise.

She feels that now that she knows more about what casual sex is all about, she can choose when and how she participates in it. For Anne, casual sex is deliberately engaged in, which contrasts with many other women's experiences of casual sex as something that 'just happens'.

Women who take up sexual agency in this way move beyond the permissiveness discourse because they are not just giving themselves permission to participate in sex. They are creating experiences and situations to satisfy their own sexual desires. They do this not by changing the dominant discourses that govern heterosexual casual sex, but by creating spaces within those discourses and subtly challenging them to allow them to cater to their own needs.

The negotiation of heterosexual casual sex is a nuanced process laden with hegemonic and often contradictory discourses. Often, there is the sense that casual sex is not really negotiated at all, that it just happens when two people are together at the bar drinking. Running parallel to this discourse are the male sexual drive discourse and the sexual permissiveness discourse. The male sexual drive discourse is used to create a model of casual sex governed by notions of male sexual desire as being ever-present and never satisfied. This discourse simultaneously silences women's sexual desires and assumes that women play a passive role in sexual relations. For casual sex to take place, the sexual permissiveness discourse is deployed, allowing women to desire and participate in sex as long as it is the version of sex in the male sexual drive discourse—that is, penetrative sex with 'no strings attached'. A few women however, position themselves within the have/hold discourse and expect that after casual sex the possibility for a friendship or relationship still exists.

Within these discourses that privilege male desire, women have been able to carve out ways to negotiate casual sex that takes into consideration their own desires. Women will place limits on the sexual activity or leave after their needs have been met. Sometimes women will take an even more active role in designing and orchestrating their own casual sex experiences that satisfy their desires. Women are adapting by recognizing that casual sex is often controlled by male sexual desire, then choosing when and how they participate in casual sex to get their own desires met.

Conclusion

When discussing issues of casual sex, YAJs first turn to a discourse of 'it just happens' and suggest that casual sex is a serendipitous event. However, through their stories the male sexual drive discourse is the dominant discourse operating in this environment. Casual sex is driven by the assumption that men are perpetually in search of sex. Perhaps surprisingly, the women deploy the have/hold discourse and report that one reason they engage in casual sex is for the possibility of developing a relationship with their casual partner. Finally, casual sex is dependent on the sexual permissiveness discourse that suggests that casual sex is permissible for both women and men (at least within the confines of the male sexual drive discourse). Finally, within these discourses women exert power through their choice in partners, by setting limits and by taking what may be considered a typically masculine role and actively pursuing casual sex.

References

Hollway, W. 1984. 'Gender Difference and the Production of Subjectivity', in J. Henriques, W. Hollway, C. Urwin, C. Venn, and V. Walkerdine, eds., *Changing the Subject: Psychology, Social Regulation and Subjectivity*, pp. 227–63. New York: Routledge.

CHAPTER 15

Same-Sex Marriage and Canadian Relationship Recognition: One Step Forward and Two Steps Back. A Critical Liberationist Perspective

Nick Mulé

Introduction

Same-sex marriage in Canada brought forth an important legal sanctioning of same-sex couples with social implications for their public recognition and legitimacy. The purpose of this paper is to deconstruct the platforms posited by sexually diverse proponents of same-sex marriage and their allies from a critical liberationist perspective. Arguments put forth on this issue in the literature are reviewed, and how the debate was restricted in Canada to focus exclusively on traditional/couplist and neo-liberal views is exposed. Injecting a critical liberationist perspective expands the narrowed frameworks of the debate, deepening the discourse in Canada and beyond. By moving beyond equality-based arguments, the very platforms utilized by the proponents of same-sex marriage are interrogated in light of a broader social justice approach that highlights and questions the privileges of marriage (LaSala, 2007; Mulé, 2006) and seeks recognition of a variety of relationships. Proponents argue that extending marital rights to same-sex couples achieves equality, whereas I argue that this 'achievement' is at the expense of equity in recognizing many other kinds of relationships—an outcome that is contrary to the ideals of social justice.

A Critical Liberationist Perspective

The analysis herein is guided by a critical liberationist perspective utilizing a queer lens. By critical, I mean there is an obligation to deconstruct existing social structures in order to interrogate degrees of equality, equity, and benefits, and then provide options to address any levels of oppression found therein (Mulé, 2008). A liberationist ethos speaks to individuals having the right to define for themselves who they are and how they live their lives with the impact of contributing to society's diversity (Hay & Roscoe, 1996; Warner, 2002), rather than being shaped by society to fit hegemonic roles and expectations and thus being marginalized if they fail to do so (Altman, 1971; Mulé, 2006). The queer lens being applied comes from a non-heterosexual and non-gender binary approach, in which the lived experiences of lesbians, gays, bisexuals, transgender, transsexual, two-spirit, intersex, queer, and/or questioning is an acknowledged reality despite society's heterosexist structures.

Institution of Marriage Questioned

'Marriage creates a two-tier system that allows the state to regulate relationships' (Ettelbrick, 1997, p. 167). In essence, by extending marriage to Canadian same-sex couples the state has been invited back into their bedrooms. Proponents of same-sex marriage, in effect, accept the regime of marriage and thus its monopoly, rather than reject 'the regime of marriage . . . [as] a means of transcending the traditional church/state monopoly on relationship options' (Butler, 2001a, p. 58).

During the debates on same-sex marriage in Canada, alternate ideas about relationship recognition were advanced by some organizations. The Law Commission of Canada (LCC) (2001) acknowledged that although recognition and support of personal adult caring and interdependent relationships is an important objective of the state (which has expanded rights and obligations for adult relationships), the state's legal recognition of relationships has focused on conjugal relationships only. LCC espoused broader values in calling for a more expanded approach to relationships: 'Instead of focusing mainly on married couples and couples deemed to be "marriage-like", governments should establish registration schemes to facilitate the private ordering of both conjugal and non-conjugal relationships' (LCC, 2001, p. 131). LCC proposed civil registration for adults regardless of relationship type that would require subscribing to a series of associated legal rights and obligations.

Similarly, the Coalition for Lesbian and Gay Rights in Ontario (CLGRO) proposed that the state should exit the business of marriage and that the institution of marriage continue to exist under the auspices of religious institutions, thus challenging marriage's state sanctioning. This would result in marriages having no legal implications, privileges, or special status (CLGRO, 2003). This proposal questions the institution of marriage, and shifts the systemic structure from the couple to the individual as the core unit, with allowance made for dependents (e.g., children, the aged, and people with (dis)abilities), thereby undercutting traditional epistemological perspectives in the process. CLGRO called for the system to be reformed by placing the individual at the core, choosing who they would register as their significant other(s), without restrictions as to relationships being sexual, conjugal, or limited to two people. CLGRO advocated for a systemic reformation that would both legally and socially recognize diverse forms of relationships, which would end the current two-tier system of relationship recognition. 'There should be no hierarchy of legally recognized relationships, such as placing marriage at a higher level than common-law relationships or non-conjugal relationships' (CLGRO, 2003, p. 2). Proposed is a broader analysis that goes beyond equality, illuminating the pursuit of same-sex marriage as contributing to the privileging of those that choose to marry, while marginalizing those that do not.

Extending Marriage to Same-Sex Couples

Varying themes have been used in arguing for the extension of marriage to same-sex couples. Marital status and its continuity between private and public spheres, hierarchy, and power are similarly understood in family and society and have been argued from both pre-modern (Smith & Windes, 2000) and modern (Sullivan, 1995) perspectives. By exposing heterosexual extended family and friends to a same-sex marital coupling, traditional concepts of marriage are challenged (Cox, 1997). Others argue liberationist concepts exist within same-sex marriage. For example, the disruption of traditional gendered and hierarchical definitions of marriage (Hunter, 1995) and the ushering in of same-sex partners both in public and private societal realms challenges heterosexist concepts of the family (Calhoun, 2000). Such perspectives are problematic for their oversight of class and power differentials within same-sex relationships and for centralizing marriage and family in their concepts of citizenship (Boyd & Young, 2003). Same-sex marriage nevertheless remains enframed in traditional heterosexual couplist structures of marriage. In other words, within the familiar institution of marriage, the structuring of the couple remains, with the only change being from opposite to same-sex parties.

These arguments may challenge traditional conceptualizations based on man/woman but they do not challenge general society as other types of relationships are simply not part of the equation. Critical liberationist perspectives assist us in understanding the breadth and depth of relationships recognition. Warner (1999) posits three liberationist principles regarding same-sex marriage: that the institution of marriage is idealized; that a variety of intimate relationships need to be affirmed and respected; and the application of straight cultural norms to queer lives needs to be resisted. Clearly, same-sex marriage will not address sexual prejudice, nor achieve social acceptance or broad personal fulfillment. Furthermore, a queer theoretical approach calls us to address sexual minority oppression by destabilizing gender

and sexual categories (Butler, 2001a); therefore, some suggest a resistance to domestication by highlighting uniqueness of difference over assimilationism (Robson, 1998). Also, a counter-cultural perspective reveals how same-sex marriage contributes to a heteronormative discourse, which impacts on gay male identity that is queer-based and distinguished from the heteronormative male (Grindstaff, 2003).

One Step Forward, Two Steps Back: Equality Arguments versus Critical Liberationist Perspectives

Internationally, Canada became the fourth country to legislatively permit same-sex couples to marry, preceded by the Netherlands, Belgium, and Spain (EGALE Canada, 2006). The process to arrive at such legislation was driven by the work of activist organizations such as EGALECanada (a Canadian LGBT lobby group) and its offshoot, Canadians for Equal Marriage—proponents of the initiative within Canadian sexually diverse communities. On the surface, allowing same-sex couples to marry paints a picture of a progressive piece of legislation that lifts a blatant form of discrimination from a marginalized population—one step forward. For sexually diverse populations it represents recognition of same-sex relationships equal to that of opposite-sex relationships with added material benefits found in tax law, spousal benefits, survivor pensions, and so on. To many Canadians, this decision symbolically represented Canada's commitment to a more inclusive society. The world generally views Canada as a progressive country. When viewing the issue from an equality perspective, within which the debates were framed, the outcome is a significant one, with implications for the recognition of relationships and how families are constituted within Canadian society, sexually diverse populations therein as well as at the international level conceptually.

However, applying a critical examination from a liberationist perspective reveals that the equality arguments and strategy in effect sets Canada's recognition of relationships two steps back. This transpired through the polarized public debates that were limited to an equality framework. An equality framework is premised on equal treatment of all people, in this case permitting same-sex couples access to the heterosexually defined institution of marriage. Proponents were made up largely of vocal members of sexually diverse communities and their supporters, and opponents generally consisted of those on the right wing of the political spectrum and/or of traditional religious views. Canadian sexually diverse proponents of same-sex marriage argued their cause via four equality-based platforms: a human rights issue narrowly defined; equality for some; inclusion, personhood, and internalized homophobia; and pro-choice for others—but problematic.

A Human Rights Issue Narrowly Defined

The argument 'It's a fight for human rights' was promulgated by the Canadians for Equal Marriage campaign, further suggesting Canada could take the lead in international human rights with the legalization of same-sex marriage ('It's a Fight for Human Rights', n.d., p. 1). Bourassa and Varnell (2002, p. 16), both active members of this campaign, also see the issue as one of human rights with discriminatory implications, for which 'homosexuals were second-class citizens' in the absence of being able to marry.

The extent of the human rights argument is questioned by a critical liberationist perspective as to why only certain kinds of couples (read: same-sex conjugal)—as opposed to other kinds of relationships—are elevated to a privileged status warranting the 'human rights' marriage offers. A helpful distinction between the 'rights' stance (to marry for those who choose to) and the 'justice' stance (that would capture all, including those who choose not to marry) is posited by Ettelbrick (1997). Attaining rights for a few and not correcting the power imbalances between the married and unmarried (regardless of sexual orientation) fails to serve justice (Ettelbrick, 1989).

Equality for Some

The issue of same-sex marriage has been presented in a sweeping fashion. According to Heale (2003),

'This is an issue of equality as protected by the Canadian Constitution' (p. 5), premising merely one kind of relationship recognition on equality. 'It is about fairness, mutual respect and equality,' said Gilles Marchildon, Executive Director of EGALE Canada (Canadians for Equal Marriage, 2004). A closer examination reveals that the pursuit of same-sex marriage was not about achieving equality for same-sex relationships, but rather about achieving equality for same-sex relationships most closely resembling those of the traditional/pre-modern heterosexual model. Hence, the assimilated minority members gain the advantages of an acquiescing majority, while those who refuse to assimilate are further marginalized (Eskridge, 2003). Yet, by using such sweeping language, a discourse is created within sexually diverse communities urging support for an issue of 'equality.' However, restricting the human rights perspective to liberal ideals of equality does not address how same-sex marriage generates new inequalities and negates equity in the process.

Inclusion, Personhood, and Internalized Homophobia

For many people, a sense of personhood is based upon being included in the mainstream with the majority, and that such a feeling can contribute to combating a form of internalized homophobia. Access to the institution of marriage addresses this, particularly for those who revere the social status of marriage without question. Quebec pro-same-sex marriage and gay activist Michael Hendricks called marriage the 'gold standard of social respectability' (cited in Brown, 2002, p. 12). Thus, by entering such an institution, a special and powerful social status is bestowed (Ettelbrick, 1997), elevating the couple by their mere membership: 'I feel like I've been admitted into membership of some kind of club,' said Toronto city councilor Kyle Rae, upon marrying his same-sex partner (City TV, 2004). The enduring status of marriage (Goldberg-Hiller, 2002) backed by legal recognition has caused some to perceive domestic partnership agreements as a discursive tension between the status of the former and contractual obligations of the latter. A heightened validity is associated with marital relationships

(Ettelbrick, 1997), which is substantiated by legally sanctioned and culturally supported legitimacy. This was exemplified by Metropolitan Community Church of Toronto (MCCT) in their submission to the Parliamentary Panel on Same-sex Marriage:

> Marriage also confers a status with well-recognized social significance that, rightly or wrongly, is perceived by many to be the commitment of the highest order of one person to another. As with many other Canadians, for gays and lesbians the capacity to marry and the right to marry the person of their choice are an incident of full membership in society. For gays and lesbians, a group that has been historically marginalized, marriage is also the recognition before and by the society of their 'full personhood.' (2003, p. 12)

Right from the outset of this quotation, it is made clear that the status marriage has in our society is not to be interrogated, but rather they are centring their position on acquiescence and acquisition for relational purposes and the benefit of assigning elevated status to personhood. By permitting access to the institution of marriage, some same-sex marriage proponents generalize its benefits to sweeping levels, as when gay activist Michael Leshner declared, 'Homophobia is dead legally as of today' (Mackenzie, 2003, p. 12).

Usage of terms and phrases such as 'gold standard of social respectability', 'membership', and 'social significance' submits to a socio-cultural ideology of marriage, contributing to and sustaining its elevated status in society unquestionably. A discourse is created that extends to individuals and couples with terminology such as 'full personhood', constructing a false sense of self-worth, devaluing those outside the institution. Such discourse contributes to a form of subordination to heteronormativity, underscored by internalized homophobia that serves to further marginalize individuals who have the strength to be non-conformist.

Pro-Choice for Others—But Problematic

Not all sexually diverse proponents of same-sex marriage want marriage for themselves, but have put forth the strong argument to support the choice of others to marry. Kevin Bourassa and Joe Varnell state, 'Our goal is to ensure that couples have the equal right to marry if they choose, not to advocate that all couples get married. We recognize that many people will choose not to formalize their relationship, through civil or religious marriage' (Equal Marriage, n.d.). Again, this perspective falls short of recognizing or extending benefits to relationships that are located outside of the institution of marriage. The lack of consensus on the issue in sexually diverse communities, which was rarely reported on in mainstream media, is addressed by Canadians for Equal Marriage campaign Co-chairperson, Mary Woo Sims:

> I think that even in our own community the issue is not very well understood, in that this is not about forcing individuals to get married, it's about giving people in our community who wish to marry the same choices that other Canadians have. . . . [Let's] be clear [on] what this debate is all about. (MacMullin, 2004, p. 4)

Sims provides a classic example of how to restrict the debate. By framing the context within one of confusion as to why sexually diverse communities have not reached unanimity on the issue, she attempts to clarify via the argument of choice, simultaneously curtailing the discussion within the confines of a liberal perspective. Such a reductionist approach serves to fence out a more expansive appraisal of the debate as would be taken by a liberationist perspective.

By extending choice to others, the hierarchy of relationships, which holds marital ones at the top, is maintained, not questioned. The following quotation from an 'older lesbian' attests to how effective the campaign was in its influence on sexually diverse communities: 'It's funny, I know a number of people, myself included, who support the marriage thing, but would never want it personally, and so feel we're letting down the team if we say so' (Mackenzie, 2003, p. 12). Proponents who take a pro-choice position for others, yet do not personally opt for marriage, on the outset, present as altruistic, but, simultaneously and usually unbeknownst to the proponents, contribute to the further marginalization of those who do not enter this privileged status, including themselves.

Conclusion

The legalization of same-sex marriage in Canada is seen by many as a step forward on the equality front. Yet the reductionist approach to the issue undertaken by Canadian sexually diverse proponents and their allies during the debates limited the discourse to conjugal relationships that most closely matched marital heterosexual relationships on the basis of 'equality'. This focus sent the queer movement two steps back, for it fails to encompass a broader range of relationship recognition in multicultural Canada from an equity perspective. A deconstruction of five platforms that sexually diverse proponents of same-sex marriage utilized during the debates reveals an assimilationist position that ultimately provided access into a two-tiered system that privileges marital relationships over all others. A critical analysis with a liberationist lens expands the discourse on broader relationship recognition in Canada, questioning the special status ascribed to marital relationships. According to liberationists, all relationships need to be recognized equitably, legally, economically, and socioculturally if we are to create a level playing field.

References

Alderson, K.G. (2004). A phenomenological investigation of same-sex marriage. *The Canadian Journal of Human Sexuality, 13*(2), 107–122.

Altman, D. (1971). *Homosexual oppression and liberation.* New York: Outerbridge & Deinstfrey.

Auchmuty, R. (2004). Same-sex marriage revived: Feminist critique and legal strategy. *Feminism & Psychology, 14*(1), 101–126.

Auger, J.A. (2003). *Passing through: The end-of-life decisions of lesbians and gay men.* Halifax, NS: Fernwood.

Bourassa, K., & Varnell, J. (2002). *Just married: Gay marriage and the expansion of human rights.* Ontario: Doubleday Canada.

Boyd, S.B. (1999). Family, law and sexuality: Feminist engagements. *International Journal of Social & Legal Studies, 8*(3), 369–390.

Boyd, S.B., & Young, C.F.L. (2003). 'From same-sex to no sex'?: Trends towards recognition of (same-sex) relationships in Canada. *Seattle Journal for Social Justice, 1*(3), 757–793.

Brown, E. (2002, June 20). Civil unions, how romantic. Toronto: *fab.*, pp. 12.

Butler, J. (2001a). There is a person here: An interview with Judith Butler (Compiled by M.S. Breen, W.J. Blumenfeld, with S. Baer, R.A. Brookey, L. Hall, V. Kirby, D.H. Miller, R. Shail, & N. Wilson). *International Journal of Sexuality and Gender Studies, 6*(1/2), 7–23.

Butler, J. (2001b). *Is kinship always already heterosexual? Inaugural lecture presented to the Center for the Study of Sexual Culture.* April 25. Berkeley: University of California.

Calhoun, C. (2000). *Feminism, the family, and the politics of the closet: Lesbian and gay displacement.* Oxford and New York: Oxford University Press.

Canadians for Equal Marriage. (2004, April 28). *News release: Canadians for Equal Marriage to respond to opponents' Big Bucks Campaign.* Ottawa: Canadians for Equal Marriage.

Canadians for Equal Marriage. (n.d.). Abolishing civil marriage: Nobody wins. Retrieved April 19, 2004, from www.equal-marriage.ca/info/abolish.pdf.

Canadians for Equal Marriage. (n.d.). It's a fight for human rights. Retrieved April 19, 2004, from www.equal-marriage.ca/releases/Canadians_for_Equal_Marriage_Campaign.pdf.

Christopher, M. C. (2005). Is marriage obsolete? *Law Now, 29*, 6.

City TV. (2004, April 3). *Pride and joy.* Toronto: City TV.

Coalition for Lesbian and Gay Rights in Ontario (CLGRO). (2002). August. *News release: The state has no business in the marriages of the nation.* Toronto: Author.

Coalition for Lesbian and Gay Rights in Ontario (CLGRO). (2003, April 10). *Presentation to the Federal Consultation on Same-Sex Marriage.* Toronto: Author.

Coalition for Lesbian and Gay Rights in Ontario (CLGRO). (2004). *Lesbian, gay and bisexual liberation in the 2000s.* Toronto: Author.

Coates, J., & Sullivan, R. (2005). Achieving competent family practice with same-sex parents: Some promising directions. *Journal of* GLBT *Family Studies*, *1*(2), 89–113.

Cox, B. J. (1997). A (personal) essay on same-sex marriage. In R.M. Baird and S.E. Rosenbaum (Eds.), *Same-sex marriage: The moral and legal debate* (pp. 27–29). Amherst, NY: Prometheus Books.

Donovan, C. (2004). Why reach for the moon? Because the stars aren't enough. *Feminism & Psychology*, *14*(1), 24–29.

EGALE Canada. (2003, August 14). News release: Abolishing civil marriage: Nobody wins. Retrieved April 19, 2004, from www.egale.ca/printer.asp?lang=E&item=205&version=EN.

EGALE Canada. (2006). *Equal marriage*. Retrieved April 29, 2006, from www.egale.ca/index.asp?lang=E&menu=30&item=983.

Equal Marriage for Same-Sex Couples. (n.d.). Introduction. Retrieved April 19, 2004, from www.samesexmarriage.ca/introduction.htm.

Eskridge, W.N., Jr. (1996). *The case for same-sex marriage: From sexual liberty to civilized commitment*. New York: The Free Press.

Eskridge, W.N., Jr. (2002). *Equality practice: Civil unions and the future of gay rights*. London: Routledge.

Eskridge, W.N., Jr. (2003). The same-sex-marriage debate and three conceptions of equality. In L.D. Wardle, M. Strasser, W.C. Duncan, & D. Orgon Coolidge (Eds.), *Marriage and same-sex unions: A debate* (pp. 167–185). Westport, CT: Praeger Publishers.

Ettelbrick, P. (1989). Since when is marriage a path to liberation? In A. Sullivan (Ed.), *Same-sex marriage: Pro and con* (pp. 121–128). New York: Random House.

Ettelbrick, P.L. (1992). Since when is marriage a path to liberation? In S. Sherman (Ed.), *Lesbian and gay marriage* (pp. 20–26). Philadelphia: Temple University Press.

Ettelbrick, P.L. (1997). Since when is marriage a path to liberation? In R.M. Baird, & S.E. Rosenbaum (Eds.), *Same-sex marriage. The moral and legal debate* (pp. 164–168). New York: Prometheus Books.

Goldberg-Hiller, J. (2002). *The limits to union: Same-sex marriage and the politics of civil rights*. Ann Arbor, MI: The University of Michigan Press.

Grindstaff, D. (2003). Queering marriage: An ideographic interrogation of heteronormative subjectivity. *Journal of Homosexuality*, *45*(2/3/4), 257–275.

Hay, H., & Roscoe, W. (Eds.) (1996). Radically gay: Gay liberation in the words of its founder. Boston: Beacon Press.

Heale, R. (2003). Divided we fall. *OutLooks* (October), p. 5.

Hunter, N. D. (1995). Marriage, law and gender: A feminist inquiry. In L. Duggan & N. D. Hunter (Eds.), *Sex wars: Sexual dissent and political culture* (pp. 107–122). New York and London: Routledge.

Janson, G. R. (2002). Family counseling and referral with gay, lesbian, bisexual, and transgendered clients: Ethical considerations. *The Family Journal*, *10*, 328–333.

LaSala, M. C. (2007). Too many eggs in the wrong basket: A queer critique of the same-sex marriage movement (Commentary). *Social Work*, *52*(2), 181–183.

Law Commission of Canada. (2001). *Beyond conjugality: Recognizing and supporting close personal adult relationships*. Ottawa: Law Commission of Canada.

Mackenzie, I. (2003). Canadians cheer US decision. *Xtra!* (November 27), p. 13.

MacMullin, G. (2004). Hoping to woo the voters. *OutLooks* (February), p. 4.

Maynard, S. (2000). Modernization or liberation? *Capital Xtra!* (March 17), p. 19.

McClellan, D. L. (1997). Second parent adoption in lesbian families: Legalizing the reality of the child. Brandeis University: Unpublished.

Metropolitan Community Church of Toronto (MCCT). (2003). *Submission of the Metropolitan Community Church of Toronto Executive Summary*. Toronto: Author.

Mohr, R. D. (1997). The case for gay marriage. In R.M. Baird & S.E. Rosenbaum (Eds.), *Same-sex marriage: The moral and legal debate* (pp. 84–104). Amherst, NY: Prometheus Books.

Mossman, M.J. (1994). Running hard to stand still: The paradox of family law reform. *Dalhousie Law Journal*, *17*, pp. 5–34.

Mulé, N. J. (2006). Equality's limitations, liberation's challenges: Considerations for queer movement strategizing. *Canadian Online Journal of Queer Studies in Education*, *2*(1). Available at http://jqstudies.oise.utoronto.ca/journal/viewarticle.php?id=26.

Mulé, N. J. (2008). Demarcating gender and sexual diversity on the structural landscape of social work. *Critical Social Work*, 9(1). Available at www.criticalsocialwork.com/units/socialwork/critical.nsf/982f0e5f06b5c9a285256d6e006cff78/ebb5ace61ebf5d368525744c00802bdf?OpenDocument.

Ontario Association of Social Workers (OASW) & Canadian Association of Social Workers (CASW). (2003). Statement of support for legal recognition of same-sex unions. Toronto: Author.

Phelan, S. (2001). *Sexual strangers: Gays, lesbians and dilemmas of citizenship*. Philadelphia: Temple University Press.

Robinson, S. (2004, January 15). *News release: Robinson slams Martin and Cotler 'backtracking' on equality for gay and lesbian couples; Calls for liberals to respect court rulings on same-sex marriage and pension rights*. Ottawa: Author.

Robson, R. (1998). *Sappho goes to law school*. New York: Columbia University Press.

Rubin, G.S. (1993). Thinking sex: Notes for a radical theory of the politics of sexuality. In H. Abelove, M.A. Barale, & D.M. Halperin (Eds.), *The lesbian and gay studies reader* (pp. 3–44). New York: Routledge.

Smith, R.R., & Windes, R.R. (2000). *Progay/antigay: The rhetorical war over sexuality*. Thousand Oaks, CA: Sage.

Sullivan, A. (1995). *Virtually normal: An argument about homosexuality*. New York: Knopf.

Tully, C.T. (1994). To boldly go where no one has gone before: The legalization of lesbian and gay marriages. *Journal of Gay and Lesbian Social Services*, 30(2), 73–87.

Vallee, D. (2003). Same-sex marriage: Why knot? Here's why not. *The Toronto Star* (June 23), A21.

Walters, S.D. (2001). Take my domestic partner, please: Gays and marriage in the era of the visible. In M. Bernstein and R. Reinmann (Eds.), *Queer families, queer politics: Challenging culture and the state* (pp. 338–357). New York: Columbia University Press.

Warner, M. (1999). Normal and normaller: Beyond gay marriage. *GLQ: A Journal of Lesbian and Gay Studies*, 5, 119–171.

Warner, T. (2002). *Never going back: A history of queer activism in Canada*. Toronto: University of Toronto.

Webb, R.A. (2005). Overview of same-sex marriage in the U.S.: The struggle for civil rights and equality. National Association of Social Workers (NASW). Retrieved October 21, 2007, from www.socialworkers.org/diversity/lgb/062005.asp.

Yep, G. A., Lovaas, K. E., & Elia, J. P. (2003). A critical appraisal of assimilationist and radical ideologies underlying same-sex marriage in LGBT communities in the United States. *Journal of Homosexuality*, 45(1), 45–64.

QUESTIONS FOR CRITICAL THOUGHT

1. Sexual relationships are intensely intimate, individualized, and personal, yet they exist within a gender-differentiated world. How does gender influence the ways that men and women experience sexual intimacy and closeness?

2. Beres identifies several gendered discourses that her participants invoked when they talked about their casual sex experiences. Have you seen these discourses or others presented elsewhere? Which ones appear in your experience to be most powerful?

3. In your experience, or in the experiences of people you know, are long-term, intimate relationships gendered differently from short-term, casual relationships?

4. What do you think about marriage between two people of the same sex? What are some arguments for and against it? Do you agree with Mule that the entire institution of marriage is problematic?

PART V

The Gendered Family

A re families 'in crisis'? Are traditional arrangements collapsing under the weight of contemporary trends ranging from relaxed sexual attitudes, increased divorce, and women's entry into the labour force to rap music and violence in the media? The persistence of public argument about family values, the idea that 'the family' is somehow in decline, the emergence of new family forms: all of these phenomena underscore the centrality of families to the reproduction of social life and to gender identity. In 1985, S.F. Berk described families as 'gender factories', and while the factory metaphor is perhaps a bit too mechanical for the complex and often contradictory gender work that goes on in families, it does emphasize the important role families play in the creation and constant re-creation of gender.

Although the 'typical' family represented in 1950s television sitcoms—composed of breadwinner father, housewife mother, and 2.5 happy, well-adjusted children—is the empirical reality for less than 10 per cent of all households, it remains the cultural ideal against which contemporary family compositions are measured. And some would like to see us 'return' to as close as possible an approximation of that imagined idealized model—perhaps by restricting access to easy divorce or restricting women's entry into the labour force, or by promoting sexual abstinence and delegitimating homosexuality.

Others, though, view the problems with the family differently. The disjunctures between the demands of the workplace and the demands (and desires) of home are evident in Gillian Ranson's account of women engineers who find that motherhood marks a major turning point in their relationship with their high-intensity, high-skill careers. Childbearing and raising children do not fit easily into the professional world—at least not the intensive-mothering form of child-raising that most North Americans have learned to value.

Janet Salaff and Arent Greve glimpse into the lives of immigrant families from China, and show that these mothers and fathers face similar challenges as they attempt to create the kind of environment for their children which they see as the most valuable. The mothers take on the lion's share of the caregiving work, and carry it out within dense female networks of relatives and in-laws that extend across countries and continents, thereby 'globalizing' the traditional feminine work of care.

Family life consists of more than just caring for children, of course. As Anne Martin-Mathews demonstrates, caregiving work in families is often needed to help the elderly and the ill, as well as the young. For many families, the actual activities of caregiving and care-receiving do not fit neatly into stereotypes about women as the caring sex. The physical maintenance of the home has also been an arena of contestation between men and women, although this is an arena in which changes are happening. Sociologist Scott Coltrane discusses the relationship between housework, childcare, and the status of women in society: the more housework and childcare women do, the lower their status. As a result, he suggests that sharing housework and childcare is not only a way for husbands and wives to enact more egalitarian relationships, but also a way to ensure that the next generation will maintain egalitarian attitudes.

From the future to the past—Eliane Leslau Silverman looks back to the early days of the twentieth century and lets elderly Alberta women tell their own stories of getting married and beginning their own families. Their accounts depict a world in which marriage and family life was powerfully gendered, and gendered in very different ways from today.

CHAPTER 16

No Longer 'One of the Boys': Negotiations with Motherhood, as Prospect or Reality, among Women in Engineering[1]

Gillian Ranson

Women who train and work as professional engineers in Canada and other industrialized countries are women operating on male turf. Unlike professions such as medicine and law, both of which are much closer to gender parity, engineering remains 'archetypically masculine' (Wajcman, 1991: 145). In spite of nearly two decades of 'women into engineering' campaigns supported by government and industry, the numbers of women entering engineering have been described as 'derisory in most countries' (Faulkner, 2000: 92). The Canadian Council of Professional Engineers (CCPE) notes that, though the proportion of women in Canadian engineering schools increased annually after 1972, in the last few years it has levelled off at about 20 per cent (CCPE, 2003). While hardly derisory, these numbers fall far short of gender parity.

Retention of women in engineering over the long haul is also likely to be a problem given that the growth in numbers of those actually practising the profession is among women in their late twenties and early thirties (CCPE, 1998). These women are also at the age where family formation becomes salient. The arrival of children seems to be one critical point at which women, but not men, leave the profession, move to part-time work, and in many other ways put their careers 'on the back burner' (Ranson, 1998, 2000).

Motherhood, it seems clear, is a significant watershed, and one that policy-makers and others concerned about retaining women in engineering should take seriously. But the reasons why it is such a watershed—and hence what needs to be done to compensate for its effects—may be more complicated than the conventional explanations about work and family balance suggest. A more elaborated explanation is that motherhood, as embodied and as material experience, exposes a major fallacy inherent in the liberal discourses of equality and gender neutrality, which establish the terms for women's entry into male-dominated occupations and workplaces in the first place. These terms allow women to enter, not as women, but as conceptual men (Snitow, 1990: 26). This conceptual cover is blown when they become, or think about becoming, mothers. For many women (especially those who themselves internalize the gender neutrality discourse), actual or prospective motherhood compels them to confront identities as 'engineer' and 'mother' that may be 'mutually incongruous' (Jorgenson, 2000: 7) and require complex negotiation and management.

In this paper I examine this more nuanced explanation, and explore its implications for all women in male-dominated occupations and workplaces who face the challenges of being 'travellers in a male world' (Marshall, 1984; Gherardi, 1996).

Women in a Man's World

Recent women entrants to male-dominated occupations have had more legal, and, increasingly, cultural support for their presence on male turf. But while the terms of their participation have changed somewhat, difficulties persist. A 1992 report by the Canadian Committee on Women in Engineering cited many stories of sexism, systemic discrimination and workplace inequality, and a series of 'common and difficult' barriers faced by women engineers (Canadian Committee on Women in Engineering, 1992: 60).

Why should such barriers persist, especially in a discursive climate of gender equality and 'family-friendly' workplaces? Acker (1990) contends that organizations are not gender-neutral spaces that women may enter on the same footing as men; neither can a 'job' be defined as abstract and gender-neutral, performed by an abstract and disembodied 'worker' who exists only in relation to the job. Acker's widely cited argument is that in the real world of actual workers, the closest

approximation to the disembodied worker who exists only for the job is 'the male worker whose life centers on his full-time, life-long job, while his wife or another woman takes care of his personal needs and his children' (Acker, 1990: 149).

Acker's description was, until recently, a good fit for most engineers. Recent initiatives to get women into engineering have usually been predicated on the assumption that 'women must be modified to fit into engineering, not the other way round' (Faulkner, 2000: 93). In ethnographic research on engineering women in a variety of educational and work settings, Eisenhart and Finkel (1998) found that organizational expectations regarding commitment to workplace activities and the worker identity favoured people who were able to put work demands first. At the same time, these expectations were perceived by everyone concerned, women and men alike, as gender-neutral. The researchers came to view gender neutrality as a socially and culturally constructed discourse that 'confers legitimacy on women's professional contribution only when they act like men' and 'makes discussion of women's distinctive issues virtually impossible' (Eisenhart and Finkel, 1998: 181).

Mothers in a Man's World

Motherhood as a barrier to women's career progress in engineering is demonstrated in much research through the 1990s. Studies in the United States (McIlwee and Robinson, 1992), Britain (Devine, 1992; Evetts, 1994, 1996; Corcoran-Nantes and Roberts, 1995; Wajcman, 1998) and Canada (Ranson, 1998, 2000) all point to the challenges for women in combining 'masculine' professional work and motherhood. They may find themselves, as noted earlier, in workplaces in which a discourse of gender neutrality masks clearly masculinist expectations about work performance and career progress. At the same time, they confront cultural expectations about mothers, framed around a dominant ideology of 'intensive mothering' (Hays, 1996; Arendell, 2000) that directly contradicts workplace expectations.

In contrast, the men with whom these women work are not subject to the same expectations regarding their family involvement. These men are much more likely than their women colleagues to have partners who can take on the bulk of family responsibilities (Wajcman, 1998; Ranson, 2000).[2] For most men, the prevailing cultural expectation is that they will be responsible for their family's financial provision, whether or not their contribution is supplemented by working partners, and whether or not they are also involved caregivers (Christiansen and Palkovitz, 2001; Ranson, 2001).

Organizational responses in the form of 'family-friendly' policies and programs would seem to be the way to overcome this under-resourcing. But research evidence suggests they are not helping nearly as much as company rhetoric and popular discourse would suggest. While policies like parental leave or flexible work schedules are generally couched in gender-neutral terms, and are purported to be directed to both women and men, in practice their take-up by men has been minimal (Andrews and Bailyn, 1993; Pleck, 1993; Rapoport and Bailyn, 1996; Hochschild, 1997). This constitutes women as the prime beneficiaries of such policies, and further entrenches the idea that they are special concessions or benefits for women (Jones and Causer, 1995; Lewis, 1997) rather than rights to which all workers are entitled.

Managing Gender

If women's entry to male occupational turf is largely based on liberal assumptions that women are for practical purposes the same as men, it follows that women themselves will need to 'manage gender' in order to fit themselves into existing organizational cultures and structures (Rubin, 1997: 31). Whatever their standing as 'conceptual men', real-life embodied women must negotiate feminine subjectivity as well.[3] This is neatly illustrated by one of Miller's (2004) interviewees, a woman engineer working in the same city as the women in this study:

> When you go to the field, you don't take a purse because you're really rubbing that female helplessness thing in, and you put all your junk—the female hygiene stuff—in your

little pockets. Another thing you do when you work downtown is you always wear wide skirts because sometimes you're going to be going to the field in the afternoon. And you can wear high heels to the office but keep a pair of flat loafers there . . . (Miller, 2004: 54).

While some of the women engineers in a 1999 study by Kvande did indeed, as noted above, strive to be 'one of the boys', others drew on other discourses (or, in Kvande's terms, constructed other femininities) that corresponded to a view of themselves as *different from*, not the same as their male colleagues. Kvande found that the women who saw themselves in this way were invariably women with children. Jorgenson, whose research (2000, 2002) focused particularly on the ways women engineers with children managed the potentially contradictory discourses of motherhood and engineering, found similar complexity. Sometimes the women positioned themselves as competent career-oriented professionals, sometimes as caring mothers, but usually with an awareness of the incompatibility of the mother–engineer identities. As one of her interviewees commented, 'I didn't want to try to be the perfect engineer because I knew I wanted a family' (Jorgenson, 2002: 370).

Jorgenson's work summarizes the position outlined at the start of the paper, that women enter engineering work as 'conceptual men', and that motherhood is, in many cases, a 'defining moment', separating mothers from others.

'Conceptual Men', Alternative Subjectivities, and Motherhood in Engineering

Women without Children

Sally, who was 41 and childless, provides a good example of the sort of long-term engineering careers available to competent and highly motivated women able to be single-minded about their professional work. This was not the case for the younger women, who still needed to confront the possibility of motherhood. Among these women, particular understandings both of motherhood and engineering work framed talk that was also significantly shaped by age and family or relationship circumstance.

The experience of Sally—a senior manager in a major oil company—provides a link to the issue of motherhood because she attributed her career success to the fact that—not from choice—she didn't have children. Sally noted that despite her company's public claims to being 'family-friendly', the 'day-to-day business environment' included the perception that to get ahead 'you've got to put in the long hours' and be 'willing to sacrifice'. Asked if she thought more women in the organization would make a difference, she said: 'I think that may be the sort of thing that *keeps* women from making a difference.' She was explicit about the difference it had made to her career: 'Because I don't have the child connection . . . I have been able to, if need be, go the extra mile, every time they've asked.'

The single women's responses to the prospect of motherhood were provisional and speculative, since all saw a permanent relationship as a prerequisite. For example, Rosemary, four years post-graduation, commented:

I'm probably indifferent either way, you know. I think it would depend on my spouse. Like, if I met somebody and they wanted kids, then I would be open to having one, maybe two. And hopefully maybe they would like to adopt children rather than (laughter) . . . I just can't see myself just, just staying home and being a mom. . . . So, but if, hey, my previous boyfriend, he was more than happy to be a stay-at-home dad. So that, that's a fit for me as well.

In this way, at the hypothetical level at least, she constructed a family scenario that would allow her to remain 'one of the boys'. This scenario did not challenge the 'intensive' version of mothering that would remove her from the workplace. Instead, Rosemary discursively nominated her hypothetical partner as the full-time caregiver, and gave herself a family role similar to those of her male colleagues. In other words, she positioned herself as a conceptual 'father'.

Like Rosemary, Julia was also 27 and four years past graduation. Though she did not self-identify as 'one of the boys' in the way Rosemary did, she was relishing the hands-on, technical, outdoor nature of her fieldwork job. But she also saw this way of working as contingent:

[N]ow I don't have the five-year to ten-year plan. I mean, between you and I, I would love to be a stay-at-home mom. . . . But, I'm not married. And I don't have any kids. So *until then*, I'm going to do the best job that I can, and follow my career, and if it happens, it happens. If it doesn't, it doesn't (emphasis added).

Julia's vision of motherhood included the view that 'if you have children . . . somebody should be at home'—and she was clear that, in her family, unlike Rosemary's, she would be that somebody. She presented this version of mothering as incompatible with engineering work: 'If I could work from home, or if I could work part-time, then that would be my ideal. But in engineering, you don't seem to be able to do that. . . .'

Other single, childless women, with more work experience than Julia, took her story to another level: children needed care that mothers should provide and that they, as mothers, would potentially be willing to provide; in the absence of these family obligations, they were devoting their energies to engineering work; this engineering work was getting to be of a kind and at a level that would not easily accommodate maternal responsibilities. Thus, for example, Sarah—a 34-year-old engineer who had recently been promoted to manage a major energy project for her company—expressed excitement that this project could be 'a stepping stone' to 'a lot more exciting projects'. Asked if she thought she would be able to combine her present job with children and family responsibilities, Sarah said:

I think I would. I know women that do do that here but they have to have a very understanding spouse that's more flexible. It's very difficult to do this job and have a spouse that's doing exactly the same thing with exactly the same sort of aspirations, I think.

Sarah's immediate qualification of the possibility of a work–family balance in her current job (by positioning herself, like Rosemary, as a father) was qualified still further by her comment later that she 'couldn't go on maternity leave in the next two years' even if she wanted to, and that she had 'sort of accepted the fact that [having children] might not happen'. Sarah had recognized, in Wajcman's (1996) terms, the 'domestic basis for the managerial career'.

Different versions of the engineering–motherhood balance came from women who were in permanent relationships with men, and who were all anticipating having children sooner or later. These women were in two groups. When interviewed, four were recent graduates, within six years of graduation, and all were in their twenties. Three were a little older and more experienced (all were 34 and had 12 years of engineering experience behind them).

Among the younger four, the ideology of intensive mothering appeared in comments rejecting nannies or daycare as strategies enabling full-time work while having young children. But they also rejected the stay-at-home mother option; all planned to work part-time when their children were young. They all assumed that part-time work would be viable, even when—as in Sheila's case—there was some evidence from a colleague working an 80 per cent schedule that it might be hard to manage. (Sheila commented, 'I honestly think that she's a little bit less organized and that I could probably handle it a little better.') These women also expressed a strong sense of entitlement with respect to what their employer ought to do for them. And they were united in their conviction that their partners—all of whom were also engineers—would share the childcare responsibilities, likely also moving to part-time work to do so. This conviction was striking, given their collective experience of working in resoundingly masculinist workplace cultures where men, for the most part, were able to delegate their family responsibilities, and where male engineers working less than full-time were almost unheard of.

The three older women were characteristic of many women in male-dominated occupations in having deferred childbearing (see Ranson, 1998). All three spoke about their work, and their current

workplaces, in terms that clearly indicated career success: a raise or stock options whenever she thought about leaving (Marcie); promotion from a junior position to the same grade as her male colleagues (Helen); a senior management position in a company she had helped to grow (Shelley). All three intended to keep working after having children, and all three, in different ways, planned to make their experience and seniority work for them as they thought about accommodating their jobs to family responsibilities. As Shelley said:

I've been with the company for a long time and I've always been a very good employee. As a result I'm paid well now, and I have a lot of responsibility and respect [within] the company. And, you know, that's my money to cash in when I need to negotiate a deal. . . . A position of strength to bargain from is always a good thing.

What seems to be the case is that this position of strength is achieved by proof of successful career performance according to male standards—in other words, by women paying their dues as 'conceptual men'. This is not to suggest that these women achieved their success by aligning themselves with men. For example, some of the experience that earned Helen her current job was gained in an overtly sexist work environment that she was 'not ever going to be a part of'. It is also not to suggest that 'male standards' are uniform. For example, most of Shelley's male colleagues and superiors were about her age; she suggested that their relative youth made them less conventional. But in every case, the standards in place were standards established by men. Having met those standards, women felt freer to negotiate as women for changes they needed to accommodate their family responsibilities.

To summarize, the women without children produced a number of different scenarios for the way motherhood might combine with engineering: motherhood viewed as incompatible with engineering, and chosen as its alternative; motherhood refused, delegated, or privatized to enable the continuation of the engineering career; motherhood and engineering combined by means of modified work arrangements (earned by male-defined career success), and the equal participation of husbands and partners. Of these scenarios, only the first assumed that motherhood and engineering were truly 'mutually incongruous', and this was not a common position. But the 'strong' view of intensive mothering it implied appeared in more diluted form in all the accounts. This, in turn, shaped how women thought they would need to accommodate their work. Unless (as in Rosemary's case) they planned to become 'fathers', motherhood was seen as putting an end to business as usual.

Women with Children

The choices and accommodations anticipated by the childless women turned out to be a generally accurate summary of the routes the mothers took. As with the mothers in Kvande's study, though, they were generally more likely to position themselves as women, differently situated from their current or former male colleagues.

Five of the women gave up full-time engineering work at or shortly after the arrival of their children. At the time they were interviewed, two were not in paid employment at all, and spoke as if a return to engineering was unlikely. Holly commented: 'As soon as I had a baby, my total perspective changed.' For Jenny, the other stay-at-home mother, her first baby's arrival signalled not so much a change of perspective as the opportunity to retreat gratefully from a world she had never wholeheartedly embraced. Jenny's choice was motherhood over engineering:

> It's not a door that I've closed and I don't have bad memories. Although what I hear about engineering now . . . I think, oh, man, I don't want to get into that any more. I really don't.

The others had had longer and more conventionally successful careers as engineers before having children. All undertook intermittent consulting contracts, but at the time they were interviewed, none were working more than a day or so a week. Kate, at home with her first child, (aged nine months at the time of the interview) framed her stay-at-home-mom status as 'a wonderful break'

after having worked in engineering for 15 years. The baby was long-awaited. She commented: 'I didn't sort of have huge expectations of it but when we finally did [have] him, I just thought, oh, why wouldn't I just kind of stay and enjoy him?' Kate had worked long enough, and recently enough, that the engineer identity was still strong ('even though I'm not working I'll always be an engineer'). But asked whether she would be an engineer 10 years down the road, she replied, 'Probably not.'

Lisa's work history was similar to Kate's. She had worked full-time for 10 years for one company, then switched to part-time with the birth of her first child. But half-time work with a second child heightened the tension between work and family responsibilities:

> I wasn't doing a good job with anything. . . . If it had gone on any longer I would have regretted it and you can't live your life like that. You've just got to do what you know you can.

Like Julia, cited earlier, Lisa had broader aspirations about family and motherhood, to which this decision conformed:

> I really wanted to be the one with the babies. I wanted to nurse them, I wanted to raise them. . . . It would have been a sacrifice to not be home with them, to me. I really wanted to do that. It was the life experience I wanted to have.

While for all four women, the commitment to motherhood rather than engineering could be construed as voluntary, for Ellie, the fifth woman in the group, it was not. At the time she was interviewed she was recovering from two very difficult pregnancies, residual physical problems following childbirth, and an extremely demanding second baby. ('I think I literally lost my mind', she commented.) In Rothman's (1994) terms, she was experiencing the 'embodied challenges' to working like a man—challenges she resisted as much as she could. Echoes of the energetic and driven women engineers described by Kate appeared in her talk of working while pregnant and sick, or doing from her hospital bed the work her (female) replacement was supposed to be doing. Ellie spoke optimistically about returning to work: 'I do want to work. I really enjoy working. I never wanted really to be a stay-at-home.' The clear implication was that when she was physically able, she would pick up her working life.

Six of the women with children continued to work full-time, or close to full-time, in engineering jobs. But the conscious downplaying of career goals in order to accommodate family responsibilities expressed by Lisa was evident in the talk of these women as well. It was also reflected in their practices—a shift in the kind of work being done to something perceived to be less stressful (Linda), a refusal of promotion in order to remain in a familiar and manageable work environment (Joanne), a move from permanent employment to consulting as a means to achieve flexibility (Kelly), the use of a pregnancy to signal a shifting of gears after a successful corporate career (Hilary), cutting back to four instead of five days a week (Shauna). These work arrangements were accompanied by talk that linked them to family benefits.

The third group of mothers is those whose careers appeared on the surface to have been less affected by motherhood. Given the way these women were working, and the jobs they were doing, they could be described as mothers in careers more often associated with men. The nine women in this group had all reached senior levels of management and/or technical specialty. But in this group also, the balance of motherhood and career was complicated and fluid. It was also in this group that the most vivid images of 'conceptual men' becoming mothers emerged. Cassie was one example. As a woman who had always been able to work as 'one of the boys', Cassie downplayed issues of gender in the workplace, noting that she had never experienced 'discrimination, or anything like that', and was 'not a supporter of affirmative action-type programs'. She said she thought 'opportunities go to those people who are willing to work for them'. But this perspective was challenged by an unplanned pregnancy at a time when she was making dramatic career progress.

Carla's case is worth noting because it is such a good example of the discursive positioning of

the 'professional engineer' and the (very much embodied) mother. When Carla returned to work after her first maternity leave, she tried to breastfeed her baby during her lunch break as a way to continue nursing. She said:

> Well, I tried it for two weeks, but then my milk supply was so big, it was just like . . . you know, here I am a professional engineer and my boobs are leaking all over the place and I just couldn't, couldn't do that.

Asked if those around her at work were supportive, she replied, 'Well, I didn't really talk about it with anybody. It was kind of a private thing.' Carla's acknowledgment of the incongruity of 'professional engineers' breast-feeding, and of breast-feeding itself as belonging in the private domain, hinted at the subjective shifts she also negotiated. Carla's career choices were constrained by her family's need for her income. Like many men also, she was the family breadwinner, in a position to delegate family work to her partner. Unlike most men, however, she expressed unease about this arrangement. Her interview was interspersed with comments that clearly indicated what Smith (1987) would call a bifurcated consciousness, divided between a focus on her work (which she enjoyed), and preoccupation with a domestic life over which she had reluctantly surrendered control. 'There are really times that I long to be the stay-at-home parent,' she commented.

For other women, there was a more conscious crossing over from a family focus to a more explicit career orientation. Zoe responded to an appeal by a friend to leave her flexible consulting arrangement and lead a small company; Ingrid's long-time male mentor asked her to return to work part-time, two months after her second child was born. Ingrid spoke of having planned not to return to work until the children were in school. But the part-time work quickly turned to full-time, then a partnership. Her account combined expressions of her enjoyment of her job with regrets about its costs.

> I think once a woman works, it's hard not to work. It's hard to stay home and not have that

challenge. . . . Knowing that other people are advancing, advancing, advancing. . . . The downside is the time. You don't know (if you raised) your kids yourself. I don't consider, myself, that I've raised my kids . . . I consider that they spend more time with their babysitter than they do with me, right? I consider that and now it's more time at school than with me, right? So I consider myself kind of the secondary raiser, kind of in their lives, my husband and I.

But in this group of mothers there were also those whose accounts were much less conflicted. For example, Denise had her first and only child, at 35. She took 20 weeks of maternity leave, the maximum her company allowed—'and honestly, I was dying to get back to work.' She commented:

> It didn't change much in my life. I still worked the same hours. I was still the same person at work as I was before. Just because I have a full-time nanny during the day, I was pretty uninterrupted, having a child, compared to what it could be.

To summarize, the 20 women with children followed fairly closely the paths anticipated by the childless women engineers described earlier with respect to the combination of engineering and motherhood. A very few voluntarily 'chose' motherhood. All the others negotiated a balance between being an engineer and being a mother that was both discursive and practical. For some of these negotiators, the balance was achieved by a conscious gearing down on the work side—but usually only after careers had been established and dues paid. For the others, it was achieved (as just noted) by means of privatizing and delegating family responsibilities in order to maintain career progress.

Conclusion

This study has proceeded from the assumption that motherhood is a watershed for women in engineering, and has explored what was described at the start of the paper as a more nuanced explanation for why this might be the case: that women enter engineering jobs as 'conceptual men', and that problems arise because mothers can't *be* conceptual men.

What it means to work as a 'conceptual man' is not self-evident. In this paper I chose to see women engineers working in this way if they were doing the same kind of work, in the same conditions, for the same hours, and with the same general expectations about quality of performance as their male colleagues. Another part of the definition was that this work was done in workplaces dominated by men—a condition that was more than met in every case. I also tried to distinguish between *working as* a conceptual man, and *aligning oneself*, or *discursively positioning oneself*, with men. On the basis of this definition, all of the women without children were working as conceptual men. Often, though not invariably, they also positioned themselves as 'one of the boys'—though this positioning was seldom sustained and consistent. Nine of the 20 women with children were also working as conceptual men—though they were much less likely to position themselves with 'the boys'.

In my discussion of these nine, and in comments about the plans of some of the childless women also proposing to delegate to partners or otherwise privatize their family responsibilities, I have suggested that these women were or would become 'fathers'. This proposition is not entirely theoretical. In a separate study (Ranson, 2001) I explored the ways the men with children interviewed for the same engineering project balanced work and family responsibilities. Serious accommodation to family responsibilities generally took two forms: a choice of work (generally office, rather that field-based, with predictable hours); or downshifting from an intensive work focus to a more relaxed pace—usually the choice of men who had achieved considerable career success first. But for all of these men, the balance of work and family still typically involved working days of 8–10 hours, and in almost every case, also involved a partner working part-time or not in paid employment, and available to pick up the slack. Access to this private infrastructure of support characterized almost all the fathers. For those mothers who have access to something similar, the 'father' analogy has some merit.

For the mothers, 'downshifting' to accommodate children went much further: an opting out of engineering, temporarily or permanently, or a reduction in work hours. Fathers never employed these strategies; indeed, men with young families working less than full-time never emerged in the larger study. This is why such strategies come to be identified with women, and why so-called 'family-friendly' organizational policies purporting to help employees balance work and family responsibilities come to be perceived as helping women fit in to men's workplaces. As noted by researchers cited earlier (Jones and Causer, 1995; Lewis, 1997; Rubin, 1997; Liff and Ward, 2001), these policies may become another organizational device for differentiating women from 'the boys'—and mothers from fathers.

Notes

1. The author would like to thank Marilyn Porter and the CRSA reviewers for very helpful comments on an earlier version of the paper. This manuscript was first submitted in September 2003 and accepted in March 2005.
2. In the larger project from which the present study is drawn, only 25 per cent of fathers in engineering jobs had partners who also worked full-time, compared to 92 per cent of the engineering mothers.
3. I am grateful to the anonymous reviewer who urged that this point be made more explicit.

References

Acker, J. 1990. 'Hierarchies, Jobs, Bodies: A Theory of Gendered Organizations', *Gender & Society* 4, 2: 139–58.

Andrews, A., and L. Bailyn. 1993. 'Segmentation and Synergy: Two Models of Linking Work and Family', in J. Hood, ed., *Men, Work and Family*, pp. 262–75. Newbury Park, CA: Sage.

Arendell, T. 2000. 'Conceiving and Investigating Motherhood: The Decade's Scholarship', *Journal of Marriage and Family* 62, 4: 1192–207.

Canadian Committee on Women and Engineering. 1992. *More than Just Numbers*. Fredericton: University of New Brunswick.

Canadian Council of Professional Engineers. 1998. *National Survey of the Canadian Engineering Profession in 1997*. Ottawa: Canadian Council of Professional Engineers.

———. 2003. 'Women in Engineering'. Available at www.ccpe.ca/e/prog_women_1.cfm.

Christiansen, S., and R. Palkovitz. 2001. 'Why the "good provider" Role Still Matters: Providing as a Form of Paternal Involvement', *Journal of Family Issues* 22, 1: 84–106.

Corcoran-Nantes, Y. and K. Roberts. 1995. '"We've got one of those": The Peripheral Status of Women in Male-dominated Industries', *Gender, Work and Organization* 2, 1: 21–33.

Devine, F. 1992. 'Gender Segregation in the Engineering and Science Professions: A Case of Continuity and Change', *Work, Employment and Society* 6, 4: 557–75.

Eisenhart, M., and E. Finkel. 1998. *Women's Science*. Chicago, IL: University of Chicago Press.

Evetts, J. 1994. 'Women and Career in Engineering: Continuity and Change in the Organisation', *Work, Employment and Society* 8, 1: 101–12.

———. 1996. *Gender and Career in Science and Engineering*. London: Taylor & Francis Ltd.

Faulkner, W. 2000. 'The Power *and* the Pleasure? A Research Agenda for "making gender stick" to Engineers', *Science, Technology, & Human Values* 25, 1: 87–119.

Gherardi, S. 1996. 'Gendered Organizational Cultures: Narratives of Women Travellers in a Male World', *Gender, Work and Organization* 3, 4: 187–201.

Hays, S. 1996. *The Cultural Contradictions of Motherhood*. New Haven, CT: Yale University Press.

Hochschild, A. 1997. *The Time Bind*. New York: Metropolitan Books.

Jones, C., and G. Causer. 1995. '"Men don't have families": Equality and Motherhood in Technical Employment', *Gender, Work and Organization* 2, 2: 51–62.

Jorgenson, J. 2000. 'Interpreting the Intersections of Work and Family: Frame Conflicts in Women's Work', *The Electronic Journal of Communication* 10, 3–4.

——. 2002. 'Engineering Selves: Negotiating Gender and Identity in Technical Work', *Management Communication Quarterly* 15, 3: 350–80.

Kvande, E. 1999. '"In the belly of the beast": Constructing Femininities in Engineering Organizations', *European Journal of Women's Studies* 6, 3: 305–28.

Lewis, S. 1997. '"Family-friendly" Employment Policies: A Route to Changing Organizational Culture or Playing About at the Margins?', *Gender, Work and Organization* 4, 1: 13–23.

Liff, S., and K. Ward. 2001. 'Distorted Views through the Glass Ceiling: The Construction of Women's Understandings of Promotion and Senior Management Positions', *Gender, Work and Organization* 8, 1: 19–36.

Marshall, J. 1984. *Women Managers: Travellers in a Male World*. Chichester: John Wiley and Sons.

McIlwee, J., and J. Robinson. 1992. *Women in Engineering*. Albany, NY: SUNY Press.

Miller, G. 2004. 'Frontier Masculinity in the Oil Industry: The Experience of Women Engineers', *Gender, Work and Organization* 11, 1: 47–73.

Pleck, J. 1993. 'Are "family-supportive" Employer Policies Relevant to Men?', in J. Hood, ed., *Men, Work and Family*, pp. 217–37. Newbury Park, CA: Sage.

Ranson, G. 1998. 'Education, Work and Family Decision Making: Finding the "right time" to Have a Baby', *Canadian Review of Sociology and Anthropology* 35, 4: 517–33.

——. 2000. 'The Best of Both Worlds? Work, Family Life and the Retention of Women in Engineering'. Paper presented at the 8th annual conference of the Canadian Coalition of Women in Engineering, Science, Trades and Technology, St. John's, Newfoundland, 6–8 July.

——. 2001. 'Men at Work: Change—or No Change?—in the Era of the "new father"', *Men and Masculinities* 4, 1: 3–26.

Rapoport, R., and L. Bailyn. 1996. *Relinking Life and Work: Toward a Better Future*. New York: Ford Foundation.

Rothman, B. 1994. 'Beyond Mothers and Fathers: Ideology in a Patriarchal Society', in E.N. Glenn, G. Chang, and L.R. Forcie, eds., *Mothering: Ideology, Experience and Agency*, pp. 139–57. New York: Routledge.

Rubin, J. 1997. 'Gender, Equality and the Culture of Organizational Assessment', *Gender, Work and Organization* 4, 1: 24–34.

Smith, D. 1987. *The Everyday World as Problematic: A Feminist Sociology*. Toronto: University of Toronto Press.

Snitow, A. 1990. 'A Gender Diary', in M. Hirsch and E.F. Keller, eds., *Conflicts in Feminism*. New York: Routledge.

Wajcman, J. 1991. *Feminism Confronts Technology*. Cambridge: Polity Press.

——. 1996. 'The Domestic Basis for the Managerial Career', *Sociological Review* 44, 4: 609–29.

——. 1998. *Managing Like a Man*. University Park, PA: Pennsylvania State University Press.

CHAPTER 17

Can Women's Social Networks Migrate?

Janet W. Salaf and Arent Greve[1]

Introduction:
Work and Family Networks

With the globalization of production and services, professionals from Asia increasingly migrate to enrich their work experiences and their family economies in new countries (Castells, 1989; Sassen, 1991). These moves often disrupt their professional employment and family support networks, which they must mobilize anew (Portes and Borocz, 1989; Levitt and Schiller, 2003). Our 'Immigration from China' project explores how social networks bridge settlement of professionals who immigrated to Canada in the skilled worker category. We look for those features in their social networks that they share with others and those which are distinctly rooted in dual-career families. This paper analyzes how migration alters the family support system, how couples adapt to reduced social capital for childcare, and how this impedes career opportunities of skilled women in particular.

Typical People's Republic of China (PRC) immigrants to Canada are married professionals who apply to immigrate based on their skills, without having been offered jobs or preceded by other family members. In China, they had built collegial social networks during their education and careers (Lin, Ensel, and Vaughn, 1981). After immigration to Canada, to get appropriate positions they search for local work-related network partners that are rooted in the occupation, not in kinship or the ethnic enclave (Gold, 2001; Poros, 2001).

Family needs also require social network support but of a different sort. Professionals are likely to marry other professionals, and both want to develop their careers. To do so, parents with young children draw on complex support systems, which, unlike job networks, are based on kinship. Like other migrants, they also have to mobilize family-related social networks over immense physical distances (Hondagneu-Sotelo and Avila, 1997).

Social Networks: Migration and Social Support

Social networks play diverse functions in international migration (Portes and Borocz, 1989; Delechat, 2001). International migrants depend on social networks to find a job, start a business, or other career needs (Min, 1988; Burt, 1992). In addition to career exigencies, new arrivals need to find a place to live, get information and advice, emotional support, and help with childcare from others, the topic of this paper (Preston and Man, 1999; Willis and Yeoh, 2000; Parrenas, 2001; Man, 2002).

Depending on the resources that the network contacts can offer, they can provide different types of support, but one contact can rarely cover a broad range of services. Furthermore, different forms of social networks give diverse kinds of assistance over time (Poros, 2001). Therefore, people need a variety of contacts to get the kind of support they need. Childcare is one of many services that people can get through their social networks. However, this delicate type of service involves considerable trust, and only a few members of a social network can offer the different types of assistance that childcare encompasses. This can be seen when we discuss types of relations and social networks that offer these resources.

Life Course Structure

Because the biggest demands from work and family come at the same time, a crucial problem for dual-career couples is balancing their work and family careers. State-legislated family policies to support social reproduction often fail to provide effective support to dual-career families. Few countries effectively organize public childcare and employment to support dual-career families. Those that do may favour some sections of the work force with childcare more than others (Moen and Firebaugh, 1994; Buchmann and Charles, 1995).

It is typically women who try to mesh these dual work–family demands. Women may adopt sequential work and family courses, focusing more on each role at different times. They might first study, then raise children, then return to the labour force. This staggered approach often runs against the demands of expected professional career sequences. Simultaneous roles allow attention to both family and career courses. Here, role conflict takes a toll on women's ability to do both without substantial help (Moen and Yu, 1999; Walter, Heinz, and Verma, 2001). Men commonly adjust their family life to their careers, while wives employ long-term, reciprocal support strategies to bridge formal and informal structures and attain work and family goals.

The difficulties that PRC immigrants to Canada encounter when they transfer between two different social contexts are central to their reconstructing work and family lives as new immigrants. Social structures, typical ways of building careers, and state family policies designed to support social reproduction differ from one setting to another and entail considerable readjustments. Without flexible informal social networks, parents have trouble bridging formal structures, and women assume most of this integrating work.

Work–Family Roles in China

Educated Chinese women have public and private roles that are both sequential and simultaneous

(Giele, 1998). The education of young Chinese professionals and skilled workers is sequential, determined by examinations that lead from one stage to the next. State educational and job placement systems—and their own performance and interests—channel the educated elite into their adult roles. In force when most of our respondents got their first jobs, this system began to change in the 1980s following the introduction of a private labour market with great consequences for their careers (Bian, 1994; Nee and Matthews, 1996). After graduation from college, they find jobs and begin to build careers. They marry and bear a child within the first year (Whyte and Parish, 1984; Robinson, 1985). Having few children is a political requirement, allowing them to devote themselves to work. The family is now seen as a smaller, leaner, even residual unit, whose tasks have lessened (Croll, Kane, and Davin, 1985).

Women and men remain in the labour force throughout their working lives. Educated women have made inroads into demanding professional, administrative, and skilled manual occupations, although assignments are gendered and males and females work in different sectors (Ngo, 2000). With the market reforms, successful professional and skilled workers increasingly earn high incomes, rewarding women for remaining on the job (Meng and Kidd, 1997).

Women take on the primary responsibility for child rearing and other caring roles. While they downplay their careers when it conflicts with their families, institutional and personal support systems help ease balancing simultaneous careers and work family roles (Moen and Yu, 1999; Zhan and Montgomery, 2003). Chinese family policy helps parents combine public and private roles. The city and the largest state work units operate daycare and nursery school places. Although there are institutional shortages, there are adequate places for professional dual-career families. Moreover, with flexible hours, parents can use around-the-clock services.

Mutual obligations between family members also provide social capital to ease the meshing of work–family systems. These norms are traced back to the patrilineal Chinese family. Respect for broad family obligations continues but is more mutual and negotiated today, giving family members a range of social supporters (Whyte and Parish, 1984). Each generation expects to benefit, in the long run, from mutual assistance (Yang, 1996). The elder generation wants to help professional sons and daughters, substantial earners in the family, meet their work responsibilities. The professional wife's job earning potential is worth more than the time she might spend at household and other reproductive chores. At the same time, children are the whole family's responsibility (Chen, Short, and Entwisle, 2000).

Many parents of our elite couples were themselves professionals who worked in the urban state sector and retired early while still in good health. With small families themselves, grandparents are not overwhelmed with care requests. Co-residence also contributes to shared reproductive tasks. There was no private housing market until the mid-1980s, and housing—provided by their work unit—was in short supply (Walder, 1986). Couples delayed marriage until they had an apartment or accepted living with the older generation, who often had better housing than the younger generation. The seniors first give young mothers childcare help; later, they receive personal care (Zhan and Montgomery, 2003). As a result, in the 1980s, an estimated 25 per cent of younger parents lived together with their own parents (Davis, 1993; Chen et al., 2000).

In these ways, features of the wider context ease reciprocal care between generations. If proximity, social norms, and structures underlay the social exchanges between female generations, how do transnational migrants get the help they need to work from kin?

Work–Family Roles in Canada

North Americans integrate their work and family life courses in diverse patterns. Women go in and out of school and paid work at different times (Gerson, 1985; Giele, 1998; Partridge, in press). Jones, Marsden, and Tepperman (1990) point out that Canadian women adapt to paid work by individualizing their life patterns, including an increasingly fluid movement between adult statuses in domestic work, full-time and part-time work, and education.

Earlier cohorts of educated women returned to work after their children were older, often in new careers (Ginzberg, 1967). Professionally trained women today postpone having children until finishing their training. They may then stay in the labour force, finding other caregivers, paying for nannies—often new immigrants of colour, work part-time, or telework (Parrenas, 2001).

Lack of state commitment to childcare facilities contributes to this fluidity. Due to the incoherent and costly early childhood education system, Canadian childcare has become largely the private responsibility of parents (Doherty, Rose, Friendly, Lero, and Hope, 1995; Vanier Institute of the Family, 2000). Parents engage in considerable private strategizing in order to combine professional work and family roles (Hochschild, 1990). Much of this is the work of women.

Methods

To understand how they reconnect social networks to do their employment and family roles, we studied 50 dual-career couples from China over time. We contacted approximately half of our sample through a large NGO immigration agency in Toronto. The other half was composed of 'snowball' contacts, introduced by the original sample. While our small sample cannot represent the many Chinese immigrants in Toronto, our respondents are typical of emigrants from China's urban centres (Liang, 2001; Statistics Canada, 2001). With dependents to support, all needed to earn money immediately. We excluded those that originally came on student visas and investment immigrants who do not immediately enter the labour force.

Participants averaged 35 years of age at immigration, most with BA degrees or higher. Two-thirds have careers in engineering, medicine, accountancy, and computer science. Men, somewhat better educated, were concentrated in engineering and computer fields. Women were also well trained and working in careers in accounting, computers, engineering, humanities, and medicine.

In China, these parents had only a single child, as dictated to the urban elite, and had a second child while living outside China. Over half the

parents, with children 10 and under, have to find childcare in order to work.

We interviewed couples in their native language. In the first three-hour session, we gathered material on the husband's and wife's work, family histories, other personal experiences, and their social networks. Follow-up interviews and phone calls brought us up-to-date on these topics. We translated the taped interviews and analyzed them for themes, using N-Vivo, a qualitative software package. The text draws on our latest information for the respondents, unless otherwise noted. We maintained contact with nearly all respondents through December 2002 and continued to correspond with many through December 2003. In this paper, we quote directly from their comments, giving them pseudonyms and adding their gender in brackets after the comments.

Work–Family Roles in China and Canada

Social Support for Work–Family Roles in China

These parents met their range of childcare needs through complex patterns of family obligations and institutional care in China. If their elders are available, the young couples initially turn to them. Seventy-one per cent of the couples received substantial childcare help from their seniors. Grandparents might take over the entire childcare burden to help their children build their professional careers. It was a recognized career advancement if their child stayed behind with its grandparents.

Getting Help for Further Study

The help received went well beyond occasional babysitting. Although they finished their basic training before marriage, several returned to school for postgraduate studies. Wives' increased dual burden and brought several family members into play.

Cheng Li (M) was a metallurgical engineer whose parents were retired teachers. First an engineer in a large public metal works, he transferred to a trading firm in charge of technical products.

When the firm went downhill, Cheng Li returned to school for an MSc in another city. Throughout, his wife, Xing Ying, who worked as an administrative assistant, remained in her in-law's home to get help with family. Her own mother, a retired factory worker, was ill and could not care for grandchildren. Xing Ying explained: 'We could have gotten our own flat if we wanted (from the enterprise). But how could I take care of my baby on my own? I needed the help of my mother-in-law.' Xing Ying's mother-in-law continued to care for the little girl in China for two years after the couple moved to Canada. With her burden reduced, Xing Ying became a student and reoriented her career.

Studying abroad created even more demands on their kin. When his son was four-years-old, Chen Hung (M) won a coveted job in the Office of the Japanese architecture branch where he worked. His wife Ying Ying visited for a year, leaving their son in Beijing. Unable to find work in Tokyo, she returned to Beijing. A year later, she went to Holland to take an MSc in Computer Sciences.

The whole family reunited in Toronto several years later. Throughout the couple's overseas sojourns, Chen Hung's mother cared for her grandson.

Some co-ordinated their housing, further studies, and child bearing plans in an all-round support system. Liuma (F), a doctor married to Zhu Ji, an electrical engineer, lived with Liuma's parents after marriage, until Liuma's father, a plant director, arranged a nearby apartment for them. When Liuma had a son, she moved back to her parents' home, hired a babysitter, and her mother also helped after work. Liuma's family continued their help for a year after the couple immigrated to Canada and could get on their feet. She recalled, 'I never felt the burden of raising a child!'

Multiplexity

Our couples could rarely designate one grandparent to take responsibility throughout the child's early years. Grandmothers have their own life course and it was not always possible to meet patrilineal goals. As a result, most combined helpers from either side, or both, at different times. The main caregiver was usually a grandparent, the second a grandparent on the other side, or a servant. Arrangements were flexible. If they sent their child to nursery school, they might use fewer helpers. If they delayed school until kindergarten, they drew on more helpers. Of the 32 parents that gave help to their grandchildren, two-thirds were the wife's parents.

For example, QuPing (F), with a BA in social science, and her husband, Hu, a computer scientist, grew up in Beijing, and got good private firm jobs in Shenzhen. After their son was born, Hu's mother came to care for the baby. At the same time, she brought her youngest son, a recent graduate, to look for a job in Shenzhen with Hu's help. When QuPing's son was two and a half years old, he was sent to Beijing, where QuPing thought schools were better, and lived with QuPing's parents. But the boy could not adjust to the nursery school routine and returned to Shenzhen. QuPing took care of him, sent him to school in the morning, and fetched him after work. Servants were hard to find, and QuPing was afraid of bringing a stranger into her home. The many services available made it easy for QuPing to handle her household responsibilities after her child returned from school. 'There wasn't so much household work to do, so I could handle it. When we returned home late, we could easily find a place to grab a bite.'

Caring for Their Own Children

Nine per cent of our couples, primarily those with no elders available, took primary responsibility for their child. The amount of time they spent on the job was central to how they combined work and family roles. When both spouses held state sector posts, they often had a more relaxed schedule. In contrast, professional mothers who worked long hours could not squeeze in much childcare. Conditions in the private sector were especially demanding.

For instance, Hung's (F) son was born during her light teaching stint in a Communist Party College, and a flexible job freed her to care for her child for a year. When her son turned two, Hung's mother had retired from her factory job and helped look after her grandson. When, by the third year, he was old enough for nursery school, Hung and her husband shared responsibility for dropping him off and picking him up.

Many private sector and some state jobs required long hours or travel. Xu Fang (F) and her husband helped manage a branch of Xu Fang's family's private paint products firm. She '. . . didn't have Saturday or Sunday free, every day was busy.' She hired two people to take care of him.

Scaling Back

With overall responsibility for their children, despite the help of others, many women altered their professional goals. Some wives deliberately slowed their careers, taking jobs that did not demand long hours and travel or transferred to more flexible jobs to care for their children. Reluctant to leave the stable state sector, fewer moved over to private sector jobs. For instance, a couple, both engineers, grew up in large peasant households and met when both were assigned to the same factory in Beijing, far from their families. The wife recalled,

> Both of us needed to work and no one helped us to take care of our child, so I shifted to teach in a secondary technical school. Because there were winter and summer holidays, it was more convenient for me to look after a child. I didn't totally give up my major, but used it just in a supplementary way.

Education was another example; many had further training after they had married, including all the PhDs (four men, one woman). While their husbands returned to school, wives maintained the family, enabling their husbands to have both a family and career. Nevertheless, wives still continued their careers.

Wives quit their formal employment entirely and cared for their children in only three cases. However, working from home, they continued to use their professional skills in the private market. For instance, one woman quit her engineering job when one of her twin sons fell and broke his arm. She traded stocks from home, while caring for her toddlers.

Institutional Care

A minority of our respondents that used state day-care facilities for very young infants and toddlers did so when there were no kin available.

School was often strict, instilling moral training, and requiring much independence. Parents wanted their children to have intimacy and personal care. Moreover, they did not want to deny the older generation the chance to care for a grandchild. Hence, most placed their children in formal childcare institutions only after they were three or older.

Few women were on their own while caring for their children. The majority drew on their social capital. They expected to work, and their kin expected to help them work as a boost to the family earnings and future. Most got help from their personal relations or others connected through them. Past that, they could draw on the state-run crèches for childcare. By supplementing kin support with their own work and scaling back on their demanding jobs, they carried work and family responsibilities first sequentially, then simultaneously.

Social Support for Work–Family Roles in Canada

From positions of relative gender equality, where they were embedded in structures that backed their careers and family roles, wives have trouble gaining professional acknowledgment abroad. They have to get Canadian professional certification, which in several cases entails doing most of the education they have over again. They also bear much of the family responsibilities. No longer in a sequential stage as in China, if they have young children to care for, they have heavy simultaneous roles. Although their kin relations are far away, building supportive social networks for their reproductive roles is central to their career edifice, and it is their double burden.

Their Experiences as New Immigrants in Canada

Foreign-earned credentials are rarely recognized by Canadian organizations. Few immigrants locate well-paying jobs, and most revise their career goals (Spitze, 1984; Basran and Zong, 1998; Salaff, Greve, and Xu, 2002). Eighty-four of our 100 respondents have experienced downward mobility compared to their position in China.

With their professional credentials and experiences unrecognized, they need to retrain. Their choice is dyadic, both parents' skills need upgrading, both are responsible for their child and need to combine their household resources. Couples decide whether both should try to break into the labour force at the same time, each carrying simultaneous roles, caring for their children, working, and retraining. Or should they negotiate a sequential life course—going to school full-time, finding alternative care for their child, and then getting a suitable job?

By engaging in sequential roles in turn, one spouse works full-time, even at a minimum wage job, to support the family while the other returns to school to upgrade the credentials needed to adapt to the local labour market. They then switch. When the wife's English proficiency is better than her husband's and the job she seeks does not need long-term re-accreditation, she may be the first to try. If her English is worse and she has trouble fitting her technical and professional job experiences into the acceptable Canadian jobs for women, she waits. Most working parents compromise by scaling back, reducing their goals, changing jobs slowly, finding help where they can, and building new relationships in Canada—turning acquaintances into multiplex relations (Hochschild, 1990).

Most commonly, the wife's career is placed second. Without a way to care for a child, longer to go to upgrade her degree, wives are more likely to work at low-paying jobs. They shape their job search around their responsibilities to the home and hence their child's age figures in the couples' plans. To suit their family roles, those with young children take short-term, English as a Second Language (ESL) courses (a non-degree program) while their children are at school. Short-term accounting courses improve their skills and get them entry-level jobs. By going to school part-time, women combine homemaking, reproductive labour, and job preparation.

Lian (F), a former accountant, weaves her ESL study with her son's primary school hours:

How many hours do I study at school? Everyday I send my son to school at 8:30, then I go to my school from 9:15 am till 2:45 pm. When I get home, I study 10–20 minutes, then I go to pick up my son.

Developing New Supports

Those with young children share their childcare responsibilities with kin, friends, and neighbours. Migration has not severed their family relations (Boyd, 1989), and kin are the most important support for those that are upgrading their skills. Just under half had children who were born since 1993 (and are under age 10 at time of writing). Of these, 63 per cent receive care for their children from kin, a proportion close to that in China. The child's grandparents immigrate or apply for shorter-term visitors' visas to help. Parents send infants and toddlers back to China to be reared by their grandparents. Parents plan for the children to remain in China for the two years they need to take courses to re-certify in professional fields, fetching the youngster back in time to enroll in primary school in Toronto.

Immigrant mothers also mobilize friends for backup care. Former colleagues have an established base for trust. They meet others, in their course of every day life, who are embedded in similar networks and share a common background, which conveys cultural similarity. These form the new multiplex networks.

Wei Yang (F) has her new roommate as backup support for her 10-year-old daughter. Although in China she was a major in Chinese literature and is a former Vice-Principal of a high school, Wei Yang cannot get a similar job in Canada. Her husband is an 'astronaut' who manages his computer sales business in Beijing. He visits several times a year, leaving childcare entirely to the wife. A virtual sole parent, Wei Yang is reluctant to return to school or take a demanding full-time job. She first tutored her daughter and other youngsters part-time in Chinese, as a service to the Chinese community. She next sold products part-time in a multilevel marketing position. Wei Yang finally found full-time work at a Chinese job agency, as a receptionist. Her daughter, now accustomed to Toronto, walks to the nearby primary school on her own. Wei Yang's family sublets a room of a two-bedroom high-rise flat from another Chinese immigrant woman, with a daughter of the same age. Her roommate watches out for Wei Yang's child after school. Unlikely to regain a supervisory position at the level she had left in China, Wei Yang works with what is available in a Chinese environment, turning to sales and service work in the Chinese community. She finds social capital from her Chinese roommate: at age 10, her child does not need a lot of care, and her roommate helps out when needed.

Ying Ying (F) took up an invitation to live temporarily at a friend's that turned into a longer-term responsibility.

Our first summer in Toronto, my husband's friend—whose wife was still in China—invited us to stay at their place (we had just arrived and had no place to live). After a few days, their son got chicken pox. My son got it, too. So the whole summer I was busy taking care of the two boys.

Although it is part of their social capital, they cannot turn to friends for the even longer-term support needed to return to school to re-qualify for professional positions. In this manner, neighbours stand in for each other and become social capital. Many negotiate exchanges with neighbours for routine help, such as when women with a neighbour with the same aged toddler share childcare. Neighbours are also likely to give emergency help. But there are limits to what friends and neighbours can and are willing to do on a long-term basis.

Children's Roles

Children play a role in the family restructuring as well. Some parents send their child to be cared for by its grandparents. Others give up the hope for a professional job for reinvented motherhood. In the end, their children grow up quickly and help the parents.

No longer part of an on-site, three-generational household, without additional family help, mothers bear considerable household burdens (Clarkberg and Moen, 2001). Parents demand a lot from their children, justifying coming abroad as a benefit for the youngsters. Their children take on an immigration burden, becoming independent, working

hard, and assuming the reason for having left China. Children care for themselves and the family more than they had done in China. Teenagers get their first part-time jobs and they help out in the family business. They study hard; several parents proudly informed us that their child had gotten into the gifted primary school program. Older children were accepted into universities with scholarships.

A few examples show how children manage on their own. Wei Yang's (F) younger daughter goes to the neighbourhood school on her own. Ying Ying's (F) teenage son makes his own lunch in the microwave. On his summer holiday from his computer engineering studies, Jiang Jing's (M) son works in a factory and fills in the family store in the evenings.

Q: You work at the same shift as your husband, so what about your daughter?

Lei Min   (*F; with demonstrable pride*): We prepare dinner for her and bring our dinner to work. She can take care of herself. She's very independent. My husband said he didn't shed a sad tear over the hard life here, but when I told him that she got second in her class during the first semester although her English was still not so good, his happy tears mixed with the sweat of his labouring job.

When Lei Min opened a hostel for new immigrants in her home, her 14-year-old daughter spent the summer greeting guests.

Intensifying Family Roles

Some women find new family roles. In contrast to China, where bearing a second child was politically damaging for those with high standing, in Canada, two children are 'natural'. Six of the couples had a second child in Canada. Nearly all with a second child had first borne a daughter.

Hen Rong (F), a former accountant in China, became a textile labourer in Toronto. Becoming pregnant, her kin and friends pressured the couple to give birth to the second child. 'This is your last chance,' her mother admonished her pregnant daughter. Her mother had cared for the couple's eldest daughter, and the couple sponsored her to immigrate. The older woman beamed as she toted the baby boy around.

A former pharmacist, now a sales clerk, justified her second pregnancy by what she saw around her, she said, 'We see Canadians around us having a child, and so decided it was natural.' Unable to resume her profession, she finds a new role in intensified motherhood. Her church members celebrated the pregnancy with showers and gifts.

The second child not only meets a long cherished value of bearing a son for the family. The newborn turns an aborted career, with a confusing prognosis, into the respected career of motherhood. None of the new mothers re-established their careers. Without childcare support in the new location, gender roles may become entrenched (Willis and Yeoh, 2000; Lee, Chan, Bradby, and Green, 2002).

Discussion

Transnational migration affects women and men in gender-specific ways and places a heavier load of responsibility on women's shoulders. This occurs both in the home and in the host countries, but migration makes this integration work difficult. Women assume more work because they undertake the meshing of work and family systems. Taken-for-granted work institutions, retirement schemes, and formal and informal childcare are rarely well integrated. When they do not easily come together, women's personal actions make these arrangements run in an expected manner. Women must organize support that requires creative reorganization of their social capital, under the new conditions.

Because work and family institutions are organized differently in every country, when catapulted into the new social system, new immigrants' experiences conflict in timing of work and family life courses. In China, professionals completed training before bearing and rearing children, following the sequential life course model. Most drew on multiplex ties to make work–family obligations function while they built their careers. They also obtained public institutional support for childcare, thus lessening the many activities they had to do simultaneously.

Arriving as professionals in Canada, where their qualifications are not recognized, with small children to care for and a household to run, they have heavy burdens. They must both re-qualify and mobilize support for their family roles at the same time. The formal and informal institutions, and personally constructed arrangements that provide childcare support, differ from those in China. When the social arrangements in Canada do not match their needs, women either leave the labour force or call on previous agreements, turning to their multiplex arrangements. They may bring their parents to Canada or send their children to China. For many, social capital is transnational.

Transnational motherhood is not limited to the working-class poor but also is known by middle-class, highly educated Chinese. Professional, career-oriented Chinese immigrants command a future promise of good resources and earnings for their wider families if they get support. They bring their mothers and mothers-in-law or send their children back to China. For some women, this support lets them reconstitute their careers. Others suffer considerable downward professional mobility. Transnational social capital facilitates but does not guarantee a rejuvenated career.

Work–family role conflicts are public issues needing institutional solutions, but few countries define them this way (Mills, 1957; Folbre, 2001). Societies rarely acknowledge the informal work that people do to mesh institutional structures. People draw on personal relations to resolve inconsistent demands. The plight of international migrants outlines the problems encountered in using personal solutions to meet public issues.

Note

1. We acknowledge gratefully the support of the 'migration from China' project by The Social Sciences and Humanities Council of Canada.

Several centres provided generous homes for our research team. The Centre for Urban and Community Studies, University of Toronto,

The Centre for Asian Studies, The University of Hong Kong provided us with helpful support. We wish to thank Stephanie Tang and staff of the CICS for their unstinting help, the many people who generously shared their views and experiences with us. Lynn Xu, Su Zhang, Yan Liu, Ada Choi, Tracy Kennedy, He Huang, and Heather Jiang supplied talented research assistance for this paper. Eleonore Kofinan, Evie Tastsoglou, and an anonymous reader for Women's Studies International Forum gave helpful suggestions.

References

Basran, G.S., and L. Zong. 1998. 'Devaluation of Foreign Credentials as Perceived by Visible Minority Professional Immigrants', *Canadian Ethnic Studies* 30, 3: 7–23.

Bian, Y. 1994. *Work and Inequality in Urban China*. New York: SUNY Press.

Boyd, M. 1989. 'Family and Personal Networks in International Migration: Recent Developments and New Agendas', *International Migration Review* 23: 638–70.

Buchmann, M., and M. Charles. 1995. 'Organizational and Institutional in the Process of Gender Stratification: Comparing Social Arrangements in Six European Countries', *International Journal of Sociology* 25: 66–95.

Burt, R.S. 1992. *Structural Holes*. Cambridge, MA: Harvard University Press.

Castells, M. 1989. *The Informational City*. Oxford, UK: Blackwell.

Chen, F., S.E. Short, and B. Entwisle. 2000. 'The Impact of Grandparental Proximity on Maternal Childcare in China', *Population Research and Policy Review* 19: 571–90.

Clarkberg, M., and P. Moen. 2001. 'Understanding the Time-squeeze: Married Couples' Preferred and Actual Work-hour Strategies', *American Behavioral Scientist* 44: 1115–136.

Croll, E., P. Kane, and D. Davin, eds. 1985. *Chinas One Child Family Policy*. London: Macmillan.

Davis, D. 1993. 'Financial Security of Urban Retirees', *Journal of Cross-cultural Gerontology* 8: 179–95.

Delechat, C. 2001. 'International Migration Dynamics: The Role of Experience and Social Networks', *Labour* 15: 457–86.

Doherty, G., R. Rose, M. Friendly, D. Lero, and S. Hope. 1995. *Childcare: Canada Can't Work without It*. Toronto: Irwin.

Folbre, N. 2001. *The Invisible Heart: Economics and Family Values*. New York: The New Press.

Gerson, K. 1985. *Hard Choices: How Women Decide about Work, Career, and Motherhood*. Berkeley, CA: University of California Press.

Giele, J.Z. 1998. 'Innovation in the Typical Life Course', in G.H. Elder and J. Giele, eds., *Methods of Life Course Research: Qualitative and Quantitative Approaches*, pp. 231–63. Thousand Oaks, CA: Sage Publications.

Ginzberg, E. 1967. *Life Styles of Educated Women*. New York: Columbia University Press.

Gold, S.J. 2001. 'Gender, Class, and Network: Social Structure and Migration Patterns among Transnational Israelis', *Global Networks* 1: 57–78.

Heinz, W.R., H. Kruger, and A. Verma, eds. 2001. *Restructuring Work and the Life Course*. Toronto: University of Toronto Press.

Hochschild, A.R. 1990. *The Second Shift*. New York: Avon.

Hondagneu-Sotelo, P., and E. Avila. 1997. '"I'm here, but I'm there": The Meanings of Latina Transnational Motherhood', *Gender and Society* 2: 548–71.

Jones, C.L., L. Marsden, and L. Tepperman. 1990. *Lives of Their Own: The Individualization of Women's Lives*. Don Mills, ON: Oxford University Press.

Lee, M., A. Chan, H. Bradby, and G. Green. 2002. 'Chinese Migrant Women and Families in Britain', *Women's Studies International Forum* 25: 607–18.

Levitt, P., and N.G. Schiller. 2003. *Transnational Perspectives on Migration: Conceptualizing Simultaneity*. CMD Working Paper #03-09j. The Center for Migration and Migration and Development Working Paper Series. Princeton, NJ: Princeton University.

Liang, Z. 2001. 'Demography of Illicit Migration from China: A Sending Country's Perspective', *Sociological Forum* 16: 677–701.

Lin, N., W.M. Ensel, and J.C. Vaughn. 1981. 'Social Resources and the Strength of Weak Ties: Structural Factors in Occupational Status Attainment', *American Sociological Review* 46: 393–405.

Man, G. 2002. 'Globalization and the Erosion of the Welfare State: Effects on Chinese Immigrant Women', *Canadian Woman Studies* 21/22, 4/1: 26–32.

Meng, X., and M.P. Kidd. 1997. 'Labor Market Reform and the Changing Structure of Wage Determination in China's State Sector during the 1980s', *Journal of Comparative Economics* 25: 403–21.

Mills, C.W. 1957. *The Sociological Imagination*. New York: Oxford University Press.

Min, P.G. 1988. *Ethnic Business Enterprise: Korean Small Business in Atlanta*. New York: Center for Migration Studies.

Moen, P., and F.M. Firebaugh. 1994. 'Family Policies and Effective Families: A Life Course Perspective', *The International Journal of Sociology and Social Policy* 14: 29–52.

Moen, P., and Y. Yu. 1999. 'Having it All: Overall Work/Life Success in Two-earner Families', *Research in the Sociology of Work* 7: 109–39.

Nee, V., and R. Matthews. 1996. 'Market Transition and Societal Transformation in Reforming State Socialism', *Annual Review of Sociology* 22: 401–35.

Ngo, H. 2000. 'Trends in Occupational Sex Segregation in Urban China'. Paper delivered at the annual meeting of the NACSA, Washington, DC.

Parrenas, R.S. 2001. 'Mothering from a Distance: Emotions, Gender, and Inter-generational Relations in Filipino Transnational Families', *Feminist Studies* 27: 361–90.

Partridge, M. In press. *Managing the Struggle: Career Strategies of University-educated Women*. Toronto: University of Toronto Press.

Poros, M.V. 2001. 'The Role of Migrant Networks in Linking Local Labour Markets: The Case of Asian Indian Migration to New York and London', *Global Networks* 1: 243–59.

Portes, A., and J. Borocz. 1989. 'Contemporary Immigration: Theoretical Perspectives on Its Determinants and Modes of Incorporation', *International Migration Review* 23: 606–30.

Preston, V., and G. Man. 1999. 'Employment Experiences of Chinese Immigrant Women: An Exploration of Diversity', *Canadian Woman Studies* 19, 3: 115–22.

Robinson, J.C. 1985. 'Of Women and Washing Machines: Employment, Housework, and the Reproduction of Motherhood in Socialist China', *The China Quarterly* 101: 32–57.

Salaff, J.W., A. Greve, and L. Xu. 2002. 'Paths into the Economy: Structural Barriers and the Job Hunt for Professional PRC Migrants in Canada', *International Journal of Human Resource Management* 13: 450–64.

Sassen, S. 1991. *The Global City: New York, London, and Tokyo*. Princeton, NJ: Princeton University Press.

Spitze, G. 1984. 'The Effect of Family Migration on Wives' Employment: How Long Does it Last?', *Social Science Quarterly* 46: 21–36.

Statistics Canada. 2001. *Facts and Figures: Immigration Overview 2001*. Available at www.cic.gc.ca./english/pdf/pub/facts2001.pdf (accessed 22 September 2002).

Vanier Institute of the Family. 2000. *Profiling Canada's Families: II*. Ottawa. Available at www.vifamily.calpubs/p2.htm (accessed 22 September 2002).

Walder, A.G. 1986. *Communist Neo-traditionalism: Work and Authority in Chinese Industry*. Berkeley, CA: University of California Press.

Whyte, M.K., and W.L. Parish. 1984. *Urban Life in Contemporary China*. Chicago: University of Chicago Press.

Willis, K., and B. Yeoh. 2000. 'Gender and Transnational Household Strategies: Singaporean Migration to China', *Regional Studies* 34: 253–64.

Yang, H. 1996. 'The Distributive Norm of Monetary Support to Older Parents: A Look at a Township in China', *Journal of Marriage and the Family* 58: 404–14.

Zhan, H.J., and R.J.V. Montgomery. 2003. 'Gender and Elder Care in China: The Influence of Filial Piety and Structural Constraints', *Gender and Society* 17: 209–29.

CHAPTER 18

Situating 'Home' at the Nexus of Public and Private Spheres: Aging, Gender, and Home Support Work in Canada

Anne Martin-Matthews

Introduction

This article considers issues of gender in the relationship between elderly clients and home support workers and in the triangulated relationship between an old person, their family member(s) and home support workers.

Home Care and Home Support Work in Canada

In recent decades, Canada's health care system, like that of much of the world, has embraced the concept of community and home care (Shapiro, 2002, 2003). The transition from hospital and institution-based care for both post-acute and chronic health conditions has involved 'sending care closer to home' (Armstrong and Armstrong, 2004: 21–3), making relatively routine the proffering of a public service in a private place.

It is estimated that one million people in Canada use home care services annually (Shapiro, 2002). Several distinct groups of workers are included under the heading of home care workers. Many have professional training and qualifications as nurses, care managers, physiotherapists, occupational therapists and social workers. However, most home care workers are 'unregulated workers' who provide non-professional services in the form of personal assistance with daily activities, such as bathing, dressing, grooming and light household tasks that help to maintain a safe and supportive home. They are variously known across Canada as home support workers, personal care workers, home helps and, until recently, 'homemakers'.

These workers are the focus of this article, and are referred to as home support workers throughout.

The estimated 32,000 home support workers in Canada in 2001 provided approximately 70–80 percent of home care needs, including both personal care (bathing, toileting) and instrumental needs (food preparation, laundry). Despite ongoing problems with low pay, little or no job progression, lack of pay for travel time between clients and often unpredictable hours of work, home support workers in Canada average eight to nine years of employment in this sector (The Home Care Sector Study Corporation, 2003).

Home Care Research and Family Biography

In the 1990s, I conducted research through four home support agencies in rural and small-town Ontario, Canada.

However, in 1999, my research interest in home support workers shifted dramatically when home care became part of my family biography. With my mother's experience of a debilitating stroke, and the building of a new home to accommodate her new life as a person with left side flaccid paralysis, confined to a wheelchair and dependent on others for all her physical needs, home care workers entered my family life. My mother receives home care services up to 30 hours a week, every week of the year—supplementing the care provided also at home by my father and two sisters (one co-residing, one living nearby) and, periodically, as distance permits, my brothers and me. I live 3000 miles away on the opposite coast of Canada.

Throughout a six-year biography that now includes the community-based health care service that I had previously studied, I have reflected anew on the research questions and issues relevant to an understanding of home as the site of care work, both paid and unpaid. I have had many private conversations with a succession of home support workers about their training, their motivations for employment in this sector, the challenges and rewards of their work and their concerns as women and as workers. I have listened to my mother grapple with how to approach these strangers who attend to her in the most intimate settings. I have heard my father lament the loss of autonomy in his own home and its 'invasion' by a succession of women employed to care. I have spent countless hours talking with my sisters about how to manage the home care situation, the turnover of workers, their variation in abilities and the impact of their personalities on the home life experience of my parents and others in my family. I have also had the experience of making telephone calls to 'home', and having a home support worker answer the call. With this stranger (to me) then telling me about how *my* family members are doing, at such times I have thought to myself: who *is* this person?

In this process, the focus of my research enquiries has changed. I now have new lenses with which to look again at my own data, at those earlier studies I conducted. Looking now with the lens of autobiography and personal experience.

Through these new lenses, my focus has shifted to explore the meaning of home as the site of care, not just as a physical structure but also as a complex symbolic concept. Looked at in this way, the data reveal issues of possession and control of the territory of home, giving rise to concerns about boundaries and spatial familiarity and attendant efforts to make sense of the 'stranger' in private places. Issues of gendered care and gendered space emerge as important to this focus. The context and frame for these enquiries is the recognition of home care as situated at the intersections of the public and private spheres and of paid and unpaid labour (Martin-Matthews and Phillips, 2003).

A Focus on Home and the Lens of Gender

A unique aspect of home care is that the workplace of the care provider is the home of the care recipient. While the implications of locale are rarely noted in texts about home care in the health and medical sciences or even in policy discussions of home and community-based services, sociology and social geography understand the significance of the locus of activity. In the context of postmodernity, Giddens argues that 'locales are thoroughly penetrated by and shaped in terms of social influences quite distant from them. What structures the locale is not simply that which is present on the scene; the "visible form" of the locale conceals the distanciated relations which determine its nature' (Giddens, 1991: 18–19). With home care now dominating my family biography, I have observed how the penetration into the place of 'home' of public policies as interpreted by local health authorities, agencies and case managers, occurs through the behaviours and practices of home care workers whose work locale is the client's home. The offering of a public service in private space exemplifies these distanciated relations that determine the nature of home care from the perspective of the older person.

Although the interpersonal dimension of home involves social interaction within and across its physical boundaries, the concepts of privacy and familiarity are inherently part of what home means: 'a haven and place of order, "insideness" and belonging' (Dill, 1991:230). My approach has also been informed by interpretations of home as a refuge from the outside world, 'a place where one can control the level of social interaction, and a place for privacy and independence' (Després, 1991: 98).

Methods

First, interviews were conducted with home care workers and their elderly clients in Ontario, Canada, at two points in time in the 1990s, 12–18 months apart. The study involved 150 home care workers interviewed in Phase I, with 137 of them reinterviewed in Phase II. Of these 137 women, 33 were no longer employed in home support at the second interview, but were included in the study because of their insights into retention issues in home care employment. Second, 155 elderly clients of home care services were interviewed in Phase I, with 118 of them interviewed again in Phase II (14 of these 118 were former clients of home care services by the time of the second interview). These home care clients ranged in age from 57 to 95 years, with an average age of 78 years. They had lived in their present community for an average of 35 years and had been receiving home care services from one month to eight years.

Third, as part of the thesis research project of a graduate student, interviews were conducted with 39 adult children identified as primary caregivers to an elderly parent who had participated in the home care client interviews (von Hof, 1991). There were 26 daughters, 7 daughters-in-law and 6 sons in that study, ranging in age from 23 to 63, with an average age of 51 years.

Finally, data are drawn from participant observation and field notes collected in Newfoundland, Canada, in interactions and meetings with home support workers, case managers, elderly home care recipients and family members. The analysis is also informed by meetings with individual home care supervisors and agencies as part of a project currently being launched in British Columbia, Canada (www.nexushomecare.arts.ubc.ca).

Gender is relevant to these analyses in a number of ways that are both implicit and explicit. It is implicit in terms of the context of home support services delivery, since all the case managers, agency personnel and home support workers participating in these studies are women. Gender is therefore difficult to interrogate in this context largely because it is so overwhelmingly *assumed* that women deliver these services. In the accounts of the clients of these services, gender is relevant because, as Twigg (2004: 65) notes, 'deep old age is predominantly female'. Reflecting this, 77 per cent of the elderly clients were women. Most of these women (58 per cent) were widowed and had lived alone an average of 14 years. Among the men, all but two were married and co-resided with their wives.

Home as the Site of Care: The Meaning of Place and Space

Perspectives of Elderly Clients: Boundary Control and the Significance of Home

Three broad themes were identified by elderly clients in their references to home as the site of care: issues of territory and boundary; control and co-operation; and the symbolic significance of home.

Issues of territory and boundary were typically expressed in terms of the necessity of bringing 'strangers' into one's own home, giving over one's privacy and sharing of the physical place:

> I think homemakers are a wonderful idea. I know my family wouldn't want to be bothered by this—having strangers around their home for hours every week—but they haven't been laid up as much as I have. (Woman, age 80, home care received seven years)

Control and co-operation also emerged as themes. Reflecting Russell's observations (in this issue) about gender differences in the meaning of home as a 'psychosocial bastion', it is notable that none of the comments concerning this issue is made by men, even though men constitute 23 per cent of the respondents in the study of elderly clients of home support services:

> The lack of privacy [does bother me]. I had two homemakers who eavesdropped every time the phone rang. (Woman, age 57, home care received two years)

For many elderly home care clients, however, there is a trade-off: by having someone come into their own home to work, they are enabled to remain in their home for longer than they would otherwise. Issues of boundary, territory, control and co-operation are dealt with in this larger context:

> Having a homemaker helps keep people in their own homes. It's worth it—the training new people, the constant revolving door with new people coming into my home and my having to explain everything to each one all over again. I

don't like that, but I know what the alternative is. (Woman, age 79, home care received three years)

As the literature on home as a haven indicates, there are dimensions of inside- and outside-ness in individual accounts of having individuals come 'into' the private space of home. Although some women did comment on what the home support workers bring into the home from 'outside', it is noteworthy that the two men who were solitary inhabitants of their homes both mentioned this:

They are cheerful. They are pleasant when they come in. They tell me what is happening outside. They go ahead and do the work. (Man, age 69, receiving home care for three years)

The theme of the symbolic significance of and attachment to home is also evident in the accounts of many elderly home care clients. It is particularly notable when these individuals speak positively about their home support worker: the highest praise for the labour of home support workers invokes the language of pride of place and 'home'. However, none of the men made reference to this:

She does everything she can to make me comfortable. . . . Mary is a very devoted person. It is like her own home, she takes very good care of it. (Woman, age 75, home care received one-and-a-half years)

In these accounts, issues of boundary, territory, and sharing of physical space with a home support worker were more frequently expressed as problematic by older women than by men. For men, references to space and place were not framed in terms of privacy and control, but rather in terms of what home support workers were able to bring into the home from the outside world.

Perspectives of Family Members: Gendered Care and Gendered Space

Among the family members interviewed, the verbatim accounts of adult sons identified the relationship between gendered filial care and the territoriality of certain types of space when home is the site of care. No women (daughters and daughters-in-law) made such comments, and we can speculate that this was because no space within the dwelling is 'off limits' for them in their roles as carers. Just as care is gendered, spatial access within the dwelling is also frequently gendered (particularly in terms of who else is occupying the space at a particular time). In answer to a question about what impact the presence of a home care worker had had on the kind of assistance provided by the adult child, several sons noted this:

It's my mother's house, even though I grew up in it. I haven't been in her bedroom or bathroom for years, not since she needed that personal care. My sisters and the home care women go in there. They do what they need to do to help Mom with that kind of stuff. That's all off-limits to me. Fine with me. I help out with the yard work and the kitchen stuff, like when the fridge breaks. That's my territory. (Son, age 51, mother receiving home care nine years)

My mother's pretty private about herself, and she doesn't get me involved in the personal care. Good thing too. I don't even go near that part of her place, her apartment when she's in there with the worker. Fixed the plumbing in there once, that's all. (Son, age 47, mother receiving home care three years)

These gendered patterns of access to these private spheres within the home reflect the range of care that women, typically, provide to other women. Twigg (2004) has observed that care work is quintessentially gendered work in that it is performed predominantly by women, and constructed around gendered identities. The verbatim accounts of these sons reflect my own observation that because 'bodywork', as described by Twigg (2004), is typically performed by women as home support workers and women as daughters and daughters-in-law, they have differential access (than do men, and especially sons) to those private spheres of the home in which this body work occurs.

Reflecting the findings of earlier studies of the gendered nature of filial care (Campbell and

Martin-Matthews, 2003; Martin-Matthews and Campbell, 1995), sons and sons-in-law largely confined their helping behaviours to the outside, to yard work, and to the more public spaces within the home. By their own accounts, the more private spaces in the dwelling (spaces connected to body work) were not within the sons' realm of activities because they did not (and were not expected to) provide this type of care. In the verbatim accounts from the interviews and in my own participant observations, there were implicit gender taboos about care (especially body work) and of gendered access to private space that were equally self-imposed by female caregivers and the home support workers.

It is clear that there are psychological, social, and emotional boundaries to be negotiated as family members move beyond the give-and-take of 'typical' family relationships over the life course, to assume responsibilities that are defined as 'caregiving'. So too are there physical boundaries—and access to physical spaces imbued with meaning—to be negotiated (and renegotiated) within families. When home is the site of care, new boundaries may emerge within domestic spaces; these boundaries reflect a system of (gendered) meanings about spaces within the household and private spaces within the home.

Home as the Site of Care: Negotiating (Contingent) Relationships

Home as the site of care is about more than the meaning of and utilization of space. Analyses of the verbatim accounts of older home care clients, home support workers and family members identified other issues: the definition of the worker–client relationship; its contingent nature; issues of isolation, security, and constraints when home is the site of care; and blurring the boundaries of paid/unpaid and trained labour. Issues of gender figure in a number of these accounts.

Perspectives of Elderly Clients: Friendship and the Boundaries of Paid Labour

In the interviews with elderly clients, they were asked whether they saw the home support worker as an employee, as a friend, or as some combination

of both. Fully 39 per cent considered the home support worker to be primarily a friend; 18 per cent as an employee; 27 per cent as both employee and friend; 3 per cent 'like family'; 6 per cent indicated all three; and 6 per cent identified, at least one of their home support workers as both a friend and 'like family'. The men receiving services were significantly more likely to consider the home support worker as an employee and no men saw her primarily as a friend (although several noted that she was a 'friend' to their wives). However, several men used the language of a family tie in describing their home support worker, describing her as 'like my own daughter' (man, age 85, receiving home care for two years). Nevertheless, for the majority of male clients, interaction with the home support worker was mediated by their wives.

Among elderly women who described their home care worker either as a friend or a combination of employee and friend, there were issues to be negotiated in the interaction however. Some were more equivocal than others:

> It depends on the day. Most of the time we get along, and I call her Jody. But some days, I want to let her know to keep her distance and I call her by her married name, Mrs S___. I depend on her, so what else can I do to let her know that she's in my house and some days I just need . . . my space, I suppose. (Woman, age 77, receiving home care six years)

Others were clear as to the nature of the relationship as outside the bounds of friendship:

> I like her enough. She's good to me, and kind, and she works hard. But she's not the sort of person I would choose as a friend, to go on an outing with, that sort of thing. (Woman, age 76, receiving home care five years)

For others, an awareness of the power differential between the dependent client and the worker characterized the relationship:

> She's always eager to go rushing out the door. I'm not as important to her as other things in

her life. (Woman, age 76, receiving home care one year)

For elderly clients, therefore, the relationship between home support workers and the client is a complex one. The presence of a stranger in the household is frequently made sense of through a refraining to the language of friendship or fictive kin. But, nevertheless, there are frequent reminders of the limits of this refraining, especially when workers rotate and the paid work period ends.

Perspectives of Home Support Workers: Couple and Gender Dynamics

Among the elderly clients interviewed, in only 15 per cent of the households were the husband and wife both clients of home care services, whereas home support workers had many situations where a client and a non-client spouse or family member co-resided. When home is the site of care, the relationship between the client and the home support worker is highly contingent on the dynamic between the couple, and between the home support worker and the non-client spouse. Gender factored into these relationships. In the verbatim accounts of the home support workers, the only references to difficult relations with non-client spouses involved the husbands of female clients:

I had to leave one couple. He screamed at me while I was washing her hair; said I'd pushed her, which was just not true. I'd had to intervene several times during a fight between the husband and wife. The husband interfered with everything I did, said I used too much water doing laundry. There was no pleasing him. I asked to be relieved. (Woman, age 43, employed in home care three-and-a-half years)

However, male clients were not uniformly viewed as more difficult. For example, one worker noted that 'Men are easier to please. They usually appreciate what you do for them' (woman, age 37, employed in home care four years).

The non-client spouse or co-resident family member plays a pivotal role in the contingent relationship between the client and the home support

worker. While agencies may see the non-client co-resider as essentially 'neutral' in the delivery of services to the client, in practice (and in my own experience as participant observer) the non-client plays a role within the home that home support workers find facilitating, hindering or ambivalent:

I don't know what I would do if Mrs M___ wasn't there to help me cajole him into the bath tub and to let me do the bathing of him. She jollies him too when he's out of sorts. Makes a real difference to my day. It helps me get the job done in the time it's supposed to take. (Woman, age 41, employed in home care nine years)

Other family members who were not co-resident also influenced both the nature of the care work and the relationship between the client and home support worker:

It really bothers me when sometimes Mrs R___ asks me to do some extra cooking or washing and I know it is not for her, it's for her daughter who's having company over or something, or needs an extra hand with the laundry. (Woman, age 47, employed in home care three years)

Home support workers spoke at length about their relationships with their elderly clients, identifying a range of issues reflecting care and concern for clients, and a keen sense of the contingent nature of the relationship:

You get so attached to these elderly people. It will kill me when this dear old lady I am caring for dies. (Woman, age 46, employed in home care two years)

Other workers see their relationship extending beyond the elderly client to include a role in bridging between the elder and his or her kin:

I inform the children . . . you act as a liaison officer or a colleague between the person you're caring for and their relatives. Some relatives really appreciate it. (Woman, age 55, employed in home care two years)

However, others invoke the language of space and territory, in proceeding more cautiously in relation to family members:

> You're in their home, and their sphere, so knowing your place is an issue sometimes. With one client, . . . I felt she should be in a nursing home because the family just kept her in a chair in front of the TV. When I bathed her, she was so frail (bones cracking), etc. But the home support worker is not to advise the family caregiver that it's time to place their parent in a nursing home. It's a difficult situation. I know that she needs better care. (Woman, age 40, employed in home care five years)

Perspectives of Home Support Workers: Boundaries of Labour and Training

In the interviews, a quarter of the elderly clients reported contact with their home support worker outside the worker's official hours of employment. Most of this interaction took place as social visits or outings. The remainder were for a variety of reasons: when they wanted the worker to pick up groceries for them; to ask the worker for transportation; and, on occasion, when the worker phoned the client to check on the client's health:

> The cutback in hours is a problem. I know she needs more help than she's getting. She relies on me. So sometimes I go back on weekends on my own, and run errands for her. This puts me in a dilemma because if the agency knew . . . and my husband thinks I'm just being taken advantage of . . . but what am I to do, if she's got no one else to do it? (Woman, age 47, employed in home care seven years)

Home support workers in Canada contribute an average of 2.6 hours of unpaid work per week (The Home Care Sector Study Corporation, 2003). While this assistance may be voluntarily given, these personal arrangements may also be exploitative for either the provider or the recipient, especially if there are no other options (Armstrong and Armstrong, 2004). Issues of gender are implicit in the clients' accounts of these unpaid contributions by women who are 'really nice girls' who 'treat me like their mother'. For some clients, this includes expectations of nurturing assistance beyond the hours of paid care. However, gender-based assumptions and values were also reflected in the comments of home support workers as well.

> It disturbs me when a client with a capable daughter is receiving services. (Woman, age 41, employed in home care four years)

For home support workers, the negotiation of relationships in the home thus included a broad array of issues, from couple and gender dynamics, to agency policies and guidelines, to concerns about safety and isolation, to the blurring of the boundaries between paid and unpaid labour.

Perspectives of Family Members: Supplementing Care and Training Workers

When family members made explicit reference to the impact of home care workers on their parent's lives or on their own, it was to extol the benefits of home care in terms of how it facilitated their ability to continue in employment themselves, or to note how it had improved their own relationship with their parent and more positively focus the time they spent together:

> When I don't have to worry about basic home living for my elderly relatives, more time can be spent with them giving moral and emotional support. (Daughter, age 42, parents receiving home care two years)

> Home care allowed my wife to provide emotional support rather than be a full-time cook and housekeeper. (Man, aged 79, receiving home care three years)

In the blurring of boundaries between the public and the private sphere, 'women who are paid carers may find themselves teaching women, in minutes, how to do what took them years of training to learn, making it more difficult to distinguish both the work and the workers' (Armstrong and Armstrong, 2004: 27). There was certainly evidence of this in the accounts of family members as they described, for example, being taught to insert a catheter, so that they could, as unpaid carers, assist with a medical procedure previously done by trained professionals.

Several home support workers acknowledged the vital role of family members in 'training' them to provide better care. Most instances of informal carers providing such 'training' were reported in terms of wives and daughters demonstrating to the home support worker their skills in knowing how to work with the client. However, husbands too showed the workers how their wives liked to be helped to walk, or have their food cut and served. Thus, in cases where formal training is inadequate to the task, or where it requires idiosyncratic knowledge of the client or environment, the unpaid and 'informal' (typically female) carer or family member may train the paid 'formal' carer. In the context of care in the home, the blurring of the public and private spheres of responsibility takes many forms.

Summary and Conclusions

This article has discussed a variety of ways in which home care workers are positioned at the centre of a web of contacts bridging the private world of family, providing care to an old person and the public world of services (care, health, welfare benefits). Working at the 'unregulated' end of the home care continuum, these women are poorly paid, have minimal training and their labours are largely invisible in the context of public discourse about home care.

The qualitative data informing this article are derived from verbatim accounts of home support workers, elderly clients and family members of clients as they describe the context of 'home' as the site of care. Home support workers identified as problematic, the balancing of agency guidelines and the unmet needs of elderly clients. For elderly clients, a key issue was the negotiation of relationships with successive 'strangers' entering the private sphere of their home. Other elderly clients noted issues of negotiation of longer-term relationships with home support workers as employee and/or friend.

The accounts of workers, clients and family members indicate the particular relevance of gender to the meaning of home, to issues of territory and control, to the relationship between care work (especially body work) and space, and to issues of security and isolation.

In situating home at the nexus of the private and the public spheres, this article has also considered what Giddens (1991) has called the distanciated relations that shape the contingent nature of home support work and of the provider–client interaction within the private sphere of the home. Framed within the context of governmental home care policies and agency guidelines, for elderly clients 'the worker embodies both what the system can and cannot do for them' (Bowdie and Turwoski, 1986: 44). For workers, employer policies and regulations often challenge their ability to address the unmet needs of clients—and may contribute to a blurring of the boundaries between paid and unpaid care work.

The gendered lens of this researcher's autobiography was the catalyst for the conceptualization of home as situated at the nexus of the private and public spheres when home is the site of care. Several of the themes identified, such as the relationship between gendered care and the gendering of space, and the contingent nature of the worker–client relationship, reflect my experience of home care in my family biography.

Caught in the midst of policy debates about the future and funding of home care, there are elders and those who care for them, often struggling to respond to the immediacy of needs in the context of a system down-sizing or in flux. The challenges at the heart of these debates unwittingly enter their lives in the form of case managers, home care professionals and, most typically, poorly paid, educated and often immigrant women employed as home support workers (see Da Roit, this issue, pp. 251–269). The practices and procedures, and rules and regulations forged by governments and implemented by agencies in response to these policy debates enter the most intimate and private spheres of their personal spaces, when community-based care is, in the words of Armstrong and Armstrong (2004), brought 'closer to home'.

Acknowledgments

The author acknowledges the support of a visiting professorship awarded by the British Academy in the writing of this article. Sara Arber provided valuable insights that encouraged a refocusing of this article. I also thank Judith Phillips, Carolyn Rosenthal and especially Joanie Sims-Gould for their helpful and constructive comments and contributions to my thinking about these issues.

References

Armstrong, P. and Armstrong, H. (2004) 'Thinking It Through: Women, Work and Caring in the New Millennium', in K.R. Grant, C. Amaratunga, P. Armstrong, M. Boscoe, A. Pederson and K. Willson (eds.) *Caring For/Caring About: Women, Home Care and Unpaid Caregiving*, pp. 5–43. Aurora, Ontario: Garamond Press.

Aronson, J. (2004) '"Just Fed and Watered": Women's Experiences of the Gutting of Home Care in Ontario', in K.R. Grant, C. Amaratunga, P. Armstrong, M. Boscoe, A. Pederson and K. Willson (eds.) *Caring For/Caring About: Women, Home Care and Unpaid Caregiving*, pp. 167–83. Aurora, Ontario: Garamond Press.

Bowdie, R. and Turwoski, A. (1986) 'The Problems of Providing Services to the Elderly in Their Own Homes', in A.O. Pelham and W.F. Clark (eds.) *Managing Home Care for the Elderly*, pp. 31–46. New York: Springer.

Campbell, L.D. and Martin-Matthews, A. (2003) 'The Gendered Nature of Men's Filial Care', *Journal of Gerontology: Social Sciences* 58B(6): S350–S358.

Després, C. (1991) 'The Meaning of Home: Literature Review and Directions for Future Research and Theoretical Development', *The Journal of Architectural and Planning Research* 8(2): 96–114.

Dill, A.E.P. (1991) 'Transformations of Home: The Formal and Informal Process of Home Care Planning', in J.F. Gubrium and A. Sankar (eds.) *The Home Care Experience: Ethnography and Policy*, pp. 227–51. Newbury Park, CA: Sage.

Giddens, A. (1991) *The Consequences of Modernity*. Cambridge: Polity Press.

Hagestad, G.O. (1996) 'On-Time, Off-Time, Out of Time? Reflections on Continuity and Discontinuity from an Illness Process', in V.L. Bengtson and B. Neugarten (eds.) *Adulthood and Aging: Research on Continuities and Discontinuities*, pp. 204–28. New York: Springer.

Karner, T.X. (1998) 'Professional Caring: Homecare Workers as Fictive Kin', *Journal of Aging Studies* 12(1): 69–82.

Katz, C. and Monk, J. (1993) *Full Circles: Geographies of Women over the Life Course*. London and New York: Routledge.

Martin-Matthews, A. and Campbell, L.D. (1995) 'Gender Roles, Employment and Informal Care', in S. Arber and J. Ginn (eds.) *Connecting Gender and Ageing*, pp. 129–43. Milton Keynes: Open University Press.

Martin-Matthews, A. and Phillips, J.E. (2003) 'Home Care Work in Canada and England: Comparative Perspectives of Home Care Workers on Relationship Issues in the Provision of Home-Based Services to Elderly Persons', paper presented at the annual conference of the Gerontological Society of America, San Diego.

Martin-Matthews, A. and Wakefield, S. (1993) *Report of the Homemaker Services to the Elderly: Provider Characteristics and Client Benefit*. Toronto: Ontario Ministry of Community and Social Services.

Ray, R.E. (1999) 'Researching to Transgress: The Need for Critical Feminism in Gerontology', *Journal of Women and Aging* 11(2/3): 171–84.

Rowles, G. and Chaudury, H. (eds.) (2005) *Home and Identity in Late Life: International Perspectives*. New York: Springer.

Rubenstein, R.L. (1990) 'Culture and Disorder in the Home Care Experience: The Home as Sickroom', in J.F. Gubrium and A. Sankar (eds.) *The Home Care Experience: Ethnography and Policy*, pp. 37–57. Newbury Park, CA: Sage.

Shanas, E. and Sussman, M.B. (1977) *Family, Bureaucracy and the Elderly*. Durham, NC: Duke University Press.

Shapiro, E. (2002) *The Health Care Transition Fund Synthesis Series: Home Care*, Cat. H13–6/2002–2 Ottawa: Minister of Public Works and Government Services Canada; at: www.hc-sc.gc.ca

Shapiro, E. (2003) 'The Romanow Commission Reports and Home Care', *Canadian Journal on Aging* 22(1): 13–17.

The Home Care Sector Study Corporation (2003) *Canadian Home Care Human Resources Study:*

Synthesis Report. Toronto: Home Care Sector Study Corporation; at: www.homecarestudy.ca.

Twigg, J. (2004) 'The Body, Gender and Age: Feminist Insights in Social Gerontology', *Journal of Aging Studies* 18(1): 59–73.

Von Hof, T. (1991) 'Homemaker Services to the Elderly: Impact on Family Caregivers', unpublished MSc. thesis, Department of Family Studies, University of Guelph, Ontario.

CHAPTER 19

Household Labour and the Routine Production of Gender

Scott Coltrane

Motherhood is often perceived as the quintessence of womanhood. The everyday tasks of mothering are taken to be 'natural' expressions of femininity, and the routine care of home and children is seen to provide opportunities for women to express and reaffirm their gendered relation to men and to the world. The traditional tasks of fatherhood, in contrast, are limited to begetting, protecting, and providing for children. While fathers typically derive a gendered sense of self from these activities, their masculinity is even more dependent on *not* doing the things that mothers do. What happens, then, when fathers share with mothers those tasks that we define as expressing the true nature of womanhood?

This chapter describes how a sample of 20 dual-earner couples talk about sharing housework and childcare. Since marriage is one of the least scripted or most undefined interaction situations, the marital conversation is particularly important to a couple's shared sense of reality. I investigate these parents' construction of gender by examining their talk about negotiations over who does what around the house; how these divisions of labour influence their perceptions of self and other; how they conceive of gender-appropriate behaviour; and how they handle inconsistencies between their own views and those of the people around them. Drawing on the parents' accounts of the planning, allocation, and performance of childcare and housework, I illustrate how gender

is produced through everyday practices and how adults are socialized by routine activity.

Gender as an Accomplishment

Candace West and Don Zimmerman (1987) suggest that gender is a routine, methodical, and recurring accomplishment. 'Doing gender' involves a complex of socially guided perceptual, interactional, and micropolitical activities that cast particular pursuits as expressions of masculine and feminine 'natures'. Rather than viewing gender as a property of individuals, West and Zimmerman conceive of it as an emergent feature of social situations that results from and legitimates gender inequality. Similarly, Sarah Fenstermaker Berk (1985: 204, emphasis in original) suggests that housework and child care

> can become the occasion for producing commodities (e.g., clean children, clean laundry, and new light switches) and a reaffirmation of one's *gendered* relation to the work and to the world. In short, the 'shoulds' of gender ideals are fused with the 'musts' of efficient household production. The result may be something resembling a 'gendered' household-production function.

If appropriately doing gender serves to sustain and legitimate existing gender relations, would inappropriate gender activity challenge that legitimacy? Or, as West and Zimmerman (1987: 146) suggest, when people fail to do gender appropriately, are their individual characters, motives, and predispositions called into question? If doing gender is unavoidable and people are held accountable for its production, how might people initiate and sustain atypical gender behaviours?

By investigating how couples share childcare and housework, I explore (1) the sorts of dyadic and group interactions that facilitate the sharing of household labour; (2) how couples describe the requirements of parenting and how they evaluate men's developing capacities for nurturing; and (3) the impact of sharing domestic labour on conceptions of gender.

The Sample

To find couples who shared childcare, I initially contacted schools and day care centres in several suburban California communities. Using snowball-sampling techniques, I selected 20 moderate-to middle-income dual-earner couples with children. To compensate for gaps in the existing literature and to enhance comparisons between sample families, I included couples if they were the biological parents of at least two school-aged children, they were both employed at least halftime, and both identified the father as assuming significant responsibility for routine childcare. I observed families in their homes and interviewed fathers and mothers separately, at least once, and as many as five times. I recorded the interviews and transcribed them for coding and constant comparative analysis.

The parents were primarily in their late thirties and had been living together for an average of 10 years. All wives and 17 of 20 husbands attended some college and most couples married later and had children later than others in their birth cohort. The median age at marriage for the mothers was 23; for fathers, 26. Median age at first birth for mothers was 27; for fathers, 30. Fifteen of 20 fathers were at least one year older than their wives. Median gross annual income was $40,000, with three families under $25,000 and three over $65,000. Sixteen of the couples had two children and four had three children. Over two-thirds of

the families had both sons and daughters, but four families had two sons and no daughters, and two families had two daughters and no sons. The children's ages ranged from four to fourteen, with 80 per cent between the ages of five and eleven and with a median age of seven.

Mothers were more likely than fathers to hold professional or technical jobs, although most were employed in female-dominated occupations with relatively limited upward mobility and moderate pay. Over three-quarters held jobs in the 'helping' professions: seven mothers were nurses, five were teachers, and four were social workers or counsellors. Other occupations for the mothers were administrator, laboratory technician, filmmaker, and bookbinder. Sample fathers held both blue-collar and white collar jobs, with concentrations in construction (3), maintenance (2), sales (3), business (3), teaching (3), delivery (4), and computers (2). Like most dual-earner wives, sample mothers earned, on average, less than half of what their husband's did, and worked an average of eight fewer hours per week. Eleven mothers (55 per cent), but only five fathers (25 per cent) were employed less than 40 hours per week. In nine of 20 families, mothers were employed at least as many hours as fathers, but in only four families did the mother's earnings approach or exceed those of her husband.

Developing Shared Parenting

Two-thirds of the parents indicated that current divisions of labour were accomplished by making minor practical adjustments to what they perceived as an already fairly equal division of labour. A common sentiment was expressed by one father who commented:

> Since we've both always been working since we've been married, we've typically shared everything as far as all the working—I mean all the housework responsibilities as well as child care responsibilities. So it's a pattern that was set up before the kids were even thought of.

Nevertheless, a full three-quarters of the couples reported that the mother performed much more of the early infant care. All of the mothers and only about half of the fathers reported that they initially reduced their hours of employment after having children. About a third of the fathers said they increased their employment hours to compensate for the loss of income that resulted from their wives taking time off work before or after the births of their children.

In talking about becoming parents, most of the fathers stressed the importance of their involvement in conception decisions, the birth process, and early infant care to later assumption of childcare duties. Most couples planned the births of their children jointly and intentionally. Eighty per cent reported that they mutually decided to have children, with two couples reporting that the wife desired children more than the husband and two reporting that the husband was more eager than the wife to become a parent. For many families, the husband's commitment to participate fully in childrearing was a precondition of the birth decision. One mother described how she and her husband decided to have children.

> Shared parenting was sort of part of the decision. When we decided to have children, we realized that we were both going to be involved with our work, so it was part of the plan from the very beginning. As a matter of fact, I thought that we only could have the one and he convinced me that we could handle two and promised to really help (laughs), which he really has, but two children is a lot more work than you realize (laughs).

By promising to assume partial responsibility for childrearing, most husbands influenced their wives' initial decision to have children, the subsequent decision to have another child, and the decision of whether and when to return to work. Almost all of the mothers indicated that they had always assumed that they would have children, and most also assumed that they would return to paid employment before the children were in school. Half of the mothers did return to work within six months of the birth of their first child.

All but one of the fathers were present at the births of their children and most talked about the importance of the birth experience, using terms like 'incredible', 'magical', 'moving', 'wonderful', and 'exciting'. While most claimed that they played an important part in the birth process by providing emotional support to their wives or acting as labour coaches, a few considered their involvement to be inconsequential. Comments included, 'I felt a little bit necessary and a lot unnecessary,' and 'I didn't bug her too much and I might have helped a little.' Three quarters of the fathers reported that they were 'very involved' with their newborns, even though the mother provided most of the daily care for the first few months. Over two-thirds of the mothers breastfed their infants. Half of the fathers reported that they got up in the night to soothe their babies, and many described their early infant care experience in terms that mothers typically use to describe 'bonding' with newborns. The intensity of father–infant interaction was discussed by fathers as enabling them to experience a new and different level of intimacy and was depicted as 'deep emotional trust', 'very interior', 'drawing me in', and 'making it difficult to deal with the outside world'.

About half of the fathers referred to the experience of being involved in the delivery and in early infant care as a necessary part of their assuming responsibility for later childcare. Many described a process in which the actual performance of care-taking duties provided them with the self-confidence and skills to feel that they knew what they were doing. They described their time alone with the baby as especially helpful in building their sense of competence as a shared primary caretaker. One man said,

> I felt I needed to start from the beginning. Then I learned how to walk them at night and not be totally p.o.'ed at them and not feel that it was an infringement. It was something I *got* to do in some sense, along with changing diapers and all these things. It was certainly not repulsive and in some ways I really liked it a lot. It was not something innate, it was something to be learned. I managed to start at the beginning. If you *don't* start at the beginning then you're sort of left behind.

This father, like almost all of the others, talked about having to learn how to nurture and care for his children. He also stressed how important it was to 'start at the beginning'. While all fathers intentionally shared routine childcare as the children approached school age, only half of the fathers attempted to assume a major share of daily infant care, and only five couples described the father as an equal caregiver for children under one year old. These early caregiving fathers described their involvement in infant care as explicitly planned:

> She nursed both of them completely, for at least five or six months. So, my role was—we agreed on this—my role was the other direct intervention, like changing, and getting them up and walking them, and putting them back to sleep. For instance, she would nurse them but I would bring them to the bed afterward and change them if necessary, and get them back to sleep. . . . I really initiated those other kinds of care aspects so that I could be involved. I continued that on through infant and toddler and preschool classes that we would go to, even though I would usually be the only father there.

This man's wife offered a similar account, commenting that 'except for breast-feeding, he always provided the same things that I did—the emotional closeness and the attention.'

Another early caregiving father described how he and his wife 'very consciously' attempted to equalize the amount of time they spent with their children when they were infants: 'In both cases we very consciously made the decision that we wanted it to be a mutual process, so that from the start we shared, and all I didn't do was breast-feed. And I really would say that was the only distinction.' His wife also described their infant care arrangements as 'equal', and commented that other people did not comprehend the extent of his participation:

> I think that nobody really understood that Jennifer had two mothers. The burden of proof was always on me that he was literally being a mother. He wasn't nursing, but he was getting

up in the night to bring her to me, to change her poop, which is a lot more energy than nursing in the middle of the night. You have to get up and do all that, I mean get awake. So his sleep was interrupted, and yet within a week or two, at his work situation, it was expected that he was back to normal, and he never went back to normal. He was part of the same family that I was.

This was the only couple who talked about instituting, for a limited time, an explicit record-keeping system to ensure that they shared child care equally.

> [Father]: We were committed to the principle of sharing and we would have schedules, keep hours, so that we had a pretty good sense that we were even, both in terms of the commitment to the principle as well as we wanted to in fact be equal. We would keep records in a log—one might say in a real compulsive way—so that we knew what had happened when the other person was on.
>
> [Mother]: When the second one came we tried to keep to the log of hours and very quickly we threw it out completely. It was too complex.

Practicality and Flexibility

Both early-and later-sharing families identified practical considerations and flexibility as keys to equitable divisions of household labour. Most did not have explicit records or schedules for childcare or housework. For example, one early-involved father reported that practical divisions of labour evolved 'naturally':

> Whoever cooks doesn't have to do the dishes. If for some reason she cooks and I don't do the dishes, she'll say something about it, certainly. Even though we never explicitly agreed that's how we do it, that's how we do it. The person who doesn't cook does the dishes. We don't even know who's going to cook a lot of the time. We just get it that we can do it. We act in good faith.

Couples who did not begin sharing routine childcare until after infancy were even more likely to describe their division of labour as practical solutions to shortages of time. For example, one mother described sharing household tasks as 'the only logical thing to do', and her husband said, 'It's the only practical way we could do it.' Other fathers describe practical and flexible arrangements based on the constraints of employment scheduling:

> Her work schedule is more demanding and takes up a lot of evening time, so I think I do a lot of the every day routines, and she does a lot of the less frequent things. Like I might do more of the cooking and meal preparation, but she is the one that does the grocery shopping. An awful lot of what gets done gets done because the person is home first. That's been our standing rule for who fixes dinner. Typically, I get home before she does so I fix dinner, but that isn't a fixed rule. She gets home first, then she fixes dinner. Making the beds and doing the laundry just falls on me because I've got more time during the day to do it. And the yardwork and cuttin' all the wood, I do that. And so I'm endin' up doin' more around here than her just because I think I've got more time.

While mothers were more likely than fathers to report that talk was an important part of sharing household labour, most couples reported that they spent little time planning or arguing about who was going to do what around the house. Typical procedures for allocating domestic chores were described as 'ad hoc,' illustrated by one mother's discussion of cooking:

> Things with us have happened pretty easily as far as what gets done by who. It happened without having to have a schedule or deciding—you know—like cooking. We never decided that he would do all the cooking; it just kind of ended up that way. Every once in a while when he doesn't feel like cooking he'll say, 'Would you cook tonight?' 'Sure, fine.' But normally I don't offer to cook. I say, 'What are we having for dinner?'

In general, divisions of labour in sample families were described as flexible and changing. One mother talked about how routine adjustments in task allocation were satisfying to her: 'Once you're comfortable in your roles and division of tasks for a few months then it seems like the needs change a little bit and you have to change a little bit and you have to regroup. That's what keeps it interesting. I think that's why it's satisfying.'

Underlying Ideology

While ad hoc divisions of labour were described as being practical solutions to time shortages, there were two major ideological underpinnings to the sharing of housework and childcare: child-centredness and equity ideals. While those who attempted to share infant care tended to have more elaborate vocabularies for talking about these issues, later sharing couples also referred to them. For instance, all couples provided accounts that focused on the sanctity of childhood and most stressed the impossibility of mothers 'doing it all'.

Couples were child-centred in that they placed a high value on their children's well-being, defined parenting as an important and serious undertaking, and organized most of their non-employed hours around their children. For instance, one father described how his social life revolved around his children:

> Basically if the other people don't have kids and if they aren't involved with the kids, then we aren't involved with them. It's as simple as that. The guys I know at work that are single or don't have children my age don't come over because then we have nothing in common. They're kind of the central driving force in my life.

While about half of the couples (11 of 20) had paid for ongoing out-of-home childcare, and three-quarters had regularly used some form of paid childcare, most of the parents said that they spent more time with their children than the other dual-earner parents in their neighbourhoods. One father commented that he and his wife had structured their lives around personally taking care of their children:

An awful lot of the way we've structured our lives has been based around our reluctance to have someone else raise our children. We just really didn't want the kids to be raised from 7:30 in the morning 'till 4:30 or 5:00 in the afternoon by somebody else. So we've structured the last ten years around that issue.

Many parents also advocated treating children as inexperienced equals or 'little people', rather than as inferior beings in need of authoritarian training. For example, an ex-military father employed in computer research stated, 'We don't discipline much. Generally the way it works is kind of like bargaining. They know that there are consequences to whatever actions they take, and we try and make sure they know what the consequences are before they have a chance to take the action.' Another father described his moral stance concerning children's rights:

I'm not assuming—when I'm talking about parent–child stuff—that there's an inequality. Yes, there are a lot of differences in terms of time spent in this world, but our assumption has been, with both children, that we're peers. And so that's how we are with them. So, if they say something and they're holding fast to some position, we do not say, 'You do this because we're the parent and you're the child.'

About half of the parents talked directly about such equity ideals as applied to children.

Concerning women's rights, 80 per cent of fathers and 90 per cent of mothers agreed that women were disadvantaged in our society, but only two mothers and one father mentioned equal rights or the women's movement as motivators for sharing household labour. Most did not identify themselves as feminists, and a few offered derogatory comments about 'those women's libbers'. Nevertheless, almost all parents indicated that no one should be forced to perform a specific task because they were a man or a woman. This implicit equity ideal was evidenced by mothers and fathers using time availability, rather than gender, to assign most household tasks.

Divisions of Household Labour

Contributions to 64 household tasks were assessed by having fathers and mothers each sort cards on a five-point scale to indicate who most often performed them (see Table 19.1). Frequently performed tasks, such as meal preparation, laundry, sweeping, or putting children to bed, were judged for the two weeks preceding the interviews. Less frequently performed tasks, such as window washing, tax preparation, or car repair, were judged as to who typically performed them.

Some differences occurred between mothers' and fathers' accounts of household task allocation, but there was general agreement on who did what.

Table 19.1 shows that in the majority of families, most household tasks were seen as shared. Thirty-seven of 64 tasks (58 per cent), including all direct childcare, most household business, meal preparation, kitchen clean-up, and about half of other housecleaning tasks were reported to be shared about equally by fathers and mothers. Nevertheless, almost a quarter (15) of the tasks were performed principally by the mothers, including most clothes care, meal planning, kin-keeping, and some of the more onerous repetitive housecleaning. Just under one-fifth (12) of the tasks were performed principally by the fathers. These included the majority of the occasional outside chores such as home repair, car maintenance, lawn care, and taking out the trash. As a group, sample couples can thus be characterized as sharing an unusually high proportion of housework and childcare, but still partially conforming to a traditional division of household labour. The fathers and mothers in this study are pioneers in that they divided household tasks differently than their parents did, differently from most others in their age cohort, and from most families studied in time-use research.

Managing versus Helping

Household divisions of labour in these families also can be described in terms of who takes responsibility for planning and initiating various tasks. In every family there were at least six frequently performed household chores over which the mother

Table 19.1 Household tasks by person most often performing them

	Mother More	Fathers and Mother Equally	Father More
Cleaning	Mopping Sweeping Dusting Cleaning bathroom sink Cleaning toilet	Vacuuming Cleaning tub/shower Making beds Picking up toys Tidying living room Hanging up clothes Washing windows Spring cleaning	Taking out trash Cleaning porch
Cooking	Planning menus Grocery shopping Baking	Preparing lunch Cooking dinner Making snacks Washing dishes Putting dishes away Wiping kitchen counters Putting food away	Preparing breakfast
Clothes	Laundry Hand laundry Ironing Sewing Buying clothes	Shoe care	
Household		Running errands Decorating Interior painting General yardwork Gardening	Household repairs Exterior painting Car maintenance Car repair Washing car Watering lawn Mowing lawn Cleaning rain gutters
Finance, Social	Writing or phoning relatives/friends	Deciding major purchases Paying bills Preparing taxes Handling insurance Planning couple dates	Investments
Children	Arranging baby-sitters	Waking children Helping children dress Helping children bathe Putting children to bed Supervising children Disciplining children Driving children Taking children to doctor Caring for sick children Playing with children Planning outings	

Note: Tasks were sorted separately by fathers and mothers according to relative frequency of performance: (1) Mother mostly or always, (2) Mother more than father, (3) Father and mother about equal, (4) Father more than mother, (5) Father mostly or always. For each task a mean ranking by couple was computed with 1.00–2.49 = Mother, 2.50–3.50 = Shared, 3.51–5.0 = Father. If over 50 per cent of families ranked a task as performed by one spouse more than the other, the task is listed under that spouse, otherwise tasks are listed as shared. N = 20 couples.

retained almost exclusive managerial control. That is, mothers noticed when the chore needed doing and made sure that someone adequately performed it. In general, mothers were more likely than fathers to act as managers for cooking, cleaning, and child-care, but over half of the couples shared responsibility in these areas. In all households the father was responsible for initiating and managing at least a few chores traditionally performed by mothers.

Based on participants' accounts of strategies for allocating household labour, I classified twelve couples as sharing responsibility for household labour and eight couples as reflecting manager–helper dynamics. Helper husbands often waited to be told what to do, when to do it, and how it should be done. While they invariably expressed a desire to perform their 'fair share' of housekeeping and child-rearing, they were less likely than the other fathers to assume responsibility for anticipating and planning these activities. Manager–helper couples sometimes referred to the fathers' contributions as 'helping' the mother.

When asked what they liked most about their husband's housework, about half of the mothers focused on their husband's self-responsibility: voluntarily doing work without being prodded. They commented, 'He does the everyday stuff' and 'I don't have to ask him.' The other mothers praised their husbands for particular skills with comments such as 'I love his spaghetti' or 'He's great at cleaning the bathroom.' In spite of such praise, three-fourths of the mothers said that what bothered them most about their husband's housework was the need to remind him to perform certain tasks, and some complained of having to 'train him' to correctly perform the chores. About a third of the fathers complained that their wives either didn't notice when things should be done or that *their* standards were too low. Although the extent of domestic task sharing varied considerably among couples, 90 per cent of both mothers and fathers independently reported that their divisions of labour were 'fair'.

Some mothers found it difficult to share authority for household management. For instance, one mother said, 'There's a certain control you have when you do the shopping and the cooking and I don't know if I'm ready to relinquish that control.'

Another mother, who shares most childcare and housework with her husband, admitted that 'in general, household organization is something that I think I take over.' In discussing how they divide housework, she commented on how she notices more than her husband does:

> He does what he sees needs to be done. That would include basic cleaning kinds of things. However, there are some detailed kinds of things that he doesn't see that I feel need to be done, and in those cases I have to ask him to do things. He thinks some of the details are less important and I'm not sure, that might be a difference between men and women.

Like many of the mothers who maintained a managerial position in the household, this mother attributed an observed difference in domestic perceptiveness to an essential difference between women and men. By contrast, mothers who did not act as household managers were unlikely to link housecleaning styles to essential gender differences.

Many mothers talked about adjusting their housecleaning standards over the course of their marriage and trying to feel less responsible for being 'the perfect homemaker'. By partially relinquishing managerial duties and accepting their husband's housecleaning standards, some mothers reported that they were able to do less daily housework and focus more on occasional, thorough cleaning or adding 'finishing touches'. A mother with two nursing jobs, whose husband delivered newspapers, commented:

> He'll handle the surface things no problem, and I get down and do the nitty gritty. And I do it when it bugs me or when I have the time. It's not anything that we talk about usually. Sometimes if I feel like things are piling up, he'll say 'Well, make me a list,' and I will. And he'll do it. There are some things that he just doesn't notice and that's fine: he handles the day-to-day stuff. He'll do things, like for me cleaning off the table—for him it's getting everything off it; for me it's putting the

tablecloth on, putting the flowers on, putting the candles on. That's the kind of stuff I do and I like that; it's not that I want him to start.

This list-making mother illustrates that responsibility for managing housework sometimes remained in the mother's domain, even if the father performed more of the actual tasks.

Responsibility for managing childcare, on the other hand, was more likely to be shared. Planning and initiating 'direct' childcare, including supervision, discipline and play, was typically an equal enterprise. Sharing responsibility for 'indirect' childcare, including clothing, cleaning, and feeding, was less common, but was still shared in over half of the families. When they cooked, cleaned, or tended to the children, fathers in these families did not talk of 'helping' the mother; they spoke of fulfilling their responsibilities as equal partners and parents. For example, one father described how he and his wife divided both direct and indirect child care:

> My philosophy is that they are my children and everything is my responsibility, and I think she approaches it the same way too. So when something needs to be done, it's whoever is close does it . . . whoever it is convenient for. And we do keep a sense of what the other's recent efforts are, and try to provide some balance, but without actually counting how many times you've done this and I've done that.

In spite of reported efforts to relinquish total control over managing home and children, mothers were more likely than fathers to report that they would be embarrassed if unexpected company came over and the house was a mess (80 per cent versus 60 per cent). When asked to compare themselves directly to their spouse, almost two-thirds of both mothers and fathers reported that the mother would be more embarrassed than the father. Some mothers reported emotional reactions to the house being a mess that were similar to those they experienced when their husbands 'dressed the kids funny'. The women were more likely to focus on the children 'looking nice', particularly when they were going to be seen in public. Mothers' greater

embarrassment over the kemptness of home or children might reflect their sense of mothering as part of women's essential nature.

Adult Socialization through Childrearing

Parents shared in creating and sustaining a worldview through the performance and evaluation of childrearing. Most reported that parenting was their primary topic of conversation, exemplified by one father's comment: 'That's what we mostly discuss when we're not with our kids—either when we're going to sleep or when we have time alone—is how we feel about how we're taking care of them.' Others commented that their spouse helped them to recognize unwanted patterns of interaction by focusing on parenting practices. For instance, one father remarked,

> I'm not sure I could do it as a one-parent family, cause I wouldn't have the person, the other person saying, 'Hey, look at that, that's so much like what you do with your own family.' In a one-parent family, you don't have that, you don't have the other person putting out that stuff, you have to find it all out on your own and I'm not sure you can.

Usually the father was described as being transformed by the parenting experience and developing increased sensitivity. This was especially true of discourse between parents who were trying to convert a more traditional division of family labour into a more egalitarian one. A self-employed construction worker said his level of concern for child safety was heightened after he rearranged his work to do half of the parenting:

> There's a difference in being at the park with the kids since we went on the schedule. Before it was, like, 'Sure, jump off the jungle bars.' But when you're totally responsible for them, and you know that if they sprained an ankle or something you have to pick up the slack, it's like you have more investment in the kid and

you don't want to see them hurt and you don't want to see them crying. I find myself being a lot more cautious.

Mothers also reported that their husbands began to notice subtle cues from the children as a result of being with them on a regular basis. The wife of the construction worker quoted above commented that she had not anticipated many of the changes that emerged from sharing routine childcare.

I used to worry about the kids a lot more. I would say in the last year it's evened itself out quite a bit. That was an interesting kind of thing in sharing that started to happen that I hadn't anticipated. I suppose when you go into this your expectations about what will happen—that you won't take your kids to day care, that they'll be with their dad, and they'll get certain things from their dad and won't that be nice, and he won't have to worry about his hours—but then it starts creeping into other areas that you didn't have any way of knowing it was going to have an impact. When he began to raise issues about the kids or check in on them at school when they were sick, I thought, 'Well, that's my job, what are you talking about that for?' or, 'Oh my god. I didn't notice that!' Where did he get the intuitive sense to know what needed to be done? It wasn't there before. A whole lot of visible things happened.

Increased sensitivity on the part of the fathers, and their enhanced competence as parents, was typically evaluated by adopting a vocabulary of motives and feelings similar to the mothers', created and sustained through an ongoing dialogue about the children: a dialogue that grew out of the routine child care practices. Another mother described how her husband had 'the right temperament' for parenting, but had to learn how to notice the little things that she felt her daughters needed:

When it comes to the two of us as parents, I feel that my husband's parenting skills are probably superior to mine, just because of his calm rationale. But maybe that's not what

little girls need all the time. He doesn't tend to be the one that tells them how gorgeous they look when they dress up, which they really like, and I see these things, I see when they're putting in a little extra effort. He's getting better as we grow in our relationship, as the kids grow in their relationship with him.

Like many fathers in this study, this one was characterized as developing sensitivity to the children by relying on interactions with his wife. She 'sees things' which he has to learn to recognize. Thus, while he may have 'superior' parenting skills, he must learn something subtle from her. His reliance on her expertise suggests that his 'calm rationale' is insufficient to make him 'maternal' in the way that she is. Her ability to notice things, and his inattention to them, serves to render them both accountable: parenting remains an essential part of her nature, but is a learned capacity for him. Couples talked about fathers being socialized, as adults, to become nurturing parents. This talking with their wives about childcare helped husbands construct and sustain images of themselves as competent fathers.

Greater paternal competence was also reported to enhance marital interaction. Fathers were often characterized as paying increased attention to emotional cues from their wives and engaging in more reciprocal communication. Taking responsibility for routine household labour offered some men the opportunity to better understand their mother's lives as well. For instance, one involved father who did most of the housework suggested that he could sometimes derive pleasure from cleaning the bathroom or picking up a sock if he looked at it as an act of caring for his family:

It makes it a different job, to place it in a context of being an expression of caring about a collective life together. It's at that moment that I'm maybe closest to understanding what my mother and other women of my mother's generation, and other women now, have felt about being housewives and being at home, being themselves. I think I emotionally understand the satisfaction and the gratification of being a homemaker.

More frequently, however, sharing childcare and housework helped fathers understand its drudgery. One father who is employed as a carpenter explained how assuming more responsibility for housework motivated him to encourage his wife to buy whatever she needs to make housework easier.

> It was real interesting when I started doing more housework. Being in construction, when I needed a tool, I bought the tool. And when I vacuum floors, I look at this piece of shit, I mean I can't vacuum the floor with this and feel good about it, it's not doing a good job. So I get a good vacuum system. So I have more appreciation for housecleaning. When I clean the tubs, I want something that is going to clean the tubs; I don't want to work extra hard. You know I have a kind of sponge to use for cleaning the tubs. So I have more of an appreciation for what she had to do. I tell her 'If you know of something that's going to make it easier, let's get it.'

Most sample fathers reported that performance of childcare, in and of itself, increased their commitment to both parenting and housework. All of the fathers had been involved in some housework before the birth of their children, but many indicated that their awareness and performance of housework increased in conjunction with their involvement in parenting. They reported that as they spent more time in the house alone with their children, they assumed more responsibility for cooking and cleaning. Fathers also noted that as they became more involved in the daily aspects of parenting, and in the face of their wives' absence and relinquishment of total responsibility for housekeeping, they became more aware that certain tasks needed doing and they were more likely to perform them. This was conditioned by the amount of time fathers spent on the job, but more than half reported that they increased their contributions to household labour when their children were under 10 years old. This did not always mean that fathers' relative proportion of household tasks increased, because mothers were also doing more in response to an expanding total household workload.

Gender Attributions

Approximately half of both mothers and fathers volunteered that men and women brought something unique to childcare, and many stressed that they did not consider their own parenting skills to be identical to those of their spouse. One mother whose husband had recently increased the amount of time he spent with their school-aged children commented: 'Anybody can slap together a cream cheese and cucumber sandwich and a glass of milk and a few chips and call it lunch, but the ability to see that your child is troubled about something, or to be able to help them work through a conflict with a friend, that is really much different.' A list-making mother who provided less childcare and did less housework than her husband described herself as 'more intimate and gentle', and her husband as 'rough and out there'. Like many others she emphasized that mothers and fathers provide 'a balance' for their children. She described how she had to come to terms with her expectations that her husband would 'mother' the way that she did:

> One of the things that I found I was expecting from him when he started doing so much here and I was gone so much, I was expecting him to mother the kids. And you know, I had to get over that one pretty quick and really accept him doing the things the way he did them as his way, and that being just fine with me. He wasn't mothering the kids, he was fathering the kids. It was just that he was the role of the mother as far as the chores and all that stuff.

A mother who managed and performed most of the housework and childcare used different reasoning to make similar claims about essential differences between women and men. In contrast to the mothers quoted above, this mother suggested that men could nurture, but not perform daily childcare:

> Nurturance is one thing, actual care is another thing. I think if a father had to—like all of a sudden the wife was gone, he could nurture it with the love that it needed. But he might

not change the diapers often enough, or he might not give 'em a bath often enough and he might not think of the perfect food to feed. But as far as nurturing, I think he's capable of caring. . . . If the situation is the mother is there and he didn't have to, then he would trust the woman to.

This mother concluded, 'The woman has it more in her genes to be more equipped for nurturing.' Thus many of the manager–helper couples legitimated their divisions of labour and reaffirmed the 'naturalness' of essential gender differences.

Parents who equally shared the responsibility for direct and indirect childcare, on the other hand, were more likely to see similarities in their relationships with their children. They all reported that their children were emotionally 'close' to both parents. When asked who his children went to when they were hurt or upset, one early- and equal-sharing father commented: 'They'll go to either of us, that is pretty indistinguishable.' Mothers and fathers who equally shared most direct childcare reported that their children typically called for the parent with whom they had most recently spent time, and frequently called her mother 'daddy' or the father 'mommy,' using the gendered form to signify 'parent'. Most often, parents indicated that their children would turn to 'whoever's closest' or 'whoever they've been with', thus linking physical closeness with emotional closeness. In-home observations of family interactions confirmed such reports.

The central feature of these and other parental accounts is that shared activities formed an emotional connection between parent and child. Shared activities were also instrumental in constructing images of fathers as competent, nurturing caregivers. Two-thirds of both mothers and fathers expressed the belief that men could care for children's emotional needs as well as women. When asked whether men, in general, could nurture like women, mothers used their husbands as examples. One said, 'I don't necessarily think that that skill comes with a sex type. Some women nurture better than others, some men nurture better than other men. I think that those skills can come when either person is

willing to have the confidence and commitment to prioritize them.'

However, the parents who were the most successful at sharing childcare were the most likely to claim that men could nurture like women. Those who sustained manager–helper dynamics in childcare tended to invoke the images of 'maternal instincts' and alluded to natural differences between men and women. In contrast, more equal divisions of household labour were typically accompanied by an ideology of gender *similarity* rather than gender difference. The direction of causality is twofold: (1) those who believed that men could nurture like women seriously attempted to share all aspects of child care, and (2) the successful practice of sharing child care facilitated the development of beliefs that men could nurture like women.

Normalizing Atypical Behaviour

Mothers and fathers reported that women friends, most of whom were in more traditional marriages or were single, idealized their shared-parenting arrangements. About two-thirds of sample mothers reported that their women friends told them that they were extremely fortunate, and labelled their husbands 'wonderful', 'fantastic', 'incredible', or otherwise out of the ordinary. Some mothers said that women friends were 'jealous', 'envious', or 'amazed', and that they 'admired' and 'supported' their efforts at sharing domestic chores.

Both mothers and fathers said that the father received more credit for his family involvement than the mother did, because it was expected that she would perform childcare and housework. Since parenting is assumed to be 'only natural' for women, fathers were frequently praised for performing a task that would go unnoticed if a mother had performed it:

I think I get less praise because people automatically assume that, you know, the mother's *supposed* to do the childcare. And he gets a lot of praise because he's the visible one. Oh, I think that he gets far more praise. I can bust my butt at that school and all he has to do is show up in the parking lot and everybody's all *gah gah* over him. I don't get resentful about that—I think it's funny and I think it's sad.

While the fathers admitted that they enjoyed such praise, many indicated that they did not take these direct or implied compliments very seriously.

I get more credit than she does, because it's so unusual that the father's at home and involved in the family. I realize what it is: it's prejudice. The strokes feel real nice, but I don't take them too seriously. I'm sort of proud of it in a way that I don't really like. It's nothing to be proud of, except that I'm glad to be doing it and I think it's kind of neat because it hasn't been the style traditionally. I kind of like that, but I know that it means nothing.

These comments reveal that fathers appreciated praise, but actively discounted compliments received from those in dissimilar situations. The fathers' everyday parenting experiences led them to view parenthood as drudgery as well as fulfillment. They described their sense of parental responsibility as taken-for-granted and did not consider it to be out of the ordinary or something worthy of special praise. Fathers sometimes reported being puzzled by compliments from their wives' acquaintances and judged them to be inappropriate. When I asked one what kinds of reactions he received when his children were infants, he said,

They all thought it was really wonderful. They thought she'd really appreciate how wonderful it was and how different that was for her to father. They'd say, 'You ought to know how lucky you are, he's doing so much.' I just felt like I'm doing what any person should do. Just like shouldn't anybody be this interested in their child? No big deal.

Another father said he resented all the special attention he received when he was out with his infant son:

Constant going shopping and having women stop me and say 'Oh it's so good to see you fathers.' I was no longer an individual: I was this generic father who was now a liberated father who could take care of his child. I actually didn't like it. I felt after a while that I wanted the time and the quality of my relationship with my child at that point, what was visible in public, to simply be accepted as what you do. It didn't strike me as worthy of recognition, and it pissed me off a lot that women in particular would show this sort of appreciation, which I think is well-intentioned, but which also tended to put a frame around the whole thing as though somehow this was an experience that could be extracted from one's regular life. It wasn't. It was going shopping with my son in a snuggly or on the backpack was what I was doing. It wasn't somehow this event that always had to be called attention to.

Thus fathers discounted and normalized extreme reactions to their divisions of labour and interpreted them in a way that supported the 'natural' character of what they were doing.

One mother commented on a pattern that was typically mentioned by both parents: domestic divisions of labour were 'normal' to those who were attempting something similar, and 'amazing' to those who were not: 'All the local friends here think it's amazing. They call him "Mr Mom" and tell me how lucky I am. I'm waiting for someone to tell me how lucky *he* is. I have several friends at work who have very similar arrangements and they just feel that it's normal.'

Because fathers assumed traditional mothering functions, they often had more social contact with mothers than with other fathers. They talked about being the only fathers at children's lessons, parent classes and meetings, at the laundromat, or in the market. One father said it took mothers there a while before they believed he really shared a range of household tasks.

At first they ask me, 'Is this your day off?' And I say, 'If it's the day off for me, why isn't it the day off for you?' 'Well, I work 24 hours a day!' And I say, 'Yeah, right. I got my wash done and hung out and the beds made.' It takes the mother a couple of times to realize that I really do that stuff.

In general, fathers resisted attempts by other people to compare them to traditional fathers, and often compared themselves directly to their wives, or to other mothers.

Fathers tended to be employed in occupations predominantly composed of men, and in those settings were often discouraged from talking about family or children. Several fathers reported that people at their place of employment could not understand why they did 'women's work', and a few mentioned that co-workers would be disappointed when they would repeatedly turn down invitations to go out 'with the boys' for a drink. One of three self-employed carpenters in the study said that he would sometimes conceal that he was leaving work to do something with his children because he worried about negative reactions from employers or co-workers:

> I would say reactions that we've got—in business, like if I leave a job somewhere that I'm on and mention that I'm going to coach soccer, my son's soccer game, yeah. I have felt people kind of stiffen, like, I was more shirking my job, you know, such a small thing to leave work for, getting home, racing home for. I got to the point with some people where I didn't necessarily mention what I was leaving for, just because I didn't need for them to think that I was being irresponsible about their work, I mean, I just decided it wasn't their business. If I didn't know them well enough to feel that they were supportive. I would just say, 'I have to leave early today'—never lie, if they asked me a question. I'd tell them the answer—but not volunteer it. And, maybe in some cases, I feel like, you know, you really have to be a little careful about being too *groovy* too, that what it is that you're doing is just so wonderful. 'I'm a father, I'm going to go be with my children.' It isn't like that, you know. I don't do it for what people think of me; I do it because I enjoy it.

Some fathers said co-workers perceived their talk of spending time with their children as indications that they were not 'serious' about their work. They reported receiving indirect messages that *providing* for the family was primary and *being with* the family was secondary. Fathers avoided negative workplace sanctions by selectively revealing the extent of their family involvement.

Many fathers selected their current jobs because the work schedule was flexible, or so they could take time off to care for their children. For instance, even though most fathers worked full-time, two-thirds had some daytime hours off, as exemplified by teachers, mail carriers, and self-employed carpenters. Similarly, most fathers avoided extra, work-related tasks or overtime hours in order to maximize time spent with their children. One computer technician said that he was prepared to accept possible imputations of non-seriousness:

> I kind of tend to choose my jobs. When I go to a job interview, I explain to people that I have a family and the family's very important to me. Some companies expect you to work a lot of overtime or work weekends, and I told them that I don't have to accept that sort of thing. I may not have gotten all the jobs I ever might have had because of it, but it's something that I bring up at the job interview and let them know that my family comes first.

The same father admitted that it is sometimes a 'blessing' that his wife works evenings at a local hospital, because it allows him to justify leaving his job on time:

> At five o'clock or five thirty at night, when there are a lot of people that are still going to be at work for an hour or two more. I go 'Adios!' [laughs]. I mean, I *can't* stay. I've gotta pick up the kids. And there are times when I feel real guilty about leaving my fellow workers behind when I know they're gonna be there for another hour or so. About a block from work I go 'God, this is great!' [laughs].

Over half of the study participants also indicated that their own mothers or fathers reacted negatively to their divisions of labour. Parents were described as 'confused', 'bemused', and 'befuddled', and it was said that they 'lack understanding' or 'think it's a little strange'. One mother reported that her parents and in-laws wouldn't 'dare to criticize' their situation because 'times have changed', but she sensed their underlying worry and concern:

> I think both sides of the family think it's fine because it's popular now. They don't dare—I mean if we were doing this thirty years ago, they would dare to criticize. In a way, now they don't. I think both sides feel it's a little strange. I thought my mom was totally sympathetic and no problem, but when I was going to go away for a week and my husband was going to take care of the kids, she said something to my sister about how she didn't think I should do it. There's a little underlying tension about it, I think.

Other study participants reported that disagreements with parents were common, particularly if they revolved around trying to change childrearing practices their own parents had used.

Many couples reported that initial negative reactions from parents turned more positive over time as they saw that the children were 'turning out all right', that the couple was still together after an average of 10 years, and that the men were still employed. This last point, that parents were primarily concerned with their son's or son-in-law's provider responsibilities, highlights how observers typically evaluated the couple's task sharing. A number of study participants mentioned that they thought their parents wanted the wife to quit work and stay home with the children and that the husband should 'make up the difference'. Most mentioned, however, that parents were more concerned that the husband continue to be the provider than they were that the wife made 'extra money' or that the husband 'helped out' at home.

> In the beginning there was a real strong sense that I was in the space of my husband's duty.

That came from his parents pretty strongly. The only way that they have been able to come to grips with this in any fashion is because he has also been financially successful. If he had decided, you know, 'Outside work is not for me, I'm going to stay home with the kids and she's going to work.' I think there would have been a whole lot more talk than there was. I think it's because he did both and was successful that it was okay.

Another mother noted that parental acceptance of shared parenting did not necessarily entail acceptance of the woman as provider:

> There is a funny dynamic that happens. It's not really about childcare, where I don't think in our families—with our parents—I don't get enough credit for being the breadwinner. Well they're still critical of him for not earning as much money as I do. In a way they've accepted him as being an active parenting father more than they've accepted me being a breadwinner.

Here again, the 'essential nature' of men is taken to be that of provider. If the men remain providers, they are still accountable as men, even if they take an active part in childcare.

Discussion

This brief exploration into the social construction of shared parenting in 20 dual-earner families illustrates how more equal domestic gender relations arise and under what conditions they flourish. All couples described flexible and practical task-allocation procedures that were responses to shortages of time. All families were child-centred in that they placed a high value on their children's well-being, defined parenting as an important and serious undertaking, and organized most of their non-employed time around their children. Besides being well educated and delaying childbearing until their late twenties or early thirties, couples who shared most of the responsibility for household labour tended to involve the father in routine child care from the children's early infancy. As Sara Ruddick (1982) has noted, the everyday aspects of child care and housework help share ways of thinking, feeling, and acting that become associated with what it means to be a mother. My findings suggest that when domestic activities are equally shared, 'maternal thinking' develops in fathers, too, and

the social meaning of gender begins to change. This de-emphasizes notions of gender as personality and locates it in social interaction.

To treat gender as the 'cause' of household division of labour overlooks its emergent character and fails to acknowledge how it is, in fact, implicated in precisely such routine practices.

References

Berk, S.F. 1985. *The Gender Factory*. New York: Plenum.

Ruddick, S. 1982. 'Maternal Thinking', in B. Thorne and M. Yalom, eds., *Rethinking the Family*, pp. 76–94. New York: Longman.

West, C., and D.H. Zimmerman. 1987. 'Doing Gender', *Gender & Society* 1: 125–51.

CHAPTER 20

The Last Best West: Women on the Alberta Frontier, 1880–1930

Eliane Leslau Silverman

Eliane Leslau Silverman interviewed older Albertan women about their experiences in the early decades of the twentieth century for her book *The Last Best West*. The selection below is taken from her chapter on love, sex, and marriage. Silverman's observations are interspersed with excerpts from her interviews.

Women and Men

Once childhood was over, there was still much for a girl to learn. Young women had to further refine their knowledge of the behaviour and sense of self appropriate to their femaleness. Part of that knowledge, gained during their adolescent years, was their sexuality. They needed to find out about what most of them called 'the facts of life': menstruation, conception, and pregnancy. The next stage lay in experiencing these biological realities as they matured in their twenties, for most of them married and had children, often more children than they wanted. In growing toward adulthood, they would need to learn too about men, how to adapt themselves to men's needs, how to suppress their

own, and sometimes how to acknowledge their own desires.

The women with whom I spoke were quite frank and open about the first stage of their adolescent lives, even if embarrassed at times and delicate in their language, using euphemisms or simply leaving words unspoken. Their occasional reticence revealed a lot about their socialization as women: they had learned to conceal their bodies, even to be ashamed of them. Where variety informed other aspects of their lives, where experiences were so varied, a curious similarity pervaded women's recollections of how they had first learned that they had female bodies. 'Learning' perhaps implies more consciousness than is accurate, for rather than knowledge, it is adolescent ignorance and female shame that emerge from their accounts.

My first menstruation came on the day of the Sunday School picnic, and I was very much put out. I can remember my mother saying that every woman has the same thing; she explained why, real quickly, and that was it. I was told just that I was growing up and there would be a change.

Relatives and peers hinted now and again, indicated that 'something would happen', and that this mystery of blood had something to do with becoming a woman.

The Métis mothers used to tell us to expect it; it's a sign of blood and that's a sign you're a girl. But I wouldn't tell my mother. I thought it was dirty. Everybody goes through that. I went to the bathroom and saw this blood, and started washing my clothes and hid them before my parents came home. I was scared something happened. That same year—I was thirteen—I was in the convent and the same thing happened. I woke up and my sheet was full of spots. No pad they gave you, just bloomers. You had to wash your things. The sister let you sleep that morning. I thought I was doing something wrong. You feel guilty.

In Russia I knew nothing about this. I was hiding it and I was scared, scared to let anybody know this was happening to me.

The hints about menstruation were usually imprecise; the menstrual taboo was powerful in frontier society. The menarche, the beginning of menstruation, was a moment denied, relegated to a realm where fear and shame ruled. Women learned at an early age to hide signs of their femaleness, their bodies, and their selves, agreeing obediently to play parts in scripts they had not written.

My aunt told me about menstruating when I was about nine years old. She was sixteen. For four years I worried about it. She had explained that some day this would come and not to be frightened. So every day of my life,

for those four years, I'd look to see if everything was all right.

I was thirteen and in the classroom. We were dismissed and I got up; I had on a white summer dress. The girl behind me pulled me back into my seat and whispered to me, 'Don't get up. I'll get my coat for you.' 'Why?' 'You've got something red on your dress.' The teacher dismissed the class and I sat there. She said, 'Rosalind, why aren't you leaving?' 'I can't.' 'You'd better go.' I put my head down on the desk and started to cry. The teacher came down and pulled me by the arm, trying to pull me out of the desk. I just hung on to the desk. She couldn't figure out what in the world was wrong. By this time Bonnie came back. She had to go home to get her coat. That's why it took so long. The teacher suddenly realized and left me alone. That was grim, what I had to learn as I grew up.

Many of the women, suffused with shame at what they saw to be nasty but also inevitable, were prepared by that shame to suppress voices inside themselves that called for self-love and pride. Not all of them, of course, were prevented from joy or productivity or creativity. Margaret Jones, with her usual good humour and quick intelligence, channelled her curiosity into a world that for her grew larger and larger.

Mother was very shy about acquainting one with the facts of life. She did say, 'Someday, there'll be blood on your nightgown; let me know.' And I thought that had to do with something mysterious. That day one of my friends told me that babies are carried around in the mother's abdomen. I told my mother that, and she at least told me the word womb, but that was about all the instruction I had. I find that passing on gossip at school was the commonest method of instruction.

I started out to read Darwin with the purpose of finding out what was what. The more I found out about controversies surrounding books, the more likely I was to read them. Of course Darwin and the rest of them assumed that people knew everything about the facts of life, so they didn't mention that. However, the most vivid religious experience I ever had was when I finished Darwin's *Descent of Man*. I can't think of anything that influenced me more deeply than that. I got out of bed and thanked God for evolution. It confirmed everything that was beautiful.

Things came together in a nutty sort of way. The first year I was teaching I had a nice, quiet old gelding to ride. He was a darling, even when he bounced me off. I was no athlete as you can imagine! He would come back and sniff at me and you could almost hear him saying, 'It's come loose again.' The next year they didn't want this heavy horse out of service so I got a little mare. Her name was Lady. She galloped much more and didn't bother to see why I'd come loose. I didn't know the horse was in heat. A stallion came into the yard after her and I realized almost immediately what he wanted. The stallion chased my poor Lady and caught her. I can still see those hooves up above my head. I got two or three of the bigger boys to help me, and we managed to get Lady away from the stallion. I trembled: what would the owners say when I got home? As a matter of fact, they were delighted to have an extra free colt.

My big aim was to keep the kids in my classes from knowing what was happening, for I still thought about my mother's statements about it being naughty to know too much. I've had many experiences that have made me realize how wrong I was.

Most women learned that it was just as well not to know too much, and especially not to talk about sexuality. They learned to become ashamed and to think of themselves as unlovable. Most of them, if they learned it at all, discovered their own desires late in their lives, often only after sexuality no longer seemed to threaten.

Sexuality was indeed threatening, not much to be welcomed in a world in which sensuality played a small role. Pleasure in scents, in touches, might be acknowledged when aroused by baking bread or by

the yellow crocuses emerging through wind-crusted snow, but rarely did frontier women express sexual pleasure, inappropriate in their frontier culture, which demanded reticence. An adult woman's life, entered into with some repulsion and much ignorance, would be an uneasy life for a long time.

How did I actually find out about sexual activity between men and women? It must have been from a neighbour child. She must have said something because I can remember when I was twelve years old we had a small house, and Father sometimes came home quite late because of his job. I woke up and I heard some kind of sound. I can remember the chills that went up and down me, the chills of recognition, really chills of horror. As far as sexual information was concerned, I think I was deprived, but not much more than the other people my age. We just had to stumble along. The worst of it was that I just loved to have a man's arms around me. That was everything to me as I got older. Being hugged and kissed was just the most marvellous thing that could happen to me. But I couldn't ever admit this to my friends. I think it would have been much better if we had all said, 'Isn't that just it?' But we didn't. This marvellous part of growing up would have been so much easier. Instead, I thought there was something wrong with me.

Prohibitions against contact with men were freely passed along, though rarely explained. Either fathers or mothers might convey the rules. Whether Scandinavian, Ukrainian, or Anglo-Canadian, ethnic background seemed not to alter the lessons that parents wanted to impress on their daughters.

Sex was not a discussed topic. My father once said, 'Thelma, I don't want you to do anything with anybody else that you wouldn't do right here in the living room.' I didn't know what he was talking about, so I just said, 'No, of course not, Dad.'

Mother used to tell me after I was a little bit older, 'You're going around with the boys;

don't ever give in because then you'll be pregnant. Don't let them touch you.' So I can tell you, when a boy touched me, I sprang back. I remember one fellow said to me, 'What's the matter? You got a spring?'

We were so naive it was pitiful. My grandmother taught me the Ten Commandments. When we came to 'Thou shalt not commit adultery,' I asked, 'Grandma, what's adultery?' She slapped me! Then she said, 'Never ask that question again.' All she ever told me later was, 'Keep the young men at arm's length.' That was her way of telling me to protect myself.

The questions about birth were answered by a variety of fairy tales the settlers brought with them: the usual cabbage patch, doctor's bag, and haystack babies whose first cries resounding through the house caused children to scurry about looking for the new kittens.

I was so dumb I thought the doctor brought babies. One afternoon Mom was outdoors. She was feeling bad so she was out in the chicken yard walking around, because I guess she was going to have the baby. Well, my cousin said, 'You know what's the matter with your mother?' 'What?' 'She's going to have a baby.' 'You're crazy,' I said.

Then my aunt came over. We were upstairs and we could hear a baby crying. All of a sudden Dad comes upstairs, and he says, 'Girls, are you awake?' 'Yes,' I said. 'There's a baby, isn't there?' 'Yes, you better come and see your little sister.'

Girls moved toward adult life—more precisely, toward marriage, by which they would be defined as grown women. The tentative glances at boys or men, slowly reaching out to communicate with them, were a major, if mysterious, part of their adolescence.

I know when my husband was courting me he had just a little buggy and a horse. I'd be so scared of that horse. I met him the first time at the third house from our place. It was just

a shack with two rooms. They were moving it, and I was watching, and he was watching me. I didn't know that at the time. Later on I met him at a dance and he says, 'You're the girl that was watching,' and I said, 'Yes, they took our playhouse away.' It was empty so long that we used to go out there and play house and hide-and-go-seek. I felt so sorry for that house when they moved it. But another house sprang up there.

Boys began by filling only a small compartment of a young girl's life. Later, their presence loomed larger, as Barbara West of Calgary recalled.

I had my first beau when I was sixteen. He was a nice Catholic boy. I went with him for years, but I didn't marry him. He used to take me to the old Pantages every Saturday; that was the vaudeville, and then he'd come home and have dinner. He got his money's worth, really. And then Sunday nights: Sunday was church night for everybody and I don't think it was for religion. It was to meet your boyfriend and then you'd walk home with him. We'd sit around the dining room table playing some foolish game, but Mother and Father were in the next room. I fell out with him later.

Girls became increasingly aware that their future lives depended on their interaction with men. They could barely envision a life on their own—and quite sensibly, since so few doors were open to single women. They began to go out with men and invite them home, most often with the expectation of marriage. Certainly, parents expected that this would be the end result. Very few of the women remained single; most of their parents had encouraged them to marry in almost the same breath as they warned against intimacy with boys. In the countryside or in the city, young women needed men, if only to ensure some kind of economic future, apart from a desire for intimacy. Yet those very people who would be so essential in their lives were also so mysterious, so different from themselves. One's behaviour had to alter in their presence, sometimes in very puzzling ways. Arleen MacKnight, who grew up in an isolated hamlet in the north and later went to Athabasca to work, found herself treated in a way that made her feel unlike herself. She found when going out with men that she was expected to act different from her accustomed mode. Relating with men meant relating with people who had grown up with different expectations and life experiences. But they were the ones who could set the terms of the relationship; most women could only agree to them.

My mother married the oldest brother. He had a younger brother, Tom; Mother said I'd be safe with him. He would be about twenty, I guess, and I would be sixteen. I was never treated so royally in my life. It seemed that he took a very great liking to me and I wasn't used to this. It was like a prince conducting a queen. I thought, 'Boy, I guess I'm some kid.' He went off to the army then, and I left town to work in a real estate office.

There was a man in the office who was a—what do you call a man who examines rocks?—a geologist. He used to phone a girl called Madeleine. There was something about her; the girls that I was living with were altogether different. I guess perhaps she was older, more sophisticated. She told him on the phone, 'Tell the girl that's in your office to come over this evening, too.' The gentleman asked me if he could take me over to Madeleine's. I was a little nervous because these people were older. I didn't know that when you are introduced to a young man, you just don't jump up and shake hands with him. This geologist, Leonard, said, 'You're not supposed to do that. When you're introduced to a man, you only say, 'How do you do?' If you jump up and shake hands with him that shows that you're terribly interested in him.' I said I somehow felt like shaking hands with the man. 'Oh,' he said, 'you really have to be trained in etiquette. I'll have to teach you.' And I thought, 'You don't need to bother . . .'

He took me out to dinner and in fact he proposed marriage. Of course he was going to have to train me to live up to his position, and he was about fifteen years older than me,

and he'd been in the war. He said, 'I would like to buy you a ring and we could be engaged.' I answered that I was engaged to someone who was in the army now. Though Tom and I hadn't any formal engagement, the fact remained that I wasn't going to take up with anybody else until I saw what happened to him or saw how he felt.

Maybe I did need some teaching. I probably did. But I've never jumped up and shaken hands with a man since that day. Still, I don't know what harm there is in it.

Courtship eventually led to marriage, a union that sometimes followed more quickly than the couple expected, as Evelyn Appleby recalled.

I guess back then girls and boys were sneaking around together at all ages, the same as they do today, you know, and there were goings on just the same as they do today. It wasn't accepted the same; it went under cover but it was certainly being done. They were the flappers, you know, and they'd be all dressed up and get most of the dances; they had a wonderful time and we were quite envious of them. Their parents weren't bothered too much about them, I don't think.

Certainly, there were girls pregnant before they married. But they were usually with the person they had been courting with. They would go out with a boy and get married. There was a certain amount of embarrassment if a person had to get married. Some people marked on the calendar when they got married so they'd know. It wasn't the accepted thing it is today, of course. There might have been some common-law people, sure, but young people weren't shacking up; it was down at the bush or someplace else. But I don't think there was so much of it because you knew everybody. I even knew the dogs' names, so you couldn't get away with very much.

Other courtships lasted longer, and some marriages were very carefully planned, as the following excerpts indicate. The first was recalled by May Potter, a Mormon from Utah who came to a Mormon community near Lethbridge with her college degree in teaching. Her marriage lasted for over 65 years of friendship and companionship.

I began teaching in 1912. I taught for four years. One of the students in my class was a young man, but older than I was. In fact, I had a winter course in which I taught men who were old enough to be my father because in the wintertime there was not much for a man to do, and a good many of them had lost out on their educational opportunities, so they came back and took this winter course. He showed such wonderful capacity that I was just thrilled to have him in the class. I could see that there was a man who had the potential of being an outstanding man. It was his logical presentation of anything, a logical sequence of thinking. I realized that he had a naturally trained mind. He got interested in me, and I was naturally interested in him. So when he proposed I said, 'Now, I do not want to marry you until you have your degree.' All my life I never wanted to be in a position of the woman up here and the man down there. The man should have the ability to inspire confidence in his wife, and she should be able to appreciate him. Now, if she's had no education and he's had no education, Lord save them.

When girls were educated beyond high school, either at university or at normal school, their marriages tended to be postponed. They delayed them because the women enjoyed their work, or because their fiancés, usually similarly educated, felt they could not yet afford to marry.

Very seldom did my classmates at university marry right away. The boys had to get established in their professions and everyone was poor as church mice, you know, so the girls taught or something until the boy was ready. Then they gave up their jobs and proceeded to propagate the species!

Class, family, and education often helped to determine who could marry whom. Marriages were sometimes a family's or society's expressions of suitability.

I know when we were kids we used to wonder about the teachers, if they ever went out with a man, or if they ever had boyfriends. The teachers around here didn't marry until pretty late, some in the fifties. I suppose probably being a teacher, and the men being mostly miners, perhaps they wouldn't dare ask the school teachers.

After the war, when the men came back, a lot of people were getting married. I met my husband when I was working in a hospital in Edmonton, where I continued to work for a couple of years after the war, so I did have a long engagement. In those days, men went to the fathers for permission. It was so different from now. There was none of this carelessness that there is today.

Millie Melnyk insisted on marriage on her own terms: 'I won't marry unless it's the one I love.' Resisting an arranged marriage was more difficult for her than for May Potter, who was well educated, or Constance Palmer, whose lengthy engagement was permitted by the habits of her class. Millie Melnyk had to struggle alone against parents and a society that insisted on marriage—any marriage.

I had an awful lot of boyfriends, young and old. The young ones were like brothers. There was one young fellow that I really kind of liked, and probably would have got to love, but my father didn't care for him. My mother used to be worried; I was seventeen, going on eighteen. She was worried I was going to be an old maid. She says, 'You're too choosy; you're picking.' I says, 'If I live to forty I won't marry unless it's the one I love.' I wanted somebody that I could really love. There was one fellow from Hillcrest who used to come, and friends of my father said to me, 'I have a lovely boy for you,' and all that. I was working then; I came home from work and we sat on the bed in the bedroom and talked a bit. And the first thing, he's asking me to marry him. I said, 'I don't know you.' He had lovely teeth, but he was kind of bald. He was a very nice person. 'How about writing?' So his friend began writing for him. I remember he sent me a big box of chocolates, five pounds, for Christmas. I was really furious. I didn't want to take anything from a person. I gave it to my brothers. By then I knew what I didn't want. But I didn't know how to get off the hook because my father and my mother liked him. There were others before that I had refused and I had a hard time getting them to go. Oh gosh, did I have trouble!

Well, later I went to this concert. We had good plays, too, and an orchestra. And there was a young fellow; he was kind of shy and standing in a doorway. I wasn't interested in anybody else. How was I going to meet him? I stepped up to him and I said, 'The concert was beautiful.' This is where I began, because he had played the mandolin. So when he went back to his mining town, what did I do? I thought of it in my mind when I went to bed and I think I gave it a week or two, a good week anyway. And I thought, 'It wouldn't hurt me to write and tell him how nice the concert was, and if he cared to write back I would write again.'

So I wrote this letter. Of course I tore up quite a few pages, but I finally wrote it so it didn't sound like I was trying to get him. It was just a perfectly friendly letter, just, 'Dear friend' and 'lovely concert.' And I got a letter inside of a week. He wrote and asked if a person wanted to farm, how would I . . .? He didn't put it right there, but I read between the lines very well. I wrote back and said, 'If a person loves the man she's getting married to, she'll go anywhere.'

He could read English, and I could read Ukrainian. After that, I bought a mandolin for myself and I started going to school to learn more Ukrainian. About three months later he came back. I met him at the station. I walked with him right through the prairies. Well, I promised I would marry him and then I

thought, 'Gee, what if my mom and dad don't like him?' So I had plans to get some clothes and elope. I didn't even tell this woman I was doing housework for because I thought, 'Who knows if he comes for me or not?' I was proud, I guess. It happens my father knew all about him; he and my uncles found out all about him, that he was a driver at the mines. We had a civil wedding.

Henrietta Crow, a Cree woman whose family left the far north early in the century for a hamlet near Slave Lake, had no choice whatsoever. Her marriage was arranged by her parents in 1915, as her own mother's had been a generation before.

Your parents choose the guy you going to marry. You don't even know the man. Here comes your husband; I was fifteen. The first dance I went to, when I was fifteen, with old Mrs. Williamson; her daughters were just young girls. Sara was my best friend so their mother came and asked my mother if I could come to the dance. But my mother had to talk to my dad first. Finally, after a week, my dad agrees so I can go with the old lady and her daughters. We walked all the way there, about six miles, to go dancing. The first dance I ever went to was at Grouard, maybe 1915.

After that dance, Sunday after, some people came to visit my mother and they were having dinner. I was in the kitchen washing dishes and all at once I heard my mother say, 'Oh yes, she'll marry him.' And that's it. And I'm wondering who was going to marry who. And it was me they were talking about. If you go tell your daughter now today, I don't know what she'd tell you. I didn't know anything about it. I was only fifteen. I still thought I was a kid, staying at home, never been with any guys, never been anywhere, know nothing, milking cows, get a pail of water, wash floor. And sewing all the time; your mother tells you, you do this and that. And all of a sudden you're getting married a year from now.

And all this time I thought it's not going to happen; they're just talking. About three months later I saw this guy come in; that's the man I'm going to marry. He sat there talking to my dad. I didn't even look at him, really. I didn't care to see him. I went to the kitchen. He's talking to my mom and dad. I didn't like him. Not like today; girls look at guys. We never used to care.

At that dance, I danced with him once. He talked to me; I don't know if I talked to him. Then I had to go sit down beside the old lady. So that was all. She'd let her daughters go with guys, take them home, but me, no, because my mother wasn't there and my dad said, 'Nobody can walk you home.' I said, 'I don't want nobody to walk me home.' I was scared of men, because I had never talked to any. That's the only time I talked to him; he came over about three months' time and sat there talking to my mom and dad, but I didn't talk to him. I went to the kitchen and stayed there all by myself. He's across the floor and I'm across here. Mostly it happened like that those days. My mother was married like that.

A very few women did not marry at all; some of them relished their freedom. Others, like Lizzie Helm, felt that in not marrying they were sacrificing something, 'at least that's what a lot have told me.' At another level, it seemed throughout her conversation that her self-esteem derived largely from that sacrifice, from looking after her brothers and her father, and from not having to confront the strangeness of men, of whom she confessed herself frightened.

I watched Mother so much. Learning about the house came to me from watching her. I used to cook, sometimes bake the bread. I can remember putting those little loaves in—we called it a Dutch loaf in those days—and I'd push in one of those minty candies and that was Father's. We had my father twenty years after Mother passed away. You see, I promised him the day she passed away to look after him. I did; I couldn't be married even if I was missing something. What would my brothers have done? They've been good to me. Richard

said the last time he was up here, he said, 'If it hadn't been for you, Dad would never have stayed.' They might all have gone back to England or to British Columbia. So I've really in one way sacrificed; that's what a lot have told me. But I'm not sorry because the boys have been good to me. To be truthful, I think I was scared by men, kind of shy.

By contrast, Jehanne Casgrain was absolutely delighted by her marriages—all three of them! Now eighty-four, with sparkling, intelligent eyes and soft pink cheeks, slight and small, she has a husband 25 years younger than herself. She was the daughter of a couple who migrated from Quebec to Wisconsin and then to Alberta, there to establish a town still homogeneous today, French and Catholic. Today she is as lively and talkative as she must have been at her first wedding, 75 years ago.

It was a little log church right over there where I was married in 1911. You see, I was just fourteen on the day I was married; not a baby, I was mature. The years were quite full for me. Of course, now I'm older. My health is not so good. I can't do what I used to, but like I say, now I married a younger man than I am. While I was young I married an older man, and now I married a younger one!

Few marriages were undertaken in such a zestful spirit. More often, the women expressed something like resignation, as Inez Wood did.

We used to come for the weekend to my mother's and sleep there. That's how my first son was born in the same house where I was born. He was a seven-month baby. Everybody had seven-month babies. I don't remember if I wanted to get married, but love is a many splendoured thing, eh?

Many accounts of getting engaged and married were oddly free of intensity, of either positive or negative emotions. One might almost add marriage to death and taxes as an inevitable, but not necessarily a joyous event.

My husband was out here in western Canada a long time. He went over to England in the war and he used to write me when he was away, because I knew him when he was a boy in St. John's. He'd tell me how he was. I didn't have any idea that I was going to marry him. He came home from war, and he still used to write me from the west and tell me the news. When he asked me to marry him, that was in a letter too, and he sent me the money to come out. Mother didn't like it very well, me going out so far by myself.

Wedding ceremonies and receptions usually conformed to ethnic tradition. Ceremonial occasions tended to be the instances in women's lives that were least changed by the frontier. Rural and urban people attempted to reproduce in ceremonies, through foods and customs, what they had left behind. Tradition provided the occasion with a sense of public validation. Marriages, births, and deaths were treated as events that were sanctioned by the community, and attended by neighbours and relatives. As nearly as possible, weddings resembled those of the old country, wherever that might be.

My wedding lasted for three days. I was twenty. An old-fashioned wedding. Imagine anybody having a hundred guests in a small house. My mother and her friends cooked for quite a few days, and no fridges then. She would run up and down from that cellar. They used to make really beautiful food.

Bob's mother put on a little wedding for us; with Bob having the grocery store, he was well known in the district. See, my parents were both dead. This probably accounts for the idea that I wasn't too lonesome when I come out here. As far as the reception goes, it was small, just the relatives.

I bought a suit in Lethbridge, a beautiful log cabin brown suit; of course they were wearing the skirts to the ankles in those days. I bought the hat, too, and I paid twenty-five dollars for it; in those days that was high. I

was all in brown, and the hat had lovely, bright flowers on it, and a veil.

I was at my aunt's place when I went to two weddings. One was in a hall and another in a thatched cottage. I was more Canadian, talked English; the others talked Ukrainian. All of a sudden crowds of people were going down to the spring with the bride and groom, and the violin playing. 'Gee, what are they going to the spring for?' 'Just an old custom,' somebody said. That's all I got until I told my mother when I came home.

Then she explained to me about the customs of the old country. The matron of honour and the best man, or an older man or woman—not too old, but older—would go to the spring during the wedding, and the bride is supposed to give—well, at that time people didn't wear panties, but whatever it was, to show. My mother said in the old country, the girls used to be smart; if they'd had their period before, or else would use a chicken's blood if they did fool around with some of the boys.

A wedding marked the community's formalized approval of an event that had meaning for the whole society. The marriage itself was private. The relationship between a husband and a wife would evolve over the years. It became a structure built of many parts, including the economic circumstances facing a couple, their characters and dispositions, and their expectations of marriage, of themselves, and of each other. Some marriages worked well, satisfying both emotional needs and the urge for intimacy. Others caused women great bitterness and sorrow.

We never had a scrap of any description. Of course he was the boss, and if he said anything I didn't dispute him. If I wanted to do it, I did it, and if I didn't I pleased myself about it. As I always told him, he thought he was the boss. No use arguing with a man if he thinks he's the boss.

Her dad was against her. She was the one that picked her man, but he was a real boozer when he was young. She was sorry later on in years. She's still stuck with the same one; he's a little better now. These old guys have different ways and then you clash; settled in their ways. But then sometimes to settle an argument you shut up; you have to.

My husband was kind of old-fashioned. He didn't even think a person should belong to women's clubs or anything like that. He thought there was too much pettiness in it. 'Oh well,' I said, 'you can't be worrying about that all the time. You have to go for what you get out of it yourself.' But I didn't join. I don't know why; he might have had something to do with it. But we just tried to consider each other's feelings.

My grandmother had come from a rich Irish family. She didn't love this man; it was a made-marriage. She said she had never kissed him before she married him. He brought her to the United States away from all she had. They settled on this farm and they were fortunate that she was among these Pennsylvania Dutch people. But she said as far as love went, there wasn't any there. She accepted his children but, the way she put it, 'I cried a lap full of tears for twenty years.' Every day for twenty years she cried a lap full of tears.

This English lady in the Peace country thought she was so superior. She had two little girls, and she was teaching them to speak in the English way, not with this horrible Canadian accent we have. I ran into her years later at Innisfail. There she could go to her own church, the Anglican, and she taught music. She wouldn't farm. Her husband bought a hog farm out of Innisfail and went back and forth from the farm to look after things. So I don't think she ever felt he was quite on the same level.

When the crops were good, my dad was generally in pretty good shape. He would take Mom for a walk, but the trouble was he would get her so worked up about how good things were going to be, and he always overestimated—because he wanted it all so

badly—the bushels he was going to get. Mom faced that right then; she learned very soon to let him dream, but she knew that there still wasn't going to be enough money for a pair of sheets for the bed.

My husband was real rough. Sometimes he didn't talk. I dig whole garden up when he was uptown. He went all around there and I thought now he will come and tell me, 'You have good job done and thanks for the job.' He never said boo. His father was same; he said he was never like his father, but he was the same. I told him, 'You worse than your father,' and then he was so mad. Then he don't talk days to me. My husband was very hard to me.

He's more than eight years older than me. When we got married was the first night he was ever close to me. I didn't feel like getting married. I didn't even want to put on my clothes, didn't even curl my hair; nothing. I guess I looked so ugly when I got married. I didn't like it. I had to fight him for three nights before he can get close to me. I didn't want a man, until his sister came down and talked to me real good. I never did care for him. But when I had kids I cared for my kids. That's all I lived for is the kids. I didn't care for him; he can go out. He can do anything he wants. Comes home with women, I didn't care.

You had to pretty well hang on in those days, no matter how bad it was. Having a roof over your head was better than nothing at all. There was plenty of fighting and quarrelling, I can remember, and screaming and yelling. You can understand it, nerves and tension and all. But they realized that they had to maintain the home and if they broke up, the wife couldn't manage alone, the husband couldn't manage alone. I think they were all pretty tired and they didn't have much time to think about doing anything else but working and sleeping.

I got married sixteen. Never went out with boys. Only saw him two times. Never been with another man, and he died nineteen years ago. Always alone; don't like nobody. I used to tell my husband, 'As soon as I die I suppose you'll live with another woman,' and he used to promise he'd never. Same with me. The priest calls me a nun! Just about! He was a good man. Never hit me, never.

My parents were equal partners always. There was no feeling that women were inferior as far as our dad was concerned. There was stability and they gave us confidence and assurance, and of course there was confidence in God. They believed in God, they believed in His Son, they believed in the power of the Spirit. I think perhaps they taught us leadership for men, but they never made any difference between male and female otherwise. But they expected a man to take the lead. It didn't make the woman an inferior being as far as our family was concerned. God meant them to work together.

My husband was a miner when we first got married, for about six months. He said, 'I'd just as soon be a farmer.' I'd rather have a little less money than see him go down that hole. You go down so deep and I couldn't stand seeing him come home being so tired. So I worked out with him for wages until we got on our own. We didn't have any children so he was my husband and baby. I kind of spoiled him a little. I wish he was here now.

Out there on the farm we used to be up at five in the morning and sometimes went until twelve at night. When it was time to go in and get supper ready my husband used to say, 'Take it easy. Rest a bit; I'll run in and get the kettle on.' He had half a mile to go to the house. By the time I got in the kettle was on and the supper was on and all we had to do was sit down and eat. He never said, 'You do this,' and I never said, 'You do that.' Fifty-seven years we worked together.

Working together: that was what it was all about. Women expected marriage to be a working partnership. It might provide them with love and intimacy, affection and warmth, loneliness and isolation, or anger and bitterness. All these were experienced as part of marriage. If frontier women expressed sincere devotion and loving loyalty to their husbands, some of them also cried 'a lapful of tears.' Certainly, intimacy was preferable to distance and loneliness. Love, however, was not what marriage meant. Before 1929, its primary purpose was not emotional. Rather, it was a working partnership designed for survival, productivity, and reproduction. The marriage of two people was the means for economic survival. Friendship might result from a couple's working together. Respect might unite them. However, deprivation, poverty, isolation, or downright meanness could make married life unpleasant, and even violent. Society and culture had deemed that a husband, as head of the unit, was in control and had to be obeyed. The lessons girls learned in their adolescence and during courtship taught them not that marriage would bring happiness or romance, but that marriage meant survival for themselves and the children they would have.

QUESTIONS FOR CRITICAL THOUGHT

1. What is your vision of ideal family life? Would your parents, siblings, and peers share that vision?

2. Ranson suggests that taking care of children is at odds with the demands of paid work, especially for women. Do you share her implicit pessimism about combining childcare and paid work?

3. The domestic division of labour still favours men with more leisure time than women, despite significant changes in recent decades. Why don't men do more around the house? What are the costs and rewards—for both men and women—of a lopsided distribution of household work?

4. What do you make of the accounts of work division and emotional sharing in the stories told by the women Silverman interviewed? Are there any aspects that appeal to you? Are there any aspects which you would find unacceptable in your own life?

5. Can you foresee a future in which all Canadian families will be shared-care families as described by Coltrane? What social changes would have to happen for this to become a reality?

6. Think about a parent with whom you share a gender. In what ways do you think your life will be different from his or hers? In what ways would you like your life to be different from his or hers?

PART VI

The Gendered Classroom

Along with the family, educational institutions—from primary schools to secondary schools, colleges, universities, and professional schools—are central arenas in which gender is reproduced. Students learn more than the formal curriculum—they learn what the society considers appropriate behaviour for men and women. And for adults, educational institutions are gendered workplaces, where the inequalities found in other institutions are also found.

From the earliest grades, students' experiences in the classroom differ by gender. Boys are more likely to interrupt, to be called upon by teachers, and to have any misbehaviour overlooked. Girls are more likely to remain obedient and quiet and to live up to (or down to) teachers' expectations. However, most of the gendering work of schools is done outside the classroom and the formal curriculum. Ellen Jordan and Angela Cowan explore the ways in which children's unstructured play re-creates gender stereotypes, while Sarah de Leeuw explores the environment of Canada's notorious residential schools for Aboriginal children, demonstrating how gendered and racialized experiences were built into the very structure of these schools.

Most of you who are reading this book have left primary and secondary schooling behind, and are currently immersed in post-secondary education. Your experiences as students may resonate with the work of both Tracey Lindberg and Brenda Beagan, who investigate everyday life in and out of the classroom. Lindberg and Beagan examine different types of education, but both find that the experience of being a student is profoundly shaped not just by gender but also by other social identities. Gender is by no means the only factor that shapes students' experiences of belonging or not belonging in school, but works in combination with other aspects of personal identity based in social categories such as race, class, and sexuality.

CHAPTER 21

Warrior Narratives in the Kindergarten Classroom: Renegotiating the Social Contract?

Ellen Jordan and Angela Cowan

Since the beginning of second-wave feminism, the separation between the public (masculine) world of politics and the economy and the private (feminine) world of the family and personal life has been seen as highly significant in establishing gender difference and inequality (Eisenstein, 1984). Twenty years of feminist research and speculation have refined our understanding of this divide and how it has been developed and reproduced. One particularly striking and influential account is given by Carole Pateman in her book *The Sexual Contract* (1988).

Pateman's broad argument is that in the modern world, the world since the Enlightenment, a 'civil society' has been established. In this civil society, patriarchy has been replaced by a fratriarchy, which is equally male and oppressive of women. Men now rule not as fathers but as brothers, able to compete with one another, but presenting a united front against those outside the group. It is the brothers who control the public world of the state, politics, and the economy. Women have been given token access to this world because the discourses of liberty and universalism made this difficult to refuse, but to take part, they must conform to the rules established to suit the brothers.

This public world in which the brothers operate together is conceptualized as separate from the personal and emotional. One is a realm where there is little physicality—everything is done rationally, bureaucratically, according to contracts that the brothers accept as legitimate. Violence in this realm is severely controlled by agents of the state, except that the brothers are sometimes called upon for the supreme sacrifice of dying to preserve freedom. The social contract redefines the brawling and feuding

long seen as essential characteristics of masculinity as deviant, even criminal, while the rest of physicality—sexuality, reproduction of the body, daily and intergenerationally—is left in the private sphere. Pateman quotes Robert Unger, 'The dichotomy of the public and private life is still another corollary of the separation of understanding and desire. . . . When reasoning, [men] belong to a public world. . . . When desiring, however, men are private beings' (Pateman, 1989: 48).

This is now widely accepted as the way men understand and experience their world. On the other hand, almost no attempt has been made to look at how it is that they take these views on board, or why the public/private divide is so much more deeply entrenched in men's lived experience than in women's. This article looks at one strand in the complex web of experiences through which this is achieved. A major site where this occurs is the school, one of the institutions particularly characteristic of the civil society that emerged with the Enlightenment (Foucault, 1980: 55–7). The school does not deliberately condition boys and not girls into this dichotomy, but it is, we believe, a site where what Giddens (1984: 10–13) has called a 'cycle of practice' introduces little boys to the public/private division.

The article is based on weekly observations in a kindergarten classroom. We examine what happens in the early days of school when the children encounter the expectations of the school with their already established conceptions of gender. The early months of school are a period when a great deal of negotiating between the children's personal agendas and the teacher's expectations has to take place, where a great deal of what Genovese (1972) has described as accommodation and resistance must be involved.

In this article, we focus on a particular contest, which, although never specifically stated, is central to the children's accommodation to school: little boys' determination to explore certain narratives of masculinity with which they are already familiar— guns, fighting, fast cars—and the teacher's attempts to outlaw their importation into the classroom setting. We argue that what occurs is a contest between two definitions of masculinity: what we have chosen to call 'warrior narratives' and the discourses of civil society—rationality, responsibility, and decorum— that are the basis of school discipline.

By 'warrior narratives', we mean narratives that assume that violence is legitimate and justified when it occurs within a struggle between good and evil. There is a tradition of such narratives, stretching from Hercules and Beowulf to Superman and Dirty Harry, where the male is depicted as the warrior, the knight-errant, the superhero, the good guy (usually called a 'goody' by Australian children), often supported by brothers in arms, and always opposed to some evil figure, such as a monster, a giant, a villain, a criminal, or, very simply, in Australian parlance, a 'baddy'. There is also a connection, it is now often suggested, between these narratives and the activity that has come to epitomize the physical expression of masculinity in the modern era: sport (Duthie, 1980; Crosset, 1990; Messner, 1992). It is as sport that the physicality and desire usually lived out in the private sphere are permitted a ritualized public presence. Even though the violence once characteristic of the warrior has, in civil society and as part of the social contract, become the prerogative of the state, it can still be re-enacted symbolically in countless sporting encounters. The mantle of the warrior is inherited by the sportsman.

The school discipline that seeks to outlaw these narratives is, we would suggest, very much a product of modernity. Bowles and Gintis have argued that 'the structure of social relations in education not only inures the student to the discipline of the work place, but develops the types of personal demeanour, modes of self-presentation, self-image, and social-class identifications which are the crucial ingredients

of job adequacy' (1976: 131). The school is seeking to introduce the children to the behaviour appropriate to the civil society of the modern world.

An accommodation does eventually take place, this article argues, through a recognition of the split between the public and the private. Most boys learn to accept that the way to power and respectability is through acceptance of the conventions of civil society. They also learn that warrior narratives are not a part of this world; they can only be experienced symbolically as fantasy or sport. The outcome, we will suggest, is that little boys learn that these narratives must be left behind in the private world of desire when they participate in the public world of reason.

The Study

The school where this study was conducted serves an old-established suburb in a country town in New South Wales, Australia. The children are predominantly Australian born and English speaking, but come from socioeconomic backgrounds ranging from professional to welfare recipient. We carried out this research in a classroom run by a teacher who is widely acknowledged as one of the finest and most successful kindergarten teachers in our region. She is an admired practitioner of free play, process writing, and creativity. There was no gender definition of games in her classroom. Groups composed of both girls and boys had turns at playing in the Doll Corner, in the Construction Area, and on the Car Mat.

The research method used was non-participant observation, the classic mode for the sociological study of children in schools (Burgess 1984; Thorne 1986; Goodenough 1987). The group of children described came to school for the first time in February 1993. The observation sessions began within a fortnight of the children entering school and were conducted during 'free activity' time, a period lasting for about an hour. At first we observed twice a week, but then settled to a weekly visit, although there were some weeks when it was inconvenient for the teacher to accommodate an observer.

The observation was non-interactive. The observer stationed herself as unobtrusively as possible, usually seated on a kindergarten-sized chair, near one of the play stations. She made pencil notes of events, with particular attention to accurately recording the words spoken by the children, and wrote up detailed narratives from the notes, supplemented by memory, on reaching home. She discouraged attention from the children by rising and leaving the area if she was drawn by them into any interaction.

This project thus employed a methodology that was ethnographic and open-ended. It was nevertheless guided by certain theories, drawn from the work on gender of Jean Anyon, Barrie Thorne, and R.W. Connell, of the nature of social interaction and its part in creating personal identity and in reproducing the structures of a society.

Anyon has adapted the conceptions of accommodation and resistance developed by Genovese (1972) to understanding how women live with gender. Genovese argued that slaves in the American South accommodated to their contradictory situation by using certain of its aspects, for example, exposure to the Christian religion, to validate a sense of self-worth and dignity. Christian beliefs then allowed them to take a critical view of slavery, which in turn legitimated certain forms of resistance (Anyon, 1983). Anyon lists a variety of ways in which women accommodate to and resist prescriptions of appropriate feminine behaviour, arguing for a significant level of choice and agency (Anyon, 1983).

Thorne argues that the processes of social life, the form and nature of the interactions, as well as the choices of the actors, should be the object of analysis. She writes, 'In this book I begin not with individuals, although they certainly appear in the account, but with *group life*—with social relations, the organization and meanings of social situations, the collective practices through which children ad adults create and re-create gender in their daily interactions' (1993: 4).

These daily interactions, Connell (1987) has suggested mesh to form what Giddens (1984) has called 'cyclical practices'. Daily interactions are neither random nor specific to particular locations. They are repeated and re-created in similar settings throughout a society. Similar needs recur, similar discourses are available, and so similar solutions to problems are adopted; thus, actions performed and discourses adopted to achieve particular ends in particular situations have the unintended consequence of producing uniformities of gendered behaviour in individuals.

In looking at the patterns of accommodation and resistance that emerge when the warrior narratives that little boys have adapted from television encounter the discipline of the classroom, we believe we have uncovered one of the cyclical practices of modernity that reveal the social contract to these boys.

Warrior Narratives in the Doll Corner

In the first weeks of the children's school experience, the Doll Corner was the area where the most elaborate acting out of warrior narratives was observed. The Doll Corner in this classroom was a small room with a glass-panelled door opening off the main area. Its furnishings—stove, sink, dolls' cots, and so on—were an attempt at a literal re-creation of a domestic setting, revealing the school's definition of children's play as a preparation for adult life. It was an area where the acting out of 'pretend' games was acceptable.

Much of the boys' play in the area was domestic:

Jimmy and Tyler were jointly ironing a tablecloth. 'Look at the sheet is burnt, I've burnt it,' declared Tyler, waving the toy iron above his head. 'I'm telling Mrs Sandison,' said Jimmy worriedly. 'No, I tricked you. It's not really burnt. See,' explained Tyler, showing Jimmy the black pattern on the cloth (23 February 1993).

'Where is the baby, the baby boy?' Justin asked, as he helped Harvey and Malcolm settle some restless teddy babies. 'Give them some potion.' Justin pretended to force feed a teddy, asking 'Do you want to drink this potion?' (4 March 1993).

On the other hand, there were attempts from the beginning by some of the boys and one of the girls to use this area for non-domestic games and, in the case of the boys, for games based on warrior narratives, involving fighting, destruction, goodies, and baddies.

The play started off quietly, Winston cuddled a teddy bear, then settled it in a bed. Just as Winston tucked in his bear, Mac snatched the teddy out of bed and swung it around his head in circles. 'Don't hurt him, give him back,' pleaded Winston, trying vainly to retrieve the teddy. The two boys were circling the small table in the center of the room. As he ran, Mac started to karate chop the teddy on the arm, and then threw it on the floor and jumped on it. He then snatched up a plastic knife, 'This is a sword. Ted is dead. They all are.' He sliced the knife across the teddy's tummy, repeating the action on the bodies of two stuffed dogs. Winston grabbed the two dogs, and with a dog in each hand, staged a dog fight. 'They are alive again' (10 February 1993).

Three boys were busily stuffing teddies into the cupboard through the sink opening. 'They're in jail. They can't escape,' said Malcolm. 'Let's pour water over them.' 'Don't do that. It'll hurt them,' shouted Winston, rushing into the Doll Corner. 'Go away, Winston. You're not in our group,' said Malcolm (12 February 1993).

The boys even imported goodies and baddies into a classic ghost scenario initiated by one of the girls:

'I'm the father,' Tyler declared. 'I'm the mother,' said Alanna. 'Let's pretend it's a stormy night and I'm afraid. Let's pretend a ghost has come to steal the dog.' Tyler nodded and placed the sheet over his head. Tyler moaned, 'ooooOOOOOOOOAHHHH!!!' and moved his outstretched arms toward Alanna. Jamie joined the game and grabbed a sheet from the doll's cradle, 'I'm the goody ghost.' 'So am I,' said Tyler. They giggled and wrestled each other to the floor. 'No! you're the baddy ghost,' said Jamie. Meanwhile, Alanna was making ghostly noises and moving around the boys. 'Did you like the game? Let's play it again,' she suggested (23 February 1993).

In the first two incidents, there was some conflict between the narratives being invoked by Winston and those used by the other boys. For Winston, the stuffed toys were the weak whom he must protect knight-errant style. For the other boys, they could be set up as the baddies whom it was legitimate for the hero to attack. Both were versions of a warrior narrative.

The gender difference in the use of these narratives has been noted by a number of observers (Paley, 1984; Clark, 1989; Thorne, 1993). Whereas even the most timid, least physically aggressive boys—Winston in this study is typical—are drawn to identifying with the heroes of these narratives, girls show almost no interest in them at this early age. The strong-willed and assertive girls in our study, as in others (Clark, 1990; Walkerdine, 1990), sought power by commandeering the role of mother, teacher, or shopkeeper, while even the highly imaginative Alanna, although she enlivened the more mundane fantasies of the other children with ghosts, old widow women, and magical mirrors, seems not to have been attracted by warrior heroes.[1]

Warrior narratives, it would seem, have a powerful attraction for little boys, which they lack for little girls. Why and how this occurs remains unexplored in early childhood research, perhaps because data for such an explanation are not available to those doing research in institutional settings. Those undertaking ethnographic research in preschools find the warrior narratives already in possession in these sites (Paley, 1984; Davies, 1989). In this research, gender difference in the appeal of warrior narratives has to be taken as a given—the data gathered are not suitable for constructing theories of origins; thus, the task of determining an explanation would seem to lie within the province of those investigating and theorizing gender differentiation during infancy, and perhaps, specifically, of those working in the tradition of feminist psychoanalysis pioneered by Dinnerstein (1977) and Chodorow (1978). Nevertheless, even though the cause may remain obscure, there can be little argument that in the English-speaking world for at least the last hundred years—think of Tom Sawyer playing Robin Hood and the pirates and Indians in J.M. Barrie's *Peter Pan*—boys have built these narratives into their conceptions of the masculine.

Accommodation through *Bricolage*

The school classroom, even one as committed to freedom and self-actualization as this, makes little provision for the enactment of these narratives. The classroom equipment invites children to play house, farm, and shop, to construct cities and roads, and to journey through them with toy cars, but there is no overt invitation to explore warrior narratives.

In the first few weeks of school, the little boys un-self-consciously set about redressing this omission. The method they used was what is known as *bricolage*—the transformation of objects from one use to another for symbolic purposes (Hebdige, 1979). The first site was the Doll Corner. Our records for the early weeks contain a number of examples of boys rejecting the usages ascribed to the various Doll Corner objects by the teacher and by the makers of equipment and assigning a different meaning to them. This became evident very early with their use of the toy baby carriages (called 'prams' in Australia). For the girls, the baby carriages were just that, but for many of the boys they very quickly became surrogate cars:

Mac threw a doll into the largest pram in the Doll Corner. He walked the pram out past a group of his friends who were playing 'crashes' on the Car Mat. Three of the five boys turned and watched him wheeling the pram toward the classroom door. Mac performed a sharp three-point turn; raced his pram past the Car Mat group, striking one boy on the head with the pram wheel (10 February 1993).

'Brrrrmmmmmm, brrrrrmmmmm,' Tyler's revving engine noises grew louder as he rocked the pram back and forth with sharp jerking movements. The engine noise grew quieter as he left the Doll Corner and wheeled the pram around the classroom. He started to run with the pram when the teacher could not observe him (23 March 1993).

The boys transformed other objects into masculine appurtenances: knives and tongs became weapons, the dolls' beds became boats, and so on.

Mac tried to engage Winston in a sword fight using Doll Corner plastic knives. Winston backed away, but Mac persisted. Winston took a knife but continued to back away from Mac. He then put down the knife, and ran away half-screaming (semi-seriously, unsure of the situation) for his teacher (10 February 1993).

In the literature on youth subcultures, bricolage is seen as a characteristic of modes of resistance. Hebdige writes:

It is through the distinctive rituals of consumption, through style, that the subculture at once reveals its 'secret' identity and communicates its forbidden meanings. It is predominantly the way commodities are used in subculture which mark the subculture off from more orthodox cultural formations. . . . The concept of *bricolage* can be used to explain how subcultural styles are constructed (1979: 103).

In these early weeks, however, the boys did not appear to be aware that they were doing anything more than establishing an accommodation between their needs and the classroom environment.

This mode of accommodation was rejected by the teacher, however, who practised a gentle, but steady, discouragement of such bricolage. Even though the objects in this space are not really irons, beds, and cooking pots, she made strong efforts to assert their cultural meaning, instructing the children in the 'proper' use of the equipment and attempting to control their behaviour by questions like 'Would you do that with a tea towel in your house?' 'Cats never climb up on the benches in *my* house.' It was thus impressed upon the children that warrior narratives were inappropriate in this space.

The children, our observations suggest, accepted her guidance, and we found no importation of warrior narratives into the Doll Corner after the first few weeks. There were a number of elaborate and exciting narratives devised, but they were all, to some degree, related to the domestic environment. For example, on April 20, Justin and Nigel used one of the baby carriages as a four-wheel drive, packed it with equipment and went off for a camping trip, setting out a picnic with Doll Corner tablecloths, knives, forks, and plates when they arrived. On May 18, Matthew, Malcolm, Nigel, and Jonathan were dogs being fed in the Doll Corner. They then complained of the flies, and Jonathan picked up the toy telephone and said, 'Flycatcher! Flycatcher! Come and catch some flies. They are everywhere.' On June 1, the following was recorded:

'We don't want our nappies [diapers] changed,' Aaron informed Celia, the mum in the game. 'I'm poohing all over your clothes mum,' Mac declared, as he grunted and positioned himself over the dress-up box. Celia cast a despairing glance in Mac's direction, and went on dressing a doll. 'I am too; poohing all over your clothes mum,' said Aaron. 'Now mum will have to clean it all up and change my nappy,' he informed Mac, giggling. He turned to the dad [Nigel], and said in a baby voice, 'Googoo; give him [Mac] the feather duster.' 'No! give him the feather duster; he did the longest one all over the clothes,' Mac said to Nigel (1 June 1993).

Although exciting and imaginative games continued, the bricolage virtually disappeared from the Doll Corner. The intention of the designer of the Doll Corner equipment was increasingly respected. Food for the camping trip was bought from the shop the teacher had set up and consumed using the Doll Corner equipment. The space invaded by flies was a domestic space, and appropriate means, calling in expert help by telephone, were used to deal with the problem. Chairs and tables were chairs and tables, clothes were clothes and could be fouled by appropriate inhabitants of a domestic space, babies. Only the baby carriages continued to have an ambiguous status, to maintain the ability to be transformed into vehicles of other kinds.

The warrior narratives—sword play, baddies in jail, pirates, and so on—did not vanish from the boys' imaginative world, but, as the later observations show, the site gradually moved from the Doll Corner to the Construction Area and the Car Mat. By the third week in March (that is, after about six weeks at school), the observer noticed the boys consistently using the construction toys to develop these narratives. The bricolage was now restricted to the more amorphously defined construction materials.

Tyler was busy constructing an object out of five pieces of plastic straw (clever sticks). 'This is a water pistol. Everyone's gonna get wet,' he cried as he moved into the Doll Corner pretending to wet people. The game shifted to guns and bullets between Tyler and two other boys. 'I've got a bigger gun,' Roger said, showing off his square block object. 'Mine's more longer. Ehehehehehehehe, got you,' Winston yelled to Roger, brandishing a plastic straw gun. 'I'll kill your gun,' Mac said, pushing Winston's gun away. 'No Mac. You broke it. No,' cried Winston (23 March 1993).

Two of the boys picked up swords made out of blue-and red-colored plastic squares they had displayed on the cupboard. 'This is my sword,' Jamie explained to Tyler. 'My jumper [sweater] holds it in. Whichever color is at the bottom, well that's the color it shoots out. Whoever is bad, we shoot with power out of it.' 'Come on Tyler,' he went on. 'Get your sword. Let's go get some baddies' (30 March 1993).

The toy cars on the Car Mat were also pressed into the service of warrior narratives:

Justin, Brendan, and Jonathan were busy on the Car Mat. The game involved police cars that were chasing baddies who had drunk 'too much beers'. Justin explained to Jonathan why his car had the word 'DOG' written on the front. 'These are different police cars, for catching robbers taking money' (4 March 1993).

Three boys, Harvey, Maurice, and Marshall, were on the Car Mat. 'Here comes the baddies,' Harvey shouted, spinning a toy car around the mat. 'Crasssshhhhh everywhere.' He crashed his car into the other boys' cars and they responded with laughter. 'I killed a baddie everyone,' said Maurice, crashing his cars into another group of cars (24 May 1993).

The boys were proposing a new accommodation, a new adaptation of classroom materials to the needs of their warrior narratives.

Classroom Rules and Resistance

Once again the teacher would not accept the accommodation proposed. Warrior narratives provoked what she considered inappropriate public behaviour in the miniature civil society of her classroom. Her aim was to create a 'free' environment where children could work independently, learn at their own pace, and explore their own interests, but creating such an environment involved its own form of social contract, its own version of the state's appropriation of violence. From the very first day, she began to establish a series of classroom rules that imposed constraints on violent or disruptive activity.

The belief underlying her practice was that firmly established classroom rules make genuine free play possible, rather than restricting the range of play opportunities. Her emphasis on 'proper' use of equipment was intended to stop it being damaged and consequently withdrawn from use. She had rules of 'no running' and 'no shouting' that allowed children to work and play safely on the floor of the classroom, even though other children were using equipment or toys that demanded movement, and ensured that the noise level was low enough for children to talk at length to one another as part of their games.

One of the outcomes of these rules was the virtual outlawing of a whole series of games that groups of children usually want to initiate when they are playing together, games of speed and body contact, of gross motor self-expression and skill. This prohibition affected both girls and boys and was justified by setting up a version of public and private spaces: The classroom was not the proper place for such activities, they 'belong' in the playground.[2] The combined experience of many teachers has shown that it is almost impossible

for children to play games involving car crashes and guns without violating these rules; therefore, in this classroom, as in many others (Paley, 1984), these games were, in effect, banned.

These rules were then policed by the children themselves, as the following interchange shows:

'Eeeeeeheeeeeeeheeeeh!' Tyler leapt about the room. A couple of girls were saying, 'Stop it Tyler' but he persisted. Jane warned, 'You're not allowed to have guns.' Tyler responded saying, 'It's not a gun. It's a water pistol, and that's not a gun.' 'Not allowed to have water pistol guns,' Tony reiterated to Tyler. 'Yes, it's a water pistol,' shouted Tyler. Jane informed the teacher, who responded stating, 'no guns, even if they are water pistols.' Tyler made a spear out of Clever Sticks, straight after the banning of gun play (23 March 1993).

The boys, however, were not prepared to abandon their warrior narratives. Unlike gross motor activities such as wrestling and football, they were not prepared to see them relegated to the playground, but the limitations on their expression and the teacher disapproval they evoked led the boys to explore them surreptitiously; they found ways of introducing them that did not violate rules about running and shouting.

As time passed, the games became less visible. The warrior narratives were not so much acted out as talked through, using the toy cars and the construction materials as a prompt and a basis:

Tyler was showing his plastic straw construction to Luke. 'This is a Samurai Man and this is his hat. A Samurai Man fights in Japan and they fight with the Ninja. The bad guys who use cannons and guns. My Samurai is captain of the Samurai and he is going to kill the sergeant of the bad guys. He is going to sneak up on him with a knife and kill him' (1 June 1993).

Malcolm and Aaron had built boats with Lego blocks and were explaining the various components to Roger. 'This ship can go faster,' Malcolm explained. 'He [a plastic man] is the boss of the ship. Mine is a goody boat. They are not baddies.' 'Mine's a steam shovel boat. It has wheels,' said Aaron. 'There it goes in the river and it has to go to a big shed where all the steam shovels are stopping' (11 June 1993).

It also became apparent that there was something covert about this play. The cars were crashed quietly. The guns were being transformed into water pistols. Swords were concealed under jumpers and only used when the teacher's back was turned. When the constructed objects were displayed to the class, their potential as players in a fighting game was concealed under a more mundane description. For example:

Prior to the free play, the children were taking turns to explain the Clever Stick and Lego Block constructions they had made the previous afternoon. I listened to Tyler describe his Lego robot to the class: 'This is a transformer robot. It can do things and turn into everything.' During free play, Tyler played with the same robot explaining its capacities to Winston: 'This is a terminator ship. It can kill. It can turn into a robot and the top pops off' (23 March 1993).

Children even protested to one another that they were not making weapons, 'This isn't a gun, it's a lookout,' 'This isn't a place for bullets, it's for petrol.'

The warrior narratives, it would seem, went underground and became part of a 'deviant' masculine subculture with the characteristic 'secret' identity and hidden meanings (Hebdige, 1979). The boys were no longer seeking accommodation but practicing hidden resistance. The classroom, they were learning, was not a place where it was acceptable to explore their gender identity through fantasy.

This, however, was a message that only the boys were receiving. The girls' gender-specific fantasies (Paley, 1984; Davies, 1989) of nurturing and self-display—mothers, nurses, brides, princesses—were accommodated easily within the classroom. They could be played out without contravening the rules of the miniature civil society. Although certain delightful activities—eating,

running, hugging, and kissing (Best, 1983)— might be excluded from this public sphere, they were not ones by means of which their femininity, and thus their subjectivity, their conception of the self, was defined.

Masculinity, the School Regime, and the Social Contract

We suggest that this conflict between warrior narratives and school rules is likely to form part of the experience of most boys growing up in the industrialized world. The commitment to such narratives was not only nearly 100 per cent among the boys we observed, but similar commitment is, as was argued above, common in other sites. On the other hand, the pressure to preserve a decorous classroom is strong in all teachers (with the possible exception of those teaching in 'alternative' schools) and has been since the beginnings of compulsory education. Indeed, it is only in classrooms where there is the balance of freedom and constraint we observed that such narratives are likely to surface at all. In more formal situations, they would be defined as deviant and forced underground from the boys' first entry into school.

If this is a widely recurring pattern, the question then arises: Is it of little significance or is it what Giddens (1984) would call one of the 'cyclical practices' that reproduce the structures of our society? The answer really depends on how little boys 'read' the outlawing of their warrior narratives. If they see it as simply one of the broad constraints of school against which they are continually negotiating, then perhaps it has no significance. If, on the other hand, it has in their minds a crucial connection to the definition of gender, to the creation of their own masculine identity, to where they position particular sites and practices on a masculine to feminine continuum, then the ostracism of warrior narratives may mean that they define the school environment as feminine.

There is considerable evidence that some primary school children do in fact make this categorization (Best, 1983; Brophy, 1985; Clark, 1990), and we suggest here that the outlawry of the masculine narrative contributes to this. Research by Willis (1977) and Walker (1988) in high schools has revealed a culture of resistance based on definitions of masculinity as *antagonistic* to the demands of the school, which are construed as feminine by the resisters. It might therefore seem plausible to see the underground perpetuation of the warrior narrative as an early expression of this resistance and one that gives some legitimacy to the resisters' claims that the school is feminine.

Is the school regime that outlaws the warrior narratives really feminine? We would argue, rather, that the regime being imposed is based on a male ideal, an outcome of the Enlightenment and compulsory schooling. Michel Foucault has pointed out that the development of this particular regime in schools coincided with the emergence of the prison, the hospital, the army barracks, and the factory (Foucault, 1980). Although teachers in the first years of school are predominantly female, the regime they impose is perpetuated by male teachers (Brophy, 1985), and this preference is endorsed by powerful and influential males in the society at large. The kind of demeanour and self-management that teachers are trying to inculcate in the early school years is the behaviour expected in male-dominated public arenas like boardrooms, courtrooms, and union mass meetings.[3]

Connell (1989) and Willis (1977) provide evidence that by adolescence, boys from all classes, particularly if they are ambitious, come to regard acquiescence in the school's demands as compatible with constructing a masculine identity. Connell writes:

> Some working class boys embrace a project of mobility in which they construct a masculinity organized around themes of rationality and responsibility. This is closely connected with the 'certification' function of the upper levels of the education system and to a key form of masculinity among professionals (1989: 291).

Rationality and responsibility are, as Weber argued long ago, the primary characteristics of the modern society theorized by the Enlightenment thinkers as based on a social contract. This prized rationality has been converted, in practice, into a bureaucratized legal system where 'responsible' acceptance by the population of the rules of civil society obviates the need for individuals to use physical violence in gaining their ends or protecting their rights, and where, if such violence is necessary, it is exercised by the state (Weber, 1978). In civil society, the warrior is obsolete, his activities redefined bureaucratically and performed by the police and the military.

The teacher in whose classroom our observation was conducted demonstrated a strong commitment to rationality and responsibility. For example, she devoted a great deal of time to showing that there was a cause and effect link between the behaviour forbidden by her classroom rules and classroom accidents. Each time an accident occurred, she asked the children to determine the cause of the accident, its result, and how it could have been prevented. The implication throughout was that children must take responsibility for the outcomes of their actions.

Mac accidentally struck a boy, who was lying on the floor, in the head with a pram wheel. He was screaming around with a pram, the victim was playing on the Car Mat and lying down to obtain a bird's eye view of a car crash. Mac rushed past the group and collected Justin on the side of the head. Tears and confusion ensued. The teacher's reaction was to see to Justin, then stop all play and gain children's attention, speaking first to Mac and Justin plus Justin's group:

T.   How did Justin get hurt?
M.   [No answer]
T.   Mac, what happened?
M.   I was wheeling the pram and Justin was in the way.
T.   Were you running?
M.   I was wheeling the pram.

The teacher now addresses the whole class:

T.   Stop working everyone, eyes to me and listen. Someone has just been hurt because someone didn't remember the classroom rules. What are they, Harvey?

(Harvey was listening intently and she wanted someone who could answer the question at this point).

H.   No running in the classroom.
T.   Why?

Other children offer an answer.

Chn.   Because someone will get hurt.
T.   Yes, and that is what happened. Mac was going too quickly with the pram and Justin was injured. Now how can we stop this happening next time?
Chn.   No running in the classroom, only walk (10 February 1993).

Malcolm, walking, bumped Winston on the head with a construction toy. The teacher intervened.

T.   [To Malcolm and Winston] What happened?
W.   Malcolm hit me on the head.
M.   But it was an accident. I didn't mean it. I didn't really hurt him.
T.   How did it happen?
M.   It was an accident.
W.   He [Malcolm] hit me.
T.   Malcolm, I know you didn't mean to hurt Winston, so how did it happen?
M.   I didn't mean it.
T.   I know you didn't mean it, Malcolm, but why did Winston get hurt?
Chn.   Malcolm was running.
M.   No I wasn't.
T.   See where everyone was sitting? There is hardly enough room for children to walk. Children working on the floor must remember to leave a walking path so that other children can move safely around the room. Otherwise someone will be hurt, and that's what has happened today (23 February 1993).

This public-sphere masculinity of rationality and responsibility, of civil society, of the social contract is not the masculinity that the boys are bringing into the classroom through their warrior narratives. They are using a different, much older version—not the male as responsible citizen, the producer, and consumer who keeps the capitalist system going, the breadwinner, and caring father of a family. Their earliest vision of masculinity is the male as warrior, the bonded male who goes out with his mates and meets the dangers of the world, the male who attacks and defeats other males characterized as baddies, the male who turns the natural products of the earth into weapons to carry out these purposes.

We would argue, nevertheless, that those boys who aspire to become one of the brothers who wield power in the public world of civil society ultimately realize that conformity to rationality and responsibility, to the demands of the school, is the price they must pay. They realize that although the girls can expect one day to become the brides and mothers of their pretend games, the boys will never, except perhaps in time of war, be allowed to act out the part of warrior hero in reality.

On the other hand, the school softens the transition for them by endorsing and encouraging the classic modern transformation and domestication of the warrior narrative, sport (Connell, 1987; Messner, 1992). In the school where this observation was conducted, large playground areas are set aside for lunchtime cricket, soccer, and basketball; by the age of seven, most boys are joining in these games. The message is conveyed to them that if they behave like citizens in the classroom, they can become warriors on the sports oval.

Gradually, we would suggest, little boys get the message that resistance is not the only way to live out warrior masculinity. If they accept a public/ private division of life, it can be accommodated within the private sphere; thus, it becomes possible for those boys who aspire to respectability, figuring in civil society as one of the brothers, to accept that the school regime and its expectations are masculine and to reject the attempts of the 'resisters' to define it (and them) as feminine. They adopt the masculinity of rationality and responsibility as that appropriate to the public sphere, while the earlier, deeply appealing masculinity of the warrior narratives can still be experienced through symbolic re-enactment on the sports field.

Conclusion

We are not, of course, suggesting that this is the only way in which the public/private division becomes part of the lived awareness of little boys. We do, however, believe that we have teased out one strand of the manner in which they encounter it. We have suggested that the classroom is a major site where little boys are introduced to the masculinity of rationality and responsibility characteristic of the brothers in civil society; we have been looking at a 'cycle of practice' where, in classroom after classroom, generation after generation, the mode of masculinity typified in the warrior narratives is first driven underground and then transferred to the sports field. We are, we would suggest, seeing, renegotiated, for each generation and in each boy's own life, the conception of the 'social contract' that is characteristic of the era of modernity, of the Enlightenment, of democracy, and of capitalism. We are watching, re-enacted, the transformation of violence and power as exercised by body over body, to control through surveillance and rules (Foucault, 1977, 1984), the move from domination by individual superiors to acquiescence in a public sphere of decorum and rationality (Pateman, 1988).

Yet, this is a social *contract*, and there is another side to the bargain. Although they learn that they must give up their warrior narratives of masculinity in the public sphere, where rationality and responsibility hold sway, they also learn that in return they may preserve them in the private realm of desire as fantasy, as bricolage, as a symbolic survival that is appropriate to the spaces of leisure and self-indulgence, the playground, the backyard, the television set, the sports field. Although this is too large an issue to be explored in detail here, there may even be a re-enactment in the school setting of what Pateman (1988) has defined as the sexual contract, the male right to dominate women in return for accepting the constraints of civil society. Is this, perhaps, established for both boys and girls by means of the endemic misogyny—invasion of girls' space (Thorne, 1986, 1993), overt expressions of aversion and disgust (Goodenough, 1987; D'Arcy, 1990), disparaging sexual innuendo (Best, 1983; Goodenough, 1987; Clark, 1990)—noted by so many observers in the classrooms and playgrounds of modernity? Are girls being contained by the boys' actions within a more restricted, ultimately a private, sphere because, in the boys' eyes, they have not earned access to the public sphere by sharing their ordeal of repression, resistance, and ultimate symbolic accommodation of their gender-defining fantasies?

Notes

The research on which this article is based was funded by the Research Management Committee of the University of Newcastle. The observation was conducted at East Maitland Public School and the authors would like to thank the principal, teachers, and children involved for making our observer so welcome.

1. Some ethnographic studies describe a 'tomboy' who wants to join in the boys' games (Best, 1983; Davies, 1989; Thorne, 1993), although in our experience, such girls are rare, rarer even than the boys who play by choice with girls. The girls' rejection of the warrior narratives does not appear to be simply the result of the fact that the characters are usually men. Bronwyn Davies, when she read the role-reversal story *Rita the Rescuer* to preschoolers, found that many boys identified strongly with Rita ('they flex their muscles to show how strong they are and fall to wrestling each other on the floor to display their strength'), whereas for most girls, Rita remained 'other' (Davies, 1989: 57–8).

2. This would seem to reverse the usual parallel of outdoor/indoor with public/private. This further suggests that the everyday equation of 'public' with 'visible' may not be appropriate for the specialized use of the term in sociological discussions of the public/private division. Behaviour in the street may be more visible than what goes on in a courtroom, but it is nevertheless acceptable

for the street behaviour to be, to a greater degree, personal, private, and driven by 'desire'.

3. There are some groups of men who continue to reject these modes of modernity throughout their lives. Andrew Metcalfe, in his study of an Australian mining community, has identified two broad categories of miner, the 'respectable', and the 'larrikin' (an Australian slang expression carrying implications of non-conformism, irreverence, and impudence). The first are committed to the procedural decorums of union meetings, sporting and hobby clubs, welfare groups, and so on; the others relate more strongly to the less disciplined masculinity of the pub, the brawl, and the race-track (Metcalfe, 1988). This distinction is very similar to that noted by Paul Willis in England between the 'ear'oles' and the 'lads' in a working-class secondary school (Willis, 1977). It needs to be noted that this is not a *class* difference and that demographically the groups are identical. What distinguishes them is, as Metcalfe points out, their relative commitment to the respectable modes of accommodation and resistance characteristic of civil society of larrikin modes with a much longer history, perhaps even their acceptance or rejection of the social contract.

References

Anyon, J. 1983. 'Intersections of Gender and Class: Accommodation and Resistance by Working-class Ideologies', in S. Walker and L. Barton, eds., *Gender, Class and Education*. Barcombe, Sussex: and Affluent Females to Contradictory Sex-role Falmer.

Best, R. 1983. *We've All Got Scars: What Girls and Boys Learn in Elementary School*. Bloomington: Indiana University Press.

Bowles, S., and H. Gintis. 1976. *Schooling in Capitalist America: Educational Reform and the Contradictions of Economic Life*. London: Routledge and Kegan Paul.

Brophy, J.E. 1985. 'Interactions of Male and Female Students with Male and Female Teachers', in L.C. Wilkinson and C.B. Marrett, eds., *Gender Influences in Classroom Interaction*. New York: Academic Press.

Burgess, R.G., ed. 1984. *The Research Process in Educational Settings: Ten Case Studies*. Lewes: Falmer.

Chodorow, N. 1978. *The Reproduction of Mothering: Psychoanalysis and the Sociology of Gender*. Berkeley: University of California Press.

Clark, M. 1989. 'Anastasia is a Normal Developer because She is Unique', *Oxford Review of Education* 15: 243–55.

———. 1990. *The Great Divide: Gender in the Primary School*. Melbourne: Curriculum Corporation.

Connell, R.W. 1987. *Gender and Power: Society, the Person and Sexual Politics*. Sydney: Allen and Unwin.

———. 1989. 'Cool Guys, Swots and Wimps: The Interplay of Masculinity and Education', *Oxford Review of Education* 15: 291–303.

Crosset, T. 1990. 'Masculinity, Sexuality, and the Development of Early Modern Sport', in M.E. Messner and D.F. Sabo, eds., *Sport, Men and the Gender Order*. Champaign, IL: Human Kinetics Books.

D'Arcy, S. 1990. 'Towards a Non-sexist Primary Classroom', in E. Tutchell, ed., *Dolls and Dungarees: Gender Issues in the Primary School Curriculum*. Milton Keynes: Open University Press.

Davies, B. 1989. *Frogs and Snails and Feminist Tales: Preschool Children and Gender*. Sydney: Allen and Unwin.

Dinnerstein, M. 1977. *The Mermaid and the Minotaur: Sexual Arrangements and Human Malaise*. New York: Harper and Row.

Duthie, J.H. 1980. 'Athletics: The Ritual of a Technological Society?', in H.B. Schwartzman, ed., *Play and Culture*. West Point, NY: Leisure.

Eisenstein, H. 1984. *Contemporary Feminist Thought*. London: Unwin Paperbacks.

Foucault, M. 1977. *Discipline and Punish: The Birth of the Prison*, A. Sheridan, trans. New York: Pantheon.

———. 1980. 'Body/power', in C. Gordon, ed., *power/knowledge: Selected Interviews and Other Writings 1972–1977*. Brighton: Harvester.

———. 1984. 'Truth and Power', in P. Rabinow, *The Foucault Reader*. New York: Pantheon.

Genovese, E.E. 1972. *Roll, Jordan, Roll: The World the Slaves Made*. New York: Pantheon.

Giddens, A. 1984. *The Constitution of Society. Outline of the Theory of Structuration*. Berkeley: University of California Press.

Goodenough, Ruth Gallagher. 1987. 'Small Group Culture and the Emergence of Sexist Behaviour:

A Comparative Study of Four Children's Groups', in G. Spindler and L. Spindler, eds., *Interpretive Ethnography of Education*. Hillsdale, NJ: Lawrence Erlbaum.

Hebdige, D. 1979. *Subculture: The Meaning of Style*. London: Methuen.

Messner, M.E. 1992. *Power at Play: Sports and the Problem of Masculinity*. Boston: Beacon.

Metcalfe, A. 1988. *For Freedom and Dignity: Historical Agency and Class Structure in the Coalfields of NSW*. Sydney: Allen and Unwin.

Paley, V.G. 1984. *Boys and Girls: Superheroes in the Doll Corner*. Chicago: University of Chicago Press.

Pateman, C. 1988. *The Sexual Contract*. Oxford: Polity.

————. 1989. 'The Fraternal Social Contract', in *The Disorder of Women*. Cambridge: Polity.

Thorne, B. 1986. 'Girls and Boys Together . . . But Mostly Apart: Gender Arrangements in Elementary Schools', in W.W. Hartup and Z. Rubin, eds., *Relationships and Development*. Hillsdale, NJ: Lawrence Erlbaum.

————. 1993. *Gender Play: Girls and Boys in School*. New Brunswick, NJ: Rutgers University Press.

Walker, J.C. 1988. *Louts and Legends: Male Youth Culture in an Inner-city School*. Sydney: Allen and Unwin.

Walkerdine, V. 1990. *Schoolgirl Fictions*. London: Verso.

Weber, M. 1978. *Selections in Translation*. W.G. Runciman, ed. and E. Matthews, trans. Cambridge: Cambridge University Press.

Willis, P. 1977. *Learning to Labour: How Working Class Kids Get Working Class Jobs*. Farnborough: Saxon House.

CHAPTER 22

Intimate Colonialisms: The Material and Experienced Places of British Columbia's Residential Schools

Sarah de Leeuw

Introduction

While there is a growing literature on residential schools in BC (Redford 1979-80; Haig-Brown 1988; Sterling 1992; Raibmon 1996; Woods 1996; Neylan 2000), little geographic notice has been given to colonialism as it was embedded, embodied, and enacted through these schools. In this article, I argue that the relatively small and intimate geographies of residential schools offer important insights into colonial projects in BC. I begin with a brief history of the province's residential schools, followed by a discussion of theories of place as a means to conceptualize colonialism. I then explore how both the material and the non-physical geographies of residential schools sought to shape and transform First Nations children while simultaneously acting as sites within which First Nations

subjects asserted agency and indigeneity. First Nations published testimonies[1] provide the primary referent through which experiences of place are explored. Theoretical discussions concerning the 'nested place'[2] nature of BC's residential schools and their occupants allow both to be examined as singular subjects and as places of multiplicity and plurality within the colonial contest. This plurality becomes apparent, in part, when First Nations students' narratives of trauma and victimization within the schools are juxtaposed with narratives of active student resistance and expressions of creative agency within the same locations. Although the testimonies considered in the first section of the article portray residential schooling primarily as a traumatic and disciplining effort imposed upon First Nations students, in the second section of the article I am interested in disrupting, or troubling, the narrative of uncontested colonial imposition. Consequently, I conclude the article with a consideration of how nested place, First Nations' resistances and Euro-colonial concepts of gender are circulating today with reference to a Dakelh woman (and former residential school student) under consideration for beatification in northern BC.

Place, as geographers have long observed, is a complex and contested concept. Nevertheless, broad agreement holds that place has an intimacy and 'known-ness' that the concept of space can lack. Furthermore, ongoing discussions concerning place have expanded the concept far beyond that of a small, contained, site within a more encompassing or universal space. Although place certainly carries with it the resonance of 'locale', it is incorrect to assume a material neutrality to the concept (Massey 1994). Indeed, as Agnew (1887) insists, place is precisely where 'social relations are constituted' (26) and as Keith and Pile (1993) have argued, place must be theorized as 'no longer passive, no longer fixed, no longer unidialectical . . . but, still, in a very real sense about location and locatedness' (5). Furthermore, social and political ideologies are made to function, are put into practice and are understood, in part through their emplacement (Cresswell 1996). As Casey (1997) suggests, place can be a generative event and may be understood as 'an active source of presencing [where] within its close embrace, things get located and begin to happen' (63).

Place no longer suggests rigid containment or boundary but rather, taking its lead from the permeability of the organic body, 'extends to the world without end . . . ingresses into the world in its entirety and draws that world back into itself. Thanks to this power, place is to be recognized as an un-delimited, de-totalized expansiveness, resonating regionally throughout the unknown as well as the known universe' (336). That conceptualizations of place might take direction from considerations of the body, or indeed that the body is a politicized place unto itself, is a concept not overlooked by feminist geographers. McDowell (1999), for instance, argues that the body is the most intimate of places while simultaneously embodying crucial sites of political, economic, and cultural struggles. The body, as Smith (1993) argues, is the place where one subject joins

or separates from another and where 'the culturally dominant and the culturally marginalized are assigned their 'proper' places' (10).

BC's residential schools, and the bodies of both the First Nations children and colonial subjects who occupied them, might thus be theorized as places within broader colonial narratives where the material and the ideological are inextricably linked. The enfolded combination of these places might be further understood as simultaneously supporting and defying the larger colonial contest in which all were situated. In other words, the relatively small places of BC's residential schools (and the smaller body-places within the schools) may be understood as multi-directional and permeable sites nested within, yet crucial to, larger spatial colonial projects. Theorizing the nestedness of residential schools, and of those who occupied them, resonates with Malpas's (1999) philosophy that subjectivity is embedded, or nested, within place and that place is narrated both by those subjects who occupy and make sense of it and by events and social interactions which also construct it. It is through this conceptualization of nested place that BC's residential schools become both places experienced within the colonial contest and places narrated by the in situ subjects, who have agency, whom the colonial process sought through education to assimilate and transform into non-indigenous peoples.

Intimate Places of Colonialism: Residential Schools in British Columbia

British Columbia's residential schools operated between 1861 and 1984. The majority of the schools were (and remain) clustered in the southwest region of the province. Of the 18, nine were operated (in partnership with the federal government) by the Roman Catholic Church while the remaining nine were operated by the United, Methodist and Anglican Churches (Figure 22.1). While both day and boarding schools operated across Canada prior to the 1876 Indian Act and the Davin Report (1879), the vast majority of schools in British Columbia opened after both of

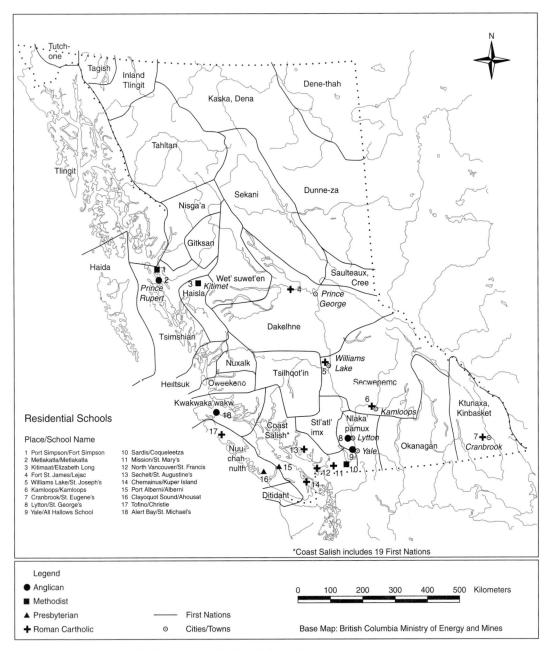

Figure 22.1 Residential Schools in British Columbia

these colonial education milestones were in place. Seventeen of the 18 schools opened post the 1876 Indian Act while 15 of British Columbia's residential schools opened and operated after Davin's report was tabled in 1879. Most BC residential schools, therefore, operated within a clear assimilativist policy framework: residential education was a means both to break Aboriginal children's links with their communities and cultures and a means to absorb them into a dominant society (Titley

1986). The built and material structures of the province's residential schools, in addition to the curricular and ideological content delivered within the schools, might thus be theorized as physical and non-material 'placial' realizations of larger colonial endeavours toward Aboriginal peoples.

Architecturally and materially, BC's residential schools transmitted a colonial narrative of non-Aboriginal domination and superiority over First Nations peoples. As the Nuu-chah-nulth Tribal Council (1996) has attested, residential schools which Nuu-chah-nulth people attended were:

> often laid out on or near the top of a hill, giving them an imposing, looming, even scary appearance in the eyes of young Nuu-chah-nulth children new to such places. The comparatively huge residential school buildings implied an importance above and beyond that of any local traditional authority, including that of the highest ranked Chief. On their first day at Indian Residential Schools, along with the trauma of being separated from their parents, Nuu-chah-nulth students new to the schools faced the realization that physical conditions, at those institutions, were very different than those they were used to in their home villages (27–28).

Similarly, an anonymous testimony by a former Kamloops Indian Residential School student, published by the Secwepemc Cultural Education Society (2000), recollects the school as physically overwhelming and powerfully disorienting. The student recalls:

> When I got to the residential school [Kamloops], it looked huge. I remember thinking, how am I ever going to find my way around here, everything's so big. When Father was talking to me, it seemed to be hollow and echoing. It seemed strange, you could smell the polish of the floors, it seemed so different. When I got upstairs the lights were out and it was dark in there. When I finally knelt down [to pray], I disappeared under the bed, it was so high. . . . I remember laying there and crying and crying (182).

Far, then, from functioning as mere containers through which colonial narratives were delivered, residential school buildings and grounds were colonial geographies in which First Nations students were enveloped. The buildings ensured First Nations students, from the moment they set eyes upon the places of their 'education', were spatially disoriented in a place designed to exclude and expunge indigeneity. The materiality of the schools produced, in situ, the power and supremacy of a Euro-colonial presence in BC. First Nations students were not only dwarfed within a colonially built environment, they were materially reminded in their every movement that their lives and culture were subordinated to a more imposing and powerful force making effort to overtake and transform them as indigenous peoples.

Aboriginal girls and young women were particularly susceptible to the bodily implantation of colonialism. This was a consciously articulated policy amongst colonial administrators and was expressed in sentiments such as the 'great forces of intermarriage and education will finally overcome the lingering traces of native custom and tradition' (Duncan Campbell Scott, quoted in Titley 1986, 34). If Nicolas Flood Davin envisioned residential schools as, metaphorically, womb like places where Aboriginal children would receive the 'care of a mother' and if the Superintendent of Indian Affairs conflated intermarriage and education as the two ways to overcome Aboriginal custom and tradition, it should perhaps come as little surprise that the testimonies of former residential school students include (albeit very scant) recollections of pregnancy and abortion within the schools. Although sexual assault and forced impregnation were by no means policy imperatives of the colonial Canadian government, a climate of subordinating First Nations physical and emotional worth, in combination with scant monitoring of the schools, may have conspired to produce the environment that Eddy Jules of Kamloops Indian Residential School recalls:

> When I was in Senior B, I used to hear about girls getting pregnant down the other end of the building. They'd get pregnant, but they

would never have kids, you know. And the thing was, they'd bring somebody in from over town who'd do an abortion, I guess. We used to hear it. It used to be really scary, hearing them open up the incinerator after what was going on. Ninety percent of it, I think, was from the supervisor knocking up our people because to them we were nothing (Secwepemc 2000, 74).

Jules' account must be read carefully and thoughtfully, particularly because, as he acknowledges, boys and girls were separated by place within the schools and his knowledge is thus not firsthand. Pregnancy in Canadian residential schools is almost entirely unrecorded in the research and literature about the schools. Reference, particularly by women, to impregnation is almost non-existent in testimonial literatures. This is likely attributable to both the tremendous shame factor involved for First Nations women and, as David Adams (1995) points out with reference to American boarding schools, to 'superintendents [who] were generally hesitant to talk about such matters for the simple reason that it reflected poorly on their management abilities. There is no record of how many girls were quietly dropped from the rolls [of boarding schools] for reasons of pregnancy' (180). While Mary-Ellen Kelm's (1996; 1998) detailed accounts of unhealth in BC's residential schools do not mention pregnancy, she does note that transforming First Nations cultures 'meant capturing bodies first: indeed, residential schooling had, at its very core, the desire to physically supervise, contain and control the population of First Nations' youth' (1996: 53) and that former students struggled with seeing 'their bodies as sites of sinfulness rather than beauty . . . both as the long-term result of an anti-body Christian education and, more traumatically, of sexual abuse' (78). Eddy Jules himself offers perhaps the most poignant explanation as to why so little about pregnancy in the schools is recorded. He states '. . . I was scared. I think most of the kids realized what was going on, but there was nothing we could do. We couldn't say anything because nobody would believe us. We'd talk about it, you know' (Secwepemc 2000, 75). Little doubt exists that sexual abuses occurred in British

Columbia's residential schools. Ecumenical apologies, court rulings, confessions of perpetrators and innumerable First Nations testimonies corroborate this (Buti 2001; Canada 2003). It is not unreasonable to extrapolate from these evidences that pregnancies did occur in British Columbia's residential schools and that Eddy Jules' memories offer insight into school realities. The colonial project in BC was certainly practiced through nested place strategies; the residential schools themselves, the subjects contained by the schools and, finally, the most intimate of places within the bodies of young First Nations peoples.

The gendered specificity of colonialism's project in BC was encoded within residential school architecture. Boys' dorms were separated from girls' dorms and, while this division would have been common to many non-Aboriginal boarding schools of the late nineteenth and early twentieth century in BC, what was unique about Indian residential schools was the heightened social segregation and familial breakdown which resulted from that material separation of genders. Gender division served two functions within residential schools: separating members of First Nations families and entrenching Euro-colonial gender ideals. A former student of Christie Indian Residential school and a Hesquia-asksup member of the Nuu-chah-nulth Nation observes that gender separation in the school resulted in her being

torn apart from them [siblings]. The windows were painted up so that we couldn't see our relatives, or our brothers. I never knew anyone [because] they always had us divided from others. They always made us forget our own family! Well, they did! We weren't allowed to speak to our own brother! (Nuu-chah-nulth 1996, 17).

Barbara Amos, another member of the Nuu-chah-nulth Nation and former student of Alberni Indian Residential School, recalls that gender separation was not confined to dorm rooms, remembering that the school was 'really strict . . . like girls on one side and boys on the other side. And that's how we ate too . . . We never ate together like a family' (Nuu-chah-nulth 1996, 21). Robert Cootes recalls that the gendered limitations and place separations imposed on students at Alberni Residential School were very much about breaking family bonds, stating that:

> throughout the night a half dozen, dozen kids would be crying, you know . . . just whimpering [about wanting family] . . . Oh yeah, I had three sisters and a brother there . . . we got punished for even talking to them! We couldn't even look at them! Couldn't go five feet within the fence without getting punished for it, [because] my sisters lived on the other side of the fence (Nuu-chah-nulth 1996, 26).

Place, particularly place as gendered and segregated, functioned within residential school to separate families and erode familial ties, furthering the colonial goals of assimilating and transforming Aboriginal peoples.

The materiality of residential schools was also inherent to the propagation of Euro-colonial ideals about the Victorian domestic ideals, which were enacted and became entrenched through the curriculum and the structuring of place. Teaching and enforcing Euro-appropriate domestic skills, including keeping a clean house, cooking scheduled meals and performing as a dedicated wife and mother, were all part of a civilizing mission enforced on colonized subjects The Euro-colonial project in Canada had a specific vision of civilizing Aboriginal women. This vision included imaging Aboriginal women as embodiments of colonial femininity, inclusive of traits popularized through the cult of the domestic, arguably with an anticipated outcome of disrupting the cycle of Aboriginal culture (i.e., disrupting Aboriginal motherhood and mothering) and ultimately eliminating indigeneity from a settler landscape (Adams 1995; Jago 1998).

Within the curricular policy document developed by the Oblate Fathers Indian and Eskimo Welfare Commission (1958) to address cross-Canada challenges in the residential school system, an entire section is devoted to vocational training for girls (home economics and household sciences). An imagination and vision of transforming Aboriginal girls into embodiments of Euro-colonial femininity is strikingly articulated:

> Throughout her contact with household science, the young girl discovers, by observation and practice, the secrets of sewing, knitting, and cooking. She is also taught to develop good habits and receives some training in the care of infants and sick people. This training should also teach her, apart from the practical knowledge necessary for the accomplishment of her daily duties, the love of the work she will be called upon to perform later in her own home (1958, 75).

The colonially envisioned future home of First Nations girls was a home consistent with Euro-colonial concepts of domestic space. The curricular ideology concerning home consequently focused on kitchens, dining rooms and sewing rooms, all of which were reflected in the teaching environment of residential schools. Kitchens and dining halls, as well as sewing, washing and ironing rooms became the places where Euro-colonial ideals of femininity were constructed, enforced and rewarded within Indian Residential Schools in British Columbia. At St. Mary's Indian Residential School, girls were responsible for sewing their own clothing (always consistent with European and settler styles), for sewing boys clothing, for sewing school costumes and for making all domestic materials including sheets and curtains (Glavin 2002). The same was true in the Kamloops Indian Residential School, where former student Janie Marchand recalls 'I used to make dresses and make underwear, you know, slips and vests and stuff like that for winter. . . . I learned how to sew, I learned how to crochet and I learned how to darn. I could darn socks really good' (Secwepemc 2000, 45). In St. Mary's, Kamloops, and Williams Lake Indian Residential Schools, the girls' sewing was a means by which the schools could raise much-needed operating funds (Furniss 1992). It also further differentiated boys from girls. At all three schools, sewing occurred in monitored spaces where a strict segregation of the sexes was enforced (boys were not allowed in sewing or washing rooms). Kitchens were also places where Euro-colonial imaginings and enforcement of femininity occurred. Like sewing and washing rooms, kitchens were a girl's domain (Nuu-chah-nulth 1996). Boys were prevented from entering them. Aboriginal girls were schooled in European culinary practices, were trained in colonial concepts of hygiene and, importantly, had enforced upon them concepts of servitude toward the colonial class (Hare and Barman 2006). When Euro-colonial femininity was acceptably performed by Aboriginal girls within scheduled places (these were scrutinized by female members of residential school staff) (Glavin 2003), girls were rewarded with authorization to partake in rituals that were also consistent with a domesticizing narrative. One such reward was to allow girls the privilege of preparing a meal and inviting fellow male students to eat it with them, thus allowing girls further opportunity to display newly learned manners and domestic etiquette (Adams 1995).

While Euro-colonial visions of domesticity and femininity were conceived and enforced within Indian residential school rooms, the visions were also inscribed upon the bodies of Aboriginal girls, notably through curriculum concerned with hygiene and health, fashion and behaviour. As a means of ensuring Aboriginal girls' bodies conformed to idealized concepts of femininity, girls were taught to properly wear hats and gloves, how to style their hair and how to appear appropriately modest and humble (Glavin 2003). In 'before and after' photographs of girls, 'savages' shed buckskin, feathers, robes and moccasins; the long black hair was shorn or bobbed or twisted into identical, 'manageable' styles; [and] pinafores, stiff starched collars, stockings and black oxfords [all] signified the 'new woman' (Lomawaima 1993, 229). Barbara Amos who attended Christie Indian Residential School testifies that 'another thing about Christie is the way they cut your hair. From what I remember, I didn't like it. 'Cause I had long hair when I went there [and] they cut my hair . . . and it always had to be up here, short . . . and we always had to have our hair curled' (Nuu-chah-nulth 1996, 64). Diane Sandy, a former student of Kamloops Indian Residential School, recalls that:

dress was a tunic, a maroon colored tunic and you wore, either you got black bloomers or you got white ones, brown socks. That first week at school . . . they put us in a line up and . . . cut our hair short. So, most of our hairdos that first year was straight cut and bangs, and some of us had long hair. We all cried seeing all the hair being cut off, put in a big pile there. Very strict, very, very, strict (Sewepemc 2000).

The bodies of young First Nations women were sites where the material and the ideological converged, through fashion inscription, through teaching and curricular intent, and through the rooms in which the students were schooled. A multi-directional relationship between material, bodily, and experiential places must thus have existed in the colonial geographies of BC's residential schools. Recognizing the multi-directional nature of a relationship suggests that, just as the colonial project asserted itself onto and into Aboriginal students, so to did First Nations children respond to and alter the project that worked so hard to contain them.

In Place Resistances: Aboriginal Students Respond to British Columbia's Residential Schools

The goal of residential schooling was to eliminate Aboriginality from the Canadian landscape by assimilating and transforming of Aboriginal peoples. Colonial policy-makers and educators on the front lines of 'Indian education' undertook efforts to implement this goal through deliberate and effective uses of place. Twelve years after the last residential school was closed in BC, however, Phil Fontaine, the National Chief of the Assembly of First Nations (AFN), observed of the residential schooling process that 'our lands were taken, our children brutalized and our languages, governments, religions, and ways of living stifled. But miraculously, we survived and here we are today, standing before you, strong and determined to reclaim our birthright in the Canadian Confederation' (Fontaine 1998, 2). How then, in the face of such focused efforts by Euro-colonialists, did First Nations ensure the failure of educational processes designed to eliminate them as peoples? More than 20 years ago, James Redford (1979–80) offered a succinctly simple observation about residential schooling in British Columbia: 'Any relationship is a mutual and perpetually changing phenomenon; to examine the contributions of only one of its participants [the colonists] is to see not half a picture, but a gravely distorted image' (55–56). The image of colonialism's project in residential school was clear for First Nations students. Colonial teachers were actively attempting to inflict colonial education upon and into students. Steve Charleson, a former student, remembers clearly that 'they wanted to change us . . . [because] it seemed like they hated us, you know, it seemed like we were always hated just for being [who] we were' (Nuu-chah-nulth 1996, 112). In spite of considerable pressure to behave otherwise, First Nations students asserted cultural sovereignty and strength. Students resisted through and within the very places designed to subordinate them and, additionally, students resisted with the intimate places into which colonialism was attempting so aggressively to insert itself: their bodies.

Evidence of First Nations students' rejection of residential schooling is attainable, in part, both through school records of student infractions and through stories articulated by former residential school students. At Coqualeetza Residential School in Chilliwack students' in-place struggles against colonial schooling resulted in an exhaustive list of punishable offences. The list suggests to just what lengths First Nations children would go in order both to combat their assimilative education and to actively transform their schooling environments. Everything from 'breaking bounds' to 'setting fire to the boy's dorm' and from 'pulling carrots' to 'breaking plaster' were listed as punishable offences along a spectrum from 'public reprimands' to 'lashes' and 'confinement/humiliation' (Woods 1996). First Nations students must have thus been active in responding to the materialized Euro-colonial parameters in which they were confined: they broke physical bounds meant to contain them and they burnt the buildings and rooms meant to impart upon students the dominance over them of a colonial project. In other words, students *used* the very places (residential schools) claimed by the colonial project in order to disrupt the material articulations of colonialism. Students also bodily resisted colonial education through 'offences' listed by Coqualeetza as 'talking Indian', 'playing in school', 'Indian dancing' and 'insolence'. When First Nations students spoke their Native tongues and danced in manners antithetical to the regulations of a residential school, they were deploying their bodies in physical defiance of colonialism's project in BC. They were, in effect, performing and asserting the simultaneous instantiations of resistance that every act of domination conjures (Scott 1990).

Acknowledgments

I am thankful to the Nuu-chah-nulth Tribal Council and the Secwepemc Cultural Education Society who, respectively, provided me copies of locally published testimonial literatures and access to their private archives. I am also thankful to staff and librarians at the Williams Lake Community Archives and the Archives of Deschatelets of the Oblates of Mary Immaculate for their willingness to grant me access to their collections. Both Anne Godlewska and Audrey Kobayashi have provided invaluable guidance and assistance, as have two anonymous reviewers. Mary and Dionys de Leeuw, Luke Eades, Emilie Cameron and David Fortin have all assisted, tremendously, in the development and writing of this article. This article evolved from a presentation given at the 2005 Annual General Meeting of the Canadian Association of Geographers in London, Ontario. I am thankful both to the organizers of that session, Laura Cameron and Caroline Desbiens, and to all those who provided feedback on that early draft. The research was made possible through Canada Graduate Scholarship funding provided by the Social Sciences and Humanities Research Council of Canada (SSHRC).

Notes

1. A number of indigenous scholars (Smith 1999; Castellano 2004; Schnarch 2004) have made compelling arguments concerning the problematics of non-indigenous researchers conducting research on or about indigenous peoples and issues. The difficulties are exceptionally acute, argue these scholars, when indigenous peoples are asked to share stories and knowledge, particularly if it concerns traumatic events that illicit painful memories, which are then removed from the research subjects' control. Concurrent with my appreciation of these positions is my interest in Gayatri Spivak's question as to whether or not the subaltern can speak. By 'speaking' Spivak states she does not mean 'talking' but rather an engagement in 'a transaction between speaker and listener' (Spivak 1996: 289). My use of (primarily) First Nations *published* testimonial literatures concerning experiences in British Columbian residential schools is an attempt both to address my discomfort with research reliant on interviewing (and potentially re-traumatizing) people about their experiences in residential schools and also an attempt to ensure that the voices of those who experienced the colonial project in residential schools first hand are not just spoken voices, but are voices listened to in a processes of understanding colonialism in British Columbia.

2. As I explore further on in the article, the concept of nested place (Malpas 1999) suggests a layering or imbrication of relationships within and between places of different scales. Divisions and boundaries blur, for instance, between private and public worlds. Places of multiple scales and sizes are understood not only to constitute each other, but to be inextricable from each other.

References

Adams, D.W. 1995 *Education for Extinction: American Indians and the Boarding School Experience, 1875–1928* (Lawrence, KS: University of Kansas Press).

Agnew, J.A. 1987 *Place and Politics: The Geographical Meditation of State and Society* (Winchester, MA: Allen and Unwin).

Barmen, J., Hebert, Y., and McCaskill, D. 1986 'The legacy of the past: An overview' in *Indian Education in Canada: Volume 1—The Legacy*, eds. J. Barmen, Y. Hebert, and D. McCaskill (Vancouver: UBC Press) 1–22.

Bhabha, H.K. 1994 *The Location of Culture* (London: Routledge).

Blake, L.A. 1999 'Pastoral power, governmentality and cultures of order in nineteenth-century British Columbia' *Transactions of the Institute of British Geography* 24, 79–93.

Brealey, K. 1995 'Mapping them "out": Euro-Canadian cartography and the appropriation of the Nuxalk and Ts'ilhqot'in First Nations' territories, 1793–1916' *The Canadian Geographer/Le Géographe canadien* 39(2), 140–168.

Buti, A. December 2001. 'Responding to the legacy of Canadian residential schools' *Murdoch University Electronic Journal of Law* 8(8), no pagination.

Byrn, J. April 15, 2002 'Rose Prince, A Quiet Soul' *The BC Catholic*. Available at http://bcc.rcav. org/02-04-15/fp2.htm, accessed November 2003 (Vancouver: Archdiocese of Vancouver), no pagination.

Canada, Government of. 2003 'The Residential School System Historical Overview' Available at www.irsr-rqpi.gc.ca/english/history.html, accessed July 2005 (Ottawa: Indian Residential Schools Resolution Canada), no pagination.

———. Department of Citizenship and Immigration. September 1952 *Indian School Bulletin* 7(1) (Ottawa: Education Division Indian Affairs Branch. Archives Deschatelets Collections).

———. Department of Indian and Northern Affairs. 1996 The Royal Commission on Aboriginal Peoples (Ottawa, Canada).

———. Department of Mines and Resources. (10 October 1946) *Indian School Bulletin* 1(1) (Ottawa: Welfare and Training Service, Indian Affairs Branch. Archives Deschatelets Collections).

———. and Davin, N.F. March 14th, *1879 Report on Industrial Schools for Indians and Half-Breeds* (Ottawa, Canada).

Cariboo Indian School. 1964 *My Heart Is Glad*. Williams Lake, British Columbia. Personal Collections: gift to the author from former residential school student.

————. 1965 *My Heart Is Glad Book II*. Williams Lake, British Columbia Personal Collections: Originals held by Williams Lake Community Archives: Williams Lake, British Columbia.

Carney, R. 1995 'Aboriginal residential schools before confederation: the early experience' *Historical Studies* 61, 13–40.

Casey, E. 1997 *The Fate of Place: A Philosophical Inquiry* (Berkeley: University of California Press).

Castellano, M.B. 2004 'Ethics of aboriginal research' *Journal of Aboriginal Health* 1(1), 98–114.

Chalmers, G.F. 2000 'Art education in "Indian" residential schools in British Columbia' *Canadian Review of Art Education* 27(1), 21–35.

Churchill, W. 2004 *Kill the Indian, Save the Child: The Genocidal Impact of American Indian Residential Schools* (San Francisco: City Lights Books).

Clayton, D.W. *2000 Islands of Truth: The Imperial Fashioning of Vancouver Island* (Vancouver: UBC Press).

Cresswell, T. 1996 *In Place Out of Place: Geography, Ideology, and Transgression* (Minneapolis: University of Minnesota Press).

Fiske, J. 1989 'Life at Lejac' in *Sa Ts'e: Historical Perspectives on Northern British Columbia*, ed. Thomas Thorner (Prince George: College of New Caledonia Press) 235–72.

Fontaine, P. March 1998 'A new beginning: national chief's remarks on the government's RCAP response' in *Residential School Update* (Ottawa: The Assembly of First Nations Secretariat).

Foucault, M. 1991 'Questions of method' in *The Foucault Effect: Studies in Governmentality with Two Lectures and an Interview with Michel Foucault*, eds. G. Burchell, C. Gordon, and P. Miller (Toronto: Harvester Wheatsheaf).

Fournier, S., and Crey, E. 1997 *Stolen from Our Embrace: The Abduction of First Nations Children and the Restoration of Aboriginal Communities* (Vancouver: Douglas & McIntyre).

Frideres, J. S. 1998 *Aboriginal Peoples in Canada: Contemporary Conflicts* (5th Edition). (Scarborough, ON: Prentice-Hall Canada Inc).

Furniss, E. 1992 *Victims of Benevolence: Discipline and Death at the Williams Lake Indian Residential School, 1891–1920* (Williams Lake, BC: The Cariboo Tribal Council).

Glavin, T., and former students of St. Mary's. 2002 Amongst God's Own: The Enduring Legacy of St. Mary's Mission (Mission, BC: Longhouse Publishing).

Haig-Brown, C. 1988 *Resistance and Renewal: Surviving the Indian Residential Schools* (Vancouver: Arsenal Pulp Press).

Hare, J., and Barman, J. 2006 'Good intentions gone awry: from protection to confinement in Emma Crosby's home for Aboriginal girls' in *With Good Intentions: Euro-Canadian and Aboriginal Relations in Colonial Canada*, eds. C. Haig-Brown, and D. A. Nock (Vancouver: UBC Press) 179–98.

Harris, C. March 2004 'How did colonialism dispossess? Comments from an edge of empire' *Annals of the Association of American Geographers* 94(1), 165–182.

————. 2002 *Making Native Space: Colonialism, Resistance, and Reserves in British Columbia* (Vancouver: UBC Press).

————. Autumn/Winter, 1997/98 'Social power and cultural change in pre-colonial British Columbia' *B.C. Studies* 115/116, 45–82.

Harris, D. 2001 *Fish, Law, and Colonialism: The Legal Capture of Salmon in British Columbia* (Toronto: University of Toronto Press).

Jago, J. 1998 'Genocide, Culture, Law Aboriginal Child Removals in Australia and Canada' Unpublished Thesis (Vancouver: University of British Columbia).

Keith, M., and Pile, S. 1993 'Introduction Part 1: the politics of place' in *Place and the Politics of Identity*, eds. Michael Keith, and Steve Pile (New York: Routledge) 1–21.

Kobayashi, A., and Peake, L. 2000 'Racism out of place: thoughts on whiteness and an antiracist geography in the new millennium' *Annals of the Association of American Geographers* 90(2), 392–403.

Lomawaima, K. T. May, 1993 'Domesticity in the federal Indian schools: the power of authority over mind and body' *American Ethnologist* 20(2), 227–240.

Llewellyn, J. J. 2002 'Dealing with the legacy of Native residential school abuse in Canada: Litigation, ADR, and restorative justice' *University of Toronto Law Journal* 52, 253–300.

Malpas, J. 1999 *Place and Experience: A Philosophical Topography* (New York: Cambridge University Press).

Massey, D. 1994 *Space, Place and Gender* (Cambridge: Polity Press in association with Blackwell Publishers).

McClintock, A. 1995 *Imperial Leather: Race, Gender and Sexuality in the Colonial Contest* (New York: Routledge).

McDowell, L. 1999 *Gender, Identity, and Place: Understanding Feminist Geographies* (Minneapolis: University of Minnesota Press).

Milloy, J. *1999 A National Crime: The Canadian Government and the Residential School System, 1879–1986* (Winnipeg: University of Manitoba Press).

Morris, P., and Fondahl, G. 2002 'Negotiating the production of space in Tl'azt'en Territory, Northern British Columbia' *The Canadian Geographer/Le Géographe canadien* 46(2), 108–25.

Neylan, S. 2000 'Longhouses, schoolrooms, and workers' cottages: nineteenth-century protestant mission to the Tsimshian and the transformation of class through religion' *Journal of the Canadian Historical Association* 11, 51–86.

———. 2003 *The Heavens Are Changing: Nineteenth-Century Protestant Missions and Tsimshian Christianity* (Montréal and Kingston: McGill-Queen's University Press).

Nuu-Chah-Nulth Tribal Council. 1996 *Indian Residential Schools: The Nuu-chah-nulth Experience*, Printed in Canada.

Oblate Fathers in Canada, Department of Indian and Eskimo Welfare Commission. *1958 Residential Education for Indian Acculturation* (Ottawa, Canada).

Razack, S. 2004 *Dark Threats and White Knights: The Somalia Affair, Peacekeeping and the New Imperialism* (Toronto: University of Toronto Press).

Raibmon, P. Summer 1996 'A new understanding of things Indian': George Raley's negotiation of the residential school experience' *B.C. Studies* 110, 69–96.

Redford, J. 1979/1980 'Attendance at Indian residential schools in British Columbia, 1890–1920' *B.C. Studies* 44, 41–56.

Said, E. 1994 *Culture and Imperialism* (New York: Vintage Books).

Sangster, J. 2002 'She Is Hostile to Our Ways': First Nations Girls Sentenced to the Ontario Training School for Girls, 1933–1960' *Law and History Review* 20(2), 59–96.

Schnarch, B. 2004 'Ownership, control, access, and possession (OCAP) or self-determination applied to research: a critical analysis of contemporary first nations research and some options for first nations communities' *Journal of Aboriginal Health* 1(1), 80–95.

Scott, J. C. 1990 *Domination and the Arts of Resistance: Hidden Transcripts* (New Haven: Yale University Press).

Secwepemc Cultural Education Society. 2000 *Behind Closed Doors: Stories from the Kamloops Indian Residential School* (Penticton, BC: Theytus Books).

Smith, D.G. 2001 'The 'policy of aggressive civilization' and projects of governance in Roman Catholic industrial schools for Native peoples in Canada, 1870–95' *Anthropologica* 43(2), 253.

Smith, L.T. 1999 *Decolonizing Methodologies: Research and Indigenous Peoples* (New York: Zed Books).

Smith, S. 1993 *Subjectivity, Identity and the Body: Women's Autobiographical Practices in the Twentieth Century* (Indianapolis Press: Indiana University Press).

Sparke, M. 1998 'A map that roared and an original atlas: Canada, cartography, and the narration of nation' *Annals of the Association of American Geographers* 88(3), 463–95.

Spivak, G.C. 1996 'Subaltern talk: interview with the editors, 29 October 1993' in *The Spivak Reader*, eds. D. Landry and G. Maclean (New York: Routledge).

Sterling, S. 1992 *My Name Is Seepeetza* (Toronto: Groundwood Books)

Tennant, P. 1990 *Aboriginal Peoples and Politics: The Indian Land Question in British Columbia, 1849–1989* (Vancouver: UBC Press).

Thomas, N. 1994 *Colonialism's Culture: Anthropology, Travel and the Government* (Princeton, NJ: Princeton University Press).

Titley, B. E. 1986 *A Narrow Vision: Duncan Campbell Scott and the Administration of Indian Affairs in Canada* (Vancouver: UBC Press).

van Dongen, M. July 2003 'Press Release—Catholic Women's League, British Columbia/Yukon Provincial Convention 2003' Available at www.cwl.bc.ca/bcykinfo.html, accessed November 2003. The Catholic Women's League of Canada, no pagination.

Woods, J. 1996 *I Remind Until I Fall: An Examination of Space, Memory and Experience at the Coqualeetza Residential School and Indian Hospital* (Vancouver: Unpublished Thesis).

CHAPTER 23

What Do You Call an Indian Woman with a Law Degree? Nine Aboriginal Women at the University of Saskatchewan College of Law Speak Out

Tracey Lindberg

I write this paper with an unsteady hand and with my heart beating in my head.[1] It is a very difficult thing to do—to evaluate legal education as it has affected First Nations women in the College of Law. I feel liberated since I am finally able to write as I want to with heart, spirit, and mind. I speak as an Indian. I speak as a woman. I speak as an Indian woman. I begin with a story.

I didn't go to Grace Adam's funeral. I didn't think I could talk to her family. She had four daughters and one son—the most giving and the strongest person, and a very lonely person. I'm not quite sure where I fit in. All I know is that they loved everyone, cared for the Earth, and celebrated the Creator.

She was an amazing woman, you know—one of the first Indian women in the province of Saskatchewan to graduate from Lebret Residential School, one of the first Indian women to obtain a university degree, one of the best teachers in the province. She was the closest many of us had come to meeting pure goodness. This woman typified for me what education for First Nations people could be like. She studied hard, learned new information, and adapted it to apply understandings of 'Indianness'. Learning was not limited to her formal education. She continued learning for the rest of her life. Her time spent at university was just a part of it. She taught her children traditional values and skills and let them learn formal education when they entered their learning phase. She was the most Indian person I had ever met. She worked hard in a world filled with much more enmity toward Indian woman than I will ever know. She

always gave, constantly worked for change, and believed each person had value.

I want so much to describe effectively the story of being an Indian woman in a non-Indian, male educational setting. I want the story to be true and strong. I want it to reflect that I am here because of Grace Adam. My daughters may come here because of me. My story involves much beauty and celebration. Yet, it is written with somewhat more cynicism and bitterness than existed three years ago when I first began this journey.

First Nations women are best at telling the stories of our first days:

> I overhead two women in the back of Torts discussing who was and was not Indian in the classroom. The assessment was based purely on physical attributes. More distressing and painful than that was the fact that we were objectified and examined like some foreign entity in 'their' class. I was hurt, alone and labeled by women I was to spend the next three years with. I remember that every time I speak with either of them.

Nine Aboriginal women,[2] including myself, have chosen to share our experiences in law school. I am fortunate to be the person compiling and presenting these experiences. The majority of Aboriginal women in the College of Law at the University of Saskatchewan are over 25 years of age. Three of the respondents are Métis women. The remainder are Treaty Indian women representing Indian Nations. Many have children. The few of us without partners or children are a distinct minority. The support system we provide for each other extends to the community as well. Many of us have met previously (through the Native Law Summer Program, employment, and political or social organizations). This support has been an undeniable factor in our continued success and presence in law school.

> I am fortunate because I know I can rely on the other Indian people I met through the summer program. It is not academic support. The presence of other Indian people in the college makes me feel visible. I thought I would vanish in law school . . . somehow become White. With other Aboriginal people here I am constantly reminded that I am here for many important and good reasons.

The contributors to this article co-operated with the knowledge that their statements and understandings would be compiled and presented as an assessment of legal education in Saskatchewan as it affects Aboriginal women. Our comments have been edited as little as possible to ensure that the truth, beauty, and, at times, rawness, are fully evident. It may hurt to read these pages. This pain is reflective of the anger and silent screaming that some of us have had to bear and suppress. These pages are also filled with support, strength, and wisdom. It will feel good to read them. Of the women polled, the majority state that they are glad to be law students. We offer our comments, critiques, and feelings not as a negative allegory of our experiences, but as an expression of our understandings of legal education. As 'outsiders' (Sheppard and Westpahl, 1992), we are able to see patterns of belief or behaviour that are difficult to detect for those immersed in the college.

Our view necessarily includes a careful examination of the accommodation of Aboriginal women in the curriculum, class teachings, materials, and understandings of law school.[3] The comments were solicited by questionnaires distributed by hand to each Aboriginal woman in the college. Participants were given the option of answering anonymously or meeting with the author to discuss their responses. Most chose to discuss the questionnaire in person.

We leave the following words to you and to your interpretation. The onus of learning about Indian and Aboriginal peoples too often comes to lie on those who are being defined. We hope our words will aid in your learning. We will facilitate your knowledge, but you must take responsibility for your own education.

Aboriginal women come to law school for a variety of reasons:

> [I came to law school] on a dare from someone.

> I was particularly optimistic. I came here to change everyone's views about Indians. I mean it. I would change professorial teaching styles, the textbooks, non-Indian students and even the laws! I was going to teach the world about an alternative mode of justice. I guess I really didn't come here to learn.

> I came to law school because I've always wanted to be a lawyer. If I am going to make a difference in the world—a law degree will help me.

> For career reasons. A law degree offers many choices.

> Because of the way I was treated by males in the justice system.

> I was arrested once protesting at Indian Affairs. When I was begin photographed and fingerprinted I asked the officer in charge why this process was being used. He said, 'Because you'll be back.' I kept that in my head while I wrote the LSAT and when I applied to law school.

There are times when as Aboriginal women, we find ourselves alienated from the learning processes. Many of the Aboriginal women interviewed found that, in part, the alienation was related to perceptions of their race based on physical attributes:

> I am able to be perceived as an Aboriginal person. This affects me in two very major ways: I cannot be a member of the very real boys club;

I am to be an expert on all Aboriginal groups and all Aboriginal concerns.

I am perceived and received as a First Nations female. Therefore, my interaction is based on who I am.

[Other's perception of me as a First Nation member] has kept me form interacting with certain people in the college. You get vibes from some people so you in turn treat them as invisible as well. Once you do that I find some of these people take notice and are annoyed by it, probably because I am not a visible minority.

I find that my look limits somewhat the people who associate with me. It is not chic or trendy to befriend an Aboriginal. I enter each situation open to new ideas and people. I request the same. I find that I do not receive this. I think there are probably all sorts of stereotypes and concerns that come with this brown skin. We are all affirmative action, we are all from reserves on a scholarship, who had a great GPA. I feel proud of how I look but I am distressed at being a brown page in their [other law students'] previously written book of experiences. I sometimes feel like I am on the outside looking in.

In many situations, we associate with, and locate near, other Aboriginal people. In many cases, the group that provides the most support includes Aboriginal peoples. The majority of Aboriginal women at the College of Law do not separate gender from origin. Aboriginal women make up a strong portion of the circle. We perform an important role in racial and cultural self-determination. Therefore, issues of racism and community wellness are often our major concern.

Sisterhood in the college, in many cases, is a secondary concern to nationhood. As Aboriginal people, we find ourselves in the position of being a bridge between two worlds. Our interaction, therefore, takes place with many people of differing world views, including Aboriginal and non-Aboriginal people. Since our support within the college varies, some of us interact principally with other Aboriginal students.

Aboriginal women in the college find it difficult to stay connected. Many of us study with, or socialize predominantly with, Aboriginal males in the college. Many of the males are single with no dependants or have partners who assume the childcare responsibilities. We associate with other Aboriginal people in situations where we need support: exam periods, community and family concerns, and assignment due dates. This behaviour is known as taking comfort into the room with you (Monture, 1986).

The support I received from Aboriginals whether male or female is moral and personal. [We are all concerned with] how to make the system work for us and who and what can work for us (the oppressed).

I find myself drawn to minority group members (lesbians, gays, other First Nations members). I was never a very strong feminist, but there is merit to a somewhat common oppressive background. I find the Aboriginal men found their voices a lot easier than Aboriginal women in the college. I have only been present during one incident of an Aboriginal woman speaking out in class. It seems like we are the first to be asked for our opinions on Aboriginal issues and dismissed in many other situations.

In my Advanced Constitutional Law class the professor announced we were to have a discussion the next day on First Nations constitutional concerns. As he read the reading list I felt more and more depressed and I couldn't figure out why. Another woman in class asked why all the assigned readings were written by non-Aboriginal males. I wanted to hug her. She made sure that I didn't disappear in that class.

There is a general sense that we [all law students] share a common experience, but I received support specifically from both Aboriginal men and women both academically and personally and I cherish it.

My main support in the college from Aboriginals has come from Aboriginal men. We keep each other sane at exam time and can discuss issues of race and even gender that are lacking in class. Aboriginal women are important to my life at law school and in general—but there is no one woman who has been a support group for school. They are good friends and good sounding boards for life though.

I have been told that women were created out of the bone of a buffalo—this is how integral Aboriginal women are to life. We were created with strength in mind—sinewy and rare. We were not made as a mate for one person, nor are we made from one person. Our strength supports all life. Because of this, we have distinct roles as Aboriginal women. We each have the same responsibilities to protect the children and their children.

However, every Aboriginal woman does not consider this gender differentiation—this feminine side of the earth—to mean that we must join together for that reason alone.

I feel that Aboriginal women in law school are not as connected to one another as they should be; outside of law school, I have managed to maintain contact and communication with the Aboriginal organizations and attend and participate in events such as conferences, social events and so forth.

There are so few of us that it is hard to bond just on the basis of race. All people of all cultures have interesting and complicated histories. I think we tend to connect with the people who are the most like us. This includes more than race and gender. While I certainly fell connected to all the Aboriginal students, as a single female with no dependants I share many traits and characteristics of other single females in the college.

I am connected to some Aboriginal students and not to others—applies to women or men.

In some classes I sit with Aboriginal students . . . our interaction is distinct because of shared experiences and confidences.

Another reason identified for this strong affiliating with Aboriginal people lies in the fact that almost all of the Aboriginal women interviewed found that non-Aboriginal students' knowledge of Aboriginal issues and understandings was quite low. This is the result of an education system that does not convey the understandings, needs, and legal positions of Aboriginal peoples and systems to the people who most need to understand it— non-Aboriginal students.[4]

In my world, you have to deal with Aboriginal people every day. I do not understand why this is not so in a college professing to be on the cutting edge of society. Aboriginal women possess untold stories and understandings. We come from areas where there is a 100 per cent Aboriginal population. We come from homes where families raised eight children. We have concepts of property and self-determination that could make others richer through the telling. I think that as Aboriginal women we have a story that is both the same as, and different from, shared. Most of us have found that the majority of the college's students are empathetic and open-minded towards Aboriginal issues, and we believe that they are 'fertile ground' for planting new seeds of knowledge about Aboriginal people.

I have found two people in the college who are constantly trying to understand, to really get around the concept of Aboriginal rights. They do this not for curiosity, for classroom purposes, or to settle their fears. They do this because they respect Aboriginal people and accept that the responsibility for keeping Aboriginal peoples and issues alive is their concern as well.

I have heard the only two women on a hockey trip called 'clan mothers' as a joke in the college newspaper. I just found the objectification so thoughtless and unkind. . . . I couldn't bring myself to mention it.

Most people recognize that a great deal of this knowledge deficit could be minimized if professors, administrators, and other staff realized that teaching from a variety of perspectives is beneficial to classroom settings. In many Aboriginal communities, elders and teachers bear a great responsibility of ensuring that the people/students are well prepared for life. This includes stories of other cultures, their understandings, and the importance of respect for all people. What kind of lives are Aboriginal law students being prepared for?

I have had two completely awful contacts with college professors. In the first, one of my professors was unable to defuse a potentially damaging conversation about Aboriginal women. One of the students commented that 'Indian men only hit Indian women when they are drunk.' This was said in a jovial and accepting tone. Several other women in the class spoke for me as I was incoherent with weariness and pain. In the second situation, a professor questioned two of eleven presentations in a class belligerently and very condescendingly. The two presentations were both on issues of Aboriginal title that adopted a point of view that differed with that of the professor. Only one faculty member was sympathetic to my concern. Other comments I received from the faculty were 'Professor X is one of the most sympathetic professors in the college', 'Professor X is just brusque,' and the advice I received was to 'write your best paper' based on the presentation. Although the professor was approached eventually I am disillusioned with the process of taking professors to task for their behaviour.

The general impression was that there were some 'informed' professors, yet many others who were unable to convey to their classes that Aboriginal issues were often distinct and very much a reality. In the few instances where Aboriginal issues were discussed, the possibility of a female interpretation was often ignored. We found ourselves immersed in invisibility. Aboriginal issues and concerns, we believe, would be considered more seriously

and addressed more frequently if there was an Aboriginal faculty member on staff.

This problem of little or no attention to gender resulted in two widely talked about class discussions in the College of Law last year. In one discussion, Aboriginal men spoke for all Aboriginal people, necessitating the request by Aboriginal women in the class that there be an opportunity for the concerns of Aboriginal women to be expressed by themselves. The other discussion, which took place in a small-group seminar class on Aboriginal law, involved a similar exclusion of Aboriginal women from the debate. In each situation, the distinct concerns of Aboriginal women were initially addressed only by Aboriginal men. In response, Aboriginal women found their voices and insisted that there were distinct issues that affected Aboriginal women.

The issue of gender differences in Aboriginal communities has become a subject that both Aboriginal and non-Aboriginal people prefer not to discuss. The truth is that women have always had a separate and equal position in politics, labour, and familial tasks. Equality as an ideal has different meanings for Aboriginal people. Aboriginal women are an essential and important part of the circle, the continuity of life. We are a part of fire, of water. We are elemental and essentially intrinsic to the continuance of life. We have our roles, different and the same, which match perfectly with those of our men. Yet somehow we are overlooked. We are elemental, and we need to reclaim our place. We are women. We are Aboriginal. But to draw a sharp line between these two characteristics makes sense only in theorists' minds.

Aboriginal politics demands a role for Aboriginal women. I think that the Aboriginal community is slow to get the message of the importance of women's roles and involvement in society and especially in politics. As with everything else, women see problems and solutions from a different perspective—which is just as valid and as important. We need a voice, and a political voice often carries farther.

I never see us as a Women's Struggle. Sisterhood, to me, most often will be secondary to nationhood. We have an unclaimed seat at the circle of Aboriginal politics. This is something we have tried and tried to discuss with other Aboriginal people. It seems the only time that Aboriginal political issues come to the forefront is when there is perceived infighting. I hope that Aboriginal issues from a women's perspective will soon be addressed. I am not yet willing to confer authority upon women's groups to speak for us.

It is widely recognized that many non-Aboriginal people do not think about, understand, or define reality in the same way that some Aboriginal people do (Monture, 1986). Certain situations and class discussions include introductory information that introduces and explains differing perspective. For example, in an environmental law class, it is made clear that corporations have different perspectives than other entities in society. The corporations' perspective is often alluded to. However, though this courtesy is extended to a fictional entity, it is not extended to Aboriginal people very often. It is even more rarely extended to Aboriginal women. As Aboriginal women, we enter our criminal law classes with the knowledge that the majority of female offenders in this province are Aboriginal women. We also recognize that there Aboriginal women prisoners are pre-judged as 'violent, uncontrollable, and unmanageable' in some prisons (Sugar and Fox, 1990). Yet I have never heard an introductory lecture on systemic discrimination. There are many ways for a professor to convey that Aboriginal women don't matter and that includes silence (Boyle, 1986).[5] I have never once heard the term 'institutionalized racism', cross a professor's lips. Yet I sit, I read, and I wonder each time we discuss an Aboriginal offender: what is everyone in this room thinking? It is not a good feeling. I feel indignant, angry, and afraid. I hope everyone in the room who is aware of these issues knows that I am Indian. I want no one to notice me and everyone to notice me. I hope no one will make a painful statement. It is an open wound to my being. This is my personhood (Monture, 1986), and we are dismembering it. Its main organs are taken out: the facts, the issues, and the ratio.

It is difficult to find the strengths in a college where many of us feel alienated, separate, and invisibly brown. Many of us only participate in seminar or limited-enrolment classes. Theory classes also encourage different perspectives, and many upper-year Aboriginal women feel comfortable speaking out in these classes. Large classes where the professor uses a Socratic teaching style were widely criticized as intimidating, [and] uncomfortable.

There is a great deal of uncertainly that surrounds us as Aboriginal in law school. We have few predecessors to look for advice. None of us are second-generation lawyers. Some of us are the daughters and granddaughters of trappers. Coming to law school is similar to moving to a foreign country, learning a new culture and language. We proceed by trial and error. As a result, we are often quiet, sometimes ill at ease, and occasionally frightened.

In property when Aboriginal title was starting I did not know how the class would respond; I felt responsible for the whole Aboriginal people—but it turned out okay and there was no need to defend my people.

I am never comfortable when called upon. It doesn't matter how well I am prepared. I will offer information when I feel there is a point that needs to be raised. I never speak just to comment on a case or give my opinion. It there is an alternate way to interpret a situation I will try to bring that up.

I try really hard to make sure I am prepared. This whole 'lazy Indian' image really is alive and at work in this college. It is especially evident in the statements I have heard regarding Aboriginal people in the part-time program.

We find ourselves making choices based on a complex set of values. These values, it seems, are based upon how connected we are with the Aboriginal communities of interest to which we belong. In turn, this connection is based on our goals for the future. In establishing goals, all the Aboriginal women who responded stated that their connection to their communities of interest was central in goal determination and occupational choice:

> I will work in any capacity to facilitate the advancement of Aboriginal self-determination. I hope this does not leave me in an urban centre, but realistically it might. I want to take my information and training and better educate myself in traditional learning (teachings of the community, elders, and other involved in self-determination).

> I plan to stay in Saskatoon and work with the community here.

> If not to my reserve, to other Native communities.

> I feel best about speaking at Bridging Week in front of all the first year students. I told them that I know we are called squaws and that when some people see us they think 'squaw'. I am proudest of telling them to see people, not colours, and to think Indian person—not Indian. I have tried my best to eradicate labeling and naming.

It is very evident among most of my Aboriginal women colleagues that law school is a portion of their lives and not the entirety of it. We are very proud of balancing family, partners, careers, community, and studies. The balance most of us accomplish is welcome and sometimes difficult to achieve. All but one of the respondents have familial support and obligations in addition to their studies. Balancing becomes an implicit and important part of our lives as family and community shift positions in our web of responsibilities.

> I feel terribly guilty for not committing any time to social or cultural concerns (like I did before law school).

> I had to miss conferences, ceremonies, and elders talks that I love to go to—for something that I am not even sure that I like.

> [I make time for] spiritual and extended family, children's social well-being, which call

for frequent trips to Regina and rez. Lots of time, money, and support are required, not to mention family emergencies.

> [There is pressure on an Aboriginal woman that there is not on an Aboriginal man], women are still expected to do it all but I need a wife too. Not in the sexual sense but someone to do all or at least some of my duties.

> Considering the funding conditions put on me by Indian Affairs I have no choice but to go full-time to get full funding. Otherwise it would be full-time work and part-time studies.

Overt racism is something that few of the Aboriginal women had actually seen, heard, or experienced from law school peers. Yet a very strong majority of the women interviewed believed that there were racial slurs and understandings at work in the College of Law.

> I heard one male student jokingly saying that he was from [an urban centre with a very high Aboriginal population] and that because he was from that town it was okay if he transgressed the limits of the law because it was all relative. He stated that he could not be penalized because 'he only shot one or two Indians.' I did not say a word. It is too scary to approach someone who feels confident enough about that belief to say it in a normal tone of voice.

> I am quite sure there are [racist statements] in the college.

> I am not likely to be made privy to the confidences of people who dislike other people on the basis of skin colour. My friends have told me of a few instances. It is hard to sleep sometimes.

Yet, as Aboriginal women we have an ongoing responsibility to seven unborn generations of children. This responsibility includes making sure that they do not have to bear this weight. It includes ensuring that barriers that barriers that existed for us as Aboriginal women are knocked down so that our children do not have to break them down. It is in this spirit that the Aboriginal women in the University of Saskatchewan College of Law mad their recommendations in the questionnaire.

There is a perception in law school that Aboriginal people in law school are not there on our merits. We are taking the spot of deserving candidates. We are lower achievers and undeserving of a position in the college. All people should compete for spaces on the same basis. These prejudiced views extend to and touch every Aboriginal woman who goes to law school. Patricia Monture wrote of this sentiment:

> Remembering back to my first day of law school, I was confronted in the lounge by another student, who with some hostility explained that perhaps one of his friends was not present because of me. And this made him angry because the only reason I could have reached the hallowed halls of the law school was by virtue of a special access program (Monture, 1990).

I have found this to be true in my experience as well.

Many of the legal concepts that we learn in law school are contrary to Aboriginal traditional notions of justice. All of the contributors to the questionnaire are in agreement that the Canadian legal system has a duty to respect Aboriginal peoples. This respect can be fostered by:

> displaying genuine commitment to and support of our dreams and aspirations of self-determination and by the willingness to listen to and implement the innovative idea conveyed by First Nations people in response to issues that directly affect us as a nation.

There is also concern regarding the exclusion of Aboriginal people and, particularly, Aboriginal women, from the curriculum. In my first year, my only memorable experiences with Aboriginal people in the justice system were confined to a duress defence (because Aboriginal people are, of course, unable to fully comprehend the complexities of a contract) and a drug-trafficking offence. As future lawyers, we all depend narrowly on our experiences in law school as a basis for future understanding and learning. I trust the ability of others to exclude information that is culturally biased, but I question all people's abilities to include information that is excluded. This includes hypotheticals that incorporate Aboriginal women as well as Aboriginal men. I have been present in two classes where there were serious attempts to linguistically include women in hypotheticals (Boyle, 1986). My pride and the feelings of inclusion were very strong. I felt my invisibility by exclusion warp for a moment. I was the same as, and different from, every person in the room. I felt included and important. It is such a small thing, but it chips away at the massive base of oppression.

We are always Aboriginal. We are always women. We are not allowed the luxury of turning our pain on and off (Monture, 1986).[6] But we bear it and we proceed. More importantly, we succeed. Many of the Aboriginal women currently in law school still consider themselves very attuned to the needs and goals of the Aboriginal community. In addition, there are more Aboriginal women in the University of Saskatchewan College of Law at this time than in any year in recent memory. We succeed in the management of studies, community interaction, and family. There can be no greater success story than that.

The essence of this paper is this: we have accepted the responsibility of educating ourselves. We have risen to the challenge of remaining Aboriginal in the search for knowledge in a system that challenges our make-up. We respect the wisdom that we have gained. We honour the teachers who have tried to change a vision of their world in order to include other worlds. We have found ourselves immersed in a value system that is strange and foreign to many of us. We have struggled academically, personally, and in innumerable other ways to include, or at least to respect, your vision of the world. It is your turn.

True success in law school includes ensuring that parity, fairness, and respect are maintained at all times. It is your turn to ensure that the infliction of racism, the appropriation of pain, and the disrespect of alternative viewpoints and understandings ends. Patricia Monture wrote of this responsibility:

When are those of you who inflict racism, who appropriate pain, who speak with no knowledge or respect when you ought to listen and accept, going to take hard looks at yourself instead of at me. How can you continue to look at me to carry what is your responsibility? And when I speak and the brutality of my experience hurts you, you hide behind your hurt. You point the finger at me and you claim I hurt you. I will not carry your responsibility anymore. Your pain is unfortunate. But do not look at me to soften it. Look to yourself (1986: 168).

We persevere and we struggle on. For many of us, the most difficult aspect of our experience is dealing with the ignorance of others. For Aboriginal women who are law students, as it was for Grace Adam, the struggle is a hard-fought one. We do not, in all cases, reject our legal education. We do, however, refuse to bear the burdens of a system that will not evolve. We continue to break the path initially walked by women like Grace Adam—our Women.

Notes

1. Because there are so few of us, many Aboriginal academics and professionals must play multiple roles in the achievement of our goals. Telling this story was important enough that I wanted to undertake to gather the stories, but I also wanted to be one of the voices that was heard. I do not profess to be impartial as I am a participant. I do not profess to be apolitical as this is personal and, as such, politicized.

2. The phrase 'Aboriginal women' is utilized throughout this article to indicate the distinct and multi-facial component and also the cultural affinity, of the respondents. This may yield a certain homogeneity that is by no means indicative of our multiplicity of experiences, understandings, or feelings about law school. However, the term does encompass the unity of nations that binds the respondents together.

3. This examination is based, in great part, on the approach taken by Catherine Weiss and Louise Melling, 'The Legal Education of Twenty

Women', *Stanford Law Review* 40 (1988): 1299. We adapted and revised the questionnaire used in that article (Ibid., Appendix A at 1360). In particular, we employed terms of racial specificity and of race/gender duality. Our questionnaire is contained in the appendix to this article.

4. Mari Matsuda has written that: 'a system that ignores outsiders' perspectives artificially restricts and stultifies the scholarly imagination.' Mari Matsuda, 'Affirmative Action and Legal Knowledge: Planting Seeds in Plowed-Up Ground' *Harvard Women's Legal Journal* 2 (1988): 1 at 3.

5. Boyle discusses silence after a pro-woman comment is made. I think it is relevant that complete silence regarding any issue that concerns all students dismisses certain defined groups of people.

6. At a conference that Monture attended, she heard of a discussion where an individual stated that 'the pain of minority people is like television, we can turn it on and off as we want to.' This is a luxury that Aboriginal people are usually not allowed.

References

Boyle, C. 1986. 'Teaching Law As If Women Really Mattered or What About the Washroom?', *Canadian Journal of Women and the Law* 2, 1: 96 at 99.

Matsuda, M. 1988. 'Affirmative Action and Legal Knowledge: Planting Seeds in Plowed-Up Ground', *Harvard Women's Legal Journal* 2: 1 at 3.

Monture, P.A. 1986. 'Ka-Nin-Geh-Heh-E-Sa-Nonh-Yah-Gah', *Canadian Journal of Women and the Law* 2, 1: 159 at 161.

———. 1990. 'Now That the Door Is Open: First Nations and the Law School Experience' *Queen's Law Journal* 15: 179 at 205.

Sugar, F., and L. Fox. 1990. 'Nistum Peyako Seht'wanin Iskwewak: Breaking Chains', *Canadian Journal of Women and the Law* 3, 2: 465 at 469.

Sheppard, C., and S. Westpahl. 1992. 'Equity and the University: Learning from Women's Experience', *Canadian Journal of Women and the Law* 5, 1: 8.

Weiss, C., and L. Melling. 1988. 'The Legal Education of Twenty Women', *Stanford Law Review* 40: 1299.

CHAPTER 24

Micro Inequities and Everyday Inequalities: 'Race', Gender, Sexuality, and Class in Medical School[1]

Brenda Beagan

Elements in the students' background do not exert any decisive influence . . . in medical school. Such background factors may have indirect influence in many ways, but the problems of the student role are so pressing . . . that the perspectives developed are much more apt to reflect the pressures of the immediate school situation than of ideas associated with prior roles and experiences (Becker et al., 1961: 47).

In this passage from *Boys in White*, a classic study of medical professional socialization, Howard Becker and his colleagues insist that social characteristics such as gender, 'race',[2] culture, social class, sexual orientation, and religion have little or no impact on medical student experiences. Social differences become background variables in the face of an overwhelming medical student culture. In their study, conducted in 1956–7, about 5 per cent of the students in any class were women and 5 per cent to 7 per cent were non-white (1961: 60).[3] They really were *boys* in white—in fact they were *white* boys in white.

Over the next 40 years the profile of the typical North American medical school class changed considerably. By 1993, 42 per cent of medical students in the United States were women (Bickel and Kopriva, 1993). In Canada, women's proportion of medical school classes increased from 9 per cent in 1957–8 to 49 per cent by 1997–8 (Association of Canadian Medical Colleges, 1998). By 1991–2 African American, Native American, Mexican American, Puerto Rican, other Hispanic, and Asian or Pacific Islander students made up 27 per cent of all medical students in the United States (Jonas et

al., 1992; c.f., Foster, 1996). In Canada statistics on the 'race' of medical students are not available. As well, medical students are somewhat older and better educated upon entry than they were in previous years (Gray and Reudy, 1998: 1047). Evidence also indicates there are more openly-identified gay/lesbian/bisexual medical students. There are currently gay and lesbian student caucuses in medical schools, a Canadian gay and lesbian medical student e-mail list, a gay and lesbian committee of the American Medical Student Association (Oriel et al., 1996), and recent journal articles addressing the concerns of gays and lesbians in medicine (Wallick et al., 1992; Rose, 1994; Cook et al., 1995; Oriel et al., 1996; Druzin et al., 1998; Klamen et al., 1999; Risdon et al., 2000).

In short, the medical student population is far less homogeneous than when Becker et al. (1961) conducted their research 40 years ago.[4] What is the impact of this increased diversity in the student population? Linda Grant (1988) suggests that who you are when you enter medicine affects the extent to which you 'fit in' during medical school. She argues that all schools have their own 'latent culture', which dictates the boundaries of appropriate behaviour: 'Those who share the latent culture have a sense of belonging; those who do not may feel alienated and marginal' (Grant, 1988: 109).

Current research supports this position. Women medical students, for example, perceive more gender discrimination than do male students and are substantially more likely to be sexually harassed by clinicians, faculty, and/or patients (Grant, 1988; Dickstein, 1993; Hostler and Gressard, 1993; Komaromy et al., 1993; Bickel, 1994; Moscarello et al., 1994; Schulte and Kay, 1994; Bickel and Ruffin,

1995; Bergen et al., 1996). Studies have documented 'micro inequities' (Haslett and Lipman, 1997) based in gender, including gender-exclusive language, absence of parental leave policies, gender-biased illustrations in medical texts, sexist jokes in class and at school social events, male students being called doctor while women are not, women being mistaken for nurses, being called 'girls', being ignored by instructors (Dickstein, 1993; Lenhart, 1993; Bickel, 1994; Kirk, 1994; Mendelsohn et al., 1994; Guyatt et al., 1997). Taken together all of these factors lead to a gendered climate in medical school that may cause women to feel less welcome, more marginal.

Similarly, racial or ethnic harassment and discrimination have been experienced by 20 per cent of medical students (Baldwin et al., 1991) and 23 per cent of residents (Baldwin et al., 1994) in the United States.[5] There is less evidence about the more subtle processes that might construct a racialized medical school climate, nevertheless, one recent ethnography of a British medical school depicts a high degree of racial segregation in extracurricular activities, suggesting the marginalization of students of colour (Sinclair, 1997). Not surprisingly, perhaps, racialized minority students tend to have higher attrition rates than white students, take longer to complete undergraduate training, and are more likely to switch specialties or drop out of residency programs (Lee, 1992; Babbott et al., 1994; Campos-Outcalt et al., 1994; McManus et al., 1996).

Class-based cultural norms that may predominate in medical training remain under examined. In a Canadian study with 80 medical students one of the two who self-identified as working-class joked that the hardest thing for him to learn at medical school was 'the wine and cheeses' (Haas and Shaffir, 1987: 23).

Recent investigations into the impact of sexual orientation in medical school suggest that homophobic attitudes are as prevalent among medical students and faculty members as in the general population (Klamen et al., 1999). Thus students who identify as gay, lesbian, or bisexual may feel more marginalized in medical school than do heterosexually-identified students. National surveys found 40 per cent of general internists and 50 per cent of internal medicine residents witnessed homophobic[6] remarks by fellow physicians, nurses, other health care workers, and patients (Cook et al., 1995; vanIneveld et al., 1996). An American study found that although 67 per cent of family practice residency program directors showed attitudes supportive to gay men and lesbians, 25 per cent would rank residency applicants lower if they were known to be gay or lesbian (Oriel et al., 1996). In addition, 46 per cent of the gay/lesbian/bisexual students surveyed had experienced discrimination based on sexual orientation during medical school, and most hid or planned to hide their homosexuality during their residency application process.

Most medical schools today have an institutional commitment to equality, which has led to the reduction or eradication of overt discrimination in admissions (Cole, 1986) and to the establishment of policies and procedures to address harassment and discrimination. Even in the absence of blatant discrimination, however, an institution may have an overall climate that welcomes some participants more than others. The research presented here sought to investigate the micro-level interactional processes through which the dominant culture of an institution may be conveyed, with attendant messages of inclusion and exclusion. This study did not set out to determine the *existence* of social inequalities based on gender, 'race', class, and sexual orientation; instead it explicates processes through which, in one particular educational institution, such inequalities are enacted.

Research Methods and Participants

In this study, three complementary strategies were employed: A survey of an entire third-year class (123 students) at one medical school; interviews with 25 students from that class; and interviews with 23 faculty members from the same medical school.[7] In a traditional medical curriculum the third year is a key transition point for students as they move out of the classrooms and into the hospital wards and clinics (Becker et al., 1961; Coombs, 1978; Broadhead, 1983; Haas and Shaffir, 1987; Konner, 1987). The increased interactions with staff and patients reflect the students back to themselves as 'doctors' (Coombs, 1978: 227; Konner, 1987; Shapiro, 1987). Such interactions can simultaneously enforce gendered and racialized notions of who fits best with common ideas of 'doctor' by refusing to reinforce some students' emerging self-conceptions as physicians (Gamble, 1990; Rucker, 1992; Dickstein, 1993; Lenhart, 1993; Bickel, 1994; Kirk, 1994; Mendelsohn et al., 1994; Blackstock, 1996).

The characteristics of students who completed the survey are indicated in Table 24.1. The sample was highly heterogeneous. Half the respondents had no religious affiliation (51 per cent) while the remainder were Christian (36 per cent), Sikh (6 per cent), Hindu (3 per cent) and Jewish (3 per cent). Twenty respondents (28 per cent) considered themselves members of minority groups, almost all identifying as Asian, Chinese, Indo-Canadian, and South Asian. The 25 students interviewed were

Table 24.1 Characteristics of the samples

Characteristic	Student survey sample (N = 72)	Student interviews sample (N = 25)	Faculty interviews sample (N = 23)
Gender			
Female	36 (50%)	14 (56%)	5 (22%)
Male	36 (50%)	11 (44%)	18 (78%)
Age			
Mean age	27 years	28 years	51 years
Range	24–40 years	23–40 years	36–67 years
Race/Ethnicity*			
Euro-Canadian	38 (53%)	18 (72%)	23 (100%)
Asian	15 (21%)	6 (24%)	
South Asian	6 (8%)		
Jewish	2 (3%)	1 (4%)	
Aboriginal	1 (1%)		
Not given	10 (14%)		
First Language			
English	52 (72%)	23 (92%)	21 (91%)
Not English	20 (28%)	2 (8%)	2 (9%)
Social class background**			
Upper/Upper-Middle	36 (50%)	14 (56%)	
Lower-Middle	23 (32%)	6 (24%)	
Working/Poor	11 (15%)	5 (20%)	
Other	2 (3%)		
Sexual orientation			
Heterosexual	71 (99%)	24 (96%)	13 (56%)
Homosexual	1 (1%)	1 (4%)	2 (9%)
Unknown			8 (35%)

* Includes 'Canadian', British, Scottish, Irish, American, German, Scandinavian, Polish, Italian, Portuguese, Oceanic. Asian includes Chinese, Japanese, Korean, Taiwanese, Indonesian, Malaysian. South Asian includes Indian, Punjabi, Pakistani.
** Self-described

slightly less heterogeneous; most were of European Canadian heritage and they were more likely to be married or living with a partner. The class from which these samples were taken was 48 per cent female and approximately 66 per cent Caucasian, 22 per cent Asian, 11 per cent Indo-Canadian, and 1 per cent African heritage.[8]

The purposive sample of faculty members and administrators tended to be male and of European heritage—not unlike the majority of faculty in this school. The length of time working at this medical school ranged from 3 to 29 years, averaging 15 years. Five were academic faculty, teaching the basic sciences;[9] the rest were clinical faculty.[10] Ten faculty members had administrative positions.

Everyday Inequalities and Micro Inequities

The notion of everyday inequalities is useful for understanding the micro-level processes through which inequities of racism, sexism, heterosexism, and classism are experienced and perpetuated in Canadian society, where most citizens express commitment to democratic principles of justice, equality, tolerance, and fairness. Studying the contrasts between America and the Netherlands, Dutch sociologist Philomena Essed developed the concept of 'everyday racism', a form of racism distinctively structured in 'practices that infiltrate everyday life and become part of what is seen as "normal" by the dominant group', even in the context of formal commitment to equality (1991: 288).

Recent work has begun to develop analyses that parallel Essed's everyday racism in other areas, particularly gender and sexuality. Nijole Benokraitis (1997a) has edited a collection of case studies analyzing what she terms 'subtle sexism'. By this she means the 'unequal and harmful treatment of women' that has been internalized as 'normal', 'natural', or 'acceptable' (Benokraitis, 1997b: 11). It can be intentional or unintentional and, as Lisa Frehill found in her study of engineering, it is consistent with normative expectations of male–female interactions: 'Although subtle sexist behaviour may be unintentional or "friendly", it

still reinforces the boundaries between men and women' (1997: 126).

In their case study of women in law, Haslett and Lipman (1997) outline instances of hostile humour, isolation, diminishing, devaluation, and discouragement that cumulatively exclude women, rendering them less confident and productive. As was the case with everyday racism, the power of these practices, which Haslett and Lipman term 'micro inequities', lies in their repetition and 'aggregate burden'.

> Taken individually, each instance of an innuendo or hostile humor may strike one as being minor and not worth 'calling someone on it'; however, the daily, cumulative burden of continuously experiencing such micro inequities is significant . . . Over time . . . micro inequities constitute a formidable barrier to performance, productivity, and advancement (Haslett and Lipman, 1997: 51).

The individually trivial nature of such practices makes them particularly difficult to address effectively.

The perpetuation of structural arrangements of inequality is accomplished through 'ongoing, everyday, taken-far-granted practices that are rooted in cultural habit' (O'Brien, 1998: 25). Understanding, then, demands inquiry focused on the interactional processes that perpetually alter or counter existing structural arrangements. Inquiry must focus on the ways even those of us committed to equality practice inequality in our everyday interactions. The research presented here is an illustration of such inquiry. It investigates the everyday inequalities and micro inequities through which the dominant culture of one medical school is maintained despite an institutional commitment to equality of opportunity.

Everyday Racism

In interviews, both faculty and students generally indicated that 'race' and racism really are not issues in medical school. Nonetheless, many students then went on to describe racist incidents, most of which occurred during rural practice placements or elective rotations in other schools: 'People there were quite racist against Natives.'

> Mark[11]:   Last summer when we did a rural practice elective out in the community I heard a few things about East Indian students who had trouble with the more redneck kind of attitudes. Older, white people in the communities might say something offensive.

In keeping with the notion of everyday racism, overt racist incidents were not very common, yet 'race' appears to affect the extent to which students feel they fit in during medical school, with 45 per cent of 'minority' students indicating they 'fit in' well, compared with 58 per cent of non-minority students. Racialized minority students were slightly more likely than others to agree that 'race' affects how students are treated by other medical staff, and that it affects the degree of respect from patients. The day-to-day importance of 'race' and culture were also highest for minority students. Furthermore, 25 per cent of students who identified as members of minority groups indicated that their racial or cultural background had a negative effect on their experiences at medical school, compared to only 4 per cent of non-minority students. Interestingly, minority students were also more likely to indicate that their race/culture had a positive impact; in contrast 84 per cent of non-minority students experienced their race as neutral. In interviews students explained that being Chinese is often an advantage in a city with a large Chinese patient population.

The most apparent form of everyday racism was racist jokes. About half (52 per cent) of the survey respondents indicated they heard 'offensive jokes' in medical school; the most common category of such jokes was those concerning 'race or ethnicity' (see Table 24.2).[12] For example:

> Sean: This guy had gone through the windshield of his car and they made some comment about, 'Oh, he was DWC. And I said, what's DWC? And they said, 'Driving While Chinese'. And that was the first day I was

there. And that's on the wards, and walking along the halls, so anybody could hear it. One of the residents said that to a doctor and the doctor laughed and said, 'Oh, that was a good one. I never heard that before.'

Table 24.2 Survey findings concerning offensive jokes

Question: **What type of jokes do you hear in medical school that you find offensive?**

Jokes about:	Frequency
Ethnic/racial groups	22
Gender	19
Particular patient types	19
Gays and lesbians	14
Height or weight	12
Religious groups	10
Cadavers	7
'Crude' topics	3
Age	2

As Nancy indicates, it can be very awkward for students to deal with racist comments when they come from attending physicians or senior residents who are in a position of power over students.

> Nancy: We had a Native man come in and told us he wasn't feeling well or whatever. And we went into the other room and the doctor said, 'So do you think this is a dumb Indian or a smart Indian?' And I went, 'What?!' . . . This is a person I'm supposed to be learning from so I can't say, 'What kind of a stupid questions are you asking me here?!' I've got to be with him for another three weeks and try and get a reference letter out of him, so I can't cut him down.

Two white students suggested they heard more overt racism than did students from racialized minority groups, since they were 'included in all the jokes' and were assumed to be like-minded because they are white: 'I was supposed to be one of them.'

Everyday Sexism

Neither male nor female students, on average, thought gender had much impact on their experiences of medical school, although the day-to-day importance of gender was greatest for women. Women also demonstrate more polarization than men; 54 per cent of women said gender is important to how they think about themselves, while a significant minority (23 per cent) said it was very unimportant. A certain ambiguity became apparent in the interviews, where most students stated that gender is really not an issue in medical school; classes are almost exactly gender balanced and everyone gets treated similarly. Having said this, however, most women and some men then went on to give examples of how gender does make a difference, ranging from quite blatant sexism and sexual harassment to a more subtle climate of gendered expectations that may make things intangibly easier for male students.

One woman was in a small clinical group with three male classmates; they were greeted every day by the attending physician with, 'Good morning, gentlemen.' Again, in the terms of everyday sexism, this minor, perhaps trivial incident may have a cumulative effect over time, conveying a repeated message of marginalization. Other students described incidents of outright sexual harassment. For example, when one woman was serving as a model patient for a demonstration the male clinician inappropriately fondled and commented on her buttocks in front of the whole class.

Far more subtle is the impact of an overall gendered climate, a series of gendered assumptions and expectations that can make life in medical school more comfortable and inviting for male students. One woman described 'low-level slightly irritating stuff', that is 'just somehow not inclusive or something, or not valuing me the way I would.' For example, students confront a lingering societal assumption that doctor *equals* man. Two male students suggested this assumption facilitates rapport with patients and eases their way through the medical hierarchy.

Mark: Perhaps I bond better with the students and the residents and the staff members just because I come from the same background as the other doctors do. . . . I've often felt, because I fit like a stereotyped white that patients might see me as a bit more trustworthy. A bit more what they'd like to see. Who they want to see.

This assumption that doctors are male may be reinforced by the fact that women students are less likely to be called doctor by other health care staff or by patients. Both students and faculty reported that women students and clinicians are still frequently mistaken for nurses. Fifty-seven per cent of the women surveyed were occasionally or regularly called doctor by someone other than family or friends, compared with 78 per cent of the men; 14 per cent of the women were *never* called doctor compared with 0 per cent of the men, Again, though being called 'Miss' while your male peers are called 'doctor' is in itself trivial, the effect can be cumulative. Perhaps consequently, almost half (6 of 14) of the women students interviewed indicated that they do not identify themselves as medical students in casual social settings outside school lest they be seen as putting on airs. None of the male students indicated this.

Constructing a professional appearance is another key element of medical socialization (Beagan, 2001), and one that is highly gendered. Both male and female survey respondents had concerns about their appearances. While male students dealt with those concerns by shaving, wearing a shirt with a collar, perhaps adding a tie, women's concerns were both more extensive and more complex. Women worried about style, accessories, body shapes, hair and make-up, about looking well-dressed without appearing too provocative, too feminine or simply incompetent: 'Is it professional enough? Competent looking? . . . I do not want to appear sexy on the job' (Survey comment, female). In the interviews, both women students and clinicians talked about dressing to earn respect; deliberately constructing an image that conveys desired messages. In contrast, the men took this for granted.

One of the most obvious areas where gender affects medical education *is* in students' choice of future career directions. Women were under-represented among those considering anesthesiology, surgery, and internal medicine, all highly paid specialties. Women were over-represented among those considering obstetrics and gynecology, psychiatry, family medicine, and pediatrics, some of the lowest paid fields of medicine. Some faculty members argued that unless there are active moves to keep women out of specific specialties gender is not an issue. Indeed for 89 per cent of male students, gender was *not* an important consideration when choosing their future specialty; for 43 per cent of women it *was* an important or very important factor (see Table 24.3).

One specialty, surgery, illustrates the complexity of gendering institutional climates. Only 28 per cent of women surveyed were considering surgery or surgical subspecialties. Students commented on the absence of women role-models, and described surgery as 'a man's world', a macho field.

> *Becky:*   It's still fairly intimidating for females to go into. . . . It's really sort of old-school, very male oriented, a boy's club. And I think that as a female I

wouldn't cope well in that. Lots of guys, if there's a woman there they won't do their usual jokes and banter between them. Or if they *do* do it, then you have to stand there and listen to it, which I wouldn't really want to either.

Even the material realities of an operating room contribute to the masculine climate of surgery, as one male surgeon outlined (c.f., Cassell, 1996).

In addition to a masculine atmosphere several women students ruled out surgery because they could not see how the long hours and intense call schedule would fit with having a family. Women rated parental and marital status as far more important considerations in career choice than did male students (see Table 24.3). Virtually every woman interviewed had concerns about fitting together career and family life, which guided them away from some specialties and toward others.

> *Nancy:*   I worry about balancing my family life. I worry about when I'm going to have children. How I'm going to put my children and my husband into a full-time career, with him having a full-time career. I don't want to have

Table 24.3 Gender-related concerns in specialty considerations

Question: How important are the following factors to you in choosing your future specialty? (1 = Not important, 5 = Very important)

	1	2	3	4	5
Gender					
Female %	26	14	17	31	12
Male %	67	22	8	3	0
$\lambda = 0.26$					
Parental status					
Female %	9	3	11	23	54
Male %	19	14	14	31	22
$\lambda = 0.17$					
Marital or relationship status					
Female %	9	3	6	37	46
Male %	19	6	17	36	22
$\lambda = 0.14$					

children who know their nanny better than they know me. I'm in that position that I think a lot of women are in, of wanting to be able to do it all and feeling inadequate when you can't. Wanting to be a full-time mom and have a nice house and be able to keep it up and do the grocery shopping and do the laundry and still work full-time and be there for all your patients and also be a good wife to your husband. And I know something's got to give and I'm not sure where it's going to be. I hope it's not my children.

While the women students were almost universally concerned with how a career would fit with expected family roles, virtually none of the men interviewed had thought about this.

Again, as was the case with everyday racism, the point is not that women face unusually high levels of sexism in medical school. Rather, this research illustrates the subtle processes of everyday sexism, interactional processes that construct the role of medical student or physician as somewhat more suited to a man than a woman. Women have to work to construct a professional appearance, to look feminine yet competent, to earn respect.

Women students choose career paths that avoid overly masculinized environments, opting for lower paid specialties that will allow them to be good wives and mothers without sacrificing their careers. When attending physicians routinely call women medical students 'Miss' while addressing their male peers as 'doctor', and when patients routinely call women students 'nurse', those trivial incidents occur *on top* of a pattern of micro inequities (Haslett and Lipman, 1997), as part of daily processes of gendering medicine.

Everyday Heterosexism

The experience of being identifiably gay or lesbian in this medical school seemed to depend a great deal on the dominant tone of each class. Being openly gay might lead to isolation one year, while the next entering class might be very supportive

of an openly gay classmate. The two clinicians interviewed who identified as gay said their sexual orientation had been a source of difficulty and marginalization for them in medical school. They had to decide how 'out' to be, and how much to suppress that part of their identity. They both see gay and lesbian students today facing similar struggles.

The one gay student who responded to the survey noted that his sexual orientation is a source of great stress. One aspect of that stress is homophobia expressed by other medical personnel. Students and physicians indicated that jokes about gays and lesbians were common.

While there are some sanctions for staff who make harassing comments, homophobic comments from patients leave students with little recourse. One clinician indicated that students just have to learn to handle it.

> *Dr F:* As a physician you will be called the 'F-word' [fag]. You will be told that you're going to get punched if you don't leave. And if you're gay or of different orientation, they might tell you, 'Hey, you take it in the ass and I'm not gonna talk to you.' It will happen. And I think it's part of [students'] education—how to deal with it.

As was the case with racist jokes and comments, students are placed in a particularly awkward position when homophobic jokes or slurs come from their patients.

Students may also face some degree of homophobia from their classmates.[13] Two students identified their heterosexuality as an advantage, commenting that it would be difficult to be gay or lesbian in their class.

> *Robin:* I see huge homophobia. I'm not gay, but out of a hundred and twenty people, statistically there's gonna be a few gay or lesbian people in my class. And no one will admit to it. . . . They obviously don't feel comfortable saying that. . . . One of my colleagues in first year had someone scribble 'fag' on

his nametag on his desk. . . . I think people try to avoid standing out in any way and I guess one way to stand out is to be gay.

It only takes a few instances such as that described by Robin to have an effect. Even if just a few students are vocally homophobic, that may be sufficient to cause gay and lesbian students in the class to feel unsafe.

Students and faculty who identified as gay described leading highly segregated lives during medical school, keeping their school lives separate from their lives in gay and lesbian communities. Several faculty members argued that this segregation and 'closeting' is a necessary survival strategy, as being out can be costly in terms of desired jobs. One gay clinician described a student coming out gradually by his third year of medical school, 'then slipping back in during fourth year, because he was afraid—and, I hate to say it . . . my feeling is that he's probably right. If he were gay and out he probably wouldn't get into a surgical residency' (c.f. Oriel et al., 1996). Even if the risks of being out are more perceived than real, one clinician pointed out that 'you're giving up an awful lot if you're wrong, if you feel that, "Gee they would accept me," and find out they won't.' Finally, one faculty member suggested sexual orientation may even influence residency choices, as he sees gay and lesbian students trying to identify which fields might be safest for them to be out (c.f., Risdon, Cook, and Willms, 2000). Again, this process, like the process of women students choosing not to enter surgery, is one of self-elimination. The realm of the possible becomes defined through cultural habit, excluding some options from consideration.

> Jason: What I've experienced is a lot of— not overt homophobia, well, a *little* overt homophobia, especially by a vocal sect in the class. . . . Among the teaching faculty there's some homophobia, just underneath the surface. They never come out and say it, they're always politically correct, but you know it's there. Fellow students—I

guess that's one of the reasons why I also feel more distant from a lot of people in the class. . . . If somebody talks about what they did on the weekend, if I did party I'm not going to tell them that I went to one of the gay bars.

Again, what is described here is not an unusually high degree of homophobia or heterosexism, nor even a set of hostile practices *intended* to exclude, discriminate, or harm. It is, rather, the experience of not quite fitting in with the dominant culture that surrounds you, of being marginalized. Everyday heterosexism, like everyday racism and sexism, is not life-threatening—although gay and lesbian students never know when it might be accompanied by a more virulent homophobia. From the simple assumption that everyone around you is heterosexual, to teasing about (hetero)sex at school social gatherings, to laughing at or making homophobic jokes, to not challenging homophobic remarks, to declining residency applications from openly gay students (Oriel et al., 1996), again the micro inequities of everyday heterosexism consist of the repetition of numerous small practices.

Everyday Classism

In Canada, the extremes of poverty and wealth are mitigated by our redistributive social welfare system. Widely accessible student loans mean university education—including medical education—and subsequent upward mobility are available to anyone willing to incur that level of debt. But social class is not just about money. Class also operates on the more subtle level of cultural capital and social capital: knowing the right people, being able to make the right sort of small talk, having the right hobbies and playing the right sports, knowing the right fork to use, and having the right clothes, accent, and demeanour.

Students from working class or impoverished families also described a significant struggle to construct the professional appearance expected in medicine. The 'right look' felt wrong for them. One woman noted that the very first time she felt she actually belonged in medical school was during a third-year elective in a clinic for low-income patients: 'I had the thrill of my lifetime at the Clinic. I could just dress in what's in my closet and not feel bad about it. And I could talk my natural way. And I *totally* fit in over there!'

There was considerable agreement among students and faculty that students from upper- or upper-middle-class backgrounds, especially the children of doctors, find it easiest to fit in at medical school and may adopt a student physician identity more readily. A third (31 per cent) of the students surveyed agreed that, 'students who come from upper-class backgrounds find it easier to fit in during medical training'—a belief held most strongly by students from working-class and impoverished family backgrounds. Poor and working-class students were more likely to believe their class background had a negative impact during medical school. One student wrote simply: 'I cannot relate to many of my classmates who come from very wealthy, Anglo-Saxon backgrounds' (Survey comment).

Two clinicians who came from working-class families said they never fit in during medical school and they continue to feel marginalized as physicians.

> *Dr P.:* [One] reason that I had a very difficult time [in medical school] is that I come from a working-class family, the only person in my extended family to finish high-school, to go to university. . . . That puts me in a very difference spot than the upper-middle-class white male, whose father was a doctor, who like the medical school, who was part of the 'in group' at the school and who is now part of the 'in group' as faculty.

One clinician was moved to tears during our interview when she recognized that the extreme isolation she felt as a working-class medical student 30 years ago has never really lessened.

Conclusions

This research in a single Canadian medical school illustrates the complexity of everyday racism, classism, sexism, and heterosexism. Well beyond blatant

forms of discrimination (practices already targeted by formal anti-discrimination policies and procedures) more covert and more subtle forms of marginalization maintain and reproduce an institutional climate that is more welcoming to some participants than others. Micro-level everyday practices of inclusion and exclusion cumulatively convey messages about who does and who does not truly belong. The interactional processes of everyday inequalities maintain hierarchies even within this group of relatively elite students and faculty.

As Jodi O'Brien (1998) suggests, the practices of everyday inequalities are often mindless, unknowing, and habitual. The power of these micro inequities is that they are seen as normal, natural, or acceptable. The majority of the participants in this research would say that gender, 'race', sexual orientation, and class are not issues in their medical school. In a society imbued with belief in meritocracy, these students and faculty have made it very near the top. They have a vested interest in denying categorically based injustices in favour of individual merit and equal opportunity. Yet the fact that the micro inequities illustrated here are at odds with the equality of opportunity expressly endorsed by the institution does not make them less damaging for marginalized and alienated students.

In contrast it suggests that ensuring equality of opportunity is not enough. Simply getting in to a school, an occupation, or a profession in which members of your social group have historically been under-represented, does not ensure that your experience there will be equitable. There may still be significant barriers to full participation. In his examination of a Canadian aboriginal teacher education program, Rick Hesch (1994: 201) argues that although students construct the program to meet their own needs as best they can, they do so in the face of 'fundamentally punishing conditions' that serve to limit their achievements. Those punishing conditions arise in the intersection of institutional expectations about students' roles with socio-cultural expectations about their private lives; there is a privileging of particular class-based and Eurocentric forms of knowledge that implicitly marginalizes them or pushes them toward assimilation. Similarly, although medical education provides an avenue for members of subordinated social groups to achieve upward mobility, in doing so they confront an institution that privileges particular cultural habits and knowledge forms. It simultaneously reproduces the inclusions and exclusions of racism, sexism, heterosexism, and classism. That institutional climate is maintained through daily subtle practices whose effects taken individually may be considered trivial, but taken cumulatively convey a message about who does and who does not belong. What remains to be seen in further research is what impact—if any—these micro inequities and everyday inequalities and their messages of marginality have on medical practitioners in their work lives.

Notes

1. I would like to thank Bethan Lloyd for comments on earlier versions of this work, and the anonymous CJS reviewers for their detailed reading and helpful comments. The research was supported by doctoral fellowships from the Social Sciences and Humanities Research Council of Canada, and the Izaak Killam Memorial Foundation.

2. The term 'race' is enclosed in quotation marks to indicate its status as a social construct rather than an ontologically valid category. Social constructs are nonetheless real in their consequences. The routine use of the term 'race' as if it actually exists in our daily social worlds makes it difficult to investigate the social relations of racialization without reference to the term—even as that helps to perpetuate its presumed validity.

3. Calculated based on the descriptive statistics given by Becker et al.: 'Each class contains a number of women, ordinarily around five . . . as well as a small number of American Negroes, possibly four or five' (1961: 60). They give the entering class size for one year, 1958, as 94 new students (1961: 53). Assuming class sizes are fairly constant, I estimate the percentages above.

4. Yet even very recent research has failed to problematize the impact of social differences among students, perpetuating the image of a generic medical student (e.g., Sinclair, 1997).

5. This research is bolstered by a growing body of personal accounts about racism in medical school (Blackstock, 1996; Gamble, 1990; Rucker, 1992). Research on the experiences of racialized minority students in Canada is virtually non-existent.

6. By 'homophobia' I mean fear and hatred of or, more mildly, hostility and condemnation directed toward people known or believed to be gay, lesbian, or bisexual. By 'heterosexism' I mean the overwhelming assumption that the world is and must be heterosexual, and the systemic display of power and privilege that establish heterosexuality as the irrefutable norm—by extension establishing homosexuality as deviance. Heterosexism centres on oblivion about/denial of the very existence of gays and lesbians. Homophobia is a more active form of intolerance and hostility.

7. The medical school where the research was conducted is not identified. This was an agreement made with the administration of the school in order to gain access to the research site. That decontextualizes the research and leaves the degree of generalizability to other medical schools an empirical question. The school followed a traditional undergraduate curriculum and was located in a large Canadian city with a racially and ethnically diverse population.

8. Subjective assessment of class photos shows that since the early 1980s about 30 per cent of each class at this school would be considered 'visible minority' students.

9. They represented anatomy, biochemistry, physiology, and pharmacology.

10. Their clinical areas included renal, pulmonary, pediatrics and pediatric oncology, medical genetics, family practice, surgery, neurology, ethics, internal medicine, infectious disease, endocrinology, anesthesia, and psychiatry.

11. All names used are pseudonyms.

12. Unfortunately, we cannot know from the data whether they had heard one such joke or heard them daily.

13. Again, whether the level of homophobia in medical school is higher or lower than in the rest of the society is not the point. The point is simply that students who identify as, or are identified as, gay or lesbian have distinctive experiences in medical school in part because they have to deal with homophobia from patients, staff, faculty, and classmates. It makes their experience of school different from that of students identified as heterosexual.

References

Association of Canadian Medical Colleges. 1998. *Canadian Medical Education Statistics* 20.

Baldwin, D.C., Jr., S.R. Daugherty, and B.D. Rowley. 1994. 'Emotional Impact of Medical School and Residency', *Academic Medicine* 69 Supplement: S19–21.

Baldwin, D.C., S.R. Daugherty, and E.J. Eckenfels. 1991. 'Student Perceptions of Mistreatment and Harassment during Medical School: A Survey in 10 United States Schools', *Western Journal of Medicine* 155: 140–5.

Beagan, B.L. 2001. 'Even if I don't know what I'm doing I can make it *look* like I know what I'm doing': Becoming a doctor in the 1990s', *Canadian Review of Sociology and Anthropology* 39, 3: 275–92.

Becker, H.S., B. Geer, A.L. Strauss, and E.C. Hughes. 1961. *Boys in White: Student Culture in Medical School*. Chicago: University of Chicago Press.

Benokraitis, N.E., ed. 1997a. *Subtle Sexism: Current Practice and Prospects for Change*. Thousand Oaks, CA: Sage.

———. 1997b. 'Sex Discrimination in the 21st Century', in N.V. Benokraitis, ed., *Subtle Sexism: Current Practice and Prospects for Change*, pp. 5–33. Thousand Oaks, CA: Sage.

Bergen, M.R., C.M. Guarino, and C.D. Jacobs. 1996. 'A Climate Survey for Medical Students', *Evaluation and the Health Professions* 19: 30–47.

Bickel, J. 1994. 'Special Needs and Affinities of Women Medical Students', in E.S. More and M.A. Milligan, eds., *The Empathetic Practitioner: Empathy, Gender and Medicine*, pp. 237–49. New Brunswick, NJ: Rutgers Press.

Bickel, J. and A. Ruffin. 1995. 'Gender-Associated Differences in Matriculating and Graduating Medical Students', *Academic Medicine* 70: 552–9.

Bickel, J., and P.R. Kopriva. 1993. 'A Statistical Perspective on Gender in Medicine', *Journal of the American Medical Women's Association* 48: 141–4.

Blackstock, D.G. 1996. 'A Black Woman in Medicine', in D. Wear, ed., *Women in Medical Education: An Anthology of Experience*, pp. 75–80. New York, SUNY Press.

Broadhead, R. 1983. *The Private Lives and Professional Identities of Medical Students*. New Brunswick, NJ: Transaction.

Cassel, J. 1996. 'The Woman in the Surgeon's Body: Understanding Difference', *American Anthropologist* 98: 41–53.

Cole, S. 1986. 'Sex Discrimination and Admission to Medical School, 1929–1984', *American Journal of Sociology* 92: 549–67.

Cook, D.I., L.E. Griffith, M. Cohen, G.H. Guyatt, and B. O'Brien. 1995. 'Discrimination and Abuse Experienced by General Internists in Canada', *Journal of General Internal Medicine* 10: 565–72.

Coombs, R.H. 1978. *Mastering Medicine*. New York: Free Press. Dickstein, L.J. 1993. 'Gender Bias in Medical Education: Twenty Vignettes and Recommended Responses', *Journal of the American Medical Women's Association* 48: 152–62.

Druzin, P., I. Shrier, M. Yacowar, and M. Rossognol. 1998. 'Discrimination against Gay, Lesbian and Bisexual Family Physicians by Patients', *Canadian Medical Association Journal* 158: 593–7.

Essed, P. 1991. *Understanding Everyday Racism: An Interdisciplinary Theory*. New York: Sage.

Foster, H.W. 1996. 'Reaching Parity for Minority Medical Residents: A Possibility or a Pipe Dream?', *Journal of the National Medical Association* 88: 17–21.

Frehill. L.M. 1997. 'Subtle Sexism in Engineering', in N.V. Benokraitis, ed., *Subtle Sexism: Current Practice and Prospects for Change*, pp. 117–35. Thousand Oaks, CA: Sage.

Gamble, V.N. 1990. 'On Becoming a Physician: A Dream Not Deferred', in E.C. White, ed., *The Black Women's Health Book: Speaking for Ourselves*, pp. 52–64. Seattle, WA: Seal Press.

Grant, L. 1988. 'The Gender Climate of Medical School: Perspectives of Women and Men Students', *Journal of the American Medical Women's Association* 43: 109–19.

Gray, J.D., and J. Reudy. 1998. 'Undergraduate and Postgraduate Medical Education in Canada', *Canadian Medical Association Journal* 58: 1047–50.

Guyatt, G.H., D.J. Cook, L. Griffith, S.D. Walter, C. Risdon, and J. Liukus. 1997. 'Attitudes toward the Use of Gender-Inclusive Language Among Residency Trainees', *Canadian Medical Association Journal* 156: 1289–93.

Haas, J., and W. Shaffir. 1987. *Becoming Doctors: The Adoption of a Cloak of Competence*. Greenwich, CT: JAI Press.

Haslett, B.B., and S. Lipman. 1997. 'Micro Inequities: Up Close and Personal', in N.V. Benokraitis, ed., *Subtle Sexism: Current Practice and Prospects for Change*, pp. 34–53. Thousand Oaks, CA: Sage.

Hesch, R. 1994. 'Cultural Production and Cultural Reproduction in Aboriginal Preservice Teacher Education', in L. Erwin and D. MacLennan, eds., *Sociology of Education in Canada: Critical Perspectives on Theory, Research and Practice*. Mississauga: Copp Clark Longman: 200–19.

Hostler, S.L., and R.R.P. Gressard. 1993. 'Perceptions of the Gender Fairness of the Medical Education Environment', *Journal of the American Medical Women's Association* 48: 51–4.

Jonas, H.S., S.A. Etzel, and B. Barzansky. 1992. 'Educational Programs in US Medical Schools', *Journal of the American Medical Association* 268: 1083–90.

Kirk, J. 1994. 'A Feminist Analysis of Women in Medical Schools', in B.S. Bolaria and H.D. Dickenson, eds., *Health, Illness, and Health Care in Canada, 2nd edition*, pp. 158–82. Toronto: Harcourt Brace.

Klamen, D.L, L.S. Grossman, and D.R. Kopacz. 1999. 'Medical Student Homophobia', *Journal of Homosexuality* 37: 53–63.

Komaromy, M., A.B. Bindman, R.J. Haber, and M.A. Sande. 1993. 'Sexual Harassment in Medical Training', *The New England Journal of Medicine* 328: 322–6.

Konner, M. 1987. *Becoming a Doctor: A Journey of Initiation in Medical School*. New York: Viking.

Lenhart, S. 1993. 'Gender Discrimination: A Health and Career Development Problem for Women Physicians', *Journal of the American Medical Women's Association* 4, 8: 155–9.

Mendelsohn, K.D., L.Z. Neiman, K. Isaacs, S. Lee, and S.P. Levison. 1994. 'Sex and Gender Bias in Anatomy and Physical Diagnosis Text Illustrations', *Journal of the American Medical Association* 272: 1267–70.

Moscarello, R., K.J. Margittai, and M. Rissi. 1994. 'Differences in Abuse Reported by Female and Male Canadian Medical Students', *Canadian Medical Association Journal* 150: 357–63.

O'Brien, J. 1998. 'Introduction: Differences and Inequities', in J. O'Brien and J.A. Howard, eds., *Everyday Inequalities: Critical Inquiries*, pp. 1–39. Malden, MA: Blackwell.

Oriel, K.A., D.J. Madlon-Kay, D. Govaker, and D.J. Mersey. 1996. 'Gay and Lesbian Physicians in Training: Family Practice Program Directors' Attitudes and Students' Perceptions of Bias', *Family Medicine* 28: 720–5.

Risdon, C., D. Cook, and D. Willms. 2000. 'Gay and Lesbian Physicians in Training: A Qualitative Study', *Canadian Medical Association Journal* 162: 331–4.

Rose, L. 1994. 'Homophobia among Doctors', *British Medical Journal* 308: 586–7.

Rucker, C.S. 1992. 'Wrestling with Ignorance', *Journal of the American Medical Association* 267: 2392.

Schulte, H.M., and J. Kay. 1994. 'Medical Students' Perceptions of Patient-Initiated Sexual Behavior', *Academic Medicine* 69: 842–6.

Shapiro, M. 1987. *Getting Doctored: Critical Reflections on Becoming a Physician*. Toronto, ON: Between the Lines.

Sinclair, S. 1997. *Making Doctors: An Institutional Apprenticeship*. New York: Berg.

vanIneveld, C.H., D.J. Cook, S.L. Kane, and D. King. 1996. 'Discrimination and Abuse in Internal Medicine Residency', *Journal of General Internal Medicine* 11: 401–5.

Wallick, M.M., K.M. Cambre, and M.H. Townsend. 1992. 'How the Topic of Homosexuality Is Taught at US Medical Schools', *Academic Medicine* 67: 601–3.

QUESTIONS FOR CRITICAL THOUGHT

1. Educational institutions include not only classrooms and curriculums, but also locker rooms, cliques, playgrounds, and other sites of informal education about what gender means. What did you learn about gender at school outside the classroom?

2. One proposed solution to the problem of gender polarization in schools is the creation of same-sex schools. Would you send your son or daughter to a same-sex school? What would be some of the advantages? What about disadvantages?

3. De Leeuw interviewed people many years after their time in British Columbia residential schools, but their memories of these schools were detailed and profound. What gendered or racialized meanings do we retain from schooling, even after our memories of the formal curriculum have faded?

4. Is there a connection between gender inequities and other kinds of 'micro inequities', as discussed by both Beagan and Lindberg?

5. Jordan and Cowan identify 'warrior narratives' as one form of unstructured dramatic play among young children. Can you identify any other such narratives from your own experiences with children's play?

6. If young children's play reinforces gender stereotypes, should parents or educators be concerned? Should we try to explicitly 'teach' gender equality?

PART VII

The Gendered Workplace

Perhaps the most drastic social change in industrial countries in the twentieth century was the entry of women into the workplace. The nineteenth-century ideology of 'separate spheres'—the breadwinner husband and the homemaker wife—has slowly and steadily evaporated. While only 20 per cent of women, and only 4 per cent of married women, worked outside the home in 1900, more than 75 per cent did so by 1995, including 60 per cent of married women. Despite the collapse of the doctrine of separate spheres—work and home—the workplace remains a dramatically divided world where women and men rarely do the same jobs in the same place for the same pay. Occupational sex segregation, persistent sex discrimination, and wage disparities are all significant problems faced by working women. These disparities are least evident at the beginning of men's and women's working lives, widening slowly as time goes by and as other life events, particularly childbearing, exert different pressures on women and on men. This section, thus, should be read in conjunction with the section on the gendered family in order to appreciate the double impact of work life and family life in shaping differences and inequalities. Men and women are distributed non-randomly through the workforce, with different genders clustered in different sectors and different types of jobs. This clustering leads to certain jobs and sectors acquiring gendered reputations as 'men's work' or 'women's work'.

In recent years, women have made significant inroads into career areas that were formerly bastions of masculinity, such as medicine or law. Men, however, have been much less likely to 'desegregate' female-dominated occupations such as nursery-school teaching or cosmetology. For those men who do enter female-dominated fields, negotiating the pitfalls of being the 'wrong' sex for the job means finding one's professional way through a minefield of gender and sexuality, as Joan Evans discusses. The male nurses in Evans's work judge themselves, and are judged by others, by their adherence to or deviation from a feminized norm of caring.

At the other end of spectrum, the firefighters interviewed by Shelley Pacholok inhabit an occupational world characterized by the hallmarks of stereotypical masculinity—risk, danger, strength and protecting others. However, as Pacholok demonstrates, masculinity is not embedded in the work itself, but is constructed through discourse and representations as the different groups of firefighters talk about their work and rank themselves against their peers.

Workplace experiences are marked by race and class (among other social categories), which combine with gender to produce distinctive forms of masculinity and femininity. Pamela Sugiman looks backwards to the shop floors of Ontario auto manufacturing plants in the 1940s. She demonstrates how ideas about gender and masculinity combined with racialized hierarchies within the plants to produce experiences and careers for black men that were very different from those of either their white or female colleagues. Black men were able to find work in the auto plants and solidarity in the labour union at a time when women, white or black, faced major obstacles; but institutionalized racism meant that they were never treated as fully equal to white men.

For most people, 'work' and 'home' are separate, and the challenges in one realm do not dominate life in the other. However, for some workers, their home *is* their workplace. Bernadette Stiell and Kim England examine the lives of live-in domestic workers, for whom the wall dividing home from work has collapsed. Although these female workers live in close quarters with their same-gender employers, hierarchies based on class and racial categories overshadow their physical proximity and their gender commonalities, just as in Sugiman's auto plants.

CHAPTER 25

Cautious Caregivers: Gender Stereotypes and the Sexualization of Men Nurses' Touch

Joan A. Evans

Introduction

Caring for and about others is historically associated with women and nursing, and more than any other quality it captures the process and goal of nurses' work (MacDougall, 1997). Despite this association, men are now entering the profession in record numbers (Halloran and Welton, 1994; Zurlinden 1998) and challenging the stereotype that men are inappropriate in the caregiver role or incapable of providing compassionate and sensitive care. The nursing literature suggests that the desire to be of help and care for others is a major reason men chose nursing as a career (Taylor et al.,

1983; Skevington and Dawkes, 1988; Galbraith, 1991; Cyr, 1992; Kelly et al., 1996; MacDougall, 1997). Once in the profession, however, prevailing gender stereotypes of men as sexual aggressors and men nurses as gay, negatively influence the ability of men nurses to develop comfortable and trusting relationships with their patients (Mathieson, 1991; Lodge et al., 1997). The sexualization of men nurses' touch provides insight into how gender stereotypes create discomfort and suspicion on the part of patients. This, in turn, impacts on men nurses' perceptions of their own safety while performing intimate and caregiving tasks. This situation ultimately impacts on the ability of men nurses to perform the very work they came into nursing to do.

The Study

Aim

The overall aim of this research was to explore the experience of men nurses and the gendered and sexed relations that structure different experiences for women and men in the same profession. The definition of masculinity used in this study is based on Connell's (1987) sociology of masculinity work. Meanings of masculinity are demonstrated through practices that capture the performative nature of gender. Connell's definition moves us away from the essentialist notion that a relatively stable masculine essence exists that defines men and differentiates them from a feminine essence that defines women (Petersen, 1998).

When theorizing about men and masculinity, we now talk of masculinities, rather than masculinity (Connell, 1987, 1995; Hearn and Morgan, 1990) because masculinity is not uniform. This concept is reflected in the notion of hegemony and the dominance in society of certain forms and practices of masculinity. Men nurses, by virtue of their participation in 'women's work', may not measure up to the hegemonic standard as evidenced by the stigma of homosexuality that surrounds them.

Method

Participants

Eight men Registered Nurses practising in the province of Nova Scotia, Canada, were selected to participate in this research using a convenience sampling technique. Because men are a highly visible minority in nursing, demographic data have been purposefully kept vague to protect the identities of the participants. Their ages ranged from late-twenties to mid-fifties, and years of nursing practice ranged from 7 to 32 years. Areas of nursing practice included community health nursing, mental health nursing, medical-surgical, and general duty nursing. Three participants were in a leadership role; two had a baccalaureate degree. Six participants were married, and two lived with a partner. One participant was an 'out' gay man.

Data were collected in 1998 in two rounds of semi-structured interviews.

Findings

The theme of men nurses as cautious caregivers emerged as one of four themes that characterized the experience of participants. The findings presented offer insight into the experience of men in nursing, but are not intended to be generalizable.

Affirmation of Caring

The participants in this research affirmed the importance of caring and traits such as compassion, empathy, and honesty as those that gave meaning to their lives as nurses. They generally also supported the perception that men and women nurses' caring styles were not the same. As one participant noted, 'We have our ways of getting it across without putting that female bent or lean on it.' Participants did not agree, however, on the ways in which women's and men's expressions of caring differed and they expressed conflicting opinions about whether men nurses were more task-orientated, more gentle, or more caring. One participant characterized the difference between women and men nurses by describing women's caring as 'warm fuzzies' and more 'touchy feelie'. These were not necessarily negative descriptors; however, most participants commented that men nurses generally used touch less than their women colleagues.

For most participants, humour and camaraderie were identified as important expressions of their caring practice. Humour in particular, added warmth and helped patients relax and feel more comfortable with them as men. Despite an acknowledgment that humour needed to be patient-specific, its character and purpose was different when it was used with men patients and in the presence of men only. In such instances, humour was described as important in relieving male anxiety. It was also a comfortable approach to men patients and a way to be more of a friend or 'buddy' to them. Men patients in turn joked with men nurses and enjoyed the freedom of sharing things with another man that a woman might find inappropriate or offensive. The masculine nature of such humour is evidenced by its 'male only' character as 'when a female staff would come in, we wouldn't continue on with it.'

The Problematic Nature of Men Nurses' Touch

Touch was one expression of caring that all participants identified as important, if not central, to their practice as nurses. Touch was also acknowledged, however, to be a practice that sometimes did not come naturally to them as men. One participant described his hands as 'rough hands' before he became a nurse. Another spoke of the newness of touching people 'because that wasn't part of my existence to that point'. Despite the newness of some caring expressions, touching and comforting others was acknowledged to be rewarding for participants and patients.

Whether the purpose of touch is to perform a procedure or provide comfort, an overriding theme is that for men nurses touching patients, particularly women patients, is potentially dangerous. Participants voiced concern that women patients might be uncomfortable and/or misinterpret their touch—a situation that in turn might lead to accusations of inappropriate behaviour or sexual molestation. The fear of misunderstandings and accusations related to touching patients resulted in participants being cautious and vigilant: 'I have to be careful what I'm doing . . . because of the possibility of somebody saying that I did something wrong, or rape, or I touched her wrong—that's always there.' Another participant commented that: 'You are very vulnerable, particularly if you're alone—and even in a ward situation. You have to be very careful that you assess the situation and know that this might be an inappropriate place to touch.'

The perception that men nurses are unable to defend themselves against patient accusations of inappropriate behaviour compounded participants' sense of themselves as vulnerable caregivers. As pointed out by one participant, 'It's my word against theirs.' Another participant who acknowledged the difficulty of defending himself commented that there were situations where he deemed it was too unsafe to touch.

Assessing When It Is Safe to Touch

Knowing when it is safe to touch and what the touch should consist of is based on a careful assessment of each patient situation. When the patient was a man, decisions regarding touch were guided by an accepted masculine norm, or what one participant referred to as a 'code' of understanding. This code is illustrated by the comment, 'Large men don't wash a healthy man's back—code.'

How far participants could go before violating the 'code' or crossing the line was dependent on the illness acuity of the male patient. As one noted, 'If you are sick, you don't mind a guy being there, you don't care who is doing anything.' It was also influenced by the age of the patient as participants generally described feeling more comfortable with older men who were less 'macho' and more receptive to expressions of compassion. They were less comfortable touching young people, particularly teens, who they perceived were more preoccupied with the possibility that a man nurse might be gay.

Participants commented that despite it being acceptable for women nurses to touch men and women patients, it was not as acceptable for men nurses to do the same. This aura of unacceptability was noted to impact not only on patients' perceptions of men nurses' touch, but also women nurses' perceptions. One participant commented that a woman colleague reported him to a supervisor when he reassured a distraught, partially dressed woman patient by putting his hand on her shoulder. Another was accused of molesting a newborn boy by the father who discovered him changing the baby's diaper. Incidents such as these left a lasting impression and reminded participants that touching patients was potentially dangerous work.

Strategizing to Protect Oneself from Accusations

As a result of the fear of being wrongfully accused of inappropriate touch, participants described six strategies they used to reduce this risk.

Strategy no. 1: Taking the time to build trust before touching. This was particularly important when interacting with women patients.

Strategy no. 2: Maintaining a degree of formality by shaking the hand of a patient. This set the tone of the interaction and provided an opportunity to assess patient comfort.

Strategy no. 3: Projecting the traditional image of a nurse to legitimize the role of men as nurses. This included wearing a white uniform.

Strategy no. 4: Working in teams with women colleagues in situations deemed to be unsafe. Such situations included checking female patients on night shifts, entering a room with teenage girls, or performing a procedure on a female that required intimate touching.

Strategy no. 5: Delegating tasks that required intimate touching of women patients. Participants traded off tasks with women nurses to ensure patient comfort and their own safety.

Strategy no. 6: Modifying procedural techniques to minimize patient exposure and the need for intimate touching. One participant commented that he might try to convince a female patient that the best intramuscular injection site was the thigh, 'not the butt'.

Discussion

Going against the Grain: Men Caregivers

Despite research that suggests men choose careers in nursing to help others (Taylor et al., 1983; Skevington and Dawkes, 1988; Cyr, 1992; Kelly et al., 1996; MacDougall, 1997), men nurses tend to gravitate to nursing specialties that require less intimate patient touching (Williams, 1989, 1995; Kauppinen-Toropainen and Lammi, 1993). The participants in this study support this tendency, and only two currently worked at the bedside in a role that required intimate caregiving. The remaining six, despite having worked at the bedside, were now in positions that required less touching and more psychological patient care. In some of these positions, however, participants continued to express vulnerability. This was especially so for

those in psychiatry: 'Touch takes on a whole new meaning that it didn't have in medicine or in med-surg. . . . It's never straight forward here. If I have someone who I know has a full-blown personality disorder, I won't even be caught in the same room alone with them.'

In order to avoid uncomfortable situations, men nurses distance themselves from traditional nursing roles and the caring ideology of nursing (Egeland and Brown, 1989; Kauppinen-Toropainen and Lammi, 1993). They are also tracked into elite specialty and leadership positions considered more congruent with prevailing notions of masculinity (Williams, 1995; Evans, 1997). The result is that power and prestige tend to be associated with small numbers of men in the profession (Porter, 1992; Ryan and Porter, 1993; Villeneuve, 1994). At the heart of this situation are gender stereotypes and the belief that men are inappropriate in caregiver roles.

Feminization of Caring

Participant accounts draw attention to differences between societal and nursing expectations of men in relation to expressions of caring. They spoke of the newness of touching with caring hands and learning to feel comfortable touching others. The need to learn to care and/or develop comfort with expressions of caring previously not practised, is supported in the nursing literature. In a study of 20 men nursing students in a baccalaureate nursing program, Paterson et al. (1996) found that men nursing students feared they would never be able to touch clients or openly display emotions because they had learned all their lives that such behaviours were effeminate and emasculating (32). Similarly, Streubert (1994) reported that men nursing students were confronted with the task of having to learn caring skills that were unique to them. They consequently struggled with the need to consciously divest themselves of their macho image as they learned to express caring in sensitive and demonstrative ways that women educators and nurses expected (Paterson et al., 1996).

Research conducted by Okrainec (1994) further highlights the notion that men and women judge the caring practices of men against a feminine norm. Okrainec surveyed 117 men and 121 women nursing students in the province of Alberta, Canada, and reported that 25 per cent of both men and women felt that women were superior in caring; 20 per cent of men and 25 per cent of women rated women superior to men in terms of empathy (104); and 50 per cent of men and 66 per cent of women rated women superior to men in ability to express feelings (103). Differences in perceptions between women and men students are noteworthy, given Okrainec's comment that most men and women nursing students thought that a caring attitude was equal in both sexes.

In the absence of an acknowledgment that expressions of caring include a wide range of possible behaviours that reflect the personalities of individual nurses and specifics of each client situation, theorizing about caring will be likely to continue to be based on stereotypical notions of masculine and feminine behaviours. Even more problematic, men nurses' expressions of caring will continue to be conceptualized as unique or special because they either fall outside the masculine stereotype, or conversely, within the feminine one. The implication of such stereotyping is that it perpetuates an artificial separation of the masculine and feminine and polarizes masculinity and femininity.

Maintaining Masculinity

For men in patriarchal culture, perpetuating the polarization of masculinity and femininity is an important practice of masculinity, as the maintenance of masculinity is predicated on the separation of all that is male and masculine from all that is female (Williams, 1989). Williams (1989) and Kauppinen-Toropainen and Lammi (1993) suggest that, for men nurses, this separation is accomplished by emphasizing different caring styles as a means of distinguishing the contribution of men nurses from that of women.

Maintaining masculinity through humour

Participants in this study demonstrate how humour as a practice of caring also constitutes a practice of masculinity. Participants commented that many of the jokes they shared with men clients were bawdy and sexist in nature and not appropriate for women. In this context, the practice of humour and its 'male

only' character can be understood to be an important means of (re)affirming masculinity. This conclusion is supported by ethnographic research about the role of humour in young men in two British schools. Researchers Kehily and Nayak (1997) suggest that humorous exchanges among young men have an unfeminine and exclusively 'straight' character to them and are constitutive of heterosexual masculine identities. As such, humorous exchanges among men can also be conceptualized as practices of male bonding, as 'men recognize and reinforce one another's bona fide membership in the male gender' and remind one another that 'they were not born women' (Frank, 1992: 57).

Sexualization of men nurses' touch

Men learn early in their nursing career that, despite being in an occupation that requires compassion and caring, touch as an expression of that compassion and caring exposes them to the risk of misinterpretation and accusations of inappropriate behaviour (Glasper and Campbell, 1994; Paterson et al., 1996). Unlike women's touch, which is considered a natural extension of women's traditional caregiver role, men's touch is surrounded with suspicion that implies that men nurses' motives for touching are not care-oriented, but sexual in nature.

Participants in this study were well aware of their vulnerability when they touched patients. Similarly, Streubert (1994) found that men nursing students dreaded how women clients might feel about having them as nurses. They consequently struggled with learning appropriate ways to care and touch that would avoid the problem of clients thinking that a man was seducing them (Paterson et al., 1996). Several practices described by participants indicate that, with experience, men nurses can and do develop strategies that allow them to care for patients and ensure their own safety. Such strategies reflect the notion that men who see themselves operating outside the hegemony of masculinity are fine-tuned to the necessary practices to protect themselves (Frank, 1992).

The sexualization of men nurses' touch is particularly evident in the area of obstetric nursing, where the nature of touch is extremely intimate. Situations in which obstetric or gynecological women patients refuse to be cared for by men nurses or men nursing students provide valuable insight into the sexualized character of men nurses' touch. An ethnographic study by Morin et al. (1999) of 32 women obstetric patients revealed that most women were accepting of men nurses. Those women who refused them, however, cited reasons that were often sexual in nature.

An interesting observation by Morin et al. (1999) is that men nurses who are older, married, and have children are generally more accepted as caregivers by women patients (85). This can be attributed to perceptions by women patients that such qualities make men nurses sexually safer and hence more comfortable to be around. Continuing with this line of theorizing, it follows that practices which contribute to the perception of men nurses as sexually safe would be employed by them to put women patients at ease. This conclusion may be evidenced by men nurses' practice of wearing a traditional nurse uniform. Mangan (1994) suggests that the nursing uniform strengthens and promotes the image of men as conforming to the expectations of the larger nursing group. This association may be important in helping men nurses project a genuine desire to care for others as one means of reducing the risk of accusations of inappropriate touch.

Discussion

Gender Stereotypes: A No-Win Situation

The need for men nurses to project conformity in relation to a traditional nursing image may not apply to all patient populations. In situations where men nurses provide intimate care to men, sexual safety for men patients may depend on the degree to which men nurses project hegemonic masculinity. The nurse uniform, because it projects a feminine image, may consequently have a negative influence on the acceptance of men nurses by men patients. It is interesting to note that only two of the participants in this research wore a nurse uniform. Both worked at the bedside in positions that required intimate patient touching.

For most participants, the need to minimize suspicions of gayness and project a masculine identity with men patients was facilitated by a 'code'

of understanding among men that was grounded in the heterosexist or homophobic principle that men do not touch other men without a legitimate need. The concept of need, as pointed out by participants, was complex and depended on factors such as patient age and illness acuity. They mentioned that they were more comfortable touching men who were acutely ill because they were too sick to care about what anyone did to them. They also found that older men were more comfortable being touched by another man because they were less macho.

Men Nurses as Failed Caregivers

The stigma associated with the stereotype of men nurses as gay is compounded by the stereotype that gay men are also sexual deviants and sexual predators (Levine, 1992). In situations where men nurses provide intimate care to children, the sexualization of men's touch consequently assumes a more sinister character that fuels suspicion that men nurses are pedophiles. Glasper and Campbell (1994) suggest that any intimate procedure conducted by men nurses on children is now suspicious as a result of a British nurse being convicted of sexually assaulting a child in his care. An interesting observation in light of this situation is that the behaviour of one man nurse has not been attributed to an individual deviation, but to all men nurses as a group.

The notion of blaming all men nurses for the transgressions of a few is also raised by Bush (1976). She notes the tendency of some patients to blame individual men nurses when they are perceived to fail in the performance of a technical skill. When a man nurse is perceived to fail in an affective area, however, men nurses as a group are blamed. This situation can be understood as a consequence of traditional gender stereotypes and the belief that men are inappropriate and unable to function as well as women in caring roles.

Conclusion

The gendered nature of men nurses' caring interactions reveals the ways in which gender stereotypes create contradictory and complex situations of acceptance, rejection, and suspicion of men as nurturers and caregivers. Here the stereotype of men as sexual aggressors creates suspicion that men are at the bedside for reasons other than a genuine desire to help others. When this stereotype is compounded by the stereotype that men nurses are gay, the caring practices of men nurses are viewed with suspicion in situations where there is intimate touching, not only of women patients, but of men and children as well. In each of these patient situations, men nurses are caught up in complex and contradictory gender relations that situate them in stigmatizing roles vulnerable to accusations of inappropriate touch.

Gender relations are complex and do not lend themselves to 'quick fixes' or recommendations that are easily implemented. The challenge in nursing is to acknowledge the power and pervasiveness of gender relations and the role they play in all nurses' lives. The answer to reducing the suspicion that surrounds men nurses' caring practice lies in challenging prevailing gender stereotypes that situate men in deviant positions when they do not conform to the hegemonic masculine standard. This challenge cannot be taken up by women nurses or men nurses alone. Meaningful change will need to be grounded in an ethos of alliance-building between women nurses and men nurses. This alliance-building needs to begin with dialogue in our nursing classrooms and workplaces if we are to begin to reveal the gendered nature of our thinking, our practices, and our institutions in the interests of revaluing caring and interpersonal skills that challenge hegemonic masculinity.

References

Connell, R.W. 1987. *Gender and Power. Society, the Person and Sexual Politics.* Stanford, CA: Stanford University Press.

———. 1995. *Masculinities.* Cambridge: Polity.

Cyr, J. 1992. 'Males in Nursing', *Nursing Managements* 23: 54–5.

Egeland, J., and J. Brown. 1989. 'Men in Nursing: Their Fields of Employment, Preferred Fields of Practice and Role Strain', *Health Services Research* 24: 693–707.

Evans, J. (1997). 'Men in Nursing: Issues of Gender Segregation and Hidden Advantage', *Journal of Advanced Nursing* 26: 226–31.

Frank, B. 1992. 'Straight/Strait Jackets for Masculinity: Educating for "Real" Men', *Atlantis* 18: 47–59.

Galbraith, M. 1991. 'Attracting Men to Nursing: What Will They Find Important in Their Career', *Journal of Nursing Education* 30: 182–6.

Glasper, A., and S. Campbell. 1994. 'Beyond the Clothier Inquiry', *Nursing Standard* 8: 18–19.

Halloran, E., and J. Welton. 1994. 'Why Aren't There More Men in Nursing' in J. McCloskey and H. Grace, eds., *Current Issues in Nursing*, 4th edn, pp. 683–91. Toronto: Moshy.

Hearn, J., and D. Morgan. 1990. 'Men, Masculinities and Social Theory', in J. Hearn and D. Morgan, eds., *Men, Masculinities and Social Theory*, pp. 1–18. Boston: Unwin-Hyman.

Kauppinen-Toropainen, K., and J. Lammi. 1993. 'Men in Female-dominated Occupations: A Cross Cultural Comparison', in C. Williams, ed., *Doing 'Women's Work'*, pp. 91–112. London: Sage.

Kehily, M.J., and A. Navak. 1997. 'Lads and Laughter: Humor and the Production of Heterosexual Hierarchies', *Gender and Education* 9: 69–87.

Kelly, N., M. Shoemaker, and T. Steele. 1996. 'The Experience of Being a Male Student Nurse', *Journal of Nursing Education* 35: 170–4.

Levine, M. 1992. 'The Status of Gay Men in the Workplace', in M. Kimmel and M. Messner, eds., *In Men's Lives,* 2nd edn, pp. 251–66. Toronto: Maxwell MacMillan Canada.

Lodge, N., J. Mallett, P. Blake, and I. Fryatt. 1997. 'A Study to Ascertain Gynecological Patients' Perceived Levels of Endorsement with Physical and Psychological Care Given by Female and Male Nurses', *Journal of Advanced Nursing* 25: 893–907.

MacDougall, G. 1997. 'Caring—A Masculine Perspective', *Journal of Advanced Nursing* 25, 809–13.

Mangan, P. 1994. 'Private Lives', *Nursing Times* 90: 60–4.

Mathieson, E. 1991. 'A Question of Gender', *Nursing Times* 87: 31–2.

Morin, K., B. Patterson, B. Kurtz, and B. Brzowski. 1999. 'Mothers' Responses to Care Given by Male Nursing Students During and After Birth', *Image: Journal or Nursing Scholarship* 31: 83–7.

Okrainec, G. 1994. 'Perceptions of Nursing Education Held by Male Nursing Students', *Western Journal or Nursing Research* 16: 94–107.

Paterson, B., S. Tschikota, M. Crawford, M. Saydak, P. Venkatesh, and T. Aronowitz. 1996. 'Learning to Care: Gender Issues for Male Nursing Students', *Canadian Journal of Nursing Research* 28: 25–39.

Petersen, A. 1998. *Unmasking the Masculine: Men and 'Identity' in a Skeptical Age.* London: Sage.

Porter, S. 1992. 'Women in a Women's Job: The Gendered Experience of Nurses', *Sociology of Health and Illness* 14: 510–27.

Ryan, S., and S. Porter. 1993. 'Men in Nursing: A Cautionary Comparative Critique', *Nursing Outlook* 41: 262–7.

Skevington, S., and D. Dawkes. 1988. 'Fred Nightingale', *Nursing Times* 84: 49–51.

Streubert, H. 1994. 'Male Nursing Students' Perceptions of Clinical Experience', *Nurse Educator* 19: 28–32.

Taylor, E., R. Dwiggins, M. Albert, and J. Dearner. 1983. 'Male Nurses: What They Think About Themselves—and Others', *RN* 46: 61–4.

Villeneuve, M. 1994. 'Recruiting and Retaining Men in Nursing: A Review of the Literature', *Journal of Professional Nursing* 10: 217–28.

Williams, C. 1989. *Gender Differences at Work: Women and Men in Nontraditional Occupations.* Berkeley, CA: University of California Press.

———. 1995. 'Hidden Advantages for Men in Nursing', *Nursing Administration Quarterly* 19: 63–70.

Zurlinden, J. 1998. 'Are Men a Step Higher on the Nursing Ladder of Success?', *Nursing Spectrum* 10A: 4–5, 12.

CHAPTER 26

Gendered Strategies of the Self: Navigating Hierarchy and Contesting Masculinities

Shelley Pacholok

In the summer and autumn of 2003 wildfires in British Columbia, Canada, caused widespread damage to forests, wildlife, animal habitat, homes, suburban neighbourhoods, and tribal lands, the likes of which were unparalleled in recent decades. From a monetary and safety perspective the costs were enormous. The cost of battling with fires in British Columbia was $6 million per day in August 2003 (CTV, 2003). Also, tragically, one air tanker and one helicopter crashed, killing three firefighters. Of the hundreds of fires that occurred that year, the Okanagan Mountain Park fire in Kelowna, British Columbia was especially destructive. It was described by the Ministry of Forests (Ministry of Forests Protection Branch, 2003b) as 'the most significant interface wildfire[1] event in B.C. history'. The fire destroyed 255 houses, forced 26,000 people from their homes (Canadian Press, 2003), burned a significant portion of a national historic site (Heritage Society of British Columbia, 2004), and scorched virtually all of Okanagan Mountain park (CHBC TV, 2003), ultimately resulting in a state of emergency. Almost 65,000 acres of land and forest were burned (Ministry of Forests Protection Branch, 2003a). As the city fire chief explained, 'Last night was probably the roughest night in Kelowna firefighting history I would say. We got hammered pretty good. These losses are staggering'. (Canadian Press, 2003).

During this natural disaster firefighters were forced to contend with two challenging situations. First, by and large they felt that they lost the battle against the fire, something that they stressed they were not accustomed to. The occupational culture of firefighting values winning—defined as controlling or exterminating fire and preventing losses to property and other valued resources. Because millions of dollars of property and resources were destroyed, the firefighters' occupational identities were threatened by the losses. They were also faced with a social hierarchy in which some firefighting groups were granted more prestige, rewards and status than other groups.

In this article I focus on the 'strategies of self' (Sherman, 2005, p. 133) that firefighters invoked to secure power and prestige in the face of this hierarchy. For example, in an effort to position their own group as superior, firefighters often attempted to undermine the credibility of firefighters from other groups. Notably, even firefighters who were lauded as heroes and had relatively high status engaged in these practices. I argue that we cannot fully understand these responses unless we take into account gender: specifically, the ways in which masculinity is implicated in the social dynamics between predominantly male firefighting groups. Building on previous research on boundary work and comparative strategies of self, I explore how masculinity is embedded in these processes; an issue largely overlooked in the literature to date.

Literature Review

Boundary Work

Michèle Lamont's (1992, 2000) research on working and upper-middle class men in the USA and France sheds some light on firefighters' inter-group dynamics. Extending Gieryn's (1983) concept of boundary work to include the identity process by which people differentiate themselves from others (Lamont, 1992), she finds that actors use a comparative self to situate themselves as superior vis-à-vis other groups. In particular, Lamont argues that working-class men define their worth and dignity using a moral measuring stick, which they use to draw moral boundaries between themselves and those to whom they feel superior (Lamont, 2000). For example, she finds that among American working-class men a strong work ethic, a disciplined self, protection, and responsibility are venerated and used to draw distinctions.

Strategies of Self

Building on Lamont's work, Rachel Sherman (2005, 2006) examines boundary work and the notion of a comparative self in an occupational context. She explores how interactive service workers in luxury hotels manage to maintain dignity and power while performing service work that positions them as subordinate in relation to socially and materially privileged hotel guests. She finds that workers use comparisons and judgments of guests and co-workers to place themselves at the top of symbolic hierarchies of competence, authority, status, need, morality, intelligence, and cultural capital. For example, workers evaluate guests on the basis of their intelligence, reframing guests' demands as indicators of incompetence and indicative of an inferior social status. In drawing these symbolic boundaries workers are able to effectively portray themselves as superior to those to whom they provide services. Finally, Sherman finds that the strategies workers use to construct superior selves are often fluid (that is, dependent on context), and contradictory (for example, workers constituted guests as inferior through both critique and empathy).

Theorizing Masculinities

Contemporary theoretical approaches to gender relations, and masculinity in particular, provide a number of pertinent insights. Firstly, differences among men shape the ways they experience and enact gender. Masculinity is profoundly influenced by social structures such as race, class, age, and sexuality, and these structures affect men in different ways. In addition, masculinity is historically and culturally contingent. So there is not one pattern of masculinity found everywhere, rather there are masculinities (Connell, 1995; Kimmel, 1994). In addition, some masculinities are deemed culturally superior to others; hegemonic masculinity is the most honoured or desired at a particular time and in a particular setting. Hegemonic masculinity cannot exist unless there are subordinated Others (that is, women and marginalized men) who are constructed as deficient in some way. As a result, hegemonic masculinity upholds power and status inequalities both between men and women, and among men (Connell, 1995, 2000).

The main patterns of contemporary hegemonic masculinity in Western societies include the connection of masculinity with toughness and competitiveness, the subordination of women and the marginalization of gay men (Connell, 1995). In addition, appropriately masculine men are supposed to (a) remain calm and reliable in a crisis, and hold their emotions in check, (b) be aggressive and take risks, (c) repudiate anything even remotely related to femininity and (d) strive for power, success and wealth (for example, see Brannon, 1976; Goffman, 1963; Kimmel, 1994). While few men actually meet all these normative standards, hegemonic masculinity is the benchmark against which all men are measured. Moreover, according to Kimmel (1994), it is other men who do the evaluating:

> We are under the constant careful scrutiny of other men. Other men watch us, rank us, grant our acceptance into the realm of manhood. Manhood is demonstrated for other men's approval. It is other men who evaluate the performance. (p. 130)

A further theoretical insight is that hegemonic masculinity cannot be reduced to a simple model of cultural control, as the notion of hegemony implies an active struggle for dominance (Connell and Messerschmidt, 2005). Therefore, while hegemonic masculinity is the standard against which all other masculinities are measured, the position at the top of the hierarchy is never secure and is always contestable (Connell, 1995). As Monaghan (2002) stresses, 'Male hierarchy is never static or guaranteed; it is processual, contested and requires the continual . . . (re)production of situational dominance, authority, and subordination' (p. 530). Further, masculinities are collective. As they are sustained and enacted by individuals, groups and institutions, these struggles occur at both individual and group levels (Connell, 2000). Because masculinity is fragile and contested (Connell, 1995; Kimmel, 1994) it must constantly be proved (Kaufman, 2001). Herein lies the key to understanding why firefighters with high status construct superior selves: ascendancy is never guaranteed; therefore, they must continually work to maintain their status vis-à-vis other men and prove that they are, in fact, appropriately masculine and therefore superior.

Connell's concept of hegemonic masculinity has been widely applied in gender-related research; however, the concept has also been criticized on a number of fronts (Connell and Messerschmidt, 2005). A number of critiques are germane to this discussion. The first points to a tendency to essentialize differences between men and women (Peterson, 2003). Connell and Messerschmidt (2005) note that the concept has often been misinterpreted and misused, and acknowledge that a great deal of essentializing has occurred in the literature, despite the fact that the concept of hegemonic masculinity was formulated in an anti-essentialist way:

> Masculinity is not a fixed entity embedded in the body or personality traits of individuals. Masculinities are configurations of practice that are accomplished in social action and, therefore, can differ according to the gender relations in a particular social setting. (2005, p. 836)

While I focus here on men's strategies for engaging with masculinity, my position is not an essentialist one. In another piece (Pacholok, 2007, unpublished) I discuss how the women firefighters in my study sometimes constructed gender on masculine terms, for example, by positioning themselves as more competent at symbolically masculine tasks than their male colleagues. This demonstrates that individual women can practise masculinities just as individual men can practise femininities (Connell, 1995); a finding also borne out in the broader literature on gender and work (for example, see Iacuone, 2005). However, because almost all the participants in my study are men, I speak mainly about patterns of masculinity construction among men.

Secondly, the concept of hegemonic masculinity has received criticism for tending to dichotomize men's and women's experiences (Brod, 1994), making it seem as though women are peripheral to hegemonic masculinity. The solution to this problem is to return to a focus on a relational approach to gender (Connell and Messerschmidt, 2005). Because gender is accomplished in interactions with others, and often defined by what one is not, what is considered to be masculine is defined in oppositional relation to understandings of what is feminine (Connell, 1995; Connell and Messerschmidt, 2005; Kimmel, 1994).

Finally, Wetherell and Edley (1999) assert that Connell's (1995, 2000) work on hegemonic masculinity has proved useful for understanding the broad social context of gender relations but has not been developed in a way that accounts for the social psychological reproduction of masculine identity. Therefore, more micro-level analyses are required to understand men's strategies for negotiating identities in everyday practice. They conclude that masculinity is a way that men position themselves through psycho-discursive practices—that is, men come to identify and create masculine identity through talk.

Synthesis: Gendered Strategies of Self

I argue that in order to make sense of the ways in which workers navigate status hierarchies we must theorize gender. Lamont (2000) sows this seed in her research on working-class men, noting that historically dominant conceptions of masculinity are embedded in the moral standards of hard work and protection that her participants used to evaluate themselves and others. I make a stronger claim, arguing that the actual work of constructing and maintaining boundaries and superior occupational selves (that is, the process itself) is an inherently gendered one. Because hegemonic masculinity is relational it requires actors to draw boundaries and create superior selves that delineate 'us' (superior men) from 'them' (marginalized Others). Further, while Sherman's (2005) idea of flexible, contradictory strategies of self is consistent with theorizing on masculinity (for example, see Connell and Messerschmidt, 2005), she does not examine how gender is embedded in the accomplishment of boundary work and selfhood. In this article I build on Lamont's (1992, 2000) and Sherman's (2005, 2006) work by considering how gender is implicated in the process of boundary work and comparative strategies of self.

In particular, I examine how the firefighting efforts were organized and the role played by the media in cultivating the hierarchy. Media analyses are routinely undertaken by gender scholars from a broad range of fields, as a considerable body of research indicates that the ways in which the media frame events has implications for the social construction of gender, especially in the aftermath of a tragedy or disaster (Drew, 2004; Grewal, 2003; Projansky, 1998). After discussing how the social hierarchy developed during the fire, I examine how the firefighters negotiated the hierarchy and the ways in which their strategies of self were gendered. Finally, I reflect on the broader implications of these findings, including the personal costs to the firefighters involved and the consequences of this on the long-term allocation of material resources.

Method

Sample

Following Cornwell et al. (2003), key informants were identified through newspaper accounts of the fires. These informants were located and contacted by phone or e-mail. They were asked to participate in the study and also asked to provide the names of additional firefighters who were then contacted for interviews. I used this snowball technique to generate the remainder of the interview contacts.

Because the Okanagan Mountain Park fire was an interface fire, a number of different groups of firefighters were involved in the firefighting efforts. Four groups of firefighters fought on the front lines of the fire: (a) structural firefighters, (b) wildland firefighters, (c) pilots and (d) heavy equipment operators. Table 25.1 provides a brief description of each group.

All four groups of firefighters are relatively homogenous in terms of their sexuality,[2] racial, ethnic, and gender diversity.[3] This is especially true for structural firefighters and heavy equipment operators, most of whom are white men. In addition, all the pilots in the sample are white men, although I was told that there were two women employed on a contract basis.

Wildland firefighters are a more diverse group, as there are a number of Native[4] crews working for the forest service. However, like structural firefighters, pilots and heavy equipment operators, most wildland firefighters are white. There are also more women working as wildland firefighters, although they only constitute approximately 20 per cent of the firefighters hired each year.

These groups also vary along several important dimensions. For example, wildland firefighters are largely composed of seasonal workers, structural firefighters (not including volunteers) are employed full-time all year round, while heavy equipment operators and pilots often work on a contract basis. Wildland firefighting tends to attract students or other young people who have other jobs in the off-season, heavy equipment operators usually work in the construction, logging or forest products industries and structural firefighters often have a background in the trades.

Data Collection

Between June and December 2004 I travelled to Kelowna to do fieldwork on three separate occasions. I conducted informal observations at a number of sites including four City of Kelowna fire halls, three branch offices of the forestry department, two air tanker centres and one helicopter base.

I also completed in-depth interviews with firefighters and informal interviews with a number of other people involved in the firefighting efforts (for example, fire centre dispatchers). I utilized photo-elicitation techniques (Curry, 1986; Harper, 2000) in many of the interviews, using pictures of the fire and destroyed homes as a way to facilitate discussion.

The participants were asked to choose a location where they felt comfortable doing the interview. As a result the interviews took place in a wide variety of settings including coffee shops, outdoor parks, workplaces and homes. However, most interviews were conducted at the participant's place of work. The interviews lasted from just over 30 minutes to two and a half hours, with the typical interview lasting from one to one and a half hours.

I chose to focus on interviews because I was primarily interested in the ways in which gendered strategies of self were accomplished through discourse. Wetherell and Edley (1999) and Connell and Messerschmidt (2005) note that masculinities do not exist as settled character structures, or types but as positions in discourse—in the ways that men situate themselves through discursive practices.

Like Wetherell and Edley (1999) I am wedded to the notion that selves are produced through, rather than simply described by, language. As they explain:

We chose discourse as a site for investigating men's identities because we are persuaded of the central role discursive practices play in the constitution of subjectivity. That is, what it means to be a person, the formulation of an internal life, an identity and a way of being in the world develop as external public dialogue moves inside to form the 'voices of the mind' (p. 337).

While talk plays a central role in the creation of self, it can also provide knowledge of social life. According to an interactionist perspective (Miller and Glassner, 1997), the discourse that emerges from the interview is situated in social worlds that exist outside the interview context. Participants draw on cultural narratives to explain their actions and make them understandable to others. Therefore, interactionist researchers are able to learn about and produce authentic accounts of respondents' social worlds by studying narratives that emerge in the interview. In short, studying discourse allows the researcher to better understand the social world of the participants.

Discursive practices shed light on social worlds and highlight the symbolic dimension of hegemonic masculinity, but discursive research cannot stand alone because gender relations are also constituted in, and shape, nondiscursive practices, such as waged labour, sexuality and childcare (Connell, 2001; Connell and Messerschmidt, 2005). In an effort to capture some of the non-discursive practices that shaped firefighters' experiences, I examined elements of the structural and cultural context in which the fire occurred by analyzing the organization of the firefighting efforts and the ways in which the media framed the event and the people involved in it.

Besides providing a window into the self and knowledge of the participants' social worlds, the interviews allowed me to gather data from a larger number of firefighters than methods like participant observation, thereby improving the reliability of my comparisons (Lamont, 2000) between firefighters from different occupational groups. On the other hand, a limitation of this method is that participants may not reveal all their practices and behaviour in interviews; consequently, I cannot know for certain whether their behaviour differed from their interview talk.

To document the newspaper coverage of the fire I conducted archival work at the Kelowna library. I examined all the fire-related articles in the two major local newspapers, The *Kelowna Daily Courier and Capital News* from 20 August to 25 September 2003. I also retrieved articles from electronic news sources. The newspaper accounts revealed that a number of people in administrative positions played key roles in the event. For example, it became clear that relations with the media had implications for the ways in which the hierarchy emerged.

As a result I chose to interview two media relations people from the forestry department (both of whom had been wildland firefighters prior to entering media relations). However, most of the sample consists of firefighters and their supervisors. The sample size for each group reflects the fact that wildland firefighters were the largest group who fought the fire, followed by structural firefighters, heavy equipment operators and pilots (although the proportions are not directly comparable). The final sample is also a result of participants' accessibility and theoretical and snowball sampling. Because most of my sample are wildland and structural firefighters, my analyses are based primarily on firefighters from these two groups.

Findings

Over the course of the fire and in the weeks and months that followed, a social hierarchy became apparent—one in which City of Kelowna firefighters received more recognition, rewards and status from the media and the public than other firefighting groups.[5] This generated a great deal of animosity between the firefighters. While these were largely unsolicited, I heard numerous disparaging comments that were often, although not exclusively, directed at the City of Kelowna firefighters, especially the fire chief, who was a favourite target.

In addition, firefighters from all groups made a concerted effort to frame their own work group as superior (that is, the ones who put themselves in the most danger, worked the hardest under the most difficult conditions and were the most skilled, did the best job and so on), while simultaneously positioning the other groups as inferior. The following quote from Greg,[6] a veteran forestry firefighter who was a supervisor during the fire, is representative of comments I heard from many of his colleagues. Greg revealed his frustration at what he felt was unfair recognition of the City of Kelowna firefighters and the lack of praise for forestry firefighters and equipment operators who were 'really' the ones who took on the most important and dangerous firefighting tasks:

I think the role, and what was accomplished by our people, on the ground, doesn't get the attention that it deserves. And I think that has a real psychological impact on our firefighters, and our equipment operators. I think that the glory all goes to the [structural] fire departments. . . . Our guys are out there, and I'm not just saying this, this isn't biased, this is my personal observation from the first 10, 12 days of the Okanagan fire. . . . Our staff, our crews, the forest service crews, were the last people out, after the fire department had left. Our guys were the ones who held and maintained that fire guard on the south side. It wasn't the [Kelowna] fire department who did that. It was our staff that did that, our firefighter personnel who held the line. It was our staff who risked themselves in injury, in maintaining that line. It was our front line folks and equipment operators that put in that [fire] guard, that worked through the heat and the dust and the hot and the dry. It's our people who do all of that. Those equipment operators chug away, day and night sometimes, 24 hours a day, and they get very little recognition. The glory all goes to the [Kelowna] fire department. And that in itself has a huge impact to the morale. And somehow the credit has to go where it rightfully belongs.

Two processes contributed to the formation of this hierarchy: the structural organization of the firefighting efforts and the media coverage of the fire. I discuss each of these in turn below. This is followed by a discussion of the firefighters' strategies for managing the hierarchy.

Access and Reward: The Structural Organization of Fire Fighting

During the fire several staging areas were set up where firefighting crews were organized and given instructions before heading out to the fire zone. The staging areas for the heavy equipment operators and wildland firefighters were on the outskirts of the city, as these sites were in close proximity to the areas where the wildland firefighting crews were working (usually deep in the forest, especially at the beginning of the fire). Pilots were dispatched from regional airport bases. The wildland firefighters' command post was set up at the Okanagan Mountain Park headquarters, located in a small town about 50 kilometres south of Kelowna.

In contrast, the structural firefighters were located at the main fire hall right in the heart of the city. The main fire hall was also where the emergency operations centre was situated. This centre housed many administrative personnel who were part of the firefighting efforts and, as a result, attracted a large number of reporters. The geographical location of the main fire hall and the fact that structural firefighters fought the fire within the city limits meant that they were much more accessible to reporters, both on and off duty.

These institutional arrangements facilitated relationships with the media that resulted in more coverage for structural firefighters. As Greg noted, 'The people that [the media] interview, because they're readily available, are the people in the fire department, in the halls.' Many other non-structural firefighters also pointed out that because structural firefighters were accessible to the media they received a great deal of coverage. For example, Bob, a 30-year veteran with the forestry service, pointed out:

> You know [the media] could go to the number one fire hall, and they could corner some fireman and they could see the trucks and all of that. You know we tried to make the fire line available to media people but it was all, you know you gotta watch for safety there too,

right? So we had escorted tours at different times, and different times we'd take them up and let them take some pictures from the air or whatever. . . . I mean it wasn't as open as the fire hall was, sort of thing.

Bob notes that safety concerns were another obstacle that made gaining access to wildland firefighters more difficult. If reporters wanted to interview wildland firefighters they had to go to the staging area, which was out of town, or to the fire zone, which was not always feasible due to safety issues. Because the main fire hall was also more accessible to the public, most of the donations to the firefighting efforts arrived there. Structural firefighters received everything from truckloads of food to cases of cold beer. In contrast, two heavy equipment operators remarked that they were not provided with any food, even when they were on duty for 12 hours or more. In addition, at the main fire hall volunteers were on hand to provide free massages, make sandwiches and provide moral support. Meanwhile, most of the wildland firefighters and pilots were stationed in base camps far from the centre of the city.

Lionel, an air attack officer who supervised pilots during the fire revealed that he and his crew members resented the structural firefighters because of the special treatment that they received:

> And, I know that there was a, lots of, ah, you know, 'well, those poor [structural] fire guys'. They're kind of, 'oh yeah, poor babies', you know. They're getting back rubs, they're getting beers. We can't have any beers on base. You know, we don't get any of that stuff. And there's no recognition. So a certain amount of, what do you call it, dissension? Oh yeah, the poor structural guys.

The general sentiment of the non-structural firefighters was that structural firefighters received preferential treatment in a number of areas. The organizational arrangements of the firefighting efforts were directly related not only to the amount of resources and support available (or not available) to the different groups of firefighters but to the amount of media exposure that each group received.

The Making of Heroes

Based on newspaper accounts, it appears that structural firefighters (especially the fire chief) did receive considerably more print media coverage than any other groups or individuals who were involved in the firefighting efforts. Technical fire information was obtained both from forest service information officers and the chief of the Kelowna fire department.

However, most of the firefighter personal interest stories were about structural firefighters and, most often, the Kelowna fire chief. While there were several articles about wildland firefighters, equipment operators and pilots, for the most part they appeared near the end of the fire. For example, over two weeks after the fire started one headline in the *Kelowna Daily Courier* exclaimed, 'Unsung heroes: heavy equipment operators have put their lives on the line fighting the Okanagan Mountain blaze, but respect has been hard to find' (Poulsen, 2003b). Even the army, brought in to provide support services to the front line firefighters, such as putting out hot spots and performing mop-up duties, received a relatively large share of media coverage.

Chris is a crew leader employed by a wildland firefighting contract company, and his perception of the media coverage is consistent with this finding. He noted that, as a result of the unequal coverage, the public gave more credit to the structural firefighters than the wildland firefighters. He also commented that as a result of these events the forestry service eventually hired more media relations people:

> And [the presence of additional media relations people] I think came directly out of Kelowna, for the most part. Because of the war between the structural and the forestry. Because of the huge battle, and we saw who won in the hearts of the people because there was the media again. And it wasn't, it was all the media on them, and then none of the media on [us], so if you only hear one side of the story, you're going to vote what?

According to Chris structural firefighters not only fared better than wildland firefighters in terms of media coverage, they won another important battle—the recognition, support and adoration of the public. Chris was not alone in his sentiments: numerous other wildland firefighters were also critical of the coverage provided by the media.

Conversely, a number of structural firefighters complained that they had received, and still continued to receive, more attention than they desired. Several mentioned that they were 'hounded' by reporters and one veteran called the event 'the fire that never goes away' in reference to the donations that continued to arrive at the fire hall and the praise still directed their way even one year after the fire. Another explained that while he appreciated the public support it was also overwhelming, 'After a while you just, you know, you feel like if one more stranger comes up and hugs me I'm gonna drop kick 'em'.

The Media as Reputational Entrepreneurs: Firefighters and Heroic Masculinity

The goal of the news media is to create and retain reader interest (Altheide, 2001). One way to accomplish this is through human interest stories, which are designed to attract readers and retain their loyalty. Successful human interest stories create 'collective attention' and encourage 'shared identification' among audience members (Fine and White, 2002, p. 57). Both during the fire and in the weeks that followed, the print media covered numerous human interest stories about firefighters. Both of the local newspapers drew on dominant cultural discourses and symbols of heroism in these stories.

Many framed firefighters as heroes, either explicitly (through the use of the word hero), or implicitly (by referring to firefighters as courageous, selfless and so on). In addition, the *Daily Courier* printed pull-out posters that read, 'Thanks for being our heroes!' and urged readers to 'show your gratitude and display this poster in your window'. The media have been involved in the business of hero-making for more than two centuries (Houchin Winfield, 2003), and this event was no exception.

Again, many of these stories involved the Kelowna fire chief and, to a lesser degree, the structural firefighters who worked for him. Perhaps, in light of the valorization of structural firefighters as heroes in the wake of 9/11 (Langewiesche, 2002; Lorber, 2002), which occurred only two years before the fire, it was strategic for the media to portray structural firefighters as heroes. They want to generate and retain interest and are successful only to the extent that their readers identify with the principal characters and settings (Fine and White, 2002). People tend to selectively perceive information, focusing on details that most readily fit into familiar frames of reference (Fisher, 1997).

Consequently, the media may have favoured the structural fire department because they recognized that their audience would identify more readily with structural firefighters as heroes, while wildland firefighters, being a more diverse group, including more women and First Nations firefighters, would not fit quite so readily into a heroism frame. In an effort to promote readers' direct identification with characters, the media acted as 'reputational entrepreneurs'—that is, they shaped the reputations of structural firefighters in ways that benefited their own interests (Fine, 1996, p. 1162). Here we can also see how demographic differences between wildland firefighters and structural firefighters played a role in the status hierarchy through the workings of the media.

Embedded in the heroism rhetoric were hegemonic constructions of masculinity. It is no secret that media representations enforce and reproduce culturally dominant gender norms, symbols, ideologies, and stereotypes (Dworkin and Wachs, 2000; Howard and Prividera, 2004). Since the use of conventional categories and familiar roles conveys stability, this may be especially true during times of crisis (Lorber, 2002). In addition, the media have a vested interest in supporting culturally dominant conceptions of manliness because they want readers to connect with the characters in their stories, as noted above.

Following are several examples that illustrate the ways in which the media implicitly championed hegemonic masculinity in their coverage of the fire. Two days after Black Friday one headline declared, 'Hard fought battle: for every home lost, firefighters

saved two, says weary fire chief' (Plant, 2003). The body of the article was punctuated by references to the danger that firefighters placed themselves in ('the fire prompted fierce firefighting that could have turned deadly'), including injuries sustained. It also relayed an incident where firefighters were trapped by the flames; however, the reporter was quick to note that 'once [the] flames died down, the men fought their way back in and put out spot fires.' Several days later, Capital News, reporting on the story of the trapped firefighters, printed the following headline, 'Training and experience kept trapped firefighters calm' (Watters, 2003). Another headline in the *Daily Courier* exclaimed, 'Hot stuff: studly forest fire point men are not just a couple of hosers' (Seymour, 2003).

These are only several examples among many in which the media implicitly referenced culturally dominant ideals of masculinity such as strength, aggression, courage in the face of danger, heterosexuality and stoicism. As in other tragedies, the media used this event to protect and articulate dominant gender narratives (Projansky, 1998). The media's own boundary work evoked and perpetuated the parameters of manhood that ultimately provided a context of support for the dynamic reproduction of hegemonic masculinity.[7] Here we can see how the collective actions of the media worked to (re)inscribe symbolic boundaries around hegemonic masculinity, which ultimately allowed the gendered strategies of self invoked by structural firefighters to take hold. I elaborate on this process in the following section.

On the whole the public appeared to embrace the new heroes. They enthusiastically participated in a yellow ribbon campaign, posted signs of gratitude around the city, attended public events to honour firefighters, supported a number of fundraising causes and donated a generous amount of time and money to the firefighting efforts.

Wildland firefighters, on the other hand, often expressed mixed emotions about the hero atmosphere that permeated the town, as they did not feel that the praise was necessarily directed at them (despite the fact that there were some signs and media stories that targeted non-structural firefighters). When asked how he felt about seeing the signs, Josh, a 22-year-old wildland firefighter in his third season as a crew member, remarked:

> Um, yeah, we saw [the signs] every time we drove in. And, like here at the [forestry] base there's somewhat, there's some animosity between us and the KFD, the Kelowna fire department. . . . Like, because they stopped the fire when it was all in the houses, they kind of got the glory. And it's, like, we all know, we couldn't do anything when it's in that kind of [forest conditions]. . . . So it was, kind of, like, well we did all this work and, despite our efforts, this is going to happen and you can't stop it. You know, we had posters and stuff but as it started kind of slowing down we were kind of, you know, we were back to doing our job and those guys are still kind of in the glory.

So, according to Josh, not only did the structural firefighters receive more credit because they were battling with house fires, they stayed in the limelight when the wildland firefighters went off to fight forest fires in other areas. As Josh and his colleagues were largely overlooked in the media coverage of the fire, perhaps it is not surprising that they were somewhat skeptical about the heroism messages that permeated the local media. It is also possible that the placement of the signs signalled that they were directed at structural firefighters, as one wildland firefighting supervisor noted that signs were erected in front of the structural firefighters' fire halls and other locations where structural firefighters could be expected to see them.

In contrast, most of the structural firefighters seemed to recognize that the heroism narrative was directed at them. One newly recruited firefighter, Jeff, maintained that being called a hero was a great 'morale booster'; however, he quickly added, 'I don't think there's anyone who wants to be called a hero or anything, like it's just, you know that's what we're paid to do.' All the structural firefighters denied being heroes and gave the trite answer that what they did was just 'part of the job'.

Social convention may have precluded structural firefighters from self-identifying as heroes, but their narratives often revealed an implicit perception that they perform courageous, if not heroic, acts in the work that they do every day.

Following are statements from three veteran firefighters who denied being heroes:

> If somebody goes in to save a child or a mother or a grandmother, then I that's the risk that we run. We pull people out of burning buildings. We did it the other day, where we pulled a guy out, maybe 5 months ago, out of a burning building, right. Risking their [sic] lives, it's what we do, right?

> Those people that are in that burning building, the only chance they have is you. The only chance they have for survival is how efficiently and how professionally you do your job. If they're not already deceased. But you know, if they're viable, or if there's something, if they're savable then you're their only chance.

> It's nice to be recognized, but I don't know what the definition of hero is. We, the guys out here, do really dangerous, successful, heroic deeds nearly every day.

So while the structural firefighters claimed to reject the hero label, a hero-like narrative was woven into many of their accounts of their regular duties. The heroism rhetoric that was disseminated through the local media exacerbated the hierarchy among firefighters, as it favoured the fire chief and other structural firefighters. In addition, the hierarchy was perpetuated by the perceptions of the firefighters themselves. Many wildland firefighters seemed to believe that the media praise was directed solely at the structural firefighters and their chief. The structural firefighters, while denying that they were heroes, viewed their job as one that requires selfless acts on a regular basis.

Contesting Credibility

In navigating the status hierarchy that was exacerbated by the organization of the firefighting efforts and the media coverage of the fire, the firefighters constructed boundaries in an attempt to distinguish their group from the others. Obviously, occupational boundaries between the firefighting groups were in place long before the fire happened.

There were also status differences between wildland and structural firefighters before the fire began. For example, a high ranking administrator in the forestry department mentioned that in years past some structural fire departments were reluctant to receive forest fire training from wildland firefighters because they were seasonal workers and viewed as less professional. In addition, wildland firefighters, loggers and pilots do not have the same cultural capital as structural firefighters because structural firefighters have been granted heroic status by the media and the public in the wake of 9/11. My argument here is that the hierarchy was exacerbated, rather than created, by the events surrounding the fire, and that the firefighters responded by strengthening and reinforcing these boundaries by undermining the competence of those outside of their occupational group.

They accomplished this by adopting a measuring stick of firefighting competence that was variously deemed to include remaining calm in a crisis, using aggressive tactics, controlling emotions and exterminating fire (the latter two criteria falling under the more general category of 'repudiating the feminine' below). The firefighters drew on these criteria to demonstrate that their group was superior to other firefighting groups. Because these standards are analogous to culturally dominant ideals of masculinity, undermining firefighting competence simultaneously undermined the masculine integrity of the targeted group. These strategies are indicative of the importance of hegemonic masculinity to firefighters, as workers often judge members of other groups to be deficient in respect to the criteria they value most (Lamont, 2000).

The firefighters' gendered strategies of self not only reinforced occupational boundaries but created boundaries that delineated the difference between 'us' (the competent firefighters and 'real' men) and 'them' (inferior firefighters and subordinate men). Ultimately, these tactics were attempts to erode the credibility of the firefighting group to which they were directed. In the following section I provide examples of firefighters' narratives in order to demonstrate these social dynamics. Note

that these individual narratives contain group referents (that is, we, they, us, them) that serve to remind us that while it is individuals who engage in strategies of self in an effort to construct superior selves, these tactics also work to demarcate and enforce boundaries between groups.

Calm and Reliable in Crisis

According to Josh, the young wildland firefighter who remarked earlier that the structural firefighters 'got all the glory', the wildland crew leaders were calm under pressure, while the structural firefighters fell apart:

> We had some [crew leaders] . . . who have both seen huge fire. But nothing like this. And they were just rock solid. They said, 'No worries, get in [the vehicles], we'll get you all through.' Everybody else was panicked. Like the Kelowna Fire department was just wiggy.

One of the crew leaders that Josh was referring to, Chris, explained that there were two occasions when he instructed structural firefighters to leave an area for safety reasons and, due to their ignorance of forest fire behaviour, they resisted. However, according to Chris, there were other times when they 'took off' when it was safe, which resulted in the loss of houses:

> There were times when the structure guys again . . . the times they would leave an area when it was safe, and then homes would go. And you'd say, 'Well, where the hell did they go?' So then you get on the radio and you start telling them, 'No, you guys, it is safe there. I know what the fire is doing, I know where it is, and I know where it's going to do. If you're there right now you can save a couple.' But no, of course they weren't.

Structural firefighters used similar tactics to portray wildland firefighters in an unflattering manner. For example, this structural firefighter seemed to genuinely delight in relaying a story where wildland firefighters apparently pulled back from the front line of the fire while the structural firefighters stayed:

> And I remember we were up in the Rimrock area when the fire broke through. . . . So we're sitting there, and we know it's coming because you can hear it, the heat, the wind, the smoke, the dust, everything. The forestry guys you know, they're all in there. And then all of the sudden we heard these whistles. And that's an emergency signal for the forestry to get the hell out. So all of these whistles, you can just hear them going right across the mountain side, and we're kind of listening and then we're like, 'What the hell is that?' And it looked like rats jumping off a burning ship [chuckles]. These guys were running as hard as they could out of the forest, by us, and down the hill and they're gone. And we're sitting there going, 'I think it's coming. You guys ready?' Oh yeah!

Mark's narrative positions his group as the competent firefighters—the real men who stayed to fight the fire. In contrast, according to Mark, the wildland firefighters ran away when things got bad. This implies that the structural firefighters were brave while the others were not. Structural firefighters, rational, fearless and calm under pressure, were ready to take on the fire, and ultimately, as Mark noted later in the interview, it was these men who put it out.

Mark's narrative is especially potent when placed in the context of the occupational culture of structural firefighting; a culture in which running away is a reprehensible act. An upper level administrator confided that it was difficult when structural firefighters had to retreat from the fire (presumably for safety reasons), because they felt that they were running away,

> 'They had to pull out of [the fire zone]. And that's like running from something. And they're not used to running from anything. You know, like, even when it makes common sense it just doesn't happen that often.'

In fact running away is so scorned that one firefighter ended up on stress leave as a result,

You know I'm not even privy to all of it, but I'm sure some of them ran, you know. . . . Like, I know one that did. And he went off on stress leave. Like, he just couldn't live with himself, eh? And I don't know if he'll ever be the same.

Given this occupational imperative, claiming that wildland firefighters ran away, as Mark did, is a serious insult that directly undermines their credibility, both as firefighters and as men.

Aggression and Risk Taking

Greg, the wildland supervisor who earlier criticized the media coverage of the fire, explained that it was actually his people who put themselves in harm's way:

> While the fire department did a great job on the structure side of it, and I don't want to take anything away from anyone, anywhere on the structural side, but when it came to the actual front line of those fires and the people who put themselves at risk, it was our people under there.

In this passage Greg discursively positions his crew (and himself, by association) as the real firefighters—the men who put themselves at risk and got the job done. One wildland firefighter went public with this claim, stating that structural firefighters disappeared when the blaze was burning near his property: 'I hate to be cynical, but I don't have a good word to say about them. You need passion and adrenaline to fight a fire. Their tolerance of risk was minimal' (Poulsen, 2003a).

The Kelowna fire chief vehemently denied these accusations and after an internal review an upper-level manager from the Ministry of Forests issued an apology, which was reported in the local media. Many structural firefighters also talked about the perils associated with their job, but they tended to view risk and danger as an everyday part of their job, as their discourse about heroism indicated. In both cases the implication is that firefighting competence requires taking risks, and (implicitly) those who are willing to take those risks are the most masculine.

Repudiating the Feminine

Firefighters also accomplished competence negatively; that is, they inferred that other firefighters were incompetent by associating them with characteristics stereotypically associated with femininity. Undermining masculinity is often achieved by implying that the person in question has qualities associated with femininity (for example, see Iacuone, 2005). This tactic is apparent in all the following narratives, although the discourse varied by occupational group. It is well established that masculinity construction is intertwined with the occupational settings in which men labour (Cheng, 1996; Collinson and Hearn, 1996; Meyer, 1999; Pierce, 1995; Prokos and Padavic, 2002). Since each group of firefighters worked in different occupations, they sometimes used disparate discourses to distance themselves from femininity or liken others to women.

One veteran firefighter, Richard, who had recently moved into an administrative position, explained the differences between structural and wildland firefighters in the following way:

[The wildland firefighters'] job is more containment. Structural firefighters are aggressive, we don't take loss very well. Forestry firefighters are more tactical, they're more like army guys. They're willing to take some losses to get some gains, if that makes sense to you? I mean, they're willing to give up a 100 acres of wildland and burn it themselves to stop the fire. Where we would never burn the house down to save another house. We would try and save that house and we would try and save the other house. That's the mental make-up of a structural firefighter versus a forestry guy, right? Forestry guys are like, okay, we'll build a guard here of dirt, and then we'll burn all this off so it doesn't come here, right. So we'll sacrifice some, to get some. Where structural firefighters are not about sacrificing anything.

Here structural firefighters are portrayed as aggressive, uncompromising and unwilling to lose, and forestry firefighters as less aggressive (maybe even passive) and prepared to lose (at least some of the time). Clearly this rhetoric positions structural firefighters as better firefighters, while equating the mental make-up of wildland firefighters with characteristics typically associated with femininity, such as passivity (Adler et al., 1992; Gonick, 2006). Richard points to firefighting tactics specific to each occupation and uses these as resources to construct the competence and masculinity of structural firefighters as superior to that of wildland firefighters.

It is worth noting that while Richard compares wildland firefighters to 'army guys', who are typically associated with aggressive masculinity (Jeffreys, 2007), the comparison suggests otherwise in this case, as the army were largely cast as support workers brought in for the ignoble job of mop-up duty.

Several forestry firefighters' accounts pointed to the mental state of structural firefighters and an emotional display by the fire chief, in a way that challenged their masculinity. In a well-publicized statement to the media the fire chief broke down in tears while relaying the events of Black Friday. On numerous occasions wildland firefighters mentioned this event even though I did not inquire about it. The chief's emotions, or 'crocodile tears' as several called it, were depicted in a derogatory manner.

In a similar vein one of the heavy equipment operators ridiculed structural firefighters who took stress leave or were otherwise having difficulty dealing with the fire. As emotions (except perhaps anger) are equated with femininity (Bird, 1996; Rubin, 2004), they are something to be disparaged. Wildland firefighters' accounts revealed disdain for public displays of emotion and their caustic remarks called into question the fire chief's masculinity.

Discussion

These findings indicate that the status hierarchy that became evident over the course of the Okanagan Mountain Park fire was due, at least in part, to the structural organization of the firefighting efforts and the ways in which the media covered the fire. The central location of the main fire hall and the fact that structural firefighters fought the fire within the city limits meant that they were more accessible to the media and, in turn, received more favourable media coverage. The media culti-vated narratives consistent with hegemonic mas-culinity and heroism. Heroism did not appear to resonate with wildland or structural firefighters but the narratives of structural firefighters were often saturated with hero-like imagery.

In an effort to maintain their place at the top of the hierarchy structural firefighters reinforced the boundary between themselves and other groups by discursively positioning others, especially wildland firefighters, as less competent and implicitly as less manly. Wildland firefighters, equipment operators and pilots attempted to secure their place at the top of the hierarchy using similar tactics. These strategies were attempts to diminish the credibility of the out-group in question.

The firefighters could have told different stor-ies and could have drawn on different explana-tions for some of these events.[8] For example, the structural firefighters could have argued that the wildland firefighters were younger and less experi-enced, or even less professional, to explain their apparent lack of aggression. Similarly, the wildland firefighters could have pointed out that the struc-tural firefighters simply had different training and responsibilities, which would explain why they may have been uneasy in some situations. Instead, firefighters used narratives that implied directly, and indirectly, that their group was the most com-petent, in terms of firefighting and masculinity, while those from other groups were less so.

What was most notable in my study was that the structural firefighters, who had a relatively high social status, also employed strategies of the superior self. The fact that the structural firefight-ers used these strategies at all provides evidence to support Connell's (1995) claim that hegemonic masculinity is not statically reproduced, but rather, is always contested. If hegemonic masculinity is a given these tactics would not be required for those with the most power and status.

However, because the positions at the top of the gender hierarchy are never secure, even those with power (in this case, structural firefighters) are compelled to engage in practices that refute the integrity of those they perceive as Other. It is only by theorizing gender—masculinity dynamics that

involve active struggles for dominance and the con-stant need to prove one's masculinity—that we can explain why the firefighters responded to the status hierarchy in the ways that they did.

We also saw that gendered strategies of self are not only used individually to construct superior selves, they are collective efforts that serve a col-lective end: defining and imposing boundaries between groups. The boundary work of the media, which bounded the parameters of heroism and manhood, enabled the structural firefighters' claims to competence and hegemonic masculinity to take hold. If it appears that groups are essential-ized as a result of strategies of self and boundary work, it is because that is precisely their intent. Essentializing is 'the making of doctrinal claims that certain good or bad traits inhere in all who share an identity' (Schwalbe and Mason-Schrock, 1996, p. 124). Each group of firefighters attempted to demonstrate that their group was populated by exemplars of masculinity and firefighting com-petence because they wanted to show that their group members were all of a certain character and quality, while others were not.

Firefighters did not appear to be cognizant of their boundary work and strategies of self, but as Sherman (2005) insightfully observes, 'strategy' does not necessarily imply an intentional or explicit act (referring to Bourdieu, 1990); rather, strategies may be functional to the worker's interest in estab-lishing superiority. Furthermore, boundaries may be reinforced in the unnoticed habits and language of everyday life (Fuchs Epstein, 1992). Despite the possible lack of intention, the effects of boundary work and strategies that elevate one's own status at the expense of others are no less harmful.

Firstly, boundaries based on real or perceived differences result in inequality (Fuchs Epstein, 1992). Sherman (2005) maintains that the luxury hotel workers in her study unwittingly legitimated inequality between themselves and hotel guests because their strategies established the guests' entitlement to their labour as legitimate. Similarly, the gendered strategies of self utilized by these firefighters had the unfortunate effect of reinfor-cing the hierarchies between groups. Ironically, rather than challenging inequities, the firefighters' strategies sustained the very disparities that those at the bottom of the hierarchy were so incensed about; namely, that they did not get the respect and recognition that they felt they deserved.

Second, symbolic 'credibility contests' (Lamont and Molnar, 2002, p. 179) involving claims to hegemonic masculinity have symbolic and material implications for inequality. Symbolically, men who embody hegemonic masculinity are given honour, prestige, and authority (Connell, 1995). Materially, men who best exemplify this ideal are granted political and material resources. For example, men at the top of the gender hierarchy earn, on average, higher salaries than women and marginalized men, and are more likely to have political power; resources that can then be used to further their own agendas.

In other words, there are material rewards for those who win symbolic battles. Groups that can claim hegemonic masculinity are able to use their status to gain material resources. In this case, structural firefighters were able to convert their collective social capital into material rewards. With the help of their union representative, the fire chief and the media, the structural firefighters successfully rallied the public and city hall and secured a pay raise less than one year after the fire.[9] The firefighters deliberately referred to the fire and their status as heroes to argue that they deserved a salary increase.[10] The fire chief, who became a local and national celebrity, also reaped many rewards. He was featured on the cover of a prominent national magazine, received an honorary degree and numerous gifts and awards, was invited to do public speaking engagements all over the country and was asked to run for political office (which he declined).

Importantly, there were also costs associated with being on, or striving for, the top. Research indicates that hegemonic masculinity comes at a personal cost to men who wholeheartedly embrace it. For example, impoverished emotional relationships (Kaufman, 2001; Rubin, 2004) dysfunctional sexual relations (Gerschick and Miller, 2001), risk-taking (Courtenay, 2000; Iacuone, 2005), and negative health outcomes (Sabo, 2004) have been linked to hegemonic masculinity construction. Barrett (1996) also posits that strategies to elevate one's own status at the expense of others result in

a Catch-22 situation that does not bode well for establishing a stable sense of masculinity:

> Preoccupation with differentiating self and discounting others creates an enduring sense of subjective insecurity. This persistent sense of fragility and precariousness generates a greater need to display worth. Such defensive posturing—differentiating self by out-performing others, validating self by negating others—is not only unlikely to lead to the achievement of a secure identity, it creates the very social conditions that drive men to strive for a chance to demonstrate exceptionality (p. 141).

Consistent with these findings, many firefighters noted that the fire and its aftermath was a difficult experience. In addition, there were long-term consequences for some. Several were on stress leave at the time of the interviews, at least one firefighter resigned, one senior member retired shortly after the fire, the fire chief retired two years later (at the age of 56), some were having marital difficulties, a number were on medication to reduce stress and a least two senior firefighters were diagnosed with post-traumatic stress disorder. There were also a handful of firefighters who chose to leave their jobs a year or more after the fire, citing the fire as one reason for their decision.

It appears, in the words of the fire chief, this fire did have a 'bad effect' on many of the firefighters. I suggest at least some of these bad effects were related to the gendered strategies of self that the firefighters employed in their efforts to attain superior status and reinforce occupational and symbolic boundaries. By theorizing gendered strategies of self and the group dynamics involved in boundary work, we can more clearly see the mechanisms through which workers' efforts to negotiate status hierarchies are translated into differential costs and rewards, something unexplored in organizational theory to date.

Acknowledgments

I would like to thank Steve Lopez, Tim Curry, Townsand Price-Spratlen, Liana Sayer, numerous other colleagues at the Ohio State University, and three anonymous reviewers for comments and suggestions that helped further develop the ideas in this article. This research was supported by the Social Sciences and Humanities Research Council of Canada.

Notes

1. The wildland–urban interface is the geographical point where the wilderness and urban development meet. In the interface, structures and vegetation are close enough for a wildfire to spread to structures or a structural fire to ignite trees and vegetation (Ministry of Forests Protection Branch, 2004).
2. In terms of sexuality, most of the firefighters who were interviewed appeared to identify as heterosexual, as many mentioned wives or girlfriends in the interviews. However, as sexuality is often invisible (especially in homophobic environments), I cannot say with certainty that all of the firefighters were heterosexual.
3. There were hundreds of women in both paid and volunteer positions who worked many hours during the crisis. However, as in other disaster settings (for example, see Fothergill, 2004), they were relegated primarily to 'support' roles, such as serving food, and finding temporary housing. As a result, most of the firefighters whom I interviewed were men. However, I did interview several women firefighters, and I explore their strategies for accomplishing gender in another article.
4. 'Native' crew is the term utilized by the forestry service to denote crews that primarily comprise First Nations people.
5. There were also divisions in these groups. However, due to space limitations these intra-group divisions are not discussed here.
6. All names are pseudonyms.
7. I am indebted to an anonymous reviewer for this idea.
8. This is especially true since I did not query firefighters about the competence of other firefighting groups. In fact, it was a topic that I tried to avoid. There were several lawsuits in process at the time and I had promised gatekeepers that I would not point fingers or place blame in my research.
9. The wildland firefighters' organization also received some resources (such as more crew positions) as a result of the fire. However, I was told by a number of people that these were primarily resources that had been cut in recent years and had simply been reinstated.
10. Some firefighters expressed discomfort with this strategy, but it was one that the group utilized nonetheless.

References

Adler, P., Kless, S. and Adler, P. (1992) Socialization to gender roles: popularity among elementary school boys and girls. *Sociology of Education*, 65,3, 169–87.

Altheide, D. (2001) *Creating Fear: News and the Construction of Crisis*. New York: Aldine De Gruyter.

Alvesson, M. (1998) Gender relations and identity at work: a case study of masculinities and femininities in an advertising agency. *Human Relations*, 51,8, 969–1005.

Barrett, F. (1996) The organizational construction of hegemonic masculinity: the case of the US Navy. *Gender, Work & Organization*, 3,3, 129–42.

Berg, B.L. (2001) *Qualitative Research Methods for the Social Sciences* 4th edn. Needham Heights, MA: Allyn and Bacon.

Bird, S. (1996) Welcome to the men's club: homosociality and the maintenance of hegemonic masculinity. *Gender & Society*, 10,2, 120–32.

Bourdieu, P. (1990) *The Logic of Practice*. Stanford, CA: Stanford University Press.

Brannon, R. (1976) The male sex role—and what it's done for us lately. In Brannon, R. and David, D. (eds.) *The Forty-nine Percent Majority*, pp. 1–40. Reading, MA: Addison-Wesley.

Brod, H. (1994) Some thoughts on some histories of some masculinities: Jews and other others. In Brod, H. and Kaufman, M. (eds.) *Theorizing Masculinities*, pp. 82–96. Thousand Oaks, CA: Sage.

Canadian Press (2003) Fire razes more than 200 homes in Kelowna, B.C. Available online at www.ctv.ca/servlet/ArticleNews/print?band=generican

darchive=CTVNewsanddate=2 Last consulted 15 February 2004.

CHBC TV (2003) Fire cools a little. Available online at www.chbc.com.news/articles_files/6812/news_14_6812.shtml Last consulted 15 February 2004.

Cheng, C. (1996) *Masculinities in Organizations.* Thousand Oaks, CA: Sage.

Cmap Tools (n.d.) Home page. Available online at http://cmap.ihmc.us Last consulted 27 March 2009.

Collinson, D. and Hearn, J. (1996) *Men as Managers, Managers as Men.* London: Sage.

Connell, R.W. (1995) *Masculinities.* Berkeley, CA: University of California Press.

Connell, R.W. (2000) *The Men and the Boys.* Berkeley, CA: University of California Press.

Connell, R.W. (2001) Introduction and overview. *Feminism and Psychology,* 11,1, 5–9.

Connell, R.W. and Messerschmidt, J.W. (2005) Hegemonic masculinity: rethinking the concept. *Gender & Society,* 19,6, 829–59.

Cornwell, B., Curry, T.J. and Schwirian, K. (2003) Revisiting Norton Long's ecology of games: a network approach. *City and Community,* 2,2, 121–42.

Courtenay, W. (2000) Constructions of masculinity and their influence on men's well-being: a theory of gender and health. *Social Science and Medicine,* 50,10, 1385–401.

CTV (2003) Support from public keeps B.C. fire crews going. Available online at www.ctv.ca/servlet/ArticleNews/print?brand=genericandarchive=CTVNewsanddate=2 Last consulted 15 February 2004.

Curry, T. (1986) A visual method of studying sports: the photo-elicitation interview. *Sociology of Sport Journal,* 3,3, 204–16.

Drew, J. (2004) Identity crisis: gender, public discourse, and 9/11. *Women and Language,* 27,2, 71–7.

Dworkin, S. and Wachs, F. (2000) The morality/manhood paradox. In McKay, J., Messner, M.A. and Sabo, D.F. (eds.) *Masculinities, Gender Relations, and Sport,* pp. 47–66. Thousand Oaks, CA, Sage Publications.

Fine, G.A. (1996) Reputational entrepreneurs and the memory of incompetence: melting supporters, partisan warriors, and images of President Harding. *American Journal of Sociology,* 101,5, 1159–93.

Fine, G.A. and White, R. (2002) Creating collective attention in the public domain: human interest narratives and the rescue of Floyd Collins. *Social Forces,* 81,1, 57–85.

Fisher, K. (1997) Locating frames in the discursive universe. *Sociological Research Online,* 2,3.

Fothergill, A. (2004) *Heads above Water: Gender, Class, and Family in the Grand Forks Flood.* Albany, NY: State University of New York Press.

Fuchs Epstein, C. (1992) Tinkerbells and pinups: the construction and reconstruction of gender boundaries at work. In Lamont, M. and Fournier, M. (eds.) *Cultivating Differences: Symbolic Boundaries and the Making of Inequality,* pp. 232–56. Chicago, IL: University of Chicago Press.

Gerschick, T. and Miller, A.S. (2001) Coming to terms: masculinity and physical disability. In Kimmel, M.S. and Messner, M.A. (eds.) *Men's Lives,* pp. 392–406. Boston, MA: Allyn and Bacon.

Gieryn, T.F. (1983) Boundary work and the demarcation of science from non-science: strains and interest in professional ideologies of scientists. *American Sociological Review,* 48,6, 781–95.

Glaser, B.G. (1992) *Emergence vs. Forcing. Basics of Grounded Theory Analysis,* Mill Valley, CA: Sociology Press.

Glaser, B.G. and Strauss, A.L. (1967) *The Discovery of Grounded Theory: Strategies for Qualitative Research.* Chicago, IL: Aldine.

Goffman, B. (1963) *Stigma; Notes on the Management of Spoiled Identity.* Englewood Cliffs, NJ: Prentice-Hall.

Gonick, M. (2006) Between 'girl power' and 'reviving Ophelia': constituting the neoliberal girl subject. *NWSA Journal,* 18,2, 1–23.

Grewal, I. (2003) Transnational America: race, gender and citizenship after 9/11. *Social Identities,* 9,4, 535–61.

Harper, D. (2000) Reimagining visual methods. In Denzin, N.K. and Lincoln, Y.S. (eds.) *Handbook of Qualitative Methods* 2nd edn, pp. 717–32. Thousand Oaks, CA: Sage.

Heritage Society of British Columbia (2004) Rebuilding the Myra Canyon trestles. Available online at www.heritagebc.ca/nl_article4.htm Last consulted 15 February 2004.

Hill Collins, P. (2000) *Black Feminist Thought* 2nd edn. New York: Routledge.

Holstein, J.A. and Gubrium, J.F. (1997) The active interview. In Silverman, D. (ed.) *Qualitative*

Research: Theory, Method and Practice, pp. 140–62. London: Sage.

Houchin Winfield, B. (2003) The press response to the corps of discovery: the making of heroes in an egalitarian age. *Journalism and Mass Communication Quarterly*, 80,4, 866–83.

Howard, J.W. and Prividera, L. (2004) Rescuing patriarchy or saving 'Jessica Lynch': the rhetorical construction of the American woman soldier. *Women and Language*, 27,2, 89–97.

Iacuone, D. (2005) 'Real men are tough guys': hegemonic masculinity and safety in the construction industry. *The Journal of Men's Studies*, 13,2, 247–66.

Jeffreys, S. (2007) Double jeopardy: women, the US military and the war in Iraq. *Women's Studies International Forum*, 30,1, 16–25.

Kaufman, M. (2001) The construction of masculinity and the triad of men's violence. In Kimmel, M.S. and Messner, M.A. (eds.) *Men's Lives*. 5th edn, pp. 4–18. Needham Heights, MA: Allyn and Bacon.

Kimmel, M.S. (1994) Masculinities as homophobia: fear, shame, and silence in the construction of gender identity. In Brod, H. and Kaufman, M. (eds.) *Theorizing Masculinities*, pp. 119–41. Thousand Oaks, CA: Sage.

Lamont, M. (1992) *Money, Morals, and Manners: The Culture of the French and American Upper-Middle Class*. Chicago, IL: University of Chicago Press.

Lamont, M. (2000) *The Dignity of Working Men: Morality and the Boundaries of Race, Class, and Immigration*. Cambridge, MA: Harvard University Press.

Lamont, M. and Molnar, V. (2002) The study of boundaries in the social sciences. *Annual Review of Sociology*, 28, 167–95.

Langewiesche, W. (2002) *American Ground: Unbuilding the World Trade Center*. New York: North Point Press.

Lois, J. (2003) *Heroic Efforts: The Emotional Culture of Search and Rescue Volunteers*. New York: New York University Press.

Lorber, J. (2002) Heroes, warriors, and burqas: a feminist sociologist's reflections on September 11. *Sociological Forum*, 17,3, 377–96.

Meyer, S. (1999) Work, play, and power: masculine culture on the shop floor; 1930–1960. *Men and Masculinities*, 2,2, 115–34.

Miller, J. and Glassner, B. (1997) The 'inside' and the 'outside': finding realities in interviews. In Silverman, D. (ed.) *Qualitative Research: Theory, Method and Practice*, pp. 99–112. London: Sage.

Ministry of Forests Protection Branch (2003a) Fire review summary for Okanagan Mountain Fire. Available online at www.for.gov.bc.ca/protect/reports/2003review/okanagan%5Ffire%5Freview%5Fk50628.pdf Last consulted 20 January 2004.

Ministry of Forests Protection Branch (2003b) Large wildfires. Available online at www.for.gov.bc.ca/protect/reports/LargeFires.htm Last consulted 1 October 2004.

Ministry of Forests Protection Branch (2004) Interface fires and safety. Available online at www.for.gov.bc.ca/protect/FAQ/interface.htm#32 Last consulted 1 October 2004.

Monaghan, L. (2002) Embodying gender, work and organization: solidarity, cool loyalties and contested hierarchy in a masculinist occupation. *Gender, Work & Organization*, 9,5, 504–36.

Pacholok, S. (2007) Masculinities in crisis: a case study of the Mountain Park fire. Unpublished PhD. Sociology Department, The Ohio State University: Columbus.

Peterson, A. (2003) Research on men and masculinities: some implications of recent theory for future work. *Men and Masculinities*, 6,1, 54–69.

Pierce, J. (1995) *Gender Trials: Emotional Lives in Contemporary Law Firms*. Berkeley, CA: University of California Press.

Plant, D. (2003) Hard fought battle. *Okanagan Sunday*, Kelowna.

Poulsen, C. (2003a) Fire actions under scope. *The Daily Courier*, Kelowna.

Poulsen, C. (2003b) Unsung heroes: heavy equipment operators put their lives on the line fighting the Okanagan Mountain blaze, but respect has been hard to find. *The Daily Courier*, Kelowna.

Projansky, S. (1998) Girls who act like women who fly: Jessica Dubroff as cultural troublemaker. *Signs: Journal of Women in Culture and Society*, 23,3, 771–808.

Prokos, A. and Padavic, I. (2002) 'There oughtta be a law against bitches': masculinity lessons in police academy training. *Gender, Work & Organization*, 9,4, 439–59.

Rubin, L. (2004) The approach–avoidance dance: men, women, and intimacy. In Kimmel, M. and Messner, M. (eds.) *Men's Lives* 5th edn, pp. 409–15. Boston, MA: Allyn and Bacon.

Sabo, D.F. (2004) Masculinities and men's health: moving toward post-Superman era prevention. In Kimmel, M.S. and Messner, M.A. (eds.) *Men's Lives* 5th edn, pp. 347–61. Boston, MA: Allyn and Bacon.

Schwalbe, M. and Mason-Schrock, D. (1996) Identity work as group process. In Markovsky, B., Lovaglia, M. and Simon, R. (eds.) *Advances in Group Processes*, pp. 115–49. Greenwich, CT, JAI Press.

Seymour, R. (2003) Hot stuff. *Daily Courier*, Kelowna.

Sherman, R. (2005) Producing the superior self: strategic comparison and symbolic boundaries among luxury hotel workers. *Ethnography*, 6,2, 131–58.

Sherman, R. (2006) *Class Acts*. Berkeley, CA: University of California Press.

Strauss, A. and Corbin, J. (1998) *Basics of Qualitative Research: Techniques and Procedures for Developing Grounded Theory*. Thousand Oaks, CA, Sage.

Strauss, A.L. (1987) *Qualitative Analysis for Social Scientists*. Cambridge: Cambridge University Press.

Watters, A. (2003) Training and experience kept trapped firefighters calm. *Capital News*, Kelowna.

Wetherell, M. and Edley, N. (1999) Negotiating hegemonic masculinity: imaginary positions and psycho-discursive practices. *Feminism and Psychology*, 9,3, 335–56.

CHAPTER 27

Privilege and Oppression: The Configuration of Race, Gender, and Class in Southern Ontario Auto Plants, 1939 to 1949[1]

Pamela Sugiman

This paper offers an examination of the ways in which the matrix of race, gender, and class has structured the automobile manufacturing industry of southern Ontario, a work setting that has long been racialized and gendered. Since the beginnings of the industry, white men have dominated the auto-manufacturing workforce. Anyone who was not white and male was in the minority, different, an intruder, treated as unequal. In the auto plants of southern Ontario, two such 'minorities' existed. One, small groups of women, many of whom were born in Canada of Anglo-Celtic and Eastern European descent, worked in McKinnon Industries of St Catharines, Ontario, and the General Motors Company of Canada's (GM) manufacturing facility in Oshawa, Ontario.[2] Two, even smaller pockets of black men, mostly Canadian-born, were concentrated in janitorial jobs and various types of foundry work in McKinnon Industries and the Ford Motor Company of Canada, as well as some smaller auto foundries in Windsor.[3]

In earlier research, I documented the experiences of white, women auto workers, tracing changes in both their position in the industry and their perceptions and politics over the course of several decades (Sugiman, 1994). This study is an attempt to reconstruct a small part of the lives of black men, on the job and in their union, at a time when their numerical presence in the auto plants was at its peak, throughout the Second World War and into the post-war period.[4] It is based on a review of union documents, as well as the oral testimonies of 12 black men who were employed in the industry during these years.[5]

In spite of the scant numbers of black men in the plants, auto manufacturers drew on widespread cultural beliefs about race and gender, and exploited and reinforced the structural inequalities that working-class blacks faced in wartime southern Ontario. Employers manipulated these beliefs in hiring workers, allocating them to jobs, and establishing the terms of their employment.

In doing so, management was central to the construction of difference among workers—a notable achievement given the striking social homogeneity of the workforce as a whole.

An understanding of the social meaning of racial and sexual difference is central to an analysis of the workplace, working people, and their struggles. When we recognize these differences, we uncover many parallel, but separate working-class realities. The distinctive experiences of black men in the industry can be attributed to the particular ways in which race, gender, and class, both as subjectivities and social processes, have converged at different moments and touched the lives of workers, as well as shaped the larger historical scenario.

Constructing Difference among Auto Workers

Though data on the demographic composition of auto plants in Canada is based largely on anecdotal evidence, it is undeniable that employers used race and sex as criteria in filling jobs. Prior to the Second World War, in the pre-union period, sizable communities of black families lived in the auto towns of St Catharines and Windsor. St Catharines, a small city near Niagara Falls, was the home of McKinnon Industries. Windsor, a mid-sized city that is situated across the river from Detroit, was the location of the Ford Motor Company of Canada, Chrysler Canada, and a number of affiliated auto foundries such as Auto Specialties, Walker Metal Products, and Malleable Iron.

Despite the strong presence of the auto companies in their communities, however, most blacks understood that auto employment was unattainable to them. Before the Second World War, only a handful of blacks worked in auto.[6]

With the outbreak of the Second World War, employers were forced to alter their hiring policies in response to stepped-up production demands and the temporary departure of many prime-age, white, male employees. Thus, the doors to the auto plants opened a crack for some of those workers who had long been on the outside. For instance, during this time, Ford hired a number of Chinese men in its Windsor plant. Proud of this move, company publicists featured a photograph of each of their 56 Chinese workers in its monthly magazine, *Ford Times*. Ford described the employment of these men as a patriotic gesture in the context of war.[7]

None of the companies, however, offered employment to black women. According to a report by Lyle Talbot, former Ford employee and president of the anti-racist organization, the Windsor Council on Group Relations, at a time when many employers badly needed to replenish their diminishing supply of workers, 'the doors of virtually every factory in the Windsor area were closed tight against coloured girls and women.'[8] The Second World War 'broke the barrier' for 'coloured *men*' only (Interview #12, 1995).

Richard Nicholson worked in the foundry in St Catharines for 36 years. He remembers his entry into the company:

> I heard the rumour . . . that McKinnon Industries was hiring blacks. . . . They were looking for *coloured people* to work in the foundry so I went down there to Ontario Street and 'bingo!' I got hired right away because I was a big lad and everything (emphasis added).

'Foundries Is Made for Black Men'

Auto makers took special measures to locate black male labourers largely because they wanted them to fill the most undesirable jobs in the plants—jobs that few white men wanted. In the auto plants of Ontario, racial segregation was never enforced as a matter of company policy, nor was it written into collective agreements (as it had been in the US). Yet management used informal, unspoken means of exclusion to place blacks in one of three areas: the heat treat, the powerhouse, or the foundry. Within various departments or divisions, some black men could also find work as janitors. According to Lyle Talbot, who temporarily worked in each of these jobs, they were all bad places to be. The powerhouse was dirty.

> [T]hey'd get all kinds of soot from the smoke. . . . In the powerhouse, there was a big pile of coal out in the yard, and big transformers

that were run by coal, heat. Black men worked in a tunnel where the coal was brought in on a conveyor from the coal pile into the big furnaces that generated the heat for the power. The men had to make sure that the coal did not fall off the conveyor going through.

The 'heat treat's the same thing', Talbot added. This is where they treated the metal with heat in long ovens. The worst of the three areas, however, was the foundry—'where all the heavy, slugging, dirty work' went on.[9] The vast majority of the black workforce was situated in the foundry.[10] And there, along with Armenians, they typically performed the least desirable job of iron pouring.

The men poured their own iron and you had to go out and shift the moulds—had a plate on top about that thick and go on top of the moulds for them to pour the iron. Sometimes they'd be pouring and the mould would be bad and as they poured in the iron would burst out the side and sometimes, as soon as that iron, just a drop, would hit . . . the concrete it would look like fireworks (Interview #12, 1995).

GM worker Richard Nicholson commented on the relationship between race and job allocation:

In 1938 . . . when I went to General Motors, they hired us blacks for one reason. They didn't lie to you. When they hired me, they told me . . . 'We got a job for you in the foundry. It's a hot job. It's a hard job.' . . . [T]hey kept calling in blacks, more blacks. They would've hired more blacks if they could have got 'em because that was where you were supposed to be—right there in the foundry.

Compounding the labour force requirements of auto manufacturers and the dire economic straits of most black workers, employers upheld a particular vision of black masculinity that rested in part on the belief that a 'coloured man' was most suited to hard, dirty, and physically demanding jobs.[11] Before foundries became highly automated,

many of the operations required enormous physical strength (lifting castings and pouring iron, for example). And the dominant cultural image of a black man was that of a strong, robust, and muscular worker. Moreover, foundry work was performed at extraordinarily high temperatures and thus demanded tremendous physical stamina. Some company officials claimed that coloured men, in particular, could endure these excesses because of a genetic predisposition to withstand heat (Interview #1, 1990; Interview #7, 1994). According to auto worker Cassell Smith,

At that time the foundry there was smoky and dusty and the workers they'd get in there wouldn't stay long. . . . So they decided, we [black men] could stand it . . . that was the purpose of it because they figured, being black, you know, you could stand the heat . . . that they're all the same . . . people in Africa stand a lot of heat.

Exhibiting a racialized paternalism, some managers publicly showcased 'their' hard-working black employees. In doing so, they presented black masculinity in a hyperbolic form—using a racial stereotype to magnify the image of the unskilled working man.[12] In the eyes of some observers in the plants, these men were little more than powerful, labouring bodies. GM foundry employee Richard Nicholson recounted,

. . . quite a few white people come over and watch you work. Take pictures. They've got pictures of me down there now. Take pictures of us doing this heavy job. And they'd just sit back and say, 'Look at them guys work!' Visitors . . . the foremen or the general foreman [would] bring people in and say, 'Let's show you how we do it—how our boys do it.' They all look at one another and they used to be taking pictures of us guys all the time—the kind of work we was doin' (Interview #1, 1990).

These men were highlighted for displaying manly brawn and to some extent they themselves expressed pride in their ability to perform work that involved remarkably high levels of physical exertion.[13] Yet at the same time, black men were objectified by employers. Managers who put the men on public display for performing hard, dirty, hazardous labour—work that they had little choice but to perform—paradoxically reinforced the notion that black males possessed a heightened masculinity while at the same time they emasculated these men in denying their 'humanness', in constructing them as 'beasts of burden'. Employers contributed to the construction of a racialized masculinity, a masculinity that embodied racial and class subordination.

The Privileges of Manhood

Being a man, however, did bring with it some privileges. It was because of their *sex* that these men were hired in the auto industry. As noted, even during the Second World War, black women faced formidable obstacles in finding any kind of factory employment in Windsor and elsewhere in Canada. Their sexual status furthermore ensured that black men would possess specific job rights, rights that were denied the small numbers of white women who had been allowed to work in some auto plants largely because of their privilege as a race.

Assumed to be breadwinners, black men held departmental, and ultimately plant-wide seniority rights, received the same wages and piece rates, and in theory, could occupy the same job classifications as all other male auto workers. There is no evidence that during these years, any of the local collective agreements between the UAW and the Big Three auto makers in Canada openly made distinctions among workers on the basis of *race*. GM worker Richard Nicholson explained that in the past, differences in monetary rewards among the male workforce were based on an employee's family responsibilities only:

> The white boys I worked with and the black boys, we'd always see one another's cheque. . . . We all get the same [pay]. . . . The only difference would be in deductions. If you have more kids than the other guy, you have a dollar or two more because they didn't take as much money off ya.

Married or single, male auto workers received higher than average wages for working-class men because of the successful efforts of the UAW to secure a family wage. The family wage demand was premised on the assumption that workers (men only) must be paid a relatively high rate because of their responsibility, as head of a household, for the economic welfare of a wife and children.[14] It was this ideology of the male breadwinner that in turn provided the rationale for women's lower rates of pay. In the words of Windsor-based auto worker Howard Olbey, in the Ford Motor Company, 'it was all man to man.'

In this particular historic context, and specifically in this sphere of social life—the paid work setting—the social meaning of gender (manhood) and race (blackness), and their configuration, permitted the elevation of black men to the *formal status* of white working-class men.

'We're All Brothers with the Union'

The vehicle by which all male auto workers secured various rights and entitlements in the workplace was the UAW, and there was a strong connection between belonging to the union and being a working-class man. Masculine bonds strengthened union ties and, in turn, union affiliation and masculinized class-based allegiances played an important part in reinforcing gender-based solidarities among these groups of men. Indeed, it is difficult to disentangle unionism from 'brotherhood' during these years. The industrial trade union was very much a masculine institution, not only because the vast majority of UAW members and leaders were men, but also because these men built their unionism around a place in the sexual division of familial labour, recreational pursuits, cultural forms of expression, strategies of resistance, and a political agenda that spoke to many of the shared experiences of working-class men (Sugiman, 1994).

Women auto workers clearly expressed strong loyalties to the union. They played an important part in building the UAW. Though female members were under-represented in the UAW leadership, seldom held an elected position, and rarely voiced their views in local union forums, they regularly attended union meetings and faithfully performed their duty as 'foot soldiers' in the early strikes and sit-downs. Notwithstanding these loyalties, however, most women felt marginalized in union politics and subordinate to their UAW brothers. Women auto workers viewed the UAW of the 1940s as a distinctly masculine enterprise. 'That was men,' one woman auto worker matter-of-factly said about the union (as cited in Sugiman, 1994).

Black men, too, had an ambivalent relationship to the UAW. After all, white men dominated the upper echelons of the union bureaucracy, few of whom challenged the informal discriminatory measures that kept black workers in perilous foundry jobs and out of the preferred skilled trades.[15] Yet black men's awareness of racist undercurrents within the labour movement did not diminish their strong commitment to industrial unionism and (unlike women members) they became actively involved in mainstream union politics at the local level. In fact, during the Second World War, their level of UAW office-holding was notably high in proportion to their numbers in the plants.

The union allegiances of black men were strengthened by the UAW International's ideological commitment to racial equality as a basic principle of industrial unionism. For decades, the discussion of race among Canadian workers has been dominated, and perhaps inhibited, by this largely American discourse.[16] In response to the persistent demands of African-American rank and file workers (Boyle, 1995), heightened racial strife in UAW-organized plants, locals, and in American cities generally, as well as the passage of US federal civil rights legislation during the war and post-war years,[17] the UAW International office took a clear stand against racial discrimination.[18] During the 1940s, the union created an International Fair Employment Practices and Anti-Discrimination Department (FEPC), made local FEPCs mandatory, and appointed a (limited) number of women and black men on the International staff, mainly in fair practices, organizing, and education departments.[19]

To the UAW, racial discrimination was a serious matter with clear moral, political, and economic ramifications. First, UAW discourse on race was highly moralistic, and was expressed in passionate, emotional language. Appealing to workers' basic sense of right and wrong, and underscoring the moral authority of industrial unionism, official UAW statements espoused an essential immorality of racism in industry. In policy statements and public addresses, UAW International leaders posited racial discrimination as 'cancerous', 'evil', 'infectious', a 'poison', and 'an act against humanity'.[20] They argued that any good trade unionist should take a stand against racism as a matter of good conscience, and out of a commitment to one of the most fundamental philosophies of their union—that of 'brotherhood'.

UAW records contain a series of diatribes by leaders asserting that it was 'illogical' and 'stupid' for trade unionists to foster or maintain racial divisions between workers because of the potential impact of such divisions on the economic security of white male workers, the future bargaining power of the union, and labour solidarity.[21]

Most black workers believed that the union contract could be used as a tool to protect their rights, in spite of the actions or inaction, prejudices or indifference, of individual men. The collective agreement was a tool for the achievement of a better life, a measure of dignity, and equal opportunity at work—an instrument that, when pressured, some (white) union leaders would put to use. According to John Milben, a foundry worker for thirty-one years, 'The union was a hundred percent behind us. . . . Fairness. We're all brothers with the union.'

Race, Brotherhood, and Resistance

From the beginnings of the auto industry in Canada, employers have contributed to the *construction of difference* within the working class. These differences were based on race, gender, and family status, as well as skill. While auto manufacturers hired white male breadwinners to fill the vast majority of jobs in the industry, they also recruited extremely small numbers of black men (and white women) to perform work that many white men either rejected or were temporarily unavailable to perform. While these two groups of workers met a need on the part of capitalists, management clearly regarded each as marginal to the industry, different, and unequal to the core workforce. Both black men and white women were defined as the 'other', a socially-created category that was itself broken down along lines of race and gender.

The history of black men in auto work is one of many contradictions. Such contradictions are the outcome of the changing configuration of race, gender, and social class. While black men were intruders in the homogeneous white world of the auto plants, their status as wage-earning men/union brothers accorded them various rights and entitlements that were denied (white) women workers. The social and political implications of race in these settings permitted black men to be elevated to the formal status of white men, a status that was based on gender privilege, and class, and gender solidarities.

Formal equal rights in union contracts (equal wages and equal seniority rights), though, did not shield black men from face-to-face indignities on the plant floor, nor did they protect the men from the hazards of working in bad jobs, or the economic impact of stunted opportunities within the firm. Gender and class shaped the content of the racism that these men experienced; they did not protect them from it.

Race and gender shape working-class experience. Whiteness and masculinity were undeniably central features of auto work. The primacy of one of these constructs over the others has sometimes been debated, but this is not at issue here for there is no neat formula that can be consistently applied to understand their alliance. It is more useful to observe how the racialization of gender and the gendering of race have changed over time, and have taken on meaning in different spheres of social existence. When we examine the ever-changing nexus of race, gender and class, we understand the relationship not merely as one of multiple oppressions, but as something more complex—one in which people can be simultaneously victims and agents; privileged and oppressed.

Notes

1. This is a revised version of a paper presented at the Annual Meeting of the American Historical Association, 2–5 January 1997. For comments on earlier drafts of this paper, I would like to thank Robert Storey, Joan Sangster, and Alice Kessler-Harris, and four anonymous reviewers for *Labour/Le Travail*. Thanks also to Hassan Yussuff, students in the caw Workers of Colour Leadership Training Programme, and the many workers who graciously agreed to share with me their stories. This research was funded by an Arts Research Board grant and a Labour Studies Programme research grant at McMaster University.

2. McKinnon Industries was originally a subsidiary of General Motors and later became a General Motors plant.

3. Small numbers of Armenian, Chinese, and Chinese-Canadian workers were also employed in the southern Ontario auto industry during the Second World War. However, I have chosen to focus here on black workers because they represented the largest minority, with the longest history in the plants.

4. Unlike their American counterparts, these workers were so few in number, so seemingly marginal to either the company or the union, that their unique histories have never been traced. Paradoxically, they are workers whose difference made them highly visible in the workplace; yet this difference has rendered them largely invisible in Canadian labour history. Currently, there are no published scholarly accounts of the ways in which race has been used in structuring the auto industry in Canada. In comparison, one can find a number of studies of gender and race relations in the American auto industry, as well as in the UAW International Office, and regional and local UAW offices in the United States. See for example, K. Tucker Anderson, 'Last Hired, First Fired: Black Women Workers during World War II', *Journal of American History* 69, 1 (June 1982): 82–97; L. Bailer, 'Negro Labor in the American Automobile Industry', Unpublished PhD Dissertation, University of Michigan, 1943; K. Boyle, '"There are No Union Sorrows That the Union Can't Heal": The Struggle for Racial Equality in the United Automobile Workers,

1940–1960', *Labor History* 36, 1 (Winter 1995): 5–23; N. Gabin, *Feminism in the Labor Movement: Women and the United Automobile Workers, 1935–1975* (Ithaca, NY: Cornell University Press, 1990); J.A. Geschwender, 'The League of Revolutionary Black Workers: Problems Confronting Black Marxist-Leninist Organizations', *Journal of Ethnic Studies* 2, 3 (Fall 1974): 1–23; sections in S. Jefferys, *Management and Managed: Fifty Years of Crisis at Chrysler* (New York: Cambridge University Press, 1986); sections in Alex Lichtenstein, 'Labor Radicalism, Race Relations, and Anticommunism in Miami During the 1940s', Paper presented at the Annual Meeting of the Organization of American Historians, Washington, DC, 30 March 1995; M. May, 'The Historical Problem of the Family Wage: The Ford Motor Company and the Five Dollar Day', *Feminist Studies* 8, 2 (Summer 1982): 399–424; A. Meier, and E. Rudwick, *Black Detroit and the Rise of the UAW* (New York: Oxford University Press, 1979); R. Milkman, *Gender at Work: The Dynamics of Job Segregation by Sex during World War II* (Urbana: University of Illinois Press, 1987); B.J. Widick, 'Black Workers: Double Discontents', in B. Widick, ed., *Auto Work and Its Discontents* (Baltimore: John Hopkins University Press, 1976), 52–60.

5. It was extremely difficult to locate black men who had worked in the auto industry during the period of study. Given the harsh conditions of their work, a sizeable number of these workers left the auto industry after the Second World War. Also, many of the men who remained in the plants suffered from serious health problems such as silicosis. Man of these men had died before this project was undertaken. By the time all the interviews for this study were completed, several participants had died.

6. White women too have had a long presence in the auto industry, and likewise they constituted a small minority. Of the Big Three auto makers, General Motors consistently employed the largest number of females. In 1918, women comprised less than 6 per cent of GM's total hourly workforce. But between 1942 and 1943, the number of women employees increased dramatically. In 1942, GM's Oshawa plant employed only 200 women, but by March 1943, this figure had risen to 400 out of a total workforce of 4,000. Rapid expansion of production as well as growing wartime labour shortages drew even more women into McKinnon Industries. According to UAW estimates, the female workforce in McKinnon rose from 600 in 1942 to 1,200 out of a total workforce of 4,500 in 1943. Where previously women had made up about 8 per cent of the total personnel, their proportion increased to 25 per cent.

7. 'Gung Ho', *Ford Times* 3, 5 (October 1943): 12–14; 'Heart Strings Stretch From Windsor 'Round the World . . .', *Ford Times* 2, 2 (November 1942): 3–4. In contrast, in June 1944, the National Selective Service of Canada (NSS) requested that McKinnon Industries employ a small number of Japanese-Canadian men. One Japanese-Canadian man had already been employed in the foundry. However, the UAW Local 199 Bargaining Committee opposed the hiring of Canadian-born 'Japs', and recommended that the matter be taken up with both the NSS and the company and that it be discussed further by District Council 26. Archives of Labor and Urban Affairs (ALUA), Box 11, UAW Region 7 Toronto Sub-Regional Office, Local 199 Report to District Council 26 Meeting, Minutes (June 1944), 8–11.

8. Lyle Talbot Private Collection, untitled document (March 1950). During the Second World War, a small group of black persons based in Toronto challenged the discriminatory practices of the National Selective Service in recruiting workers for essential war industries. See J.W. Walker, *Racial Discrimination in Canada: The Black Experience*, Canadian Historical Association Booklet 41 (Ottawa 1985), 17. This stands in contrast to the situation in the United States. In the US, labour market shortages during the Second World War were so great, and the black population much more sizeable than in Canada, that both black women and men began to get jobs in the auto industry. For example, Chrysler went from 0 black women to approximately 5,000 in April 1945. See B. Widick, 'Black Workers: Double Discontents', 93. In the mid-1960s one black female was employed in Chrysler Canada's administrative office. In Oshawa, the home of General Motors of Canada, there was no black community from which to draw workers.

9. For a discussion of foundry work in early twentieth century Canada, see C. Heron, 'The

Craftsman: Hamilton's Metal Workers in the Early Twentieth Century', *Labour/Le Travailleur* 6 (Autumn 1980): 7–48. Decoufle and Wood examine mortality patterns among workers in a grey iron foundry for the period 1938 to 1967. The authors highlight the connection between foundry employment and race. P. Decoufle and D.J. Wood, 'Mortality Patterns Among Workers in a Gray Iron Foundry', *American Journal of Epidemiology* 109, 6 (1979): 667–75; see also, E.S. Gibson, R.H. Martin, and J.N. Lockington, 'Lung Cancer Mortality in a Steel Foundry', *Journal of Occupational Medicine* 19, 12 (December 1977): 807–12.

10. Black men in the US were also concentrated in foundry work, as well as wet-sanding operations, material handling, and janitorial assignments. See K. Boyle, '"There Are No Sorrows"', 8; B. Widick, 'Black Workers: Double Discontents', 53.

11. For a discussion of race and images of masculinity in the contemporary period, see among others, R. Staples, 'Masculinity and Race: The Dual Dilemma of Black Men', *Journal of Social Issues* 34, 1 (1978): 169–83.

12. This idea was articulated by *Labour/Le Travail* reviewer #2.

13. In his account of metal workers in Hamilton, Ontario during the early twentieth century, Heron argues that the pride of moulders in steel foundries 'fed on the physical demands of the work, which was notoriously heavy, dirty, and unhealthy'. See C. Heron, 'The Craftsman', 11.

14. For a more detailed discussion of the family wage, see B. Bradbury, *Working Families: Age, Gender, and Daily Survival in Industrializing Montreal* (Toronto: McClelland and Stewart, 1993), chapter 3; N. Gabin, *Feminism in the Labor Movement*; M. May, 'Bread before Roses: American Workingmen, Labor Unions, and the Family Wage', in R. Milkman, ed., *Women, Work, and Protest: A Century of U.S. Women's Labor History* (Boston: Routledge and Keegan Paul, 1985), 1–21; R. Milkman, *Gender at Work*; J. Parr, *The Gender of Breadwinners: Women, Men, and Change in Two Industrial Towns, 1880–1950* (Toronto: University of Toronto Press, 1990); B. Palmer, *Working-Class Experience: Rethinking the History of Canadian Labour, 1800—1991* (Toronto: McClelland and Stewart, 1992).

15. The level of participation of workers of colour, however, dropped in the following decades. To this day, workers of colour remain underrepresented in the Canadian Auto Workers Union, especially in local office.

16. Although racism was a reality in Canada, the experience of Canadian auto workers was distinctive. As noted, blacks constituted a tiny minority in Canadian UAW plants relative to American firms, particularly in comparison to US cities such as Detroit. Thus, in Canada, there was no strong and politically powerful contingency to fight for racial equality. Furthermore, this small group of workers was concentrated in a very narrow range of jobs. Likewise, they were minorities within their communities. Importantly, because of the hidden nature of the discrimination they faced, because racism in Canadian auto plants was less extreme and less overt than in the United States, many people believed that race discrimination was exclusively an American problem. See for example, L.E. Talbot, 'The Distinctive Character of Racism in Canada', ma thesis, University of Windsor (1982); James W. St.G. Walker, *Racial Discrimination in Canada: The Black Experience*, Canadian Historical Association Historical Booklet 41 (Ottawa 1985). UAW Canadian Region leaders therefore seldom addressed the issue of race. For this reason, the focus of this discussion is the resistance activities of rank and file workers themselves.

17. For example, on 25 June 1941, the US government issued Presidential Executive Order 8802, which reaffirmed the policy of full participation in defence programs by all persons regardless of race, creed, colour, or national origin. See ALUA, UAW Research Department Collection, Box 9, File: 9–24, Discrimination Against Negroes in Employment, 1942–7, 'Executive Order 8802.'

18. For example, ALUA, Emil Mazey Collection, Box 11, File: 11-6, FEPC, 1946–47-2, 'William Oliver to All Local Union Officers and Fair Practices Committees' (4 September 1947); ALUA, Emil Mazey Collection, Box 11, File: 11-6, FEPC, 1946–47-2, 'Fair Practices and Anti-Discrimination Department Article 25'.

19. For example, ALUA, UAW Canadian Region Series III Collection, Box 70, File: 7, District Council, 1940, 'Minutes, District Council 26 Meeting' (13–14 January 1940); ALUA, George Addes Collection, Box 82, File: 82-24, 'Order Creating UAW-CIO Fair Practices Committee'. Created in

1944, the overriding goal of the Fair Practices and Anti-Discrimination Department was to unite workers, regardless of religion, race, creed, colour, political affiliation, or nationality. It was to accomplish this aim by addressing workers' complaints of discrimination, publicizing UAW no-discrimination policies and guidelines for handling discrimination cases, setting up and activizing local FEPCs, conducting workplace audits to determine composition by sex and race in the plants, and educating workers through various programmes, conferences, radio addresses, and the Department's monthly publication, *Ammunition*.

20 See for example, ALUA, UAW Research Department Collection, Box 9, File: 9-24, Discrimination Against Negroes in Employment, 1942–47,

'R.J. Thomas to All UAW-CIO Executive Board Members and Department Heads, November 25, 1943'; ALUA, UAW Research Department Collection, Box 18, File: Minorities, 1942–47, 1 of 2, 'UAW Fight Against Intolerance', Address by George W. Crockett, Director, UAW-CIO Fair Practices Committee 4 November, 1945.

21. For example, ALUA, UAW Research Department Collection, Box 11, File: 11-20, Fair Practices and Anti-Discrimination Department, 1947–58, 'Summer School Course in Workers Education'; ALUA, Emil Mazey Collection, Box 11, File: 11-6, FEPC, 1946–47-2, 'First Annual Summary of Activities of the International UAW-CIO Fair Practices Committee'; 'UAW Seeks to Prevent Hiring Discrimination', *Michigan Chronicle*, 8 September 1945.

References

Boyle, K. 1995. '"There Are No Union Sorrows That the Union Can't Heal": The Struggle for Racial Equality in the United Automobile Workers, 1940–1960', *Labor History* 36, 1 (Winter): 5–23.

Sugiman, P. 1994. *Labour's Dilemma: The Gender Politics of Workers in Canada, 1937–1979*. Toronto: University of Toronto Press.

CHAPTER 28

Domestic Distinctions: Constructing Difference among Paid Domestic Workers in Toronto[1]

Bernadette Stiell and Kim England

Have you seen the movie *Mary Poppins*? There's a song that says that if you can find the good things, then everything else is ok. What she says is actually amazing. The kids love it too. It's my theme song to keep me going sometimes. That is our song, the nanny song. 'You find the fun and the job's a game.' That's exactly it, 'a spoonful of sugar helps the medicine go down', that's it literally, and figuratively speaking. A pat on the back goes a long way. But I didn't get that at all. That's the reason why I was

unhappy [with her previous employer]. (Silke, a 30-year-old German woman employed as a 'domestic worker in Toronto.)

Silke came to Toronto in 1986 to work as a nanny. She is one of more than 90,000 women who have arrived in Canada over the past 15 years under two federal government programs (the Foreign Domestic Movement program, 1981–92, and the Live-in Caregivers Program, 1992 to the present). These programs require that domestic workers/

caregivers be 'live-ins' at their employer's homes for their first two years in Canada. Silke had a difficult relationship with her employer, partly as a result of the contradictions and ambiguities associated with her 'workplace' being her employer's 'home'. In this paper we explore how paid domestic workers in Toronto, including Silke, negotiate the dynamics of their employer–employee relation.

As in Canada as a whole, live-in paid domestic work in Toronto is usually the work of migrant or immigrant women, especially 'third world' women of colour. However, most employers are white. Thus, our investigation of the employer–employee work relation hinges on an exploration of difference and diversity. Recent discussions in feminist studies stress the simultaneous and inseparable operation of various social relations of difference. In other words, social relations of difference are not merely additive; instead the experience of one transforms the experience of the others. Taken together, gender, 'race'/ethnicity, class, and so on form interlocking, relational systems of oppression and privilege within which there are a multiplicity of identities, which in turn gain meaning in relation to other identities (Spelman, 1988; hooks, 1989; Hill-Collins, 1990; McDowell, 1991; Kobayashi and Peake, 1994; Ruddick, 1996). In this paper we explore the experiential pluralities of women in paid domestic work.

Toward a Household Geography of Paid Domestic Work

Blurring the 'Public'/'Private' and 'Home'/'Work' Divides

Since 1981, Canada's federal policies have strictly stipulated that foreign domestic workers can only enter Canada if they 'live-in' for two years. Various advocacy groups have lobbied to remove the live-in requirement, but the government insists that the demand is only for live-in domestic workers, and that live-out jobs in domestic work can be easily filled by workers already in Canada (Employment and Immigration Canada, 1991, 1992). Live-in domestic work represents a peculiar form of paid employment and employer–employee relations.

First and foremost, the domestic worker's 'workplace' is her employer's home, with its high degree of personalism in a 'private' (as opposed to the more usual 'public') domain of work. So, live-in paid domestic work blurs the boundaries between 'home' and 'work' and 'public' and 'private', which in turn complicates the employer–employee relation. Secondly, the work relation is shaped by intimacy, affective labour, ideologies of the family, as well as public discourse about 'good mothering'. It is a work relation summarized by the notion that it is a 'labour of love' and that paid domestic workers are Like One of the Family (Childress, 1956).[2] Thirdly, that the boundary of public and private is blurred and even undefined, means that live-in domestic work can lead to exploitation (Rollins, 1985; Colen, 1989; Arat-Koç, 1992; Ng, 1993; Bakan and Stasiulis, 1994; Gregson and Lowe, 1994; Thornton-Dill, 1994). For example, Arat-Koç and Villasin (1990) found that 65 per cent of the domestic workers they surveyed in the Toronto area were routinely required to work overtime, 44 per cent of whom received no compensation.

When an employee is legally required to live-in as part of her job, work relations are complicated by antagonisms and ambiguities based on the merging of public 'work' and private 'home' spheres, and the emotional complexities of trying to simultaneously maintain both a personal relationship and a work relationship.

The literature on the experience of paid domestic workers highlights a set of commonalities. It tends to be characterized by oppressive material conditions, including isolation, loneliness, powerlessness, and invisibility. Even for the live-out domestic workers (who form the focus of many non-Canadian studies), exploitation is a frequent experience, imposed by long working hours, unpaid overtime, and limited time off. For some domestic workers, working in what they see as a low-status occupation means that stigma, low self-esteem, and low self-worth are also relatively common. In part, these experiences relate to the asymmetrical power relations between the domestic worker and her employer (Cock, 1980; Gaitskell et al., 1984; Rollins, 1985; Glenn, 1986, 1992; Bradshaw-Camball and Cohen, 1988;

Colen, 1989; Romero, 1992; Thornton-Dill, 1994; Mattingley, 1996). The characteristics and experiences of domestic work are further exacerbated when the domestic worker is 'living in'. Certainly, significant improvement in work experience is reported when the 'live-in' arrangement is removed (Colen, 1989; Romero, 1992). This is clearly the case in the US where the trend towards live-out, 'day-work', multiple employers and more formal work schedules has decreased the intensity of isolation, dependence and exploitation which are still features of live-in domestic work in Canada.

In Canada, at least, there is evidence that strongly suggests that paid domestic work has become racialized. Key to the process of racialization is the ideology that a domestic worker's relative worth is judged relative to the poverty (or wealth) of her country of origin. European women seem to be accorded more prestige than 'third world' women. Moreover, it seems that Europeans may receive higher pay, better treatment, and be regarded as 'nannies' in the strictest sense of doing mainly childcare. 'Third world' women may receive less pay and be treated less well, while being deemed 'domestics' who are expected to do extensive housework as well as childcare (Arat-Koç, 1992; Bakan and Stasiulis, 1994, 1995).

Employer–Employee Relations

Previous studies indicate that women are more likely to hire domestic workers if they are unable to negotiate an equitable division of domestic labour with their male partners (Rollins, 1985; Hertz, 1986; Arat-Koç, 1992; Ng, 1993; Gregson and Lowe, 1994). In other words, despite the growth in women's employment, women continue to be largely responsible for domestic work whether as paid domestic workers, or as 'managers' of domestic workers they hire. However, the gender commonality between employer and employee is often marked by myriad differences. For example, that immigrant women of colour are over-represented among domestic workers is naturalized as their being predisposed to domestic work (Rollins, 1985; Glenn, 1992; Macklin, 1992; Ng, 1993; Bakan and Stasiulis, 1995). Macklin (1992) demonstrates this point with the example

of Mary, the white Canadian employer of Delia, a Filipina domestic worker:

> Mary [can] objectify Delia in various ways that are influenced, but not precluded, by gender. For example, Mary can hardly claim that Delia is ideally suited to domestic work because she is a woman without impugning herself, but she can fall back on Filipino women being 'naturally' hard working, subservient, loyal, tidy housekeepers and 'good with children'. In this context, race, ethnicity and culture conjoin with sex to create a sub-category of women whose subordination other women can rationalize by projecting onto them the stereotypical 'feminine' qualities that patriarchy has used against women generally (1992: 754).

Of course, not all employer–employee relations in paid domestic work are exploitative and abusive. Bradshaw-Camball and Cohen (1988) suggest that the range and variety of employer–employee relations can be placed along two intersecting continua: one representing the domestic worker's 'sense of self-worth', the other representing the employer's 'concern with equity and fairness'. So, for instance, potentially exploitative work relations may result from an employer with little 'concern with equity and fairness' employing a domestic worker with a low 'sense of self-worth'. The employer's and domestic worker's location on these continua are mediated by issues of identity. Employers of domestic workers in Toronto are more likely to be white and middle-class and, most commonly, anglophone. On the other hand, domestic workers are frequently of a different 'race'/ethnicity, country of origin, immigration/ citizenship status, and language, and these differences can alter the complexion of employer–employee relations.

In this paper, we take the first word/third world dichotomy as a starting point. However, we want to avoid an over-emphasis on the fixed and oppositional categories of black/white dichotomy of 'race'. This is particularly important in the case of foreign domestic workers in Canada, because if the more subtle differences of language are not accentuated, Filipinas might not be differentiated from

Afro-Caribbeans (the two largest groups of foreign domestic workers in Canada). In light of the diversity among Canada's foreign domestic workers, we look at a number of groups of paid domestic workers in Toronto. Our analysis highlights the simultaneous operation of systems of difference (gender, 'race'/ethnicity, class, language, and so on) that texture the experience of paid domestic workers, and emphasizes that within these interlocking systems there are a range of locations with varying degrees of power and marginality.

Background to the Study

The empirical portion of our paper is based on our collaborative analysis of 18 lengthy, in-depth interviews conducted by Bernadette with women who were, or had been, paid domestic workers in Toronto (see Table 28.1; the women are identified by pseudonyms). The women were reached through notices in the offices of INTERCEDE and 'snowballing'. The women interviewed came from

nine countries of origin—Canada, England, France, Germany, Hungary, Eire, Jamaica, Philippines, and Thailand. In no way do we contend that this small sample is representative of all domestic workers in Toronto; rather, we believe these 18 women reflect some of the diverse identifies and experiences of this varied group of workers. The majority of the women were in their twenties and thirties, and all but two were single (the two who were married were also the only ones with children). One was Canadian, five were landed immigrants; of the others, five were on open permits (an immigration status between a temporary work permit and landed immigrant), and seven were on temporary work permits. Most of the women were live-ins, but three were live-outs and another three (who were no longer on temporary work permits) had recently left paid domestic work.

I (Bernadette) conducted the interviews, and quickly realized that my own identity was a significant factor in the subtle and not too subtle interactions between myself and the participants. My

Table 28.1 Characteristics of domestic workers interviewed

Pseudonym	Country of Origin	'Race'	First Language	Age (years)	Marital Status	Children	Year of arrival	Immigration Status	Live-in or Live-out
Barb	Canada	White	English	24	Single	0	N/A	Citizen	Live-in
Kath	England	White	English	22	Single	0	1989	Open	Live-in
Karen	England	White	English	23	Single	0	1993	Temp	Live-in
Sue	England	White	English	23	Single	0	1993	Temp	Live-in
Maryse	France	White	French	27	Single	0	1991	Temp	Live-in
Ingrid	Germany	White	German	29	Single	0	1991	Temp	Live-out
Silke	Germany	White	German	30	Single	0	1986	Landed	Live-out
Alena	Hungary	White	Hungarian	26	Single	0	1991	Open	Live-in
Anna	Hungary	White	Hingarian	27	Divorced	0	1990	Open	Live-out
Maggie	Eire	White	English	29	Single	0	1986	Landed	Live-in
Cynthia	Jamaica	Non-white	English	30	Single	0	1991	Temp	Live-in
Felicity	Jamaica	Non	English	35	Married	2	1992	Temp	Live-in
Edith	Philippines	Non	Tagalog	50s	Single	0	1986	Landed	House-keeper
Joan	Philippines	Non	Tagalog	32	Married	1	1987	Landed	Cashier[*]
Jocie	Philippines	Non	Tagalog	34	Single	0	1989	Open	Live-in
Naomi	Philippines	Non	Tagalog	28	Single	0	1991	Open	Live-in
Wilma	Philippines	Non	Tagalog	30	Single	0	1990	Open	Cashier[*]
Amy	Thailand	Non	Thai	30	Single	0	1989	Landed	Cashier[*]

* Woman with open/landed immigrant status who no longer works as a paid domestic worker.

country of origin (England), language and accent (southeast English), 'race' and culture (British West Indian), education (graduate student at the University of Toronto), and, of course, gender, all to some extent affected the negotiation of the 'betweenness' of the researcher–researched relationship. I was able to relate with great ease with the English and Irish women. We chatted quite generally about our shared experience of being 'Anglos' in Canada. There were also partial points of connection between the Jamaican women and myself in terms of a shared 'West Indian' identity—they disclosed a number of experiences and opinions that I do not believe they would have so readily revealed to a Canadian or white English interviewer. At the same time, however, there were occasions when I realized they had assumed rather too much common ground and I was unable to appreciate fully the more subtle nuances of everything they said because I am not Jamaican. Perhaps the greatest social distance was between the Filipina women and myself, which was in part due to a lack of shared language fluency and my unfamiliarity with their culture (all the interviews were conducted in English).

Employer–Employee Relations and the Construction of Difference

A number of major themes emerged from the interviews regarding the relationship between the paid domestic workers and their middle-class employers. In particular, we look at the domestic workers' experiences of living-in, being 'one of the family' and the degree of respect, dignity, and self-worth they feel. We not only consider these experiences around issues of class and 'race'/ethnicity, but in terms of domestic workers' immigration/citizenship status, country of origin (or nationality), and language.

Living-in

Living-in means you are on call 24 hours a day. Living-in means if (the employers) feel like going to a party at 10 o'clock, then that's ok, the nanny's there. And you don't get paid for that (Felicity, Jamaican).

More than any other issue that emerged from the interviews, the living-in requirement was unanimously cited as being especially problematic. However, this was not the case for every woman interviewed. As a white, anglophone Canadian, Barb was not required to live-in. She saw living-in as an opportunity to live away from her parents that enabled her to continue living in a comfortable middle-class home (something she could not afford if she was in a different occupation). Regardless of their motivations for coming to Canada or their long-term immigration goals, all the women who entered Canada as domestic workers/caregivers were legally required to live-in their employer's home for their first two years in Canada. Corroborating previous studies, we found that regardless of their identities, most of the women interviewed felt that they had experienced some level of exploitation through excessively long working hours, overtime without pay, restricted days off, or performing tasks outside their contract—all of which they attributed wholly or partially to their living-in. As Joan (Filipina) and Felicity (Jamaican) put it:

When you live-in they can demand a lot, because they see that you're there. In the night, if they want something to eat or drink, they will call you. As long as they are awake, then you have to stay awake with them too (Joan, Filipina).

I knew it wasn't going to be easy living in someone else's home. What I didn't prepare myself for was the subtle abuses. . . . Living-in means they come in at 5:30 pm, but you keep the kids until they've finished supper. Then you clean up, after you clean up, they might decide they want to go for ice cream or coffee, but you are still working. When you even mention that you're supposed to get overtime pay, they say 'You're a trouble-maker.' They say no one has ever asked for that before (Felicity, Jamaican).

Although exploitation was a general feeling, it is interesting to observe the ways in which different groups of domestic workers experienced these problems and how they were able to deal with them. One important issue was the perceived need to remain in an unsuitable job. When the English NNEB-trained[3] nannies reported enduring poor working or living conditions it was usually in their first job, which was often arranged before their arrival in Canada. These jobs often fell short of their expectations, but they remained with these employers in the pursuit of a good reference for their next job. As Kath described:

> My first job changed, that's why I was only there for a year. It was awful. They changed a lot of things once I got here . . . they wanted a housekeeper and they took the car away from me, extended my hours, but that just wasn't on. When I tried to talk to them about it they said they'd deal with it later, but later never came. When you're at college they drum it into you that you have to do your first year, you have to get that experience and then a good reference. They don't tell you how easy it is to get another job over here. So I stuck it out, I was unhappy, but I did it (Kath, English).

For a number of the 'third world' women, it was their desire to apply for landed immigrant status that may have led them to put up with intolerable conditions and treatment from their employers. In a number of instances, domestic work provided much-needed remittance to support children and relatives in their homeland. Changing jobs entailed bureaucratic delays, considerable expense, and could reduce their chances of being viewed as reliable and hard-working when they came to submit their application for landed-immigrant status. Lack of freedom to change jobs, negotiate with employers or even complain about their treatment was expressed by a number of 'third world' women, including Cynthia and Jocie:

> Each time you have to change jobs, you pay Immigration $100. . . . It doesn't look good on your record—that's why a lot of people take the abuse, you can't be bothered changing this and that. And then the probability of you meeting someone who is decent is 0.000000 up to infinity 1 (Cynthia, Jamaican).

> There's less problem [with Filipinas], because they don't complain. Even though they get into trouble, they just stay quiet. You know why? Because they don't want to get bad record from government. They want their immigration status (Jocie, Filipina).

For most, living-in contributed to the feelings of isolation and loneliness associated with their job. Joan (a Filipina carer of an elderly couple) remarked that 'when you live-in, you feel lonely, when you don't see anybody, just this old couple'; and Amy (Thai) said that: 'My first employer never made me feel as if their home was mine. I missed my family. I became very lonesome and they wouldn't allow my friends to visit.' Many of the domestic workers said that they felt like an intruder in their employer's house. For example, paid domestic workers are often segregated to selected areas of the household at specific times of the day—a practice that Romero (1992) terms 'spatial deference' (also see Glenn, 1992). Cynthia (Jamaican) illustrated this concept when she talked of her employer's insistence on family privacy extending to making Cynthia wait until they had finished eating the meal that she had prepared, before 'crawling out of my room to get something to eat'. Of course, 'spatial deference' highlights the use of space to reinforce the invisibility expected of domestic workers when their services were not required; and the 'non-person', invisible identity domestic workers are expected to assume emphasizes the significance of geography at the household scale.

Typically, the women resented living-in because it often engendered a feeling of being trapped and also impinged upon their independence as adults. This was summed up by Joyce (Filipina): 'I'm living under someone else's rules' and Ingrid (German): 'I don't have to tell them where I'm going or what I'm doing all the time, but they ask anyway.' Such feelings were exacerbated by the family's lack of respect for the domestic worker's privacy and space, especially when they have to share a bathroom, or if their bedrooms are all on the same floor. Immigration Canada states that employers should 'provide accommodation which ensures privacy, such as a private room with a lock on the door,' for which room and board is deducted monthly (Employment and Immigration Canada, 1992). Six of the women said that in at least one job they had bedroom doors without locks, which sometimes resulted in members of the family entering without knocking. Generally, living-in was less resented in more equitable, respectful employer–employee relationships, and the more privacy and freedom the women had, the more content they tended to be living-in. Once in a 'good job', compromises were less frequent and usually compensated, and/or appreciated.

'Like One of the Family'?

> You're supposed to feel so privileged to be part of their family that you overlook everything else (Cynthia, Jamaican).

The interviews indicated that 'living-in' was an almost uniformly problematic experience for the women, but that the experience of being 'like one of the family' was less even. The emotional involvement of domestic workers in private households can result in mutual friendships with the employers. Rollins (1985) even uses the term 'maternalism' to convey the highly gendered and personal nature of this type of work relation, where women's supportive, nurturing roles alter the power dynamic. While nationality, 'race'/ ethnicity, and class differences are very significant, the extent and way in which personalism is experienced obviously also depends on the personalities of the individual domestic worker and her employer. However, we think the interviews suggest that more equitable, mutually supportive, and respectful relationships were most often experienced where there was greater similarity in the identities of the domestic worker and her employer.

More than any other group, the white anglophones (Canadian, English, and Irish) reported having more informal and symmetrical relationships with their employers, sometimes describing their employers as 'friends', or feeling that they are considered to be 'like one of the family'. As Barb (Canadian) told Bernadette:

> Sometimes we go from being like best friends to employer–employee. There's a line you can't cross when you're in this job. It's kinda weird, sometimes you're really good friends, and sometimes you can just say the wrong thing, if you are not in the friendship mode (Barb, Canadian).

However, being 'like one of the family' was also interpreted by some of the woman as a means of extracting further unpaid physical and affective labour, without the genuine caring and respect associated with familial relationships. Gregson and Lowe (1994) describe such relations as false kinship ties. Felicity expresses her disdain at what she felt were false displays of affection and kinship from her white employer:

> What I can't deal with is the idea that because I mop their floors, I'm stupid. They can do anything they want to me. They don't have to respect you, but they come with this disguise, 'Oh, you're part of the family.' They hug you. I don't want to be hugged! For God's sake, I'm your employee, treat me like an employee! I don't want to be hugged. But that's their way of trying to outsmart you. It's emotional blackmail. You're meant to think, 'This nice white lady, she's hugging me.' Then I'm supposed to take everything they dish out. I don't want that. I just want to be respected as a worker, with an employer–employee relationship (Felicity, Jamaican).

Both Jamaican women with whom Bernadette spoke objected to what they considered to be a patronizing emotional association. Their comments also reflect Rollins' (1985) and Romero's (1992) observations that personalism across racial lines is often advantageous to the employer. Women of colour can become safe confidants for their middle class, white employers, as they each tend to have entirely different social networks. The inherent power relation means that the middle-class, white employer need not fear rebuttal, disapproval or rejection.

Of course, no matter how symmetrical the employer–employee relationship, there still remains a status differential in terms of the work relation. Maryse (French) came to Canada as a nanny to learn English. In her first job she had difficulties based on her language ability. However, in her present job, class has emerged as a prominent factor in her relationship with her employer, who does not have a paid job outside the home:

> She's not from a rich family, but, because she's married to a neuro-surgeon, she feels she must live a good life . . . she's not a bad person, she's just snobby, and because of that it makes a big difference. She's a woman, she says 'It's because I pay (you) I need everything, you have to give me everything.' And she's really demanding. When she wants something, she wants it now. She's just like a spoilt kid (Maryse, French).

We see the intersection of gender and class as very evident here. Asymmetric power relations are enforced because Maryse's employer feels that she should be able to purchase obedience through her husband's class position and her status as his wife. The gendered character of the domestic division of labour also comes into play as the employer sees herself as paying Maryse to do 'her' chores. Moreover, it seems to us that the deference inherent in this type of work relation may have placed the employer in a position of power not otherwise available to her as a 'housewife'. This power differential seemed to have been internalized by Maryse who said: 'You feel like a real slave. . . . I feel extremely humiliated sometimes. I know I shouldn't take it that way, but it's the way I feel'.

The introduction of 'race'/ethnicity differences into an already asymmetrical relationship multiplies the subtleties of those differences already inherent in class difference. Cynthia and Felicity (Jamaicans) both told Bernadette that they had experienced racism (as well as classism), often in quite overt and complex ways. Felicity maintained that racism was fundamental to explaining her situation, although she clearly understood that it is impossible to untangle 'race' from other structures of differentiation.

> Sometimes when they treat you badly, it's because you're black, and they really just don't

have any respect for you as a human being, no matter how educated, well-spoken, and no matter how good you are with the kids. But it's also because they pay you to be in their house that makes it even worse, you become nothing in their eyes. I can't tell you why, there are so many reasons, but they happen together, we come as one package. . . . They just abuse, abuse, abuse you. It doesn't matter how intelligent you may appear to be, they just look at you as a black helper. . . . Colour doesn't have any respect for class. They will still see you as a helper, no matter what (Felicity, Jamaican).

In short, intimacy, affective labour, and a high degree of personalism often veil the asymmetrical class relation associated with paid domestic employment. However, we think the interviews also reveal that the class relation is constructed in relation to interlocking systems of 'race'/ethnicity and gender.

Respect, Dignity, and Self-Worth

> I'm pretty well respected . . . what you say goes, and they're willing to come around to what you want. Well this one (her current employer), more than the first one. They know what you're capable of. She's always had NNEBs. She knows what to expect (Kath, English).

Respect and dignity are fundamental to a person's feeling of self-worth and self-esteem, and are important in defining the dynamics of the social relations of paid domestic work. It does seem that the degree of respect experienced by different groups of domestic workers is highly variable and nuanced, with the overriding significant factor being the precise nature of each employer– employee relation—the attitude of the employer to her employee, and the ability of each domestic worker to be assertive in a given situation. The relative presence or absence of respect in the employer–employee work relation can also indicate the level of asymmetry in the power relation. Bradshaw-Camball and Cohen's (1988) concepts of the employer's 'concern with equity and fairness' versus the employee's 'sense of self-worth' are useful here.

As a white, anglophone Canadian, Barb shared the same citizenship and (at least in terms of her family background) class position as her employer. So, relative to the foreign domestic workers Bernadette interviewed, Barb experienced the most symmetrical power relations with her employer.

My dad is not poor. I am not a poor person, I'm basically pretty privileged. My boss finds it weird that I'm on the same social scale as she is. I'm not impressed by the car she drives, or the house she lives in, so in a way that is different. I'm Canadian, I speak near-perfect English, and I'm educated . . . (our relationship) is pretty good. Having me was a bit of an adjustment because she was used to having a Filipina nanny, and to have someone who understands everything she says to me, and someone who's not going to fight her exactly, but not meekly let her walk all over me, was a big change for her. Sometimes we have our altercations over it. Other than that she really likes me, and I really like her (Barb, Canadian).

Barb's confident and assertive personality must be placed in the broader context of her identity. Barb makes the interconnections between numerous systems of difference when explaining her reasonably symmetrical work relation. She does not stress her class background alone. Her country of origin (including its relative wealth), citizenship, language, and education intersect to construct her relatively privileged position. Indeed, the openly contested nature of this work relation appears to have presented more challenges for Barb's employer, who had been in a position of clear authority and control with her previous Filipina employee. As Barb put it: 'The difference with me is that I have more choice, more freedom. Tomorrow if I think "well, screw you", I can walk out the door and go home.' Barb became a nanny because she 'loves kids', but she only saw her job as 'something to do for now'. We argue that Barb's secure social, economic, and political status as a Canadian, without immigration or employment restrictions, helped create a much more equitable power relation between her and her employer.

The other groups of foreign domestic workers seldom expressed the same level of friendship with, or respect from their employers. English language difficulties can distance non-anglophone domestic workers (even those from Europe) from the mutual respect or intimacy of personal friendship. Although they often talked about respect and mutuality, the non-anglophone domestic workers also talked of being made to feel 'stupid' because of language and communication difficulties:

These employers respect me, they respect what I have to say about the children, what I think should happen. They respect me (but sometimes) I think they must think that we are pretty stupid. . . . They really underestimated my intelligence, which is really insulting (Silke, German).

However, it seemed to us that the non-anglophone Europeans often challenged their employers when they 'underestimated their intelligence'. As Anna (Hungarian) told Bernadette, 'If your English is not that great, they think you're as stupid as your English is. But the first time you show that you are not, they know it!' We feel it is important to differentiate between East and West Europeans. For instance, Anna and Alena (Hungarians) experienced further degrees of isolation and alienation based on their transition from a socialist background to the Western culture of Canada. Alena felt that her employer had been especially neglectful of her responsibilities towards her foreign employee, and was insensitive to Alena's 'culture shock'. She felt that this, combined with her feelings of powerlessness and her employer's apparent lack of respect for her needs, prevented Alena from objecting to her employer's demands for emotional support:

She's a single mother, when she comes home after a hard day, I am her spouse! When she talks to me about her troubles, all her hard times at work, somewhere behind that (is) 'what an easy life you've got'. Sometimes she wants to comfort me and say 'I know how hard your day can be', but basically, I know what she thinks. Many times we ended up talking, imagine, I am desperate to get to my room. . . . I am willing to listen to her, but I'm very bothered by the fact that I'm paid there (and) she's still the boss actually, no matter how friendly she is. (And the) fact that she can use those things against you (in day-to-day confrontations and negotiations, or even with Employment and Immigration Canada), if I start talking about my problems (Alena, Hungarian).

This situation is clearly not a mutually supportive emotional relationship. The asymmetric power relation is obvious, and it is only the emotional needs of the employer that are being met, with little consideration for the boundaries of the work relation, or Alena's personal needs.

'Race'/ethnicity differences further reinforced feelings of language inferiority, particularly if the employers did not seem to respect their employees efforts to learn English. Moreover, having their intellect demeaned was a particularly familiar experience for the Thai and Filipina women, as Amy (Thai) and Joan (Filipina) show:

I didn't get on well with my employer. I couldn't speak English well. After seven months things got better, but they think you are stupid because you can't speak English, so they over-work you, they think you don't know the rules. . . . I was so upset when I heard them call me stupid. That made me determined to learn to speak English (Amy, Thai).

The interviews are full of statements that illustrate that the stereotype of the uneducated, poor, 'third world' domestic worker of colour, who cannot speak English is so persuasive and potent that it can lead to their educational achievements or middle-class background being discounted. Joan described her previous job:

At my last employer, her daughter—she were talking to me, asking me about life in the Philippines. . . . And I was telling her, I never worked as a domestic back home. All of my family are educated, all the children

and everything. And she felt that because she was not educated, she was just a high school graduate, working in Bell Canada, she felt like I am over her. She said to me, even though you are educated, they don't acknowledge your education here and you still belong to poor country. That's what she told me! I don't say anything, because I think I hurt her feelings in some way. She had to find some way to put me down. I just don't say anything. I feel bad, but I just don't say anything. I just keep quiet (Joan, Filipina).

It is evident that Joan disrupted and challenged the 'third world domestic' stereotype. This family member reasserted an asymmetric power relation by reconstructing Joan as a 'third word domestic' by discounting her worth, achievements and background as 'inferior' to her own.

As with personalism, a 'sense of self-worth' is dependent on a number of structural factors, including 'race'/ethnicity, class, education, and training, as well as other factors such as personality, life experience, support networks and family responsibilities. Similarly, the employer's 'concern with equity and fairness' can also be related to her own and her employee's identity, personality, and life experiences. Overall, the interviews indicated to us that the white anglophones generally appeared to have a higher degree of confidence and a stronger 'sense of self-worth', enabling them to be more assertive, while non-anglophones and women of colour experienced increasing degrees of difficulty in negotiating their position and gaining their employer's respect.

Conclusions

Our paper illustrates how paid domestic workers' experiences of the employer–employee relation are mediated through an interlocking, relational system of difference, particularly gender, class, 'race'/ethnicity, immigration/citizenship status, and language. Commonalities of gender and occupation by domestic workers are cross-cut by locations of privilege and marginality in terms of class, citizenship/immigration status, 'race'/ethnicity, country of origin, training, and language. The most privileged was the white, anglophone Canadian who experienced the most freedom, choice, and power, which meant she had a much more secure, symmetrical relationship with her employer compared to many of her foreign counterparts. Of the foreign domestic workers interviewed, the specific articulation of systems of difference led to a range of experiences of the extent of asymmetry in employer–employee power relations, with the greatest symmetry tending to be in those situations where the employee and employer held more similar positions in the social relations of difference.

However, we also want to emphasize that many of the women interviewed shared a number of common concerns. Almost all the domestic workers had, at some stage, experienced difficulties related to living-in, especially in dealing with employers who frequently demanded additional duties not stated on their contracts. But those who are less marginalized tended to be better able to negotiate these situations. Their locations in the systems of difference often related to their 'sense of self-worth' in terms of their occupation and their experience of respect. One result tended to be that anglophone 'nannies', unlike 'third world' 'domestic workers' were more likely to find jobs with better hours and less or no housework.

We have attempted to provide insights into the dynamic, complex, and interrelated character of the processes that shape employer–employee relations marked by the antagonisms, contradictions, and ambiguities associated with a 'workplace' being someone else's 'home'. We have stressed that specific articulations of difference (as well as the specific context and the individual personalities involved) produce difference constellations of experiences of live-in paid domestic work.

Notes

1. We thank the staff and volunteers of intercede for their time and access to their resources. We also thank women who participated in this research: they are identified by pseudonyms. We are grateful to Kevin Cox, Nancy Duncan, Linda McDowell, Lynn Staeheli and the three reviewers for their helpful comments on an earlier version of this paper. Bernadette Stiell was partly funded by the Canadian Memorial Foundation.

2. Alice Childress's book is a fictional account that draws on lived experiences from the everyday lives of African American domestic workers.

3. The NNEB (National Nursery Examination Board) diploma is offered only in Britain. It is a two-year, post-secondary training program and is one of the most widely recognized qualifications in childcare.

References

Arat-koç, S. 1992. 'In the Privacy of Our Own Home: Foreign Domestic Workers as Solution to the Crisis of the Domestic Sphere in Canada', in M.P. Connelly and P. Armstrong, eds., *Feminism in Action: Studies in Political Economy*, pp. 149–75. Toronto: Canadian Studies Press.

Arat-koç, S., and F. Villansin. 1990. 'Report and Recommendations on the Foreign Domestic Movement Program'. Submitted to the Ministry of Employment and Immigration on behalf of intercede, Toronto Organization for Domestic Workers' Rights.

Bakan, A.B., and D. Stasiulis. 1994. 'Foreign Domestic Worker Policy in Canada and the Social Boundaries of Modern Citizenship', *Science and Society* 58: 7–33.

———. 1995. 'Making the Match: Domestic Placement Agencies and the Racialization of Women's Household Work', *Signs* 20: 303–35.

Bradshaw-Cambrall, P., and R. Cohen. 1988. 'Feminists: Explorers or Exploiters', *Women and Environments* 11: 8–10.

Childress, A. 1956. *Like One of the Family*. Brooklyn, NY: Independence.

Cock, J. 1980. *Maids and Madams: A Study in the Politics of Exploitation*. Johannesburg: Raven Press.

Colen, S. 1989. '"Just a little respect": West Indian Domestic Workers in New York City', in E.M.

Chaney and M.G. Castro, eds., *Muchachas No More: Household Workers in Latin America and the Caribbean*, pp. 171–94. Philadelphia: Temple University Press.

Employment and Immigration Canada. 1991. *Foreign Domestic Workers: Preliminary Statistical Highlight Report*. Ottawa: Employment and Immigration Canada.

———. 1992. *The Live-in Caregiver Program: Information for Employers and Live-in Caregivers from Abroad*. Ottawa: Employment and Immigration Canada.

Gaitskell, D., J. Kimble, M. Manconachie, and E. Unterhalther. 1984. 'Class, Race, and Gender: Domestic Workers in South Africa', *Review of African Political Economy* 27/28: 86–108.

Glenn, E.N. 1986. *Issei, Nisei, War Bride: Three Generations of Japanese American Women and Domestic Service*. Philadelphia: Temple University Press.

———. 1992. 'From Servitude to Service Work: Historical Continuities in the Racial Division of Paid Reproductive Labor', *Signs* 18: 1–43.

Gregson, N., and M. Lowe. 1994. *Servicing the Middle Classes: Class, Gender and Waged Domestic Work in Contemporary Britain*. London and New York: Routledge.

Hertz, R. 1986. *More Equal Than Others: Women and Men in Dual-career Marriages*. Berkeley, CA: University of California Press.

Hill-Collins, P. 1990. *Black Feminist Thought: Knowledge, Consciousness and the Politics of Empowerment*. London and New York: Routledge.

hooks, b. 1989. *Talking Back—Thinking Feminist, Thinking Black*. Boston: South End Press.

Kobayashi, A., and L. Peake. 1994. 'Unnatural Discourse: 'Race' and Gender in Geography', *Gender, Place and Culture* 1: 225–43.

Macklin, A. 1992. 'Foreign Domestic Worker: Surrogate Housewife or Mail Order Bride?', *McGill Law Journal* 37: 681–760.

Mattingley, D. 1996. 'Domestic Service, Migration, and Local Labor Markets on the US–Mexican Border', PhD dissertation. Graduate School of Geography, Clark University, Worcester, MA.

McDowell, L. 1991. 'The Baby and the Bath Water: Diversity, Deconstruction and Feminist Theory in Geography', *Geoforum* 22: 123–33.

Ng, R. 1993. 'Racism, Sexism, and Immigrant Women', in B. Sadra, L. Code, and L. Dorney, eds., *Changing Patterns: Women in Canada*, pp. 279–301. Toronto: McClelland and Stewart.

Rollins, J. 1985. *Between Women: Domestics and Their Employers*. Philadelphia: Temple University Press.

Romero, M. 1992. *Maid in the USA*. London and New York: Routledge.

Ruddick, S. 1996. 'Constructing Difference in Public Spaces: Race, Class, and Gender as Interlocking Systems', *Urban Geography* 17: 132–51.

Spelman, E. 1988. *Inessential Woman: Problems of Exclusion in Feminist Thought*. Boston: Beacon Books.

Thornton-Dill, B. 1994. *Across Boundaries of Class and Race: An Exploration of the Relationship between Work and Family among Black Female Domestic Servants*. New York: Garland Publishing.

QUESTIONS FOR CRITICAL THOUGHT

1. Are you currently training for a particular type of work, or do you have a particular career in mind? Do you expect that your gender will influence your success in this career?

2. If you work with people of different genders, whether in a part-time or full-time job, how do you think gender might affect workplace experiences? If your workplace is dominated by one gender, why is that the case?

3. Why do you think women still make less money in their paid jobs than men? Is it because of individual choices or systematic barriers? Or both? Or neither?

4. The male nurses that Evans studied were clearly considered unusual for working in a field dominated by women. Are there any kinds of work that you think would be difficult for you, or that you would not want to take, because of your gender?

5. What workplaces have you encountered as a worker, customer, or visitor that are dominated by one sex or the other? What workplaces have you encountered that are more equally divided between the sexes?

6. As Stiell and England suggest, the division between 'work' and 'home' is not always straightforward. How do you distinguish between these two spheres? In what ways is home like work, or work like home?

PART VIII

The Gendered Media

The idea of Canada as a media-saturated society has become a cliché, and pop sociology accounts of how the media influence ideas and behaviours abound. In the most simplistic of these accounts, men and women imitate the images of masculinity and femininity that they see on their screens and in their pages, so that young women aspire to being sexually provocative and skinny, while young men take on the macho trappings of violence.

The authors in this section go beyond this monkey-see-monkey-do approach to media and gender to examine how gender is constituted and represented in media products, focusing on the products (or 'mediated texts') themselves. Ideas about gender appear in ways that are not obvious or overt, and are often much more complex than they might seem at first glance.

Christie Barron and Dany Lacombe examine the ways that violence among girls has become a spectacle in news media, presented as shocking and horrific. They use the concept of a 'moral panic' to make the case that the attention given to extreme and isolated cases of murderous girls such as those who killed Reena Virk is a manifestation of profound social ambivalence about girls who are strong, tough, and sometimes 'nasty'—girls who, in other words, are just like boys.

Toughness and strength (although not 'nastiness'!) are also at issue in Elizabeth Gidengil and Johanna Everett's analysis of how party leaders' debates have been covered on Canadian TV. They use a detailed, highly specific accounting of metaphors and descriptive phrases, comparing them with observed behaviours, to argue that even in a world where women have been prime ministers and party leaders, TV news coverage is not gender-blind. They note that female politicians who show any assertiveness tend to be described as aggressive attackers, while the familiar language of heroic sports metaphors is reserved for male politicians only.

Sports metaphors get another workout in Stacey Lorenz and Geraint Osborne's look backwards at the early days of hockey in the nineteenth century. They demonstrate both the persistence of sports as an arena for defining and displaying hegemonic masculinity—men as tough, relentless, and immune to pain—and the various types of normative masculinity available to men, from the respectable middle-class head of household to the 'rowdy roughs' who populated the hockey rink and the stands.

The first three articles in this section address the reinforcement of stereotypes about gender in the mainstream media. In her contribution, Alison Jacques examines how such media responded to a subculture driven by the explicit deconstruction and rejection of these stereotypes, in the form of the 'riot grrl' movement of the 1990s. She highlights the contradictions and ambivalences of this media treatment, whereby opinion leaders such as *Seventeen* and *Rolling Stone* spread the word about the 'grrls', while simultaneously repackaging the 'riot grrl' concept into tame, non-threatening commodities.

CHAPTER 29

Moral Panic and the Nasty Girl

Christie Barron and Dany Lacombe

Female violence became a topic of much discussion in the mid-1990s in the wake of the gruesome sexual murders of teenagers by the infamous Ontario couple Paul Bernardo and Karla Homolka. But it was the murder of Reena Virk by a group of mostly female teens, in a suburb of Victoria in November 1997, which led Canadians to believe that something had gone terribly wrong with teenage girls. The belief that girl violence is rampant is a social construction. According to Statistics Canada, the annual youth charge rate for violent crime dropped 5 per cent in 1999, signalling a decline for the fourth year in a row (Statistics Canada, 2000). Moreover, Doob and Sprott (1998) have shown that the severity of youth violence did not change in the first half of the 1990s. Questioning the federal government's concern about the increase in girls' participation in violent and gang-related activities, Reitsma-Street (1999: 350) indicates that the number of girls charged for murder and attempted murder has been constant for the past 20 years and that such charges are infrequent. Although statistics indicate a phenomenal increase in the number of young women charged with minor or moderate assault over the past 10 years (from 710 charged under the Juvenile Delinquents Act in 1980 to 4,434 under the Young Offenders Act in 1995–6), several researchers indicate that the increase is more a reflection of the youth justice system's change in policy and charging practices than a 'real' change in behaviour (Doob and Sprott, 1998; Reitsma-Street, 1999). Yet the

public continues to believe that youth violence, particularly girl violence, is increasing at an alarming rate and necessitates immediate attention (Chesney-Lind and Brown, 1999: 171). This perception begs the important question: Why, despite evidence to the contrary, are recent isolated incidents of female violence interpreted as a sign that today's girls have become increasingly 'nasty'?

We argue that the recent alarm over girl violence is the product of a moral panic that has had a significant impact on social, educational, and legal policy-making. Drawing on the moral panic and risk society literature, as well as the work of Michel Foucault, this paper examines how the recent concern with girl violence emerged; what effects that concern has had on policy-making in particularly and on society in general; and why the panic over young females is occurring today.

How the Nasty Girl Emerged

All moral panics identify and denounce a personal agent responsible for the condition that is generating widespread public concern. As Schissel explains, 'Folk devils are inherently deviant and are presumed to be self-seeking, out of control and in danger of undermining the stability of society . . .' (1997: 30). Hence, during the 'warning phase' of a panic there are predictions of impending doom, sensitization to cues of danger, frequent overreactions, and rumours speculating about what is happening or what will happen (Cohen, 1980: 144–8). Subsequently, a large part of the public becomes sensitized to the threat, and, as in the case of the Nasty Girl, when confronted with an actual act of girl violence their perception of danger and risk solidifies.

It is not surprising, therefore, that the beating and murder of 14-year-old Reena Virk by a group of seven girls and one boy would become the event that provided evidence that girl violence had become a significant problem in Canada. On 14 November 1997, Virk, 'a pudgy East Indian girl trying desperately to fit in', (Cernetig, Laghi, Matas, and McInnes, 1997: A1) was on her way back to her foster home when friends asked her to join them under the bridge, a popular hangout. According to trial testimony, an argument broke out and accusations were directed at Virk for spreading rumours about one of the girls, talking to another's boyfriend, and rifling through the address book of another (Tafler, 1998: 20). The news that Virk was beaten to death by a youth group, part of 'a teen subculture where girls pretending to be members of L.A. street gangs fight each other,' shocked the country. According to *The Globe and Mail*, Reena's death became: 'A national tragedy' (Cernetig et al., 1997: A1).

Central to the creation of a climate of fear is statistical manipulation of crime data to establish the amplitude of girl violence. As journalist N. Nolan astutely recognizes in her analysis of the media reporting of the Virk case: 'Experts and authors were appearing on TV and radio talk shows trumpeting— with the solemn self-importance that always accompanies adult laments about the various wickedness of youth—the shocking fact that, according to the Canadian Centre for Justice Statistics, crime by young girls had increased 200 per cent since 1986' (1998: 32). However, most articles failed to recognize that the increase was in reference to minor assaults, such as pushing or slapping, which did not cause serious injury. Doob and Sprott explain, 'One would, we believe, have more confidence that this increase reflected a change in girls' behaviour if it were to have shown up in the 'most serious' category of assaults' (1998: 192).[1] At the time of Virk's murder, girls were still far less involved than

boys in all levels of assault and only 4.5 per cent of youths charged with a homicide offence were female (1998: 192). Moreover, according to more recent official statistics, the rate of male youth crime is almost three times higher than the female rate and, in 1999, the violent crime rate dropped (–6.5 per cent) for female youths (Statistics Canada, 2000). Yet, inflated statistics about girl violence are usually assumed to be factual because, as Cohen (1980) explains, they are voiced by 'socially accredited experts' whose expertise alone serves to legitimize the moral panic.

Historically, as Klein (1995) details, female offenders were described by experts as masculinized monsters (Lombroso, 1920), insensitive and lacking moral values (Thomas, 1907), envious of men due to lack of a penis (Freud, 1933), psychologically maladjusted (Pollack, 1950), and promiscuous (Davis, 1961) (all as cited in Madriz, 1997: 26). Moreover, conceptions of morality increasingly became central to the identification and supervision of 'dangerous' females. As the legitimate guardians of the moral sphere, middle-class women, in particular, participated in social purity movements that succeeded in criminalizing females who used their sexuality to survive. The reformers' efforts to rescue 'fallen women' and 'delinquent girls' from the harmful effects of industrial capitalism indicate how the bourgeois preoccupation with uplifting moral standards became central to the supervision of working-class girls.

Such reform movements also led to the establishment of child welfare agencies and the creation of juvenile justice systems. The youth criminal court evolved as a judicial parent or 'parens patriae' that signalled the increasing involvement of the state in regulating and rehabilitating adolescent behaviour (Geller, 1987: 116). Girls, in particular, were deemed vulnerable and were incarcerated for status offences for their own protection, both from themselves and others. In the mid-twentieth century, the popularization of psychology helped foster a shift in the understanding of unruly girls and women: from being inherently bad or immoral they became inherently mad (Faith and Jiwani, 2002: 87). As Myers and Sangster uncovered in their study of Canadian reform schools for girls from 1930–60, the 'girl problem' was construction by 'psychologists, penal workers, administrators and nuns whose preconceived expert knowledge about the nature of young women shaped their reconstructions of delinquent girls' rebellions within a language of irrationality, incredulity, and pathology' (2001: 669).

Overall, the dominant idea throughout most of the twentieth century was that females who offend are rejecting their feminine role and are emulating their male counterpart. Consequently, many criminologists feared the impact of the 1960s women's movement on the feminine role.

Lacking from media analyses of female violence is the considerable impact of structural factors, including institutional racism, and economic and social inequality in the life of young female offenders and their victims. As Faith and Jiwani contend: 'Significantly absent in the range of explanations put forward by the media was Reena Virk's marginalized positioning vis-à-vis those who had beaten and killed her. The issue of race and racism was either absent from the media discourse or presented in terms of her inability to fit in' (2002: 101–2). In a re-examination of her research data, Artz (2004) draws on social interdependence theory to acknowledge the importance of social structures in girls' use of violence because they 'provide us with clues as to how people may be interpreting self and world and how they may be morally positioned with regard to their actions' (Artz, 2004: 104).

In summary, we have drawn on the moral panic literature to examine the recent preoccupation with the violent girl. We argued that through distortion, exaggeration, and statistical manipulation of data, as well as expert evidence, the media was able to construct a new breed of female, the Nasty Girl, who has become one of our current folk devils. This construction is not without consequences: 'We want assurances that what happened to Reena couldn't happen to anybody else' asserts the popular magazine *Chatelaine*, because 'after all, next time it might be my daughter or yours who is the victim' (Martin, 1998: 71). In a climate of fear, Schissel (1997: 30) reminds us, it is easier 'for average citizens to become embroiled in the alarm over [folk devils] and to call for harsh justice.'

Unfortunately, the reforms resorted to in a time of panic often fail to address the real source of public anxiety. It is to those reforms that we now turn.

The Effects of the Moral Panic on Policy-Making

The panic over the Nasty Girl has had a significant impact on legal, educational, and social policy in Canada. The result has been an increase in both formal and informal mechanisms of control. While proposals for legal reform mostly consist of repressive measures targeted at delinquent youths, social and educational programs contain informal mechanisms of control targeting society more generally. As we show in this section, proposals for reform are not only disciplinary mechanisms of power acting on the body of the individual delinquent; they are also part of the more recent governmental techniques of power which regulate and mange free individuals through the fostering of a culture of risk management, public safety, and security consciousness (Foucault, 1982; Cohen, 1985; O'Malley, 1996; Garland, 1997).

While harsh legal policy is aimed at incapacitating both violent boys and girls, informal mechanisms of control targeting young girls in particular have also resulted from the panic over girl violence. These mechanisms, however, did not emerge from within the centre of the criminal justice apparatus; rather, they evolved at the margins of society, through the work of social agencies, activists, and experts who helped create a consensus about the problem of girl violence. This groundwork has produced new definitions of violence and new methods of controlling both young females and society in general.

The new rationality and concern actively seeks the participation of authorities in the informal control of girls. For example, Pepler and Sedighdeilami's caution that 'Girls in families with violence, ineffective parenting, and high levels of conflict should be identified for supportive interventions' (1998: iii) encourages school staff to observe and detect signs of risk in girls. The popular magazine *Today's Parent*, in an article entitled,

'When the Tough Get Going . . . the Going Gets Tough: How to Deal with Bullies', promotes parents becoming detectives through continuous observation of their children, since bullying is an 'underground activity'. Stuart Auty, president of the Canadian Safe School Network, is known to give parents his expert advice on how to steer children away from violence, including basic strategies such as 'knowing your kid, staying connected and providing them with opportunities to develop their self-esteem, as well as establishing limits and consequences when rules are broken' (cited in Martin, 1998: 77). While it is ironic that mainstream parental and educational advice is now repackaged as state-of-the-art technology to prevent bullying, we see in this strategy a sign of the current shift in crime control policy that Foucauldian scholars have identified as 'government-at-a-distance' (Rose and Miller, 1992; Garland, 1997).

As we know from Foucault's studies of the asylum, the prison, and sexuality, power—which he also refers to as 'governmentality'—is better understood as a rationality evolving from the margins of society than as one concentrated exclusively in its centre, the state. It is in the interstice between the state and the individual—that is to say, in the social field occupied by the school, the hospital, the juvenile court, and social workers' and psychologists' offices, that different forms of rationality emerge and produce their disciplinary and regulatory effects onto the social body. Diverse professionals and agencies come together to govern the behaviour and mentality of both those who pose problems, such as the violent girl, and those they can enlist in the management of the violent girl. While the strategies of power produced in those 'centres of governance' (Garland, 1997: 179–80) have disciplinary effects meant to break and tame those at the receiving end, some act through the subjects for the purpose of creating a 'responsibilized autonomy' in them. For example, since Virk's death, expert advice encourages parents, teachers, and youth to change their behaviour and self-image to bring them into line with socially approved desires and identities, and, in the process, ensure the good functioning of the family and the school. The participation of these individuals in the management of the violent girl does not rely on force, but rests instead upon an alliance expert authorities, which is grounded in what Garland perceives as 'willingness of individuals—whether as family members, or workers, citizens—to exercise a 'responsibilized' autonomy, and to pursue interests and desires in ways which are socially approved and legally sanctioned' (1997: 180). This strategy of governmental power, Garland continues, characterizes most current crime control policy:

> State authorities . . . seek to enlist other agencies and individuals to form a chain of coordinated action that reaches into criminogenic situations, prompting crime-control conduct on the part of 'responsibilized' actors (see Garland, 1996). Central to this strategy is the attempt to ensure that all the agencies and individuals who are in a position to contribute to these crime-reducing ends come to see it as being in their interests to do so. 'Government' is thus extended and enhanced by the creation of 'governors' and 'guardians' in the space between the state and the offender (Garland, 1997: 188).

Youths are particularly targeted by this strategy of power grounded in a 'responsibilized' autonomy. For example, as part of its 'Taking a Stand' program, the BC government made available a toll-free, province-wide phone number to 'prevent crime and violence and to offer youth a safe, confidential means to obtain information and help.' The 'Youth against Violence Line' wallet card distributed to schools invites young people to phone in and report incidents where they feel 'scared', 'threatened' or 'don't know what to do'. Similarly, the Police force of a suburb of Victoria, BC, launched a program named 'Solid Rock', in which police officers or actors perform skits to convince young people that teenagers who go to the authorities rather than putting up with bullies are not rats but exemplary, responsible citizens (McInnes, 1998: A4). We see in these well-intentioned government programs an attempt to help youth become not only law-abiding citizens, but *homo prudens* (O'Malley, 1996) too, thus enticing them in the creation of a culture of risk management in which they learn to fear youth and think of themselves as potential victims (Ericson and Haggerty, 1997). These programs illustrate the profound change in current crime control policy Garland foresaw: 'The new programmes of action are directed not toward individual offenders, but toward the conduct of potential victims, to vulnerable situations, and to those routines of everyday life which create criminal opportunities as an unintended by-product' (Garland, 1996: 451). Hence, we need to understand the moral panic about the violent girl or youth in general as a process that leads not only to the containment and transformation of violent girls and boys, but also to the increased self-discipline and regulation of all youths, who learn to think of themselves as potential victims of bullying.'

To summarize, the policies and programs stemming from the moral panic about violent girls include repressive measures towards violent youth that are deployed by the crime-control apparatus. They also include more informal mechanisms of crime control directed at society, which are deployed by a 'government-at-a-distance'. While repressive measures stem from traditional crime-control agencies, such as the police or prisons, informal control operates rather indirectly or 'at a distance' by fostering the co-operation of non-state organizations and private individuals (Garland, 1997: 188). Through the actions of various experts involved in the fight against bullies, parents, teachers, young people and, specifically, girls are encouraged to become responsible and prudent individuals. To this effect, policies and programs seek to make them recognize their responsibility in reducing crime and persuade them to change their behaviour to reduce criminal opportunities (Garland, 1996: 453).

Why Is the Panic Happening Today?

Why did the reaction to girl violence take the particular form and intensity it did during the late 1990s? The moral panic literature emphasizes that, during a panic, the anxieties the public experiences are real, but their reaction is often misplaced. Hence, the object of the panic, the violent girl, is not always the source of people's anxiety.

In psychoanalytical terms, she is more likely to be the object of a projection, rather than the source of concern and fear. As one media article stated, the murder of Virk resulted in 'a profound self-examination and fear among Canadians that society's rules are undergoing unsettling change' (Mitchell, 1997: A1). This section attempts to situate the moral panic about girl-violence in its larger social and political context, in order, to uncover some of the anxieties that propelled it to become symbolically attached to aggressive girls. We follow this discussion with a brief examination of the way policies aimed at violent girls could better attempt to address the problems young girls face today.

We start our attempt at contextualizing the moral panic over the violent girl by examining the larger structural forces characterizing our present. According to Young (1999), the transition from modernity (the 'Golden Age' of the post-war period) to the present late modernity (late 1960s and onwards) resulted in significant structural and psychological changes that produced social anxieties. The shift primarily entailed a movement from an inclusive to an exclusive society: from a society that incorporated its members and enjoyed full (male) employment, rising affluence, stable families and conformity, to an exclusive society arising from changes in the labour force. These changes included a shift from a more social-based, communitarian labour force to one of individualism stemming from the new knowledge-based, technology, society. As late-modern society became increasingly characterized by plurality of values, self-reflexivity, multiculturalism, and scientific and political relativism, the solid foundation of modernity began to melt. Material certainty and shared values shattered, leaving us with a heightened sense of risk and uncertainties. In such a precarious climate, crime acquires a powerful symbolic value. If we could only control crime better, we would bring safety into one aspect of our disrupted lives. It is not surprising that our quest for security often translates into a projection of our fears onto specific scapegoats, who are made responsible for our feelings of insecurity.

What social anxieties are projected onto the violent girl today? What threat to societal values has she come to represent. In the wake of the

Virk case, it was not difficult to find newspaper articles emphasizing the dangers of the rise in 'Girl Power'. A pullout section of the *Vancouver Province*, for example, had a picture of the petite head of the popular sitcom character Ally McBeal superimposed on the body of Rambo. While she smiles innocently at the camera, her muscular arms are holding a machine gun. The caption reads: 'It's a girrrl's world: Yikes! It's only a matter of time before women take over' (Bacchus, 1998). Although Bacchus writes in a tongue-in-cheek manner, he outlines 'evidence' of a shift from patriarchy to matriarchy: the Spice Girls, Buffy the Vampire Slayer, angry chanteuses like Alanis Morissette, Xena, the Lilith Fair, the WNBA, Martha Stewart, Rosie O'Donnell, and the Women's Television Network. While Bacchus quickly clarifies that women have not achieved superiority or even equality in the workplace, the evidence of the shift to matriarchy he posits is in the form of a change 'in spirit'. The mantra of this spirit, Bacchus claims, is 'Go girl!' (Bacchus, 1998).

The media sensationalized the spirit of girl power by positing it as the cause of girl violence. Showing insightful reflexivity, Nolan suggests that '[f]ollowing long-standing misogynist traditions, they've made the assumption that the behaviour of a few reveals the brutality of all girls and that increased freedom for women—brought about specifically by feminism—is responsible for the supposed rise in young women's violence' (1998: 32). Girl power, the source of social anxieties, is the real nasty here; the moral panic over the statistically insignificant Nasty Girl is a projection of a desire to retrieve a patriarchal social order characterized by gender conformity.

While a segment of our society is increasingly worried about the ill effect of the spirit of girl power and engrossed in attacking popular culture and in developing policies to transform all girls into good girls, another segment is capitalizing on girl power to turn a profit. 'Bad girls = big bucks' claims the *Vancouver Sun* (Todd, 2001: A17). It is not the first time folk devils become prey to commercial exploitation and are given a greater ethos than they originally possessed (Cohen, 1980: 140, 176). Today, young girls are implored by marketers and the media to dress like adults and to express sexual, aggressive confidence (Clark, 1999: 47). Under the headline 'Hollywood discovers girl power', *USA Today* acknowledges that 'where the girls are is where Hollywood wants to be' (Bacchus, 1998: B1). And whereas girls were previously sex symbols in the background of beverage advertisements, they are now staring down the camera lens as they 'growl': 'This is our beer' (Bacchus, 1998: B3).

The spirit of girl power is paradoxically what policies and programming for violent girls aim at transforming through the adoption of anger management skills based on a cognitive behavioural model. Programs that encourage control, empathy, self-esteem, communication, and social skills are important, yet they do little in addressing the wider social context in which girl power takes place, as well as the desire for autonomy and the consumerism it creates. These techniques assume individual pathology and are based on a punishment–correction model that has failed repeatedly to reform (Foucault, 1979). Moreover, while most current programs to curb girl-violence are founded on cognitive skills training and risk technologies, we also believe there has been insufficient critical evaluation of actuarial practices with youth. As Lupton (1999: 2) argues, the technico-scientific approach to risk ignores how 'risk' can be a sociocultural phenomenon in its own right. In a study on girls incarcerated for violent offences in Saskatchewan, one of us questions if actuarial techniques depoliticize the process of social control by assisting in the efficient management of the offender, rather than addressing social conditions requiring reform (Barron, forthcoming).

An alternative approach to address violence would be to focus on gender, race, and class-specific initiatives that appeal to the realities of young females. Chesney-Lind and Brown (1999) argue that because girl violence differs from boy violence in magnitude and quality, the traditional approaches to treatment and models of law enforcement are inappropriate for girls. They, and others, call for programs that recognize factors that marginalize girls, including the extensiveness of girl victimization, and the complicating factors of culture, racism, and social and economic inequality, which may contribute to violent behaviour

(Jiwani, 1998; Chesney-Lind and Brown, 1999; Jackson, 2004).

Conclusion

Discussing the construction of the Nasty Girl as a moral panic should not negate a search for positive reforms nor undermine the devastation resulting from rare acts of female aggression and violence. Although it can be argued that the call of gender-based programs would confirm the amplitude of girl violence, it cannot be denied that young females are incarcerated for violent acts and have

different life experience and needs than those of males. Perhaps the most promising recommendations for female programming include giving girls a voice in program design, implementation and evaluation in order to address the wider context in which violence takes place. We maintain that, in addition to gender, the interlocking systems of oppression in young women's lives must be considered. Acknowledging and responding to the connections between racism, sexism, ableism, homophobia, and economic inequality is a challenge to the philosophical underpinnings of the criminal justice and education systems.

Note

1. Doob and Sprott also bring to our attention the problems associated with statistics on minor offences among youth by revealing how their increase is more related to institutional changes in reporting policies than in an actual increase in violence. For example, the Ontario Ministry of Education requested that education boards develop violence-prevention policies and implementation plans for reporting and recording violent incidents by September 1994. Increasingly, policies of 'zero tolerance' of violence in the schools mandate that all cases of violence be brought to court. According to Doob and Sprott, 'Such policies can be expected to result in increased numbers of minor cases of violence—these are the cases that are likely to have been ignored in the past' (1998: 188).

References

Anon. 1996. 'When the Tough Get Going . . . the Going Gets Tough: How to Deal with Bullies', *Today's Parent* 13, 7: 66–70.

Anon. 1997. 'In Reena's World, Being a "Slut" Can Get you Killed', *Toronto Star*, 6 December: E1, E4.

Artz, S. 2004. 'Revisiting the Moral Domain: Using Social Interdependence Theory to Understand Adolescent Girls' Perspectives on the Use of Violence', in M. Moretti, C. Odgers, and J. Jackson, eds., *Girls and Aggression: Contributing Factors and Intervention Principles*, pp. 101–13. New York: Springer.

Bacchus, L. 1998. 'It's a Girrrl's World', Vancouver Province, 2 August: B1–B3.

Barron, C. (forthcoming). 'Nasty Girl: The Impact of the Risk Society on Female Young Offenders'. PhD dissertation, Simon Fraser University, School of Criminology, Burnaby, BC.

Cernetig, M., B. Laghi, R. Matas, and C. McInnes. 1997. 'Reena Virk's Short Life and Lonely Death; Swept Away: A 14 year-old Girl Beaten by the Very Teens She Wanted as Friends was Left to the Cold Salt-water', *The Globe and Mail*, 27 November: A1.

Chesney-Lind, M., and M. Brown. 1999. 'Girls and Violence: An Overview', in D. Flannery and C.R. Huff, eds., *Youth Violence: Prevention, Intervention and Social Policy*. Washington, DC: American Psychiatric Press.

Clark, A. 1999. 'How Teens Got the Power: Gen Y Has the Cash, the Cool—and a Burgeoning Consumer Culture', *Maclean's* 22 March: 42–9.

Cohen, S. 1980. *Folk Devils and Moral Panics: The Creation of the Mods and Rockers*. New York: St Martin's Press.

Cohen, S. 1985. *Visions of Social Control*. New York: Oxford University Press.

Doob, A., and J.B. Sprott. 1998. 'Is the "Quality" of Youth Violence Becoming More Serious?', *Canadian Journal of Criminology and Criminal*

Justice 40, 2: 185–94. Ericson, R., and K. Haggerty. 1997. *Policing the Risk Society*. Toronto: University of Toronto Press.

Faith, K., and Y. Jiwani. 2002. 'The Social Construction of "Dangerous" Girls and Women', in B. Schissel and C. Brooks, eds., *Marginality and Condemnation: An Introduction to Critical Criminology*, pp. 83–107. Halifax: Fernwood Publishing.

Foucault, M. 1979. *Discipline and Punish: The Birth of the Prison*. New York: Vintage Books.

———. 1982. *The Subject and Power*, 2nd ed., H.L. Dreyfus and P. Rabinow, eds. Chicago: Chicago University Press.

Garland, D. 1996. 'The Limits of the Sovereign State: Strategies of Crime Control in Contemporary Society', *British Journal of Criminology* 36, 4: 445–71.

———. 1997. '"Governmentality" and the Problem of Crime: Foucault, Criminology, Sociology', *Theoretical Criminology* 1, 2: 173–214.

Geller, G. 1987. '"Young Women in Conflict with the Law', in E. Adelberg and C. Currie, eds., *Too Few to Count: Canadian Women in Conflict with the Law*, pp. 113–26. Vancouver: Press Gang Publishers.

Jackson, M.A. 2004. 'Race, Gender, and Aggression: The Impact of Sociocultural Factors on Girls', in M. Moretti, C. Odgers, and J. Jackson, eds., *Girls and Aggression: Contributing Factors and Intervention Principles*, pp. 82–99. New York: Kluwer Academic/Plenum Publishers.

Lupton, D. 1999. *Risk and Sociocultural Theory: New Directions and Perspectives*. Cambridge, UK: Cambridge University Press.

Madriz, E. 1997. *Nothing Bad Happens to Good Girls*. Berkeley, CA: University of California Press.

Martin, S. 1998. 'Murder in Victoria: Why did Reena Virk Die?', *Chatelaine*, May: 70–7.

McInnes, C. 1998. 'Police Probe Gang Assault of Nanaimo Teen', *The Globe and Mail*, 12 March: A4.

Mitchell, A. 1997. 'Virk's Death Triggers Painful Questions: Girls' Involvement "Exacerbates Rage"', *The Globe and Mail*, 28 Nov: A1, A8.

Myers, T., and J. Sangster. 2001. 'Retorts, Runaways and Riots: Patterns of Resistance in Canadian Reform Schools for Girls, 1930–60', *Journal of Social History* 34, 3: 669–97.

Nolan, N. 1998. 'Girl Crazy: After the Brutal Murder of Reena Virk, the Media Whipped the Country into a Frenzy Over a Supposed "Girl Crime Wave"', *This Magazine*, 31, 5 (March/April): 30–5.

O'Malley, P. 1996. 'Risk and Responsibility', in A. Barry, T. Osborne, and N. Rose, eds., *Foucault and Political Reason*, pp. 189–208. Chicago: Chicago University Press.

Pepler, D.J., and F. Sedighdeilami. 1998. *Aggressive Girls in Canada*. Working Papers. Hull, QC: Applied Research Branch, Strategic Policy, Human Resources Development Canada.

Reitsma-Street, M. 1999. 'Justice for Canadian Girls: A 1990s Update', *Canadian Journal of Criminology and Criminal Justice* 41, 3: 335–64.

Rose, N., and P. Miller. 1992. 'Political Power Beyond the State: Problematics of Government', *British Journal of Sociology* 43, 2: 173–205.

Schissel, B. 1997. *Blaming Children: Youth Crime, Moral Panics and the Politics of Hate*. Halifax: Fernwood Publishing.

Statistics Canada. 2000. 'Crime Statistics', *The Daily*. 18 July. Available at www.statcan.ca/Daily/English1000718/d00718a.htm.

Tafler, S. 1998. 'Who was Reena Virk?' *Saturday Night*, 113, 3: 15–22.

Todd, D. 2001. 'Bad Girls = Big Bucks', *The Vancouver Sun*, 26 January: A17.

Young, J. 1999. *The Exclusive Society*. London: Sage.

CHAPTER 30

Unconventional Politicians: Gender and Media Coverage of Canadian Leaders' Debates, 1993, 1997, 2000

Elisabeth Gidengil and Joanna Everitt

Television news has been likened to a 'masculine soap opera' (Fiske, 1987: 308). Nowhere is this more apparent than in the metaphors that are used to (re)construct politics. News reports are regularly presented using a 'masculine narrative' (Rakow and Kranich, 1991: 8), filled with images of the battlefield and the sports arena. The use of this stereotypically masculine imagery raises important questions about the coverage of women engaged in political activity. Given the critical importance of leader evaluations to vote choice in Canada (Blais et al., 2002, chapter 12; Gidengil et al., 2000), this article focuses on the gendered nature of news coverage of party leaders in the 1993, 1997, and 2000 Canadian elections.

This investigation compares the women's coverage with their actual behaviour, by focusing on the English-language televised leaders' debates and their subsequent coverage in the nightly news. This enables us to overcome a serious potential challenge: if women are covered differently, does this really reflect the gendered nature of news coverage or is it simply that the women *did* behave differently? Finally, we draw on Annabelle Sreberny-Mohammadi and Karen Ross's notion of gendered mediation (1996; see also Ross and Sreberny, 2000) to cast a fresh light on the three questions that have dominated the growing literature on women, politics and the media: visibility, stereotyping, and framing.

Women are typically less visible in the news than their male counterparts. For example, François-Pierre Gingras (1995) found that female politicians received markedly less coverage in Ottawa area newspapers in 1991 than their numbers warranted. This parallels Kim Fridkin Kahn's (1994) finding

that female gubernatorial and Senate candidates in the United States received less news coverage than their male counterparts and Pippa Norris's (1997) finding that female leaders worldwide were mentioned in significantly fewer stories in international news media than the men who preceded or succeeded them (see also Kahn and Goldenberg, 1991). And even when women were visible, their coverage tended to be rather narrowly focused, dwelling on their viability and framing their issue competencies and/or personality traits in stereotypically feminine terms. For example, Kahn and Goldenberg (1991) found that coverage of female candidates was more likely to focus on how they were doing in the polls and how well their campaigns were being run, and when their issue positions were covered, the focus tended to be on issues like education rather than the economy or foreign policy.[1] More generally, there is evidence that the media apply sex-specific narrative frames when covering female politicians and that female politicians are subject to harsher evaluative criteria. When Tremblay and Bélanger (1997) examined the portrayal of party leaders in political cartoons in major Canadian newspapers during the 1993 election, for example, they found that over one half of the cartoons in which the two female leaders appeared portrayed them in sex-typed ways as witches, say, or Cinderellas. Similarly, Robinson and Saint-Jean (1991, 1995) report that depictions of female politicians in Canada have relied on a succession of sex-based stereotypes evolving from 'spinster' to 'superwoman' and 'one of the boys' (see also Norris, 1997; and Ross, 1995).

Even when women are not being framed in stereotypically feminine terms, though, gender biases may still be present. These biases are more subtle, but they are also more insidious because they are embedded in the conventional language of political news. This is the key insight of the gendered mediation thesis: '. . . the way in which politics is reported is significantly determined by a male-oriented agenda that privileges the practice of politics as an essentially male pursuit. The image and language of mediated politics, therefore, supports the status quo (male as norm) and regards women politicians as novelties' (Ross and Sreberny, 2000: 93). The gendered mediation thesis continues the focus on stereotyping and framing, but now the central concern is the implications for female politicians of being framed in stereotypically masculine ways. These implications revolve around the extent and nature of women's visibility in the news. If women fail to conform to the traditional masculine norms of political behaviour, their visibility will suffer, but if they do try to conform, any behaviour that runs counter to deeply rooted conceptions of the feminine norm may well receive disproportionate attention in the news.

Metaphors and Gendered Mediation

As Gunther Kress notes, 'All reporting is mediation' (1983a; see also Kress, 1983b; and Geis, 1987). It is media personnel who decide who or what gets covered and, equally important, *how* they are covered. Kress goes on to highlight the critical role that language plays in the mediation process 'by supplying the categories which may be imposed by the reporter on the event' (1983a, 120). This is not a neutral process. On the contrary, 'words represent categorizations of the world *from a point of view*' (125; emphasis added). When that point of view incorporates gendered assumptions about politics and politicians, the mediation process itself is necessarily gendered.

This is reflected in the choice of metaphors that are used to (re)construct political behaviour. Metaphors are literary devices that are used to enrich our speech or prose. However, 'Unlike literature, news stories use metaphors that are so conventional that they have become clichés and their metaphorical nature is consequently unrecognized' (Fiske, 1987: 291; see also Blankenship 1976; Blankenship

and Kang, 1991; Gingras, 1997; and Mumby and Spitzack, 1985). Election campaigns are routinely framed as battles between warring camps and party leaders as boxers going for the knockout punch.

These 'cliché metaphors' abound in television news reports for a variety of reasons. First, there is the medium. Television journalists and news writers must compress their stories into many fewer words than newspaper journalists. Thomas Patterson and Robert McClure have made the point succinctly: an entire evening newscast will typically contain fewer words than the front page of a quality newspaper (1976: 55). Constructing politics in the conventional language of conflict and confrontation offers a ready way of simplifying the news story to fit the constraints of the medium.[2] Moreover, 'the tyranny of the deadline requires the speed and efficiency that only conventions make possible' (Fiske, 1987: 282).

Then there are prevailing news values. Television newscasts are competing for an audience, not just with rival network newscasts, but with entertainment and sports programming on other channels. This means that 'news has to be popular, it has to produce an audience' (Fiske, 1987: 281). It bears emphasis that the audience for news is disproportionately male. Stories that involve conflict are seen as enhancing the entertainment value of the news and this is reflected in the frequent resort in political reporting to images of the boxing ring, the sports arena, the battlefield and the back alley brawl (see Bell, 1991; Fiske, 1987: 286; Gingras, 1997; Lawrence, 2000; Mendelsohn, 1993; Patterson, 1980; Taras, 1990: 100-08).

However, the factors shaping the choice of language go much deeper than the commercial constraints of the medium and prevailing news values. As Liesbet van Zoonen emphasizes, the 'gendered structure of news production' affects the meaning that is encoded into media discourses (1994: 43).[3] Despite the entry of more women into the profession, television news remains a male-dominated sphere, and its norms, values, and conventions continue not merely to reflect, but to reinforce, that fact. At the same time, television news personnel are part of a larger society in which the conception (whether conscious or not) of politics as a male preserve remains deeply rooted, not least because politics is still predominantly a man's world. These larger cultural assumptions influence news coverage, even as that coverage subtly perpetuates them. It is not surprising, then that 'gendered assumptions about politicians are manifest in the discourses used by the media' (Ross and Sreberny, 2000: 89).

These same factors also help to explain why framing female politicians in the conventional language of the news can result in sex-differentiated coverage. Conflictual behaviour is newsworthy in itself, but conflictive behaviour on the part of women is especially newsworthy because it fulfils a second news value, the value variously referred to as 'unexpectedness' or 'surprisingness' (Bell, 1991; Fiske, 1987: 286). When women behave combatively, they are behaving unexpectedly since that behaviour contravenes deeply rooted and often unconscious notions of how women are supposed to behave.

This implies that confrontational behaviour on the part of a female party leader will tend to receive more coverage than comparable behaviour on the part of her male counterparts. This tendency will be reinforced by the 'basic schema incompatability' (Butler and Geis, 1990: 48) that unexpected behaviour presents. As Alice H. Eagly and her colleagues (1992) explain, the effect is to accentuate or to exaggerate the counter-stereotypical behaviour. On the other hand, if a female party leader does not behave aggressively, her visibility may well suffer. Such low key behaviour fails not one, but two key tests of newsworthiness: it is neither conflictual nor unexpected.

Our initial work on the 1993 televised leaders' debates enabled us to provide some support for these arguments (Gidengil and Everitt, 1999, 2000). Not only was the language of news coverage gendered, its imagery littered with references to the battlefield, the back alley and the sports arena, but this masculine imagery was applied in ways that clearly differed according to the leaders' sex. In contrast to their male counterparts, both the Conservative party leader, Kim Campbell, and Audrey McLaughlin, the leader of the New Democratic party, were portrayed in much more confrontational terms than their actual behaviour in the debates themselves would seem to warrant.

Of the two women, McLaughlin clearly adopted a less combative debating style, and what was striking about her coverage was simply how little she received. Tellingly, though, the coverage that she did receive focused disproportionately on displays of confrontational behaviour.

However, the fact that we were looking at a single election left a number of important questions unanswered. First, it is possible that Campbell's coverage reflected not her gender, but the fact that she was the incumbent prime minister. As Robinson and Shehan observe, 'being the incumbent may almost inevitably mean the toughest press of all' (1983: 139). Second, it is possible that Campbell's treatment was a manifestation of the 'rise-and-fall' phenomenon. This is the 'cycle of boom-and-bust coverage' that was first observed during presidential primaries in the United States in which 'candidacies are first touted and then examined more critically' (Zaller and Hunt, 1994, 1995). As Robinson and Shehan note, the media 'correct for their early favourable coverage . . . by growing tougher on candidates they perceive themselves as having helped, either in terms of access or in tone. Those who do well in the news media in the beginning pay for it as the calendar moves on' (1983: 128). Mendelsohn and Nadeau (1999) have shown that coverage of Campbell followed a very similar trajectory as the honeymoon period following her selection as leader gave way to the partisan environment of the campaign. Finally, we need to ask whether the sex-differentiated treatment persists when female party leaders are no longer such a novelty on the electoral scene.

Comparing coverage across the 1993, 1997, and 2000 elections enables us to address these questions. We can compare Prime Minister Campbell's coverage in 1993 with Liberal prime minister Jean Chrétien's in 1997 and 2000 in order to assess whether Campbell's coverage was simply typical of that accorded an incumbent prime minister. Similarly, we can evaluate whether her coverage was just another manifestation of the rise-and-fall phenomenon by comparing her coverage with Canadian Alliance leader Stockwell Day's in 2000. Of all the new party leaders since Campbell, his treatment by the media would seem to bear the strongest traces of the boom-and-bust cycle. Finally, we can assess the novelty factor by comparing McLaughlin's coverage in 1993 with Alexa McDonough's coverage in 1997 and then again in 2000. The fact that the two women were leading the NDP means that we can eliminate party label as an alternative explanation for any differences in their coverage.

Data and Methods

Our analysis focuses on coverage of the English-language debates on the public Canadian Broadcasting Corporation and privately owned CTV.[4] For 1993, we examine coverage on the nightly news on October 4, immediately following the debate, and on October 5. No stories mentioning the debate were run after this date. In 1997, the French-language debate took an unexpected turn when Claire Lamarche, the debate moderator, collapsed 30 minutes before the scheduled end of the debate. The concluding segment of the debate was postponed until almost a week later and this extended the period of time in which reporters reviewed the English debate. Hence, the analysis of the 1997 election includes any mention of the leaders' performances in the English debate between May 12 and May 18. For the 2000 election, we analyze coverage on the evening news broadcasts of November 9, immediately following the debate, and November 10. The debate was not covered in subsequent newscasts.

In order to test our propositions about the impact of gendered mediation we need a systematic assessment of just how combatively each leader behaved. Following the procedures employed by Denis Monière (1994) in his analysis of the 1993 French-language debate, we use five indicators of aggressive debating behaviour—namely, addressing another leader as 'you' or by name, how often each leader was shown interrupting, and how often each leader was shown pointing a finger or clenching a fist (see also Tiemans, et al., 1985).[5] There is an obvious hierarchy to this behaviour: addressing remarks directly to another leader rather than to the moderator or the audience is patently less aggressive than pointing a finger at another leader or clenching a fist to emphasize a point.

The coding of the English-language debate in each election was performed by a graduate student in Communication Studies at McGill University.

We then compare the leaders' behaviour in the debates with the coverage that they received. We focus on the metaphors used to characterize each leader's behaviour. If gendered mediation was occurring, it should be apparent in the choice of imagery used by reporters and news anchors. The gendered mediation thesis implies that these choices will reflect a deeply rooted conception of politics as a male preserve. As a result, we expect 'masculine' images of warfare, violence, and sports to predominate in post-debate coverage and we expect that the choice of metaphors will over-emphasize combative behaviour on the part of the female leaders. This will be especially evident when women are new to the electoral scene. At the same time, the gendered mediation thesis implies that women who fail to conform to the dominant confrontational norms will tend to receive less attention from the media because they are harder to fit into the conventional frames. Lacking the crucial ingredients of both conflict and unexpectedness, their behaviour will simply not qualify as very newsworthy.

Debate Behaviour

Prime Minister Campbell was clearly the more combative of the two women in the 1993 English debate (see Figure 30.1). Indeed, she rivalled Chrétien (11 times) in her use of the most aggressive type of debating behaviour, gesturing a dozen times with her fist clenched. Still, she ranked behind both Chrétien (61 times) and Reform Party leader Preston Manning (55 times) when it came to finger-pointing (43 times) and behind both Manning (67) and Bloc Québécois leader Lucien Bouchard (35) when it came to interrupting other speakers (31). And she was the least aggressive of all in her use of personal forms of address.

As the prime minister going into that election, it is important to compare Campbell's performance with Chrétien's in 1997 and 2000. On every dimension save finger-pointing, Campbell was less combative than Chrétien. It is also instructive to compare Campbell's behaviour in the 1993 debate with her Conservative successors' behaviour in the 1997 and 2000 debates. In 1997, Jean Charest was less likely to engage in finger-pointing (17 times), but this was true of all five leaders in that debate. At the same time, he was just as likely to interrupt other speakers (29) as Campbell had been in 1993 and he was even more given to fist-clenching (17). He was also much more likely to address other leaders by name (51). Similarly, in the 2000 debate, Joe Clark was as combative as Campbell had been. Indeed, he was more combative when it came to addressing other leaders as 'you' (91 times) and using their names (33). The one exception was finger-pointing, but again all five leaders were less given to finger-pointing than their counterparts had been in 1993.

Audrey McLaughlin's debating style in 1993 was much more low-key than Campbell's. To the extent that she behaved combatively, that combativeness took the form of engaging directly with the other leaders (as opposed to addressing her remarks to the panel or to the audience). She was second only to Manning (63 times) in her use of 'you' (54) and she was even more likely (26) than Manning (21) to address the other leaders by name. But in contrast to Manning, she was much less likely to resort to the more confrontational forms of behaviour. She was the least likely to interrupt another leader (22 times) or to engage in finger-pointing (24), and she gestured with a clenched fist only once.

McLaughlin's successor as NDP leader, Alexa McDonough, adopted a more combative stance in the 1997 debate. She was more likely than McLaughlin to interrupt other speakers (29 times) and to use a clenched fist (7), while being just as prone as her predecessor to addressing other leaders as 'you' (55) and using their names (24).

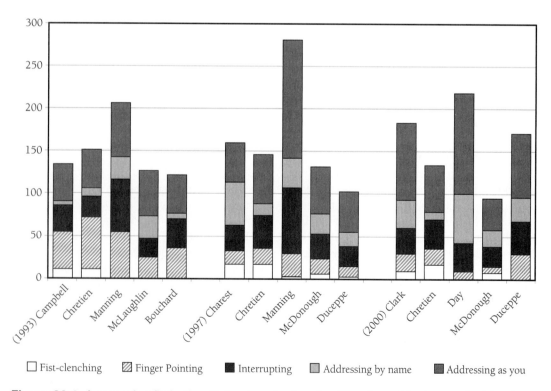

Figure 30.1 Aggressive Debating Behaviour by Leader (Number of Instances by Type)

However, she interrupted much less often than Manning (77) did in 1997 and she engaged in much less finger-pointing (17) than he did (26 times). Meanwhile, Charest (17) and Chrétien (16) were both much more likely to clench their fists as they made their points than McDonough was. In fact, there was not a single indicator of confrontational behaviour on which McDonough ranked first or even second.

In the 2000 debate, McDonough reverted to a more low-key style of debating. She was the least likely to address other leaders as 'you' (37 times) and used their names less frequently (19) than all but Chrétien (9). She was also the least likely to interrupt (25) or to point her finger at other leaders (5). However, there was one notable exception to this pattern: McDonough clenched her fist (9) almost as often as Clark did (10). Still, it was Chrétien who was most given to using this gesture as he spoke (16).

The key point is that McLaughlin and McDonough alike generally engaged in less confrontational behaviour than their male counterparts in all three debates. Campbell, meanwhile, clearly opted for a more combative style of debating in 1993. That said, it would be difficult to argue that she was the most aggressive of the leaders in the 1993 debate or that she was more confrontational than her party's leaders or the incumbent prime minister in the 1997 and 2000 debates. This makes a comparison of their coverage all the more revealing.

When female politicians engage in confrontational behaviour, they are violating deeply held notions of how women should behave. The gendered mediation thesis suggests that the unexpectedness of this behaviour will make it especially newsworthy. If this argument is correct, we should expect to see extensive news coverage of Campbell's displays of combativeness, with these displays receiving more coverage than similar behaviour on the part of her male counterparts. On the other hand, we should expect much more perfunctory coverage of both McLaughlin and McDonough. When women conform to expectations and adopt a more low-key approach than their male counterparts, as McLaughlin and McDonough did, the gendered mediation thesis

predicts that they will attract little media attention. Lacking as it does the critical ingredients of either conflict or unexpectedness, such behaviour is just not particularly newsworthy. However, the coverage that they do receive will tend to play up any instances of confrontational behaviour. This should be particularly true of McLaughlin's coverage in 1993, given the novelty of women participating in the leaders' debate.

Metaphoric Language

A systematic analysis of the imagery used in reporting on the leaders' debates enables us to test these propositions. Identifying metaphoric language is no easy task. The definition of the term 'metaphor' is deceptively simple: 'the application of a word or phrase to an object or concept it does not literally denote, suggesting comparison to that object or concept.'[6] In practice, though, deciding what is and what is not metaphorical language is far from easy. Some metaphors have entered so completely into common parlance that they have become 'dead metaphors' and we no longer recognize their non-literal application. Indeed, the argument can be made that all language is ultimately metaphoric (Booth, 1978; Davidson, 1978). Our solution was to employ graduate students in English to identify every 'live' metaphor used in post-debate coverage. These metaphors were then classified into categories that were established on the basis of the frequency of occurrence of different types of imagery.[7] The classification was performed blind to the identity of the leaders. A total of 184 metaphors were identified in coverage of the 1993 debate, 178 in coverage of the 1997 debate, and 92 in coverage of the 2000 debate. The number was much lower in 2000 because coverage of the outcome of the United States presidential election reduced the amount of attention given to the leaders' debate.

At the heart of the gendered mediation thesis is the notion that the news is a masculine narrative, dominated by stereotypically masculine images. This is certainly true of television news coverage of the leaders' debates in recent Canadian elections (see Figure 30.2). In 1993, almost one-third of the metaphors (30 percent) used in reports on the

English debate employed the language of warfare. While the proportion was lower in coverage of the 1997 (22 per cent) and 2000 English debates (16 per cent), these debates were still constructed as 'bloody battles'. Some leaders went 'on the offensive' as they 'attacked on all fronts', while others were 'dodging attacks' as they came 'under fire from all sides'. Leaders tried to avoid 'taking bad hits' as the 'verbal guns rattled away'. When the leaders were not battling, they were 'feuding' and 'fighting' and 'ganging up on one another'. Some were left 'verbally beaten and bruised' as they got a 'rough going-over'. If the debates were not battles or brawls, they were sports or games. This imagery was especially common in coverage of the 2000 debate (40 per cent). The most common metaphors drew on stereotypically masculine sports like boxing, baseball, football and the traditional Canadian sport of hockey. Some leaders 'sparred', while others 'duked it out'. There were 'no knock out punches' but there were 'a lot of shots on net' as the leaders 'faced off'.

Of the four most frequently used types of imagery (warfare, sports and games, general violence, and theatre and show business), only the theatre and show business category can be considered gender-neutral. When the debates were constructed as plays or performances, they became 'made-for-TV political drama'. There were 'dramatic moments' as leaders tried to 'steal the spotlight'. Clearly, though, the coverage of all three debates was dominated by the stereotypically masculine metaphors.[8] The proportion was highest in coverage of the 2000 debate, with 68 per cent of the metaphors drawing on images of the battlefield, the sports arena or backstreet violence, but even in coverage of the 1997 debate, these images still accounted for 54 per cent of the total metaphors used.

Liesbet Van Zoonen has linked the gendered nature of media coverage to the 'pervasive commercial logic of the media' (1994: 61). As she observes, public and private broadcasters are increasingly subject to the same logic as they compete for market shares. In a similar vein, Marc Raboy refers to the 'hybridization of public broadcasting' in Canada, noting that the CBC has 'to compete with the private sector directly, for audiences, for advertisers . . .' (1996: 117). One result is a style

of reporting on CBC that is shaped 'as much by the need to entertain as to inform' (Taras, 1991: 171). Accordingly, we should expect to see similarities in the prevalence of stereotypically masculine imagery on CBC and CTV. This is indeed the case. The main difference between the two networks in this regard is that the proportion of sports metaphors was higher in CTV's debate coverage in all three elections. Even on CBC, though, at least one half of the metaphors used to (re)construct the debates drew on stereotypically masculine imagery.[9]

As we noted earlier, the gendered nature of news coverage reflects more than the prevailing news values and the constraints of the medium. The gendered mediation thesis points to what van Zoonen terms the 'gendered structure of news production' (1994: 50). She argues that this structure perpetuates 'a particular kind of gendered professionalism' whereby female journalists come to internalize the prevailing norms and conventions of news production. It is important to ask, then, whether the metaphorical mix was affected by the sex of the journalist. Initially, the results seem inconsistent. Female journalists used more stereotypically masculine imagery (75 per cent) than their male counterparts (67 per cent) when they covered the 2000 debate, but fewer stereotypically masculine images (52 per cent and 46 per cent) than their male counterparts (67 per cent and 59 per cent) in their coverage of the 1993 and 1997 debates. It turns out that this apparent inconsistency can be explained by the networks for which the journalists were working. In 1993 and 1997, the female journalists were almost all on CBC, whereas in 2000 they were almost all on CTV. This neatly illustrates van Zoonen's point that the expression of 'gendered professionalism' is conditioned by the organizational context. However, the larger point remains that the language of television news is heavily gendered, regardless of network and regardless of the journalists' sex.

The critical question from the perspective of gendered mediation is whether this language was applied in a sex-differentiated fashion. It clearly was in 1993 (see Figure 30.3). Although Campbell was no more aggressive than the other leaders, she was the most likely to be portrayed as a warrior

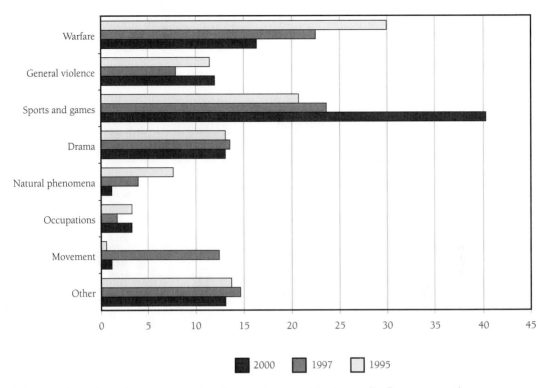

Figure 30.2 Metaphorical Construction of Leaders' Debates (in Percentages)

doing battle or as a street-fighter. Indeed, 69 per cent of the metaphors used to characterize her participation in the debates relied on images of violence, compared with only 42 per cent for Chrétien and 41 per cent for Manning. Even more striking was the extent to which attack metaphors were used in Campbell's post-debate coverage. Fully one-third (34 per cent) of the metaphors applied to Campbell employed images of attacking. For all his finger-pointing and interrupting of other speakers, not a single attack metaphor was applied to Manning in 1993. Similarly, for all his finger-pointing and fist-clenching, not a single attack metaphor was applied to Chrétien.

The contrast with coverage of Charest in 1997 and Clark in 2000 highlights the asymmetrical treatment of Campbell. During the 1997 debate, Charest clenched his fist more often than his Conservative predecessor had in 1993 and yet only 9 per cent of the metaphors used in his post-debate coverage drew on images of warfare or violent acts

in general. Even more tellingly, only two metaphors (4 per cent) portrayed him as being on the attack.[10] Instead, Charest was portrayed as a player who was in the game (26 per cent) or a performer who was on the stage (28 per cent). Post-debate coverage of the Conservative leader in 2000 tells a similar story. Of the 12 metaphors applied to Clark, half (6) drew on sports and games imagery and only three drew on images of warfare and violence. And, despite his combative debating style, only one attack metaphor was used in his coverage.

A comparison with the coverage received by Chrétien in 1997 and 2000 is also illuminating. Going into the 1993 election, Campbell was prime minister, and we have to consider the possibility that her coverage was simply typical of that accorded the incumbent. In 1997 and 2000, Chrétien was the incumbent, and like Campbell, a significant proportion of his coverage did draw heavily on images of violence (51 per cent in 1997 and 50 per cent in 2000). In neither year, though,

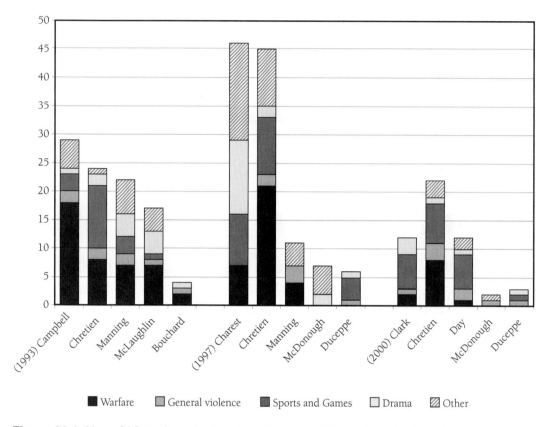

Figure 30.3 Use of Metaphors by Leader (Number of Metaphors by Type)

did the use of this imagery rival Campbell's coverage in 1993 (69 per cent). And, in contrast to Campbell, he was portrayed as being on the defensive (38 per cent in 1997 and 27 per cent in 2000) rather than on the attack. Indeed, in 1997, only two metaphors portrayed him as attacking and in 2000 only a single metaphor did so. This is despite the fact that in both years he ranked first or second in the frequency of interrupting, finger-pointing, and fist clenching in the debates themselves.

Finally, there is the coverage of Day in the 2000 debate. While the Alliance leader was less likely to point his finger than Manning had been in the two previous debates, and he did not gesture with his fist clenched, Day frequently interrupted other speakers and addressed his remarks directly to them (see Figure 30.1). However, only three of the twelve metaphors used in his coverage portrayed

him as being involved in any sort of conflict and not one single metaphor showed him as being on the attack. If the 'rise-and-fall' phenomenon was playing itself out in coverage of Day, this did not appear to affect the type of imagery that was used in his debate coverage.

Of all the leaders in all three elections, it was Campbell whose coverage contained the highest proportion of images of warfare and violence, and yet she was by no means the most aggressive of the leaders in any of the debates. It is hard to avoid the conclusion that television news coverage did indeed play up Campbell's aggressive behaviour in the 1993 debates, just as the gendered mediation thesis predicted.

Similarly, media coverage of the 1993 debates focused disproportionately on McLaughlin's displays of confrontational behaviour. True, metaphors of warfare and violence were used less frequently (47 per cent) in her coverage than in Campbell's, but like Campbell, she was portrayed as being on the attack much more frequently (29 per cent) than her male counterparts, despite her generally low-key debating style. In fact, 15 of the 16 attack metaphors used in coverage of the 1993 debate referred to one or other of the two women. What really stands out about McLaughlin's coverage, though, is that there was so little of it.

This was even more the case in 1997 and 2000, when the novelty of female party leaders had worn off. Only seven instances of metaphorical language were found for McDonough in the entire coverage of the 1997 debates. None of those images drew on stereotypically masculine activities.[11] In 2000, a systematic coding of McDonough's post-debate coverage turned up a mere two metaphors. Tellingly, one of these two metaphors had her 'hammering' Chrétien. This lack of coverage is consistent with the gendered mediation thesis: McDonough's debating style just did not qualify her as being very newsworthy. Like McLaughlin in 1993, she was certainly combative at times, but once the novelty of a female leader wears off, it seems, media coverage is less likely to play up the instances of confrontational behaviour.

Discussion

The metaphors used in coverage of recent televised leaders' debates confirm that television news remains a 'masculine narrative'. Stereotypically masculine imagery predominates. As the gendered mediation thesis predicts, this imagery served to highlight counter-stereotypical behaviour on the part of the two women who took part in the 1993 English televised leaders' debate.

The coverage of that debate focused disproportionately on Campbell's confrontational behaviour. It is striking that not one single attack metaphor was applied to either Manning or Chrétien, despite their aggressive debating style. Extending the comparisons across the two subsequent debates confirms that Campbell's coverage cannot be explained by the fact that she was the incumbent. Nor can it be explained by the fact that she was well into the 'bust'

stage of a 'boom-and-bust cycle' of media coverage, otherwise we might have expected to see at least traces of a similar pattern in Day's debate coverage in 2000. That we do not, lends credence to the notion of gendered mediation.

McLaughlin's coverage also portrayed her as behaving quite aggressively, and yet she was the least likely to engage in finger-pointing or to interrupt other leaders, and she only clenched her fist once during the debate. The asymmetrical treatment is underlined by the fact that not one metaphor portrayed either Manning or Chrétien as being on the attack, even though their debating style was clearly more confrontational than McLaughlin's. The use of attack metaphors in covering McLaughlin is the more striking given that she did not receive a great deal of coverage. The lack of visibility accorded her successor in television news reports of both the 1997 and 2000 debates underscores the way that the 'masculine' framing of television news may serve to marginalize women who fail to behave as combatively as some of their male counterparts. By 2000, the novelty of a woman leading the NDP had worn off and McDonough was barely visible in post-debate coverage.

Of course, we cannot rule out the possibility that the treatment of the NDP header is simply an example of 'hopeless cases' getting 'hopeless coverage' (Robinson and Shehan, 1983, 76). It bears emphasis, though, that in 1997 Charest was leading a party with a mere two seats in the House of Commons and his party ended up winning one less seat than McDonough's party. Similarly, in 2000 the NDP came out one seat ahead of Clark's Conservatives. However, as Shannon Sampert and Linda Trimble astutely observe, 'Clark, as a male leader who had played the game (and won) before, was more likely to be perceived as within the [game] frame' (2003).

The following excerpt from CTV's coverage of the 2000 debate illustrates how the dominant 'masculine' framing of television news can work to reduce women's visibility. This is how reporter Craig Oliver chose to word his report:

Jean Chrétien clearly tonight got into a stick-swinging melée with four opponents. He got hammered hard. He left the ice bent and battered, but he was standing. He skated off. And in that sense, I don't think it changed the scoreboard any. Joe Clark was firing at both goals at both ends of the ice, sniping at everyone, but there were no McSorleys although very close to it. This was about as rough a game of verbal hockey as you can get. . . . Stockwell Day conducted himself pretty well, but there were no breakaways through an open net. He took a lot of shots on net, quite a few of them somehow just seemed to miss.

When a reporter adopts the language of ice hockey to tell his story, is it any surprise that he neglects to comment on the performance of the lone female participant? Women simply do not form part of the frame of reference. Like the boxing ring, the professional ice hockey arena is still very much a male preserve.

The exclusion of McDonough from this game narrative is not an isolated example. Sports imagery was used less frequently in covering all three women, implying that the women were somehow perceived as not really belonging in the 'game' of politics. As journalist Ellen Goodman noted during the 1984 US presidential campaign,

The sports metaphor is a macho metaphor whether it is used to convince voters that [Democratic vice-presidential candidate Geraldine] Ferraro is one of the guys or that Ronald Reagan still has the old one-two. When media coverage is dominated by such 'macho metaphors', women politicians may be subtly disadvantaged. The not-too-subliminal message is that politics is just another game men play. (Goodman, 1984: 19)[12]

In the language of ice hockey, the viewer is left with the impression that McDonough did not 'make the cut' and was simply 'warming the bench'. This phenomenon is not confined to television news. Sampert and Trimble show how the 'gendered game framing' of headlines in *The Globe and Mail* and *The National Post* during the 2000 election campaign also served to marginalize McDonough.[13]

Finally, Oliver's report underlines the difference in the way that confrontational behaviour on the part of the men was constructed. When Campbell and McLaughlin behaved combatively, they were portrayed as aggressors waging war on the other participants, but similar behaviour on the part of their male counterparts was presented as if it were just part of the game. The women 'launched attacks' while the men 'took shots on net'. The effect is to play up the women's confrontational behaviour.

As the gendered mediation thesis emphasizes, gender biases are embedded in the very language of political reporting. The increase in the number of women competing for elite elected office (and in the number of women involved in news production) has done little to change the conventions of political journalism. These conventions continue to reinforce the image that politics is a man's game. The prevailing 'masculine' news frames subtly serve to highlight the 'unnatural' position of women in politics. Suggestions that a woman might 'land a blow', deliver 'a knockout punch', or even 'have a breakaway on an open net' challenge traditional social expectations of appropriate gender role behaviour. If a female party leader tries to fit in by behaving combatively, media coverage will tend to exaggerate her aggressive behaviour and she will risk appearing 'too aggressive'. On the other hand, if a female party leader fails to conform to the traditional masculine approach to politics, her behaviour is likely to receive less attention from the media than a similarly low-keyed performance by a male leader and she will risk being 'sidelined'.[14]

The implications of our findings go beyond the challenges that they pose for women competing for high elected office. As Fiske notes, 'Making sense of politics by metaphors of war or sport constructs politics as a conflict between parties and not as a public sphere serving the good of the nation' (1987: 291). One effect may be to deter many qualified women (and men) from entering electoral politics. The other effect may be to heighten democratic malaise. It would be naive to assume that the media are simply reflecting the way that politics is. On the contrary, they are active (if unknowing) participants in perpetuating the notion that politics is a game played by men.

Notes

1. See also Carroll and Schreiber (1997) and Kahn (1994). However, Kevin Smith found less evidence of sex-differentiated coverage when he examined press coverage of state-wide campaigns in the United States in 1994 (1997). There was also little evidence of stereotyping when it came to press coverage of world leaders (Norris, 1997).

2. The journalists interviewed by Gingras (1997) offered this as one of their reasons for using sports and games metaphors.

3. She is careful to avoid any suggestion that there is a necessary connection between structure and output. See also Fiske (1987, chapter 15) and Ross and Sreberny (2000).

4. We are grateful to the Fraser Institute for making transcripts of the coverage of the debates for 1993 and 1997 on both networks available to us. The Institute does not bear any responsibility for the analyses and interpretations presented here. The CBC coverage for the 2000 debates came from the CBC website. The CTV coverage for the 2000 debates came from Newscan.

5. For more details, see Gidengil and Everitt (1999). Our analysis of aggressive behaviour focuses solely on the English-language debates, but a comparison with Monière's analysis of the 1993 French debate suggests that even though the leaders were more combative in English, their relative combativeness did not change significantly. As one anonymous reviewer noted, it could be interesting to expand the coding in the future to include more subtle forms of power behaviour like stance and eye contact.

6. This definition is in Random House Webster's Electronic Dictionary, College Edition.

7. The classification was performed independently by one of us and by a research assistant. The level of inter-coder agreement was 88 percent in 1993, 85 percent in 1997, and 89 percent in 2000. Additional coders were employed to resolve the disagreements.

8. There was not a single instance of stereotypically feminine imagery in the coverage of either the 1997 or the 2000 debates. In 1993, there was a lone instance of a cooking metaphor.

9. The figures ranged from a low of 51 per cent in 1997 to a high of 60 per cent in 2000. Meanwhile, on CTV, the figures ranged from a low of 58 per cent in 1997 to a high of 75 per cent in 2000. The increased use of sports metaphors in 2000 is the more interesting in that the campaign coincided with neither hockey (1997) nor baseball (1993) playoffs.

10. Only six attack metaphors were used in the entire coverage of the 1997 debate. Ten such metaphors were applied to Campbell alone in 1993.

11. Compared with Charest (59), Chrétien (54), Manning (19), and Duceppe (20). The 1993 figures were McLaughlin (16), Campbell (58), Chrétien (37), Manning (21) and Bouchard (15).

12. Cited by Blankenship and Kang (1991).

13. They report that neither newspaper used a single sports metaphor in headlines featuring McDonough.

14. For an example of Campbell being taken to task for being too aggressive, see Gidengil and Everitt (1999). Sampert and Trimble (2003) also give a telling example of McDonough being censured for going on the attack.

References

Bell, Allan. 1991. *The Language of News Media.* Oxford: Blackwell.

Blais, André, Elisabeth Gidengil, Richard Nadeau and Neil Nevitte. 2002. *Anatomy of a Liberal Victory: Making Sense of the 2000 Canadian Election.* Peterborough: Broadview Press.

Blankenship, Jane. 1976. 'The Search for the 1972 Democratic Nomination: A Metaphorical Perspective'. In *Rhetoric and Communication*, eds. Jane Blankenship and Hermann G. Stelzner. Urbana: University of Illinois Press.

Blankenship, Jane and Jong Guen Kang. 1991. 'The 1984 Presidential and Vice-Presidential Debates: The Printed Press and "Construction by Metaphor".' *Presidential Studies Quarterly* 21: 307–18.

Booth, Wayne C. 1978. 'Metaphor as Rhetoric: The Problem of Evaluation'. In *On Metaphor*, ed. Sheldon Sacks. Chicago: University of Chicago Press. 47–70.

Butler, Doré and Florence L. Geis. 1990. 'Nonverbal Affect Responses to Male and Female Leaders: Implications for Leadership Evaluations'. *Journal of Personality and Social Psychology* 58: 48–59.

Carroll, Susan J. and Ronnee Schreiber. 1997. 'Media Coverage of Women in the 103rd Congress'. In *Women, Media, and Politics*, ed. Pippa Norris. Oxford: Oxford University Press, 131–48.

Davidson, Donald. 1978. 'What Metaphors Mean'. In *On Metaphor*, ed. Sheldon Sacks, Chicago: University of Chicago Press, 29–45.

Eagly, Alice H., Mona G. Makhijani and Bruce G. Klonsky. 1992. 'Gender and the Evaluation of Leaders: A Meta-Analysis'. *Psychological Bulletin* 111:3–22.

Fiske, John. 1987. *Television Culture*. New York: Methuen.

Geis, Michael L. 1987. *The Language of Politics*. New York: Springer-Verlag.

Gidengil, Elisabeth, André Blais, Richard Nadeau and Neil Nevitte. 2000. 'Are Leaders Becoming More Important to Vote Choice in Canada?' Paper presented at the annual meeting of the American Political Science Association, Washington.

Gidengil, Elisabeth and Joanna Everitt. 1999. 'Metaphors and Misrepresentation: Gendered Mediation in News Coverage of the 1993 Canadian Leaders' Debates'. *Press/Politics* 4,1: 48–65.

Gidengil, Elisabeth and Joanna Everitt. 2000. 'Filtering the Female: Gender Mediation in Television Coverage of the 1993 Canadian Leaders' Debates'. *Women & Politics* 21,4: 105–31.

Gidengil, Elisabeth and Joanna Everitt. forthcoming. 'Gender, Media Coverage and the Dynamics of Leader Evaluations: The Case of the 1993 Canadian Election'. In *Capturing Campaign Effects*, eds. Henry E. Brady and Richard Johnston. Ann Arbor: University of Michigan Press.

Gingras, Anne-Marie. 1997. 'Les métaphores dans le langue politique'. *Politique et Sociétés* 30: 159–71.

Gingras, François-Pierre. 1995. 'Daily Male Delivery: Women and Politics in the Daily Newspapers'. In *Gender and Politics in Contemporary Canada*, ed. François-Pierre Gingras. Toronto: Oxford University Press, 191–207.

Goodman, Ellen. 1984. 'This Sporting Election'. *Boston Globe*, October 18, 19.

Kahn, Kim Fridkin and Edie N. Goldenberg. 1991. 'Women Candidates in the News: An Examination of Gender Differences in US Senate Campaign Coverage'. *Public Opinion Quarterly* 55: 180–99.

Kahn, Kim Fridkin. 1994. 'The Distorted Mirror: Press Coverage of Women Candidates for Statewide Office'. *Journal of Politics* 56: 154–73.

Kress, Gunther. 1983a. 'Linguistic and Ideological Transformations in News Reporting'. In *Language, Image, and Media*, eds. Howard Davis and Paul Walton. Oxford: Basil Blackwell, 120–38.

Kress, Gunther. 1983b. 'Linguistic Processes and the Mediation of 'Reality': The Politics of Newspaper Language'. *International Journal of the Sociology of Language* 40: 43–57.

Lawrence, Regina G. 2000. 'Game-Framing the Issues: Tracking the Strategy Frame in Public Policy News'. *Political Communication* 17: 93–114.

Mendelsohn, Matthew. 1993. 'Television's Frames in the 1988 Canadian Election'. *Canadian Journal of Communication* 18: 149–71.

Mendelsohn, Matthew and Richard Nadeau. 1999. 'The Rise and Fall of Candidates in Canadian Election Campaigns'. *Press/Politics* 4: 63–76.

Monière, Denis. 1994. 'Le contenu du débat des chefs en français'. In *La bataille du Québec: Premier épisode Les élections fédérales de 1993*, eds. Denis Monière and Jean H. Guay. Saint-Laurent: Fides.

Mumby, D. K. and C. Spitzack. 1985 'Ideology and Television News: A Metaphoric Analysis of Political Stories'. *Central States Speech Journal* 34: 162–71

Norris, Pippa. 1997. 'Women Leaders Worldwide: A Splash of Color in the Photo Op'. In *Women, Media, and Politics*, ed. Pippa Norris. Oxford: Oxford University Press, 149–65.

Patterson, Thomas E. 1980. *The Mass Media Election: How Americans Choose Their President*. New York: Praeger.

Patterson, Thomas E. and Robert D. McClure. 1976. *The Unseeing Eye: The Myth of Television Power in National Politics*. New York: G. P. Putnam's Sons.

Raboy, Marc. 1996. 'Canada: The Hybridization of Public Broadcasting'. In *Public Broadcasting for the 21st Century*. ed. Marc Raboy. Luton: University of Luton Press.

Rakow, Lana F. and Kimberlie Kranich. 1991. 'Women as Sign in Television News'. *Journal of Communication* 41: 8–23.

Robinson, Gertrude and Armande Saint-Jean. 1991. 'Women Politicians and Their Media Coverage: A Generational Analysis'. In *Women in Canadian Politics: Toward Equity in Representation*, Volume 6 Research Studies for the Royal Commission on Electoral Reform and Party Financing. ed. Kathy Megyery. Toronto: Dundurn Press, 127–69.

Robinson, Gertrude and Armande Saint-Jean. 1995. 'The Portrayal of Women Politicians in the Media: Political Implications'. In *Gender and Politics in Contemporary Canada*. ed. François-Pierre Gingras. Toronto: Oxford University Press, 176–90.

Robinson, Michael J. and Margaret A. Shehan. 1983. *Over the Wire and On TV*. New York: Russell Sage Foundation.

Ross, Karen. 1995. 'Gender and Party Politics: How the Press Reported the Labour Leadership Campaign'. *Media, Culture & Society* 17: 499–509.

Ross, Karen and Annabelle Sreberny. 2000. 'Women in the House: Media Representation of British Politicians'. In *Gender, Politics and Communication*, eds. Annabelle Sreberny and Liesbet van Zoonen. Cresskill: Hampton Press. 79–99.

Sampert, Shannon and Linda Trimble. 2003. "Wham, Bam, No Thank You Ma'am': Gender and the Game Frame in National Newspaper Coverage of Election 2000'. In *Women and Electoral Representation in Canada*, eds. Manon Tremblay and Linda Trimble. Toronto: Oxford University Press, 211–26.

Smith, Kevin B. 1997. 'When All's Fair: Signs of Parity in Media Coverage of Female Candidates'. *Political Communication* 14: 499–509.

Sreberny-Mohammadi, Annabelle and Karen Ross. 1996. 'Women MPs and the Media: Representing the Body Politic'. *Parliamentary Affairs* 49: 103–15.

Taras, David. 1990. *The Newsmakers*. Scarborough: Nelson.

Taras, David. 1991. 'How Television Transformed the Meech Lake Negotiations'. In *After Meech Lake: Lessons for the Future*, eds. David E. Smith, Peter MacKinnon and John C. Courtney. Saskatoon: Fifth house.

Tiemans, Robert K., Susan Hellweg, Philip Kipper and Steven L. Phillips. 1985. 'An Integrative Verbal and Visual Analysis of the Carter-Reagan Debate'. *Communication Quarterly* 33: 34–42.

Tremblay, Manon and Nathalie Bélanger. 1997. 'Femmes chefs de partis politiques et caricatures éditoriales: l'élection fédérale canadienne de 1993'. *Recherches feministes* 10: 35–75.

van Zoonen, Liesbet. 1994. *Feminist Media Studies*. Thousand Oaks: Sage.

Zaller, John and Mark Hunt. 1994. 'The Rise and Fall of Candidate Perot: Unmediated Versus Mediated Politics—Part I'. *Political Communication* 11: 357–90.

Zaller, John and Mark Hunt. 1995. 'The Rise and Fall of Candidate Perot: Unmediated Versus Mediated Politics Part II'. *Political Communication* 12: 97–123.

CHAPTER 31

'Talk about Strenuous Hockey': Violence, Manhood, and the 1907 Ottawa Silver Seven–Montreal Wanderer Rivalry

Stacy L. Lorenz and Geraint B. Osborne

Contrary to some popular opinion that hockey violence is growing worse, violence has been a central part of hockey culture for more than a century. David Seglins argues that from the game's beginnings to today, 'violent forms of hockey have been tolerated, legitimized, ritualized and at times celebrated by players, fans, organizers, commentators and the Canadian state' (1995, 41). Since the late nineteenth century, violence in hockey has been accepted 'as just part of the game' (135).[1] Lawrence Scanlan writes, 'My overwhelming impression from reading the literature, from hearing the testimony of players from the early to mid-1900s, and from poring over news clippings, is that early hockey was very much like war. The blood flowed freely' (2002, 30).

The 1907 season featured a number of notable incidents of on-ice violence. Following a particularly rough match between the Ottawa Silver Seven and the Montreal Wanderers on 12 January, assault charges were brought against three members of the Ottawa team. During this game, Charles 'Baldy' Spittal, Harry Smith, and Alfred Smith were involved in separate stick attacks on Montreal players. In the first of these incidents, the *Montreal Gazette* reported that Cecil Blatchford of the Wanderers 'was smashed over the head by Spittal, a short, quick jab with the stick, that laid Bla[t]chford prone, with the blood pouring from a cut over the temple' (1907e, 2). Next, 'Harry Smith put [Ernie] Johnson down and out with a smash across the face' (2). Finally, Alf Smith attacked Hod Stuart: 'Smith skated in from centre ice and smashed the Wanderer cover-point across the temple with his stick. Stuart went down in a heap. . . . When Stuart was lying helpless on the ice, Smith was heard to remark, 'Did you get that one, Hod?' Then he skated away chuckling' (2). No player was suspended for his actions in this game. Motions for season-long and one-week suspensions were defeated by representatives of clubs in the Eastern Canada Hockey League (*Montreal Gazette* 1907d, 4; *Montreal Star* 1907b, 22); however, Montreal police later arrested Spittal and the Smiths (see Figure 31.1). The charge against Harry Smith was dismissed, but Baldy Spittal and Alf Smith were found guilty of assault. Both men were required to pay a $20 fine and $19 in costs, and the judge warned that similar offences would not be treated so leniently in the future (*Montreal Star* 1907a, 3).[2]

This article examines media narratives of hockey violence and manhood during the 1907 season in central Canada. The 1907 Ottawa Silver Seven–Montreal Wanderer rivalry is a useful case study for examining violence and masculinity in Canadian hockey prior to the First World War. The Silver Seven and the Wanderers were among Canada's leading hockey teams; games between the two clubs attracted a great deal of public attention.[3] Media coverage of the match of 12 January 1907 was especially noteworthy as newspapers constructed a number of important narratives of hockey and masculinity in response

Messrs. Alf. and Harry Smith played while under arrest, but not like this, as the 25-centers expected.

Figure 31.1 *Montreal Star*, 28 January 1907, 3. The three Ottawa players were arrested when they returned to Montreal for a match against the Montreal Victorias.

to the spectacular degree of violence in this game. A late-season rematch between the two teams prompted further discussion of the place of violent and 'strenuous' play in hockey. This essay also analyzes other game reports from the 1907 season in order to place the narratives surrounding the Ottawa–Wanderer rivalry in a broader context.

Narratives of hockey in the Canadian press during the time period of our case study described violence in the sport in terms of both 'brutal butchery' and 'strenuous spectacle'—sometimes on the same page of the newspaper. This article explores the meaning of these conflicting narratives of violent and physical play in hockey.[4] It considers hockey's appeal to players and spectators in light of the complex relationship between 'respectable' and 'rough' masculine ideals. It also assesses hockey violence in the context of changing standards and perceptions of manhood in the late nineteenth and early twentieth centuries. Hockey played an important role in the social construction of masculinity in this period. By evaluating key issues surrounding violence, gender, and class in early hockey, this research addresses important gaps in the study of Canadian sport history and the analysis of hockey and Canadian popular culture.[5]

Knowledge of the historical origins of hockey violence is not simply valuable for the insight it sheds on the past. It is also crucial to an adequate understanding of present-day hockey violence. In the wake of such incidents as Marty McSorley's 'clubbing' of Donald Brashear in February 2000 (Mickleburgh 2000) and Todd Bertuzzi's 'blind-siding' of Steve Moore with a punch from behind in March 2004 (MacIntyre 2004; Pap 2004), the National Hockey League (NHL) has faced intense criticism for its brutality. The Bertuzzi case, in particular, rekindled discussions about the problem of violence in NHL hockey. One aspect of this debate that has not received sufficient attention, however, is a historical perspective on the place of physical violence and intimidation in the game.

Hockey, Class, and Manliness

With the development of industrial capitalism and the emergence of an entrepreneurial and professional middle class during the nineteenth century, men increasingly perceived their gender identity in relation to individual achievement and economic success in the marketplace. This hegemonic ideal of 'self-made manhood' (Rotundo 1993; Howell 1995; Kimmel 1996) was championed by a rising middle class of merchants, bureaucrats, clerks, and business and professional men (Wamsley 1999; Holman 2000; Bouchier 2003). Middle-class notions of manliness were also rooted in the idea of respectability (Gorn 1986; Marks 1996; Riess 1997). According to Christopher Anstead, 'A respectable male individual had to be industrious, sober, religious, compassionate, morally upright and responsible for his own welfare and that of his family' (quoted in Bouchier 2003, 26). While this version of manly respectability carried considerable cultural authority, working-class males, in particular, challenged middle-class standards of manhood. For example, labourers in industrializing cities frequently defined their

masculine identity away from work, in the realm of leisure. As a result, a distinct working-class culture developed around such activities as drinking, gambling, fighting, and bloodsports; within groups like fire companies, street gangs, lodges, and political factions; and in such places as saloons, pool halls, theatres, and brothels (DeLottinville 1981/82; Gorn 1986; Marks 1996; Wamsley and Kossuth 2000). This culture valued masculine honour, toughness, and physical prowess; in Elliott J. Gorn's words, the working class 'inverted the bourgeois ethos with an antithetical assertion of rough male conviviality' (1986, 133).

Although there were clear differences between 'respectable' and 'rough' masculine ideals, distinctions between middle-class and working-class notions of manhood were neither simple nor rigid. Lynne Marks's examination of gender and leisure in late-nineteenth-century small-town Ontario is especially insightful in this regard. According to Marks, many young men were involved in 'less than respectable activities that were part of a certain masculine culture, predominantly a youth culture, which to some extent crossed class lines' (1996, 90). She argues that historians have underestimated the cross-class appeal of a 'rough' masculinity rooted in 'physical strength, recourse to violence, danger, and a certain wildness among youth' (90). The ideals of 'responsible, respectable breadwinner' and 'rowdy rough' co-existed in such groups as fraternal orders, fire brigades, militia companies, and sports clubs (Marks 1996, 108–25, 137–39, 211–13). Although middle-class sports associations sought to shape the manly character of young men in accordance with respectable ideals, the members of amateur sports teams sometimes pushed the boundaries of upright behaviour: 'Definitions of manly respectability were contested,' Marks writes, 'and even the most middle-class sports clubs, like their counterparts among the fraternal orders, were part of a larger masculine leisure culture and as such accepted a certain level of manly roughness' (1996, 123).[6]

The emergence of modern hockey was tied to conceptions of middle-class amateurism and 'respectable' middle-class masculinity. Prior to the First World War, organized hockey in Canada was played, developed, and controlled mainly by the male, urban, English-speaking middle class. Amateur sportsmen, social reformers, and muscular Christians regarded hockey as a 'manly' sport that instilled moral virtue and developed valuable character traits (Metcalfe 1987, 10, 13, 61–73, 96–98; Gruneau and Whitson 1993, 31–56, 193–96; Seglins 1995, 13–14, 18–31, 73–75). At the same time, however, some organizers, players, and fans embraced elements of 'rough' masculinity within the game.

Violence in hockey addressed a social need in helping Canadians to define and develop a meaningful masculinity. Although the persistence of physicality and aggression in hockey seemed to contradict the ideals of respectability at the heart of middle-class manliness, this affinity for violence is understandable in the context of a developing model of masculinity that cut across class lines. The new standard of active, muscular manhood glorified physical struggle and violent action. 'Primitive' elements in sports like hockey helped to counter the fear that over-civilization was making men weak, effeminate, and over-sophisticated. At the same time, the cross-class appeal of an aggressive masculinity based on force and danger helps to explain the popularity of 'strenuous', even 'brutal', hockey among middle-class players and spectators.

Brutal Butchery: Montreal Narratives

Media narratives of the Ottawa–Wanderer game of 12 January 1907 shed considerable light on the place of violence and roughness in hockey during the early twentieth century. Accounts of the match in the Montreal press expressed outrage at the attacks carried out by the visiting team. Newspaper headlines communicate this narrative most clearly. The *Montreal Gazette* stated on its second page, 'WANDERER WON BRUTAL CONTEST— Champions Cut Down by Ottawa, Stuck to Task and Downed Assailants.—BUT LITTLE GOOD HOCKEY.— Occasional Skill Shown in Battle Where Strength Was Requisite Quality' (1907e, 2). The game was called 'as disgraceful an exhibition of rough and brutal play as has been seen here—at least, in recent years.' The *Montreal Star*'s coverage was even more prominent and sensational. The two-column,

front-page headline read, '"THEY SHOULD EACH GET SIX MONTHS IN JAIL," IS THE OPINION AS TO SATURDAY HOCKEY BRUTALITIES—Old Players Say it was the Worst Exhibition of Butchery they Ever Saw—Mr. Recorder Weir Would have had them Arrested-Police Magistrate McMahon of Westmount Prepared to Apply the Law' (*Montreal Star* 1907g, 1). Inside the paper, the four-column headline across a lengthy, illustrated game story screamed, 'Butchery, Not Hockey, at the Arena Saturday Night' (*Montreal Star* 1907c, 10).

In an editorial titled, 'Hockey or Manslaughter?' the *Star* described the match as a 'brutal exhibition of rough play and deliberate fouling', and called for the police to treat assaults in hockey just like crimes on the street:

> The police authorities have a responsibility in the case. They know now that a hockey match is likely to result in breaches of the law, and there should be competent police officers present to put under immediate arrest any player who is guilty of an assault. An assault should be no more condoned in a rink crowded with ladies and gentlemen than on St. James street; and the arrest should be as prompt, as public and as certain as if such assault were committed on St. James street in the presence of a squad of policemen. Hockey thuggism will have to be stopped even if we send the hockey thugs to penitentiary. (1907e, 4)

The editorial page also featured a drawing of a hockey player armed with a sword, axe, knife, and gun (see Figure 31.2), accompanied by a caption which stated, 'The Ottawa hockey team may not be able to play hockey, but it can show the excited populace the latest fancy designs in attempted murder' (*Montreal Star* 1907f, 4).

Together, the *Star*'s headlines, stories, and opinions created a narrative of shocking, even criminal, violence. These dramatic depictions of on-ice atrocities not only provided a critique of violent hockey, but they also helped the newspaper to engage and attract readers.

Hockey brutality may have been repugnant— especially when perpetrated against the home

The Ottawa hockey team may not be able to play hockey, but it can show the excited populace the latest fancy designs in attempted murder.

Figure 31.2 *Montreal Star*, 14 January 1907, 4.

team—but it still demanded readers' attention. For instance, the *Star's* detailed summary of the Ottawa–Wanderer match in its sports section began with the following satiric account of the Silver Seven's trip home:

The professional Butchers' Association of Ottawa organized an excursion to Montreal on Saturday, and had a most successful and pleasant outing.

After a most entertaining exhibition of their skill and prowess, attended by about seven thousand people in the Montreal Arena, situated in the model Town of Westmount, they returned to Ottawa well satisfied with the work done.

On the train going home, speeches of congratulation were made to the winners of the spirited exhibition and prizes were awarded to the following gentlemen.

1. Mr. Spittal, Champion Meat Chopper for the artistic manner in which he cut down Cecil Blatchford of the Wanderers. . . .

2. Mr. Harry Smith, for beating Johnson into unconsciousness. . . .

3. Mr. Alf. Smith, for the elegant way in which he chopped down Hod Stuart with a lateral blow on the temple. . . .

The chairman regretted that he could not bestow any medals on Mr. Pulford, as the exhibitions of scientific ferocity of the other gentlemen were far ahead of his. He came to the conclusion that Mr. Pulford could not have been very well, but expressed the hope that he would soon recover to exhibit at many more matches some of that bloodthirstiness for which he has been known in the past, and which made him a shining example for other members of the team. (1907c, 10)

Although the writer censured the players' actions through this ironic appraisal, he also implicitly acknowledged that violence created fan interest by situating the 'butchery' within an entertaining and sensational story that would appeal to readers. There is also a tone of playfulness and exaggeration in this account that blunts the force of the reporter's criticism: a truly reprehensible crime likely would not have been analyzed in the same way.

The criticism of violent hockey is accompanied by a degree of sensationalism that serves as a reminder that 'butchery' also helped sell newspapers.

Strenuous Spectacle: Ottawa Narratives

The narratives created by Ottawa newspapers presented a very different view of the events in Montreal. The *Ottawa Evening Journal*, in particular, offered a narrative of 'strenuous spectacle' that contrasted with the narrative of 'brutal butchery' offered by the Montreal press.[7] While the Star's portrayal of hockey brutality blended horror and fascination, the Ottawa newspaper presented the sport's rougher elements as part of an absorbing, aggressive, masculine display. The *Evening Journal's* two-column headline on page two declared, 'OTTAWAS LOST TO WANDERERS—Game was Decidedly Strenuous and Several Players Were Badly Cut Up.—Cup Holders Failed to Score When Ottawas Only had Three Men on the Ice. Officials Off Color. Great Crowd in Attendance' (*Ottawa Evening Journal* 1907e, 2). The reporter who composed the game story revelled in the match's intense physicality:

> Talk about strenuous hockey. You haven't seen the real thing unless you were fortunate enough to be at the Ottawa–Wanderer game on Saturday night in Montreal. It was a hummer from start to finish and will go down into history as one of the hardest fought games on record. There was tripping, slashing and hard body checking in plenty, and it was very evident that both teams had it in for each other. Knocks were exchanged at every opportunity, and these opportunities came often. (2)

The writer emphasized the game's appeal to spectators, along with its violence:

> For people with weak hearts to go to many such matches it would be a straight case of suicide. . . . The excitement was intense throughout the entire match and at times the crowd would rise to its feet when some mixup occurred and hoot and cheer by turns. An official of the Arena said he had never seen more feeling shown or a more excited crowd in the spacious rink. . . . When the match had finished many pools of blood could be seen on the ice. (2)

According to the *Evening Journal*, fans were keenly interested in fierce, physical, and potentially dangerous hockey. Rather than being outraged by rough play, these spectators—and readers—were drawn to the 'strenuous' aspects of the sport.[8]

Although the *Evening Journal* recounted the violent incidents that would lead to criminal charges, its reporting lacked the lurid description and sardonic indignation of the Montreal coverage. For instance, the Ottawa newspaper described Spittal's attack on Blatchford in a way that suggested there was nothing extraordinary about it: 'Blatchford came down with a rush and skated into Pulford, who had fallen,

and got Harvey over the neck with his stick. Spittal saw this and retaliated, giving Blatchford a wicked clip over the head which made a nasty cut and the blood spurted over the ice. He was able to resume in about 10 minutes with his head bandaged up' (*Ottawa Evening Journal* 1907e, 2). Moreover, the fundamental distinction between the two teams—and the primary reason for the complaints coming out of Montreal—was that the Ottawas could take their lumps in manly fashion, while the Wanderers were soft and weak: 'The Ottawas were guilty of several offenses that could have been well cut out, but they got their share of the bumps,' stated the *Evening Journal*. 'The only real difference is they can take all kinds of knocks and never quit, while if a Wanderer player got any kind of a jab he had to be hurried to the dressing room for a breathing spell' (2). This willingness to administer and withstand physical punishment was a core element of the cross-class, masculine leisure culture that embraced hockey during this time period (Rotundo 1993; Marks 1996; Wamsley and Whitson 1998).

Another important dimension of the *Evening Journal*'s reporting was the emphasis placed on the role of the referee. The newspaper attributed many infractions to incompetent officiating, rather than to any malicious intent on the part of the Ottawa players: 'If the Ottawas has [sic] played a less rough game and kept on the ice instead of decorating the fence so often, there would be a different tale to tell to-day,' acknowledged the *Evening Journal* reporter. 'But then there is a good deal of reason in the methods pursued by Ottawas, as they were getting sent to the side for the most trivial offenses, in fact, at times players and spectators alike wondered what they had been ordered to the side for' (*Ottawa Evening Journal* 1907e, 2). In addition to calling a series of unjustified penalties, the referee allegedly missed—or ignored—'many a nasty jab' (2) handed out by the Wanderers. In light of the poor quality of the officials, the growing frustration of the Ottawa players was understandable. As the *Evening Journal* pointed out, 'This naturally worked up hard feeling and left the players in anything but a good frame of mind' (2). Thus, the disillusionment that resulted from inept officiating served as a logical explanation for the Ottawas' subsequent rough play:

There is no real justification for rough work, but when the officials practically make the game a farce by ordering off half your team for trivial offenses, men naturally become reckless and do many things they would not do if getting fair treatment. This was the case with the Ottawas. They thought they were getting a raw deal from the officials and well knowing that they could not beat their opponents and the officials, too, became disgusted and sailed in with a dash that threatened to put all the Wanderer team on the hospital list (2).[9]

Finally, rather than condemning the Ottawas for their reckless violence, the *Evening Journal* actually praised them for their steadfast play when competing shorthanded as a result of penalties: 'The way the men played against such odds and with the crowd hooting and calling all kinds of "nice" things at the Ottawas, shows what kind of stuff the local boys are made of,' boasted the newspaper. 'It was an exhibition of pluck that won admiration from even the people who a moment before were calling loudly for the Wanderers to put the Ottawas out of business' (2).

The *Ottawa Citizen* also cited the high calibre of the game, while implying that rough and aggressive play contributed to its quality. The *Citizen*'s sports page featured the two-column headline, 'WANDERERS AND OTTAWAS IN TERRIFIC MATCH—Senators Played Very Rough Hockey and Were Beaten Four Goals to Two.—Hod Stuart, Bla[t]chford and Johnson Badly Injured. Ottawas Heavily Penalized' (*Ottawa Citizen* 1907j, 8).[10] The game report began, 'When the big gong at the Arena sounded Saturday night for the last time, fourteen tired, worn-out athletes skated or rather dragged themselves off the ice amidst one long, continuous roar from seven thousand hockey enthusiasts who had witnessed one of the roughest and most exciting struggles on record' (8). In addition, the *Citizen*—like the *Evening Journal*—claimed that the referee treated Ottawa unfairly: 'All the blame for the unruly tactics employed fell on the shoulders of Ottawa, and the Senators, during the greater part of the second half, were forced to play three or four men against seven,' the *Citizen* reported (8).

Coverage of the Ottawa–Wanderer game and its aftermath also constructed what could be described as a 'squealing' narrative. Manly players were expected to react to rough play 'like men'. This meant accepting a certain degree of violence, tolerating pain and injury, and persevering through difficulty and danger. As a result, when complaining—or 'squealing'—about Ottawa brutality seemed to become excessive, the manliness of the Montreal players and their supporters was called into question. A member of the Ottawa executive expressed this view when he told the *Ottawa Citizen*, 'The Ottawa players received just as many blows as the Wanderers; they were black and blue after the match, but, unlike the Wanderers, they didn't lie down. Ottawa took their taps like men and the Wanderers should be the last ones on earth to put up a squeal' (*Ottawa Citizen* 1907f, 10).[11] The *Ottawa Free Press* conveyed a similar message, reporting, 'Ottawa supporters claim a moral victory, and—the truth must be told—a general satisfaction to see their favourites make the home team 'lay down' as they expressed it after the game' (quoted in Montreal Star 1907c, 10). Meanwhile, the *Toronto Telegram* offered a parallel criticism of the Montreal press: 'Saturday night when Wanderers went up against Ottawa, and got the worse of it, Montreal papers executed a squealing specialty,' claimed the *Telegram*. 'There is not the slightest doubt in the world that Ottawa plays anything but a parlour game, but the idea that Wanderers are the Alice-sit-by-the-fire team that knows no wrong is enough to make old Rameses shake with boyish laughter' (quoted in *Ottawa Evening Journal* 1907i, 2). The fear of a perception of unmanly squealing also made representatives of the Wanderer club reluctant to criticize publicly the conduct of the Ottawa players—and, in particular, to pursue suspensions for the attacks: 'It was thought that perhaps Wanderers would take the matter up themselves with the league, but there is no prospect of this,' reported the *Montreal Gazette*. 'They will let the matter rest on the report of the officials, and avoid all cause for a charge of squealing' (1907b, 2).

The spectre of squealing later played an important part in the dismissal of charges against Harry Smith. Smith had been arrested for allegedly assaulting Ernie Johnson, but when he appeared in court, 'there was not a man amongst all the witnesses called who would positively testify that he saw Smith hit Johnson with deliberate intent' (*Ottawa Evening Journal* 1907b, 1). Perhaps the most interesting testimony came from Johnson himself. Reluctant to violate hockey's manly 'code', Johnson not only declined to speak out directly against Smith, but he refused even to acknowledge that he had been injured during the game. Johnson told the court,

> There was a scrimmage, he was struck by a blow coming from somewhere, he couldn't tell where, and delivered by someone, he couldn't tell who. He never lost consciousness, he did not fall on the ice because the blow knocked him out, and it was simply to keep the blood from running onto his clothes that he remained prone on the ice. The scar at present to be seen decorating his beak-like nose was not from the blow in question, but had been received the year before. (*Montreal Star* 1907d, 1)

The conflicting Montreal and Ottawa perspectives on these issues clearly reflect a home-team bias. Accounts of the game and its aftermath were filtered through the lens of local boosterism. As a result, it is not surprising that newspapers generally supported their own city's team, while criticizing opponents from other communities (Lorenz 2003, 148–52); however, the different narratives of hockey violence surrounding the Ottawa–Wanderer match were not simply the products of civic rivalry or isolated examples of local perspectives. These narratives also spoke more broadly to different ways of experiencing and enjoying hockey, to various tensions within public perceptions of the sport, and to a more widely held ambivalence about violence in the game. For example, a newspaper story that portrayed violence as 'butchery' and 'manslaughter' would make sense to readers only if excessive violence was sometimes perceived as a significant problem in hockey. Similarly, a reporter's depiction of rough play as 'strenuous' action would resonate with readers only if violent hockey was often interpreted as exciting and admirable. At the same time, dramatic accounts of on-ice mayhem and descriptions of spectacular displays of masculine aggression were part of a broader move toward sensationalism and entertainment in news coverage—a move being made by quality dailies and people's journals alike. Thus, accounts of the Ottawa–Wanderer game provide exaggerated examples of complex narratives that were woven into hockey coverage on a regular basis.

Hard and Fast, but Clean

While the degree of violence in the Ottawa–Wanderer game was exceptional, stickwork, rough play, and fighting were far from unusual elements in turn-of-the-century hockey. Descriptions of slashing, tripping, hacking, hard checking, brawls, cuts, broken noses, and other injuries were typical features of hockey reporting by 1900 (Metcalfe 1987, 69; Seglins 1995, 41–42). As a result, newspaper readers were exposed to a number of different perspectives on hockey violence in the early twentieth century. These narratives expressed the tensions and ambivalence that were evident in coverage of the Ottawa–Wanderer match. Reporters, players, and team officials favoured 'decidedly strenuous' but 'clean' hockey. They tried to distinguish between this preferred brand of 'hard' and 'fast' hockey, and an excessively violent version of the game they called 'dirty' or, sometimes, 'rough' hockey; however, these distinctions were not easy to draw. The problem, of course, was that hard and strenuous hockey was marked by a great deal of physical, even violent, play. Body checking, collisions, slashing, intimidation, blood, and bruises were frequently applauded by hockey observers. As the *Cornwall Freeholder* noted following the death of Bud McCourt late in the 1907 season, 'The public are not blameless. They encourage good, hard play as they call it, but which really means doing anything disreputable that escapes the eye of the referee' (quoted in *Ottawa Evening Journal*, 1907g, 2).[12] The fact that 'rough' hockey could sometimes be 'clean' and at other times was considered 'dirty' also demonstrates the ambivalence toward violence that was central to perceptions of the sport.

These strains and contradictions were important dimensions of routine hockey reporting during the

1907 season. For instance, the *Ottawa Citizen*'s summary of a match between the towns of Arnprior and Renfrew described the essential elements of 'good, clean hockey': 'The game was without a doubt the fastest played in the Ottawa Valley league this season. . . . Both teams upheld their good reputation for manly playing, and while the game was well above the standard, there was an entire absence of rough work and it was, nevertheless, one of the keenest battles on record. . . . The players went at it with a vim and the checking was heavy and close, though no rough tactics were employed on either side' (1907a, 8). The *Citizen* reporter observed, 'Three of the Arnprior men were in the box at one time but only for petty offenses. . . . McMillan and Dontigny were both accidentally knocked out in the latter half and had to be carried off the ice' (8). In sum, the game was a 'keen battle' that featured 'heavy' checking, numerous penalties, and players being knocked unconscious during play—but it was not 'rough'. The *Citizen* generated a similar narrative in its description of a Federal Hockey League contest involving the Ottawa Victorias and Cornwall:

> Outside of three or four Stanley cup matches . . . nothing more exciting has been pulled off in Dey's arena than the Victoria–Cornwall Federal league fixture of Saturday night. . . . The game was hard and, at times, rough, but the long list of penalties was due to close checking and tripping rather than to deliberate dirty work. True, three of the Cornwall boys were laid out, two from heavy body-checks, and one from a blow with the puck; but all this was incidental to one of the hardest matches ever seen in the Federal league. (1907e, 8)

The Ottawa–Wanderer Rematch

Media narratives of the second meeting of the season between the Ottawa Silver Seven and the Montreal Wanderers, scheduled for Saturday, 7 March, in Ottawa, also demonstrate the tensions surrounding the cultural experience of hockey during this time period.[13] First, newspaper coverage of the rematch focussed on the high level of spectator interest in the game. When several

hundred tickets became available to the general public two days before the contest, a huge crowd gathered outside an Ottawa drugstore to purchase admission to the game. In a front-page article, the *Ottawa Evening Journal* stated, 'No more exciting scenes have been witnessed in Ottawa for many a long day than those of the early hours of this morning, when thousands of people fought for tickets for the Ottawa–Wanderer hockey match' (1907f, 1). The report continued, 'The police made several attempts to form the crowd in line and used their batons freely, but there was nothing doing. The crowd simply pushed them aside. . . . Never have so many lovers of the game contracted the hockey fever so badly as the crowd this morning' (1).

In Montreal, a large crowd gathered in front of the *Montreal Star*'s downtown office on the night of the game while the Ottawas and the Wanderers were facing off in Ottawa. These followers of hockey had assembled to listen to the progress of the game as telegraph bulletins were received by the newspaper. According to the *Star*, 'The plan of having a member of the Star editorial staff read out the report of the match as it came direct from the rinkside at Ottawa over a direct wire again proved to be exceedingly popular, and the four or five thousand people gathered literally hung upon the speaker's lips' (1907h, 3). Public interest in the game was confirmed by the size and enthusiasm of the group surrounding the newspaper building:

> There have been many great crowds in front of that office on various occasions, but the crowd on Saturday night beat everything that was ever seen, not barring election nights. It extended on St. Catherine past Metcalfe street, and across Peel street down as far as the lane that runs back of Alexander's. It was a most excited and enthusiastic crowd also. In fact, never, either in the case of hockey or lacrosse matches, has a crowd at a bulletin board in Montreal shown so much excitement. (3)[14]

The Wanderers won the match by a score of 10–6 and claimed the Eastern Canada Hockey League championship (*Ottawa Evening Journal* 1907j, 2). In contrast to the first Ottawa–Wanderer game, coverage of the rematch in Montreal and Ottawa newspapers was remarkably similar in content and tone. On the whole, media reports in both cities constructed a narrative of 'strenuous spectacle' around the contest. The only notable occurrence of excessive violence was a clash in which Ottawa's Harry Smith cut Montreal's Hod Stuart with his stick. By combining speed and skill with hard hits and physical play, the match achieved the precarious balance between strenuousness and roughness that was essential to the most exciting hockey.

The headline introducing the *Montreal Star's* coverage read, 'Wanderers' Win Stunned Ottawa—Champions Played Opponents Off Their Feet in Stirring Hockey Struggle and Retained Title of Leadership in League' (1907k, 3). The *Star* reported,

> It was a hard, rough match. The ice was heavy and on the slower surface it was easier than usual to reach the man, consequently there was a great deal of bodying and the boards often crashed from the impact of a victim. Apart from the incident in which Harry Smith figured and some of Baird's tricks, it was not a dirty game to the extent that some of the previous meetings have reached. The Ottawa men played hard, but their opponents stuck with them and it is probable that they gave as much as they took. (3)

The *Star* also praised Stuart's determination in the face of the Silver Seven's efforts to intimidate him: 'Ottawa seemed to want to get at Hod Stuart. They did land Hod, and that gentleman left a gory souvenir in Dey's Rink to mark where he fell,' wrote the *Star* reporter. 'He was "got at" early, probably after half a minute's play, but that nerved Stuart to his work, and he played the best game of this season, fully earning the high compensation given for his services' (3). In addition, the newspaper noted that police officers were present at the game in an attempt to deter the type of violence that occurred in the January meeting of the two clubs. 'However, no officer was needed,' commented the *Star* reporter, 'and the game was played to a strenuous, but not unduly rough, finish' (3).

Despite the fact that the Ottawa club lost the game, the *Ottawa Evening Journal* celebrated the quality of the match even more enthusiastically than the *Montreal Star*. The *Evening Journal's* headlines summarized the essential ingredients of an outstanding hockey game:

> WANDERERS CAPTURE CHAMPIONSHIP; DEFEATED OTTAWAS IN HARD GAME—Victory of the Montreal Team Came as One of the Biggest Surprises in Sporting Circles in Years.—One of the Fastest Games Ever Witnessed in the Capital. Wanderers Had Best of Play Nearly all the Way. Plenty of Tripping and Slashing, but Little Really Dirty Play. Great Crowd in Attendance. Police and Firemen Stationed at Rink. Score 10 to 6. (1907j, 2)

The contest featured speed, excitement, and keen competition: 'People who paid big prices for their tickets had the satisfaction of knowing that they saw one of the greatest games of hockey ever played in Canada,' claimed the *Evening Journal*. 'It was a battle royal between the giants of the hockey world, and everyone wanted to witness the struggle' (2). Most importantly, the *Evening Journal* highlighted the appeal of rough, physical hockey to fans: 'The play was of the kind that kept everyone keenly excited, being fast and hard at all stages, with plenty of heavy checking and bodying and all kinds of tripping and slashing,' enthused the *Evening Journal* writer.[15] 'The penalty list was quite a heavy one, although the offenses in the majority of cases were not very glaring. That the play was rough no one will question, but there was little really dirty work' (2). Finally, the newspaper noted that 'the officials were fair in their decisions and quick to act in case of rough play. . . . Some nasty trips and slashes escaped their notice but that is to be expected in such a strenuous and fast game' (2).

Conclusion

This study has analyzed contradictory media narratives of rough and aggressive hockey in relation to gender and class identities in late-nineteenth- and early-twentieth-century Canada. It has examined hockey violence in the context of media and spectator interest, and considered the meanings of hockey within the wider history of manhood and masculinity in North America. During the 1907 season, central Canadian newspapers created hockey narratives that combined elements of 'brutal butchery' and 'strenuous spectacle'. Narratives of hockey as 'brutal butchery' expressed outrage and concern, while revealing a degree of popular fascination with the game's violent possibilities. In contrast, accounts of hockey as 'strenuous spectacle' represented the sport as a stirring public display of masculine force and aggression. The Ottawa Silver Seven-Montreal Wanderer rivalry provided a particularly vivid forum for the expression of these complex narratives. Moreover, newspaper descriptions of games involving different teams in a variety of leagues reflected similar concerns and perceptions related to violence in hockey.

Ideals of respectable, middle-class masculinity and rough, working-class masculinity co-existed within accounts of fast, skilled, rugged, hard-hitting hockey.[16] Excitement and entertainment were equated with both speed and violence; admiration for precise and diligent work was expressed alongside approval of 'stiff' checking and jarring collisions. 'Manly' hockey was expected to be fast and clean, with no 'foul' or 'dirty' tactics; yet, tripping and slashing were regarded as legitimate parts of the game, heavy body checks were applauded, and a high level of violence was expected under the strain of a closely contested match. Even being knocked unconscious by an opponent could be considered 'incidental'. At the same time, the danger, physicality, and competitiveness of 'decidedly strenuous' hockey cultivated and reinforced standards of passionate manhood and primitive masculinity. In the culture of hockey, 'keen battles' were welcomed, and the ability to absorb pain and punishment without complaint was widely respected. As a result, both middle-class and working-class fans expected players to 'take their taps like men' and to refrain from unmanly 'squealing'.

This historical case study also reveals that contemporary hockey violence is not unique. Violence has been central to 'manly playing' since hockey's earliest days and has always garnered the attention of the media and most fans, regardless of their class origins. A proper understanding of contemporary debates and incidents, such as those involving Marty McSorley and Todd Bertuzzi, requires not only an appreciation for the current state of violence in the sport, but also an acknowledgment of its deep historical roots. By enhancing our awareness of the kinds of violence accepted in the game's formative era, this analysis of media narratives of violent and physical play during the 1907 hockey season helps us to understand more clearly the long history of accepted brutality within the sport. In addition, by demonstrating that the elimination of violence strikes at the core meanings of hockey, this article helps to explain why the hockey establishment has been so resistant to cracking down on rough play.

The justifications for violence that were articulated in the context of the Ottawa–Wanderer rivalry and the admiration of robust, rugged hockey expressed in 1907 newspaper coverage are still prominent in the culture of hockey today. The game reports examined in this case study suggest that stick-swinging incidents and aggressive hits have been regarded as ordinary aspects of 'strenuous hockey' for at least a century. Like McSorley and Bertuzzi, a number of early-twentieth-century hockey players used their sticks or fists to inflict severe, intentional blows on their opponents—yet, within the conventions of hockey, all of these players could credibly claim that they had not acted 'maliciously', and that they had merely intended to deliver the usual 'hard knocks' that are accepted within the sport. At the same time, lenient punishments for such assaults confirm that the criminal justice system and hockey leagues themselves have tolerated significant levels of savagery within the sport. For example, the outcome of the three 1907 assault cases involving members of the Ottawa Silver Seven made a powerful statement that such violent acts were simply part of the game. Similarly, Todd Bertuzzi's plea agreement, his reinstatement by the NHL, and his recent, albeit controversial, selection to the 2006 Canadian Olympic hockey squad, indicate that the threshold for 'normal' violence' in hockey continues to be extremely high—and that our willingness to accept on-ice brutality has not diminished very much in the last hundred years.

Notes

An earlier version of this essay was presented at the 2005 North American Society for Sport History conference in Green Bay, Wisconsin. The authors would like to thank Alan Metcalfe and the three anonymous reviewers for their helpful suggestions.

1. For a useful analysis of key issues surrounding violence and masculinity in hockey, both historically and in the present, see Gruneau and Whitson (1993, 175–96).
2. See also *Ottawa Evening Journal* (1907b, 1; 1907h, 1), *Montreal Star* (1907d, 1; 1907i, 6), and *Ottawa Citizen* (1907b, 8). This game and its aftermath, including the court cases involving Smith, Smith, and Spittal, are examined in Seglins (1995, 76–77, 113–24). At least three other assault charges were brought against Canadian hockey players in the early twentieth century as a result of violent incidents during games. Although four of these six cases ended in a conviction, punishment was lenient, ranging from a $3 penalty to a $20 fine. No player served jail time for knocking an opponent senseless with his stick (Seglins 1995, 145).
3. In 1907, the Ottawa Silver Seven and the Montreal Wanderers participated in Canada's most prestigious league, the Eastern Canada Amateur Hockey Association, commonly known as the Eastern Canada Hockey League. Ostensibly an amateur organization, the ECAHA was moving towards open professionalism between 1904 and 1910. In 1907, the ECAHA permitted 'declared' professionals to play in the league. See Metcalfe (1987, 168–72) and Gruneau and Whitson (1993, 72–77).
4. This essay draws upon ideas and methods utilized in other historical studies of sports media narratives. See, for example, Goldstein (1989), Oriard (1993; 2001), Welky (1997; 1998), Dyreson (1998), and Grundy (2001).
5. Studies of hockey prior to the First World War include Morrow (1981), Mott (1985), Vigneault (1986), Metcalfe (1987, 61–73), Barnes (1990), Seglins (1995), Gruneau and Whitson (1993, 31–92), Mason and Schrodt (1996), Mason (1998), Robidoux (2002), and Wilson (2005). Surprisingly, there is very little published scholarly work on the history of violence in hockey.

6. See also Bouchier (2003, 27–28, 106–07, 125–30, 133, 136–37) and Howell (1995, 4–6, 14–15).
7. The comparative framework used in this case study invites a similar approach to examining more recent incidents of violence in hockey. For example, comparisons could be made between how Vancouver newspapers narrated Todd Bertuzzi's attack on Colorado's Steve Moore, as well as Bertuzzi's subsequent reinstatement by the NHL, and how these same stories were covered by Canadian 'national' newspapers, such as *The Globe and Mail* and the *National Post*, by journalists in other Canadian cities, or by the local media in Denver, Colorado.
8. See also Seglins (1995, 54–57, 80) and Gruneau and Whitson (1993, 180–81).
9. On the tendency to blame referees for on-ice violence, see Seglins (1995, 77–78).
10. Although the Ottawa franchise was not officially known as the 'Senators' until the 1908–1909 season, this nickname was frequently used in 1907.
11. For other examples of 'squealing', see Seglins (1995, 65–66).
12. See also an editorial in the *Ottawa Citizen* (1907d, 6) and Seglins (1995, 80).
13. The Ottawa–Wanderer rematch would either settle, or set up, the championship of the Eastern Canada Hockey League. If the undefeated Wanderers won the game, they would capture the league title. If the Ottawas avenged their earlier defeat in Montreal, the two clubs would be tied in the league standings, with just one loss each. They would then play a two-game, total goal series, with one game in each city, in order to determine the league champion. The winner of the Wanderer-Ottawa match-up would also earn the right to challenge the Kenora Thistles for the Stanley Cup. See *Ottawa Evening Journal* (1907j, 2).
14. On telegraph re-enactments of hockey games in this period, see Gruneau and Whitson (1993, 84), Morrow (1981, 61–63), and Lorenz (2003, 147–48).
15. According to Daniel Mason and Barbara Schrodt, when the Montreal Wanderers played the Portage Lakes Hockey Club in Houghton, Michigan, in 1904, Houghton's local newspaper, the *Daily Mining Gazette*, described the game in

remarkably similar terms. The *Mining Gazette's* account of the match stated that 'the game had all the features which go to make hockey the most exciting sport in the world. There was slashing, body checking, terrific shooting, marvelous speed, injuries to players, combination plays' (Mason and Schrodt 1996, 61).

16. Warren Goldstein makes a similar observation in relation to baseball during the 1860s. According to Goldstein, 'The potential for disorder and violence was said to attract 'roughs', while the promise of manly displays of nerve and skill spoke to the 'respectable' patrons. This analysis was correct but it was incomplete. These differential appeals also spoke to conflicting tendencies within every member of the baseball fraternity, no matter how 'respectable', no matter how 'low" (1989, 80).

References

Barnes, John. 1983. *Sports and the Law in Canada.* Toronto: Butterworths.

———. 1988. *Sports and the Law in Canada.* 2nd ed. Toronto: Butterworths.

———. 1990. 'Two Cases of Hockey Homicide: The Crisis of a Moral Ideal'. Paper presented to the North American Society for Sport History, Banff, Alberta.

Bouchier, Nancy B. 2003. *For the Love of the Game: Amateur Sport in Small-Town Ontario, 1838–1895.* Montreal and Kingston: McGill-Queen's University Press.

Burstyn, Varda. 1999. *The Rites of Men: Manhood, Politics, and the Culture of Sport.* Toronto: University of Toronto Press.

DeLottinville, Peter. 1981–82. 'Joe Beef of Montreal: Working-Class Culture and the Tavern, 1869–1889'. *Labour/Le Travail* 8/9: 9–40.

Dyreson, Mark. 1998. *Making the American Team: Sport, Culture, and the Olympic Experience.* Urbana and Chicago: University of Illinois Press.

Goldstein, Warren. 1989. *Playing for Keeps: A History of Early Baseball.* Ithaca and London: Cornell University Press.

Gomm, R., M. Hammersley, and P. Foster. 2000. 'Case Study and Generalization'. In *Case Study and Method: Key Issues, Key Texts,* ed. R. Gomm, M. Hammersley, and P. Foster, 98–115. Thousand Oaks, CA: Sage.

Gorn, Elliott J. 1986. *The Manly Art: Bare-Knuckle Prize Fighting in America.* Ithaca: Cornell University Press.

Grundy, Pamela. 2001. *Learning to Win: Sports, Education, and Social Change in Twentieth-Century North Carolina.* Chapel Hill and London: University of North Carolina Press.

Gruneau, Richard, and David Whitson. 1993. *Hockey Night in Canada: Sport, Identities, and Cultural Politics.* Toronto: Garamond Press.

Hoganson, Kristin L. 1998. *Fighting for American Manhood: How Gender Politics Provoked the Spanish-American and Philippine-American Wars.* New Haven and London: Yale University Press.

Holman, Andrew C. 2000. *A Sense of Their Duty: Middle-Class Formation in Victorian Ontario Towns.* Montreal and Kingston: McGill-Queen's University Press.

Howell, Colin D. 1995. *Northern Sandlots: A Social History of Maritime Baseball.* Toronto: University of Toronto Press.

Kimmel, Michael. 1996. *Manhood in America: A Cultural History.* New York: Free Press.

Lorenz, Stacy L. 2003. '"In the Field of Sport at Home and Abroad": Sports Coverage in Canadian Daily Newspapers, 1850–1914'. *Sport History Review* 34 (2): 133–67.

———. 2004. 'On-Ice Violence Has Been a Part of Hockey for Almost 100 Years'. *Edmonton Journal,* 28 December, A16.

MacGregor, Roy. 2004. 'Canada's Troubled Game Suffers Yet Another Blow'. *The Globe and Mail,* 10 March, A1.

MacIntyre, Iain. 2004. 'Bertuzzi Likely to Face Wrath of League'. *Vancouver Sun,* 9 March, E3.

Mangan, J.A. 1987. 'Social Darwinism and Upper-Class Education in Late Victorian and Edwardian England'. In *Manliness and Morality: Middle-Class Masculinity in Britain and America, 1800–1940,* eds. J.A. Mangan and James Walvin, 135–59. New York: St. Martin's Press.

Marks, Lynne. 1996. *Revivals and Roller Rinks: Religion, Leisure, and Identity in Late-Nineteenth-Century Small-Town Ontario.* Toronto: University of Toronto Press.

Mason, Daniel S. 1998. 'The International Hockey League and the Professionalization of Ice Hockey, 1904–1907'. *Journal of Sport History* 25 (1): 1–17.

Mason, Daniel, and Barbara Schrodt. 1996. 'Hockey's First Professional Team: The Portage Lakes

Hockey Club of Houghton, Michigan'. *Sport History Review* 27 (1): 49–71.

McLaren, Angus. 1990. *Our Own Master Race: Eugenics in Canada, 1885–1945*. Toronto: McClelland & Stewart.

Metcalfe, Alan. 1987. *Canada Learns to Play: The Emergence of Organized Sport, 1807–1914*. Toronto: McClelland & Stewart.

Mickleburgh, Rod. 2000. 'Judge's Warning Rejected by NHL'. *The Globe and Mail*, 7 October, A1, A9.

Mitchell, J.C. 1983. 'Case and Situational Analysis'. *Sociological Review* 31:187–211.

Montreal Gazette. 1907a. 'Brilliant Hockey'. 28 January, 2.

———. 1907b. 'Game the One Topic'. 15 January, 2.

———. 1907c. 'Report to League'. 14 January, 4.

———. 1907d. 'Sluggers Go Free'. 19 January, 4.

———. 1907e. 'Wanderer Won Brutal Contest'. 14 January, 2.

Montreal Star. 1907a. 'Alf. Smith Fined Twenty and Costs'. 1 March, 3.

———. 1907b. 'A Bombshell Explodes in Eastern Hockey'. 19 January, 22.

———. 1907c. 'Butchery, Not Hockey, at the Arena Saturday Night'. 14 January, 10.

———. 1907d. 'Charge Against Smith Dismissed'. 18 February, 1.

———. 1907e. 'Hockey or Manslaughter?' 14 January, 4.

———. 1907f. 'The Ottawa Hockey Team'. 14 January, 4.

———. 1907g. "They Should Each Get Six Months in Jail', Is the Opinion as to Saturday Hockey Brutalities'. 14 January, 1.

———. 1907h. 'Tremendous Crowd at Star Bulletins'. 4 March, 3.

———. 1907i. 'Twenty Dollars Fine for Spittal'. 28 February, 6.

———. 1907j. 'Vain Regrets'. 15 January, 16.

———. 1907k. 'Wanderers' Win Stunned Ottawa'. 4 March, 3.

———. 1907l. 'Wild Rush for Seats for Saturday's Game'. 28 February, 3.

Morrow, Don. 1981. 'The Little Men of Iron: The 1902 Montreal Hockey Club'. *Canadian Journal of History of Sport* 12 (1): 51–65.

Mott, Morris. 1985. 'Flawed Games, Splendid Ceremonies: The Hockey Matches of the Winnipeg Vics, 1890–1903'. *Prairie Forum* 10 (1): 169–87.

Mrozek, Donald J. 1987. 'The Habit of Victory: The American Military and the Cult of Manliness'. In *Manliness and Morality: Middle-Class Masculinity in Britain and America, 1800–1940*, eds. J.A. Mangan and James Walvin, 220–41. New York: St. Martin's Press.

Oriard, Michael. 1993. *Reading Football: How the Popular Press Created an American Spectacle*. Chapel Hill and London: University of North Carolina Press.

———. 2001. *King Football: Sport and Spectacle in the Golden Age of Radio and Newsreels, Movies and Magazines, the Weekly and the Daily Press*. Chapel Hill and London: The University of North Carolina Press.

Ottawa Citizen. 1907a. 'Arnprior Nine; Renfrew Six'. 19 January, 8.

———. 1907b. 'Both Players Were Fined'. 1 March, 8.

———. 1907c. 'Great Fight for Hockey Tickets'. 28 February, 8.

———. 1907d. 'The Hockey Fatality'. 8 March, 6.

———. 1907e. 'Ottawa Vics Won Again'. 28 January, 8.

———. 1907f. 'Ottawas Will Drop Out'. 18 January, 10.

———. 1907g. 'Sporting Gossip'. 29 January, 8.

———. 1907h. 'Tickets for Big Game Have All Been Sold'. 1 March, 8.

———. 1907i. 'Victorias Defeated in Brilliant Match'. 28 January, 8.

———. 1907j. 'Wanderers and Ottawas in Terrific Match'. 14 January, 8.

Ottawa Evening Journal. 1907a. 'Great Rush for Tickets'. 28 February, 2.

———. 1907b. 'Harry Smith Is Acquitted'. 18 February, 1.

———. 1907c. 'Ottawa Seconds Tie with Rialtos'. 9 March, 2.

———. 1907d. 'Ottawas Beat the Victorias'. 28 January, 2.

———. 1907e. 'Ottawas Lost to Wanderers'. 14 January, 2.

———. 1907f. 'Police Used Batons Freely on the Crowd'. 28 February, 1.

———. 1907g. 'The Rules Must Be Enforced'. 11 March, 2.

———. 1907h. 'Spittal Is Found Guilty'. 28 February, 1.

———. 1907i. 'Wanderers Can Rough It Some'. 16 January, 2.

————. 1907j. 'Wanderers Capture Championship; Defeated Ottawas in Hard Game'. 4 March, 2.

Pap, Elliott. 2004. 'Outrage: Bertuzzi Faces Police Investigation, NHL Suspension for Attack on Moore'. *Edmonton Journal*, 10 March, A1.

Riess, Steven A. 1997. 'Sport and the Redefinition of Middle-Class Masculinity in Victorian America'. In *The New American Sport History: Recent Approaches and Perspectives,* ed. S.W. Pope, 173–97. Urbana and Chicago: University of Illinois Press.

Robidoux, Michael A. 2002. 'Imagining a Canadian Identity through Sport: A Historical Interpretation of Lacrosse and Hockey'. *Journal of American Folklore* 115 (456): 209–25.

Rotundo, E. Anthony. 1993. *American Manhood: Transformations in Masculinity from the Revolution to the Modern Era*. New York: BasicBooks.

Rutherford, Paul. 1975. 'The People's Press: The Emergence of the New Journalism in Canada, 1869–99'. *Canadian Historical Review* 56:169–91.

————. 1978. *The Making of the Canadian Media*. Toronto: McGraw-Hill Ryerson.

————. 1982. *A Victorian Authority: The Daily Press in Late Nineteenth-Century Canada*. Toronto: University of Toronto Press.

Scanlan, Lawrence. 2002. *Grace under Fire: The State of Our Sweet and Savage Game*. Toronto: Penguin Canada.

Seglins, David. 1995. "Just Part of the Game': Violence, Hockey and Masculinity in Central Canada, 1890–1910'. MA thesis, Queen's University.

Sotiron, Minko. 1997. *From Politics to Profit: The Commercialization of Canadian Daily Newspapers, 1890–1920*. Montreal and Kingston: McGill-Queen's University Press.

Vaughn, Diane. 1992. 'Theory Elaboration: The Heuristics of Case Analysis'. In *What Is a Case? Exploring the Foundations of Social Inquiry*, ed. C. Ragin and H. Becker, 173–202. Cambridge: Cambridge University Press.

Vigneault, Michel. 1986. 'La diffusion du Hockey à Montréal, 1895–1910'. *Canadian Journal of History of Sport* 17 (1): 60–74.

Vipond, Mary. 1989. *The Mass Media in Canada*. Toronto: James Lorimer.

Wamsley, Kevin B. 1999. 'The Public Importance of Men and the Importance of Public Men: Sport and Masculinities in Nineteenth-Century Canada'. In *Sport and Gender in Canada*, eds. Philip White and Kevin Young, 24–39. Don Mills: Oxford University Press.

Wamsley, Kevin B., and David Whitson. 1998. 'Celebrating Violent Masculinities: The Boxing Death of Luther McCarty'. *Journal of Sport History* 25 (3): 419–31.

Wamsley, Kevin B., and Robert S. Kossuth. 2000. 'Fighting It Out in Nineteenth-Century Upper Canada/Canada West: Masculinities and Physical Challenges in the Tavern'. *Journal of Sport History* 27 (3): 405–30.

Welky, David B. 1997. 'Viking Girls, Mermaids, and Little Brown Men: U.S. Journalism and the 1932 Olympics'. *Journal of Sport History* 24 (1): 24–49.

————. 1998. 'Culture, Media and Sport: The *National Police Gazette* and the Creation of an American Working-Class World'. *Culture, Sport, Society* 1 (1): 78–100.

Wilson, J.J. 2005. 'Skating to Armageddon: Canada, Hockey and the First World War'. *The International Journal of the History of Sport* 22 (3): 315–43.

Yin, R.K. 2003a. *Applications of Case Study Research*. 2nd ed. Thousand Oaks, CA: Sage.

————. 2003b. *Case Study Research: Design and Methods*. 3rd ed. Thousand Oaks, CA: Sage.

CHAPTER 32

You Can Run but You Can't Hide: The Incorporation of Riot Grrrl into Mainstream Culture

Alison Jacques

The group of young punk feminists calling itself 'riot grrrl' always struck me as a subculture built on contradiction. On the one hand, its call for a 'Revolution Girl Style Now' is basically an angrier, more urgent version of the second-wave feminist assertion that 'sisterhood is powerful'. Springing from the male-dominated terrain of punk (and male-dominated society at large), riot grrrl promoted female empowerment, expression, and 'girl love', and gave voice to many women's experiences that have traditionally been silenced. But, rather than taking the opportunity to spread its message and reach out to as many girls and women as possible through the mass media, riot grrrl opposed media coverage with a vehemence that verged on paranoia. Much of the group's energy was spent staying out of the spotlight, and its 'revolution' was therefore limited to those in the know.

I am interested in the process by which a subculture is brought to the mainstream, and I will attempt in this paper to demonstrate that riot grrrl was subject to this process of incorporation despite its attempts to resist.

Riot Grrrl: Revolution, Whose Style?

The beginnings of the riot grrrl (RG) movement can be traced to 1990 when, according to Theo Cateforis and Elena Humphreys, young women in Olympia, Washington, 'decided to react against that city's stagnant male-dominated punk scene' (320). In August 1991 the week-long International Pop Underground Convention in Washington, D.C., kicked off with Girl Day, which, in retrospect, was RG's 'coming out' party. In 1992, the three-day national Riot Grrrl Convention was held

in D.C., comprising a number of educational workshops on topics such as violence against women, fat oppression, and unlearning racism; performances by female bands and spoken word artists; and the 'All-Girl All-Night Dance Party' (Cateforis and Humphreys 320; Klein 214).

Generally speaking, RG emerged as an American-based movement comprised of young female punks who were fed up with the overwhelming maleness of punk rock, as well as being feminists who were fed up with sexism in general. The bands (e.g., Bikini Kill, Bratmobile, Heavens to Betsy) were on independent record labels. Media-savvy grrrls hooked up through self-published fanzines and word-of-mouth. Their lyrics and other writing centred on themes of sexual abuse, oppression, and body image. They attended and organized conventions and fundraisers around feminist issues. They adopted slogans like 'Revolution Girl Style Now' and 'Stop the J-Word jealousy from Killing Girl Love' (Klein 213). They took the original punk do-it-yourself approach to music-making, encouraging female peers to pick up instruments and form bands. They were overwhelmingly white, mostly middle class, many were college educated, and a large proportion identified as queer. Membership of RG was relatively small when compared to that of other subcultures, such as punk or hip hop. According to the pop-cult web site alt.culture, RG numbers were 'grossly over-inflated by a media titillated by the notion of a teenage girl army' ('rock women').

One must consider the context from which a subculture springs, as well as the context within which it is received by the mainstream, in order to avoid overstating its innovation—a tendency of early subculture theorists (see Clarke). As stated, RG was a musical and political subculture, born of punk rock and feminism. Riot grrrls were certainly not the first women in punk, nor were they the first feminists to make political music. But, as a group, they were the first to deliberately and explicitly fuse the two realms with such an aggressive, in-your-face style. A Bikini Kill performance, for example, was described as 'not just a vague, fuck-society punk gesture, but a focused critique of the [patriarchal structure of the] punk scene itself' (White 399). Several writers have noted a mid-'80s shift within punk toward a hardcore, misogynist scene that many females found hostile and unwelcoming (Cateforis and Humphreys; Gottlieb and Wald; Klein; Wald). Many riot grrrls were students or graduates of college Women's Studies programs, as well as being 'daughters of seventies women's libbers' (White 404)—feminist discourse and political action were familiar. In terms of the context within which RG was received—or, why the media would be 'titillated by the notion of a teenage girl army'—I believe it is significant that rap music was gaining widespread popularity in the late 1980s; it is possible that angry white women seemed positively charming to the media compared to angry black men.

Antagonism between RG and mainstream media is well documented (see Cateforis and Humphreys; Gottlieb and Wald; Greenblatt; Klein). The most popular version of events is that distorted or dismissive press coverage of RG led the grrrls to establish a nationwide media blackout in 1992–93. After all, according to Kathleen Hanna (Bikini Kill singer and oft-touted RG leader), 'we weren't doing what we did to gain fame, we were just trying to hook up with other freaks' (qtd. in Greenblatt 25). However, neither RG nor the media were homogenous groups and, despite the call for a media blackout, there was no monolithic RG resistance to co-optation. The relationship between the two resembled both Hebdige's oppositional model and Thornton's co-operative model. For one thing, some riot grrrls didn't mind talking to the mainstream press, and did so (see Malkin); others continued to do interviews with underground publications like *Punk Planet* and *off our*

backs. The 'alternative', but-still-mainstream teen magazine *Sassy* promoted RG to some three million readers, demonstrating that 'the media, beyond its function to control and contain this phenomenon, may also have helped to perpetuate it' (Gottlieb and Wald 265). In addition, for a political movement that wanted to reach out to alienated girls, the media-blackout strategy closed RG off to girls in smaller centres and risked defining RG as an exclusive, insular movement. Indeed, Gottlieb and Wald advise that:

> If Riot Grrrl wants to raise feminist consciousness on a large scale, then it will have to negotiate a relation to the mainstream that does not merely reify the opposition between mainstream and subculture. (271)

Although this dilemma to remain 'authentic' but risk elitism, or to reach a wider audience but to 'sell out' exists in all subcultures, I believe it was especially prevalent for RG because of the movement's foundation in both punk rock and feminism. Depending on one's perspective, each can be seen to limit RG's ability to resolve the reach-out/sell-out dilemma. On the one hand, while feminist praxis ideally involves consciousness-raising and the fostering of women's diverse voices, punk tends to be an insular scene with a high degree of subcultural capital and disdain for outsiders and commercial success; on the other hand, while punk promotes a strong D.I.Y. ethic that opens itself to amateurs, feminism traditionally has been a vehicle primarily for educated, middle-class, white women (as was RG). Discussion of this dilemma implies that there was a real choice to be made, that the scene/music in question could take or leave the path to success. However, there is the distinct possibility that RG music was ultimately unsellable: the combination of punk's abrasive sound and low production quality with the grrrls' frank feminist lyrics may not have been as attractive to the media as the grrrls themselves. Judging by the fact that the media did not champion RG music, it seems the media felt riot grrrls were better seen and not heard. As one grrrl wrote in her zine, 'The media didn't give a shit about any of the things any of the girls were saying, they just wanted to sell their paper [sic] with pictures of angry grrrls and riot grrrl fashion' (*channel seven* 4). Ultimately, media attention turned to other female rockers—women whose anger was more palatable, like Alanis Morrisette and Liz Phair. Although RG chapters still exist around North America, and continue to start up worldwide, many of these grrrls 'have no tangible connection with the women from the beginning' and the original musicians have moved on to new projects (Cateforis and Humphreys 337).

Incorporation: Grrrl for Sale

Although RG bands were never featured on the cover of *Spin* or on the *Billboard* charts, I propose that the media did their best to neutralize the ideological threat posed by RG by co-opting and trivializing the movement's very name. As well, I will argue that a particular RG system of signification—namely, the words some grrrls wrote on their bodies—was commodified and mass-(re)produced in the form of slogan T-shirts. As Hebdige points out, of course, both ideology and commerce can be seen to 'converge on the commodity form' (96). So, although I have classified appropriation of 'grrrl' as an example of the ideological form of incorporation, dissemination of the word occurred in the marketplace; at the same time, while mass-production of girl-themed T-shirts represents the commodity form of incorporation, the display of words is a behaviour with significant symbolic value and, as such, is linked to the ideological form.

The Ideological Form (an Example)

The name 'Riot Grrrl' is a deliberate manipulation of signs: the word 'riot' implies protest and aggression; the word 'girl' describes female childhood and is condescending when used to refer to a grown woman; the transformed word 'grrrl' literally includes a growl that turns the sugar-and-spice connotations of 'girl' upside-down. For the mass media, an industry that thrives on sound bites and buzz words, 'grrrl' was a commercial dream come true. Through decontextualized adoption of this word, the media effectively trivialized its origins and, in so

doing, minimized the otherness of RG. After initial reports on RG itself, the popular press used 'grrrl' to refer to any independent, noisy (white) female rock musicians, such as Kim Gordon (of Sonic Youth), L7, and Courtney Love. Then it was spread to other genres. A 1995 *Rolling Stone* article on Natalie Merchant (of 10,000 Maniacs), for example, was called 'Flower Grrrl'. The term was also taken outside the music world into general pop-cultural terrain: also in 1995, a profile of a female athlete in *Seventeen* was called 'Biker Grrrl'; in *Wired*, a story about a female computer whiz was called 'Modern Grrrl' (Cateforis and Humphreys 337). The very word with which a subculture had named its defiance was re-defined to encompass mass public femaleness. Once established as a trend, of course, it became destined for obsolescence. In 1996, a *Newsweek* article reported that 'Female rage is all the rage' ('Where the wimps are': 80); by 1998, a *Time* feature on young feminists described 'grrrl' as 'that tiresome battle growl' (Labi: 55).

The Commodity Form (an Example)

Riot grrrls were 'skilled creators of spectacle' (White 405). Music and fashion are hard to separate in any case; with RG, as with punk, hip hop, and grunge, the name refers equally to sound and style. Many grrrls used their bodies to convey bold statements in two ways: first, through 'punk fashion irony' and the juxtaposition of gendered signs (e.g., '1950s dresses with combat boots, shaved hair with lipstick, studded belts with platform heels') (Klein 222); and second, through writing politically loaded words such as rape, 'shame' (Japenga 30), 'prophet' (France 23), and 'slut' on their arms and midriffs. I believe a line can be drawn from the words that riot grrrls wrote on their bodies in the early 1990s to popular girl-themed slogans printed on T-shirts in the mid- to late '90s. A 1993 story on RG in *Seventeen* stated that grrrls 'like to "accessorize" with black Magic Markers' (Malkin: 81). In 1993, *Rolling Stone* reported on this 'new' trend, as publicly displayed by four (male) rock stars: Prince, Eddie Vedder, Shannon Hoon (of Blind Melon), Nuno Bettencourt (of Extreme)—adding, 'Riot grrrls do it, too' ('Body talk' 16). So-called 'alternative' shops were soon flooded with 'baby tees'—tight-fitting T-shirts for girls—emblazoned with sassy, sexy words like 'Tasty', 'Tart', and 'Maneater' (Heinrich B1). More recently, Porn Star became a popular T-shirt moniker and, thanks (?) to the enormous popularity and ubiquity of the Spice Girls, circa 1997, malls were flooded with 'girl power' merchandise from T-shirts to shoelaces and stickers.

T-shirts have long been popular public forums for political slogans and advertisements alike. Indeed, 'girl power' (or 'girls rule', 'girls rock', and so on) is a message—a catchy slogan, to be exact: the nature of the medium—that girls should wear on their sleeves, so to speak. Giese argues that the wearers of such T-shirts are political in that they 'are taking a risk by going public with their beliefs and are forcing everyone in sight to deal with those views' (20); however, as D'Andrade points out,

> For some people, it's a way to bypass the complexities of feminism—it's a lot easier to wear a 'girls kick ass' T-shirt than to learn how to defend yourself physically. (21)

A 'Girls Rule' T-shirt is probably no more or less a politically authentic statement than a 'Save the Whales' bumper sticker, depending on its wearer and the context of its use. Still, it is important to remember that RG was deliberately anti–consumer culture; writing on oneself with a marker is not only a political, feminist action (first, in choosing to 'deface' the feminine body which is ideally a flawless object; second, in drawing attention to issues of women's oppression through the words),

but displays the classic do-it-yourself ethic of punk. While anyone willing to mark herself has access to a felt pen and a range of words limited only to her imagination, a baby tee must be purchased at its marked-up retail cost. Whether or not its slogan is meant to be ironic, any critique of capitalism is, by definition, lost in its (mass) production.

Conclusion

Despite generalizations made for the purposes of this paper, RG was not a homogenous entity—nor was it self-contained. I suspect that many self-declared grrrls also reached beyond this movement in their tastes and style (and that other girls reached in), and it would be worthwhile to find out where RG intersected with other subcultures and the mainstream. As well, it would be interesting to compare the path of RG bands with that of women who attained commercial success in the mainstream music industry. After all, RG's inception—that is, pre–Jagged Little Pill, Lilith Fair, and the Spice Girls—preceded the amalgam of 'women in rock' that peaked at the end of the 1990s. In particular, comparisons with the more visible major-label 'angry women' (e.g., Hole, the contents of Women in Rock compilations) may determine whether 'selling out' necessarily requires that women compromise a feminist stance. The contradiction with which I opened this paper rears its head again here: it may be true that riot grrrl remains an 'authentic' and enormously empowering movement for thousands of girls, but there are millions more who might pay attention if the 'Revolution Girl Style' were indeed televised.

References

'Body Talk'. *Rolling Stone*. (6 Oct 1994): 16.

Cateforis, Theo, and Elena Humphreys. 'Constructing Communities and Identities: Riot Grrrl New York City'. *Musics of Multicultural America: A Study of Twelve Musical Communities*. Eds. K. Lornell and A.K. Rasmussen. New York: Schirmer, 1997.

channel seven. [No issue no.] 1994.

Clarke, Gary. 'Defending Ski-Jumpers: A Critique of Theories of Youth Subcultures'. *The Subcultures Reader*. Eds. Ken Gelder and Sarah Thornton. London: Routledge, 1997 [1981].

Coon, Caroline. 'The Sex Pistols'. *Rock She Wrote: Women Write about Rock, Pop, and Rap*. Eds. Evelyn McDonnell and Ann Powers. New York: Dell, 1995 [1976].

D'Andrade, Hugh. 'The Buffy Effect'. *Bitch*. (Summer 1999): 18–21, 58.

Ewen, Stuart. *All Consuming Images: The Politics of Style in Contemporary Culture*. New York: Basic Books, 1988.

'Flower Grrrl'. *Rolling Stone*. 8 (22) (July 1993): 24–5.

France, Kim. 'Grrrls at War'. *Rolling Stone*. (8–22 July 1993): 24–5.

Giese, Rachel. 'To Die For! From Ribbon-Mania to Ghetto Flavas, the Fashion Industry Is Out to Accessorize Your Dissent'. *This Magazine*. (June 1994): 17–22.

Gottlieb, Joanne, and Gayle Wald. 'Smells Like Teen Spirit: Riot Grrrls, Revolution and Women in Independent Rock'. *Microphone Fiends: Youth Music and Youth Culture*. Eds. Andrew Ross and Tricia Rose. New York: Routledge, 1994.

Greenblatt, Cathy. 'Unwilling Icons: Riot Grrrl Meets the Press'. *Border/Lines*. (Dec. 1996): 24–7.

Hebdige, Dick. *Subculture: The Meaning of Style*. London: Routledge, 1979.

Heinrich, Kim. 'tee tease'. *Calgary Herald*. (6 June 1995): B1.

Japenga, Ann. 'Punk's Girls Groups are Putting the Self Back in Self-Esteem'. *New York Times* (15 Nov. 1995): 30.

Klein, Melissa. 'Duality and Redefinition: Young Feminism and the Alternative Music Community'. *Third Wave Agenda: Being Feminist, Doing Feminism*. Eds. L. Heywood and J. Drake. Minneapolis: Univ. of Minnesota, 1997.

Labi, Nadya. 'Girl Power'. *Time* (29 June 1998): 54–6.

Malkin, Nina. 'It's a Grrrl Thing'. *Seventeen* (May 1993): 80–2.

'rock women'. alt.culture. www.altculture.com/aenries/r/rockxwx.html. Date accessed: 23 June 1999.

Rose, Tricia. 'A Style Nobody Can Deal With: Politics, Style and the Postindustrial City in Hip Hop'. *Microphone Fiends: Youth Music and Youth Culture*. Eds. A. Ross and T. Rose. New York: Routledge, 1994.

Thornton, Sarah. 'Moral Panic, the Media and British Rave Culture'. *Microphone Fiends: Youth Music and Youth Culture*. Eds. Andrew Ross and Tricia Rose. New York: Routledge, 1994.

Wald, Gayle. 'Just a Girl? Rock Music, Feminism, and the Cultural Construction of Female Youth'. *Signs: Journal of Women in Culture and Society* 23 (3), 1998: 585–610.

'Where the wimps are'. *Newsweek* (29 April 1996): 80.

White, Emily. 'Revolution Girl Style Now'. *Rock She Wrote: Women Write about Rock, Pop, and Rap*. Eds. E. McDonnell and A. Powers. New York: Dell, 1995 [1992].

QUESTIONS FOR CRITICAL THOUGHT

1. In these articles, sports emerge as a potent source of metaphors and images in the media. Where do you see sports metaphors at work?

2. How does gender subtly influence the portrayals of twenty-first-century Canadian politicians? (Compare, for example, coverage of Belinda Stronach and Michael Ignatieff, or Elizabeth May and Stockwell Day).

3. Are subcultural and countercultural movements inevitably co-opted by their incorporation into mainstream media? What individuals or groups do you know of who have balanced subversion of gender stereotypes with mass appeal?

4. The articles in this section deal primarily with "old" media, print, and television. Do you find significant differences in the representation of gender in 'old' media and 'new' media, such as YouTube or Facebook?

PART IX

Social Movements

When most people think of gender and social activism, they picture suffragists marching for women's right to vote in the 1920s, or perhaps the 'women's lib' movement of the 1960s and 1970s (in which, by the way, no bras were ever burned—the torching of lingerie was a media invention). These movements were about redistributing power among the genders, through political, economic, domestic, and cultural actions. Some may also think of the men's movement, which began in the 1980s, in which men too found themselves questioning repressive and confining norms of gender.

Some critics have tried to write off feminism as 'over and done with', now that Western women have the same legal rights and many of the same opportunities as their male counterparts. However, Candis Steenburgen argues that rumours of feminism's death are greatly exaggerated. While younger feminists today may differ from their foremothers in their tactics and in some aspects of their goals, she contends, the questioning, transformative spirit of earlier feminism lives on.

Far from being marginalized, feminism in Canada has become institutionalized, with feminist organizations carrying out invaluable work in society, from running shelters for survivors of domestic violence to advocating for training programs to help women become skilled in trades. However, this mainstreaming can have a down side, in the form of bureaucratization and the reproduction of the hierarchical structure of traditional institutions. Leona English looks at the internal workings of several feminist organizations, exploring how power is exercised both formally and informally.

Joanne Minaker and Laureen Snider examine another consequence of the transformations wrought by the feminist movement: the formation of counter-movements whose existence is premised on the idea that the pendulum has swung too far in favour of women, so that men are now the ones being marginalized and disenfranchised. One counter-movement claim is that men are victimized by domestic violence just as much as women are, and are unfairly painted as perpetrators. Minaker and Snider argue that this claim does not stand up to empirical scrutiny, and that the push to define men and women as equals in violence emerges from particular political and economic circumstances.

The term 'gender and social movements' does not refer only to social movements *about* transforming gender. Activists for a variety of causes *do* gender in the course of advocating for their goals. Miya Narushima looks at a groups of activists who push the gendering of social movements to the point of absurdity—which is precisely their intent. She profiles the Raging Grannies, older women activists for international peace, economic redistribution, and other causes, who adopt an exaggerated 'little old lady' persona, with accompanying songs and performances, to draw attention to their causes and to deflect negative responses through humour. The Grannies deftly deploy gender as a political tactic, and turn stereotypes on their heads.

CHAPTER 33

Feminism and Young Women: Still Alive and Kicking

Candis Steenbergen

Efforts to define 'feminism' and attempts to determine the boundaries of the 'women's movement' have always been problematic. Characterizing a feminist (or worse: the feminists) has been even harder. 'Feminism', as Geraldine Finn has noted, 'does not speak with one voice' (299). Feminists have always expressed their desire for social, political, economic, and cultural change in a variety of milieus. Feminist activity has always assumed a wide range of forms: from militant political activism, to silent volunteerism, to academic research and writing, to the creation of works of art, to so much more. Feminist historians acknowledge that the women's movement in Canada has always had a 'diverse, complex, and shifting reality', and agree that feminists have never followed a unified political ideology (Adamson, Briskin and McPhail 9). While all feminisms share certain characteristics, significant differences in political strategy, in vision, in attitudes towards men, in understanding the roots of women's oppression, and in setting priorities also typify the Canadian women's movement ideology (Adamson et al.; Hamilton).

Feminism itself has altered and evolved over time as the intricacies of women's positions in society have changed (Wine and Ristock; Adamson et al.). In the early moments of the contemporary women's movement, second-wave feminists identified, named, analyzed, and resisted women's

oppression, particularly as it existed in the private lives of 'ordinary' women. The decade that followed has been called 'a phase of expansion and consolidation', a period in which the women's movement grew in size and visibility, as well as in organizational and strategic terms (Tremblay).[1] In the 1980s, many of the battles fought by the mainstream women's movement concentrated on institutional policy and political change. The strategies adopted by the women's movement through all three decades were employed in reaction to the political conditions of their struggles. But they were also the result of constant internal checks and balances performed by and among women of strikingly different political persuasions (Hamilton).[2]

Feminism in the last decade has been no different. By the early 1990s, the battlegrounds for feminist struggles had altered again. As early as 1993, Manon Tremblay noted that:

Over the course of the last few years, the feminist movement has devoted itself primarily to fighting to maintain what women have gained in a climate of political conservatism, of financial austerity, and of the affirmation of a neo-conservative right wing. In addition, the antifeminist undercurrent which is currently developing in the West has led to the belief that the feminist movement has lost its raison d'etre with women now having achieved equality with men. (276)

At the beginning of the new century, Tremblay's 'undercurrent' is a commonly heard reproach of feminism and its proponents. The 'diversified, multifaceted, and enriched' nature of feminist activities has been re-interpreted (and perpetuated by popular media) as demonstrative of an antiquated, ineffectual, 'splintered and fragmented' women's movement (Hamilton 80). The evidence supporting those charges has been even more unsettling. The arrival of a number of North American publications in the very recent past—written predominantly by young, female iconoclasts—incited reports of the arrival of the next generation of feminists: self-proclaimed 'dissidents' who herald the coming of feminism's last breath.

In the United States, 'feminism's daughters' appeared in the form of Katie Roiphe's *The Morning After: Sex, Fear and Feminism* (1993), Christina Hoff Sommers' *Who Stole Feminism? How Women Have Betrayed Women* (1994), Rene Denfeld's *The New Victorians: A Young Woman's Challenge to the Old Feminist Order* (1995), and—of course—Danielle Crittenden's *What Our Mother's Didn't Tell Us: Why Happiness Eludes the Modern Woman* (1999) and Wendy Shalit's *A Return to Modesty: Discovering the Lost Virtue* (1999), to name just a few. Almost perfectly paralleling the introduction of Ally McBeal to the television-consuming public, the entrance of these young voices—all straight, white, and well-educated voices, I should add—announced the 'coming-of-age' of the heirs of the sexual revolution and the new faces of feminism. Women have made it, they say. Get over it.

Canada has not been without similar voices. In 1992, Amy Friedman published *Nothing Sacred: A Conversation with Feminism*. Using Queen's University as a model, the American-born author asserted that feminism had mutated and that she was no longer comfortable identifying with what the movement had become. Over the last 30 years, she argued, feminism has grown terrified of recognizing differences among women, and has not retained the sacredness of the personal. Individual stories, she asserted, now served only as 'fodder

for a statistical mill' (42). Friedman's agitation with academic feminism was multifaceted: she 'deplored [the] sloppy, inaccurate, lazy language' used by proponents, was angered by the promotion of 'female knowledge as distinct from male knowledge', and was dismayed by the apparent feminist belief in 'ultimate solutions' for the atrocities of the world against women (42, 44, 58). She stated:

> The new feminist rhetoric . . . was beginning to sound like other versions of revolutionary fanaticism, and revolutionary fanaticism, we all know, has sparked some of the most heinous regimes in humankind's history. No matter who the enemy. (60)

According to Friedman, feminism lost sight of its original goals and fixated on romanticized images of women as powerless victims, encouraged self-pity, and sought to gain strength in martyrdom.

In 1995, Canadian journalist Kate Fillion published *Lip Service: The Truth about Women's Darker Side in Love, Sex, and Friendship*. Fillion discussed the myth of female moral superiority, and attempted to deconstruct a number of existing stereotypes, including 'woman as victim', and 'woman as saint'. She stated that women today adhere to conflicting paradigms:

> Self-determination is what women want, but the myth of female moral superiority tells us that women cannot be actors in their own right. Apparently, women are too pure to harbor negative feelings and too virtuous to make mistakes. Agency—having some control over one's own life—is confused with happy endings. When things turn out well, women are given full credit, but when something goes wrong, we are absolved of responsibility. (318)

Based on her own observations and a handful of interviews, Fillion denounced feminists for attempting to achieve sexual liberation through the perpetuation of dangerous dichotomies and through the preservation of an age-old sexual script, and argued that, consequently, 'the common language used to discuss sexuality in the public arena . . . [has been] predicated on women's passivity and oppression' (223).

The next year, Donna LaFramboise (also a journalist) published *The Princess at the Window: A New Gender Morality*. LaFramboise attacked 'establishment feminism', that group of 'people who are recognized by society at large as legitimate feminist spokespersons' (1996: 8). Citing Ann Landers, Ms, Marilyn French, and Catherine MacKinnon, LaFramboise asserted that 'the lunatic fringe has taken over mainstream feminism' (1996: 33). Arguing that highly questionable ideas have been elevated to feminist dogma, she claimed that feminism has become extremist, self-obsessed, arrogant, and intolerant. LaFramboise was alarmed by the speed at which such 'sloppy thinking' has permeated the rhetoric of popular culture and has influenced public policy, and stated that traditional methods of examining women's issues have become obsolete (1996: 48). LaFramboise argued that feminism has perpetuated the myth of female martyrdom, stated that feminists have deliberately maintained such fictions to ensure its survival, and differentiated between 'a feminism that informs one's opinions and a feminism that dictates how one should think' (1996: 323).

Friedman, Fillion, and LaFramboise presented limited analyses of feminism's past shortcomings and future directions. All three generalized 'North American feminism' as a unit based upon their own observations, anecdotes, conversations with friends, content analyses of newspaper columns, and a variety of studies on white, heterosexual, able-bodied, educated, middle- to upper-class women. All of the authors were former students (or graduates) of women's studies departments, and all three targeted the work of feminists in the academy, yet all failed to illustrate an in-depth knowledge of feminist theory or of the history of the women's movement. All of the authors used items from the popular press, provided snippets of contentious quotations from select feminist theorists (mostly American ones), and relied heavily upon personal interviews. All three expressed concern for the current state of feminism, and all provided instances in which mainstream second-wave praxis has 'failed', but none provided viable alternatives. All three viewed tolerance and

flexibility as key elements of future strategies for the women's movement, yet none succeeded in achieving a sound blend of analysis, theory, and practice.

Feminist commentators were swift in their criticism of the three Canadian-published books, their authors, and their American counterparts. One reviewer attacked their 'highly selective, blinkered vision', and stated that their texts were little more than 'in-your-face rant[s]' supported by 'extraordinarily inflated ideas' about the prevalence and influence of feminism in Canada (Hurley). Myrna Kostash attacked Fillion for presenting second-wave feminism as 'a monolithic movement reducible to a single tendency', and suggested that this new generation believes that feminism is anti-male, and that 'mainstream feminists hate the very idea of sex with men' (1996: 13). By the year 2000, the presence of a new generation of women, concerned with little more than individual gain, the consumption of material goods, and the exertion of their own enlightened power, was branded into the public mind. The image of the 'new modern woman' of the millennium was 'bad girl', one who has rejected the 'tyranny of contemporary sexual politics' brought about by feminism and who has been aggressively taking matters into her own hands (Dennis 3).

As the last decade's media frenzy suggests, a new generation of women has emerged, aggressively analyzing, rethinking, and challenging the assumptions and strategies of feminism's diverse histories and theories. Unfortunately (but not surprisingly), the popular press pinpointed the wrong group of women. A third wave has appeared within the women's movement; a generation of young women actively addressing the complexities of women's everyday experiences and the personal and structural relations affecting them. Their critiques—as varied as the feminisms that have come before—are intended to further the feminist cause, not to slander the movement or its proponents.

Despite the mass visibility of post-feminists, young feminist women—raised with feminism as a familiar concept since their birth; the beneficiaries of many of the successes of the women's movement; and those who know that there are still challenges remaining and obstacles to be jumped for women—exist and work and resist in the millennium. And, like the 'popular kids' of their age group, many of them are vigorously engaged in exploring the intersections of sexualities, sexual pleasure, and feminism—and challenging some of the feminist strategies of the past as a result. The differences between the two, however, are significant. For one thing, most young women with legitimate concerns and critiques of feminism and the women's movement have not lined bookstore shelves with mass-market bestsellers, done the talk-show circuit, or made countless headlines. Instead, their voices appear in independently produced zines, in book reviews hidden in the backs of journals, on walls and across public advertisements, in non-mainstream publications, and in other, less conspicuous (and less financially rewarding), spaces. Third-wave feminists also understand and recognize that there is no feminist monolith, or any feminist 'establishment' trying to take all the fun out of sex.[3] As well, young women see the historical specificity of the women's movement's engagement with and inquiries into issues of sexuality and body politics. They might not be thrilled with the way things turned out and want to revisit older strategies and theories (and question and confront those who pursued them), but most have the rationale not to blindly point fingers.

Women's sexual freedom was one of the key feminist goals of the late 1960s and early 1970s, and women's right to sexual pleasure and to control their own bodies symbolized their right to social equality.[4] Women formed woman-centred collectives and organizations and utilized public spaces as forums to speak about, challenge, and try to resolve, sexual discrimination and lingering postwar repression.[5] One objective was to denounce and dispel the inaccuracies of 'those heterosexual practices predicated on the assumption of the priority of a male sexual urge and a male right to sexual pleasure' (Hamilton 65). Activists sought to expose the double standard that celebrated men for 'sowing their wild oats' and divided women as 'whores' and 'virgins'. In public and in the home, feminists challenged socially enforced domesticity,

To wrest control away from the state, the medical establishment, institutionalized religion, pharmaceutical companies, advertisers,

pornographers, institutionalized censorship, [and] the violence of men. (Pierson 98)

The struggle for reproductive rights, the revelatory discovery of the clitoris as a site of sexual response, and the publication of woman-centred journals, created 'a thrilling sense of new possibilities' for women (Tiefer 115).

By the mid-1970s, mainstream feminist praxis had turned its attention away from the personal aspects of sexuality and focused predominantly on legal, political, and social policy making and change, and in that climate 'it was virtually impossible for lesbian, bisexual, or heterosexual feminists to claim the right to sexual pleasure' (Ross 113). Concentrating instead on policy-based issues that they could mobilize around and effectively influence, the now 'mainstream' feminist movement became focused on male sexual violence, the legalities of the Divorce Act, pornography, and the political and legal battles regarding rape and sexual assault. The sexuality debates had begun to change, and analyses of sexual danger rapidly superseded discussions of women's personal empowerment, pleasure and desire.[6]

When the next generation of women came of age in the late 1980s and 1990s, sexuality was again a hot topic—one that pervaded (and continues to drench) virtually all facets of popular culture, the media, and mass-market advertising. The growth and intellectual development of young women today has been marked by a greater overall awareness of sex, sex identities, and sexualities, and a resurgent interest in the role that sexual identity plays in their everyday lives. The establishment of women's studies in schools, the inclusion (albeit paltry) of feminist and queer theory in other fields of study, and strong and vocal lesbian and gay voices have all contributed to their awareness. Young women also grew up with an expansion of cultural influences: music videos, cable TV, improved satellite communications, the Internet, and specialty magazines; all of which have affected and shaped their outlook. Advertising specifically and pop culture generally have become increasingly sexualized and young feminists have acknowledged that 'as women became more powerful in real life, their clothes got tighter and shorter in the make-believe-it's-real world of television' (Timson 52). In many ways, post-feminism emerged at an opportune moment in history: feeding off of the backlash of the '80s and utilizing the public fixation with and consumption of sexuality to their advantage.

The desire to analyze body image, self-esteem, desire, sexuality, and sexual pleasure has been strong in third-wave writings to date. To many, those pursuits have revolved around continual self-analysis and personal negotiation, an attempt to reconcile the desire to create their own version of 'femininity', and the fear of betraying their allegiance to feminism and the struggle for female empowerment. For some, that has translated into a strong defiance of pre-constructed notions of what constitutes a 'beautiful' female body and activism against fat-phobia. For others, it has meant indulging in beauty culture: fashion magazines, makeup, hair products, and slinky fashions previously viewed as fodder for the male gaze:

> For me, being a femme means that I take pride in wearing just the right shade of lipstick, drawing the perfect black line above my eyelashes, keeping my legs smooth, and smelling good. Being a femmenist means knowing I am just as attractive when I don't wear makeup, shave, or put on perfume. (delombard 29–30)

Young feminists are conscious of the use of sexuality and sexualized images of women in the media that consistently support and perpetuate traditional sex roles and sexual identities, and actively strive to make sense of manipulative media techniques in their work. A number of young feminist scholars, writers, artists, activists, and critics of the mass media have attempted to link their connection (and attraction) to the hyper-sexualized culture of consumerism and consumption with their identities as women, sexual beings, and feminists. The editors of *BITCH: Feminist Response to Pop Culture* explain the rationale:

> We are supposedly living in a new age—one that some have dubbed post-feminist. Feminism is over, they say. Just get over it. But television

demonstrates that most people still think what a woman is wearing is more important that what she's thinking. Magazines that tell us, both implicitly and explicitly, that female sexual urges are deviant while reminding us that maintaining our sex appeal is the only way to wring commitment out of a man, without which our lives will be sad and incomplete in spite of dazzling careers and intense friendships. Billboards urge us to fork over our hard-earned cash for the glittery, overpriced wares of companies that depend on our unhappiness and dissatisfaction for their profits.

The negotiation between the attractive, processed, advertised, and consumable version of female sexuality and the difficulties of translating it into a lived reality has been substantial in third-wave analyses to date. In many respects, the approach has been to acknowledge the mixed messages pervading popular culture and account for the 'problem desires' that often result. Not surprisingly, the craving for sexual empowerment has paralleled young women's questioning of reality, of the sexual revolution, and—necessarily—of their feminist 'brand'.

While young feminist perspectives regarding sexuality have just begun to emerge, much of the writing to date begins from a location similar to pro-sex feminists: where the early second-wave feminists left off. Early feminist writings that emphasized women's sexual freedom did not ignore the existence of sexual danger in many women's lives. Instead, they argued that women's sexual freedom could not occur without a more thorough sense of women's realities as well as a realization of the need for social, economic, and political rights.[7] It's just that one ended up absorbing the other. The complex sexual context of the current time has made a reconnection of the two necessary and unavoidable, and young women's activism has reflected that. In organizations and campus centres, young feminists have created pamphlets, how-to manuals, and newsletters on everything from surgical operations to enhance, sculpt, or rejuvenate the vagina, to tips on body piercing and tattooing, to info on the morning-after pill, to AIDS awareness.[8] Third-wave reactions to body politics coalesce neatly with the intentions of early second-wave discussions on the body.

In response to the often contradictory conditions surrounding women's sexual lives, young women have sought to combine radical perspectives on sexual theory with the everyday occurrences of women's lived experiences. That has translated, so far, into a reinterpretation of both personal and collective identities, an interrogation of the women's movement of the past and of the current period, as well as the creation of new visions for the future. Mariana Valverde has noted that there have traditionally been two genres used by women to talk about sex: the intellectual application of a number of abstract theoretical frameworks to women's sexual experiences and desires, and 'the confessional'. The new generation of feminists values both, and has been actively attempting to combine the two strategies in a concerted effort to work through the 'lived messiness' of women's lives. The potential that explorations of women's sexuality has is 'infinite and incalculable', but the myriad of problems, issues, and concerns facing young women also indicates that their 'sexual project is just beginning' (Crosbie xii).

Of course, the issues of sexuality and body politics covered herein are only fragments of the kinds of work that young women are currently engaged in. Like the waves that came before, the third is as difficult to define and as arduous to label and their activism has been as problematic— or more so—to pinpoint. Like their forerunners, their feminisms come in a myriad forms: they don't all adhere to the 'feminist' label, they don't follow a single agenda, they don't necessarily agree, and they don't share the same political motivations, priorities, or dreams. Their realities are as diverse, fluid, and complicated as the environment in which they resist. Whether feminism's 'third wave' overshadows post-feminist ideology in the public's eye remains to be seen, but a number of things are certain. The new generation of young feminists is emerging, reacting, and acting within a particular moment in history, just as the feminisms of the past have changed in reaction to the ideological, social, cultural, and political climates within theirs. The future of feminism in Canada is not post-feminism; it is a strongly supported, vigorously active, dynamic group of young women who are determined to flex and bend their feminisms with where the world takes them, pushing the women's movement into the next century.

Notes

1. Tremblay notes that the 1970s marked the institutionalization of the women's movement with the establishment of state organizations like the Canadian Advisory Council on the Status of Women.
2. Hamilton noted that 'feminists disagreed not only on the explanations for women's inequality, oppression, and subordination, but also on the means to transform their situation' (54).
3. For a satirical look at one woman's quest for 'the feminist establishment' (and for a job therein) see Kamen 1996.
4. The feminist interest in sexuality and sexual pleasure certainly didn't begin in the 1960s. It has always been at the forefront of feminist inquiries. For a thorough look at sexuality in the post-war years, see Adams.
5. The contemporary gay liberation movement emerged from the New Left as a unified force during this period (see Kinsman).
6. These discussions continued at the grassroots level. Mainstream feminists, the more visible, public 'face' of the women's movement, switched their focus to more political, policy-based issues.
7. It should be noted that Valverde (1995), Kinsman, and Ross have all illustrated that pro-sex feminism, gay/lesbian cultural formations, and the pursuit of sexual pleasure through 'alternative' means have always existed in Canada, and they did not dissipate when the mainstream women's movement began to target violence and policy issues more actively in the mid-1970s. They just didn't get props.
8. See AGENDER (Carleton University) and Challenge the Assumptions! Both illustrate a concern articulated in the mid-1980s, expressed in McCooey.

References

Adams, Mary Louise. *The Trouble with Normal*. Toronto: University of Toronto Press, 1997.

Adamson, Nancy, Linda Briskin, and Margaret McPhail. *Feminist Organizing for Change*. Toronto: Oxford University Press, 1988.

Bellafante, Ginia. 'Feminism: It's All About Me!' *Time Magazine* 151 (25) (29 June 1998): 48–56.

BITCH: Feminist Response to Pop Culture. www.bitch-magazine.com/mission.html.

Connell, R.W. 'Sexual Revolution'. *New Sexual Agendas*. Ed. Lynne Segal. New York: New York University Press, 1997.

Crittenden, Danielle. *What Our Mothers Didn't Tell Us: Why Happiness Eludes the Modern Woman*. New York: Simon & Schuster, 1999.

Crosbie, Lynn. *The Girl Wants To*. Toronto: Macfarlane, Walter and Ross, 1993.

delombard, jeannine. 'Femmenism'. *To Be Real: Telling the Truth and Changing the Face of Feminism*. Ed. Rebecca Walker. New York: Doubleday, 1995. 21–33.

Denfeld, Rene. *The New Victorians: A Young Woman's Challenge to the Old Feminist Order*. New York: Warner Books, 1995.

Dennis, Wendy. *Hot and Bothered*. Toronto: The Penguin Group, 1992.

Fillion, Kate. *Lip Service: The Truth about Women's Darker Side in Love, Sex, and Friendship*. Toronto: Harper Collins Publishers, 1995.

Finn, Geraldine. 'Conclusion'. *Feminism in Canada*. Eds. Angela Miles and Geraldine Finn. Montreal: Black Rose Books, 1982. 299–306.

Friedman, Amy. *Nothing Sacred: A Conversation with Feminism*. Canada: Oberon Press, 1992.

Greenglass, Esther R. *A World of Difference: Gender Roles in Perspective*. Toronto: John Wiley and Sons, 1982.

Greer, Germaine. *The Whole Woman*. London: Bantam-Dell-Doubleday, 1999.

Hamilton, Roberta. *Gendering the Vertical Mosaic*. Toronto, Copp Clark Ltd., 1996.

Hurley, Clarissa. 'Feminists Bashing Feminism: The Princess at the Window'. *The New Brunswick Reader* 17, August 1996.

Kamen, Paula. 'Acquaintance Rape: Revolution and Reaction'. *'Bad Girls'/'Good Girls': Women, Sex & Power in the Nineties*. Eds. Nan Bauer Maglin and Donna Perry. New Brunswick: Rutgers University, 1996. 137–149.

Kamen, Paula. 'Paradigm For Sale'. *Shiny Adidas Track Suits and the Death of Camp: The Best of Might Magazine*. Ed. Might Magazine. New York: Boulevard Books, 1998.

Kinsman, Gary. *The Regulation of Desire: Homo and Hetero Sexualities*. Montreal: Black Rose Books, 1996.

Kostash, Myrna. *Long Way from Home*. Toronto: James Lorimer and Co., 1980.

Kostash, Myrna. 'Dissing Feminist Sexuality'. *Canadian Forum* (September 1996): 13–17.

LaFramboise, Donna. *The Princess at the Window: A New Gender Morality*. Toronto: Penguin Books, 1996.

LaFramboise, Donna. 'Freedom, Baby'. *The National Post*, 18 March 1999: A18.

McCooey, Sharleen Johnson. 'Help Yourself'. *Herizons* 4 (1) (Jan/Feb 1986): 39.

Parr, Joy. *A Diversity of Women*. Toronto: University of Toronto Press, 1995.

Pierson, Ruth Roach. 'The Politics of the Body'. *Canadian Women's Issues: Volume 1: Strong Voices, Twenty-five Years of Women's Activism in English Canada*. Eds. Ruth Roach Pierson, Marjorie Griffin Cohen, Paula Bourne, and Philinda Masters. Toronto: James Lorimer & Company, Publishers, 1993. 98–122.

Roiphe, Katie. *The Morning After: Sex, Fear and Feminism*. Boston: Little Brown & Company, 1993.

Ross, Becki. *The House that Jill Built*. Toronto: University of Toronto Press, 1995.

Segal, Lynne. *Straight Sex: Rethinking the Politics of Pleasure*. Berkeley: University of California Press, 1994.

Shalit, Wendy. *A Return to Modesty: Discovering the Lost Virtue*. Toronto: HarperCollins Canada, 1999.

Sommers, Christina Hoff. *Who Stole Feminism? How Women Have Betrayed Women*. New York: Simon & Schuster, 1994.

Tiefer, Leonore. *Sex is Not a Natural Act and Other Essays*. Boulder: Westview Press, 1995.

Timson, Judith. 'Bimbo-Watch: Resistant to Feminism, She Just Won't Go Away'. *Maclean's* 27 November 1995: 52.

Traas, Wendy. 'Splitting Hairs: Creative Expression vs. Self-Normalization in Women's Hair Care'. Diss. Brock University, April 1999.

Tremblay, Manon. 'Gender and Society: Rights and Realities'. *Canada and the United States: Differences that Count.* Ed. David Thomas. Peterborough: Broadview Press, 1993.

Valverde, Mariana. 'If Freud Were A Woman . . .' *Broadside* 5 (6) (April 1984): 9.

Whelehan, Imelda. *Modern Feminist Thought.* New York: New York University Press, 1995.

Wine, Jeri Dawn and Janice L. Ristock. *Women and Social Change.* Toronto: James Lorimer and Company, 1991.

CHAPTER 34

A Foucauldian Reading of Learning in Feminist Nonprofit Organizations

Leona M. English

Feminist organizations, especially those in the non-profit sector, play a significant role in the development of a collective feminist consciousness and increased learning and employment opportunities for women. Ferree and Martin (1995, p. 3) note feminism has been 'a significant, though controversial, force' and that many of its positive effects have been operationalized through the concerted efforts of feminist *organizations* that have worked for changes through social action, education, lobbying, and the provision of a supportive community for local feminists.

The 10 organizations represented in this study are non-profits, which are often caricatured as less organizationally strong yet friendly alternatives to profit-making organizations. They range from women's centres and counselling services to shelters for victims of domestic violence.

It is worth noting that the organizations in this study are self-described as feminist, non-profit, and social-action oriented. They are feminist in that all share a commitment to 'end sexism, sexist exploitation and oppression' (hooks, 2000, p. viii), though they vary in emphases and orientations to feminism. They are social-action oriented in that they address social inequalities—poverty, illiteracy, violence, and so forth. They are non-profit in that they do not seek to make money or to profit from their work.

Theoretical Framing

The theoretical framing of this inquiry occurs at the intersection of several frames of thought, the first of which is a feminist reading of the literature on non-profit organizations and learning, which is generally masculinist (Block & Rosenberg, 2002), funding focused, and governance driven. The research that does focus on women in non-profits tends to reify stereotypic feminine traits and practices, reminiscent of the early stages of feminism. Fondas (1997), for example, makes the case that feminine practices such as supporting and nurturing are deliberately seeping into mainstream management discourse because they are seen to be effective in organizational leadership. Little if any attention is given in the women's organizational or non-profit literature to the power and resistance exercised by women, leaving largely unexplored the area of informal and nonformal learning.

The second theoretical underpinning is Foucauldian post-structuralism, with its emphasis on the nexus of knowledge, discourse, and power. Foucauldian post-structuralism focuses on the *technologies* (practices) *of power* and the ways in which power becomes present and capillary—that is, working its way through systems of human interaction, including but not confined to language.

This Foucauldian view of power sharpens our perception of the positive effects of power. A key idea in post-structuralism is that there is resistance to the exercises or technologies of power, such as adult education practices of team learning, facilitation, learning circles, and learning journals. Learners can resist, for instance, reproducing the adult educator's knowledge by creating their own, or they can resist intense questioning by leaving the room or staying silent. In a Foucauldian sense, the emphasis is on the how of power and not the what or the why or the when. *Discourse* is more than conversation: Discourse refers not only to what is said, but who can speak and with what authority (see Ball, 1990). Discourse can be analyzed through any meaning-making practices, and not language alone; for example, practices related to the regulation of time or dress or to the physical arrangement of space are discursively constituted. The feminist organizations that are discussed in this article offer an educational arena in which to study the intersection of power, knowledge, and discourse. Traditional forms of power such as sovereign leaders (kings, queens, bosses) have been replaced by seemingly innocuous practices such as using the circle, consensus, and voice, but they exercise power nonetheless. These technologies or practices of power produce effects (good and bad) and work to create a regime of truth (universalisms or unwritten laws).

Although Foucault and feminism have not always been seen as compatible, I use them here for the attention they bring to knowledge, power, and discourse (see McNay, 1992, for an extended discussion).

The ways in which women's learning is approached have been largely framed by gendered and stereotyped ways of knowing. Within the literature of non-profit women's organizations, women are said to 'practice a more inclusive and process-oriented leadership' (Meinhard & Foster, 2003, p. 370; see also Rosener, 1990). Research from a qualitative and Foucauldian post-structuralist perspective is needed to continue the project of addressing these stereotypes and of understanding the intricacies of power and knowledge. These three frameworks intersect in

intriguing ways in this article. Feminist readings of non-profits, Foucauldian post-structuralism, and relational learning are read over and against each other. Guided by these theoretical frameworks, especially by their points of connection, the researcher attempts to complicate the learning relationships by focusing on the learning of the women in these organizations that precede and determine the printed texts.

The Methodological Underpinnings

This researcher focused on feminist organizations in eastern Canada, interviewing eight directors and assistant directors (minimally paid) and eight board members (volunteers) to explore the complicated and often contradictory ways in which they learn in their own organizations. (See Table 34.1 for a description of the participants.) The organizations are feminist in orientation and range from women's centres, antiviolence agencies, and transition houses for victims of violence, to women's counselling services. Feminist organizations were chosen because they are explicitly action oriented and thus closer to adult education's focus on critical social action. To solicit participants, an Internet search of women's non-profit organizations in eastern Canada was conducted. Organizations were contacted via e-mail and asked if they had directors or board members who were willing to participate. Only those organizations that self-identified as feminist during the initial contact were used. In three cases, the author knew the interview participants briefly through volunteer or professional associations.

All organizations comprised only women, and all staff were women. The women interviewed range in age from 25 to 60 and have been involved from a minimum of 1 year to a maximum of 25 years (the median length of involvement was 5 years). Leaders (directors and board members) were chosen because they were most accessible and likely to be conversant in the programming and governance of the organization. Four of the board members are no longer serving on the boards but are still attached to the organizations through a membership system. Of the 16 semistructured interviews,

4 were done by e-mail, 4 in person, and 8 by telephone. Distance and available research funds determined the mode of communication; consequently, the closest interviews were done in person and those farther away were done by e-mail or telephone. The research interviews consisted of open-ended questions of how these directors and board members learn.

The 16 interviews were conducted by a range of means—telephone, in-person, and by e-mail. The format definitely influenced the responses, with the in-person interviews yielding the most helpful data. Although e-mail was expeditious, it did not allow for the probing that is necessary to get to the heart of issues of power and knowledge in this study. E-mail may have allowed participants to monitor their responses and to resist revealing any examples or thoughts that might be considered as disloyal to feminism. The e-mail responses were notably more positive and less complicated than the transcripts from the phone and in-person interviews. Yet, in the in-person interviews, there were many instances in which the women were hesitant to say anything that might be upsetting or seen as working contrary to a positive view of feminism. For instance, an executive director prefaced her comments with, 'I want to be really careful here because I don't want to dismiss the women who worked so hard.' This self-surveillance sometimes works to control their speech and causes the women to discipline themselves, as if being watched by some external force.

Table 34.1 The Participants

Pseudonym	Age Range	Position	Length of Involvement	Type of Interview
Norma	40–45	Board member	10 years	Phone
Maria	50–55	Executive director	20 years	Phone
Brenda	50–55	Executive director	20 years	Phone
Louise	35–40	Executive director	1 year	E-mail
Lisa	45–50	Executive director	10 years	E-mail
Anna	30–35	Executive director	4 years	E-mail
Marsha	45–50	Executive director	15 years	E-mail
Tish	25–30	Board member	1 year	E-mail
Helen	50–55	Executive director	20 years	Phone
Casey	55–60	Board member	25 years	Phone
Denise	40–45	Board member	10 years	Phone
Angela	45–50	Executive director	4 years	Phone
Cathy	35–40	Former board member	4 years	In person
Lorna	40–45	Former board member	3 years	In person
Dolly	55–60	Former board member	3 years	In person
Janet	40–45	Former board member	5 years	In person

Specific work contexts cannot be given as this might reveal the women's identities.

Reading the Data

The analysis of the data is guided by the methodological precautions offered by Foucault (1980, pp. 96–102) about the analysis of power and knowledge. The first is that the focus should be on examining power in local situations where it becomes capillary; this study analyses power in feminist, non-profit organizations, which all operate at the grassroots level. The second is that the focus should not be on *who* exercises power but on *how* it is exercised. In this study, the focus is on how women in feminist, non-profit organizations learn. They set out to be effective practitioners who advance the cause of women, in egalitarian, collectivist, and relational ways, and in so doing bring power into play through normalization procedures. The third is that power needs to be considered in terms of how it links people; how power circulates and creates individuals who are experiencing and exercising power, rather than acting as inanimate objects or victims. The fourth is beginning with an ascending level of analysis, from the very micro-practices of power that are utilized. In looking at the everyday practices of feminist organizations, the focus is on how technologies such as the learning circle and varying levels of knowledge of feminism create good feminists and board members as well as produce resistances. The fifth aspect of Foucault's analytic structure is the link between power and knowledge and how power is necessarily imbricated in any analysis of knowledge and learning. In this case, an analysis of the data shows how knowledge, including self-knowledge, is produced in these organizations. Feminism becomes a discipline of study, and practice is used as a disciplinary technology. These precautions guide the analysis and are directly connected to the actual data when it makes sense to do so. There are five themes developed here from what the participants said in the interviews. Rather than the traditional qualitative approach of reporting the data and then analyzing them, each of the themes is read against feminist, post-structuralist, and relational learning theory.

Intentional Learning in the Organization

Significantly, more than half of the 16 participants indicated that their learning about feminist organizations occurred informally. They learned by watching the leaders, participating in meetings, organizing events for women, and working with other members.

Board members report a considerable amount of informal learning in 'relation to personnel issues; budgeting . . . negotiation skills, finances, and fundraising'. One woman noted that her learning came through dealing with staffing issues, from finding out that sometimes there is conflict and not everyone wants to negotiate difference.

Yet, she pointed out that the women were able to work through the issues because 'it was all women on the board; women are less inclined to grandstand or to engage in impression management.' Relational learning in feminist organizations has been subjected to truth rules, in a Foucauldian sense, about how feminist organizations ought to be, rules that have arisen in women's efforts to define and support themselves, and also in their effort to effect social change.

The executive directors saw the fostering of learning as part of their mandate and as part of their commitment to feminism. Yet, the lack of funding and resources from government coffers sometimes made organized learning impossible. Some of the board members, when asked about learning opportunities, responded that they would like to have had more non-formal learning such as workshops or a stronger board orientation around roles of boards, responsibilities, limits, and legal implications of involvement. Many directors recognized their responsibility in this regard, although they did not always have the resources to put it in into effect. Typical efforts would be these, described by one director:

> My leadership is to make a sincere effort to hire competent women and then let them go do their work and then support them in doing it and to ask questions to make them think about what it is they're doing and to provide, I guess that kind of direction. . . . Try to introduce women to good resources and good text and good places where they can learn things.

In supporting this informal learning, the directors themselves resisted the frugality of government and other constraints. They exercised power through voicing support and by finding new ways to support learning. Yet, the very labelling of the leader of the women's organization as a director and, in most cases, executive director (ED) established the distinction between members (subordinates or subalterns) and managers. ED is a necessary title that enables the organization to conform to government bureaucratic funding rules (to be eligible to apply for grants, the organizations have to use government management categories such as director). The discourse of member and director is a technology of power that serves to divide and can produce complacent individuals ('let the leader do it, she is being paid') and can also effect continuous self-surveillance (she is in charge, so 'I feel her watching me'). The organization is intended to be one of shared meaning, learning, and growth, yet the management discourse reflects the needs of a bureaucracy.

Socioeconomic Context Influences: Learning about Good Feminists

By focusing on the local—in this case, non-profit, feminist—organizations, the research allows for a fuller perspective of how 'power operates at its extremities, in its ultimate destinations, with those points where it becomes capillary' (Foucault, 1980, p. 96). The geographic location on the east coast of Canada, a region known for chronic unemployment, factored into the projects the organizations chose to pursue, often issues of housing, poverty, and underfunding by government. Continuous lobbying for a piece of the pie is a particular challenge, resulting in impediments to long-term planning (see Bradshaw, Murray, and Wolpin, 1996) and resulting in a particular learning about what it means to be a good feminist in these organizations. One board member of a transition house for victims of abuse commented on the culture of her local women's resource centre, noting that

> there is an underlying belief among male-dominated government funders that women's organizations need less money because women will pick up the slack. This overwork and underpay can cause jealousy, feeling unequal, and that you are being treated differently. Our experience at the [women's organization] was that we left exhausted. Even the staff were jaded, beaten down by the system.

The power flows from government ('we don't have enough funds to give women's organizations any more money') through the directors and staff ('we don't have enough money to hire more people so we all have to pitch in and do more') through to the board members ('we all need to help with fund-raising or the whole organization will fall apart'). The power is capillary because it branches out into the extremities of the organization, teaching workaholism and victimhood and producing guilt and broken individuals, women who feel they have not done enough. 'Some women guilt others into taking on things that they cannot handle nor do they want to handle. They can "guilt" women into volunteering, even to self-detriment—financial and stress-wise,' said one board member of a community-based women's resource centre. An effect of these feelings of guilt is an increase in self-examination—turning over and over in one's mind, Did I do enough? Could I have done more? Am I lazy? It creates a woman who is doubtful and worn. Yet, there is a consistent note of optimism in the women's voices, affected to a strong degree by their commitment to the feminist organization, which in some cases has been for more than 25 years. Power, exercised here in the form of guilt, produced a desire in this board member to directly acknowledge the guilt trips and to actively resist them by saying no. She unlearned the negative messages. The resistance in this female board member was formed precisely at the point where power was exercised by another (Brookfield, 2001). The socio-economic context and the resultant lack of funding is the site of this exercise of power and resistance at the microlevel.

Women's Causes and Feminist Leanings: Learning about Feminism or Feminisms

All the organizations supposedly had feminist leanings, including an orientation to justice and structural change as well as the creation of supportive networks of women. Yet, the degree of commitment to feminism was sometimes hard to read. There is a reality, as one director of a women's crisis centre pointed out, that if 'work comes up at a women's centre [in this rural area], what will happen is that many women (feminist or not) will apply, which has implications for who is involved in the centre.' Because, as one director said, 'we're the only game in town,' there are conflicting understandings of the organization even among members.

One participant who had ambivalence about the way in which feminism was enacted, but who had been on the board and a member of a feminist organization for many years, talked about the political focus of the board:

> Because feminism is to the heart of many women's lives of those who are involved in this association, many of the women who are involved . . . don't have simple discussions—these women are so heavy. Their talk polarizes us versus them. Anyone who doesn't agree with them is the wrong person.

This type of ambivalence and varying orientations to feminism had several effects. In one of the feminist organizations, the board did not broach reproductive rights because this was a sensitive subject locally, in effect diminishing the feminist orientation of the organization. Yet, as a board member put it, she had 'learned to choose your battles', something that her own role models in larger centres rarely had to do. Her capacity to stand back and to see that the power exercised by other women in the organization served to support the status quo was an exercise of her own power, and a strategic way of using silence to dilute theirs. In a Foucauldian sense, she was able to negotiate the conflicted terrain by illuminating, if only for herself, the hidden ways that the others (in some cases, non-feminists) resisted change. In many ways, the discourse of the organization created the division between the deeply committed (those who 'choose their battles' but still remain steadfast) and those who are lukewarm about their commitment (most of these women are 'too heavy'). The man–woman binary logic that a post-structural analysis seeks to disrupt appears in other transcripts with reference to a largely female board of directors who are divided in making policy decisions related to the participation of men on the board, on committees, or at annual meetings.

Yet, the directors are very aware of this range of commitment and disparity of views. They used experience as a technology that changes how some women think and feel about feminism. One director of a women's shelter noted that learning occurs in tandem with experience:

> Sometimes they get involved, not because of the feminism but because a project that has

come up and they have applied for it, ok. But when they get here and they start to work in the environment . . . a learning curve happens. It is not imposed; it is just that their lives get opened to women's reality. . . . I think they get more passionate if they come and work here.

The experience itself, the feminist environment, and the witnessing of the barriers to women's equality serve an important learning and teaching function. It could be said that experience is a technology employed to foster these transformative learning moments; once the women come into the organizations, they are imbued with feminist thinking. The effect of the power of experience is to create a woman who has learned informally to be a good feminist.

However, not all members become compliant or are converted. Another board member of a counselling support service observed that she had a

> conflicted attitude to feminism. I read a lot about feminism and often appreciate feminist theory; I do not see it in practice by self-identified feminists. I have been in some situations where well-known feminists treat new people to the field, other researchers on women's issues, in very non-collegial, unsupportive ways.

Her ability to resist the binary of feminists and non-feminists, and to break down the walls that separate them, is post-structuralism in action (Ryan, 2001).

Learning How to Work with Conflict

Of note is how the various women perceived the atmosphere of the organization, especially when it came to resolution of conflict. The directors, by and large, saw themselves as problem solvers who describe the resolution of conflict in a relational way—'We talk it out and we discuss issues when they come up.' That sometimes makes feminist organizations challenging places because there is an upfrontness about problems and a seemingly endless willingness to talk things through. The production of this regime of truth about women as relational learners produces two connected yet contradictory effects: On one hand, it reinforces the power of feminism and of women having voice, yet on the other hand, images of cozy, unrelenting self-disclosure produce a truth effect that women are essentially relational. The latter universalizes the experience of women and learning and further contributes to women's isolation and separateness. Most would say, however, that there is consensus, or, as one woman put it, 'We agree to disagree sometimes.' On occasion, women's organizations choose not to make a policy because it will be too divisive; 'such as whether men can participate or not.' In these ways, the directors and board members are always experiencing and exercising power.

It is around issues of conflict and discussion that relational learning as an identity for women's organizations is challenged most. The universal notion of women agreeing to disagree is in contrast with the resistances that some members name. One board member of a women's resource centre, for instance, has decided not to participate in board meetings any longer because the organization has 'become top down'. Her resistance took the form of leaving—silencing herself. Another women remembered a director saying, 'You, the board, are my boss,' which was seen by the board member as 'disingenuous'. Although she 'admired the work the staff does', she is under no illusion that the board had any great influence: 'We, as a board, support, not direct, staff.'

Organizational Structures: Learning about Contradictions

Early feminist ideas (see descriptions of first- and second-wave feminists in Starr, 2000) about ideal characteristics of feminist organizations—egalitarian, relational, and supportive of voice and difference— are complicated in this analysis. In reality, as one director of a transition house notes, 'The organization is hierarchical by virtue of having an executive director and a board of directors.' A board member puts it this way: 'So then you have feminists who want flat organizations but it's so entrenched in the whole organization it creates more conflict. You are trying to oppose patriarchy within the confines of patriarchal organization.' This participant pointed out that after four years of being a board member,

she now understood that although everyone was trying to operate under feminist principles (participatory decision making, consensus), there are real-life demands of funders that the organization be hierarchical, accountable, and adhere to governmental models of organization.

Yet, the rhetoric or regime of truth of these organizations being a 'home' for all members continues. A prime example is found in how some of the board members described how their board meetings operated. One board member put it this way: 'Informal sharing would intimidate women who were embarrassed they didn't know. . . . We would sit in a circle and share how we were and I was frightened to death.' This example, a theme in at least some of the participants' narratives, speaks to the disciplinary power of the circle, where there is nowhere to hide (Brookfield, 2001), and the ways that the dominant and liberal discourse of a supposedly egalitarian structure actually served as an instrument of surveillance, a micropractice of disciplinary power. When women do tell all in the circle, as some of these participants noted was the practice in their particular organizations, they become penitents who bare all to the group, leaving themselves naked and allowing the group to hear their stories, to accumulate data on them. Foucault refers to this as pastoral power (see English, in press). In the telling or confessing, they participate in the development of dividing practices, letting people know who the authentic feminists are. Knowing this, women exercise self-discipline.

Voice and Authority: Learning How She Can Speak and Act

'What can she know?' and 'How can she speak?' and 'How can she act?' (Code, 1991) are relevant questions for any organization or learning setting. One woman, who had spent three years as a board member, described her organization as 'cliquish'. Her resistance was to leave because she did not see the setting as congenial or inclusive. Pointing to a 'core group of members who had been there for a long time,' she saw them as 'the true decision makers'. She remembered one long-time board member saying 'we need youth,' though that 'same person was hostile to youth. . . . It was intimidating really.'

This founder's syndrome (Block & Rosenberg, 2002), or the control of a seemingly consensual and democratic organization by those who have been around the longest, determines in many cases who exercises power and voice. The voice of the founder, imbued as it is with experience and 'wisdom', in effect, produces silence in some members, especially those new to the board. Another woman, who had been involved in the organization for 25 years, had silently left because the founding members embodied power and authority. The technology of the circle and the check-in at the beginning of board meeting, used as a practice of inclusion, effected fear and conformity in one of the newer board members, who felt disenfranchised by the power of experience and authority. She noted that the pressure to speak at times left her uncomfortable and anxious. Those not on the inside of the organization listen and exercise their own resistances, which may include forming alliances with other new members. In some ways, the discursive effect of 'who has the authority to speak' renders the organization more masculinist than feminist, more exclusionary than relational, and decreases the learning opportunities for new board members to become effective, productive, and feminist individuals.

Discussion

This research makes explicit the ways in which power operates, in capillary fashion, and how it is multidirectional, creating participants who learn to be 'good' feminists. In looking at the 'continuous and uninterrupted processes which subject our bodies, govern our gestures, dictate our behaviours' (Foucault, 1980, p. 97), we see the amount of learning that occurs in these feminist non-profit organizations. It allows us to trace the micropractices of power and how they create participants.

Because this research focuses on a particular area (eastern Canada), a particular type of organization (non-profit and social action), and a particular group of women (feminists), it allows for the specific study of how power operates and how it connects with knowledge production. The ways in which women learn, and the specific social practice and microtechnologies of power involved, serve as microcosm of the larger lifelong learning sphere. The technologies of power that are used here, especially the discourse of equality and voice, serve to create both compliance and resistance for feminists. Women learn to be good feminists and also reluctant feminists, who negotiate power every day. They learn to use silence, as well as strategies of compliance and resistance, to participate in the complex web of power relationships in which they are imbricated.

The data show that these feminists' learning relationships are complex and much more complicated than a simplistic humanist reading might allow for. In examining at a very local level how power, authority, and discord factor into the everyday discourse of organizations, this article contributes to an understanding of women's learning. We see also that among these women there is an articulated attempt to surface tensions and to engage in an oftentimes conflictual discourse, which does not always lead to harmony and caring. In fact, it allows two regimes of truth (caring and conflictual) to be operative at once. The learning relationships are characterized by a continuous and careful attempt to negotiate the nexus of power, knowledge, and ability among directors and board members.

References

Ball, S.J. (Ed.). (1990). *Foucault and education: Discipline and knowledge*. New York: Routledge.

Belenky, M.F., Clinchy, B., Goldberger, N., & Tarule, J. (1986). *Women's ways of knowing*. New York: Basic Books.

Block, S.R., & Rosenberg, S. (2002). Toward an understanding of founder's syndrome: An assessment of power and privilege among founders of nonprofit organizations. *Nonprofit Management and Leadership, 12*(4), 353–68.

Bordt, R.L. (1997). *The structure of women's nonprofit organizations*. Indianapolis: Indiana University Press.

Bradshaw, P., Murray, V., & Wolpin, J. (1996). Women on boards of nonprofits: What difference do they make? *Nonprofit Management and Leadership, 6*, 241–54.

Brookfield, S.D. (2001). Unmasking power: Foucault and adult learning. *The Canadian Journal for the Study of Adult Education, 15*(1), 1–23.

Brookfield, S.D. (2005). *The power of critical theory: Liberating adult learning and teaching.* San Francisco: Jossey-Bass.

Chapman, V.-L. (2003). On 'knowing one's self' self-writing, power, and ethical practice: Reflections from an adult educator. *Studies in the Education of Adults, 35*(1), 35–53.

Code, L. (1991). *What can she know? Feminist theory and the construction of knowledge.* Ithaca, NY: Cornell University Press.

DiStefano, C. (1990). Dilemmas of difference: Feminism, modernity and postmodernism. In L.J. Nicholson (Ed.), *Feminism/postmodernism* (pp. 63–82). London: Routledge.

English, L. M. (in press). Foucault, feminists and funders: A study of power and policy in feminist organizations. *Studies in the Education of Adults.*

Ferree, M.M., & Martin, P.Y. (1995). Doing the work of the movement: Feminist organizations. In M. Marx & P. Y. Martin (Eds.), *Feminist organizations: Harvest of the new women's movement* (pp. 3–23). Philadelphia: Temple University Press.

Fletcher, J.K. (1998). Relational practice: A feminist reconstruction of work. *Journal of Management Inquiry, 7*(2), 163–86.

Fondas, N. (1997). Feminization unveiled: Management qualities in contemporary writings. *Academy of Management Review, 22*(1), 257–82.

Foucault, M. (1977). *Discipline and punish: The birth of the prison.* New York: Vintage.

Foucault, M. (1980). *Power/knowledge: Selected interviews and other writings 1972–1977* (C. Gordon, Ed.). New York: Pantheon.

Gibelman, M. (2000). The nonprofit sector and gender discrimination: A preliminary investigation into the glass ceiling. *Nonprofit Management & Leadership, 10*(3), 251–69.

Goldberger, N., Tarule, J., Clinchy, B., & Belenky, M. (Eds.). (1996). *Knowledge, difference and power: Essays inspired by Women's Ways of Knowing.* New York: Basic Books.

Hayes, E., Flannery, D., with Brooke, A. K., Tisdell, E. J., & Hugo, J. M. (2000). *Women as learners: The significance of gender in adult learning.* San Francisco: Jossey-Bass.

Hercus, C. (1999). Identity, emotion, and feminist collective action. *Gender & Society, 13*(1), 34–55.

hooks, b. (2000). *Feminism is for everybody: Passionate politics.* Cambridge, MA: South End Press.

MacKeracher, D. (1996). *Making sense of adult learning.* Toronto, Canada: Culture Concepts.

McNay, L. (1992). *Foucault and feminism.* Cambridge, UK: Polity.

Meinhard, A.G., & Foster, K. (2003). Difference in the response of women's voluntary organizations to shifts in Canadian public policy. *Nonprofit and Voluntary Sector Quarterly, 32,* 366–96.

Odendahl, T., & O'Neill, M. (1994). *Women and power in the nonprofit sector.* San Francisco: Jossey-Bass.

Phillips, N., & Hardy, C. (2002). *Discourse analysis: Investigating processes of social construction* (Vol. 50, Qualitative Research Methods Series). Thousand Oaks, CA: Sage.

Rosener, J.B. (1990). Ways women lead. *Harvard Business Review, 68*(6), 109–25.

Rossiter, M. (2005). Relational learning. In L.M. English (Ed.), *International encyclopedia of adult education* (pp. 548–552). New York: Palgrave.

Ryan, A.B. (2001). *Feminist ways of knowing: Towards theorising the person for radical adult education.* Leicester, UK: National Institute of Adult Continuing Education.

Starr, C. (2000). Third wave feminism. In L. Code (Ed.), *Encyclopedia of feminist theories* (p. 474). New York: Routledge.

Tambouko, M. (2003). *Women, education and the self: A Foucauldian perspective.* London: Palgrave, Macmillan.

CHAPTER 35

Husband Abuse: Equality with a Vengeance?

Joanne C. Minaker and Laureen Snider

Introduction

The most recurrent backlash against women's safety is the myth that men are battered as often as women. . . . Of course we must have compassion for those relatively few men who are harmed by their wives and partners, but it makes logical sense to focus our attention and work on the vast problem of male violence . . . and not get side-tracked by the relatively tiny problem of male victimization. (Straton, 1994: 79–80)

This article employs the phenomenon of 'husband abuse' to analyze feminist initiatives to ameliorate and empower women through criminal-law reform.

Our original intention was to look at women as victims and as offenders today, to investigate the continuing validity (or not) of the 1994 critique. However, it soon became clear that today's realities are too complex and contradictory to allow such an analysis. Instead, we have done a case study of a phenomenon that, we argue, exemplifies these complexities: the newly discovered problem of 'husband abuse'. 'Wife battering'—the original problem constituted by 1970s feminists—has morphed into 'domestic violence' and then into 'husband abuse'. The husband-abuse argument runs counter to decades of feminist research, theory, and activism. One of the battered women's movement's key goals was to challenge the silence over woman abuse and decrease public tolerance of it. With the proliferation of 'husband abuse' discourse, feminist assumptions, research evidence, and claims—that women are more likely to be injured, that women are murdered at three times the rate of men, and that, when separated, they are eight times as likely to

be killed (Jiwani, 2000; Statistics Canada, 2005)—are under attack. As we shall show, the claim that spousal abuse is a gender-neutral phenomenon has become the new 'common sense', the dominant lens used by policy makers, media, and influential interest groups. To understand how and why this has happened, 'husband abuse' must be situated in the social, economic, and political milieu that produced it and that reinforces it to this day. This article demonstrates how the very successes of feminism, combined with neo-liberal governance, the burgeoning power of men's movements, and new communication media, have given rise to new subjects, mentalities, and practices.

1. A Case of Backlash: Male Victims and Female Abusers

Rationale and Claims: Domestic Violence as Gender Neutral

The claim/myth that domestic violence is an equal-opportunity activity—that is, women are as violent as men, women initiate violence as often as men, and male victims are as likely to be harmed as female victims—is a striking example of feminist backlash (see Cook, 1997; Macchettio, 1992; Straus, 1993). The creation of a 'female aggressor' to match male aggressors suggests mutual battering as well as an even playing field inside and outside the family. In other words, Canada has a husband-battering problem, but it remains hidden because of cultural scripts that keep men silent and because powerful women's groups overstate male-against-female violence. We do not challenge the fact that some men are victimized in the context of intimate relationships, nor do we seek to minimize their suffering.

Rather, we assert that focusing on 'female aggressors' ignores the damaging violence men inflict on other men and on women, obscures who is doing what to whom, and undermines the ideological climate feminists struggle(d) to create, wherein instances of male domination, gender inequality, and systemic violence are called into question.

This section sets out the truth claims of husband abuse, the role of the mass media (including the Internet, books, and newspaper articles), and the new common sense that has resulted. Below we identify three critical fault lines: (1) the use of tautological arguments; (2) connections to larger symbolic structures; and (3) implications. As we shall demonstrate, the problem of husband abuse is primarily a constructed and symbolic one. Our purpose is to challenge the material and ideological effects these claims have had on women's lives, particularly the decline—symbolic and financial—in support for abused women.

The first question to ask, then, is whether men really are highly vulnerable to attacks from their wives and girlfriends. Are patriarchy and sexism obsolete, no longer ongoing realities in women's lives? The term 'husband abuse' was coined back in 1978, apparently by Suzanne Steinmetz, in an article reviewing several U.S. studies and one Canadian one (the latter with a sample of 52 college students). Steinmetz reported that half of both men and women admitted using 'some form' of violence toward a partner and that 12 per cent of women admitted to being the sole aggressor. The Cycle of Violence, Steinmetz's 1977 book, was the first of what became a steady stream of writings discussing female-on-male violence. Shortly thereafter, Murray Straus and Richard Gelles (1986; Straus, Gelles, and Steinmetz 1980) published the first widely accepted 'data' appearing to confirm that domestic violence was/is indeed symmetrical. Twenty years of subsequent research built on this base.

The argument is a prototypical illustration of claims making, showing the mechanisms whereby husband abuse is discursively constructed as a real phenomenon and a pervasive social problem, thereby challenging feminist claims that asymmetrical violence within the home is the norm. Although some men are emotionally,

psychologically, or physically mistreated by their intimate partners, the bulk of the empirical evidence (Rodgers 1994; Johnson 1996; Fitzgerald 1999) indicates that female partners are abused more frequently and suffer more serious injuries (Comack, Chopyk, and Wood, 2000). But as articles in scholarly journals, newspaper reports, and websites present 'evidence' purportedly showing that husband abuse is a serious social problem, and as more and more stories of the plight of abused male victims attract disproportionate publicity, the 'problem' becomes more deeply entrenched into the public mind. Men's groups claiming expert knowledge and first-hand experience as victims appropriate and displace feminist claims. By the pervasive logic of equality discourse, if men batter women, then women (must) batter men too. Thus we see interchanges such as the following:

Q: Why haven't I heard much about this problem?

A: Lack of awareness . . . little support . . . more likely to be ridiculed than taken seriously . . . expected to take abuse 'like a man'. . . . Social messages which tell us it is OK for a woman to hit a man. . . . This 'double standard' also contributes to the under-reporting of domestic violence against men. . . . Sadly, the women's movement . . . has not been particularly supportive of abused men. ('Common Questions' n.d.)

Millions of abused husbands are out there but silenced—or so we are meant to infer. The argument goes in circles, and with each spin it seems to gain more credibility. The 'double standard' unearthed by feminist researchers takes on an entirely new meaning.

To expose this tautology, public discourse, specifically print and Internet media, must be more closely examined. Our search of Canada Newsstand, a database of events as reported in major Canadian newspapers, revealed more than 100 articles on the topic 'husband abuse', indicating its wide dissemination. Headlines like 'Violence against men deserves attention too'

(*National Post*, August 1, 2000), 'Male victims overlooked' (*Hamilton Spectator*, January 3, 2002), 'Studies shatter myth about abuse' (*USA Today*, June 22, 2003), and 'Battered men too shy to enrol' (*Calgary Herald*, December 2, 2003) are common. They make 'sense' because they are inserted into a larger symbolic structure where equality is assumed to exist and differences between men and women have disappeared. The argument reproduces rather than challenges male domination, as well as obscuring structural inequalities. It is very much about silencing feminist claims. Abuse in the home is no longer a woman's or feminist issue but a 'human issue', with men and women equally affected (McNeely and Mann 1990). Under the guise of 'completing the picture', the reality of power, control, and conflict in heterosexual intimate relationships is masked; the very essence of the problem of violence against women disappears. Advocates use terms like 'partner conflict', 'mutuality of abuse', and 'family violence' to make the problem of male battery real (Fontes, 2003).

Nor do we see groups of men working at the grassroots level to provide support, care, and services for male victims. Instead, through men's organizations and collectives, men's groups and anti-feminist critics put their energies into demonizing and punishing female aggressors, rejecting feminist claims of inequality, and challenging the gains of the battered women's movement.

Because it is hard to find convincing evidence that male victims of abuse are numerous, or that they are trivialized, disbelieved, and considered an aberration not serious enough to require social intervention (Sarantakos 1999), alternative explanations must be considered. We suggest that the prominence of the social problem of husband abuse indicates something else—a counter-movement led by pro-men's rights groups and anti-feminist women's groups aimed at re-appropriating male power and privilege lost to second-wave feminism. In an attempt to reclaim lost ideological power, husband-abuse discourse denies that the familial home is patriarchal. Gender parity validates gender-neutral policies that result in a focus on individual cases of violence, ignoring the systemic reality of male violence against women. In short, the social construction of the problem of 'husband abuse' not only calls for but has largely brought about a resurgence of gender-neutral politics.

Claims Making through Internet Culture

Ray Blumhorst is a 6 foot 1 inch, 230 pound, decorated combat veteran who served in Vietnam. Ray Blumhorst is also a battered husband. Today he walks with a limp—he says not from war wounds, but from one of his ex-wife's assaults. Blumhorst recently filed a widely reported sex discrimination lawsuit against 10 Los Angeles County domestic violence shelters for refusing to accept male victims. He says his ex-wife attacked him by surprise on numerous occasions, once throwing a heavy book stand at him, which damaged his knee and put him on crutches. (Sacks, 2003)[1]

According to MENWEB (n.d.), 835,000 men have been 'silent for too long'. The following are typical examples:

Men and women are equals in violence . . . feminists, men-against-violence-against-women activists, three levels of government, and thousands of media reports have all painted an extreme, one-sided, simple-minded portrait of domestic violence as being about a hulking brute of a man terrorizing a quivering wisp of a woman. (Laframboise, 1999)

Women are just as violent to their spouses as men, and women are almost three times more likely to initiate violence in a relationship. (Evenson and Milstone, 1999)

Still, the newest findings challenge the feminist belief that 'it is men only who cause violence' says psychologist Deborah Capaldi of the Oregon Social Learning Center. 'That is a myth' (Peterson, 1999)

Dozens of websites celebrate the new 'reality' of husband abuse. In addition to websites, numerous popular books celebrate the abused husband and aggressive wife, and many of these are promoted through the Internet. See, for example, *The Verbally Abusive Relationship* (Evans, 1996); Philip Cook's *Abused Men: The Hidden Side of Domestic Violence* (1997); and Patricia Pearson's *When She Was Bad* (1997).

These claims have gained real political power. One has only to navigate the Canadian government's website on the subject to see how completely the phenomenon of wife battering has disappeared. 'Family violence', 'spousal abuse', and 'husband abuse' are now dominant. Under the Domestic Violence link there is a 63-page collection entitled 'Directory of Services and Programs for Abused Men in Canada' alongside a 53-page document called 'Transition Houses and Shelters for Abused Women in Canada'. But a cursory search of programs for abused men listed for Edmonton, Alberta, reveals that few of these places are actually delivering services to male victims of intimate abuse. Most provide individual counselling support (for any problem, from depression to substance abuse), some are nothing more than personal answering machines, and many are listed multiple times. When one of the authors called one of these agencies requesting 'services or programs offered for men who are victims of intimate partner abuse', batterer treatment programs were mentioned first. Another revealing illustration came from the Sexual Assault Centre of Edmonton, also listed in the government's document. It turns out that more than 90 per cent of its clients are women, not men. The males they do serve are primarily victims of child abuse, and most of them were victimized by other males. If this is typical (and it appears to be), then why are these organizations listed in a directory of services and support for abused men?

Empirical Evidence: What's Justifying These Claims?

> Unfortunately, disparate, decontextualized and sometimes illegitimate findings can be easily cited and are often employed to back up fallacious claims. (Hammer, 2002: 95)

Academic research and government-commissioned studies are the primary source of legitimacy for these claims.[2] On 14 July 2005, Statistics Canada posted a statistical profile of family violence in Canada which asserts that 'an estimated 7 per cent of women and 6 per cent of men in a current or previous spousal relationship encountered spousal violence during the five years up to and including 2004' (Statistics Canada, 2005). Based on data from the 2004 General Social Survey, the report also notes that the severity of spousal violence is greater for women: 23 per cent of female victims reported the most serious forms of violence (being beaten, choked, or threatened by a gun or knife), compared to 15 per cent of men. Only 19 per cent of men indicated they suffered injuries, compared to 44 per cent of women. Proof positive of gender parity?

The 'canon' or 'edict' supporting these claims is a biography published by psychologist Martin Fiebert in 1997 and updated in 2001. For example, the article posted on www.ifeminists.com about Ray Blumhorst claims that more than 35 per cent of all domestic violence victims are men (Sacks, 2003). The article cites the bibliography mentioned above, which is said to demonstrate that 'women are as physically aggressive, or more aggressive than, men in their relationships with their spouses or male partners' (Sacks, 2003). Fiebert's bibliography is often taken as gospel and used to convey the impression that there is solid empirical grounding for husband-abuse claims. His 'extensive bibliography' has frequently been called on to demonstrate that women are as violent as men, that women initiate violence as often as men, and that male victims are as likely to be harmed as female victims. For example, on 10 July 1999, Donna Laframboise in the *National Post* asserts that 'Men and women are equals in violence.' She goes on to claim,

> According to the National Clearinghouse's wife-abuse fact sheet, 'While men, too, can be abused by a partner, research has consistently shown that the man is the victim of abuse in fewer than 10% of all incidents of partner abuse' And the moon is made of green cheese. In fact, two years ago, California State University psychologist Martin Fiebert assembled a list of 70 research studies, stretching

back to the 1970s, all concluding something quite different: That violence in married, co-habiting or dating couples is an equal-opportunity phenomenon. (Laframboise 1999)

To interrogate these claims, we went straight to the source—Martin Fiebert's 'References Examining Assaults by Women on Their Spouses or Male Intimate Partners: An Annotated Bibliography' (2005), and what we found was revealing.[3] The bibliography mixes popular publications and academic journal articles (16 from the *Journal of Interpersonal Violence* alone), published and unpublished works, new and old material (references date back to 1963), as well as including links to Internet sources (e.g., Corry, Fiebert, and Pizzey, 2002).

Of the 176 sources listed, at least 80 employed the Conflict Tactics Scale, noted for equating physical with psychological violence.[4] Another 50 sampled only college or university students in dating relationships. Nineteen sampled selective groups (e.g., only women identified as 'aggressive', only males, or military couples), and of these 11 studied high school students and youth (some as young as 10 years old). Twenty-four were review studies, many citing sources included on the primary list. Many studies cited were flawed or outdated. Three of the studies cited (Feather 1996; Gonzalez 1997; Milardo 1998) used hypothetical scenarios. For example, N.T. Feather (1996) presented participants with a hypothetical scenario in which either a husband or wife had perpetrated domestic violence and evaluated participants' reactions. The study found that most participants were more sympathetic to the wife and viewed husbands as deserving of harsher penalties. Denise Gonzalez's unpublished master's thesis (1997) surveyed 225 female college students, probing for information about histories and rationales for initiating violence and having them respond to eight conflict scenarios. Fifty-five percent of participants admitted to initiating physical aggression toward their male partners, usually as a spontaneous reaction to frustration. Milardo's (1998) research, relying on a sample of 180 college students (88 men, 72 women), found that 83 per cent of the women, but only 53 per cent of the men, indicated that

they would be 'somewhat likely' to hit their partner. This finding was based on asking participants whether they would be likely to hit a partner in several common situations in dating relationships.[5] On such slender bases, then, an equal-opportunity social problem has been created.[6]

Despite these weaknesses, Fiebert's (2001) bibliography carries impressive scholarly weight. The 'empirical evidence' he has compiled, and studies published by reputable, respected sources such as Statistics Canada, are seized, publicized, and celebrated by anti-feminist journalists and conservative men's groups.

One does not have to look far to see the results. Statistics Canada has retreated to gender-neutral 'family violence research' (DeKeseredy and Kelly 1993; DeKeseredy and Schwartz, 2003), eschewing gender-specific definitions of violence in intimate relationships employed earlier (in the Violence Against Women Survey and the Canadian National Survey on Woman Abuse in University and College Dating). As DeKeseredy and Schwartz (2003) assert, backlash politics have had a whiplash effect on workers and abuse survivors. It becomes more difficult to garner much-needed support and resources. As we will argue below, husband-abuse claims are used as a rationale to further reduce resources for women's groups, shelters, and other social-support services for female victims of male violence (Jiwani 2000).

2. Situating Husband Abuse: Analysis and Implications

Removing Male Privilege—The Successes of Feminist Movements

To understand why Canada in particular (and Anglo-American democracies overall) has been so ready to accept claims that spousal abuse is gender neutral, we must go back to 1970 and examine not the failures of feminism but its real and enduring successes. Over the past 35 years, feminists throughout the developed world have achieved remarkable victories, revolutionizing dominant institutions, laws, tolerance levels, and subjectivities. A genderquake has been launched (Wolf,

1993), the aftershocks of which will be with us for generations (Mann, 2000). Second-stage feminism first hit the public stage in Canada with the formation of the Royal Commission on the Status of Women (1967), followed by the Office of Equal Opportunity (1971) and the National Commission on the Status of Women (1972). A decade later, when statistical studies showed that formal equality had not produced substantive equality, the principle of equal pay for work of equal value was introduced in all workplaces receiving federal funding (Fudge, 2002).[7] With high-level public backing, then, feminists and their allies began the job of transforming the fabric of late-modern society as lived in the Canadian state. Building on decades of struggle, a series of statutes and legal decisions gave women new rights to abortion and birth control, to matrimonial assets and child support after divorce, and to virtually all jobs and professions. Alongside gender-specific legislation, the Canadian Charter of Rights and Freedoms, passed in 1982, officially established equal rights for all (Comack, 1999). Liberal feminists—predominantly middle-class, well-educated white women—became a force in law, academe, media, education, and professional and institutional life in Canada.

Thus much progress was made. Women's opportunities for jobs, education, benefits, affluence, and independence increased. So did women's expectations of men, and their/our unwillingness to accept or excuse bad (male) behaviour. Rape and domestic-assault laws were revised; policies banning sexual and workplace harassment became common. One predictable, indeed inevitable, response to this very successful bid for power was the emergence of resistance (Foucault, 1977; Faludi, 1991). Voices in media and government began proclaiming that the pendulum had swung too far. Men, it was claimed, were now the disadvantaged and oppressed sex.

Making Lives Harder—Dismantling the Welfare State

Resistance and resentment were reinforced by concomitant economic changes, changes that destroyed much of the social safety net and removed many of the benefits associated with

the Keynesian welfare state (Fudge and Cossman, 2002). Starting in the 1980s, powerful economic elites persuaded state actors to embark on wide-ranging programs of neo-liberal 'reform'. Citing globalization, government deficits, and the need to compete internationally with low-wage countries, these 'reforms' systematically targeted government programs, benefits, and regulations. From (un)employment insurance to minimum wage to welfare rates, benefits were reshaped or cut. Working conditions deteriorated, job and wage cuts proliferated, and unemployment increased. In the public sector, privatization—'the amalgam of neoliberal and neoconservative strategies that marks the dismantling of the welfare state' (Martin, 2002: 355)—became the one-stop solution for everything from inefficiency to deficits. Outsourcing and union-destroying 'right to work' laws began to appear. Those still employed saw fewer benefits, lower wages, and longer hours of work. At the societal level, income inequality increased. Throughout the 1990s, incomes grew exponentially for those at the top of the income distribution hierarchy, while those in the bottom quintiles suffered both real and relative declines (Schrecker, 2001). Tax law (Philips, 2002), retirement income (Condon, 2002), immigration (Macklin, 2002), and health care (Gilmore, 2002) were 'rethought', and refashioned to fit neo-liberal priorities.

While these policy shifts affected all men, women, and children, groups were differentially affected. The virtues of neo-liberalism—self-reliance, independence, marketing oneself as a product—are difficult to realize if you are poor, young, female, single, uneducated, disabled, or marginalized by race or ethnicity. When governments turn responsibilities for day care, elder care, and health care over to the private sector, those unable to pay for services are punished. When retirement income is privatized, those who have been excluded from the labour market (mothers and caregivers) and those who have never earned much (seasonal workers, immigrants, poor people) suffer most.[8]

But many men were also hard hit. Neo-liberal changes produced 'a sharp deterioration in the labour market position of young men' (Fudge and Cossman, 2002: 25). Throughout the 1980s and 1990s, unionized, well-paid, secure jobs disappeared, and young working-class men suffered—they lost earning potential, income, security, status, and power. They could no longer expect to find a secure job, bring home a 'family wage', or provide the necessities of life; both partners had to find jobs outside the home. It now takes the combined wages of two breadwinners to provide the equivalent in purchasing power to the wage one full-time breadwinner (usually male) received in 1975 (Fudge and Cossman, 2002). Women's power within and outside the home increased. Wives' benefits and entitlements were no longer tied to a wage-earning husband but, rather, depended on their own positions in the labour market. And, since job opportunities for some women (educated, middle class, white) increased throughout the 1980s and 1990s, the female partner often snagged the better job, thus reversing the dependence equation (Vosko, 2004). Real declines in wages also fuelled male anger. In the bellwether United States, 'real hourly earnings fell from 1973 to 1998'; from 1979 to 1999 income inequality increased 19 per cent; and hours of work per week rose (Vosko, 2004: 95). While Canadian unions were stronger and minimal social-safety-net provisions are still in place, daily life became more competitive, uncaring, and unequal (Fudge and Cossman, 2002). Many people—men and women—are worse off materially than they were 30 years ago. Welfare and (un)employment benefits are harder to obtain and retain, education is increasingly expensive, and 'good jobs', jobs with prospects and security, are increasingly unavailable. Those in the bottom third of the income pyramid, especially young, black, or Native people, face greater surveillance and demonization.

Results: Anti-feminist Backlash

Women's successes and male economic, political, and ideological losses, then, have provided fuel for widespread resistance and what has been called anti-feminist backlash (Faludi, 1989). Many institutions today are questioning, if not reversing, feminist-inspired initiatives: in education, boys are now portrayed as disadvantaged; in the workplace, female sexual harassment is seen as out of control.

The identity labelled 'feminist' has been transformed from badge of honour to stigma (Masuch, 2004). In 1998 Canada's federal government, the body that established the inquiries and commissions that put feminism on the policy map in the first place, eliminated all subsidies to the National Action Committee on the Status of Women (Fudge, 2002). Fathers' rights groups, claiming rampant discrimination in family courts, began demanding that laws on custody be rewritten (Mann, 2002). The United States, which exerts enormous influence on every aspect of life in Canada, faces the very real danger that its Supreme Court will abolish abortion rights won in 1973 (via Roe v. Wade). Moral panics about 'epidemics' of violent girls, female stalkers, and homicidal mothers fill newspapers and magazines, videos, and the Internet. Women and girls are depicted as the equals of men: equally violent, aggressive, and sadistic (Pearson, 1995, 1997; Dutton, 1994; Laframboise, 1996, 1998). Stories that reflect unfavourably on 'feminists' receive massive prime-time media coverage. In November 1998, for example, in a series of front-page articles, the *National Post* ran a series of articles on shelters for abused women in which 'feminists' running shelters were portrayed as self-serving, power-hungry women driven by anti-male ideology. (Note the choice of words: both 'feminist' and 'ideology' convey negative messages.) Interviews with selected shelter clients bolstered the claim (Laframboise, 1998).

Thus it is not surprising that husband abuse is widely accepted as real, or that women today are constructed as equally violent. These claims are made in the prestigious languages of science; they resonate with well-established, powerful discourses of equality and risk. Such factors facilitate their cultural penetration and make them appear both salient and relevant. As social problem and claim, husband abuse reflects and simultaneously reinforces the 'mentalities and sensibilities' of our time (Garland, 1990, 2001). Seeing the world through lenses of equality has become simple common sense. However, its effects are neither simple nor benign. Discourses of equality and risk transmit important gender-neutralizing, gender-denying messages, messages with real, often deleterious effects. Translating social issues—inequality, poverty, and racism—into risk categories where chances of victimization and criminality are expressed in statistical terms makes invisible many crucial differences. When categories such as class, race, and gender do not appear in the actuarial charts and tables of 'experts', they tend to disappear from discourse as well, or they are dismissed as yesterday's knowledge: outdated, obsolete, out of synch with modern sensibilities. Or, most serious of all, they are translated into languages that actually legitimize increased repression. Thus criminalized women with the most extensive histories of poverty, exploitation, and abuse, those who need the most humane treatment and resources to rebuild their lives, receive instead longer sentences and more punitive treatment in maximum-security environments. When converted into risk categories, their manifold and desperate needs signal 'high-risk offender' (Hannah-Moffat, 2001; Carlen, 2002).

Ironically, the claim of equality, now used against women as often as not, was formerly an organizing cry for groups seeking female empowerment. Battles to reform laws on sexual and domestic assault provided evidence showing that, in law and in courtrooms, male perpetrators were excused while female victims were blamed (in rape and sexual assault cases) or silenced and ignored (in cases of domestic assault) (Smart, 1989, 1995; Snider, 1985). Battles to end the abuse of criminalized women and to secure rights and programs for the incarcerated also made equality claims, with groups arguing that differences in treatment and opportunities for male versus female prisoners violate the Charter (Hannah-Moffat, 2001; Hannah-Moffat and Shaw, 2000). Although it quickly became apparent that equality discourse was a dangerous, two-edged sword (Smart, 1989), it was one of the few tools available at that time.

Today the compulsion to (re)discover and (re) assert equality between men and women permeates cultural, political, economic, and social life, particularly in English-language capitalist democracies. Virtually every social problem and issue has been reinterpreted in terms of gender equality. If fathers are the prime culprits in child sexual abuse, mothers must be equally likely to offend.

If boys bully, so do girls. If violent male gangs are a problem, there must be violent female gangs. And they will be found: in the United Kingdom the 'ladette' phenomenon is a media staple. With little regard for empirical evidence, female groups are portrayed as exact parallels to 'the lads', equal in size, aggression, and danger to the public (Worrall, 2002). In Canada moral panics centred on sadistic antisocial women and violent thrill-seeking girl gangs are common, fuelled by the notorious real-life examples of Karla Homolka and the murderous assault on teenager Reena Virk. And now, in the area of domestic abuse, the logic that the existence of battered wives 'proves' the existence of battered husbands, and the allied assumption that women inflict equally serious injuries and psychological damage, permeates dominant culture. However few battered husbands there actually are, they will be 'found', publicized, and hailed as examples of a reality formerly obscured by man-hating feminists.

The effect is an ongoing cultural denial of the reality of unequal victimization. Portraying spousal violence as gender neutral sends powerful political messages, messages that justify 'an ideological and moral retreat' by professionals and policy makers (Worrall, 2002: 48). Denying the victimization of women is not merely politically and culturally attractive; it is a potential money-saver. If men and women are equally likely to batter, why should governments provide specialized counsellors for rape victims or costly gender-specific programs and institutions?

However, portraying reality this way requires a highly selective reading of extant empirical literatures. Numerous studies document the long-established fact that the percentage of female batterers, child sex abusers, and violent girls is much lower than that of males; in most offences, the sex ratio discrepancy is close to 10:1 (Chesney-Lind, 1987; Daly and Chesney-Lind, 1988; DeKeseredy, 2000; Belknap, 2001). Despite much-lauded and well-publicized studies 'proving' that sexual abuse of children by mothers is almost as common as that by fathers (Welldon, 1988), in 1999 only 16 women were imprisoned for sex offences in all of England and Wales; in contrast, there were 2,492 male offenders (Worrall, 2002: 51). Another U.K.

study looking at all assault cases reported to police in 1999 found that 81 per cent were male-on-female assault and only 8 per cent were female-on-male (Stanko, 2001). A similar Canadian study found that 80 per cent of spousal violence, 75 per cent of physical child abuse, and 100 per cent of child sexual abuse involves male perpetrators (Mann, 2000: 31). Those studies of domestic violence that present evidence of gender equivalence (Straus, 1993; Straus and Gelles, 1986; Straus et al., 1980; Kennedy and Dutton, 1989) turn out, on closer analysis, to tell a very different story. Conflict scales that equate verbal and physical violence hide the fact that female violence against men is usually defensive and fail to mention that women are usually the help-seeking party (Comack et al., 2000). The fact that women victims of spousal violence are much more likely to be injured, and much more likely to suffer serial assaults, also disappears (Statistics Canada, 2005).

Implications and Conclusion

This study has shown how a new de-gendered consciousness of family violence has seized the public imagination and come to dominate policy agendas. As we have seen, feminist initiatives to force states and societies to take wife abuse seriously were successful. However, when combined with neo-liberal governance, the rising power of men's movements, and the Internet, they have given rise to new subjects—the abused husband and his binary counterpart, the battering wife. At the policy level, this has produced gender-neutral approaches to what officials now call 'family violence'.

The claim that male and female partners are equally prone to violence is made by powerful groups, resonates with discourses of equality, and reinforces constituencies promoting criminal-justice 'solutions' to all social problems. Men's movements and pro-status-quo women's groups ensure public prominence for such claims, while social-science experts confer legitimacy. The quest to discover, document, and publicize the hypothesized 'missing' male victim (and to criminalize the hypothesized female offender) can thus be situated in the social, political, and cultural conditions that produced it.

The consequences for women, particularly those disadvantaged by class and ethnicity, have been more negative than positive. The invention and celebration of 'husband abuse' makes it more difficult to deal with real power imbalances between male and female partners and easier to ignore or explain away empirical evidence showing that family violence usually means wife abuse. For men and men's groups, if women are really 'just as bad as men', it becomes acceptable—even legitimate—to avoid dealing with the causes and consequences of the still ubiquitous reality of male violence against women. When policy makers take husband-abuse claims at face value, resources allocated to rape crisis centres, shelters, and services for battered women can be reduced or eliminated. Feminist scholars are forced into defensive postures to prevent the erosion of gains already won (or so it was believed) and away from gender analyses that help us to understand and respond constructively to the realities of intimate violence. The social and cultural conditions that reinforce violent solutions create more desperate citizens, and ever more desperate social orders are ignored, silenced, or obscured. And the struggle to build safer societies becomes a battle over which sex should be punished more (Snider, 1998).

Notes

1. Glenn Sacks is a men's and fathers' issues columnist and nationally syndicated radio talk-show host in the United States.
2. The General Social Survey's 1999 Spousal Violence Data, released as part of Statistics Canada's annual Family Violence in Canada: Statistical Profile, is another example of how empirical evidence is used to support claims of male victimization and challenge the 1993 Violence Against Women Survey results.
3. Since we began the research and writing for this article, Fiebert has updated the bibliography, which previously contained 122 citations (99 empirical studies and 23 reviews and/or analyses).

4. The Conflict Tactics Scale is a problematic measurement tool for: failing to acknowledge contextual factors that underpin and increase women's vulnerability to gender-based violence; not examining the full spectrum of violence against women and ignoring the socio-economic and political context in which women live.

5. The inclusion of research by Walter DeKeseredy and Martin Schwartz (2003) is particularly fascinating, given their work in the area of violence against women and their recent publication, 'Backlash and Whiplash: A Critique of Statistics Canada's 1999 General Social Survey on Victimization' (2003), which is highly skeptical of husband-abuse claims.

6. The most striking reference included in the bibliography was Gerhart Saenger's 1955 study, 'Male and Female Relations in the American Comic Strip'. Saenger (1955) examined 20 editions of all comic strips in New York City newspapers in 1950. The results 'showed' that husbands were victims of aggression in 63 per cent of conflict situations, while wives were victims in 39 per cent of situations; wives were more aggressive in 73 per cent of domestic situations and 'equally' aggressive in 10 per cent. Men were more violent than their wives in only 17 per cent of the comics.

7. Resistance to this policy has been fierce. With feminism losing power and credibility in the 1990s and neo-liberal cost-cutting measures in full force, the federal government became increasingly reluctant to enforce this provision. Federal public-sector employees won many court victories until on 29 October 1999, the Treasury Board agreed to pay compensation to women for past injustices. But, by that time, wages and working conditions in the public sector had already been equalized: both sexes are now treated as poorly as women once were—a pyrrhic victory indeed (Fudge 2002).

8. Ironically, state intervention, portrayed as wasteful and inefficient when used to support people in need, suddenly became 'essential' when used to coerce and control (Snider 1998; Martin 2002). As people on the bottom get more desperate, the relatively privileged get more fearful. As long as 'criminals', 'welfare cheats', 'violent girls', and 'squeegee kids' are the object of repression, as long as these controls are directed against Them and not Us, coercion is legitimate and politically popular.

References

Belknap, Joan 2001 *The Invisible Woman: Gender, Crime and Justice*, 2nd ed. Belmont, CA: Wadsworth.

Carlen, Pat, ed. 2002 *Women and Punishment: The Struggle for Justice*. Collumpton, U.K.: Willan Publishing.

Chesney-Lind, Meda 1987 Girls and violence: An exploration of the gender gap in serious delinquent behaviour. In D. Corwell, I. Evans, and C. O'Donnell (eds.), *Childhood Aggression and Violence*. New York: Plenum.

Comack, Elizabeth, ed. 1999 *Locating Law: Race/Class/Gender Connections*. Halifax: Fernwood Publishing.

Comack, Elizabeth, Vanessa Chopyk, and Linda Wood 2000 *Mean Streets? The Social Locations, Gender Dynamics, and Patterns of Violent Crime in Winnipeg*. Ottawa: Canadian Centre for Policy Alternatives. www.policyalternatives.ca/documents/Manitoba_Pubs/meanstreets.pdf

Common questions about domestic abuse against men n.d. Men's Activism News Network. www.mensactivism.org/activis_files/q_and_a_flyer.pdf

Condon, Mary 2002 Privatizing pension risk: Gender, law and financial markets. In Brenda Cossman and Judy Fudge (eds.), *Privatization, Law, and the Challenge to Feminism*. Toronto: University of Toronto Press.

Cook, Philip 1997 *Abused Men: The Hidden Side of Domestic Violence*. Westport, CT: Praeger.

Corry, Charles E., Martin S. Fiebert, and Erin Pizzey 2002 Controlling domestic violence against men. www.familytx.org/research/Control_DV_against-men.pdf

Daly, Kathleen and Meda Chesney-Lind 1988 Feminism and criminology. *Justice Quarterly* 5(4): 101–43.

DeKeseredy, Walter 2000 *Women, Crime and the Canadian Criminal Justice System*. Cincinnati: Anderson.

DeKeseredy, Walter and Martin D. Schwartz 2003 Backlash and whiplash: A critique of Statistics Canada's 1999 General Social Survey on Victimization. *Online Journal of Justice Studies* 1(1). http://ojjs.icaap.org/issues/1.1/dekeseredy-schwartz.html

Dutton, Donald 1994 Patriarchy and wife assault: The ecological fallacy. *Violence and Victims* 9: 125–40.

Evans, Patricia 1996 *The Verbally Abusive Relationship: How to Recognize It and How to Respond*. Avon, MA: Adams Media.

Evenson, Brad and Carol Milstone 1999 Women emerge as aggressors in Alberta survey. *National Post*, July 10: A1.

Faludi, Susan 1991 *Backlash: The Undeclared War against American Women*. New York: Crown.

Feather, N.T. 1996 Domestic violence, gender and perceptions of justice. *Sex Roles* 35: 507–9.

Fiebert, Martin S. 2001 References examining assaults by women on their spouses or male partners: An annotated bibliography, www.batteredmen.com/fiebert.htm

Fitzgerald, Robin 1999 *Family Violence in Canada: A Statistical Profile*. Ottawa: Statistics Canada.

Foucault, Michel 1977 *Discipline and Punish: The Birth of the Prison*. Trans. Alan Sheridan. New York: Pantheon.

Fudge, Judy 2002 From segregation to privatization: Equality, the law and women public servants 1908–2001. In Brenda Cossman and Judy Fudge (eds.), *Privatization, Law, and the Challenge to Feminism*. Toronto: University of Toronto Press.

Fudge, Judy and Brenda Cossman 2002 Introduction: Privatization, law and the challenge to feminism. In Brenda Cossman and Judy Fudge (eds.), *Privatization, Law, and the Challenge to Feminism*. Toronto: University of Toronto Press.

Garland, David 1990 *Punishment and Modern Society*. Chicago: University of Chicago Press.

Garland, David 2001 *The Culture of Control*. Oxford: Oxford University Press.

Gilmore, Jane 2002 Creeping privatization in health care: Implications for women as the state redraws its role. In Brenda Cossman and Judy Fudge (eds.), *Privatization, Law, and the Challenge to Feminism*. Toronto: University of Toronto Press.

Gonzalez, Denise 1997 Why females initiate violence: A study examining the reasons behind assaults on men. Master's thesis, California State University, Long Beach.

Hammer, Rhonda 2002 *Antifeminism and Family Terrorism: A Critical Feminist Perspective*. Lanham, MD: Rowman & Littlefield.

Hannah-Moffat, Kelly 2001 *Punishment in Disguise: Penal Governance and Canadian Federal Women's Imprisonment*. Toronto: University of Toronto Press.

Hannah-Moffat, Kelly and Margaret Shaw, eds. 2000 *An Ideal Prison? Critical Essays on Women's Imprisonment in Canada*. Halifax: Fernwood Publishing.

Jiwani, Yasmine 2000 The 1999 General Social Survey on Spousal Violence: An analysis. www.harbour.sfu.ca/freda/reports/gss01.htm

Kennedy, Lesley and Donald Dutton 1989 The incidence of wife assault in Alberta. *Canadian Journal of Behavioural Sciences* 21: 40–54.

Johnson, Holly 1996 Violent Crime in Canada. *Juristat* 16.6.

Laframboise, Donna 1996 *The Princess at the Window: A New Gender Morality*. Toronto: Penguin Books.

Laframboise, Donna 1998 Battered shelters. *National Post*, November 14: B1.

Laframboise, Donna 1999 Men and women are equals in violence. *National Post*, July 10: A1.

Lupri, Eugen and Elaine Grandin 2004 *Intimate Partner Violence against Men*. Ottawa: Minister of Health.

Macchettio, John 1992 Aspects of male victimization and female aggression: Implications for counselling men. *Journal of Mental Health Counseling* 14: 375–92.

Macklin, Audrey 2002 Public entrance/private member. In Brenda Cossman and Judy Fudge (eds.), *Privatization, Law, and the Challenge to Feminism*. Toronto: University of Toronto Press.

Mann, Ruth 2000 *Who Owns Domestic Abuse? The Local Politics of a Social Problem*. Toronto: University of Toronto Press.

Mann, Ruth 2002 Emotionality and social activism. *Journal of Contemporary Ethnography* 31: 251–84.

Martin, Diane 2002 Both pitied and scorned: Child prostitution in an era of privatization. In Brenda Cossman and Judy Fudge (eds.), *Privatization, Law, and the Challenge to Feminism*. Toronto: University of Toronto Press.

Masuch, Christie 2004 Man-Haters, militants and aggressive women: Young women, media representations and feminist identity. Master's thesis, Queen's University, Kingston, ON.

McNeely, R.L. and C.R. Mann 1990 Domestic violence is a human issue. *Journal of Interpersonal Violence* 5: 129–32.

MENWEB n.d. MenWeb—Domestic Violence (home page), www. batteredmen.com

Milardo, R.M. 1998 Gender asymmetry in common couple violence. *Personal Relationships* 5: 423–43.

Pearson, Patricia 1995 Behind every successful psychopath. *Saturday Night* (October): 50–63.

Pearson, Patricia 1997 *When She Was Bad: Women's Violence and the Myth of Innocence*. Toronto: Random House.

Peterson, Karen S. 2003 Studies shatter myth about abuse. *USA Today*, June 22. www.usatoday.com/news/health/2003-06-22-abuse-usat_x.htm

Philips, Lynn 2002 Tax law and social reproduction: The gender of fiscal policy in an age of privatization. In Brenda Cossman and Judy Fudge (eds.), *Privatization, Law, and the Challenge to Feminism*. Toronto: University of Toronto Press.

Rodgers, Karen 1994 Wife Assault: The Findings of a National Survey. *Juristat* 14.9.

Sacks, Glenn 2003 Battered husbands' injuries no jokes: Men as well as women deserve shelter from domestic violence, www.ifeminists.net/introduction/editorials/2003/0617sacks.html

Saenger, Gerhart 1955 Male and female relations in the American comic strip. *Public Opinion Quarterly* 19: 195–205.

Sarantakos, Sotorios 1999 Husband abuse: Fact or fiction? *Australian Journal of Social Issues* 34: 231–52.

Schrecker, Ted 2001 From the welfare state to the no-second-chances state. In Susan Boyd, Dorothy Chunn, and Robert Menzies (eds.), *(Ab) Using Power: The Canadian Experience*. Halifax: Fernwood Publishing.

Smart, Carol 1989 *Feminism and the Power of the Law*. London: Routledge.

Smart, Carol 1995 *Law, Crime and Sexuality: Essays in Feminism*. London: Sage.

Snider, Laureen 1985 Legal reform and social control: The dangers of abolishing rape. *International Journal of Sociology of Law* 13: 337–56.

Snider, Laureen 1994 Feminism, punishment and the potential of empowerment. *Canadian Journal of Law and Society* 9(1): 75–104.

Snider, Laureen 1998 Towards safer societies: Punishment, masculinities and violence against women. *British Journal of Criminology* 38: 1–39.

Snider, Laureen 2000 The sociology of corporate crime: An obituary. *Theoretical Criminology* 4: 169–206.

Stanko, Elizabeth 2001 The day to count: Reflections on a methodology to raise awareness about the impact of domestic violence in the UK. *Criminal Justice* 1: 215–26.

Statistics Canada 2005 Family violence in Canada: A statistical profile, 2005. *The Daily*, July 14. www.statcan.ca/Daily/English/050714/td050714.htm

Steinmetz, Suzanne 1977 *The Cycle of Violence: Assertive, Aggressive and Abusive Family Interaction*. New York: Praeger.

Steinmetz, Suzanne 1978 The battered husband syndrome. *Victimology* 2: 499–509.

Straton, Jack 1994 The myth of the 'battered husband syndrome'. *Masculinities* 2: 79–82.

Straus, Murray 1993 Physical assaults by wives: A major social problem. In Richard Gelles and David Loseke (eds.), *Current Controversies on Family Violence*. London: Sage.

Straus, Murray and Richard Gelles 1986 Societal changes and change in family violence from 1975 to 1985 as revealed by two national surveys. *Journal of Marriage and the Family* 48: 465–80.

Straus, Murray, Richard Gelles, and Suzanne Steinmetz 1980 *Behind Closed Doors: Violence in the American Family*. New York: Doubleday.

Tutty, Leslie 1999 *Husband Abuse: An Overview of Research and Perspectives*. Ottawa: National Clearinghouse on Family Violence.

Welldon, Elizabeth 1988 *Mother, Madonna, Whore: The Idealization and Denigration of Motherhood*. London: Free Association Books.

Wolf, Naomi 1993 *Fire with Fire*. Toronto: Random House.

Worrall, Anne 2002 Rendering women punishable: The making of a penal crisis. In Pat Carlen (ed.), *Women and Punishment: The Struggle for Justice*. Cullompton, U.K.: Willan Publishing.

Vosko, Leah 2004 *Confronting the Norm: Gender and the International Regulation of Precarious Work*. Ottawa: Law Commission of Canada.

CHAPTER 36

A Gaggle of Raging Grannies: The Empowerment of Older Canadian Women through Social Activism

Miya Narushima

Introduction: A Portrait of the Raging Grannies Movement

A Gaggle of Grannies
(Tune: 'Side by Side')

Oh, We're just a gaggle of grannies
Urging you off of your fannies
We're telling you boys
We're sick of your toys
We want no more war
We know if you tried you could
Chretien [Canada's Prime Minister at the time
    of writing]
Change our country's direction
We're telling you now
We're angry & how
We want no more war
We really mean it
No more war
We'll say it nicely
No more war
We mean precisely
NO MORE WAR!

(Kingston Grannies, 2001)

'A Gaggle of Grannies' is a standard number sung by many Raging Grannies groups across Canada. As its lyrics depict, the Raging Grannies are groups of female social activists who are 50-plus. The history of their movement goes back to 1987, when 10 older women in a street theatre group in Victoria, British Columbia, paddled canoes to confront the big US nuclear-powered warship that had entered Canadian waters, while chanting protests songs in flamboyant 'granny' duds with flowery hats (McLaren and Brown 1991). Having successfully gained media attention and public interest, they branched out into other areas of social concern including the environment, mining, nuclear power, militarism, clear-cut logging, poverty, corporate greed, racism, sexism, and any forms of social and economic injustice.

Grannies are politically conscious but nonpartisan. Their activism is largely community-based, i.e. each local group acts independently choosing the issues that they wish to work on. Yet, they are also linked nationally through the Internet, regular newsletters, annual regional meetings and the biannual nationwide assembly that they call their 'Unconvention'. All these help them spread their network to exchange songs and strategies, while informing a wide range of updated news and social issues. Grannies often collaborate with other advocacy groups in their local communities to organize larger-scale events and protests. As a street singing and theatre troupe, they are also frequently invited to perform in a variety of community gatherings and festivals. The financial support for their activism mainly comes from the donations received in these booked appearances.

Although research on the Raging Grannies is still scarce, Hill's (2000) qualitative study of 26 Grannies in Toronto provides a thorough overview of the common characteristics of the Grannies and their values. The 'Granny psyche' as identified by Hill (2000) includes feminist values, creativity, rebelliousness, empathy, risk-taking, spirituality, and humour. Hill's Grannies are predominantly white, middle-class, well-educated grandmothers retired from such professions as social workers, nurses, teachers, university and college professors, etc. Many are lifelong activists who have been involved in labour, anti-war, civil rights, and women's liberation movements since they were in young adulthood.

From its small beginnings, the 'Raging Grannies' has become a viable political movement with chapters in more than 50 cities and towns across Canada, some in the USA and a few even in Greece and India. Why this rapid increase in popularity? Why 'Raging Grannies'? What does this kind of social activism mean to women in late adulthood, and what are its implications for an aging and lifelong learning society? To find answers to these questions, I conducted a qualitative case study of this older women's movement in Canada, combining an extensive document analysis with four months of fieldwork with two Granny groups in Ontario. In the following article, divided into five sections, I begin with a brief description of the context of a greying Canadian society and its growing numbers of older women. Second, I summarize some theories regarding later life development, women's empowerment, and multiple roles from the critical gerontology and psychodrama perspectives. Then, I outline my research methodology and procedures, followed by a presentation of my findings and analysis. The final section discusses the implications of the Grannies' activism in the light of lifelong learning.

Context: The Aging Population and Older Women

In Canada, as in many other countries, older adults over 65 are the fastest growing segment of the population. Statistics Canada (Norland 1994) has estimated that there will be more 'seniors' than any other age group in the Canadian population in 30 years, by which time the ratio of the Canadians over 65 will have almost doubled (to 22.4 per cent by 2030). This demographic shift, sometimes called 'apocalyptic demography' (Robertson 1999) or a 'ticking time bomb', has raised worries that the younger generation will have to carry too many dependent elderly on their shoulders. By lumping

'seniors' together by chronological age, however, this kind of demographic determinism overlooks various factors including socio-economic conditions, health, lifestyle, cohort difference, and gender, all of which affect an individual's aging. Given that most provinces in Canada still have a mandatory retirement system and that policy debate is monopolized by the premise of 'older people' as post-productive service recipients, opportunities to utilize the skills and strengths of older people have been limited by structural factors and entrenched patterns of discourse. In a sense older people, regardless of gender, are alienated from the mainstream, while the social roles and cultural meaning of 'old age' are neglected despite the aging population (Cole, 1992).

'Old age', however, is not gender-neutral category—it requires a gender-specific perspective. Women's longer life expectancy means that they outnumber their male counterparts in late adulthood. The life expectancy of Canadian men in 1999 was 76.3 years compared to 81.7 for their female counterparts, for example, while the sex ratio of Canadians over 65 was 75 men per 100 women (Statistics Canada, 2002, quoted in McCarten, 2002). This means that so-called aging problems—i.e. chronic illness and frailty, poverty, loneliness, abuse, and so forth—also tend to be associated more with women. Consequently, older women are likely to be pathologized and denigrated as fragile, needy recipients of welfare and health care services. In a sense, senior women face the double-jeopardy of agism and sexism (Browne, 1998).

Partly because of this kind of stereotype, older women's potential for empowerment through collective political action remains largely overlooked. Preconceptions associating old age with social disengagement leads to a misperception of political behaviour among older adults. Yet, aging is not accompanied by a decline in political and social interest, and even greater 'grey power' may develop in the years ahead, something Peterson and Somit's (1994) study of US seniors suggests. Contemporary older women can be seen as a pioneer cohort moving beyond the traditional gender stratification of society.

Research Method

This study employs a qualitative case study approach that allows me to explore the Raging Grannies movement from manifold angles. It also synchronizes with Browne's (1998) 'feminist life-span perspective on aging' analysis which advocates listening to what older women say about their lives in order to learn about their views regarding aging and the current system surrounding old age. The procedures of the study are divided into two phases. Phase I consists of document analysis including 40 microfilmed articles issued between 1988 and 2000 in various local newspapers in Canada, 116 websites (including one local Grannies group homepage), and about 200 songs collected in their song books. Based on the overview gained through phase 1, I then conducted face-to-face interviews along with participant observation of 15 women in two Grannies groups in Ontario between August and December in 2001. These two groups were selected from among nine who had responded to my help-wanted email that had circulated on the nation-wide list-serve of their organization.

I selected these two groups because neither had been studied by other researchers or journalists, and for the practical reason that they were located in suburban cities within a range of my home in Toronto, which allowed me to make frequent visits for participant observation and interviews. Both groups were originally formed six to seven years ago and were similar in terms of the socio-economic and cultural backgrounds of their members. One difference between the two groups was that one was larger (15 people) including more original members, while the other was smaller (7 people) and three of them had just joined when my fieldwork began. Although I observed more commonalities than differences between the two groups (verifying the characteristics of the movement that had engaged from my prior document analysis), it also became apparent that the proportion of new and long-time members shaped the process of forming a collective identity.

The racial and socio-economic backgrounds of participants in my study were similar to those in

Hill's (2000) study of Toronto Grannies. The 15 Grannies who I interviewed were middle-class (except for one farmer) white women whose ages ranged from mid-50s to mid-70s. Twelve were married, one divorced, and two were widows who lived by themselves. All but two were grandmothers. Four were still working full or part time (as a senior administrator in university, a pharmacist, a writer and an organic farmer), while the rest had retired from various occupations (e.g. teachers, social workers, nurses, lab technicians, secretaries, etc.). All participants spoke English as their first language although two had immigrated to Canada from other Commonwealth countries in their youth. Despite the commonalties, however, certain differences from Hill's 2000 group were noticeable. Half the Grannies in my study were facing health problems, either their own or those of close family members. In terms of my participants' history of social activism, about 60 per cent were veteran activists, whereas 40 per cent had got their feet wet in 'activism' for the first time in retirement, although most had done community volunteering.

Face-to-face interviews were conducted at participants' homes, coffee shops, event sites or workplaces depending on their preference. Each participant engaged in at least one formal video-taped interview, each of which was between 60 and 90 minutes long, semi-structured with open-ended questions. Grannies were asked to talk freely about why they joined the Grannies, what their experience was like, and how they thought it had changed them. Participant observations were conducted at each group's 'gigs' or public appearances at various occasions (e.g. Hiroshima Remembrance Day, United Nations Day, The End of Sanctions on Iraq campaign, a Town Hall meeting for anti–World Trade Organization) as well as their monthly meetings. Since the period of my fieldwork spanned the events of September 11, most of the Grannies' gigs after the incident aimed at dampening pro-war sentiment. All the interviews were transcribed and analyzed manually to identify overarching themes following the strategy for category construction suggested by Merriam (1998). I then compared and categorized these into three key areas related to my original research questions: the motivations, strategies, and processes of learning that can be seen as the outcomes of the Grannies' activism.

Theoretical Perspectives: Women's Later Life Development and Empowerment

Although developmental theories have been criticized for their age-stratified hierarchical stages of human development, concepts of developmental tasks such as 'generativity' (Erikson, 1983; Kotre, 1984; Friedan, 1993), 'ego-integrity' (Loevinger, 1973; Erikson, 1983), and 'gero-transcendence' (Tornstam, 1994) still provide philosophical directions for personal growth in later life. 'Generativity' has to do with guiding and caring for the next generation, while 'ego-integrity' is associated with the feeling of self-acceptance in old age. Later life development also requires adapting to physical limitations and social losses, while learning to 'gero-transcend' oneself through a love of humankind involves shifting one's worldview from a materialistic to a more spiritual perspective. Psychosocial development in late adulthood thus appears to be an inward-turning process. Interpreting these developmental goals from the angle of social gerontology, however, one's continuous relationship with the external social world is equally important for successful later life development. In the view of a continuity theorist like Atchley (1999), the key for later life development is to adjust one's relationships with others in society while maintaining continuity in one's own life.

Theories of gender-related adult development also provide more concrete elements to help analyze the meanings of the Grannies' movement for older women. Since Gilligan (1982) posited women's development in terms of the morality of responsibility, the value of connections, and the ability to care, there has been much debate about whether these so-called feminine attributes are essential to female psychosocial development. Caffarella and Olson (1993), based on their extensive review of empirical studies, supported and extended Gilligan's (1982) argument, noting that a connection with others, a reciprocal relationship

between the individual and her environment, and an interplay of multiple roles have more weight in women's development than that of men.

Recent studies focusing on middle-aged and older women have also suggested the importance of these gendered and role-specific resources to women's psychosocial well-being. Price's (1998) study has indicated the positive influence of feminine attributes and multiple roles on women's passage to retirement. Altschuler's (2001) study of the centrality of care-giving to older women's personal identity also argues that the provision of caring serves to extend meaning and continuity across the life span. It is important, however, to note that these feminist studies regard women's caregiving role—their work of love—as possessing a stressful and exploitative element as well. Nevertheless, it can also be meaningful for women's psychosocial well-being, a way of remaining connected to others and mastering challenges. In this context, the concept of care is expanded from something concrete and task-related to something more symbolic and ongoing that is deeply intertwined with women's lifeworld and self development.

Theories of empowerment also add another dimension to our understanding of the Raging Grannies' activism, highlighting the social and collective aspect of older women and power. Taken together, the literature in women's studies (Miller, 1991; Surrey, 1991; Browne, 1998) and later life learning (Cusack, 2000; Jarvis, 2001) suggest that 'power' for older women can be posited as the 'capacity to move or to produce change', as 'power emerging from interaction', or as the 'increased ability to engage in critical thinking and leadership'. Jarvis (2001: 125), from the perspective of later life learning, has advocated the importance of critical thinking in the empowerment of older adults by noting that 'once older adults feel free to engage in critical thought, they are empowered.'

Regarding the process of older women's empowerment, Cox and Parsons (1996), based on their social work practice, stressed the importance of a cohesive collective or group experience to problem solving. Their study (1996: 135) also suggested that older women need a safe environment for building relationships upon feelings of trust, reciprocity, and commonality which are developed through continued interaction and a sense of belonging, acceptance, affirmation, and mutual aid. What these theories imply is that women's individual empowerment and the relational context through which this empowerment emerges must always be considered simultaneously.

'Raging Grannies' as a Self-Defined Social Role

The mission statement of the Raging Grannies movement included in their songbook goes as follows:

> We are enraged about the state of the Earth we are leaving for our precious grandchildren. We are raging against the system that has allowed this to happen and the institutions that perpetuate the atrocities against our planet. As grandparents, we have a responsibility to the children and grandchildren of the future, and it is not too late for us to act. (McLaren and Brown, 1991: 4)

'Earth', 'responsibility', 'children and grandchildren', 'future', 'act'—as these words imply, the Raging Grannies frame their activism as a symbolic extension of their roles as responsible and caring grandmothers who are concerned about the future of our planet and posterity. Most Grannies I interviewed are real-life grandmothers, and they underscored the point that they are acting on behalf of their grandchildren:

> I had not been socially active in this way, but I felt, at this point in time, it was time to do something. Because I had enough anger building in me over the years over things that should be happening or not happening. I have seen so many dreams and hopes fall in the dust and then resurrect themselves. And I don't feel so shattered when something doesn't work out. I have more of a long-term view now. I think if something doesn't happen in my lifetime, it may happen in the lifetime of my grandchildren. The idea is to make a better

world for our grandchildren so that when they are growing up they will have not exactly an easier time, but a fuller life. (Granny M)

Given their passion with which they talk about issues that may harm their descendants, it is indisputable that the activism of the Grannies stems from a kind of grandmotherly love mixed with a ripened awareness about the world, and where priorities should be placed. This desire to leave a better world for future generations can be interpreted as a demonstration of a high degree of 'generativity' and 'gero-transcendence' in later life, reflecting Hill's (2000) study that found generativity at the core of the Granny psyche. Friedan (1993: 619), an advocate for social involvement in later life, suggested that 'generativity is expressed in more mundane terms whenever [senior citizens'] talents are truly used as a community resource, or where they are allowed or encouraged to use their wisdom in work with younger people.' In the current discourse on 'old age' in Western societies, however, how much encouragement do older people—in particular, older women—really receive to cultivate their generativity while contributing their talents and wisdom as a broader community resource? This is the question confronted by the Raging Grannies. Indeed, the more I got to know them, the more I was convinced that their activism extends far beyond the 'generative' acts of caring grandmothers.

The Raging Grannies can be understood as an older women's liberation movement. As Hill (2000) pointed out, their activism sends a strong feminist message about the oppression of women in a patriarchal system. My participants' 'rage' about the social devaluation of older women was loudly echoed in comments like this:

> The grannies in our society opted to be silent. Now they talk more and more about elder abuse. I think of elders as elders in the traditional indigenous sense. Most often our society sees them in the malls or in church afternoon women's groups. Nobody expects them to really do anything for society. So I think that's another thing that we are

deliberately taking on. You cannot shut us up in an old people's home, you cannot put us in a mall and expect us to buy a cup of coffee and we will be happy all day, because we know something is wrong here. (Granny L)

This comment reveals two things: an anger about the social stigma of 'older women' as 'being past, useless, and not really being involved' (Granny L), and their strong desire to keep involved in and contributing to society. Browne (1998) once posited that agism on top of sexism can radical- ize older women, mobilizing them to fight against other forms of oppression and injustice. Given the Grannies' vehemence about the social denigration of 'older women', Browne's (1998) hypothesis may be less idealistic than many assumed.

Despite the feminist nature of the Raging Grannies' movement, however, their activism exhibits a strong emphasis on caring as an affirma- tive feminine attribute.

Older Women
(Tune: 'Merry Widow Waltz')

Let us celebrate the older woman now
To the troubles in her life
She will not bow
Earning every wrinkle
Striving to be strong
Sharing laughter, friendship
All the day is long
Older women overseas, newspapers show
War and sadness in their eyes
The truth they know
Fighting for their families
Willing peace to be
Standing tall while losing all
They call to me
Older women changed this land
They won the vote
Built careers, ran corporations
And we note
Took on politicians
So to change our laws
Fighting on for justice
They win our applause!

Here's to older women
All the things they do
Nurturing, supporting, caring
Their lives through
Wisdom comes with aging
Every grey hair won
Years unfold and still we feel
We've just begun.

(Southwest Ontario Grannies, 2000: 95–96)

This song portrays the struggles, sorrows, accom- plishments of women who shared a certain period of history and culture, as well as their pride and soli- darity. Above all, it depicts older women's endorse- ment of the 'nurturing, supporting, and caring' activities that have formed the core of their identity and provide them with a sense of purpose and con- tinuity in life. The Grannies I met often suggested that 'care' was the central value generating their energy: 'Well, "raging" to me simply means being forceful about what we consider in need of correc- tion and improvement. I think it's a good strong word that means that we really "care"' (Granny H). This reminds us to avoid the simplistic dualism which sees women's caregiving as either all good or all bad, a position argued in the feminist analysis of gender-graded roles (Browne 1998, Altschuler 2001). After all, it is undeniable that caring has been essential part of these older women's self develop- ment across their entire life span (Gilligan, 1982; Caffarella and Olson, 1993; Browne, 1998; Price, 1998; Altschuler, 2001). Providing caring hands indeed seems to be a great source of joy and satis- faction for these older women. Given the import- ance of continuity in later life to cope with inevitable physical and social change (Atchley, 1999), the value of caring for older women should not be seen in black and white terms.

Given their emphasis on caring and nurturing, at first glance the Raging Grannies' image risks pro- moting the prevailing rhetoric of traditional gender roles. Ironically, however, it is these conventional norms that the Raging Grannies aim to break free of. By identifying themselves as 'raging', these older women, who are biologically and economically in the post-productive period, are trying to extend their generative 'caring' from the domestic to the social arena to establish a new social role as 'caretakers of our planet' (DeShaw of Southwest Ontario Grannies, 2000: 5). Even more unconventional is the way they take advantage of the 'granny' stereotype to achieve this goal. Like the Trojan Horse, they exploit the social perception of 'sweet little old ladies' to gain entry to otherwise inaccessible places (McLaren and Brown, 1991). In fact, their group even made the 'Anti-Canadian' list of the Royal Canadian Mounted Police for 'acts of civil disobedience'! An 83-year-old Granny once confided that 'a Granny isn't a grandmother. A Granny is a frame of mind' (Growe, 1998). Given that the social role can be 'how you like to appear to the world, not simply how the world makes you appear' (Hopcke, 1995: 23), these words suggest that what a 'Granny' is seeking is an alternative way of living and aging. Rather than withdrawing from society in retirement, the Grannies choose to engage in the world even more fully through their social and political commitment, in other words their 'rage' or 'care'.

Grannies' Dual-Layered Mask Strategies

Mask 1: Strategic Humour and Absurdity

The Raging Grannies are known for their eye-catching style with their trademark outrageous 'granny' garb and hats, and their parodic songs that match their lyrics with well-known folk, pop, rock and hymn melodies. Although both the Grannies groups I observed followed this basic general pattern, each had its own unique style of protest. These and other groups' ingenuous strategies have been reported in local newspapers across Canada. To take a few examples, to demonstrate against the Gulf War one group sang anti-militaristic songs while literally knitting a web around a tank in front of an armoury (McLaren and Brown, 1993). To raise public awareness about the dangers of pesticide and herbicide, another group dressed up like big yellow dandelions and marched into a local Saturday farmers' market, where they sang and served organic dandelion dishes (*Hamilton Spectator*, 2000). One group even joined bicycle club riders to sing against urban

pollution (Harper, 2000). As these episodes manifest, the Grannies' protest is unpredictable, witty, and funny, and even absurd at first glance.

The playfulness of their act, however, masks a serious intent. Their extravagant 'granny' duds, mocking songs, and other overtly dramatic acts are all strategies to grab an audience's attention and get their progressive message across.

> Sanctions Hokey Pokey
> We say you can't have pens
> We say you can't have toys
> We say you can't have books
> 'Cause you're Iraqi girls and boys
> The banned list also freezes
> Drugs to cure diseases
> Do we care whom this destroys? 'No!'
> The bombs the US dropped
> Were topped off with a slick
> Canadian uranium
> To make your people sick
> It gives your children cancer
> Chemo could be the answer
> But we'll make the sanctions stick!

> (Peterborough Grannies, 2002)

After hamming up this song at an event called 'End of Sanctions on Iraq Campaign', one Granny explained their strategic humour:

> Of course, you get some funny looks if you are walking around in this get-up and doing this (shrugs her shoulders). But it's entertaining, so people will take a lesson in that form. You can't just walk up to people and say, 'What do you think of the sanctions on Iraq?' But if you are doing it in this way, it just warms people up and they will accept things that they probably wouldn't accept in other ways. In addition, people are less likely to attack 'Grannies' than they would you. If you came across opinions you didn't like and the person was your grandmother, you would think 'Well, it's OK'. You are not going jump up and down. If we laugh about it, they are not going to attack us for sure. (Granny B)

The Grannies know from their life experience that preaching or talking in a structured manner on serious matters is not necessarily the best way to raise people's awareness. Instead, they use music and laughter to evoke a gut response in their audience.

Despite their approach, however, the reaction from audience is not always as they expected:

> We started to do our gig on New Year's Eve, something called the First Night in this city. And there is a big party in the malls downtown. For the first few years, they asked the Raging Grannies to sing. Because Grannies are funny, people would gather around to listen. But when they heard that we have serious messages, they would just dribble away. When we go to events where people are committed to social action, we get a great response. They like us. But generally speaking, I think most people think, 'Aren't they cute? But aren't they crazy?' I haven't got time to think about it, but that's my sense. (Granny J)

Both the Granny groups I observed seemed to be well-respected and popular among fellow community activists in both cities, with many booked performances in various events organized by local organizations. Yet, their voluntary gigs on street corners tended to be either ignored or treated as a momentary curiosity by busy passers-by despite the Grannies' zealous efforts to get them to join in by offering song sheets and sometimes even homemade cookies. Hill's (2000) study and many other articles regard the Grannies' efforts to raise public awareness about social issues as effective without offering any supporting data. I do not completely disagree with their claims. Yet, my participant observations convinced me that the Grannies' activism has a stronger influence on the older women themselves than it does on the general public.

Mask 2: The Grannies' Act and Creative Self-expression

The strategic use of political satire works not only to draw public attention but also to provide a space for older women to freely express themselves in creative and enjoyable ways. The second layer of the Grannies' 'mask' is that element of dramatic performance, symbolically implied by the fact that Grannies call their public appearances 'gigs'. It struck me that, in contrast with their outrageous and comical public image in media, many of the older women whom I met were unexpectedly gentle and rather shy when off-stage. Many mentioned the transformative influence of acting in costume:

> You need to be brave to do this, and I don't think I'm so much a brave person in public. Well, I tell you. When I dress up, like a lot of actresses say, I feel freer to sing and to speak out. It changes my personality a little. It's like make-up. When I dress up I feel I can act like a Granny (laughter). When I put on this costume, I'm braver and I'm overcoming my fear. (Granny N)

Like a 'mask', the costume provides older women with the Raging Granny's persona, thus transforming the self. On the surface, it is paradoxical that older women need the 'Granny' mask to make them feel 'less themselves' (Granny B) to do their gigs, while the aim of their action is to express themselves through raising their voice and making themselves visible. Hopcke (1995), a clinical psychologist, provides a clue to how this works by noting that putting on a mask and ritual clothing unconsciously serves to help transform oneself by lifting one from the ordinary to the transcendent, and that such an obliteration of ordinary self immediately results in self liberation. In this sense, the Grannies' flamboyance seems to provide a sense of playfulness and freedom that helps them break down the conventional behaviour of middle-class older women.

The Grannies also respond to the idea of using songs as a political weapon. Many of my participants included singing and writing poems, verses and short stories among their hobbies. Granny M, who once was a music teacher and loves singing, commented:

> I know that I've been angry with a lot of things: health care is still falling apart, the environment, the treatment of women and so forth. These things create so much anger and

frustration, like what can I do about it. Being a Granny is finding a way to control our fears and frustrations by channelling our anger into action. I find it very satisfying that we let out our emotions by writing a song and singing it loudly. (Granny M)

As this comment implies, art forms such as music, poetry, and drama make it easier and even 'therapeutic' for older women to express their anger, frustration, and fear, providing a way to convert their negative emotions into positive actions. In addition, writing and singing protest songs requires a great deal of critical thinking to analyze the social issues based on their own daily experiences, and think about actions to address the problems. In this sense, to wear a 'Granny' mask is not simply to obliterate or liberate older women through the play and joy mode; rather, it makes them take the role represented by the mask more seriously. Adopting a social persona means to become that person, that identity, and therefore take the responsibilities that come with the role (Hopcke, 1995).

The Sense of 'Us' and Collective Empowerment

Rebel in Disguise
(Tune: 'You're a Devil in Disguise'. Elvis)

I looked like a granny
I felt like a granny
I thought like a granny
Then I got wise
Now I'm a rebel in disguise
Oh yes I am
A rebel in disguise, Oh yeah
A rebel in disguise
I got off my fanny
I joined Raging Grannies
I learned it was canny
To protest LOUD
(Chorus) We are rebels in disguise
Oh yes we are
Rebels in disguise Oh Yeah

Rebels in disguise
We stand up for what's right
Sing out, day or night
We can fight a good fight
When we're inspired.

(Southwest Ontario Grannies, 2000: 13)

This song delineates the process of transition and liberation of an old woman who has joined the Raging Grannies. As one may have noticed, the subject of the verses shifts from 'I' to 'we' as the song goes on. In fact, this sense of 'us', of connection, is a dominant characteristic of the Grannies' activism. Grannies always use 'we' as subject when they are talking about their activities, not to mention in the lyrics of their songs. Four participants in my study joined their groups about the same time as I began my fieldwork. During the first month or so, they often used the third person 'the Grannies' or 'they' to mention their colleagues. Yet, they shifted to 'we' or 'other Grannies' in a relatively short period. At the same time, they were getting more involved in various aspects of Grannies' activities.

It is beyond the scope of this study to posit the extent to which the experience of Granny initiates resembles that of younger people in a similar situation. Yet, I assume there may be some differences between older and younger people in terms of the speed and the degree of adaptability. Most of the Grannies I interviewed, even new members, had been actively involved in different forms of social action (e.g., community volunteering, writing letters to politicians and newspapers, marching to support social causes, etc.) and had built up a large store of frustration and criticism throughout their lives. Therefore, although it may take more time and courage for older women to commit to this new type of activism, once they have joined, they quickly become active and devoted members. In contrast, youth may find it much easier to join a protest movement as an extension of their social network without fully grasping or even agreeing with its vision (Kilgore, 1999).

After all, it takes a lot of guts for older women to express their anger and political concerns in public or even in private, as these comments imply:

Some of my friends don't want to be with me when I dress up like a Granny. They are much too proper. I don't know what they think, but they probably cannot acknowledge this foolishness. (Granny N)

To come out with the Grannies has really almost saved my life, because I have good friends here and I can get some of this frustration out of my system from having to stay at home and not being able to speak out. Well, my husband doesn't agree with me politically at all. I always express my opinion (laughter), but he doesn't necessarily hear it. (Granny J)

For some Grannies, it was a kind of lifelong frustration they were breaking free of. They said that they had always felt isolated, or even guilty, for being critical of the social system in their rather conservative middle-class circles: 'I am no longer a little boy crying in the wilderness. I am now in a shelter under the Granny umbrella. This is where I can think that many people think as the same as I do' (Granny O). As these comments testify, the sense of 'us' provides socially conscious older women with a 'shelter' where they can talk, free of any uneasiness, about their political concerns with other women who have similar inclinations and values.

This collective identity, however, is not something that springs up naturally—rather it is carefully cultivated. In fact, both groups in my study were making efforts to make their relationship non-hierarchical, mutually respectful, harmonious, encouraging, and co-operative. Each has a couple of core members who are veteran activists with a broad social network in their communities. These are the untitled leaders who lead and encourage other members who are less experienced. Old members often give a new member their extra Granny hats as a symbolic welcome gift. One of the leaders of one Granny group explained the principles of their 'feminist inclusive approach':

We don't blame people for not being at gigs and practices. We're not negative about members who aren't willing to take part in things. We really try to be inclusive and just keep that door as open as we can. If you come, great. If you cannot come, that's OK. So we try not to be judgmental. Because we are really busy people. And I think that really helps us. (Granny H)

Another Granny leader explained her group's collective decision-making process as follows:

Our discussion is quite open. Of course, like any other group, we cannot assume everybody has the same way of thinking. There are certain things we agree on and there are other things we just don't agree on. When we disagree, we sit around and talk, and try to find a comfort level. Or we just say those who are interested join the gig. But we would also discuss it and go over some of the analysis about why some of us think it's important and why some are uncomfortable. (Granny E)

The safe environment of the Grannies' groups— characterized by collective decision-making and inclusive, non-judgmental relationships—fulfils many of the factors said to make older women's empowerment happen in a relational context (Cox and Parsons 1996). Yet what kind of personal power have Grannies gained through their activism? To get a more concrete idea, I asked them whether their activism has led to any personal changes or rewards. Granny B, who had just joined the group one month earlier, explained her personal change in this way:

I gained more self-confidence. It's just being able to declare who you are more freely. Even if nobody is listening, I'm stating who I am. Sometimes I compare it to . . . well, my daughter is gay, and she joined the gay pride parade and that was sort of the same feeling, I think. You declare to the world, this is who I am. That's very empowering. (Granny B)

For Granny R, who was suffering from a chronic illness:

It [activism] gives me a voice. The voice that the Grannies have is a gentle voice. We are not pushing people or coercing them but giving them some fun with the lesson. Oh, I feel good about it. Besides, I have a nasty chronic disease, which means I'm often sick. But it's all right. Part of what Grannying does for me is that it makes me feel I can do things. I do push harder at things than if I wasn't sick. I think being sick may even be part of why I'm a Raging Granny. I'm fighting for myself. I need to have a life, not just lie around in bed. But I've never thrown up at a Granny gig yet (laughter). (Granny R)

Granny U, who got involved in social activism around the time she turned 60, reflects:

It [activism] makes me much more aware of the power that individuals can have. Often people say, 'Oh, well, we cannot do anything about that.' That is not true. All movements started from one person's thought. That's the only way to start it and there is power in people. I think the power of people is greater than many believe. Now with globalization and lobby groups . . . it's very important for some of us to do something if there is any hope at all.

Although the answers vary depending on each woman's personal context, being a Granny has definitely affected their lives. It provides them with a sense of purpose, of contribution, and of mastery. It promotes self-help, self-acceptance, liberation, and the realization of their capacity to become an agent for change. All these can be considered essentials for psychosocial development and well-being in later life. They are also congruent with the concept of an alternative power for women advocated in the literature of both women's studies (Miller, 1991; Surrey, 1991; Browne, 1998) and later life learning (Cusack, 2000; Jarvis, 2001). The Raging Grannies' empowerment is an ongoing process through which both individuals and groups learn to be free from the conventional often internalized image of 'old age', while realizing their 'power within' and the 'power in people' (Granny M).

Implications for Later Life Learning

In this article, I have explored the Raging Grannies' movement from various angles, trying to identify what constitutes a later life learning experience and what learning means in the context of Grannies' style activism. To be a Raging Granny is to engage in an ongoing process of self-actualization and liberation both individually and collectively, while making their social concerns more visible to Canadians at the same time. Given the nature of my qualitative case study approach, it is not my intention to draw hard and fast conclusions. Yet, my findings suggest that the case of the Raging Grannies may provide some useful hints for adult educators who are making efforts to create and promote supposedly empowering programs for later life learning. It also urges us to reconsider the role of later life learning in our society.

Call Me Senior
(Tune: 'Moonshine')

Yes, I'm over fifty, and the older I grow
I never stop learning. There's lots more to know
I've got time to listen, if you need to tell
Somebody sometime, when you're going
    through hell
Chorus: Call me 'senior', call me 'oldster'
Call me 'Nana' or 'Gram'
Call me 'elderly person'
That's not all I am
Inside I am young, maybe younger than you
Becoming somebody
till finding out WHO!

(Southwest Ontario Grannies, 2000: 17)

The desire for learning and personal growth is a lifelong process, not something that fades away in later life. As the lyrics of this song suggest, the journey of an older woman who strives to be 'somebody' continues in spite of the agism she faces. The quest for an authentic self and spiritual growth, after all, goes hand in hand with such goals of later life development as 'ego-integrity' and 'transcendence' (Loevinger. 1973; Erikson, 1985 [1963], Tornstam

1994). It has been noted that some women are able to experience freedom for the very first time in their later years and get more radical and activist with age (Greer, 1991; Steinem in Growe, 2001). It is questionable whether all older women, in particular the socially disadvantaged who struggle for daily survival due to poor economic and health conditions, have this option. Nevertheless, for women like the Grannies who are relatively healthy and financially secure, this argument seems to be relevant. As some Grannies comment: 'When you are older, you aren't concerned with child-rearing, and you are not afraid to speak out because your husband might lose his job' (Wilmot, 2000); 'As a senior, you can kick up your heels and nobody is going to get in your way' (Evasuk, 1990); and 'Women of a certain age, which is our age, lose lots of self-consciousness. So we don't mind coming out and looking a bit different and a bit silly' (Granny L). The question then is how older women can make full use of this freedom and vigour for their personal as well as community development, while facing the increasing difficulties they encounter as they age. Greer (1991) once recommended that one strategy women can use to combat devaluation and gain freedom, peace, and joy in later life is the practice of solitude and reflective thought. The Grannies' activism manifests another possibility: that joy and empowerment in later life can be generated from collaborative and creative political activities with other women.

The shifting demographics of our population challenge us to reconstruct the current discourse concerning 'older women' and reassess their needs and abilities. True, older women are significant consumers of welfare benefits and health care services as a result of the problems naturally associated with advanced age. Rather than regarding them solely through a lens of pathology, however, we need to think how we can build new social mechanisms to empower them and make full use of their strengths, appreciating their potential to act as agents for social change (Browne, 1998). Adult educators need to reflect on how later life learning can take the lead in this endeavour, while reviewing the current conditions of third age education.

Moody (1988) once summarized four decades of expansion in older adults' education in the USA as: first, 'rejection', which regards educational programmes for obsolete older people as a waste of time and money; second, 'social service', which regards education as a way to keep the elderly busy; third, 'participation', which maintains that older adults should be encouraged to actively participate in community life to gain self-sufficiency; and fourth, 'self-actualization', which identifies psychological and spiritual growth as the main educational objective for older adults. More recently, Jarvis (2001: 4) has provided a thorough overview of the historical development of third age education, criticizing the quality of current third age education as still mostly 'learning for learning's sake for middle-class leisure time pursuit' with no radical perspective in spite of its tremendous growth. This overlaps Thomas's (1992: 46) bitter characterization of third age education in Canada as keeping them 'busy and, therefore, kept from mischief, particularly political mischief'. Although there are some exceptions like the innovative programs launched by the University of Third Age and the Elderhostel, the philosophy and quality of most third age education programs seems to have stagnated in Moody's (1988) third and fourth stages over the last quarter of a century. In addition, the 'lifelong learning' model being adopted in many countries today is characterized by commodified knowledge and vocational training for competition in the global economy, leaving 'post-work' generations in the margins (Withnall, 2000; Jarvis, 2001). Under such circumstances, many older people—in particular, older women—are still ghettoized as consumers of leisure and hobby-oriented learning programs, which are not necessarily helpful for their overall development. Looking at the Grannies' activism and, more generally, older women's desire to stay involved in society, even Moody's (1988) 'favourable' stages—which encourage older people's 'participation' and 'self-actualization—need to be extended one step further by fortifying the liaison between the personal and social aspects of learning. In the current discourse, the goal of third age education still lies mainly in older adults' personal growth and self-sufficiency. What is missing, however, is a vision of older adults using their knowledge, skills, and life experience to spur community development and social transformation.

The Grannies' social activism serves as an alternative model for later life learning. It encompasses community-based reciprocity, a mutual 'give and take', as the following comment by Granny I underscores:

> As we perform in public as Grannies, we don't only try to educate people. By being at the gathering today, we have learned a lot. We will take a lot of stories that we can share with our friends and family, maybe not in so a direct way, but indirectly. So we do gain as well as give by being Grannies. (Granny I)

The example of the Raging Grannies suggests that it is important to generate more opportunities for older women to involve themselves in political community activism, a social and collective learning environment to help them cultivate their creativity, critical thinking, sense of self-liberation, and well-being in late adulthood. It also exemplifies how so-called women's attributes can be turned into an advantage for older women when they are properly included in a curriculum. In these unsettled times dominated by military might, corporate greed, environmental destruction and languishing welfare and public services, it is critical that older women be encouraged to broadcast their non-violent, harmonious, caring point of view.

Of course, some questions must be asked concerning the further development of the Grannies' activism. Why are members of the Grannies so homogeneous in terms of ethnicity and class? Would it be better if they included more intergenerational activities? In particular, how can they take their 'mask' strategies one step further to better communicate their political message? Although by now Granny activities across Canada seem to have gained enough support in the media to be reported in a sympathetic way, these reports often focus on their amusing appearance rather than their message. In addition, the Grannies are, in a sense, still faceless due to their collective Granny mask. If the Raging Grannies cannot encourage a more diversified membership or find ways to take off their Granny masks when the occasion requires, then their movement will remain a shelter for socially conscious, creative, middle-class older women. Yet, the need to wear the Granny mask reflects what older women have to fight against in Canadian society. Until ordinary older women can express their social concerns unmasked, until their voices are taken seriously, the Grannies' gaggle will continue.

Acknowledgments

I would like to thank the Grannies I interviewed for their lenient collaboration and the Toyota Foundation, Tokyo, for their generous financial support for this study.

References

Altschuler, J. (2001) Meaning and centrality of caring activities among older women. *Journal of Women & Aging* 13:(3), pp. 79–99.

Atchley, R.C. (1999) *Continuity and Adaptation in Aging: Creating Positive Experiences.* (Baltimore and London: The Johns Hopkins University Press).

Browne, C.V. (1998) *Women, Feminism and Aging.* (New York: Springer).

Caffarella, R.S. and Olson, S.K. (1993) Psychosocial development of women: a critical review of the literature. *Adult Education Quarterly* 43, pp. 125–51.

Cole, T.R. (1992) *The Journey of Life.* (Cambridge, New York, Port Chester, Melbourne and Sydney: Cambridge University Press).

Cox, E.O. and Parsons, R.R. (1996) Empowerment-oriented social work practice: impact on late life relationships of women. *Journal of Women & Aging* 8:(3/4), pp. 129–43.

Cusack, S. (2000) Critical educational gerontology and the imperative to empower. In F. Glendenning (ed.) *Teaching and Learning in Later Life: Theoretical Implications* p. 61. (Aldershot, Burlington, Singapore and Sydney: Ashgate Atena).

Erikson, E.H. (1983) *Childhood and Society*, 35th anniversary edn. (New York and London: W.W. Norton & Company).

Evasuk, S. (1990) Never underestimate Granny power. *The Toronto Star*, 2 April. Friedan, B. (1993) *The Fountain of Age.* (New York: Simon & Schuster).

Greer, G. (1991) *The Change: Women, Aging, and Menopause.* (New York: Fawcett).

Growe, S.J. (1998) Raging Grannies try to make world a better place. *The Toronto Star*, 14 November.

Gilligan, C. (1982) *In a Different Voice: Growth and Change in Adult Life.* (New York: Simon & Schuster).

Hamilton Spectator (2000, 11 July) Raging Grannies protest against pesticides: virtues of dandelions touted over chemicals.

Harper, T. (2000) Grannies heckle Day. *The Toronto Star,* 29 October. Hill, L.P. (2000) The Raging Grannies: personal attributes of older women involved in popular education for social change. Unpublished MA thesis, OISE/University of Toronto.

Hopcke, R.H. (1995) *Persona: Where Sacred Meets Profane.* (Boston and London: Shambhala).

Jarvis, P. (2001) *Learning in Later Life: An Introduction for Educators & Carers.* (London: Kogan Page).

Kilgore, D.W. (1999) Understanding learning in social movements: a theory of collective learning. *International Journal of Lifelong Education* 18:(3), pp. 191–202.

Kingston Grannies (2001) Personal communication.

Kotre, J.N. (1984) *Outliving the Self: Generativity and the Interpretation of Lives.* (Baltimore and London: The Johns Hopkins University Press).

Landy, J.R. (1990) The concept of role in drama therapy. *The Arts in Psychotherapy* 17, pp. 223–30.

Landy, J.R. (1993) *Persona and Performance: The Meaning of Role in Drama, Therapy, and Everyday Life.* (London, Bristol, Pennsylvania: Jessica Kingsley).

Loevinger, J. (1976) *Ego Development.* (San Francisco: Jossey-Bass).

McCarten, J. (2002) Men gain ground in numbers game. *The Toronto Star*, 17 July.

McLaren, J. and Brown, H. (eds.) (1991) *The Raging Grannies Songbook.* (Gabriola Island, BC & Philadelphia, PA: New Society).

Merriam, S.B. (1998) *Qualitative Research and Case Study Applications in Education: Revised and Expanded from Case Study Research in Education.* (San Francisco: Jossey-Bass).

Miller, J.B. (1991) The development of women's sense of self. In J.V. Jordan, A.G. Kaplan, J.B. Miller, I.P. Striver and J.L. Surrey (eds.), *Women's Growth in Connection: Writings from the Stone Center* p. 11. (New York and London: Guilford).

Moody, H.R. (1988) *Abundance of Life: Human Development Policies for an Aging Society.* (New York: Columbia University Press).

Norland, J.A. (1994) *Profile of Canada's Seniors.* (Ottawa: Ministry of Industry, Science and Technology), Statistics Canada, No. 96-312E.

Peterborough Grannies (2001) Personal communication.

Peterson, S.A. and Somit, A. (1994) *The Political Behavior of Older Americans.* (New York and London: Garland).

Price, C.A. (1998) *Women and Retirement: The Unexplored Transition.* (New York and London: Garland).

Raging Grannies (1997) Vow. Available online: http://reseau.chebucto.ns.ca/Community Support/VOW/songs.htm.

Robertson, A. (1999) Beyond apocalyptic demography: toward a moral economy of interdependence. In M. Minkler and C. L. Estes (eds.), *Critical Gerontology: Perspective from Political and Moral Economy* p. 75. (Amityville, NY: Beywood).

Southwest Ontario Grannies (2000) *Raging Grannies' 'Carry On' Song Book*. Collected by Southwest Ontario Grannies, spring 2000.

Surrey, J.L. (1991) Relationship and empowerment. In J.V. Jordan, A.G. Kaplan, J.B. Miller, I.P. Striver, and J.L. Surrey (eds.), *Women's Growth in Connection: Writings from the Stone Center* p. 163. (New York & London: Guilford).

Thomas, A. (1992) The emergence of a new leisure class. In J.E. Thornton (ed.), *Education in the Third Age: Canadian and Japanese Perspectives* p. 39. (Vancouver, BC: Faculty of Education, University of British Columbia).

Tornstam, L. (1994) Gero-Transcendence: a theoretical and empirical exploration. In L.E. Thomas and S.A. Eisenhandler (eds.), *Aging and the Religious Dimension* p. 203. (Westport, CT: Auburn House).

Wilmot, C. (2000) Don't mess with these nice old ladies! *The Jamaica Gleaner*, 12 February. Available online: http://dev.go-jamaica.com/gleaner/20000212/cleisure/c3.html.

Withnall, A. (2000) The debate continues: integrating educational gerontology and lifelong learning. In F. Glendenning (ed.), *Teaching and Learning in Later Life: Theoretical Implications* p. 87. (Aldershot, Burlington, Singapore and Sydney: Ashgate Arena).

QUESTIONS FOR CRITICAL THOUGHT

1. Have you ever participated in any social movement? (Or perhaps you currently consider yourself a proponent of a particular cause). If so, what drew you to take part? Was there anything gendered about the movement, or about your participation?

2. Can you imagine a Raging Grandpas group? What stereotypes about masculinity might lend themselves to the sort of comic exaggeration the Grannies have taken on?

3. Minaker and Snider argue that the 'husband abuse' movement has anecdotes, not data, on its side. What makes these anecdotes so powerful and convincing if they are not backed by solid evidence?

4. Do you consider yourself a feminist? Why or why not? Have you encountered self-defined feminists in your own life?

5. If you could start your own social movement to transform one aspect of gender as it is experienced in the twenty-first century, what would you focus on, and why?

PART X

The Gender of Violence

From early childhood to old age, violence is perhaps the most obdurate, intractable gender difference we have observed. In Canada, a 2005 study of police apprehension rates found that women constituted only 18 per cent of those apprehended for crimes against persons. As the level of violence involved in the crime increases, the gender imbalance increases. At the higher end of the spectrum of physical violence, the study concluded that 'female rates for homicide, attempted murder, and sexual assault were negligible' (Statistics Canada 2008:4). 'Men are always and everywhere more likely than women to commit criminal acts,' write criminologists Michael Gottfredson and Travis Hirschi (1990: 145).

But how are we to understand this connection between men and violence? Peggy Reeves Sanday argues that it's not a question of men being innately prone to violence. She connects levels of violence to levels of gender inequality, arguing that the more unequal a society, the more rape happens. By locating the originals of rape in male domination—profound separation between masculine and feminine social spheres, low levels of male involvement in child care, women's dependence on men—Sanday lays to rest the argument that rape is simply an inevitable hazard of a gendered society. Along similar lines, Russell Dobash, R. Emerson Dobash, and their colleagues use a gendered power analysis to explain why men batter the women they say they love in far greater numbers than women hit men.

However, gender alone is not the whole story in domestic violence. As Sepali Guruge, Nazilla Khanlou, and Denise Gastaldo demonstrate, this violence does not arise from the simple fact of maleness. The authors track the important influences that ethnicity and economic class, as well as the stresses and insecurities of international migration and 'outsider' status in Canada, have on gender violence. Further, gender violence is not limited to attacks on women by men (or vice versa). Violence is also implicated in the social organization of gender when it is used to enforce the rigid gender binary, by punishing those who dare to step outside it, such as transgendered people. Viviane Namaste coined the term 'genderbashing' to describe the violence perpetrated on transgendered individuals, and argues that this form of violence is still largely invisible to the general public, even as violence against lesbians and gay men receives more and more attention.

Of course, once masculinity is identified as a risk factor for violence, we are left with the political question of what to do about it. Michael Kaufman describes the efforts of a brave group of men to stop male violence—starting from the belief that men can be honourable, strong, and assertive without taking out their frustrations on the women in their lives. Kaufman believes that men are the only ones who can end male violence, because men are the only ones who can create new, healthier meanings for masculinity.

References

Gottfredson, M., and T. Hirschi. 1990. *A General Theory of Crime*. Stanford, CA: Stanford.

Statistics Canada. 2008. 'Female Offenders in Canada', *Juristat* 28:1. Available online at www.statcan.gc.ca/pub/85-002-x/85-002-x2008001-eng.pdf.

CHAPTER 37

Rape-Prone versus Rape-Free Campus Cultures

Peggy Reeves Sanday

In *Fraternity Gang Rape* (Sanday, 1990) I describe the discourse, rituals, sexual ideology, and practices that make some fraternity environments rape-prone. The reaction of fraternity brothers to the book was decidedly mixed. Individuals in some chapters were motivated to rethink their initiation ritual and party behaviour. In sarcastic opinion pieces written for campus newspapers other people dismissed the book on the grounds that I was 'out to get' fraternities. As recently as December 1995, a young man wrote a letter to the editor of *The Washington Post* criticizing me for allegedly connecting hate speech and sexual crimes on college campuses with 'single-sex organizations'. Having set me up as the avenging witch, this young man then blames me for perpetuating the problem. My '[a]cross-the-board generalizations,' he claimed 'only make it more difficult for supportive men to become involved and stay active in the fight against these attacks.'

It is one of the tragedies of today's ideological warfare that this writer finds such an easy excuse to exempt himself from participating in the struggle to end violence against women. To make matters worse, his rationalization for opting out is based on a trumped-up charge. In the Introduction to my book, I carefully note that I am dealing with only 'a few of the many fraternities at U. and on several other campuses'. I state the case very clearly:

The sexual aggression evident in these particular cases does not mean that sexual aggression is restricted to fraternities or that all fraternities indulge in sexual aggression. Sexist attitudes and the phallo-centric mentality associated with 'pulling train' have a long history in Western society. For example, venting homoerotic desire in the gang rape of women who are treated as male property is the subject of several biblical stories. Susan Brownmiller describes instances of gang rape by men in war and in street gangs. Male bonding that rejects women and commodifies sex is evident in many other social contexts outside of universities. Thus, it would be wrong to place blame solely on fraternities. However, it is a fact also that most of the reported incidents of 'pulling train' on campus have been associated with fraternities (Sanday, 1990: 19).

As an anthropologist interested in the particulars of sexual ideologies cross-culturally, I am very wary of generalizations of any sort. In 1975 I was very disturbed to read Susan Brownmiller's claim in the opening chapter of *Against Our Will* (1975) that rape is 'a conscious process of intimidation by which all men keep all women in a state of fear' (15). This statement was inconsistent with the compelling argument she presents in subsequent chapters that rape is culturally constructed and my own subsequent research on the socio-cultural context of rape cross-culturally, which provided evidence of rape-free as well as rape-prone societies.

In this chapter, I will briefly summarize what we know about rape-prone fraternity cultures and contrast this information with what a rape-free context might look like. Since the available data are sparse my goal here is mostly programmatic, namely to encourage studies of intra-campus and cross-campus variation in the rates and correlates of sexual assault.

Rape-Prone Campus Environments

The concept of rape-free versus rape-prone comes from my study of 95 band and tribal societies in which I concluded that 47 per cent were rape-free and 18 per cent were rape-prone (Sanday, 1981). For this study I defined a rape-prone society as one in which the incidence of rape is reported by observers to be high, or rape is excused as a ceremonial expression of masculinity, or rape is an act by which men are allowed to punish or threaten women. I defined a rape-free society as one in which the act of rape is either infrequent or does not occur. I used the term 'rape-free' not to suggest that rape was entirely absent in a given society but as a label to indicate that sexual aggression is socially disapproved and punished severely. Thus, while there may be some men in all societies who might be potential rapists, there is abundant evidence from many societies that sexual aggression is rarely expressed.

Rape in tribal societies is part of a cultural configuration that includes interpersonal violence, male dominance, and sexual separation. Phallocentrism is a dominant psycho-sexual symbol in these societies and men 'use the penis to dominate their women' as Yolanda and Robert Murphy say about the Mundurucu (Sanday, 1981: 25). Rape-prone behaviour is associated with environmental insecurity and females are turned into objects to be controlled as men struggle to retain or to gain control of their environment. Behaviours and attitudes prevail that separate the sexes and force men into a posture of proving their manhood. Sexual violence is one of the ways in which men remind themselves that they are superior. As such, rape is part of a broader struggle for control in the face of difficult circumstances. Where men are in harmony with their environment, rape is usually absent.

In *Fraternity Gang Rape* I suggest that rape-prone attitudes and behaviour on American campuses are adopted by insecure young men who bond through homophobia and 'getting sex'. The homoeroticism of their bonding leads them to display their masculinity through heterosexist displays of sexual performance. The phallus becomes the dominant symbol of discourse. A fraternity brother described to me the way in which he felt accepted by the brothers while he was a pledge.

> We . . . liked to share ridiculously exaggerated sexual boasting, such as our mythical 'Sixteen Kilometre Flesh-Weapon'. . . . By including me in this perpetual, hysterical banter and sharing laughter with me, they showed their affection for me. I felt happy, confident, and loved. This really helped my feelings of loneliness and my fear of being sexually unappealing. We managed to give ourselves a satisfying substitute for sexual relations. We acted out all of the sexual tensions between us as brothers on a verbal level. Women, women everywhere, feminists, homosexuality, etc., all provided the material for the jokes (Sanday, 1990: 140–1).

Getting their information about women and sex from pornography, some brothers don't see anything wrong with forcing a woman, especially if she's drunk. After the 1983 case of alleged gang rape I describe in the book, one of the participants—a virgin at the time—told a news reporter:

> We have this Select TV in the house, and there's soft porn on every midnight. All the guys watch it and talk about it and stuff, and [gang banging] didn't seem that odd because it's something that you see and hear about all the time. I've heard stories from other fraternities about group sex and trains and stuff like that. It was just like, you know, so this is what I've heard about, this is what it's like. . . . (Sanday, 1990: 34).

Watching their buddies have sex is another favourite activity in rape-prone campus environments. A woman is targeted at a party and brothers are informed; they then hide out on the roof outside the window, or secret themselves in a closet, or look through holes in the wall. Since the goal is to supply a live pornography show for their buddies, the perpetrators in these cases may easily overlook a woman's ability to consent. They certainly don't seek her consent to being watched. It is assumed that if she came to the house to party she is prepared for anything that might happen, especially if she gets drunk. On some campuses I have been told that this practice is called 'beaching' or 'whaling'.

Taking advantage of a drunk woman is widely accepted. As a group of brothers said in a taped conversation in which they discussed the young woman in the 1983 case:

> 'She was drugged.'
> 'She drugged herself.'
>
> 'Yeah, she was responsible for her condition, and that just leaves her wide open . . . so to speak.'
> [laughter] (Sanday, 1990: 119)

In a 1990 talk show—on which I appeared with a victim of gang rape—a young man from a local university called up and admitted that the goal of all parties at his fraternity was 'To get 'em drunk and go for it.' In 1991, I read an article entitled 'Men, Alcohol, and Manipulation', in a campus newspaper from still another university. The author reported hearing several members of a fraternity talking with the bartender about an upcoming social event as follows:

> *Brother 1:* Hey, don't forget—make the women's drinks really strong.
> *Bartender:* Yeah, I won't forget. Just like usual.
> *Brother 2:* We need to get them good and drunk.
> *Bartender:* Don't worry, we'll take care of it.
> *Brother 3:* That'll loosen up some of those inhibitions.

This is the kind of discourse I would classify as rape-prone.

Getting a woman drunk to have sex in a show staged for one's buddies is tragically evident in the testimony heard in the St John's sex case tried in Queens, New York, in 1991–2. This case involved six members of the St John's University lacrosse team, who were indicted for acts ranging from unlawful imprisonment and sexual abuse to sodomy. A seventh defendant pleaded guilty and agreed to testify for immunity (see Sanday, 1996, for a description of the case and the subsequent trial). From the testimony in the case and interviews with the complainant and members of the prosecution team, I reconstructed the following scenario.

A young, naive woman student, whom I call Angela (pseudonym), accepted a ride home from school from a male friend, Michael. On the way, he stopped at the house he shares with members of the St John's lacrosse team to get gas money and invited her inside. At first she refused to go in but upon his insistence accepted the invitation. Inside she met his roommates. Left alone in the third floor bedroom, she accepted a drink from Michael:

> The drink tasted terrible. It was bitter and stung her throat. When she asked what was in it, Michael said he put a little vodka in it. When she explained that she never drank, because drinking made her sick, Michael didn't listen. Then she tried to tell him that she hadn't

eaten anything since lunch, but this did not move him. 'Vodka is a before dinner drink,' he explained, insisting that she drink it.

Finally, she gave in to his pressure and downed the contents of the first cup in a few gulps because of the bitter taste. When she finished, Michael went over to the refrigerator and brought back a large container, which he said was orange soda with vodka. He placed the container on the floor beside her feet. When Michael poured another cup, she told him, 'But Michael, I couldn't finish the first one. I don't think I will be able to finish another.' Michael said again: 'It's only vodka. It can't do anything to you, Angela.' He also said, 'You know, Angela, in college everyone does something, something wild they can look back on.'

'Something wild?' Angela asked quizzically.

'Something wild,' Michael said again. 'Something you can look back on and talk about later in life.' With the beer can that he was holding in his hand but never drank from, he hit her cup and said, 'Here's to college life.' Later, Angela blamed herself for accepting the drinks from Michael. She was caught between wanting to please the host and wanting to assert her own needs. She had tried to please him by finishing the first drink. Now, she drank the second.

Then, he poured a third drink. When she balked at drinking this one, he started getting upset and annoyed. He told her it was a special drink, made just for her. He accused her of making him waste it. He started pushing the drink up to her mouth. He put his hands over the cup and pushed it to her lips. He said, 'Oh Angela, don't make me waste it. It's only vodka. A little vodka can't do anything to you.'

By now, Angela felt dizzy and her hands were shaking. She felt lost, unable to move. She had spent a lifetime doing what she was told to avoid being punished. Here was Michael upset with her because she didn't want the drink he had made for her. She thought to herself, 'If he wants me to drink it, I'll drink it for him.' After she drank most of the third cup, Michael went to put the container back. Her head was spinning and she began to feel really sick, like she was going to vomit. She tried to tell Michael that she was sick, but he didn't seem interested in how she was feeling.

Michael sat next to her and massaged her shoulder. She would never forget his pseudo-seductive voice. She hardly knew him, and here he was talking to her like he really cared for her. It was so obviously a put-on, she was shocked by the insincerity. He kept telling her, 'You need to relax. You are too tense. If you relax, you will feel better.' She tried to get up but she was too weak and she fell back down. (Sanday, 1996: 11–12)

Testimony in the case revealed that after Angela passed out from Michael's drinks, three house members stood on the landing and watched as Michael engaged in oral sodomy. After Michael left the house, these three took their turns while visitors invited over from another lacrosse team house watched. At the trial these visitors testified that they left the room when Angela woke up and started screaming. One of the lead prosecutors speculated that they left because they realized only then that she was not consenting. They did not understand that the law applies to using drugs and alcohol as it does to using force.

Cross-Campus Variation in Rape and Sexual Coercion

In his paper, Boeringer reports that 55.7 per cent of the males in his study at a large southeastern university obtained sex by verbal harassment (i.e., 'threatening to end a relationship unless the victim consents to sex, falsely professing love, or telling the victim lies to render her more sexually receptive', the variable labelled Coercion). One-quarter of the males in Boeringer's study reported using drugs or alcohol to obtain sex (Drugs/Alcohol) and 8.6 per cent of the sample reported at least one use of force or threatened force to obtain sex (Rape).

Schwartz and Nogrady found a much lower incidence of sexual coercion and assault at their research site, a large mid-western university. These authors (private communication) reported that

18.1 per cent of the 116 males in their sample reported some form of unwanted sex: sex by pressure (6.9 per cent); forced sex play/attempted rape (5.2 per cent); or completed rape (6.0 per cent). Of the 177 women interviewed 58.6 per cent reported some form of unwanted sex; sex by pressure (24.1 per cent); forced sex play/attempted rape (14.4 per cent); and completed rape (20.1 per cent).

The effect of fraternities is quite different on the two campuses. Boeringer found that fraternity men reported a higher overall use of coercion short of physical force to obtain sex. According to Boeringer, 'fraternity members engage in significantly greater levels of sexual assault through drugging or intoxicating women to render them incapable of consent or refusal' (9). Fraternity members are also more likely than independents to use 'non-assaultative sexual coercion', or verbal pressure. 'While not criminal in nature,' Boeringer points out, 'these verbally coercive tactics are nonetheless disturbing in that they suggest a more adversarial view of sexuality in which one should use deceit and guile to "win favours" from a woman' (10). From his study, Boeringer concludes that 'fraternity members are disproportionately involved in some forms of campus sexual aggression.' Like the prosecutor in the St John's case mentioned above, he suggests that in all likelihood the process of 'working a yes out' which I describe (Sanday, 1990: 113) is viewed by fraternity members as a 'safer path to gaining sexual access to a reluctant, non-consenting woman than use of physical force' (12).

Schwartz and Nogrady found no effect of fraternity membership. The most important predictor of sexual victimization in their study involves alcohol. It is not drinking per se that they found important, but whether or not a male perceives that his friends approve of getting a woman drunk for the purpose of having sex (the Approve variable). Also important is whether a male reports that he has friends that actually engage in this behaviour (the Get Drunk variable). The drinking variable that is the most influential in predicting a man's reported sexual assault is the intensity of his drinking—that is, the number of drinks he consumes when he goes out drinking (Drinks). Thus, the authors conclude that 'the level of the

perceived male peer support system for exploiting women through alcohol, plus the amount of alcohol actually consumed by men when they drink, are the primary predictors of whether they will report themselves as sexual victimizers of women.'

The differences reported by Boeringer and Schwartz and Nogrady suggest not only that fraternities vary with respect to rape-prone behaviours but also that campuses vary with respect to overall rates of sexual assault. The latter result suggests that we need to look at cross-campus variation as well as at intra-campus variation. There are several problems that need to be addressed before either intra-campus or cross-campus variation can be established. First, in studying intra-campus variation we must be careful in reaching conclusions about the effect of such factors as drinking intensity or fraternity membership because the dependent variable is frequently lifetime prevalence rates rather than incidence in the past year.

Regarding cross-campus variation, there is the problem of comparability of studies. Boeringer (private communication), for example, measures prevalence rates in his study, while Schwartz and Nogrady (private communication) measure incidence. Since incidence rates are always lower, we cannot conclude that the campuses studied by these authors are much different. Additionally, as noted by Schwartz and Nogrady as well as by Koss (1993), victimization rates from one study to another may not be comparable because of different methodologies, definitions, questions, and sampling procedures.

Nevertheless, some trends can be noticed. The available evidence against variation is seen in the fact that Koss's 15 per cent completed rape prevalence rate in the national study of 32 campuses is replicated by other studies of college students on particular campuses. Koss and Cook (1993: 109) note, for example, that estimates of completed rape frequency in the 12 per cent range have been reported for two campuses and estimates 'as high or higher than 12 per cent for unwanted intercourse have been reported in more than 10 additional studies lacking representative sampling methods'. According to these authors 'there are no studies that have reported substantially lower or higher rates of rape among college students.'

Evidence for variation comes from Koss's analysis of the relationship of prevalence rates to the institutional parameters used to design the sample (Koss, 1988). She found that rates varied by region and by governance of the institution. Rates were twice as high at private colleges and major universities (14 per cent and 17 per cent respectively) than they were at religiously affiliated institutions (7 per cent).

Ethnicity of the respondent (but, interestingly not the respondent's family income) was also associated with prevalence rates. More white women (16 per cent) reported victimization than did Hispanic (12 per cent), black (10 per cent), or Asian women (7 per cent). These figures were almost reversed for men. Rape was reported by 4 per cent of white men, 10 per cent of black men, 7 per cent of Hispanic men, and 2 per cent of Asian men. Prevalence rates reported by men also differed by region of the country. More men in the Southeast region (6 per cent) admitted to raping compared with men in the Plains states (3 per cent) and those in the West (2 per cent) (Koss, 1988).

Intriguing evidence for cross-campus variation in rape rates and related variables comes from Koss's national study of 32 campuses. Using Koss's data I looked at prevalence and incidence rates for each of 30 campuses in her study (2 campuses were excluded because of the amount of missing information). The results show a wide discrepancy when campuses are compared. For example the campus percentages of males admitting that they have used alcohol or force to obtain sex (Koss's 1988, 11 rape variables) range from 0–10 per cent. Campus percentages of males who admit to perpetrating unwanted sex in the past year (as opposed to since the age of 14) range from 6–22 per cent. The latter percentages are higher because I computed them using all the sexual experience questions (excluding the two authority questions). Since the latter percentages are based on a question that measures incidence ('How many times in the past school year?') the results provide a measure of an dependent variable that can be compared with drinking intensity.

The Koss survey includes two questions that might be taken as measures of drinking intensity. Both questions are asked in such a fashion as to measure drinking intensity in the past year.

One asks 'How often do you drink to the point of intoxication or drunkenness?'; the other asks 'On a typical drinking occasion, how much do you usually drink?' The campus percentages of males checking the most extreme categories of the first question (1–2 or more times a week) ranges from 1–24 per cent. The campus percentages of males checking the most extreme categories of the second question (more than 5 or 6 cans of beer or other alcoholic beverages) ranges from 6–71 per cent. Since all studies—Schwartz, Boeringer, Koss, and Gaines (1993)—are unanimous on the effect of drinking, this information, perhaps more than any other, is suggestive of variation in the rape-prone nature of campus environments.

The Concept of a Rape-Free Society

Assuming that we could identify campuses on which both males and females reported a low incidence of rape and/or unwanted sex, the next question would be whether there is a significant difference in the sexual culture on these campuses compared to the more rape-prone campuses. My cross-cultural research which demonstrated differences in the character of heterosexual interaction in rape-free as opposed to rape-prone societies would suggest that the answer to this question is yes. The outstanding feature of rape-free societies is the ceremonial importance of women and the respect accorded to the contribution women make to social continuity, a respect which places men and women in relatively balanced power spheres. Rape-free societies are characterized by sexual equality and the notion that the sexes are complementary. Although the sexes may not perform the same duties or have the same rights or privileges, each is indispensable to the activities of the other.

Since 1981 when this research was published, I have spent approximately 24 months (extended over a period of 14 years) doing ethnographic research among the Minangkabau, a rape-free Indonesian society. I chose the Minangkabau because of social factors that conformed with my profile of rape-free societies. The Minangkabau are the largest and most modern matrilineal society in the world today. Women play an undisputed role in Minangkabau symbol system and daily life, especially in the villages. Among the most populous of the ethnic groups of Indonesia, the Minangkabau are not an isolated tribal society in some far off corner of the world. Banks, universities, and modern governmental buildings are found in two of the major cities of West Sumatra, the traditional homeland of the Minangkabau people. At the major universities, it is not uncommon to find Minangkabau PhDs trained in the United States. People own cars and travel by bus throughout the province. Most children go to local schools and, increasingly, many attend college.

The challenge facing me when I went to West Sumatra was first to find out whether the incidence of rape was low and, if so, to crack the cultural code that made it so. In the early years there was ample evidence from police reports and from interviews conducted all over the province that this was a rape-free society. Ethnographic research conducted in several villages provided confirmation. This research demonstrated that women are the mainstays of village life. The all-important family rice fields are inherited through the female line. Husbands live in their wives' houses. It is believed that this is the way it should be, because otherwise in the event of a divorce women and children would be left destitute. The main reason given for the matrilineal inheritance of property is that since women bear the infant and raise the child it is in keeping with the laws of nature to give women control of the ancestral property so that they will have the wherewithal to house and nurture the young.

Missing from the Minangkabau conception of sexuality is any show of interest in sex for the sake of sex alone. Sex is neither a commodity nor a notch in the male belt in this society. A man's sense of himself is not predicated by his sexual functioning. Although aggression is present, it is not linked to sex nor is it deemed a manly trait. The Minangkabau have yet to discover sex as a commodity or turn it into a fetish.

There is a cultural category for rape, which is defined as 'forced sex' and is punishable by law. Rape is conceived as something that happens in the wild, which places men who rape beyond the pale of society. In answer to my questions regarding the relative absence of rape among them compared to the United States, Minangkabau informants replied that rape was impossible in their society because custom, law, and religion forbade it and punished it severely. In the years that I worked in West Sumatra, I heard of only two cases of rape in the village where I lived. One case involved a group of males who ganged up on a young, retarded woman. In this case the leader of the group hanged himself the next day out of fear of avenging villagers. The rest of the assailants went to jail. The second case involved a local woman and a Japanese soldier during the Japanese occupation of the Second World War and after. To this day people remember the case and talk about the horror of the Japanese occupation.

In the past few years, Indonesia's entrance into the global economy has been accompanied by an amazing shift in the eroticization of popular culture seen on TV. In 1995 the signs that this culture was filtering into Minangkabau villages were very evident. To the extent that commodification and eroticization breaks down the cultural supports for its matrilineal social system, the Minangkabau sexual culture will also change. Indeed, today in the provincial capital some argue that the Minangkabau are not rape-free.

During my last field trip in 1995, I heard of many more reports of rape in the provincial capital. In the early 1990s, for example, there was a widely publicized acquaintance gang rape of a young woman by a group of boys. Interviewing court officers in the capital, I was told that this was the only case of its kind. Compared with similar cases in the United States, such as the St John's case, the outcome was still very different. While the St John's defendants were either acquitted or got probation after pleading guilty, all the defendants in the Sumatran case were convicted and sent to jail. But, one may well ask whether the criminal justice system will continue to convict defendants as tolerance for sexual coercion begins to permeate popular beliefs.

Rape-Free Campus Cultures

A rape-free campus is relatively easy to imagine, but equally hard to find. Based on anecdotal information one candidate comes to mind. On this campus everyone—administrators, faculty, and students—are on a first-name basis, which makes the atmosphere more egalitarian than most campuses. Decision making is by consensus and interpersonal interaction is guided by an ethic of respect for the individual. Those who are disrespectful of others are ostracized as campus life is motivated by a strong sense of community and the common good. No one group (such as fraternities, males, or athletes) dominates the social scene. Sexual assault is a serious offence treated with suspension or expulsion. Homophobic, racist, and sexist attitudes are virtually nonexistent. Individuals bond together in groups drawn together by mutual interests, not to turn against others. Interviews suggest that the incidence of unwanted sex on this campus is low; however, this must be corroborated by a campus-wide survey.

For information on a rape-free fraternity culture I turn to a description offered by a student who wrote a mini-ethnography on his fraternity for a class project. Another brother in the same fraternity corroborated his description after reading the ethnography and adding additional information. In the following, the fraternity is referred to by the pseudonym QRS. With their permission, the fraternity brothers are identified by name.

Noel Morrison and Josh Marcus recognize that fraternities on their campus (called U.) 'propagate sexist attitudes and provide a breeding ground for insecure acts of sexism, racism, and homophobia'. According to Noel, U.'s fraternities 'tend to be self-segregating entities which seek to maintain the inferior social position of women and minority students through exclusion' and social intolerance. QRS, however, consciously fights against this norm.

QRS is one of the oldest fraternities at U., going back at least 100 years. It was like all other fraternities at U. until 1977 when it was almost forced to disband due to insufficient numbers. At that time, a group of nine first-year males pledged as a group knowing that their numbers would give them control of house decisions. They exercised this control by rewriting the house constitution and initiation rituals. Today the brothers are proud to say that they are 'not a real fraternity'. Interestingly, although both Joel and Noel treasure their lives in QRS (because of

the fun, companionship of respected friends, and community the house offers), both feel that fraternities should be abolished.

Partly as a defence mechanism and partly to underscore their difference, QRS brothers stigmatize members of other fraternities as 'jarheads'. The word 'jarhead' is used to refer to the 'loud, obnoxious, sexist, racist, homophobic' members of U.'s fraternities. Most of the brothers in QRS do not participate in the campus inter-fraternity council and prefer to see themselves as 'a group of friends', rather than as a fraternity, and their house as 'a place to have concerts'. Parties are always open to anyone and are either free to everyone or everyone pays, contrary to parties at other houses in which men pay and women are admitted for free.

At QRS heavy drinking is not a requisite for membership and is not a part of initiation. There are no drinking games and binge drinking does not occur. While some brothers drink to get drunk more than once a week, most don't. At parties there are always brothers who watch out for women or house members who have had too much to drink. Josh stressed that 'it is clearly not acceptable for someone to take advantage of a drunk woman, because that's rape.' There is no talk in the house about getting a girl drunk to have sex, he says. Members are very aware that where there is heavy drinking someone can be taken advantage of. If a female passes out or is very drunk she is watched or escorted home. Both Josh and Noel remember an incident during a party in the fraternity next door, in which several members of QRS came to the aid of a young woman whose shirt was above her waist and who had passed out on their porch, left there perhaps by friends from the party who had deserted her. Their intervention may have saved her life. When they were unable to get her to talk, they took her to the emergency room of a nearby hospital only to learn that she was in a coma and her heart had stopped. Fortunately, they were in time and she responded to treatment.

Women are not seen as sex objects in the house, but as friends. Unlike other fraternities at U., there is no distinction drawn between 'girlfriends' and friends and there are no 'party girls'. Noel says that when he was rushing he would often hear women referred to as 'sluts' in other fraternities. However, at QRS this is unheard of. According to Josh, a brother who acted 'inappropriately' with a woman would be severely reprimanded, perhaps even expelled from the fraternity. The brothers are not afraid of strong women. There are women's studies students who are regulars at the house, along with outspoken feminists and activists. Noel quotes one of them:

> I guess there're a few brothers who make sexist jokes, but I don't know how seriously people take them. I remember last year in the middle of mid-terms I was studying late at night and was feeling sick and tired, and in a span of about five minutes, four people offered their beds to me, not as a sexual thing at all, but just because they cared.

One QRS brother started the Men's Association for Change and Openness (MACHO) and is an active participant in U's student peer-counselling group for sexual health. One brother displays a 'Refuse and Resist' sticker on his door, proclaiming, 'Date rape: cut it out or cut it off.' In a 1993 pamphlet advertising QRS as the site of the National Anarchist gathering, the brothers wrote, 'Although QRS is a frat, it is generally a friendly place, along with being a safe haven for women.'

Most interesting about QRS is its acceptance of homosexuality and bisexuality. Homophobia does not become the basis for males to prove their virility to one another. Because of its openness about sex and acceptance of homosexuality, QRS has earned the reputation on campus of being 'the gay frat' or 'faggot house'. Josh comments on this reputation and what it means to him:

> QRS's attitudes about homosexuality are complex, but fundamentally tolerant and respectful. Some brothers revel in rumours that we are the 'gay frat'. It is rumoured that a few years ago a few of the brothers were involved sexually, and one of our most involved alumni is homosexual.

Although most fraternities have had or have a few homosexual brothers, this honest acceptance of homosexuality is unusual. QRS brothers are proud of being called the 'gay frat'. Evidence of this is the humorous statement in the letters given prospective pledges offering bids, which ends with the phrase 'we are all gay'.

Conclusion

The first step in the struggle against 'hidden rape', which began in the late '60s with consciousness-raising groups (see Sanday, 1996: Chapter 8), was to recognize the problem and speak out against it. The next step was to change outmoded rape laws and assess the causes and frequency of sexual violence against women. Mary Koss's national survey of 1985 demonstrated that one in four women will experience rape or attempted rape in her lifetime. Since the '80s many other surveys have replicated her findings. The search for causes has been the subject of numerous studies, including those represented in this volume.

The next step is to go beyond the causes and study solutions. One approach would be to find naturally occurring rape-free environments on today's college campuses. QRS is one example. No rape-free campuses have been identified by research, yet I have heard descriptions from students that lead me to believe that such campuses exist. Identifying such campuses and seeking out environments like QRS is the next step for research. In this paper I have identified the kinds of problems such research must address. First, it is necessary to obtain incidence as well as prevalence data. Secondly, we need more subtle measures of the kinds of socio-cultural correlates that have been discussed in this paper: drinking intensity; using pornography to learn about sex rather than talking with one's partner; bragging about sexual conquests; setting women up to display one's masculinity to other men; heterosexism; homophobia; and using pornography as a guide to female sexuality. Finally, we need to develop a consensus on the criteria for labelling a campus either rape-free or rape-prone. If at least one in five women on a given campus say they have experienced unwanted sex in the last year, I would label the campus rape-prone. However, others may want to propose different criteria. Once a consensus is reached, the movement to make our campuses safe for women might include identifying rape-free and rape-prone campuses.

Note

This article has benefited from the comments of Mary P. Koss. I am also grateful to Koss for supplying me with the data on her 1986 study of 32 campuses. Martin D. Schwartz and Scot B. Boerginer graciously supplied me with additional data from their studies and answered my many questions. Noel Morrison played an important role by giving me permission to summarize his description of his fraternity. John Marcus, a brother in the same fraternity, was also helpful in corroborating Noel's observations and supplying a few of his own.

References

Brownmiller, S. 1975. *Against Our Will: Men, Women, and Rape*. New York: Simon and Schuster.

Koss, M.P. 1988. 'Hidden Rape: Sexual Aggression and Victimization in a National Sample of Students in Higher Education', in A.W. Burgess, ed., *Rape and Sexual Assault II*, pp. 3–25. New York: Garland.

———. 1993. 'Rape: Scope, Impact, Interventions, and Public Policy Responses', *American Psychologist* (October): 1062–9.

Koss, M.P., and J.A. Gaines. 1993. 'The Prediction of Sexual Aggression by Alcohol Use, Athletic Participation, and Fraternity Affiliation', *Journal of Interpersonal Violence* 8: 94–108.

Koss, M.P., and S.L. Cook. 1993. 'Facing the Facts: Date and Acquaintance Rape are Significant Problems for Women', in R.J. Gelles and D.R. Loseke, eds., *Current Controversies on Family Violence*, pp. 104–19. Newbury Park, CA: Sage.

Sanday, P.R. 1981. 'The Socio-cultural Context of Rape: A Cross-Cultural Study', *Journal of Social Issues* 37: 5–27.

———. 1990. *Fraternity Gang Rape: Sex, Brotherhood and Privilege on Campus*. New York: New York University Press.

———. 1996. *A Woman Scorned: Acquaintance Rape on Trial*. New York: Doubleday.

CHAPTER 38

The Myth of Sexual Symmetry in Marital Violence

Russell P. Dobash, R. Emerson Dobash, Margo Wilson, and Martin Daly

Long denied, legitimized, and made light of, wife-beating is at last the object of widespread public concern and condemnation. Extensive survey research and intensive interpretive investigations tell a common story. Violence against wives (by which term we encompass de facto as well as registered unions) is often persistent and severe, occurs in the context of continuous intimidation and coercion, and is inextricably linked to attempts to dominate and control women. Historical and contemporary investigations further reveal that this violence has been explicitly decriminalized, ignored, or treated in an ineffectual manner by criminal justice systems, by medical and social service institutions, and by communities. Increased attention to these failures has inspired increased efforts to redress them, and in many places legislative amendments have mandated arrest and made assault a crime whether the offender is married to the victim or not.

A number of researchers and commentators have suggested that assaults upon men by their wives constitute a social problem comparable in nature and magnitude to that of wife-beating. Two main bodies of evidence have been offered in support of these authors' claims that husbands and wives are similarly victimized: (1) self-reports of violent acts perpetrated and suffered by survey respondents, especially those in two US national probability samples; and (2) US homicide data. Unlike the case of violence against wives, however, the victimization of husbands allegedly continues to be denied and trivialized. 'Violence by wives has not been an object of public concern,' note Straus and Gelles (1986: 472). 'There has been no publicity, and no funds have been invested in ameliorating this problem because it has not been defined as a problem.'

We shall argue that claims of sexual symmetry in marital violence are exaggerated, and that wives' and husbands' uses of violence differ greatly, both quantitatively and qualitatively. We shall further argue that there is no reason to expect the sexes to be alike in this domain, and that efforts to avoid sexism by lumping male and female data and by the use of gender-neutral terms such as 'spouse-beating' are misguided. If violence is gendered, as it assuredly is, explicit characterization of gender's relevance to violence is essential. The alleged similarity of women and men in their use of violence in intimate relationships stands in marked contrast to men's virtual monopoly on the use of violence in other social contexts, and we challenge the proponents of the sexual symmetry thesis to develop coherent theoretical models that would account for a sexual monomorphism of violence in one social context and not in others.

A final thesis of this paper is that resolution of controversies about the 'facts' of family violence requires critical examination of theories, methods, and data, with explicit attention to the development of coherent conceptual frameworks, valid and meaningful forms of measurement, and appropriate inferential procedures. Such problems are not peculiar to this research domain, but analysis of the claims regarding violence against husbands provides an excellent example of how a particular approach to construct formation and measurement has led to misrepresentation of the phenomena under investigation.

The Claim of Sexually Symmetrical Marital Violence

Authoritative claims about the prevalence and sexual symmetry of spousal violence in America began with a 1975 US national survey in which 2,143 married or cohabiting persons were interviewed in person about their actions in the preceding year. Straus (1977–8) announced that the survey results showed that the 'marriage licence is a hitting licence', and moreover that the rates of perpetrating spousal violence, including severe violence, were higher for wives than for husbands. He concluded:

> Violence between husband and wife is far from a one way street. The old cartoons of the wife chasing the husband with a rolling pin or throwing pots and pans are closer to reality than most (and especially those with feminist sympathies) realize (Straus, 1977–8: 447–8).

In 1985, the survey was repeated by telephone with a new national probability sample including 3,520 husband–wife households, and with similar results. In each survey, the researchers interviewed either the wife or the husband (but not both) in each contacted household about how the couple settled their differences when they had a disagreement. The individual who was interviewed was presented with a list of eighteen 'acts' ranging from 'discussed an issue calmly' and 'cried' to 'threw something at him/her/you' and 'beat him/her/you up', with the addition of 'choked him/her/you' in 1985 (Straus, 1990a: 33). These acts constituted the Conflict Tactics Scales (CTS) and were intended to measure three constructs: 'Reasoning', 'Verbal Aggression', and 'Physical Aggression' or 'Violence', which was further subdivided into 'Minor Violence' and 'Severe Violence' according to a presumed potential for injury (Straus, 1979; Straus and Gelles, 1990a). Respondents were asked how frequently they had perpetrated each act in the course of 'conflicts or disagreements' with their spouses (and with one randomly selected child) within the past year, and how frequently they had been on the receiving end. Each respondent's self-reports of victimization and perpetration contributed to estimates of rates of violence by both husbands and wives.

According to both surveys, rates of violence by husbands and wives were strikingly similar. The authors estimated that in the year prior to the 1975 survey 11.6 per cent of US husbands were victims of physical violence perpetrated by their wives, while 12.1 per cent of wives were victims of their husbands' violence. In 1985, these percentages had scarcely changed, but husbands seemed more vulnerable: 12.1 per cent of husbands and 11.3 per cent of wives were victims. In both surveys, husbands were more likely to be victims of acts of 'severe violence': in 1975, 4.6 per cent of husbands were such victims versus 3.8 per cent of wives, and in 1985, 4.4 per cent of husbands versus 3.0 per cent of wives were victims. In reporting their results, the surveys' authors stressed the surprising assaultiveness of wives:

> The repeated finding that the rate of assault by women is similar to the rate by their male partners is an important and distressing aspect of violence in American families. It contrasts markedly to the behavior of women outside the family. It shows that within the family or in dating and cohabiting relationships, women are about as violent as men. (Straus and Gelles, 1990b: 104)

Others have endorsed and publicized these conclusions. For example, a recent review of marital violence concludes, with heavy reliance on Straus and Gelles's survey results, that '(a) women are more prone than men to engage in severely violent acts; (b) each year more men than women are victimized by their intimates' (McNeely and Mann, 1990: 130). One of Straus and Gelles's collaborators in the 1975 survey, Steinmetz (1977– 8), used the same survey evidence to proclaim the existence of 'battered husbands' and a 'battered husband syndrome'. She has remained one of the leading defenders of the claim that violence between men and women in the family is symmetrical. Steinmetz and her collaborators maintain that the problem is not wife-beating perpetrated by violent men, but 'violent couples' and 'violent people'. Men may be

stronger on average, argues Steinmetz, but weaponry equalizes matters, as is allegedly shown by the nearly equivalent numbers of US husbands and wives who are killed by their partners. The reason why battered husbands are inconspicuous and seemingly rare is supposedly that shame prevents them from seeking help.

Straus and his collaborators have sometimes qualified their claims that their surveys demonstrate sexual symmetry in marital violence, noting, for example, that men are usually larger and stronger than women and thus able to inflict more damage and that women are more likely to use violence in self-defence or retaliation. However, the survey results indicate a symmetry not just in the perpetration of violence but in its initiation as well, and from this further symmetry, Stets and Straus (1990: 154–5) conclude that the equal assaultiveness of husbands and wives cannot be attributed to the wives acting in self-defence, after all.

Other surveys using the CTS in the United States and in other countries have replicated the finding that wives are about as violent as husbands. The CTS has also been used to study violence in dating relationships, with the same sexually symmetrical results.

Some authors maintain not only that wives initiate violence at rates comparable to husbands, but that they rival them in the damage they inflict as well. McNeely and Robinson-Simpson (1987), for example, argue that research shows that the 'truth about domestic violence' is that 'women are as violent, if not more violent than men,' in their inclinations, in their actions, and in the damage they inflict. The most dramatic evidence invoked in this context is again the fact that wives kill: spousal homicides—for which detection should be minimally or not at all biased because homicides are nearly always discovered and recorded—produce much more nearly equivalent numbers of male and female victims in the United States than do sublethal assault data, which are subject to sampling biases when obtained from police, shelters and hospitals. According to McNeely and Mann (1990: 130), 'The average man's size and strength are neutralized by guns and knives, boiling water, bricks, fireplace pokers, and baseball bats.'

A corollary of the notion that the sexes are alike in their use of violence is that satisfactory causal accounts of violence will be gender-blind. Discussion thus focuses, for example, on the role of one's prior experiences with violence as a child, social stresses, frustration, inability to control anger, impoverished social skills, and so forth, without reference to gender. This presumption that the sexes are alike not merely in action but in the reasons for that action is occasionally explicit, such as when Shupe et al. (1987: 56) write: 'Everything we have found points to parallel processes that lead women and men to become violent. . . . Women may be more likely than men to use kitchen utensils or sewing scissors when they commit assault, but their frustrations, motives and lack of control over these feelings predictably resemble men's.'

In sum, the existence of an invisibles legion of assaulted husbands is an inference that strikes many family violence researchers as reasonable. Two lines of evidence—homicide data and the CTS survey results—suggest to those supporting the sexual-symmetry-of-violence thesis that large numbers of men are trapped in violent relationships. These men are allegedly being denied medical, social welfare, and criminal justice services because of an unwillingness to accept the evidence from homicide statistics and the CTS surveys.

Violence against Wives

Any argument that marital violence is sexually symmetrical must either dismiss or ignore a large body of contradictory evidence indicating that wives greatly outnumber husbands as victims. While CTS researchers were discovering and publicizing the mutual violence of wives and husbands, other researchers—using evidence from courts, police, and women's shelters—were finding that wives were much more likely than husbands to be victims. After an extensive review of extant research, Lystad (1975) expressed the consensus: 'The occurrence of adult violence in the home usually involves males as aggressors towards females.' This conclusion was subsequently supported by numerous further studies of divorce records, emergency room patients treated for non-accidental

injuries, police assault records, and spouses seeking assistance and refuge. Analyses of police and court records in North America and Europe have persistently indicated that women constitute 90–95 per cent of the victims of those assaults in the home reported to the criminal justice system.

Defenders of the sexual-symmetry-of-violence thesis do not deny these results, but they question their representativeness: these studies could be biased because samples of victims were self-selected. However, criminal victimization surveys using national probability samples similarly indicate that wives are much more often victimized than husbands. Such surveys in the United States, Canada, and Great Britain have been replicated in various years, with essentially the same results. Beginning in 1972 and using a panel survey method involving up to seven consecutive interviews at six-month intervals, the US National Crime Survey has generated nearly a million interviews. Gaquin's (1977–8) analysis of US National Crime Survey data for 1973–5 led her to conclude that men 'have almost no risk of being assaulted by their wives' (634–5); only 3 per cent of the violence reported from these surveys involved attacks on men by their female partners. Another analysis of the National Crime Survey data from 1973 to 1980 found that 6 per cent of spousal assault incidents were directed at men (McLeod, 1984). Schwartz (1987) re-analyzed the same victimization surveys with the addition of the 1981 and 1982 data, and found 102 men who claimed to have been victims of assaults by their wives (4 per cent of domestic assault incidents) in contrast to 1,641 women who said they were assaulted by husbands. The 1981 Canadian Urban Victimization Survey and the 1987 General Social Survey produced analogous findings, from which Johnson (1989) concluded that 'women account for 80–90 per cent of victims in assaults or sexual assaults between spouses or former spouses. In fact, the number of domestic assaults involving males was too low in both surveys to provide reliable estimates' (1–2). The 1982 and 1984 British Crime Surveys found that women accounted for all the victims of marital assaults. Self-reports of criminal victimization based on national probability surveys, while not without methodological weaknesses, are not subject to the same reporting biases as divorce, police and hospital records.

The national crime surveys also indicate that women are much more likely than men to suffer injury as a result of assaults in the home. After analyzing the results of the US National Crime Surveys, Schwartz (1987: 67) concludes, 'There are still more than 13 times as many women seeking medical care from a private physician for injuries received in a spousal assault.' This result, again, replicates the typical findings of studies of police or hospital records. For example, women constituted 94 per cent of the injury victims in an analysis of the spousal assault cases among 262 domestic disturbance calls to police in Santa Barbara County, California; moreover, the women's injuries were more serious than the men's. Berk et al. (1983: 207) conclude that 'when injuries are used as the outcome of interest, a marriage license is a hitting licence but for men only.' Brush (1990) reports that a US national probability sample survey of over 13,000 respondents in 1987–8 replicated the evident symmetry of marital violence when CTS-like questions about acts were posed, but also revealed that women were much more often injured than men (and that men down-played women's injuries).

In response, defenders of the sexual-symmetry-of-violence thesis contend that data from police, courts, hospitals, and social service agencies are suspect because men are reluctant to report physical violence by their wives. For example, Steinmetz (1977–8) asserts that husband-beating is a camouflaged social problem because men must overcome extraordinary stigma in order to report that their wives have beaten them. Similarly, Shupe et al. (1987) maintain that men are unwilling to report their wives because 'it would be unmanly or unchivalrous to go to the police for protection from a woman' (52). However, the limited available evidence does not support these authors' presumption that men are less likely to report assaults by their spouses than are women. Schwartz's (1987) analysis of the 1973–82 US National Crime Survey data found that 67.2 per cent of men and 56.8 per cent of women called the police after being assaulted by their spouses. One may protest that these high percentages imply that only a tiny proportion of the most severe spousal assaults were acknowledged as assaults by respondents to these crime surveys, but the results are nonetheless contrary to the notion that assaulted men are especially reticent. Moreover, Rouse et al. (1988), using 'act' definitions of assaults which inspired much higher proportions to acknowledge victimization, similarly report that men were likelier than women to call the police after assaults by intimate partners, both among married couples and among those dating. In addition, a sample of 337 cases of domestic violence drawn from family court cases in Ontario showed that men were more likely than women to press charges against their spouses: there were 17 times as many female victims as male victims, but only 22 per cent of women laid charges in contrast to 40 per cent of the men, and men were less likely to drop the charges, too. What those who argue that men are reluctant or ashamed to report their wives' assaults overlook is that women have their own reasons to be reticent, fearing both the loss of a jailed or alienated husband's economic support and his vengeance. Whereas the claim that husbands under-report because of shame or chivalry is largely speculative, there is considerable evidence that women report very little of the violence perpetrated by their male partners.

The CTS survey data indicating equivalent violence by wives and husbands thus stand in contradiction to injury data, to police incident reports, to help-seeking statistics, and even to other, larger, national probability sample surveys of self-reported victimization. The CTS researchers insist that their results alone are accurate because husbands' victimizations are unlikely to be detected or reported by any other method. It is therefore important to consider in detail the CTS and the data it generates.

Do CTS Data Reflect the Reality of Marital Violence?

The CTS instrument has been much used and much criticized. Critics have complained that its exclusive focus on 'acts' ignores the actors' interpretations, motivations, and intentions; that physical violence is arbitrarily delimited, excluding, for example, sexual assault and rape; that retrospective reports of the past year's events are unlikely to be accurate; that researchers' attributions of 'violence' (with resultant claims about its statistical prevalence) are based on respondents' admitting to acts described in such an impoverished manner as to conflate severe assaults with trivial gestures; that the formulaic distinction between 'minor' and 'severe violence' (whereby, for example, 'tried to hit with something' is definitionally 'severe' and 'slapped' is definitionally 'minor') constitutes a poor operationalization of severity; that the responses of aggressors and victims have been given identical evidentiary status in deriving incidence estimates, while their inconsistencies have been ignored; that the CTS omits the contexts of violence, the events precipitating it, and the sequences of events by which it progresses; and that it fails to connect outcomes, especially injury, with the acts producing them.

Straus (1990b) has defended the CTS against its critics, maintaining that the CTS addresses context with its 'verbal aggression' scale (although the assessment of 'verbal aggression' is not incident-linked with the assessment of 'violence'); that the minor-severe categorization 'is roughly parallel to the legal distinction between "simple assault" and "aggravated assault"' (58); that other measurement instruments have problems, too; and that you cannot measure everything. Above all, the defence rests on the widespread use of the instrument, on its reliability, and on its validity. That the CTS is widely used cannot be gainsaid, but whether it is reliable or valid is questionable.

Problems with the Reliability and Validity of CTS Responses

Straus (1990b: 64) claims that six studies have assessed 'the internal consistency reliability' of the CTS. One of the six (Barling and Rosenbaum, 1986) contains no such assessment, a second is unreferenced, and a third unpublished. However, a moderate degree of 'internal consistency reliability' of the CTS can probably be conceded. For example, those who admit to having 'beat up' their spouses are also likely to admit to having 'hit' them.

The crucial matter of interobserver reliability is much more problematic. The degree of concordance in couples' responses is an assay of 'interspousal reliability' (Jouriles and O'Leary, 1985), and such reliability must be high if CTS scores are to be taken at face value. For example, incidence estimates of husband-to-wife and wife-to-husband violence have been generated from national surveys in which the CTS was administered to only one adult per family, with claims of victimization and perpetration by male and female respondents all granted equal evidentiary status and summated. The validity of these widely cited incidence estimates is predicated upon interspousal reliability.

Straus (1990b: 66) considers the assessment of spousal concordance to constitute an assay of 'concurrent validity' rather than 'interspousal reliability', in effect treating each partner's report as the violence criterion that validates the other. But spousal concordance is analogous to interobserver reliability: it is a necessary, but by no means sufficient condition, for concluding that the self-reports accurately reflect reality. If couples generally produce consistent reports—Mr and Mrs Jones both indicate that he struck her, while Mr and Mrs Smith both indicate that neither has struck the other—then it is possible though by no means certain that their CTS self-reports constitute valid (veridical) information about the blows actually struck. However, if couples routinely provide discrepant CTS responses, data derived from the CTS simply cannot be valid.

In this light, studies of husband/wife concordance in CTS responses should be devastating to those who imagine that the CTS provides a valid account of the respondents' acts. In what Straus correctly calls 'the most detailed and thorough analysis of agreement between spouses in response to the CTS', Szinovacz (1983) found that 103 couples' accounts of the violence in their interactions matched to a degree little greater than chance. On several CTS items, mainly the most severe ones, agreement was actually below chance. On the item 'beat up', concordance was nil: although there were respondents of both sexes who claimed to have administered beatings and respondents of both sexes who claimed to have been on the receiving end, there was not a single couple in which one party claimed to have administered and the other to have received such a beating. In a similar study, Jouriles and O'Leary (1985) administered the CTS to 65 couples attending a marital therapy clinic, and 37 control couples from the local community. For many of the acts, the frequency and percentage data reported are impossible to reconcile; for others, Jouriles and O'Leary reported a concordance statistic (Cohen's Kappa) as equalling zero when the correct values were negative. Straus (1990b) cites this study as conferring validity on the CTS, but in fact, its results replicated Szinovacz's (1983): husband/wife agreement scarcely exceeded chance expectation and actually fell below chance on some items.

Straus (1990b) acknowledges that these and the other studies he reviews 'found large discrepancies between the reports of violence given by husbands and by wives' (69). He concludes, however, that 'validity measures of agreement between family members are within the range of validity coefficients typically reported' (71), and that 'the weakest aspect of the CTS are [sic] the scales that have received the least criticism: Reasoning and Verbal aggression' (71), by which he implies that the assessment of violence is relatively strong.

Ultimately, Straus's defence of the CTS is that the proof of the pudding is in the eating: 'The strongest evidence concerns the construct validity of the CTS. It has been used in a large number of studies producing findings that tend to be consistent with previous research (when available), consistent regardless of gender of respondent, and theoretically meaningful.' And indeed, with respect to marital violence, the CTS is capable of making certain gross discriminations. Various studies have found CTS responses to vary as a function of age, race, poverty, duration of relationship, and registered versus de facto marital unions, and these effects have generally been directionally similar to those found with less problematic measures of violence such as homicides. However, the CTS has also failed to detect certain massive differences, and we do not refer only to sex differences.

Consider the case of child abuse by stepparents versus birth parents. In various countries, including the United States, a step-parent is more likely to fatally assault a small child than is a birth parent, by a factor on the order of 100-fold; sublethal violence also exhibits huge differences in the same direction. Using the CTS, however, Gelles and Harrop (1991) were unable to detect any difference in self-reports of violence by step- versus birth parents. Users of the CTS have sometimes conceded that the results of their self-report surveys cannot provide an accurate picture of the prevalence of violence, but they have made this concession only to infer that the estimates must be gross underestimates of the true prevalence. However, the CTS's failure to differentiate the behaviour of step- versus birth parents indicates that CTS-based estimates are not just underestimates but may misrepresent between-group differences in systematically biased ways. One must be concerned, then, whether this sort of bias also arises in CTS-based comparisons between husbands and wives.

Problems with the Interpretation of CTS Responses

With the specific intention of circumventing imprecision and subjectivity in asking about such abstractions as 'violence', the CTS is confined to questions about 'acts'. Respondents are asked whether they have 'pushed' their partners, have 'slapped' them, and so forth, rather than whether they have 'assaulted' them or behaved 'violently'. This focus on 'acts' is intended to reduce problems of self-serving and biased definitional criteria on the part of the respondents. However, any gain in objectivity has been undermined by the way that CTS survey data have then been analyzed and interpreted. Any respondent who acknowledges a single instance of having 'pushed', 'grabbed', 'shoved', 'slapped', or 'hit or tried to hit' another person is deemed a perpetrator of 'violence' by the researchers, regardless of the act's context, consequences, or meaning to the parties involved. Similarly, a single instance of having 'kicked', 'bit', 'hit or tried to hit with an object', 'beat up', 'choked', 'threatened with a knife or gun', or 'used a knife or fired a gun' makes one a perpetrator of 'severe violence'.

Affirmation of any one of the 'violence' items provides the basis for estimates such as Straus and Gelles' (1990b: 97) claim that 6.8 million husbands and 6.25 million wives were spousal assault victims in the United States in 1985. Similarly, estimates of large numbers of 'beaten' or 'battered' wives and husbands have been based on affirmation of any one of the 'severe violence' items. For example, Steinmetz (1986: 734) and Straus and Gelles (1987: 638) claim on this basis that 1.8 million US women are 'beaten' by their husbands annually. But note that any man who once threw an 'object' at his wife, regardless of its nature and regardless of whether the throw missed, qualifies as having 'beaten' her; some unknown proportion of the women and men who are alleged to have been 'beaten', on the basis of their survey responses, never claimed to have been struck at all. Thus, the 'objective' scoring of the CTS not only fails to explore the meanings and intentions associated with the acts but also has in practice entailed interpretive transformations that guarantee exaggeration, misinterpretation, and ultimately trivialization of the genuine problems of violence.

Consider a 'slap'. The word encompasses anything from a slap on the hand chastizing a dinner companion for reaching for a bite of one's dessert to a tooth-loosening assault intended to punish, humiliate, and terrorize. These are not trivial distinctions; indeed, they constitute the essence of definitional issues concerning violence. Almost all definitions of violence and violent acts refer to intentions. Malevolent intent is crucial, for example, to legal definitions of 'assault' (to which supporters of the CTS have often mistakenly claimed that their 'acts' correspond; e.g., Straus, 1990b: 58). However, no one has systematically investigated how respondents vary in their subjective definitions of the 'acts' listed on the CTS. If, for example, some respondents interpret phrases such as 'tried to hit with an object' literally, then a good deal of relatively harmless behaviour surely taints the estimates of 'severe violence'. Although this problem has not been investigated systematically, one author has shown that it is potentially serious. In a study of 103 couples, Margolin (1987) found that wives surpassed husbands in their use of 'severe violence' according to the CTS, but unlike others who have obtained this result, Margolin

troubled to check its meaningfulness with more intensive interviews. She concluded:

> While CTS items appear behaviorally specific, their meanings still are open to interpretation. In one couple who endorsed the item 'kicking', for example, we discovered that the kicking took place in bed in a more kidding, than serious, fashion. Although this behavior meets the criterion for severe abuse on the CTS, neither spouse viewed it as aggressive, let alone violent. In another couple, the wife scored on severe physical aggression while the husband scored on low-level aggression only. The inquiry revealed that, after years of passively accepting the husband's repeated abuse, this wife finally decided, on one occasion, to retaliate by hitting him over the head with a wine decanter (1987: 82).

By the criteria of Steinmetz (1977–8: 501), this incident would qualify as a 'battered husband' case. But however dangerous this retaliatory blow may have been and however reprehensible or justified one may consider it, it is not 'battering', whose most basic definitional criterion is its repetitiveness. A failure to consider intentions, interpretations, and the history of the individuals' relationship is a significant shortcoming of CTS research. Only through a consideration of behaviours, intentions, and intersubjective understandings associated with specific violent events will we come to a fuller understanding of violence between men and women. Studies employing more intensive interviews and detailed case reports addressing the contexts and motivations of marital violence help unravel the assertions of those who claim the widespread existence of beaten and battered husbands. Research focusing on specific violent events shows that women almost always employ violence in defence of self and children in response to cues of imminent assault in the past and in retaliation for previous physical abuse. Proponents of the sexual-symmetry-of-violence thesis have made much of the fact that CTS surveys indicate that women 'initiate' the violence about as often as men, but a case in which a woman struck the first blow is unlikely to be the mirror image of one in which her husband 'initiated'. A noteworthy feature of the literature proclaiming the existence of battered husbands and battering wives is how little the meagre case descriptions resemble those of battered wives and battering husbands. Especially lacking in the alleged male victim cases is any indication of the sort of chronic intimidation characteristic of prototypical woman battering cases.

Any self-report method must constitute an imperfect reflection of behaviour, and the CTS is no exception. That in itself is hardly a fatal flaw. But for such an instrument to retain utility for the investigation of a particular domain such as family violence, an essential point is that its inaccuracies and misrepresentations must not be systematically related to the distinctions under investigation. The CTS's inability to detect the immense differences in violence between stepparents and birth parents, as noted above, provides strong reason to suspect that the test's shortcomings produce not just noise but systematic bias. In the case of marital violence, the other sorts of evidence reviewed in this paper indicate that there are massive differences in the use of confrontational violence against spouses by husbands versus wives, and yet the CTS has consistently failed to detect them. CTS users have taken this failure as evidence for the null hypothesis, apparently assuming that their questionnaire data have a validity that battered women's injuries and deaths lack.

Homicides

The second line of evidence that has been invoked in support of the claim that marital violence is more or less sexually symmetrical is the number of lethal outcomes:

> Data on homicide between spouses suggest that an almost equal number of wives kill their husbands as husbands kill their wives (Wolfgang, 1958). Thus it appears that men and women might have equal potential for violent marital interaction; initiate similar acts of violence; and when differences of physical strength are equalized by weapons,

commit similar amounts of spousal homicide (Steinmetz and Lucca, 1988: 241).

McNeely and Robinson-Simpson (1987: 485) elevated the latter hypothesis about the relevance of weapons to the status of a fact: 'Steinmetz observed that when weapons neutralize differences in physical strength, about as many men as women are victims of homicide.'

Steinmetz and Lucca's citation of Wolfgang refers to his finding that 53 Philadelphia men killed their wives between 1948 and 1952, while 47 women killed their husbands. This is a slender basis for such generalization, but fuller information does indeed bear Steinmetz out as regards the near equivalence of body counts in the United States: Maxfield (1989) reported that there were 10,529 wives and 7,888 husbands killed by their mates in the entire country between 1976 and 1985, a 1.3:1 ratio of female to male victims.

Husbands are indeed almost as often slain as are wives in the United States, then. However, there remain several problems with Steinmetz and Lucca's (as well as McNeely and Robinson-Simpson's) interpretation of this fact. Studies of actual cases lend no support to the facile claim that homicidal husbands and wives 'initiate similar acts of violence'. Men often kill wives after lengthy periods of prolonged physical violence accompanied by other forms of abuse and coercion; the roles in such cases are seldom if ever reversed. Men perpetrate familicidal massacres, killing spouse and children together; women do not. Men commonly hunt down and kill wives who have left them; women hardly ever behave similarly. Men kill wives as part of planned murder-suicides; analogous acts by women are almost unheard of. Men kill in response to revelations of wifely infidelity; women almost never respond similarly, though their mates are more often adulterous. The evidence is overwhelming that a large proportion of the spouse-killings perpetrated by wives, but almost none of those perpetrated by husbands, are acts of self-defence. Unlike men, women kill male partners after years of suffering physical violence, after they have exhausted all available sources of assistance, when they feel trapped, and because they fear for their own lives.

A further problem with the invocation of spousal homicide data as evidence against sex differences in marital violence is that this numerical equivalence is peculiar to the United States. Whereas the ratio of wives to husbands as homicide victims in the United States was 1.3:1, corresponding ratios from other countries are much higher: 3.3:1 for a 10-year period in Canada, for example, 4.3:1 for Great Britain, and 6:1 for Denmark. The reason why this is problematic is that US homicide data and CTS data from several countries have been invoked as complementary pieces of evidence for women's and men's equivalent uses of violence. One cannot have it both ways. If the lack of sex differences in CTS results is considered proof of sexually symmetrical violence, then homicide data must somehow be dismissed as irrelevant, since homicides generally fail to exhibit this supposedly more basic symmetry. Conversely, if US homicide counts constitute relevant evidence, the large sex differences found elsewhere surely indicate that violence is peculiarly symmetrical only in the United States, and the fact that the CTS fails to detect sex differences in other countries must then be taken to mean that the CTS is insensitive to genuine differences.

A possible way out of this dilemma is hinted at in Steinmetz and Lucca's (1988) allusion to the effect of weapons: perhaps it is the availability of guns that has neutralized men's advantage in lethal marital conflict in the United States. Gun use is indeed relatively prevalent in the US, accounting for 51 per cent of a sample of 1,706 spousal homicides in Chicago, for example, as compared to 40 per cent of 1,060 Canadian cases, 42 per cent of 395 Australian cases, and just 8 per cent of 1,204 cases in England and Wales (Wilson and Daly, 1990). Nevertheless, the plausible hypothesis that gun use can account for the different sex ratios among victims fails. When shootings and other spousal homicides are analyzed separately, national differences in the sex ratios of spousal homicide remain dramatic. For example, the ratio of wives to husbands as gunshot homicide victims in Chicago was 1.2:1, compared to 4:1 in Canada and 3.5:1 in Britain; the ratio of wives to husbands as victims of non-gun homicides was 0.8:1 in Chicago, compared to 2.9:1 in Canada and 4.5:1 in Britain (Wilson and Daly,

1990). Moreover, the near equivalence of husband and wife victims in the US antedates the contemporary prevalence of gun killings. In Wolfgang's (1958) classic study, only 34 of the 100 spousal homicide victims were shot (15 husbands and 19 wives), while 30 husbands were stabbed and 31 wives were beaten or stabbed. Whatever may explain the exceptionally similar death rates of US husbands and wives, it is not simply that guns 'equalize'.

Nor is the unusual US pattern to be explained in terms of a peculiar convergence in the United States of the sexes in their violent inclinations or capabilities across all domains and relationships. Although US data depart radically from other industrialized countries in the sex ratio of spousal homicide victimization, they do not depart similarly in the sex ratios of other sorts of homicides (Wilson and Daly, 1990). For example, in the United States, as elsewhere, men kill unrelated men about 40 times as often as women kill unrelated women.

Even among lethal acts, it is essential to discriminate among different victim–killer relationships, because motives, risk factors, and conflict typologies are relationship-specific. Steinmetz (1977–8, Steinmetz and Lucca, 1998) has invoked the occurrence of maternally perpetrated infanticides as evidence of women's violence, imagining that the fact that some women commit infanticide somehow bolsters the claim that they batter their husbands, too. But maternal infanticides are more often motivated by desperation than by hostile aggression and are often the result of acts of neglect or abandonment rather than by assault. To conflate such acts with aggressive attacks is to misunderstand their utterly distinct motives, forms, and perpetrator profiles, and the distinct social and material circumstances in which they occur.

How to Gain a Valid Account of Marital Violence?

How ought researchers to conceive of 'violence'? People differ in their views about whether a particular act was a violent one and about who was responsible. Assessments of intention and justifiability are no less relevant to the labelling of an event as 'violent' than are more directly observable considerations like the force exerted or the damage inflicted. Presumably, it is this problem of subjectivity that has inspired efforts to objectify the study of family violence by the counting of 'acts', as in the Conflict Tactics Scales.

Unfortunately, the presumed gain in objectivity achieved by asking research subjects to report only 'acts', while refraining from elaborating upon their meanings and consequences, is illusory. As noted above, couples exhibit little agreement in reporting the occurrence of acts in which both were allegedly involved, and self-reported acts sometimes fail to differentiate the behaviour of groups known to exhibit huge differences in the perpetration of violence. The implication must be that merely confining self-reports to a checklist of named acts cannot allay concerns about the validity of self-report data. We have no more reason to suppose that people will consensually and objectively label events as instances of someone having 'grabbed' or 'hit or tried to hit' or 'used a knife' (items from the CTS) than to suppose that people will consensually and objectively label events as instances of 'violence'.

If these 'acts' were scored by trained observers examining the entire event, there might be grounds for such behaviouristic austerity in measurement: whatever the virtues and limitations of behaviouristic methodology, a case can at least be made that observational data are more objective than the actors' accounts. However, when researchers have access only to self-reports, the cognitions of the actors are neither more nor less accessible to research than their actions. Failures of candour and memory threaten the validity of both sorts of self-report data, and researchers' chances of detecting such failures can only be improved by the collection of richer detail about the violent event. The behaviouristic rigour of observational research cannot be simulated by leaving data collection to the subjects, nor by active inattention to 'subjective' matters like people's perceptions of their own and others' intentions, attributions of loss of control, perceived provocations and justifications, intimidatory consequences, and so forth. Moreover, even a purely behaviouristic account

could be enriched by attending to sequences of events and subsequent behaviour rather than merely counting acts.

Enormous differences in meaning and consequence exist between a woman pummelling her laughing husband in an attempt to convey strong feelings and a man pummelling his weeping wife in an attempt to punish her for coming home late. It is not enough to acknowledge such contrasts (as CTS researchers have sometimes done), if such acknowledgments neither inform further research nor alter such conclusions as 'within the family or in dating and cohabiting relationships, women are about as violent as men' (Straus and Gelles, 1990b: 104). What is needed are forms of analysis that will lead to a comprehensive description of the violence itself as well as an explanation of it.

In order to do this, it is, at the very least, necessary to analyze the violent event in a holistic manner, with attention to the entire sequences of distinct acts as well as associated motives, intentions, and consequences, all of which must in turn be situated within the wider context of the relationship.

The Need for Theory

If the arguments and evidence that we have presented are correct, then currently fashionable claims about the symmetry of marital violence are unfounded. How is it that so many experts have been persuaded of a notion that is at once counterintuitive and counterfactual? Part of the answer, we believe, is that researchers too often operate without sound (or indeed any) theoretical visions of marital relationships, of interpersonal conflicts, or of violence.

Straus (1990a: 30), for example, introduces the task of investigating family violence by characterizing families as instances of 'social groups' and by noting that conflicts of interest are endemic to groups of individuals, 'each seeking to live out their lives in accordance with personal agendas that inevitably differ'. This is a good start, but the analysis proceeds no further. The characteristic features of families as distinct from other groups are not explored, and the particular domains within which the 'agendas' of wives and husbands conflict are not elucidated. Instead, Straus illustrates family conflicts with the hypothetical example of 'Which TV show will be watched at eight?' and discusses negotiated and coerced resolutions in terms that would be equally applicable to a conflict among male acquaintances in a bar. Such analysis obscures all that is distinctive about violence against wives, which occurs in a particular context of perceived entitlement and institutionalized power asymmetry. Moreover, marital violence occurs around recurring themes, especially male sexual jealousy and proprietariness, expectations of obedience and domestic service, and women's attempts to leave the marital relationship. In the self-consciously gender-blind literature on 'violent couples', these themes are invisible.

Those who claim that wives and husbands are equally violent have offered no conceptual framework for understanding why women and men should think and act alike. Indeed, the claim that violence is gender-neutral cannot easily be reconciled with other coincident claims. For example, many family violence researchers who propose sexual symmetry in violence attribute the inculcation and legitimation of violence to socializing processes and cultural institutions, but then overlook the fact that these processes and institutions define and treat females and males differently. If sexually differentiated socialization and entitlements play a causal role in violence, how can we understand the alleged equivalence of women's and men's violent inclinations and actions?

Another theoretical problem confronting anyone who claims that violent inclinations are sexually monomorphic concerns the oft-noted fact that men are larger than women and likelier to inflict damage by similar acts. Human passions have their own 'rationality', and it would be curious if women and men were identically motivated to initiate assaults in contexts where the expectable results were far more damaging for women. Insofar as both parties to a potentially violent transaction are aware of such differences, it is inappropriate to treat a slap (or other 'act') by one party as equivalent to a slap by the other, not only because there is an asymmetry in the damage the two slaps might inflict, but because the parties differ in the responses available to them and hence in their control over the dénouement. Women's motives may be expected to differ systematically from those of men wherever the predictable consequences of their actions differ systematically. Those who contend that women and men are equally inclined to violence need to articulate why this should be so, given the sex differences in physical traits, such as size and muscularity, affecting the probable consequences of violence.

In fact, there is a great deal of evidence that men's and women's psychologies are not at all alike in this domain. Men's violent reactions to challenges to their authority, honour, and self-esteem are well known; comparable behaviour by a woman is a curiosity. A variety of convergent evidence supports the conclusion that men (especially young men) are more specialized for and more motivated to engage in dangerous risk-taking, confrontational competition, and interpersonal violence than are women. When comparisons are confined to interactions with members of one's own sex so that size and power asymmetries are largely irrelevant, the differences between men and women in these behavioural domains are universally large.

We cannot hope to understand violence in marital, cohabiting, and dating relationships without explicit attention to the qualities that make them different from other relationships. It is a cross-culturally and historically ubiquitous aspect of human affairs that women and men form individualized unions, recognized by themselves and by others as conferring certain obligations and entitlements, such that the partners' productive and reproductive careers become intertwined. Family violence research might usefully begin by examining the consonant and discordant desires, expectations, grievances, perceived entitlements, and preoccupations of husbands and wives, and by investigating theoretically derived hypotheses about circumstantial, ecological, contextual, and demographic correlates of such conflict. Having described the conflict of interest that characterize marital relationships with explicit reference to the distinct agendas of women and men, violence researchers must proceed to an analysis that acknowledges and accounts for those gender differences. It is crucial to establish differences in the patterns of male and female violence, to thoroughly describe and explain the overall process of violent events within their immediate and wider contexts, and to analyze the reasons why conflict results in differentially violent action by women and men.

References

Barling, J., and A. Rosenbaum. 1986. 'Work Stressors and Wife Abuse', *Journal of Applied Psychology* 71: 346–8.

Berk, R.A., S.F. Berk, D.R. Loseke, and D. Rauma. 1983. 'Mutual Combat and Other Family Violence Myths', in D. Finkelhor, R.J. Gelles, G.T. Hotaling, and M.A. Straus, eds., *In The Dark Side of Families*, pp. 197–212. Beverly Hills, CA: Sage.

Brush, L.D. 1990. 'Violent Acts and Injurious Outcomes in Married Couples: Methodological Issues in the National Survey of Families and Households', *Gender and Society* 4: 56–67.

Gaquin, D.A. 1977–8. 'Spouse Abuse: Data from the National Crime Survey', *Victimology* 2: 632–43.

Gelles, R.J., and J.W. Harrop. 1991. 'The Risk of Abusive Violence among Children with Nongenetic Caretakers', *Family Relations* 40: 78–83.

Johnson, H. 1989. 'Wife Assault in Canada'. Paper presented at the Annual Meeting of the American Society of Criminology, November, Reno, NV.

Jouriles, E.N., and K.D O'Leary. 1985. 'Interspousal Reliability of Reports of Marital Violence', *Journal of Consulting and Clinical Psychology* 53: 419–21.

Lystad, M.H. 1975. 'Violence at Home: A Review of Literature', *American Journal of Orthopsychiatry* 45: 328–45.

Margolin, G. 1987. 'The Multiple Forms of Aggressiveness between Marital Partners: How Do We Identify Them?', *Journal of Marital and Family Therapy* 13: 77–84.

Maxfield, M.G. 1989. 'Circumstances in Supplementary Homicide Reports: Variety and Validity', *Criminology* 27: 671–95.

McLeod, M. 1984. 'Women against Men: An Examination of Domestic Violence Based on an Analysis of Official Data and National Victimization Data', *Justice Quarterly* 1: 171–193.

McNeely, R.L., and C.R. Mann. 1990. 'Domestic Violence is a Human Issue', *Journal of Interpersonal Violence* 5: 129–32.

McNeely, R.L., and G. Robinson-Simpson. 1987. 'The Truth about Domestic Violence: A Falsely Framed Issue', *Social Work* 32: 485–90.

Rouse, L.P., R. Ereen, and M. Howell. 1988. 'Abuse in Intimate Relationships: A Comparison of Married and Dating College Students', *Journal of Interpersonal Violence* 3: 414–29.

Schwartz, M.D. 1987. 'Gender and Injury in Spousal Assault', *Sociological Focus* 20: 61–75.

Shupe, A., W.A. Stacey, and L.R. Hazelwood. 1987. *Violent Men, Violent Couples: The Dynamics of Domestic Violence*. Lexington, MA: Lexington Books.

Steinmetz, S.K. 1977–8. 'The Battered Husband Syndrome', *Victimology* 2: 499–509.

———. 1986. 'Family Violence: Past, Present, and Future', in M.B. Sussman and S.K. Steinmetz, eds., *Handbook of Marriage and the Family*, pp. 725–65. New York: Plenum.

Steinmetz, S.K., and J.S. Lucca. 1988. 'Husband Battering', in V.B. Van Hasselt, R.L. Morrison, A.S. Bellack, and M. Hersen, eds., *Handbook of Family Violence*, pp. 233–46. New York: Plenum Press.

Stets, J.E., and M.A. Straus. 1990. 'Gender Differences in Reporting Marital Violence and Its Medical and Psychological Consequences', in M.A. Straus and R.J. Gelles, eds., *Physical Violence in American Families*, pp. 151–65. New Brunswick, NJ: Transaction Publishers.

Straus, M.A. 1977–8. 'Wife-beating: How Common, and Why?', *Victimology* 2: 443–458.

———. 1990a. 'Measuring Intrafamily Conflict and Violence: The Conflict Tactics (CT) Scales', in M.A. Straus and R.J. Gelles, eds., *Physical Violence in American Families*, pp. 29–47. New Brunswick, NJ: Transaction Publishers.

———. 1990b. 'The Conflict Tactics Scales and Its Critics: An Evaluation and New Data on Validity and Reliability', in M.A. Straus and R.J. Gelles, eds., *Physical Violence in American Families*, pp. 49–73. New Brunswick, NJ: Transaction Publishers.

Straus, Murray A., and Richard J. Gelles. 1986. 'Societal Change and Change in Family Violence from 1975 to 1985 as Revealed by Two National Surveys', *Journal of Marriage and the Family* 48: 465–80.

————. 1987. 'The Costs of Family Violence', *Public Health Reports* 102: 638–41.

Straus, M.A., and R.J. Gelles, eds. 1990a. *Physical Violence in American Families*. New Brunswick, NJ: Transaction Publishers.

————. 1990b. 'How Violent are American Families? Estimates from the National Family Violence Resurvey and Other Studies', in M.A. Straus and R.J. Gelles, eds., *Physical Violence in American Families*, pp. 95–112. New Brunswick, NJ: Transaction Publishers.

Szinovacz, M.E. 1983. 'Using Couple Data as a Methodological Tool: The Case of Marital Violence', *Journal of Marriage and the Family* 45: 633–44.

Wilson, M., and M. Daly. 1990. 'Who Kills Whom in Spouse-killings? On the Exceptional Sex Ratio of Spousal Homicides in the United States', *Criminology* 30: 189–212.

Wolfgang, M.E. 1958. *Patterns in Criminal Homicide*. Philadelphia, PA: University of Pennsylvania Press.

CHAPTER 39

Intimate Male Partner Violence in the Migration Process: Intersections of Gender, Race, and Class

Sepali Guruge, Nazilla Khanlou, and Denise Gastaldo

Introduction

Intimate partner violence is the threat of, and/or actual, physical, sexual, psychological, or verbal abuse by a current or former spouse or non-marital partner, as well as coercion, or the arbitrary deprivation of liberty that can occur in public or private life (United Nations [UN] 1993). Intimate male partner violence (IMPV) is widely acknowledged as a critical health issue for women worldwide; however, relatively little is known about its production in diverse settings and contexts. Data compiled by the World Health Organization (WHO) (2000) for IMPV across many countries has suggested that the percentage of women who had ever been physically assaulted by a male intimate partner ranged from 5.1 per cent to 67 per cent. In addition to other limitations, these statistics do not include other forms of abuse such as emotional and sexual abuse, and thus do not accurately demonstrate the prevalence and seriousness of the issue. The recent WHO (2006) study addressing some of these concerns showed that the prevalence of diverse forms of IMPV ranged from 15 per cent to 71 per cent across 10 countries (n = 24,000) and rates of

lifetime IMPV varied widely, as did women's responses to IMPV, with many factors affecting the production of IMPV. The findings reinforced the need to develop context-specific knowledge about this issue.

Background

IMPV as a Global Health Issue

The IMPV is a significant cause of morbidity and mortality for women worldwide (Heise et al. 1994), the most common physical injuries being multi-site contusions and soft tissue injuries (Muellman et al. 1996). Chronic physical health conditions linked to IMPV include neck and back pain, arthritis, headaches and migraines, hypertension, unexplained dizziness, sexually transmitted infections, chronic pelvic pain, gynecological symptoms, and gastrointestinal problems (Ratner 1995, Campbell & Lewandowski 1997, Coker et al. 2000). Mental health problems include depression, acute and chronic symptoms of anxiety, symptoms consistent with post-traumatic stress disorder, substance use/dependence and thoughts of suicide (Eby et al. 1995, Ratner 1995, Eischbach & Herbert 1997).

IMPV in the Canadian Context

The 1993 *Violence Against Women Survey*, well known in Canada, in which 12,300 randomly selected women were interviewed, showed that 51 per cent had been physically or sexually assaulted at least once since the age of 16 years, 29 per cent had been physically abused, and 8 per cent had been sexually assaulted by a male intimate partner (Rodgers 1994). According to the more recent (2000) *General Social Survey* (GSS) of over 14,000 women (over 15 years) from 10 provinces, approximately 37 per cent of women who had ever been married or ever had a male live-in intimate partner had experienced IMPV at least once. The attempts to assess IMPV prevalence in immigrant households through secondary analysis of GSS data (e.g. Hyman 2002, Ahmad et al. 2005) were constrained by the survey's limitations. Among others, it excluded those who did not speak Canada's two official languages.

Interest in IMPV in the post-migration context IMPV has recently increased in Canada. We consider this a positive move, given that more than 200,000 immigrants and refugees arrive annually, women make up about half of this number, and lack of attention to this topic limits the resources and policy attention devoted to it.

Theorizing IMPV

Numerous theories have been offered to explain why IMPV occurs. In general, they can be divided into those focusing on the individual level (e.g., based on biological and psychological explanations) and those emphasizing the relationship at the micro-, meso- or macro-systemic levels (e.g., based on social and gender perspectives). Most theories have not explored the intersectionality of migration, race, culture, gender, and class in understanding IMPV.

To overcome these limitations, we used a post-colonial feminist perspective in this study. A review of some key post-colonial feminist authors' (Memmi 1967, hooks 1984, Jayawardena 1986, Minh-Ha 1989, Collins 1990, Mohanty 1991) work indicates that there is no single post-colonial feminist perspective. However, all these perspectives emphasize the importance of understanding the historical construction of women in and from low- and middle-income countries and its consequences, and the need to recognize, as well as construct, knowledge from their perspective (Spivak 1988, McClintock 1995).

An ecosystemic framework was also used in this study. Ecosystemic frameworks help reveal how people and their environments are understood in the context of their continuous and reciprocal relationships (Loue & Faust 1998, Germain & Bloom 1999). The factors considered are: ontogenic (the individual history of the partners); micro-systemic (the family setting in which the abuse occurs); meso-systemic (the social networks in which the family participates); and macro-systemic (the culture and society-at-large).

Using an ecosystemic framework, situated in a postcolonial feminist perspective, avoids the creation of simplistic views of IMPV as relating to particular groups or to people with particular characteristics. The relevance of the two together in addressing post-migration IMPV has been discussed elsewhere (see Guruge & Khanlou, 2004).

Migration and Displacement of Sri Lankan Tamils

The estimated 188 million people living in Sri Lanka in 1998 (UN 1999) represented several different ethnic groups. As each group struggled to overcome damage from a colonial past and ongoing neo-colonialism, new forms of domination and exploitation evolved within the country. For 25 years, civil war raged between the Sri Lankan government and the Liberation Tigers of Tamil Eelam, a militant/separatist group fighting for full independence and a separate homeland for Tamils. Since 1983, many Tamils have fled the war to countries such as India, Australia, Norway, Germany, England, and the United States of America (USA). Canada is the home to the largest Sri Lankan Tamil community outside Sri Lanka.

The Study

Aim

This paper is a report of a study of Sri Lankan Tamil Canadian immigrants' perspectives on factors that contribute to IMPV in the post-migration context.

Design

An exploratory qualitative descriptive design was used.

Participants

Combining opportunity, snowball, and purposive sampling strategies, we recruited participants from October 2004 to May 2005. The data were collected through individual interviews with 16 community leaders in health and settlement work (Set 1); four focus groups with women (6–12 in each group) and another four with men (4–6 in each group) from the general Tamil community (Set 2); and individual interviews with six women who had experienced IMPV (Set 3). The purpose of selecting these groups was to capture the phenomenon from diverse viewpoints (Schensul et al. 1999). For example, community leaders were better suited to exploring macro-systemic factors, community members had knowledge of meso-factors, and abused women were better qualified to discuss their individual situations. Similarly, we wanted to hear from women and men, and women with an abuse history and those without. The underlying premise was that topics such as male violence against women cannot be understood fully by only hearing abused women's stories; we must also understand the viewpoints of the oppressors (Anderson & Hill Collins 1995) if we are to challenge the status quo, especially along the lines of multiple sites of oppression.

Data Collection

Interviews and focus groups were, on average, two hours long. The first author conducted all individual interviews (in Sets 1 and 3) ($n = 22$), except for one interview that required an interpreter. The (Set 2) focus groups with women and men were conducted in Tamil, respectively by a female and male community leader. The first author co-facilitated all eight focus group discussions ($n = 41$). The focus groups conducted in Tamil created a space for participants to voice in their own language the concerns of importance to them. According to the post-colonial feminist perspective, the idea of giving voice to those who might not be heard (e.g., due to language differences), guided this study. The individual and group discussions were guided by exploratory, open-ended questions (see Tables 39.1 and 39.2). The interviews were transcribed verbatim, and focus groups were translated and transcribed.

Ethical Considerations

Ethics approval was obtained from the appropriate university. All potential participants were informed, both via consent form and verbally, of their right to refuse to participate or answer any questions or to terminate participation at any time. Focus group participants were also made aware, in advance, of who the facilitators were. At the beginning of focus group sessions, participants were asked to respect each other's information and not to disclose identifying information about themselves. Focus group facilitators and the transcriptionists signed a confidentiality agreement.

Findings

The participants represented the demographics of the Sri Lankan Tamil community in Canada

---

Table 39.1 Examples of individual interview questions posed

What do you think about Tamil men's and women's relationships in Sri Lanka/Canada?

What do you think about wife abuse in the Tamil community? Why do you think it happens in Sri Lanka/Canada? (probe about gender, culture, class)

How do you think what happens at home between a husband and wife is influenced by their friends, family and neighbours? (probe about gender, culture, class, race)

How are the couples influenced by what is happening in Canadian culture and society? (probe about gender, culture, class, race)

Table 39.2 Examples of focus group questions asked

Please tell me about your experience about coming to live in Canada.

What was it like to build a new life here?

What would have been helpful to you and your family in getting settled in Canada?

What leads to conflicts among Tamil couples living in Canada?

How do they resolve these conflicts?

Wife abuse happens in every community and culture. Why do you think it happens in the Tamil community?

How does being in Canada shape why/how wife abuse happens?

in terms of age (range = 24–70 years), education (range = elementary school to university), length of stay in Canada (range = 1–20 years), and religion (most were Hindu) (see also Tables 39.3–39.5). Their conceptualizations of the production of IMPV are presented under four themes.

Experiences of Violence Pre-migration and during Border-Crossing

Participants in all three sets spoke about their experiences during the civil war. Many lost homes, businesses, and employment. They spoke about frequent roadside checking, bomb threats, and sounds of sirens and having to run to bunkers. Young men were arrested and tortured; some disappeared and/or died in prison. Participants from Set 1 connected men participating in, witnessing, or being victims of war violence with intolerance, anger, suspicion, and aggression at home:

Husbands being separated from wives (. . .) have been taken out for interrogation . . . having to always suspect another person, whether he is an enemy or nor. (Set 1, Participant 6)

The children grow up seeing people fighting and killing, you know. Anger and aggression becomes an acceptable way of expressing discontent with something. Which is what you have often when you come to a new place. (Set 1, Participant 10)

The second quote also implies that learned behaviour can affect how a person manages discontent or

anger. Overall, participants perceived that psychological stress and trauma from the war influenced men negatively.

Conflicts and wars increase violence against women, which is the case in Sri Lanka. In all three sets, participants spoke about the vulnerability of girls and women. Parents often feared for their daughters' safety and attempted to send them out of the country:

Unfortunately a friend of mine . . . disappeared. My family was worried that I was going to disappear. So they proposed [a marriage for] me to (. . .) from (. . .). I didn't want to marry that time. I wanted to study and get a good job, but I didn't feel safe. We hear all kinds of things happening to girls. I was missing my friend and that had a very bad effect on me. My family was scared and started to react. That is how I ended up in this situation. (Set 3, Participant 5)

Because of the country's situation, this participant agreed to marry a man who later became abusive. There had not been enough time to investigate her potential husband's background, the usual procedure in arranged marriages.

Violence was reported to occur also during border-crossing. Although Canada has made considerable efforts to accept refugees, current immigration policies make the process difficult for Tamils. For example, Tamils are unable to register with the United Nations High Commissioner for Refugees (UNHCR) to obtain refugee status while still living in

Table 39.3 Demographic characteristics of community leaders

Characteristic	
Gender	10 women, 6 men
Age group	6 (in their 30s), 5 (in their 40s), 5 (over 50 years)
Birth city	9 (Jaffna)
Decade left Sri Lanka	1 (1970s), 8 (1980s), 4 (1990s), 3 (2000s)
Lived in a third country	10
Years in Canada	1.5–20: 6 (1–5 years); 2 (6–10 years); 6 (11–15 years); 2 (16–20 years)
Level of education	Grade 10—University
Work type in Canada	Health or settlement sectors (n = 16)

Table 39.4 Demographic characteristics of focus group participants

Focus group	1 (n = 8)	2 (n = 6)	3 (n = 12)	4 (n = 5)	5 (n = 6)	6 (n = 4)
Gender	Women	Men	Women	Men	Women	Men
Age range (years)	30–63	41–50	27–65	25–62	24–69	35–69
Birth city	Jaffna	Jaffna	Jaffna	Jaffna	Jaffna	Jaffna
Years in Canada	1–10	2–12	2–11	1–11	2–11	8–18
Level of education	8–13	8–13	10–13	10–13	<8–Univ.	1.3–Univ.
Arranged marriage	All	3	8	2	4	2
Second session	Yes (n = 7)	–	–	–	–	Yes (n = 4)

Table 39.5 Demographic characteristics of abused women participants

Characteristic	
Age	25–70 years
Birth city	Mostly Jaffna (n = 5)
Years in Canada	3–12
Level of education	Grade–University
Length of marriage	2–50 years
Arranged marriage	Yes (n = 5)
Worked outside home in Sri Lanka	Yes (n = 5)
Currently employed	Yes (n = 3)
Number of children	0–5

Sri Lanka (Fuglerud 1999), and they cannot apply for a Canadian visa, for example, if they have lost necessary documents during displacement or cannot easily replace them because villages have been destroyed or evacuated. Further, family sponsorship applications in Canada are often delayed. These problems drive Tamils to other ways of reaching safety or reuniting with family members, including hiring agents who bring them to Canada, often breaking international laws. The following illustrates some of the complexity of border-crossing:

> It is because of the civil war we had to leave the country. I came here through the US. Until then, I have never been to a jail. But there, they put me in jail for a month. I was very much affected mentally due to this, as we didn't commit any crime. (Set 2, Participant 2)

Some participants highlighted evidence of violation of people's rights by those in authority in various countries as well as the unacceptable daily life conditions that some Tamils had to endure to reach their final destination. While the hope of a new home and safer place drive people to such travel, uncertainty, fear, anxiety, and stress associated with these steps were identified by participants as having a negative psychological impact on people, both short and long-term. According to most, these incidents also shaped how people view others, and whether or not they would seek help from others, for example to cope better with post-migration stressors, especially from those in authority, such as healthcare professionals, settlement workers and child welfare officers.

Gender Inequity in the Marital Institution

Coming from a patriarchal society, participants had learned gender roles in childhood and adulthood from family, neighbours, schools, workplaces, and society-at-large. In Sri Lanka men were the primary breadwinners; they often did not do household work but were responsible for household repairs and physically demanding work, such as lifting and moving. Although gendered responsibilities varied over time, among families, and across socio-economic groups, women were

primarily responsible for cooking, cleaning, and child-rearing.

After migration, Tamil men who came alone were forced to assume household tasks. However, according to participants, most men continued to perceive household responsibilities as women's domain. Most single men returned to Sri Lanka to find a suitable wife who would fulfil such expectations:

> As soon as their mother, wife, or sisters come, men expect the women to work for them. There are exceptions. (Set 1, Participant 5)

In the new context, some couples successfully negotiated household responsibilities based on who could do the tasks better/more easily, who was available at a particular time of day, and who enjoyed doing the task. Such change was perceived to be more common among those who immigrated at a younger age:

> He is young guy . . . very much a short-tempered guy. . . . I saw a change in him. He told me, 'I am helping my wife.' She has two kids. 'I am a truck driver, and she is alone, so I have to come back and clean for her . . . so I decided to take local trips instead of long-distance trips.' (Set 1, Participant 4)

Others changed because they had no choice—owing to their work commitments, timing, and so on—allowing for a more equal distribution of work between the couple. In contrast, some husbands held their wives responsible for household work even if they worked outside the home as many hours as he did and contributed equally to the family income.

Participants in Sets 1 and 2 spoke about a general perception in the community that some disciplining of the women was justified, especially to prevent bigger problems. The reasons presented included incomplete household work, suspected or real extramarital affairs, refusing husbands' requests for sex, arguing or complaining, and asking for things such as money or tasks to be completed at 'inappropriate times'. These were also the justifications used by the abusive husbands of participants in Set 3. These expectations/perceptions/responses were also shaped by the changes in post-migration social networks.

Changes in Social Networks and Supports

The Tamils were used to a social structure and networks that often strongly influenced their lives in Sri Lanka. Such networks often provided instrumental, informational, emotional, and psychological support, especially to new couples, young families, and those who were dealing with life challenges. However, post-migration social networks are usually smaller or non-existent, especially for women who often arrive sponsored by their husbands. According to most participants, even if family members were in Canada, the values that governed the expected/perceived/given support have changed since coming to a more individualistic society:

> Relationships are much tighter back home. It is not the same here. Even when we have relatives here, we would think about interfering or not [in people's personal lives by trying to help them]. (Set 2, Participant 4)

The changes in the quantity and quality of support have also changed due to the extremely busy lives they lived in Canada.

The resulting lack/loss of support has increased the household responsibilities of both spouses and their reliance on each other for support. While the latter has positive effects, such as increased communication and shared decision making between the couple without the influence or interference of family, sole reliance on one person causes tremendous stress. A participant highlighted a possible scenario:

> When there is pregnancy, when there is childbirth, they have no one to care for them, and that is the time when they need family the most. That is when the husband might feel stressed out (. . .) and move out. (Set 1, Participant 7)

Overall, participants emphasized that increases in stress resentment, and arguments about the quantity and quality of household work each spouse did contributed to conflict and abuse. If the woman's family was not in Canada, the husband also had more power over her (especially if his family was living with them or nearby). In some cases, the husband's family was reported to be the instigator or the abuser. Women's family members also were perceived to reinforce patriarchal practices. Participants in Set 2, for example, spoke about the indirect and direct pressure women themselves placed upon other women to adhere to such patriarchal practices. This idea was confirmed by a participant in Set 1:

> My mum tells me, 'Your husband is coming, now, you're talking with me, why don't you go greet your husband and serve him food?' My mother-in-law immediately stops whatever she is doing and serves food for her son. But she never told me [directly] 'Oh, you are his wife, you have to go and do things' (Set 1, Participant 3)

These changes in social networks and supports were perceived to be particularly negative for women who were not fluent in English or not in paid employment, as they were more isolated and further dependent on their husbands.

Perceptions of Changes in Social Status and Privilege: Gender and Race Lenses

Immigration to a new country is often imbued with changes in socio-economic status and privileges. A negative change in this regard is more likely for immigrants from low- and medium-income countries who move to high-income nations. According to most of our women participants, their husbands and other men in their community often were stuck in jobs that they began as stepping stones to better jobs that never materialized because of racism in the employment sector in Canada. Their accounts implied that immigrants are being used as a source of cheap labour:

> [Canada] needs people for its economy. They need people to clean their offices, clean toilets, deliver newspapers, and wash dishes in restaurants, because not that many white Canadian

people want to do these low-paying, low-status jobs. . . . So there is no real motivation for [the] government to invest in these people [immigrants] in a way that they become successful. Then who will do these types of jobs? (Set 1, Participant 1)

This participant's perception of the new forms of colonization taking place in immigrant-receiving countries in the West was in line with the perceptions of most others in Sets 1 and 2. Tamil men's downward mobility in professional and economic status led to loss of social status at home, and within their extended families, the Tamil community, and larger Canadian society. As can be gleaned from the next excerpt, patriarchal ideological values dictated that men assume the responsibilities of paying off family debts, sponsoring their wives and children for immigration, financially supporting their extended families in Sri Lanka, and paying dowries for their sisters and daughters to be married:

I borrowed money from an uncle to come here. I was worried if I could give back the loan if I get deported. Also, my siblings were back home. I was the eldest. In our culture, as you know, the girls have to be married off by the boys and we need to give dowry for that and only then we can get married. So these were all pressures on me. I have an elder sister [who needed to be married off] and I was crying about that situation. (Set 2, Participant 6)

Across interviews, participants agreed that, as part of arranged-marriage customs in Sri Lanka, women almost always married men of equal or higher educational and professional status and then enjoyed the associated living standard. One woman commented on the implications of husbands' status change on family dynamics:

Here a woman lawyer can marry a chef and it is not a problem at home. But our society is set up to say that women should always marry up or someone who is doing a better job or is better than you professionally. So, when we come here, things become upside down. You

don't know what it does to the family . . . not just to the man. (Set 1, Participant 15)

Inability to fulfil these responsibilities as well as expectations associated with their previous status demoralized men; some became depressed or turned to alcohol. In some cases, couple conflict ensued.

Discussion

Study Limitations

The study sample was limited to those who, in Canada, belonged to the lower-middle class and working class and were under 65 years of age, and it possible that those outside these criteria might perceive IMPV differently. To avoid placing them at risk, we did not speak with women who were living with abusive husbands; thus, their voices are absent from this study. The presence of community leaders as focus groups facilitators might have limited the openness with which participants spoke about the issues.

Factors Influencing Post-migration IMPV

Participants' accounts revealed a complex range of factors that influenced IMPV after migration, presented here according to the ecosystemic framework. All were specifically connected to the intersectionality of gender, race, and class, and were congruent with post-colonial thought.

Individual-level factors

The individual-level factor that we found to be key to IMPV was pre-migration exposure to war and multiple trauma. Men who experienced or engaged in violence were perceived to have mental health problems, such as low tolerance for stress (e.g. job loss) and various stimuli (e.g., loud noise at home), and symptoms of anxiety and depression. They were perceived to be more suspicious of their wives because they had learned to distrust people in general. Chambion (1989) and Penalosa (1986) noted that immigrant men's previous exposure to violence could be connected to aggressive or violent behaviour towards their wives. In a recent study by Gupta et al. (2009) involving a group of immigrant men to the USA, a statistically significant relationship between pre-migration exposure to political violence and IMPV perpetration in the post-migration context was found. However, there is limited literature on this topic.

Micro-level factors

Key micro-level factor influencing the production of IMPV post-migration included the changes in husband's and wife's socio-economic statuses. THESE changes contributed to two scenarios of post-migration family power imbalance. In the first, some husbands gained control, authority, and power within their families after migration—for example, by being sole breadwinner or through their wife's isolation and/or lack of English skill. Other researchers have also reported this scenario (e.g. Abraham's 1999, 2000 studies of South-Asian immigrants). In the second scenario, some husbands' power and authority decreased owing to the deskilling and deprofessionalization they experienced. Wives' greater access to paid (albeit low status and low paid) employment post-migration, and their relatively increased earnings, led some husbands to reassert their authority through violence. Other researchers in the USA and Canada (e.g., Krulfeld, 1994; Kulig, 1994; Morrison et al., 1999; Min, 2001; Oxman-Martinez et al., 2000; Tang & Oatley, 2002) have noted similar findings. An important contribution of our study to the literature is the recognition that the two scenarios can co-exist within the same community.

Meso-level factors

The most important meso-level factor affecting the post-migration production of IMPV was the change in social networks and supports. In Canada, Tamil couples might have no family members to help with day-to-day life, and thus rely heavily on each other. Under economic and time constraints, this situation leads to stress, resentment, and conflict. Hyman et al. (2004) reported similar findings in their study with Ethiopian-immigrant married couples in Toronto, and in their follow-up study (Hyman et al., 2006) with divorced women and men from the same community. McSpadden and Moussa (1993) also found that loss of extended family support and advice led to marital conflict among Canadian Ethiopian immigrants.

As in other communities, Tamil women are often held as the bearers of the community values and beliefs. As such, even when family members were available in Canada, they often enforced patriarchal norms and practices. Husbands' family involvement (in the absence of women's families) was noted to be particularly negative for the woman when couple conflicts occurred. Women's sole reliance on husbands and their families also increased the likelihood of a woman being abused by her husband's relatives, mainly female in-laws. Similar findings were noted in the USA among 'Asian-Americans' (Huisman, 1996), 'Asian-Indians' (Mehotra, 1999), and Mexicans (Morash et al., 2000). The Tamil community further enforced, both subtly and overtly, patriarchal rules and practices, even when some such practices were reported to have changed/are changing in Sri-Lanka. Overall, this situation gave men an upper hand over the rest of the family.

Macro-level factors

Our findings, along with those of a number of previous studies, show that post-migration factors operating at the macro-level of society, including economic insecurity resulting from non-recognition of professional/educational credentials, workplace deskilling, and racial/ethnic discrimination—added to patriarchal pressure for men to meet family and social responsibilities—pushed men to self- and family destructive behaviours such as alcohol and other addictions, and to infidelity (Perilla et al., 1994; Rhee, 1997; Morash et al., 2000; Tran & Des Jardins, 2000) as well as to engaging in abusive behaviours (George & Ramkissoon, 1998; Perry et al., 1998; Moghissi & Goodman, 1999; Abraham, 2000). In other words, our findings along with these other studies findings illuminate the connection between the social inequities and their impact on individual men and their families (i.e., how gender and class intersected with race to create conflicts and abuse post-migration). Our findings thus can be used to contest uni-factoral explanations of IMPV, such as patriarchy.

What Is Already Known about This Topic

- Numerous factors explain the production of intimate male partner violence, with little consensus on its aetiology.
- Etiological theories of violence have included psychological explanations, biological differences, sociological perspectives and feminist approaches.
- Some etiological theories explain intimate male partner violence at an individual level, while others look to the family for an explanation, and some operate at the societal level.

What This Paper Adds

- Rather than being caused by one or several factors operating within a single level of society, intimate male partner violence is produced by a complex and interrelated set of factors operating at individual, family, community, and societal levels in the pre-migration, border-crossing, and post-migration contexts.
- Production of post-migration intimate male partner violence involved experiences of violence in the pre-migration and border crossing contexts; gender inequity in the marital institution; and post-migration changes in social supports as well as in socioeconomic status and privilege.
- Women who had been married and lived with their husbands in Sri Lanka experienced wife abuse only after coming to Canada; thus, the relevance of the post-migration context in the production of intimate male partner violence should not be underestimated.

Conclusion

Post-colonial feminist perspectives are useful in understanding post-migration IMPV, which is produced by the interaction of multiple forms of inequities that men and women experience before migration, while crossing borders, and after migration that are created in the intersection of several forms of neo-colonial oppressive relations, such as racism, classism, and sexism. While we did not explore the reproduction of IMPV in this study—that is, IMPV that began before migration and continued after couples reunited, it is noteworthy that women in this study who had married and lived with their husbands in Sri-Lanka experienced abuse only after coining to Canada. Thus, we propose that post-migration IMPV can only be explained by such plurality of factors that capture the complexity of immigrants' lives in diaspora and displacement.

Acknowledgments

We acknowledge the contribution of Dr Shahrzad Mojab, thesis committee member, and Dr Ruth

Gallop, co-supervisor and thesis committee member, during the project development phase of the study.

Funding

The first author gratefully acknowledges the financial support she received for her work from the Canadian Institutes of Health Research in the form of a Doctoral Fellowship (2003–2006) and a New Investigator Award (2008–2013) in the area of Gender and Health.

Conflict of Interest

No conflict of interest has been declared by the authors.

Author Contributions

SG, NK, and DG were responsible for the study conception and design. SG performed the data collection. SG performed the data analysis. SG was responsible for the drafting of the manuscript. SG, NK, and DG made critical revisions to the paper for important intellectual content. SG and NK obtained funding. NK and DG supervised the study. SG, NK, and DG provided other contributions.

Contribution to the Paper

This paper is based on SG's doctoral dissertation defended in December 2006 at the Faculty of Nursing, University of Toronto. NK and DG supervised SG's thesis. SG drafted the paper, and NK and DG critically revised it.

References

Abraham M. (1999) Sexual abuse in South Asian immigrant marriages. *Violence Against Women* 5, 591–618.

Abraham M. (2000) Isolation as a form of marital violence: the South Asian immigrant experience. *Journal of Social Distress and the Homeless* 9, 221–36.

Ahmad F., Ali M. & Stewart D.E. (2005) Spousal abuse among Canadian immigrant women. *Journal of Immigration Health* 7, 239–46.

Anderson M.L. & Hill Collins P. (1995) *Race, Class, and Gender: An Anthology*, 2nd edn. Wadsworth, Belmont, CA.

Bryman A. (2001) *Social Research Methods*. Oxford University Press, New York.

Campbell J. & Lewandowski L. (1997) Mental and psychical health effects of intimate partner violence on women and children. *Psychiatric Clinics of North America* 20, 353–74.

Chambion A. (1989) Refugee families' experiences: three family themes—family disruption, violent trauma, and acculturation. *Journal of Strategic and Systemic Therapies* 8, 3–13.

Coker A.L., Smith P.H., Bertea F., King M.R. & McKeown R.E. (2000) Physical health consequences of physical and psychological intimate partner violence. *Archives of Family Medicine* 9, 451–57.

Collins P.H. (1990) *Black Feminist Thought: Knowledge, Consciousness, and the Politics of Empowerment*. Routledge, New York.

Eby K., Campbell I., Sullivan C. & Davidson W. (1995) Health effects of experiences of sexual violence for women with abusive partners. *Health Care for Women International* 16, 563–76.

Fischbach R. & Herbert B. (1997) Domestic violence and mental health: correlates and conundrums within and across cultures. *Social Science and Medicine* 45, 1161–76.

Fuglerud O. (1999) *Life on the Outside: The Tamil Diaspora and Long Distance Nationalism*. Pluto, London.

George U. & Ramkissoon S. (1998) Race, gender and class: interlocking oppressions in the lives of South Asian women in Canada. *Affilia* 13, 102–19.

Gerbert B., Bronstone A., Pantilat S., McPhee S., Allertun M. & Moe J. (1999) When asked, patients tell: disclosure of sensitive health-risk behaviours. *Medical Care* 37, 104–11.

Germain C.B. & Bloom M. (1999) *Human Behaviour in the Social Environment*, 2nd edn. Columbia University Press, New York.

Gupta J., Acevedo-Garcia D., Hemenway D., Decker M.R., Raj A. & Silverman J.G. (2009) Premigration exposure to political violence and perpetration of intimate partner violence among immigrant men in Boston. *American Journal of Public Health* 99, 462–69.

Guruge S. & Collins E. (2008) *Working with Women: Issues and Strategies for Mental Health Professionals*, 1st edn. Centre for Addiction and Mental Health, Toronto, ON.

Guruge S. & Gastaldo D. (2008) Violencia en la pareja e inmigración: ?Cómo ser parte de la solución? [Violence in couples and immigration: How to be part of the solution?] (Editorial) *Presencia* 8, Retrieved from www.index-f.com/presencia/n8/p8801.php on 10 January 2009.

Guruge S. & Khanlou N. (2004) Intersectionalities of influence: researching health of immigrant and refugee women. *Canadian Journal of Nursing Research* 36, 32–47.

Heise L.L., Pitanguy J. & Germain A. (1994) *Violence Against Women: The Hidden Health Burden: World Bank Discussion Papers (No. 255)*. International Bank for Reconstruction and Development/World Bank, Washington, DC.

Hooks B. (1984) *Feminist Theory: From Margin to Center*. South End, Boston.

Huisman K.A. (1996) Wife battering in Asian American communities: identifying the service needs of an overlooked segment of the U.S. population. *Violence Against Women* 2, 260–83.

Hyman I. (2002) Immigrant and visible minority women. In *Ontario Women's Health Status Report* (Stewart D.E., Cheung A., Ferris L.E., Hyman I., Cohen M. & Williams I.J., eds.), Ontario Women's Health Council, Toronto, Canada, pp. 338–58.

Hyman I., Guruge S., Mason R., Stuckless N., Gould J., Tang T., Teffera H. & Mekonnen G. (2004) Post migration changes in gender relations among Ethiopian immigrant couples in Toronto. *Canadian Journal of Nursing Research* 36(4), 74–89.

Hyman I., Guruge S., Mason R., Stuckless N., Gould J., Tang T., Teffera H. & Mekonnen G. (2006) *Post Migration Changes in Gender Relations in the Ethiopian Community in Toronto: Phase II*. Centre of Excellence for Research on Immigration and Settlement, Toronto, Canada. Retrieved from http://ceris.metropolis.net/Virtual%20Library/RFPReports/Hyman_PhaseII2004.pdf on 9 June 2006.

Jayawardena K. (1986) *Feminism and Nationalism in the Third World*. Zed Books, London.

Krulfeld R.M. (1994) Changing concepts of gender roles and identities in refugee communities. In *Reconstructing Lives, Recapturing Memory: Refugee Identity, Gender and Culture Change* (Camino L.A. & Krulfeld R.M., eds.), Gordon and Breach, Washington, DC, pp. 71–4.

Kulig J. (1994) Old traditions in a new world: changing gender relations among Cambodian refugees. In *Reconstructing Lives, Recapturing Memory: Refugee Identity, Gender and Culture Change* (Camino L.A. & Krulfeld R.M., eds.), Gordon and Breach, Washington, DC, pp. 129–46.

Lincoln Y.S. & Guba E. (1985) *Naturalistic Inquiry*. Sage, Newbury Park, CA.

Lofland J. & Lofland L.H. (1995) *Analyzing Social Settings: A Guide to Qualitative Observation and Analysis*, 3rd edn. Wadsworth, Belmont CA.

Loue S. & Faust M. (1998) Intimate partner violence among immigrants. In *Handbook of Immigrant Health* (Loue S., ed.), Plenum Press, New York, pp. 521–44.

McClintock A. (1995) *Imperial Leather*. Routledge, New York.

McLoughlin F. & Grumbach K. (1999) Screening and intervention for intimate partner abuse: practices and attitudes of primary care physicians. *Journal of the American Medical Association* 282, 468–474.

McSpadden L.A. & Moussa H. (1993) I have a name: the gender dynamics in asylum and in resettlement of Ethiopian and Eritrean refugees in North America. *Journal of Refugee Studies* 6, 203–25.

Mehotra M. (1999) The social construction of wife abuse: experiences of Asian Indian women in the United States. *Violence Against Women* 5, 619–40.

Memmi A. (1967) *The Colonizer and the Colonized*. Beacon Press, Boston.

Min P. (2001) Changes in Korean immigrants' gender role and social status, and their marital conflicts. *Sociological Forum* 16, 301–20.

Minh-Ha T.T. (1989) *Woman, Native, Other: Postcolonial Feminism*. Indiana University Press, Indianapolis.

Moghissi H. & Goodman M.J. (1999) 'Cultures of violence' and diaspora: dislocation and gendered conflict in Iranian-Canadian communities. *Humanity and Society* 23, 291–318.

Mohanty CT. (1991) Under Western eyes: feminist scholarship and colonial discourses. In *Third World Women and the Politics of Feminism* (Mohanty C.T., ed.), Indiana University Press, Bloomington, pp. 51–80.

Montalvo-Liendo N. (2008) Cross-cultural factors in disclosure of intimate partner violence: an integrated review. *Journal of Advanced Nursing* 65(1), 20–34.

Morash M., Bui H.N. & Santiago A.M. (2000) Cultural-specific gender ideology and wife abuse in Mexican-descent families. *International Review of Victimology* 7, 67–91.

Morrison F., Guruge S. & Snarr K.A. (1999) Sri Lankan Tamil immigrants in Toronto: gender, marriage patterns, and sexuality. In *Gender and Immigration* (Kelson G.A. & DeLaet D.L., eds.), New York University Press, New York, pp. 144–60.

Muellman R.L., Lenaghan P.A. & Pakieser R.A. (1996) Battered women: injury locations and types. *Annals of Emergency Medicine* 28, 486–92.

Oxman-Martinez J., Abdool S. & Loiselle-Leonard M. (2000) Immigration, women and health in Canada. *Canadian Journal of Public Health* 91, 394–95.

Penalosa F. (1986) *Central Americans in Los Angeles: Background, Language and Education* (Occasional Paper 21). Spanish Speaking Mental Health Research Center, Los Angeles, CA.

Perilla J., Bakeman R. & Norris K. (1994) Culture and domestic violence: the ecology of abused Latinas. *Violence and Victims* 9, 325–39.

Perry C.M., Shams M. & DeLeon C.C. (1998) Voices from an Afghan community. *Journal of Cultural Diversity* 5, 127–31.

Ratner P. (1995) Indicators of exposure to wife abuse. *Canadian Journal of Nursing Research* 27, 31–46.

Rhee S. (1997) Domestic violence in the Korean immigrant family. *Journal of Sociology and Social Welfare* 24, 63–77.

Rodgers K. (1994) Wife assault in Canada: the findings of a national survey. *Juristat Service Bulletin, Canadian Center for Justice Statistics* 14(9), 1–21.

Schensul S.L., Schensul J.J. & LeCompte M.D. (1999) *Essential Ethnographic Methods.* Altamira Press, Walnut Creek, CA.

Spivak G.C. (1988) Can the subaltern speak? In *Marxism and the Interpretation of Culture* (Nelson C. & Grossberg L., eds.), University of Illinois Press, Chicago, pp. 271–313.

Tang T.N. & Oatley K. (2002) *Transition and Engagement of Life Roles among Chinese Immigrant Women.* Paper presented at American Psychological Association Annual Convention, Chicago.

Tran C.G. & Des Jardins K. (2000) Domestic violence in Vietnamese refugee and Korean immigrant communities. In *Relationships among Asian American Women* (Chin J.L., ed.), American Psychological Association, Washington, DC, pp. 71–96.

Tuhiwai Smith F. (2001) *Decolonizing Methodologies: Research and Indigenous People.* University of Otago Press, Dunedin.

United Nations (1993) *Declaration on the Elimination of Violence against Women.* Canada–USA Women's Health Forum, New York, p. 6. Retrieved from www.hc-sc.gc.ca/canusa/papers/canada/english/violence.htm on 1 February 2005.

United Nations (1999) Consideration of Reports Submitted by States Parties under Article 18 of the Convention on the Elimination of All Forms of Discrimination Against Women: Third and Fourth Reports.

World Health Organization (2000) *Prevalence of Violence against Women by an Intimate Male Partner.* Retrieved from www.who.int/violence_injury_prevention/vaw/prevalence.htm on 11 June 2006.

World Health Organization (2006) Multi-country Study on Women's Health and Domestic Violence against Women. Summary Report: Initial Results on Prevalence, Health Outcomes and Women's Responses. World Health Organization, Geneva, Switzerland.

CHAPTER 40

Genderbashing: Sexuality, Gender, and the Regulation of Public Space

Viviane K. Namaste

In North America, violence against lesbians, gay men, and bisexuals is escalating at an alarming rate. A survey conducted in 1986–7 by the Philadelphia Lesbian and Gay Task Force reports that violence against lesbians and gay men in that city had doubled since 1983–4 (as cited in Valentine, 1993: 409). The United States National and Lesbian Task Force (NGLTF) documents that incidents of violence against sexual minorities increased 127 per cent from 1988 to 1993 (NGLTF, 1994: 1).

Though scholars (Comstock, 1991; von Schultess, 1992; Valentine, 1993) and community activists (Hendricks, 1993) have increasingly addressed the issue of violence against lesbians and gay men, there remains very little reflection on the function of gender within these acts of aggression. In this chapter, I argue that a perceived transgression of normative sex/gender relations motivates much of the violence against sexual minorities, and that an assault on these 'transgressive' bodies is fundamentally concerned with policing gender presentation through public and private space. I also consider the implications of this research for transsexual and transgendered people. Given that the perception of gender dissidence informs acts of queerbashing, we can deduce that those individuals who live outside normative sex/gender relations will be most at risk for assault. Finally, I examine some of the ways in which educational strategies on violence separate gender and sexuality, and thus prevent a political response that accounts for the function of gender in queerbashing. Specific examples are taken from briefs presented in November 1993 to the Quebec Human Rights Commission's public hearing in Montreal on violence and discrimination against lesbians and gay men (Demczuk, 1993; Hendricks, 1993; Namaste, 1993; Pepper, 1993).[1] I demonstrate the ways in which gender and sexuality are separated, and thus how the issue of gender is foreclosed by certain gay male community activists.

Limits of Tolerance: Gender Norms and Gender Transgressions

'Gender' refers to the roles and meanings assigned to men and women based on their presumed biological sex (Mackie, 1983). It is a social function, neither timeless nor historical. For example, we generally associate the colour pink with girls and femininity and the colour blue with boys and masculinity. There is nothing inherent in either of these colours that links them to a particular gender: pink, or turquoise, could just as easily designate masculinity. Gender is also about what men and women are supposed to do in the world—men wear pants, have short hair, can grow beards, and are considered more physically aggressive than women. Women can wear skirts, have longer hair, wear makeup, and are judged to be emotional. In Western societies, it is thought that there are

only two genders—men and women (Ortner and Whitehead, 1981).

'Sexuality', in contrast, refers to the ways in which individuals organize their erotic and sexual lives. This is generally categorized into three separate areas: heterosexuals—individuals who have sexual relations with members of the opposite sex; homosexuals—those who have sexual relations with members of the same sex; and bisexuals—people who relate erotically to both men and women (Kinsey, Pomeroy, and Martin, 1948).

In Western societies, gender and sexuality get confused. For example, when a 15-year-old boy is assaulted and called a 'faggot', he is so labelled because he has mannerisms that are considered 'effeminate'. He may or may not be gay, but he is called a 'queer' because he does not fulfill his expected gender role. A young girl can be a tomboy until the age of 11 or so, but she must then live as a more 'dainty', 'feminine' person. If she does not, she may be called a 'dyke—again, regardless of how she actually defines her sexual identity. In both examples, the presentation of gender determines how these youths are received by their peers. When people shout 'faggot' at a 15-year-old boy, they really mean that he is not a 'masculine' man. Gender and sexuality are collapsed. As Rubin points out, the merging of gender and sexuality enables some feminist theorists to write about erotic desire (Rubin, 1984: 307).

The fusion of gender and sexuality has distinct implications for the problematic of violence. The connotations of the pejorative names used against individuals who are assaulted—names like 'sissy', 'faggot', 'dyke', 'man-hater', 'queer', and 'pervert'—suggest that an attack is justified not in reaction to one's sexual identity, but to one's gender presentation. Indeed, bashers do not characteristically inquire as to the sexual identity of their potential victims, but rather make this assumption on their own. On what basis do 'queerbashers' determine who is gay, lesbian, or bisexual?

Joseph Harry's research suggests that gender should be considered an important variable in queerbashing incidents (1982, 1990). Harry found that groups of assailants involved in these crimes relied on gender cues to ascertain sexual identity.

If they judged a potential victim to be 'effeminate', for example, he was subject to attack. A related study confirms this hypothesis: 39 per cent of men surveyed who behaved in a 'feminine' manner had been physically assaulted, compared with 22 per cent of men who were 'masculine' and only 17 per cent of men who conducted themselves in a 'very masculine' fashion (Harry, 1982). According to this survey, males who are classified as 'effeminate' are more than twice as likely to experience physical violence than males whose gender presentation corresponds to social norms. A study of anti-lesbian abuse in San Francisco indicates that 12 per cent of lesbians surveyed had been punched, kicked, or otherwise physically assaulted (von Schultess, 1992). Significantly, the only justification offered related to gender:

> [F]ourteen of the women said that the only explanation for incidents they had experienced was the fact that they had short hair and were wearing trousers and in most cases were in the company of another woman (Valentine, 1993: 409).

Women and men who transgress acceptable limits of self-presentation, then, are among those most at risk for assault. Assaults against men judged to be 'effeminate' or women deemed 'masculine' reveal the ways in which gender and sexuality are intertwined. Gender is used as a cue to locate lesbians and gay men. Though the perceived transgression of gender norms motivates bashing, this affects men and women differently. The gendered construction of space—both public and private—figures centrally in these acts of aggression.

Transsexual and Transgendered People and Violence

Despite the variety of gender identities available in transgender networks, and despite the prevalence of transgendered people in other cultures, most people in Western societies assume that there are only two sexes (males and females) and two genders (men and women) (Ortner and Whitehead,

1981; Devor, 1989; Bullough and Bullough, 1993; Herdt, 1994; Feinberg, 1996). For transsexual and/or transgendered people, this poses a significant problem: a person must choose the gender to which he/she belongs and behave accordingly. Because most people believe that there are only 'men' and 'women', transgendered people need to live as one or the other in order to avoid verbal and physical harassment. In transgendered communities, this is known as the need to pass. Passing is about presenting yourself as a 'real' woman or a 'real' man—that is, as an individual whose 'original' sex is never suspected.[2] Passing means hiding the fact that you are transsexual and/or transgendered. Most people go to extraordinary lengths to live undetected as transsexuals. Electrolysis, voice therapy, the binding of breasts, mastectomy, and plastic surgery are some of the more common means employed to ensure that people pass successfully.

Given the cultural coding of gender into a binary framework, a high incidence of violence directed against TS/TG people is not surprising. Although there is very little data available on transgendered people as victims of violence, a 1992 study showed that 52 per cent of MTF transsexuals and 43 per cent of FTM transsexuals surveyed in London, England, had been physically assaulted (Tully, 1992: 266). Contrast these members with data from a 1989 American telephone poll, which revealed that 7 per cent of lesbians and gay men were victims of assault in the previous year (NGLTF, 1994). Although these samples represent two different countries, the statistical difference of violent incidents against gay/lesbian and transgender individuals is remarkable and certainly suggests that gender plays a crucial role in the attacks generally referred to as 'gaybashing'.

Although gender plays a central role in incidents of queerbashing, a collapse of gender and sexuality precludes a consideration of how this violence specifically affects transgendered people. Dorian Corey notes that contemporary gay antiviolence activists do not recognize the different ways aggression is, and has historically been, directed against transgendered people and gays:

> When the closet doors were shut [for gays, in the past], drag queens, of course, were out

there anyways. We never had a closet. Let's face it, when you put on a dress and hit the world, you're declaring what you are. . . . These children that are supposedly straight looking, they're the ones getting bashed, so now [in the 1990s] they're protesting. The girls were always getting their asses kicked. It's just a thing of who you are and what you are. (as quoted in Enigma, 1992: 35–6)

Transsexual activists have suggested that one of the ways we can respond to the function of gender in violence is by naming it directly. As an activist button proclaims, 'transsexuals get queerbashed too'. Activists also insist that we need to speak of *genderbashing*, not gaybashing. This discourse separates gender and sexuality, since their collapse prevents an appreciation of the specificity of violence against transsexual and transgendered people.

Sex Work and Transsexual/ Transgendered Public Space

'Transsexual and transgendered public space' refers to urban areas known for their transsexuals and transvestites, such as the Meat District on the border of New York's Greenwich Village, Santa Monica Boulevard in Los Angeles, or the Tenderloin in San Francisco. While gay male public space is defined through the presence of gay businesses and bars, transsexual public space reflects the areas of the city frequented by transsexual and transvestite sex workers.

Since gender and sexuality are not the same, it is not surprising that most cities have separate geographic areas known for transgendered people and lesbians/gays. Pat Califia articulates the differences between gay ghettoes and sex worker areas:

Gay ghettos operate differently than other types of sex zones. They are more likely to be residential districts for gay men as well as places where they can find entertainment. Although johns still enter gay ghettos in quest of pleasurable activities not available within the nuclear family, they have better

luck scoring if they camouflage themselves as residents of the area (1991: 14).

Because transgender areas are not tied to a notion of a resident (as in the case of gay ghettos), the ways in which the space can be defined varies. Although certain sections of the city are known for their transsexuals and transvestites, these people are usually only visible at night. New York's Meat Market District is so named because of its many meat-packaging warehouses. When these businesses close at the end of the day, transgendered sex workers come out to earn their livelihoods, and thus transform the meaning of the term 'meat' into one with explicit sexual connotations. Time of day and geographic space converge to establish a public transgender identity. For example, a Toronto sex worker interviewed in David Adkin's film *Out: Stories of Lesbian and Gay Youth* refers to the area where transgender prostitutes solicit clients as 'trannie town' (Adkin, 1993).

As Califia demonstrates, the recent emergence of gay ghettos has separated sexual minorities from transsexual prostitutes. Although bars catering to transgendered people are extremely rare, they are usually located in sex worker districts rather than in gay villages. In Montreal, for example, the transsexual/transvestite bar Café Cléopâtra is situated near the corner of Sainte-Catherine and Saint-Laurent streets, in the heart of the red-light district.[3] The bar is widely known for its prostitutes—it is a space not only where transgendered people can socialize, but where they can also earn their livings. Montreal police observe the establishment regularly. While recent years have not witnessed any official raids on the bar, it is common of officers to walk in, 'do the rounds', and inspect bar patrons, sex workers, and their prospective clients.[4]

This police harassment of transgendered people relates to the laws against prostitution. In Canada, prostitution is entirely legal, but soliciting clients is not (*Pocket Criminal Code of Canada*, 1987: 118–19). Individual officers have enormous scrutiny in the interpretation of what constitutes 'solicitation': it may be a verbal agreement about sexual acts in exchange for financial compensation, or it may be a smile or glance directed at an undercover officer.

While the latter instance would probably not be considered 'solicitation' in a court of law, officers still have the power to charge individuals with the crime and place them in custody at night (Scott, 1987). It is the communication of sexual desire that is criminalized in Canada, not sexual desire or its enactment per se. Not surprisingly, this legislation does not affect all sex workers equally. Cathy, the operator of an escort service, remarks that street prostitutes—those most visible in the public eye—are most affected by this law: 'escort services . . . have enjoyed . . . tolerance as we go tiptoeing around in the night, not bothering communities because we're not standing in people's front yards' (1987: 88–91). Research indicates that police use the soliciting law to harass prostitutes, following them down the street in a patrol car or stopping to talk with them during their work (Hankins and Gendron, n.d.).

Limits of Antiviolence Activism: Opposing Gender and Sexuality

Much of the activist response to violence against sexual and gender minorities has centered on the gay village of a particular city (see Hendricks, 1993). As most gay men are assaulted in areas demarcated as 'gay': this focus is useful. Yet such a strategy forecloses an investigation of gender and ignores the different experiences of lesbians, bisexual women, and transgendered people with respect to public space and violence. By emphasizing sexual identity, this discourse establishes an antiviolence agenda that is, at best, only somewhat useful. Consider the text of an educational poster produced by Montreal's police department (Service de police de la communauté urbaine de Montreal, or SPCUM): 'Being lesbian, gay, or bisexual is not a crime. Bashing is.' The slogan—which also appears on buttons produced by antiviolence activists in Toronto—addresses the perpetrators of violence directly, and in that, it is to be commended. Despite this direct address, however, the poster does not engage the cognitive processes at work that perpetrators use to determine who is gay, lesbian, or bisexual. In this discourse, identity is mobilized as

the ground upon which acts of violence are established. People are bashed because they are gay, lesbian, or bisexual. But we have already seen that bashing occurs due to the perception of potential victims, and that compulsory sex/gender relations figure centrally in these acts of interpretation. In this light, educational materials that address the perpetrators of violence should focus on the interpretive processes these people use to locate queerbashing victims. Because gender is the primary mechanism through which this takes place, there is a desperate need for posters, pamphlets, and presentations that outline the ways in which a binary gender system is upheld, as well as the power relations concealed within it. Through a stress on being, rather than on the perception of doing, the SPCUM poster reifies sexual identity and prevents a proper investigation of gender in the problematic of violence.

Implicitly, gender and sexuality are juxtaposed. This opposition can be witnessed in the brief presented by the SPCUM to the Quebec Human Rights Commission in association with its public hearings on violence and discrimination against lesbians and gay men (November 1993). In their brief to the commission, the SPCUM presented data on the prevalence of crime in District 33—the geographic area that includes (but is not limited to) the gay village. The borders of the village (René-Lévesque and Ontario, Amherst, and Papineau) were compared to a similar section of the city—that demarcated by the streets René-Lévesque and Ontario (north/south axis) and Amherst and Saint-Laurent (east/west). The SPCUM was interested in comparing these two sections of District 33 in order to evaluate the frequency of violent incidents (thefts, sexual assault, harassment). The areas are proportional in size, each comprising about 20 per cent of the district. Moreover, they share certain similarities in terms of the businesses, bars, and people present:

> Tous deux sont dans l'axe de la rue Ste-Catherine, rue très fréquentée de jour comme de nuit et où l'on retrouve divers commerces, restaurants, bars et salles d'amusement. On y retrouve également des activités reliées à la vente et la consommation de stupéfiants, à la

prostitution masculine et féminine contrôlée, en partie, par deux groupes des motards criminels. [Both include Sainte-Catherine Street, which is busy both day and night, and where one can find a variety of businesses, restaurants, bars, and amusement halls. One can also find activities related to the sale and consumption of drugs, as well as male and female prostitution, which is controlled, in part, by two groups of criminal bikers.] (SPCUM, 1993).

The SPCUM data indicates that between November 1991 and October 1993, a total of 1,454 crimes were recorded for the gay village—approximately 18 per cent of the total number of reported crimes in District 33 (1993: 10–11). Given that the gay village comprises 20 per cent of the district, the study implies that incidents of violence and crime correspond proportionately to geography. (However, the brief does not address the population of the gay village in relation to that of the entire district, thus associating violence with city space rather than demographics.)

The SPCUM offers comparative data to legitimate this figure. The section of District 33 to which the gay village is compared indicates 2,774 incidents of violence over the same time period, a statistic that amounts to 34 per cent of the violence in the total district (1993: 11). Since the comparison territory is relatively equal in size to that of the gay village, it is suggested that violence and crime occur more frequently in this area than in the section of the city known to be populated by gay men. By demonstrating the ways in which crime in the gay village is statistically below the proportional incidents of violence in District 33, the SPCUM attempts to dismiss activists who point to increased instances of bashing in Montreal's gay village. (The results of the SPCUM study are presented in Figure 40.1.)

There are, of course, tremendous differences in the data on violence collected by police departments and that collected by lesbian and gay community groups (Comstock, 1991; NGLTF, 1994). What is perhaps even more remarkable about the research presented by the SPCUM, however, is the way in which it forces a separation between sexuality and gender in terms of public space. The comparative section of District 33—that area bordered by Saint-Laurent, Amherst, Ontario, and Réne-Lévesque—is well known as the city's sex worker district. The city's only transsexual/transvestite bar

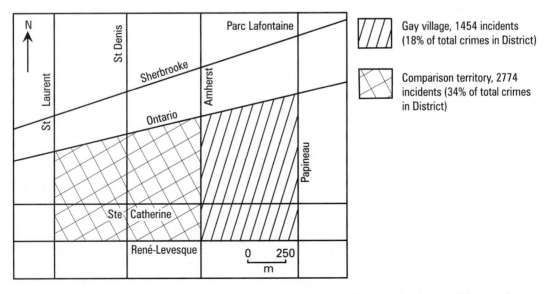

Figure 40.1 Incidents of violent crimes in two sections of Police District 33, Montreal, November 1991–October 1993 (SOURCE: SPCUM 1993, 10–11.)

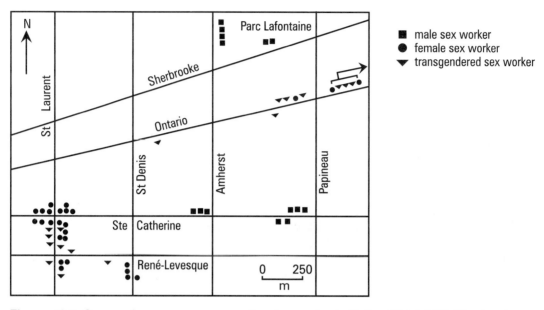

Figure 40.2 Sex-worker presence according to gender in Police District 33, Montreal, November 1991–October 1993 Note: more sex workers can be found further east on Ontario. (SOURCE: field research.)

is located here, and streets in this region are also frequented by TS/TG prostitutes.

Although the SPCUM maintains that both the gay village and this comparative section are homes to prostitutes, they do not account for the gendered breakdown of this activity. Field research conducted in the summer of 1993 indicates that most male prostitutes work in the gay village, toward Papineau; directly on its borders (Parc Lafontaine, located just above Amherst and Ontario); or in an adult cinema at the corner of Sainte-Catherine and Amherst. In contrast, most female prostitutes work on the corner of Saint-Laurent and Sainte-Catherine, on Saint-Denis, or on side streets in the vicinity. Transgendered prostitutes can also be found in this area. (The geographic location of sex workers in District 33 is depicted in Figure 40.2).

Regarding incidents of violence, most TS/TG prostitutes work in an area with a much higher frequency of criminal acts than the gay village (34 per cent versus 18 per cent). Although these statistics do not necessarily indicate that more transgendered people (proportionally) are victims of violence than gay men, it is certainly fair to stipulate

that they work in an area known for criminal activities. To present this region as a comparative sample against the gay village is, then, to juxtapose gender and sexuality. While the SPCUM attempts to dispel fears about the high incidence of violence in gay space, it offers no examination of the role gender plays either in this site or its comparative territory. Because gender is not signalled as a factor in the discussion of District 33—along with other variables including poverty and homelessness—the SPCUM assumes that crime does not vary according to the gendered dimension of public space. The focus accorded to sexuality and the gay ghetto makes it impossible to address the violence that is directed against TS/TG people—whether they are in the gay village, a sex worker zone, or elsewhere.

Conclusion

The theoretical issues presented here, especially the relations between gender and sexuality, raise additional questions as to the collection and interpretation of evidence on gendered violence. What implications does the presence of TS/TG people in public space hold in terms of violence? Do bashers drive into these areas, looking to assault a transsexual woman or a transvestite prostitute, as they often drive into gay villages in search of queerbashing victims (Comstock, 1991: 49)? Are transgendered people of colour assaulted more frequently than those who are white? What happens when transgender prostitutes enter areas demarcated as 'gay'? Are these people subject to assault because of an association between prostitution and aids, and if so, how does this relate to increased violence against those perceived to be HIV-positive (NGLTF, 1994)? Since much of the data on queerbashing indicates that it is often perpetrated by young males, usually in groups (Comstock, 1991: 65), are transgendered youth most at risk for assault? What are the specific methodological difficulties involved in collecting data on violence against transgendered people? Will these people be reluctant to report the assaults they experience to the police, as are many lesbians, gay men, and bisexuals? Given that transsexuals are incarcerated according to their 'original', biological sex (e.g., an MTF person is placed in an all-male jail), can we expect transsexuals to consider police and law enforcement officials in a favourable light?[5] Do transgendered people even inform gaybashing hotlines when they are assaulted, or do they not consider themselves part of these communities? How can we record incidents of genderbashing for the collection of hate crime statistics?[6] These are only a few of the questions that a more detailed, empirical study of violence against transgendered people would address.

In recent years, the issue of violence has received increased attention in the communities of the sexually marginalized, as well as within the academy. Although some of the research emphasizes the role of gender in violence (Harry, 1990;

von Schultess, 1992; Valentine, 1993), it has yet to explore the implications of this issue for transgendered individuals and communities. The definition of public space is intimately linked to culturally sanctioned gender identities. This has profound implications for people who live outside normative sex/gender relations: 'ordinary' public space as well as regions known as gay ghettoes are sites where the gender potential of being verbally abused, and/or physically assaulted, is remarkably high. Furthermore, although gender and sexuality are conventionally confused, such that 'effeminate' men and 'masculine' women are 'gaybashed' irrespective of their sexual identities, the variables of gender and sexuality can also be juxtaposed. Such an opposition can be quite explicit, as when middle-class gay men struggled to evict transgendered prostitutes from Vancouver's West End (Arrington, 1987). A separation of gender and sexuality can also be more subtle, as in the discourse on violence proposed by many gay male activists that privileges sexuality over gender, and hence develops a political response that is only valid for urban, middle-class gay men.

Taking up the issue of violence against sexual and gender minorities, this chapter has attempted to illustrate how some of the responses to violence preclude an adequate conceptualization of gendered aggression. Through a literature review on gender and violence, as well as a preliminary analysis on the geographic location of Montreal prostitutes in 1992, I have argued that the discourse of violence against sexual minorities excludes transsexual women. Further more, the briefs presented to the Quebec Human Rights Commission offer an engaging case study of how the social relations of gender are textually coordinated in one institution, such that transsexuals are beyond consideration.

Notes

1. Copies of these briefs are available from the Commission des droits de la personne et de la jeunesse, 360 Saint-Jacques, Montreal, QC, H2Y 1P5, Canada.

2. The issue of 'passing' has been examined from an ethnomethodological perspective within sociology. See Harold Garfinkel, *Studies in Ethnomethodology* (Englewood Cliffs, NJ:

Prentice-Hall, 1967); and Kessler and McKenna, *Gender: An Ethnomethodological Approach* (New York: John Wiley and Sons, 1978).

3. For more on the geographic area of Montreal's red-light district, see Daniel Proulx, Le Red Light de Montreal, 1945–1970 (Montreal: Boreal, 1994); and Thérèse, Limonges, *La Prostitution à Montreal: Comment, pourquoi certaines fen deviennent des prostituées: Étude sociologique et criminologique.* (Montreal: Édit de l'homme, 1967).

4. Montreal police entered Café Cleopatra with a video camera, for instance, on 13 November 1997. See Viviane Namaste, 'Évaluation des besoins: Les travesty(e)s et les transsexuel(le)s au Quebec à l'égard du vih/Sida'. Report submitted to the Centre Québécois de Coordination sur le SIDA, Montreal, May 1998. (A copy of this report is available through ASST(e)Q in care of CACTUS, 1626 rue Saint-Hubert, Montreal, QC, H2L 3Z3.)

5. For more on transgendered people in prison, see James Tee, *Health Issues of the HIV + MTF Transgendered Prison Population* (Toronto: PASAN—Prisoners' AIDS Support Action Network [489 College St, Suite 405, Toronto, ON, M6G 1A5, 416-920-9567], 1997); Maxine Petersen, Judith Stephens, Robert Dickey, and Wendy Lewis, 'Transsexuals within the Prison System: An International Survey of Correctional Services Policies', *Behavioral Sciences and the Law* 14 (1996): 219–29; and Ann Scott, 'A Brief on HIV/AIDS in the Transgendered Prison Population'. Presentation at the International Foundation for Gender Education conference, Toronto, 27 March 1998. Also see Ann Scott and Rick Lines, 'HIV/AIDS in the Male-to-Female Transsexual and Transgendered Prison Population: A Comprehensive Strategy. A Brief from PASAN. (Toronto: May 1999).

6. Documenting hate crimes against gays and lesbians is difficult because the violence must be clearly accompanied by anti-gay epithets. For instance, if a man is stabbed in the gay village and his wallet stolen, he will be considered the victim of a robbery unless the assailants called him derogatory insults relating to his perceived sexuality (see SPCUM, 'Mémoire sur la discrimination et la violence envers les gais et les lesbiennes'. Brief presented to the Quebec Human Rights Commission, November 1993. [Copy available for consultation at the Commission des droits de la personne et de la jeunesse, 360 Stain-Jacque, Montreal, QC, H2Y 1P5.]). In the case of violence against transgendered people, this criterion for documentation is questionable, since many MTF transsexuals are called 'faggot'. Programmatically, we should not have to wait until bashers decry transgendered people with the proper vocabulary before we have an adequate manner of recording such genderbashing incidents.

References

Adkin, D. 1993. *Out: Stories of Lesbian and Gay Youth.* Montreal: National Film Board of Canada.

Arrington, S. 1987. 'Community Organizing', in L. Bell, ed., *Good Girls/Bad Girls: Sex Trade Workers and Feminists Face to Face*, pp. 104–8. Toronto: Women's Press.

Bullough, B., and V. Bullough. 1993. *Cross Dressing, Sex, and Gender.* Philadelphia: University of Pennsylvania Press.

Califa, P. 1991. 'The City of Desire: Its Anatomy and Destiny', *Invert* 2, 4: 13–16.

Cathy. 1987. 'Unveiling', in L. Bell, ed., *Good Girls/Bad Girls: Feminists and Sex Trade Workers Face to Face*, pp. 88–91. Toronto: Women's Press.

Comstock, G. 1991. *Violence against Lesbians and Gay Men.* New York: Columbia University Press.

Demczuk, I. 1993. 'Des droits à reconnaître. Hétérosexisme et discrimination envers les lesbiennes'. Brief presented to the Quebec Human Rights Commission, November 1993.

Devor, H. 1989. *Gender Blending: Confronting the Limits of Duality.* Bloomington: Indiana University Press.

Enigma, A. 1992. 'Livin' Large: Dorian Corey', *Thing* 8: 35–6.

Feinberg, L. 1996. *Transgender Warriors: Making History from Joan of Arc to RuPaul.* Boston: Beacon Press.

Hankins, C., and S. Gendron. n.d. *Project Prostitution: Rapport sur les entretiens de groupes réalisés à la maison Tanguay.* Montral: Centre d'études sur le sida, Unité de santé publique, Hôpital général de Montreal.

Harry, J. 1982. 'Derivative Deviance: The Cases of Extortion, Fag-Bashing and the Shakedown of Gay Men', *Criminology* 19: 546–63.

———. 1990. 'Conceptualizing Anti-gay Violence', *Journal of Interpersonal Violence* 5: 350–8.

Hendricks, M. 1993. 'Lesbian and Gay Community Relations with the M[ontreal] U[rban] C[ommunity] Police'. Brief presented for the group Lesbiennes et Gais contre la violence to the Quebec Human Rights Commission, November 1993.

Herdt, G., ed. 1994. *Third Sex, Third Gender: Beyond Sexual Dimorphism in Culture and History*. New York: Zone Books.

Kinsey, A., W. Pomeroy, and C.E. Martin. 1948. *Sexual Behavior in the Human Male*. Philadelphia: W.B. Saunders Company.

Mackie, M. 1983. *Exploring Gender Relations*. Toronto: Butterworths.

Namaste, K. 1993. 'Transgenders and Violence: An Exploration'. Brief presented to the Quebec Human Rights Commission, November 1993.

National Gay and Lesbian Task Force (NGLTF). 1994. *Anti-gay/lesbian Violence, Victimization, and Defamation in 1993*. Washington, DC: NGLTF Policy Institute.

Ortner, S. and H. Whitehead, eds. 1981. *Sexual Meanings: The Cultural Construction of Gender and Sexuality*. Cambridge, UK: Cambridge University Press.

Pepper, D. 1993. 'Community Based Responses to Bias Crimes: Some Critical Steps'. Brief presented to the Quebec Human Rights Commission, November 1993. *Pocket Criminal Code of Canada*. 1987. Toronto: Carswell.

Rubin, G. 1984. 'Thinking Sex: Notes Towards a Radical Theory of the Politics of Sexuality', in C. Vance, ed., *Pleasure and Danger: Exploring Female Sexuality*, pp. 267–319. Boston: Routledge and Kegan Paul.

Scott, V. 1987. 'C-49: A New Wave of Oppression', in L. Bell, ed., *Good Girls/Bad Girls: Sex Trade Workers and Feminists Face to Face*, pp. 100–3. Toronto: Women's Press.

SPCUM. 1993. 'Mémoire sur la discrimination et la violence envers les gais et les lesbiennes'. Brief presented to the Quebec Human Rights Commission, November 1993.

Tully, B. 1992. *Accounting for Transsexuality and Transhomosexuality*. London: Whiting and Birch.

Valentine, G. 1993. '(Hetero)Sexing Space: Lesbian Perceptions and Experiences of Everyday Spaces', *Environment and Planning D: Society and Space* 11: 409.

von Schultess, B. 1992. 'Violence in the Streets: Anti-lesbian Assault and Harassment in San Francisco', in G. Herek and K. Berril, eds., *Hate Crimes: Confronting Violence Against Lesbians and Gay Men*, pp. 65–77. London, UK: Sage.

CHAPTER 41

The White Ribbon Campaign: Involving Men and Boys in Ending Global Violence against Women

Michael Kaufman

The need to address men, to challenge them to end the violence, should be apparent. After all, it is men, or at least some men, who are committing the violence, and meanwhile the vast majority of men have remained silent about it. Through this silence, men—as the half of humanity who have controlled social discourse, law-making, religious ideas, the police and courts, and so forth—have allowed the violence to continue.

Although the need for public education campaigns that challenge men to stop the violence seems unarguable, in most parts of the world, efforts of this sort have been infrequent or non-existent.

Public education is critical if men are to question their own attitudes and behaviour that might be part of a continuum of violence. It is critical if men are to challenge the men around them. However, I'd like to suggest that there are two prerequisites if we are going to address men and boys effectively and successfully on this issue: (1) we must actually involve them in the work to end the violence; and (2) we must do so—without playing down the extent of the problem or the importance of personal responsibility—based not on a vague sense of collective guilt or litanies about those other men who presumably are not as pure or good as us but rather on the basis of love and an appeal to goodness in men. It must be done on the basis of respect for men, even if there is absolutely no respect for the behaviour and attitude of some of those very same men. This latter point is not the focus of this article, but is the note I will end on.

In this chapter I first sketch out an analysis of the complexities of men's violence against women, an analysis that forms the basis for the strategies I am suggesting. Flowing from this analysis, I discuss why men's involvement is critical to addressing boys and men successfully on these issues. Third, I discuss the White Ribbon Campaign, a growing international effort to address and involve boys and men in ending violence against women.

The Complex Puzzle of Men's Violence

An understanding of the complex nature and causes of men's violence must form the basis of any strategic approach. Without such an understanding, we will be left with exhortations from well-meaning men or women that have little or no social or individual impact. (Indeed, I would suggest that the often-discussed high-recidivism rate of North American men who have gone through treatment programs for violence against women is the result of an incomplete analysis of the problem.)

Let me reprise my analysis of this violence, drawing on my framework of 'the seven Ps of men's violence' (Kaufman, 1999).

Patriarchal Power: The First 'P'

Individual acts of violence by men occur within what I have described as 'the triad of men's violence'. Men's violence against women does not occur in isolation but is linked to men's violence against other men and to the internalization of violence—that is, a man's violence against himself (Kaufman, 1985).

Indeed, male-dominated societies are not only based on a hierarchy of men over women but some men over other men. Violence or the threat of violence among men is a mechanism used from childhood to establish that pecking order. One result of this is that men 'internalize' violence—or perhaps, the demands of patriarchal society encourage biological instincts that otherwise might be relatively dormant or more benign.

This triad of men's violence—each form of violence helping create the others—occurs within a nurturing environment of violence: the organization and demands of patriarchal or male-dominant societies.

What gives violence its hold as a way of doing business, what has naturalized it as the de facto standard of human relations, is the way it has been articled into our ideologies and social structures. Simply put, human groups create self-perpetuating forms of social organization and ideologies that explain, give meaning to, justify, and replenish these created realities.

Violence is also built into these ideologies and structures for the simpler reason that it has brought enormous benefits to particular groups. First and foremost, violence (or at least the threat of violence) has helped confer on men (as a group) a rich set of privileges and forms of power. If indeed the original forms of social hierarchy and power are those based on sex, then this long ago formed a template for all the structured forms of power and privilege enjoyed by others as a result of social class, skin colour, age, nationality, religion, sexual orientation, or physical abilities. In such a context, violence or its threat becomes a means to ensure the continued reaping of privileges and exercise of power. It is both a result and a means to an end.

The Sense of Entitlement or Privilege: The Second 'P'

The individual experience of a man who commits violence may not revolve round his conscious desire to maintain power. His conscious experience is not the key here. Rather, as feminist analysis has repeatedly pointed out, such violence is often the logical outcome of his sense of entitlement to certain privileges. If a man beats his wife for not having dinner on the table on time, it is not only to make sure that it doesn't happen again, but is an indication of his sense of entitlement to be waited on. Or, say a man sexually assaults a woman on a date; it is about his sense of entitlement to physical pleasure even if that pleasure is entirely one-sided. In other words, it is not only inequalities of power that lead to violence, but also a conscious or more often unconscious sense of entitlement to privilege.

Permission: The Third 'P'

Whatever the complex social and psychological causes of men's violence, it would not continue if it did not receive explicit or tacit permission in social customs, legal codes, law enforcement, and certain religious teachings. In many countries, laws against wife assault or sexual assault are lax or non-existent; in many others laws are barely enforced; in still others they are absurd, such as those countries where a charge of rape can be prosecuted only if there are three male witnesses and where the testimony of the woman is not taken into account.

Meanwhile, acts of men's violence and violent aggression (in this case, usually against other men) are celebrated in sport and cinema, in literature and warfare. Not only is violence permitted, it is glamorized and rewarded.

The Paradox of Men's Power: The Fourth 'P'

It is my contention however, that these first three points—the critical components of most feminist analyses of men's violence—while central, do not adequately explain the widespread nature of men's violence, nor the connections between men's violence against women and the many forms of violence among men. Here we need to draw on the paradoxes of men's power or what I have called 'men's contradictory experiences of power' (Kaufman, 1993, 1994).

The very ways in which men have constructed their social and individual power is, paradoxically, a source of enormous fear, isolation, and pain for men themselves. If power is constructed as a capacity to dominate and control, if the capacity to act in 'powerful' ways requires the construction of a personal suit of armour and a fearful distance from others, if the very world of power and privilege removes men from the world of child-rearing and nurturance, then we are creating men whose own experience of power is fraught with crippling problems.

This is particularly so because the internalized expectations of masculinity are themselves impossible to satisfy or attain. This may well be a problem inherent in patriarchy, but it seems particularly true in an era and in cultures where rigid gender boundaries are being challenged or where there is a fear of challenge and change. Whether it is physical or financial accomplishment, or the suppression of a range of human emotions and needs, the imperatives of manhood (as opposed to the simple certainties of biological maleness) seem to require constant vigilance and work, especially for younger men.

The personal insecurities conferred by a failure to make the masculine grade, or simply the threat of failure, is enough to propel many men, particularly when they are young, into a vortex of fear, isolation, anger, self-punishment, self-hatred, and aggression.

Within such an emotional state, violence becomes a compensatory mechanism. It is a way of re-establishing the masculine equilibrium, of asserting to oneself and to others one's masculine credentials. This expression of violence usually includes a choice of a target who is physically weaker or more vulnerable. This may be a child or a woman, or it may be a social group, such as gay men, or a religious or social minority, or immigrants; the victim poses an easy target for the insecurity and rage of individual men, especially since such groups often do not receive adequate protection under the law.

What permits violence to become an individual compensatory mechanism has been the widespread acceptance of violence as a means of solving differences and asserting power and control. What makes it possible are the power and privileges men have enjoyed, things encoded in beliefs, practices, social structures, and the law.

The Psychic Armour of Manhood: The Fifth 'P'

Men's violence is also the result of a character structure that is typically based on emotional distance from others. As I and many others have suggested, the psychic structures of manhood are crated in early child-rearing environments that are often typified by the absence of fathers and adult men—or, at least by men's emotional distance. In this case, masculinity is codified by absence and constructed at the level of fantasy. But even in patriarchal cultures where fathers are more present, masculinity is codified as a rejection of the mother and femininity—that is, a rejection of the qualities associated with caregiving and nurturance. As various feminist psychoanalysts have noted, this creates rigid ego barriers, or, in metaphorical terms, a strong suit of armour.

Dr Gabor Maté draws on new research on brain development:

> There is now a large body of evidence suggesting that the infant's emotional inter-actions with its primary caregivers provide the major influence on the physiological and biochemical development of the brain regions responsible for emotional and behav-ioural self-control. When infants and young children lack parenting which is emotionally nurturing and consistently available, given in a non-stressed atmosphere, research suggests that problems of self-regulation often result. The greater the deprivations, the less optimally the orbitofrontal cortex is likely to develop and function, which a July 2000 article in *Science* suggests might be a critical factor in developing a proclivity to acts of violence (Maté, 2000).

The result of this complex and particular process of psychological development is a dampened ability for empathy (to experience what others are feeling) and an inability to experience other people's needs and feelings as necessarily relating to one's own. Acts of violence against another person are, therefore, possible.

Masculinity as a Psychic Pressure Cooker: The Sixth 'P'

Many of our dominant forms of masculinity hinge on the internalization of a range of emotions and their redirection into anger. It is not simply that men's language of emotions is often muted or that our emotional antennae and capacity for empathy are somewhat stunted. It is also that a range of natural emotions have been ruled off-limited and invalid. While this has a cultural specificity, it is rather typical for boys to learn from an early age to repress feelings of fear and pain. On the sports field we teach boys to ignore pain. At home we tell boys not to cry and to act like men. Some cultures celebrate a stoic manhood. (And, I should stress, boys learn such things for survival; hence it is important we don't blame the individual boy or man for the origins of his current behaviours, even if, at the same time, we hold him responsible for his actions.)

Of course, as humans, we still experience events that cause an emotional response. But the usual mechanisms of emotional response, from actually experiencing an emotion to letting go of the feelings, are short-circuited to varying degrees among many men. But, again for many men, the one emotion that has some validation is anger. The result is that a range of emotions are channelled into anger. While such channelling is not unique to men (nor is it the case for all men), for some men, violent responses to fear, hurt, insecurity, pain, rejection, or belittlement are not uncommon.

The Seventh 'P': Past Experiences

This all combines with more blatant experiences for some men. Far too many men around the world grew up in households where their father beat their mother. They grew up seeing violent behaviour toward women as the norm, as just the way life is lived. For some men this results in revulsion toward violence, while in others it produces a learned response. In many cases it is both: men who use violence against women often feel deep self-loathing.

The phrase 'learned response', though, is almost too simplistic. Studies have shown that boys and girls who grow up witnessing violence are far more likely to be violent themselves. Such violence may be a way of getting attention; it may be a coping mechanism, a way of externalizing impossible-to-cope-with feelings. Such patterns of behaviour continue beyond childhood: most men who end up in programs for men who use violence either witnessed abuse against their mother or experienced abuse themselves.

The past experiences of many men also include the violence they themselves have experienced. In many cultures, while boys may be only half as likely as girls to experience sexual abuse, they are twice as likely to experience physical abuse. Again, this produces no one fixed outcome, and again, such outcomes are not unique to boys. But in some cases these personal experiences instill deep patterns of confusion and frustration; boys learn that it is possible to hurt someone you love, and that only outbursts of rage can get rid of deeply imbedded feelings of pain.

Finally, there is the issue of petty violence among boys that, as a boy, doesn't seem petty at all. Boys in many cultures grow up with experiences of fighting, bullying, and brutalization. Sheer survival requires, for some, accepting and internalizing violence as a norm of behaviour.

Why Men's Involvement Is Critical

How might such an analysis inform our strategies to end violence against women? We can see, of course, that we must collectively challenge men's social and individual power, men's sense of entitlement to privilege, and the social permission most societies have given to the violence. This requires the sort of legal, judicial, educational, political, cultural, behavioural, and attitudinal changes that have been a part of feminist practice and social change over the past 30 years.

But the final four 'Ps' tell us that such an approach will, in a sense, 'rebound' off men's own experiences unless we find ways that link men's experiences with an understanding of the oppression of women.

One way of doing this is through the actual involvement of men and boys as a critical component of public education to end violence against women:

1. The challenge of ending violence against women is not simply a question of providing corrective information as we might, for example, when we educate people about the link between contaminated water and certain diseases. People in those situations can and will change their habits. Violence against women occurs because of a complex and contradictory range of factors deeply imbedded in culture, economy, law, and, most intractably, the psychic structures of masculinity. By and large, it is not the result of lack of information, although misinformation may in some cases fuel it. If the ability to dominate is a display of manhood, only by involving males in a redefinition of manhood will we effectively challenge these patterns of dominations and control.

2. Violence against women is not simply an activity easily amenable to behavioural modification. It is very different from, say, educating people about the terrible consequences of drunk driving. Such issues can be addressed largely through media campaigns and the provision of information. Ending the violence requires far more than drumming a message into men's heads.

3. Men must be involved because, more than anything else, men and boys will listen to other men and boys, far more than they will listen to the anger or pleas of women or to a disembodied media voice. This is because masculinity is created in the eyes of men. In other words, if one's manhood is most critically assessed in a homosocial environment (Kimmel, 1996; Burstyn, 1999), then it is this environment that can most readily deconstruct and reshape the dominant discourse on masculinity. Simply put, men and boys tend to look to other men and boys for their models of manly activity. This power of the male voice is part of the sexist reality (and part of our message of men is to listen to the voices of women). But if we are effectively to reach men and boys, then men and boys must be involved. This requires more than having a man's voice used in a radio ad. By involved, I mean the active participation of men and boys in anti-violence efforts, in defining and leading efforts to reach other men.

4. One reason for the effectiveness of such participation is that through participation, men and boys will feel a sense of 'ownership' in the problem. They will feel they have a personal relationship to the issue and a stake in the process of change. Such a feeling, in turn, will unleash greater energies and unlock new resources that can be used to end the violence. In other words, involving men in this work is, paradoxically, the way to address the very real concern about scarce resources (that now go to women and girls and to women's programs) being siphoned off by/to men and boys. Developing a sense of ownership means that men will develop a commitment to redirecting resources towards explicit gender issues as well as learning to address the gender dimensions of all issues.

What might such an effort—actually to address and involve men—look like? One approach is that of the White Ribbon Campaign.

The White Ribbon Campaign

In 1991 a handful of men in Canada took the first steps down a pathway whose future we did not know: we decided we had a responsibility to urge men to speak out against violence against women. We knew that most men in Canada were not violent toward women, but we also knew that the vast majority of us remained silent. Through our silence, we allowed the violence to continue.

We adopted a white ribbon as a symbol. Wearing the ribbon would neither be an act of contrition, nor a symbol of misplaced collective guilt; it did not indicate that the wearer was a great guy. Rather, wearing the ribbon was a personal pledge never to commit, condone, or remain silent about violence against women. It would be a catalyst for discussion and soul-searching. It would be a public challenge to those many men who may use violence against a wife, girlfriend, family member, or stranger. It would be a call on our policy-makers, opinion leaders, police, and courts to take seriously this national and international epidemic. And it would be an act of love for the women in our lives.

From the start, the primary goal of the WRC has been to encourage men to look at their own attitudes and behaviour and to learn to challenge other men to stop all forms of violence against women. We believe that as more men and boys take responsibility for challenging themselves and others, then the epidemic levels of violence against women will finally end.

In the past decade, we have moved beyond an idea organized from my living room, to active campaigns in schools and communities across Canada. We know of White Ribbon organizations or local White Ribbon campaigns or white ribbon distribution in Asia (India, Japan, and Vietnam), Europe (Norway, Sweden, Finland, Denmark, Spain, Belgium, Germany, and England), Africa (Namibia, Kenya, South Africa, and Morocco), the Middle East (Israel), Latin America (Brazil), Australia, and the United States. There may well be others.

The campaign is developing closer contacts with international organizations including ties with various bodies of the United Nations, in particular UNIFEM, with whom we are developing a formal partnership. (UNIFEM has proclaimed 25 November as the International Day for the Eradication of Violence Against Women.) We are working closely with women's organizations in a number of countries.

The central organizing idea of White Ribbon is this: just as the problem of violence against women is not confined to the margins of society, our efforts to reach men cannot be marginal. We know that we must find ways to involve the vast majority of men. This is in contrast to many previous efforts of pro-feminist men. Walking a narrow and cozy pathway can be nice; it is safe and you can be relatively assured that everyone around you agrees on all the important issues of the day. But there's room for only a few of you. White Ribbon wants to make room for hundreds of thousands, millions of men and boys. To do so, we have to find the highways where men travel.

Traditional progressive organizations have insisted (or at least assumed) that their members agree on virtually everything: that is, they must share a worldview. Instead, White Ribbon decided we needed agreement on one point: that men must work together and alongside women to end all forms of violence against women.

This has allowed us to pitch a tent that would bring together men from across the political, economic, and social spectrums. To be active in White Ribbon, we do not have to agree on environmental or economic issues, we do not have to agree on which political parties to support, we do not have to agree on labour or poverty issues, and so forth. Where there is no confusion is on the core issues concerning men's violence against women: we are united against wife assault, against sexual assault, against sexual harassment, against men's controlling behaviour in relationships. We are united in support to increased funding for women's programs, including women's shelters and rape crisis centres. We are united in support for men playing a greater role as nurturers and caregivers. All that is a lot to agree on and to work toward.

For me, one symbol of this type of approach was the launching of the Swedish WRC in the autumn of 1998. On a public stage, a group of men stood side-by-side to put on white ribbons and to commit themselves to working to end violence against women. There was a former social democratic prime minister standing next to the head of a right-wing taxpayers coalition, there were corporate leaders and trade unionists, and standing next to each other were the leaders of the Swedish Turkish Association and the Swedish Kurdish Association. Whatever their many areas of conflict, these men stood together, as a unitary voice of men speaking to, and challenging, their brothers.

Areas and Type of Work

One area of focus for the WRC is in the school system. We do so to reach boys whose ideas about the other sex and about themselves as men are still forming. White Ribbon has produced a series of education kits for teenagers that are now used in over a thousand junior highs and high schools across Canada, representing one million students. Many more schools hold annual White Ribbon activities during which they do educational work and raise money for local women's programs.

We also want to reach men where they work, and men and women where they shop. So a second and rapidly growing area of our work has been with corporations and trade unions. We have worked hard to develop these partnerships for several important reasons: most adult Canadians spend a good part of each day at work. A trade union or corporation can act as a transmission belt, bringing the ideas of White Ribbon to a large audience in offices and on the shop floor. The corporate partnerships also allow us to reach people as consumers.

The support of corporations and unions is also important because the WRC in Canada has chosen not to accept government funding (so as not to take money from women's programs). We rely entirely on support from these groups, foundations, and many concerned individuals.

We also work in that most nebulous of areas, the public arena. This has a number of components:

- We work with women's organizations to respond to current events, court decisions, and government policy concerning violence against women. This work includes lobbying, public demonstrations, press conferences, and letter-writing.
- Each year public relations firms donate resources to produce radio, television, and print advertisements that the media broadcast or print for free.
- For several years we have produced a large poster with a headline 'These men want to end violence against women' followed by a hundred empty lines. The posters are displayed in schools, workplaces, places of worship, union halls, and shops for men and boys to sign.
- One version of the poster (which is also produced as a magazine-sized advertisement) has signatures by a wide range of well-known Canadian men from the arts, sports, business, various ethnic communities, labour, and so forth.
- We distribute press releases, hold occasional press conferences, and write articles for newspapers on the issues of the day.
- We maintain a website and distribute a newsletter to our members and supporters.

- We have a relationship with several programs that work with men who use violence.

White Ribbon Week

The focus and signature event of the WRC in Canada is our annual White Ribbon Week—a slight misnomer as it now runs from 25 November (the International Day for the Eradication of Violence Against Women) until 6 December. The latter is the anniversary of what we in Canada call 'the Montreal Massacre', the day in 1989 when a man murdered 14 women engineering students. That day was a catalyst not only for the White Ribbon Campaign, but also for national soul-searching and action that continues to this day.

Around that time, our public service ads are broadcast on television and radio, and are printed in newspapers and magazines. We distribute white ribbons in schools, universities, places of worship, workplaces, on the street, and in selected shops. Our posters are displayed in many locations for men and boys to sign.

Although White Ribbon Week is our signature event, our office and volunteers are busy year round responding daily to requests for information, ideas and resources; organizing other activities; responding to the issues of the day; and organizing the fund-raising events that sustain the WRC and draw in new groups of men,

Supporting Women's Efforts and Women's Groups

I have already mentioned several ways we work in support of women's groups. From the outset, White Ribbon has viewed women's organizations as the experts on these issues and looks toward them for leadership in the field. This does not mean that the WRC operates as a subcommittee of women's groups. Indeed, if our agenda is to address and involve men, we feel that we have a particular expertise and insights that may or may not be shared by women's organizations. As well, we know there is a diversity of views in the women's community and the approach of White Ribbon will not please everyone

At the same time, we know that these organizations have far more knowledge of the dimensions of the problem, of legislative and judicial issues, and of issues concerning programming. We know both our volunteers and staff have a tremendous amount to learn. In a similar vein, we believe in the importance of men listening to the voices of women. This, indeed, is the lead point on our flyer 'What Every Man Can Do to End Violence against Women'.

But Based on Love?

I would like to end with a suggestion which space does not allow me to explore, but which is part of the ongoing discussions of White Ribbon.

I believe that most versions of feminism are based on the possibility of men's participation in a radically different gender order—that is, on men's ability to change. This in turn presupposes some inherent goodness of males, or at least an inherent capacity to relate to women as equals and as leaders worthy of love and respect. Such an approach hinges on the distinction between males (as a biological entity) and men/masculinity as a gender order that is predicated on men's domination, on men's practices of dominations, and on the whole contradictory experiences of that power.

What this (and the whole preceding analysis) suggests to me is that the approach of efforts such as White Ribbon must be based on respect for males (while showing no respect for harmful behaviours or attitudes). It must be based on an appeal to goodness, not simply excoriating faults, crimes, and problems. While the latter might make some of us feel superior, self-righteous, or different from men who use violence, it will do little or nothing actually to reach those men who do use violence and draw them into a process of change. It also sets up a false dichotomy between those men who actively use violence and those of us who do not (but certainly engage in various dominating and negative practices, however subtle or accepted these might at times be).

The whole analysis of the seven 'Ps' suggests that it is the crippling process inherent in the development of 'normal' hegemonic forms of manhood that is at the root of the problem of men's violence (or, at least, activates biological potentials).

Part of ending the violence is urging, pressuring, and encouraging men to heal, so that they will not continue to inflict their own pain on women, children, and other men. I say all this not simply in a feel-good, 'let's all love each other' sense, but from the entirely practical viewpoint of how change might actually happen.

I believe this is true, whether it applies to working with abusive men who use violence, or for general public education and awareness to reach men. It is this—a message of change—that invites men into a dialogue with women to end the violence, to redefine relations between the sexes and, ultimately, to redefine what it means to be a man, and that ultimately will play a role in ending the longest epidemic the people of our planet have known.

References

Burstyn, V. 1999. *The Rites of Men: Manhood, Politics and the Culture of Sport*. Toronto: University of Toronto Press.

Kaufman, M. 1985. 'The Construction of Masculinity and the Triad of Men's Violence', in M. Kaufman, ed., *Beyond Patriarchy: Essays by Men on Pleasure, Power and Change*. Don Mills, ON: Oxford University Press; Reprinted in L. O'Toole and J.R. Schiffman, eds. 1997. *Gender Violence*. New York: New York University Press.

———. 1993. *Cracking the Armour: Power, Pain and the Lives of Men*. Toronto: Viking Canada.

———. 1994. 'Men, Feminism, and Men's Contradictory Experiences of Power', in H. Brod and M. Kaufman, eds., *Theorizing Masculinities*. Thousand Oaks, CA: Sage.

———. 1999. 'The Seven Ps of Men's Violence'. Available at www.michaelkaufman.com.

Kimmel, M. 1996. *Manhood in America*. New York: Free Press.

Mate, G. 2000. 'A Solution to Violence is in Our Hands', *Globe and Mail*, 2 August.

QUESTIONS FOR CRITICAL THOUGHT

1. Do you live in a rape-prone culture? Have you ever experienced one?

2. Where do men fit into the ongoing struggle to stop violence against women? Do you agree with Kaufman's contention that the only thing that will stop male violence is a radical change of heart among men?

3. Dobash et al. jump into the heated debate about the gender division of domestic violence, and argue that marital violence is more often visited on women by men than on men by women. Why is this a contentious and controversial topic in the media, in the world of academic research, and in the world of policy-making?

4. What defines violence? Are there some acts which are considered violent and unacceptable in some contexts, but acceptable in others? Where should the line be drawn between acceptable and unacceptable conduct, especially with respect to intimate or domestic relationships?

5. How can we account for the extreme violence visited on people who don't conform to norms of what a man or a woman 'should' look or act like, as described by Namaste? How is 'genderbashing' connected to the violence perpetrated against women?

Acknowledgments

Christie Barron and Dany Lacombe, 'Moral Panic and the Nasty Girl', *Canadian Review of Sociology & Anthropology* 42, 1 (2005): 51–69.

Brenda Beagan, 'Micro Inequities and Everyday Inequalities: "Race", Gender, Sexuality, and Class in Medical School'. Reprinted by permission of the *Canadian Journal of Sociology*.

Melanie Beres, '"It Just Happens": Negotiating Casual Heterosexual Sex'. This chapter originally appeared in Beres, M.A. (2006). From *Sexual Consent to Heterosexual Casual Sex among Young Adults Living in Jasper*. Unpublished Doctoral Dissertation, University of Alberta, Edmonton, Alberta, Canada.

Susan Bordo, 'The Body and the Reproduction of Femininity'. From *Unbearable Weight: Feminism, Western Culture, and the Body*. Published by University of California Press. Copyright © 2004, The Regents of the University of California.

David M. Buss, 'Psychological Sex Differences through Sexual Selection', *American Psychologist* 50(30): 164–71.

Scott Coltrane, 'Household Labour and the Routine Production of Gender', *Social Problems* 36, 5 (1989): 473–90.

Sarah de Leeuw, 'Intimate Colonialisms: The Material and Experienced Places of British Columbia's Residential Schools', *The Canadian Geographer* 51, 3 (2007) 339–59.

Russell P. Dobash, R. Emerson Dobash, Margo Wilson, and Martin Daly, 'The Myth of Sexual Symmetry in Marital Violence', *Social Problems* 39, 1 (1992): 71–91.

Leona M. English, 'A Foucauldian Reading of Learning in Feminist Nonprofit Organizations', *Adult Education Quarterly*, Vol. 56, No. 2 (February 2006), 85–101.

Joan A. Evans, 'Cautious Caregivers: Gender Stereotypes and the Sexualization of Men Nurses' Touch', *Journal of Advanced Nursing*, 40(4): 441–8. Published by Blackwell Publishing Ltd.

Anne Fausto-Sterling, 'The Five Sexes: Why Male and Female Are Not Enough', *The Sciences* (March/April 1993).

Patricia Gagné, Richard Tewksbury, and Deanna McGaughey, 'Coming Out and Crossing Over: Identity Formation and Proclamation in a Transgender Community', *Gender & Society* (Vol. 11, No. 4), pp. 478–508, copyright 1997 by Sociologists for Women in Society.

Elisabeth Gidengil and Joanna Everitt, 'Unconventional Politicians: Gender and Media Coverage of Canadian Leaders' Debates, 1993, 1997, 2000', *Canadian Journal of Political Science* 36:3 (July–August 2003), 559–77.

Sepali Guruge, Nazilla Khanlou, and Denise Gastaldo, 'Intimate Male Partner Violence in the Migration Process: Intersections of Gender, Race, and Class', *Journal of Advanced Nursing*, Vol. 66, No. 1 (January 2010) 103–13.

Alison Jacques, 'You Can Run but You Can't Hide: The Incorporation of Riot Grrrl into Mainstream Culture', *Canadian Women's Studies*, Vol. 20/21, No. 4/1 (2001), 46–51.

Ellen Jordan and Angela Cowan, 'Warrior Narratives in the Kindergarten Classroom: Renegotiating the Social Contract?', *Gender & Society* (Vol. 9, No. 6), pp. 727–43, copyright 1995 by Sociologists for Women in Society.

Michael Kaufman, 'The White Ribbon Campaign: Involving Men and Boys in Ending Global Violence against Women'. From *A Man's World? Changing Men's Practices in a Globalized World*, Bob Pease and Keith Pringle, eds. Published by Zed Books, 2002.

Eliane Leslau Silverman, *The Last Best West: Women on the Alberta Frontier, 1880–1930*. Revised and updated edition. Excerpts from the chapter 'Women and Men'. Calgary: Fifth House, 1998, 57–77.

Tracey Lindberg, 'What Do You Call an Indian Woman with a Law Degree: Nine Aboriginal Women at the University of Saskatchewan College of Law Speak Out', *Canadian Journal of Women and the Law* 9 (1997): 301–35. Copyright © University of Toronto Press 1997. Reprinted by permission of University of Toronto Press Incorporated (www.utpjournals.com).

Judith Lorber, 'Believing Is Seeing: Biology as Ideology', *Gender & Society* (Vol. 7, No. 4), pp. 568–81, copyright 1993 by Sociologists for Women in Society.

Stacey L. Lorenz and Geraint B. Osborne, '"Talk about Strenuous Hockey": Violence, Manhood, and the 1907 Ottawa Silver Seven–Montreal Wanderer Rivalry', *Journal of Canadian Studies*, Vol. 40, No. 1 (Winter 2006), 125–56.

Anne Martin-Matthews, 'Situating "Home" at the Nexus of Public and Private Spheres: Aging, Gender, and Home Support Work in Canada', *Current Sociology*, March 2007, Vol. 55(2): 229–49.

Karen McGarry, 'Mass Media and Gender Identity in High Performance Canadian Figure Skating'. Reprinted with permission from *The Sport Journal*, Vol. 8, No. 1.

Joanne C. Minaker and Laureen Snider, 'Husband Abuse: Equality with a Vengeance?', *Canadian Journal of Criminology and Criminal Justice,* Vol. 48, No. 5 (September 2006), 753–81. Reproduced with the permission of the *Canadian Journal of Criminology and Criminal Justice.* Copyright of the Canadian Criminal Justice Association.

Nick Mulé, 'Same-Sex Marriage and Canadian Relationship Recognition: One Step Forward and Two Steps Back: A Critical Liberationist Perspective', *Journal of Gay and Lesbian Social Services*, 22: 74–90 (2010).

Viviane K. Namaste, 'Genderbashing: Sexuality, Gender, and the Regulation of the Public Space'. From *Invisible Lives: The Erasure of Transsexual and Transgendered People*, by Vivian K. Namaste. Copyright © University of Chicago Press, 2000. Reprinted by permission of the publisher.

Miya Narushima, 'A Gaggle of Raging Grannies: The Empowerment of Older Canadian Women through Social Activism', *International Journal of Lifelong Education*, Vol. 23, No. 1 (January 2004) 23–42.

Shelley Pacholok, 'Gendered Strategies of the Self: Navigating Hierarchy and Contesting Masculinities', *Gender, Work, and Organization*, Vol. 16, No. 4 (July 2009), 471–500. Journal compilation © 2009 Blackwell Publishing Ltd.

Shauna Pomerantz, Dawn H. Currie, and Deidre M. Kelly, 'Sk8ter Girls: Skateboarders, Girlhood, and Feminism in Motion', *Women's Studies International Forum* 27, 5/6 (2004): 547–57.

Gillian Ranson, 'No Longer "One of the Boys": Negotiations with Motherhood, as Prospect or Reality, among Women in Engineering', *Canadian Review of Sociology & Anthropology* 42(2) (2005): 145–66.

Peggy Reeves Sanday, 'Rape-Prone versus Rape-Free Campus Cultures', *Violence against Women* (Vol. 2, No. 2), pp. 191–208, copyright 1996 by Sociologists for Women in Society.

Tabassum F. Ruby, 'Listening to the Voices of *Hijab*', *Women's Studies International Forum* 29, 1 (2006): 54–66.

Janet W. Salaf and Arent Greve, 'Can Women's Social Networks Migrate?', *Women's Studies International Forum* 27, 2 (2004): 249–62.

Robert M. Sapolsky, 'Testosterone Rules'. Reprinted by permission of the author.

Candis Steenbergen, 'Feminism and Young Women: Still Alive and Kicking', *Canadian Women's Studies*, Vol. 20, No. 1 (Winter–Spring 2001), 6–15.

Bernadette Stiell and Kim England, 'Domestic Distinctions: Constructing Difference among Paid Domestic Workers in Toronto', *Gender, Place, and Culture* 4 (1997): 339–60.

Pamela Sugiman, 'Privilege and Oppression: The Configuration of Race, Gender, and Class in Southern Ontario Auto Plants, 1939 to 1949', *Labour/Le Travail*, North America, 47, Jan. 2001. Available at: http://www.lltjournal.ca/index.php/llt/article/view/5219. Date accessed: 24 Jan. 2011.

Nancy Theberge, '"It's Part of the Game": Physicality and the Production of Gender in Women's Hockey'. Reprinted with permission of the author.

Lily Tsui and Elena Nicoladis, 'Losing It: Similarities and Differences in First Intercourse Experiences of Men and Women'. Reprinted with permission from *The Canadian Journal of Human Sexuality*. Published by the Sex Information and Education Council of Canada.

Pamela Wakewich, 'Contours of Everyday Life: Women's Reflections on Embodiment and Health over Time'. Excerpted from *Women's Bodies/Women's Lives: Health, Well-being and Body Image*.

Candace West and Don H. Zimmerman, 'Doing Gender', *Gender & Society* (Vol. 1, No. 2), pp. 125–51, copyright 1987 by Sociologists for Women in Society.